AF544971

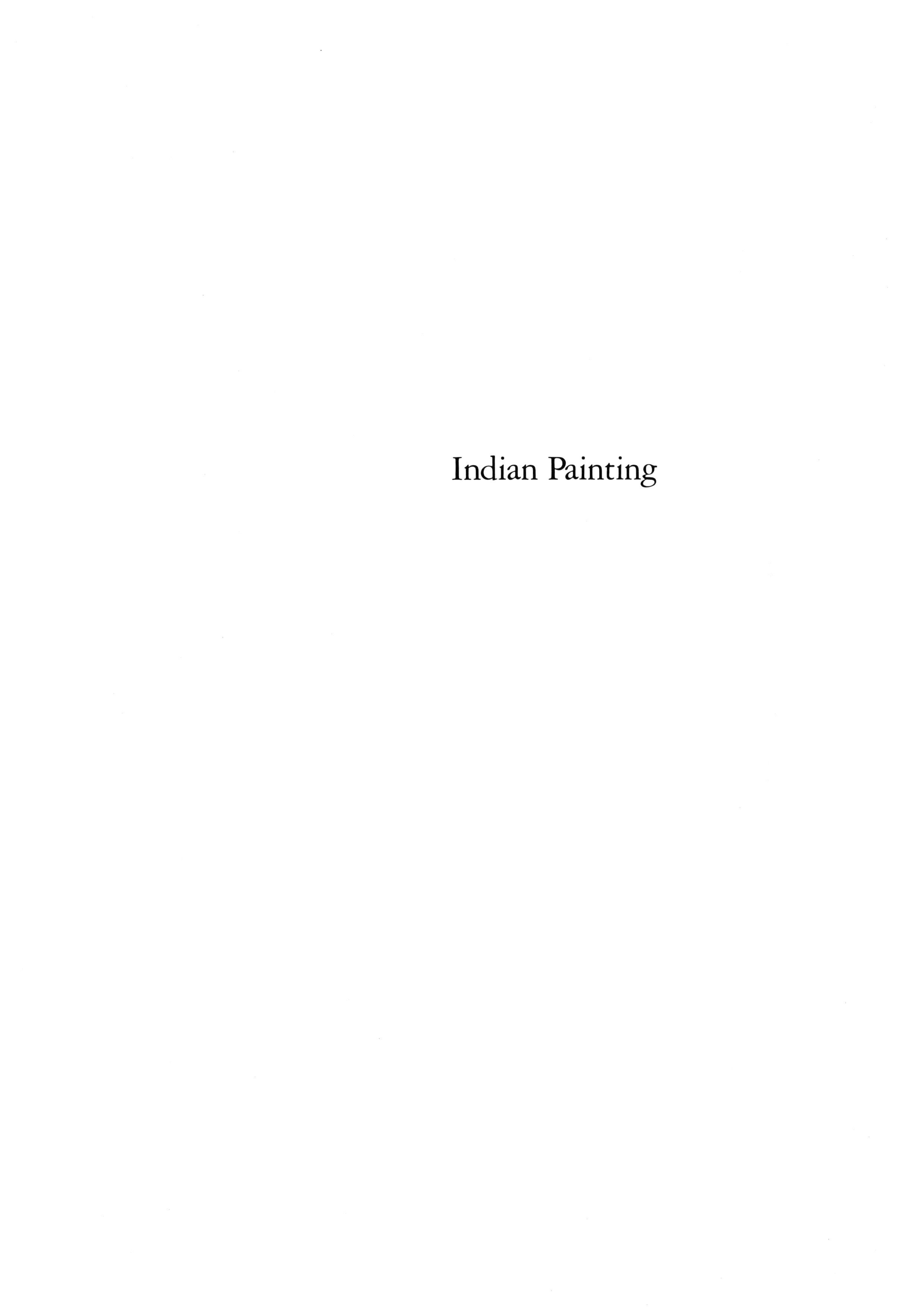

Indian Painting

Volume 1

1000–1700

Indian Painting

A Catalogue of the Los Angeles County Museum of Art Collection

Pratapaditya Pal

Los Angeles County Museum of Art

Published by the
Los Angeles County
Museum of Art
5905 Wilshire Boulevard
Los Angeles, California 90036

in association with
Mapin Publishing Pvt. Ltd.
Chidambaram
Ahmedabad 380 013 India

by arrangement with
Grantha Corporation
80 Cliffedgeway
Middletown, New Jersey
07701

Distributed worldwide
except in Asia by
Harry N. Abrams,
Incorporated, New York,
A Times Mirror Company
100 Fifth Avenue
New York, New York 10011

COVER: detail of *Prince with a Falcon,* Mughal, Akbar period, 1600–1605, [64].

Edited by Joseph N. Newland
Designed by Pamela Patrusky
Photography of the collection by Steve Oliver
Composed in Garamond Three by Andresen Graphic Services, Tucson, Arizona
Printed and bound by Nissha Printing Co., Ltd., Kyoto, Japan

This catalogue was supported by a grant from the National Endowment for the Arts.

In the transliteration of names and terms that occur frequently, diacritical marks have been omitted except in the Bibliography and Index and in the Appendix (where a stricter transliteration system is followed). Numbers in brackets, such as [45], refer to catalogue entries.

Library of Congress Cataloging-in-Publication Data

Pal, Pratapaditya.
Indian painting : a catalogue of the Los Angeles County Museum of Art collection / Pratapaditya Pal.
p. cm.
Includes bibliographical references and index.
Contents: v. 1, 1000–1700.
ISBN 0-8109-3465-5
1. Painting. Indic—Catalogs. 2. Painting—California—Los Angeles—Catalogs. 3. Los Angeles County Museum of Art—Catalogs.
I. Los Angeles County Museum of Art. II. Title.
ND1001.P33 1993
759.954'074'79494—dc20 93-317
CIP

ISBN: 81-85822-22-0 (Mapin)
ISBN: 0-944142-95-8 (Grantha)
ISBN: 0-8109-3465-5 (Abrams)

This book is presented as a benefit of your museum membership. The exhibitions and programs of the Los Angeles County Museum of Art would not be possible without your generous support.

Contents

Foreword

This is the fifth in the series of catalogues raisonnés of the museum's Indian and Southeast Asian art collection. It is the first of two volumes devoted to our large collection of Indian painting and encompasses works created between 1050 and 1700, including many fine early Mughal examples. Most of the paintings here were acquired in 1969 from the renowned collection of Nasli and Alice Heeramaneck. Many important additions, however, have been made under the guidance of Dr. Pratapaditya Pal, who has been in charge of the Indian art department for twenty-three years. (The next volume will cover eighteenth- and nineteenth-century painting and include all the museum's Rajput pictures.)

Like the four volumes that precede it, *Indian Painting* represents another stage in Dr. Pal's synthesis of the field of Asian art history and is especially valuable in its elucidation of complex questions concerning dating and iconography. Certain aspects of Indian painting have been more thoroughly investigated than others—Mughal painting, for example, has received more scholarly attention than Buddhist painting—and those issues that remain largely unresolved add to the difficulty of presenting an accessible overview of the field. The task is nevertheless one to which Dr. Pal has brought considerable expertise, and he demonstrates in the detailed catalogue entries his ability not only to synthesize previous discourse but also to provide interesting commentary on the origin and subject of individual works. In addition, the introduction to this volume, with its discussion of the history of Indian painting before 1000, makes this publication a significant general presentation of the entire spectrum of Indian painting.

Indian Painting and the series of which it is a part illuminate the significance of the museum's collection for understanding the history of Indian art and should prove useful for scholars as well as those generally interested in this great tradition of art.

MICHAEL E. SHAPIRO
Director
Los Angeles County Museum of Art

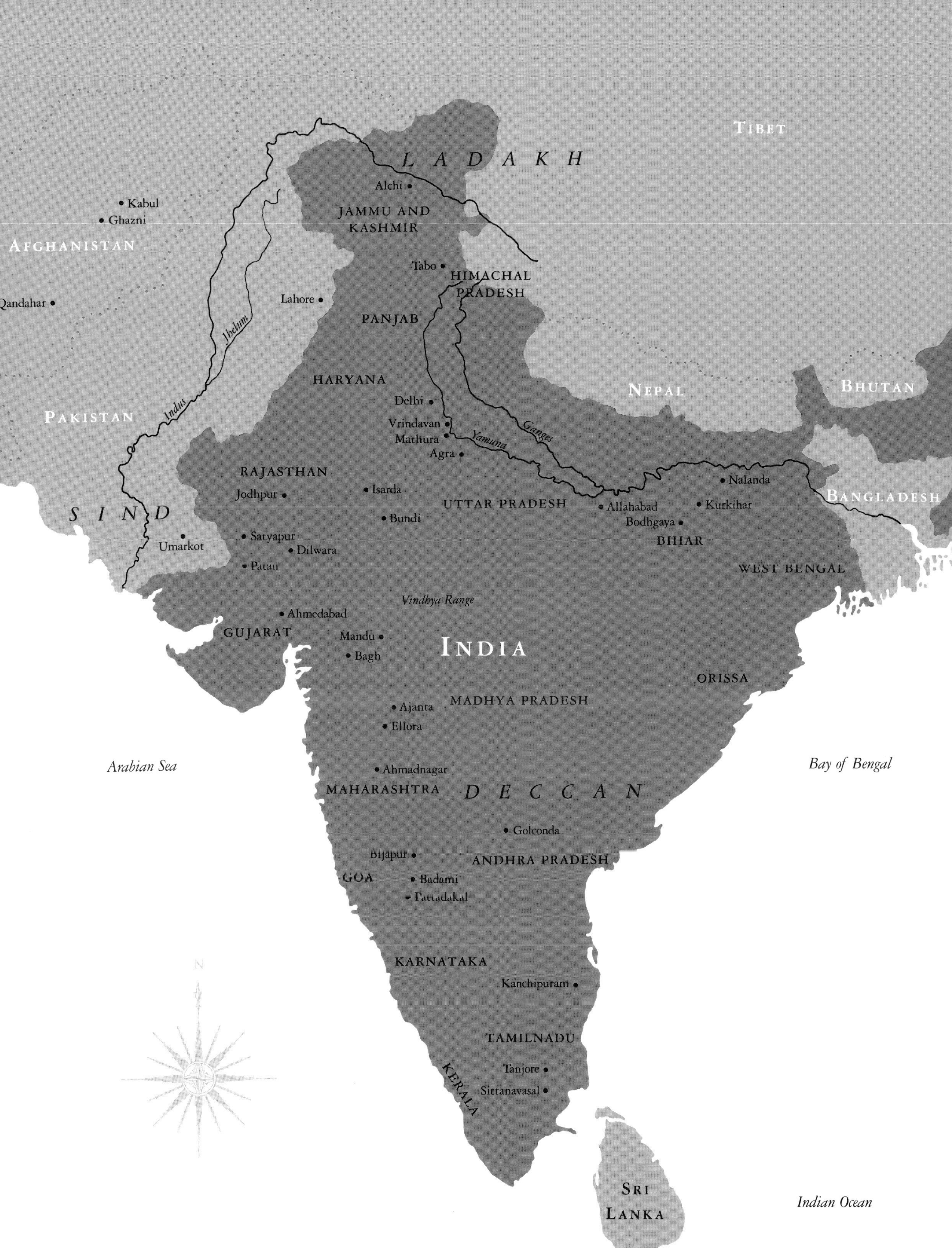

Tibet
Ladakh
Alchi
Kabul
Ghazni
Jammu and Kashmir
Afghanistan
Tabo
Himachal Pradesh
Qandahar
Lahore
Panjab
Jhelum
Haryana
Nepal
Bhutan
Delhi
Pakistan
Indus
Vrindavan
Mathura
Yamuna
Ganges
Agra
Rajasthan
Nalanda
Isarda
Jodhpur
Uttar Pradesh
Allahabad
Kurkihar
Bangladesh
Sind
Bundi
Bodhgaya
Umarkot
Satyapur
Dilwara
Bihar
Patan
West Bengal
Vindhya Range
Ahmedabad
Gujarat
Mandu
India
Bagh
Orissa
Ajanta
Madhya Pradesh
Ellora
Arabian Sea
Bay of Bengal
Ahmadnagar
Maharashtra
Deccan
Golconda
Bijapur
Andhra Pradesh
Goa
Badami
Pattadakal
Karnataka
N
Kanchipuram
Tamilnadu
Kerala
Tanjore
Sittanavasal
Sri Lanka
Indian Ocean

Preface and Acknowledgments

The first of two volumes devoted to the museum's Indian painting collection, this volume covers Buddhist and Jain manuscript illumination, illustrated books dating from the Sultanate period (c. 1200–1526), and Mughal and Deccani painting and calligraphy created between about 1550 and about 1700. The next volume will include all the Rajput pictures as well as later Mughal and Company school works. An overview of the history of Indian painting up to the time covered by the collection is given in the introduction to this volume.

The majority of the paintings in this volume were acquired in 1969 from Nasli and Alice Heeramaneck. Comprehensive as that assemblage was, there were some lacunæ, which have since been filled through both purchase and donations. The names of the donors are recognized in the individual catalogue entries, and it is a great pleasure for me to thank them all for their generous support. In addition I must also thank the dealers for bringing to our attention pictures that would otherwise have remained unknown and who have often waited patiently, as the museum acquisition process is particularly slow.

Compared with the other volumes in the series of catalogues raisonnés of the museum's Indian and Southeast Asian collection, this one has been the longest in gestation for several reasons. By the time the manuscript was completed in May 1992, the most daunting task proved to be the decipherment, transcription, and translation of the texts that accompany the paintings. Covering as the catalogue does almost seven centuries of the history of Indian painting, including early Buddhist, Jain, and a great deal of Islamic material, the textual material is in several languages. This required the cooperation of several scholars, who also had other commitments to attend to.

Many others have contributed to this catalogue directly or indirectly. While it will not be possible to name them all, it is a pleasure to express my gratitude for their cooperation. Over the years, many scholars have visited the museum and have made useful comments on the pictures. Noteworthy among them are Dr. Asok Das, Dr. B. N. Goswamy, Messrs. Karl Khandalavala, Terence McInerney, Robert Skelton, and Dr. Ellen Smart. For reading and translating the Sanskrit inscriptions in the Buddhist and Jain manuscripts, I am indebted to Dr. Gouriswar Bhattacharya. The bulk of the Persian and Arabic inscriptions were read and translated by Mr. Simon Digby and Dr. Zahra Faridany-Akhavan. However, I am also indebted to Dr. Z. A. Desai and Professor

Wheeler Thackston for additional help in resolving knotty linguistic issues. Wherever their translations have been used, the translators have been duly acknowledged. Another person outside the museum to be mentioned is Emeritus Professor Roy C. Craven, who kindly read the entire manuscript and made helpful comments.

I take great pleasure in thanking the following individuals in the museum for their moral encouragement as well as substantial material help: Victoria Blyth-Hill and Dr. John Twilley, Conservation; Dr. Bruce Davis, Prints and Drawings; Anne Diederick and Eleanor Hartman, Art Research Library; Dr. Janice Leoshko, who read the entire manuscript, Dr. Stephen A. Markel, who helped with countless details, Esther Medina, and Tom Nixon, Indian and Southeast Asian Art; Dr. Thomas W. Lentz, formerly of Ancient and Islamic Art; Edward Maeder, Costumes and Textiles; Joseph N. Newland, Dr. Susan Caroselli, and Nancy Carcione, Publications; Pamela Patrusky, Graphic Design; Steve Oliver, Photographic Services; Dr. Earl A. Powell III, formerly director. A special round of applause is due to Steve Oliver for photography, Joseph Newland for editing, and Pamela Patrusky for design.

PRATAPADITYA PAL
Senior Curator
Indian and Southeast Asian Art

NOTE: *After this book was typeset, important books on Indian painting by Dr. Amina Okada and Dr. Milo C. Beach were published. They include a number of the museum's paintings, but references to these two books could not be included in this catalogue.*

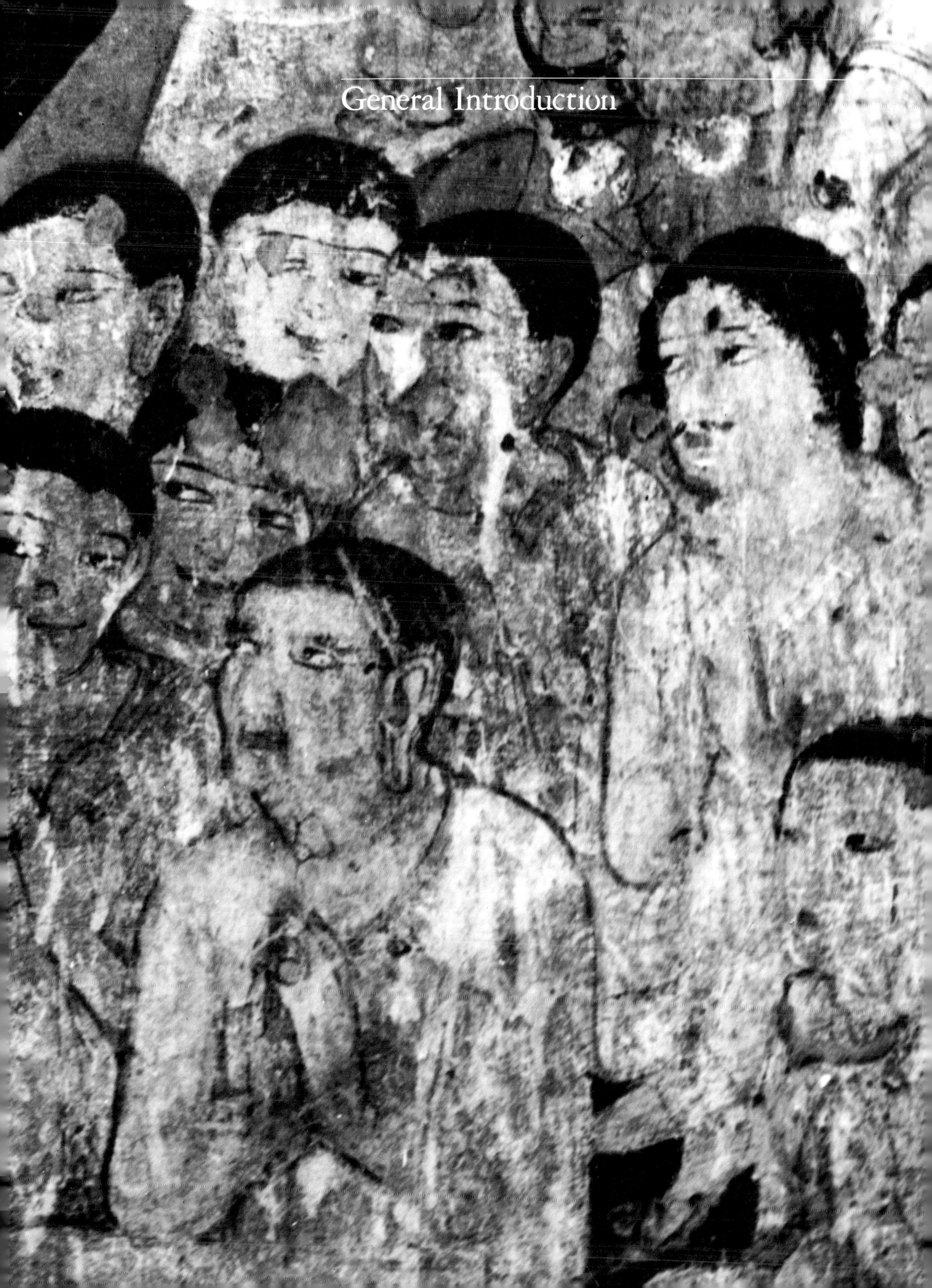

General Introduction

Drawing, shading, decorative design, and coloring
are the four basic elements in a picture.
Masters applaud superior draughtsmanship,
while connoisseurs appreciate finesse in shading.
Women prefer ornamental virtuosity,
and the general public is seduced by rich colors.
A good artist should create his picture in such a manner
that it satisfies all different tastes.

VISHNUDHARMOTTARAPURANA
Book 10, chapter 41, verses 10–12

General Introduction

The Indian paintings catalogued in this volume were executed over a period of seven centuries, from about A.D. 1000 until 1700. At the beginning of the period the subcontinent was divided into numerous kingdoms, both large and small. Only one small kingdom in Sind (Pakistan) was ruled by a Muslim dynasty; otherwise the rulers as well as the ruled followed the three religions known today as Hinduism, Buddhism, and Jainism. Hinduism was the predominant religion, but both the Buddhist and Jain communities were sizable. Although not much painting has survived from before the period, what does remain, together with literary evidence, demonstrates that murals were common in both sacred and secular buildings. Illuminated books were yet to become popular, but religious and narrative paintings on cloth were used by adherents of all three religions. Portraiture was familiar as well, but no example has survived. There were also large numbers of tribal peoples across the land, some of whom left evidence of their aesthetic activities in caves and rock-shelters.

The seven centuries during which the catalogued pictures were created can be conveniently divided into three periods: Pala, Sultanate, and Mughal. Though there were other kingdoms dominant in the north and the west during the eleventh and twelfth centuries, only the Pala dynasty, which ruled mostly in Bihar and Bengal, is relevant here. The Buddhist illuminated manuscripts in the collection were produced during their rule (c. 800–1200). If the Jains residing in the Pala kingdom used illustrated books, none has survived.

Although the Muslim ruler Mahmud of Ghazni (r. 986–1030), in present-day Afghanistan, repeatedly attacked India between 1001 and his death in 1030, the real founder of Islamic rule in northern India was Muhammad Ghori (d. 1206). After conquering Ghazni in 1173, he moved down into the subcontinent and by 1192 had brought much of the Gangetic valley under his control by defeating and killing Jaichand of Kanauj. For the next three centuries and a quarter much of northern India was ruled by Muslim rulers known as *sultans,* and hence the period is characterized as the Sultanate period.

The next period of Indian history, stretching from 1526 until 1857, is generally referred to as the Mughal period. Derived from the word *Mongol,* the expression *Mughal* is applied to the dynasty founded by Babur, who traced his descent from the Mongol Chingiz (Genghis) Khan. A Timurid prince from Ferghana in Central Asia, he defeated Ibrahim Lodi in 1526 and occupied the throne at Delhi until his death in 1530.

Babur's son Humayun lost the kingdom after ruling for a decade and fled to Iran. He regained it in 1556 but died the following year. His son Akbar (r. 1556–1605) expanded the empire from Kandahar in Afghanistan in the north to the three Deccani kingdoms of Ahmadnagar, Bijapur, and Golconda—which paid him allegiance—in the south, and from Gujarat in the west to Bengal in the east. Akbar's son Jahangir (r. 1605–27) kept most of it intact, as did his successor, Shah Jahan (r. 1628–58). The next ruler, Aurangzeb (r. 1658–1707), ultimately succeeded in vanquishing the three Deccani kingdoms and thereby extending the empire to its maximum geographical extent, but in the process he bankrupted the treasury and sowed the seed of the subsequent downfall of the empire. Thereafter, the Mughal empire disintegrated steadily until the British crown assumed sovereignty in 1858.

The works catalogued in this volume include illustrated manuscripts, both sacred and secular; religious paintings on cloth; portraits and genre pictures; as well as mythological and rhetorical works. Also discussed are a number of examples of Islamic calligraphy, which are often mounted back-to-back with pictures. With the exception of all the Buddhist and two of the Jain manuscripts, which are of palm leaves, and three paintings on cloth, all the works in the collection are on paper.[1] Although the Buddhists in eastern India stopped producing books after 1250, the Jains in the western part of the subcontinent were prolific during the Sultanate period. Illustrated books were produced for Hindu and Muslim patrons as well during this period, and a small group is included in the collection.

The largest number of paintings catalogued here belongs to the early Mughal period (1526–1707). The majority was rendered for the Mughal court, but some were produced for the independent Muslim courts that flourished in the southern region known as the Deccan plateau. Mughal and Deccani pictures were much more varied in type than those from the Sultanate period. For instance, the book illustrations of the Mughal period reveal a greater diversity of subject matter, including histories and romances. Moreover, a large number of Mughal works consists of court portraits and genre representations not encountered earlier. There are also examples of both Indian and Iranian calligraphy in the Arabic script. The paintings and the calligraphic panels were assembled in albums that served as a sort of portable picture gallery. The pictures and calligraphic panels were often surrounded by elaborately painted and ornamental borders, where one encounters some of the most spontaneous and liveliest of all Mughal genre studies.

INDIAN PAINTING BEFORE 1000

Although the museum's earliest examples of Indian painting are from the first quarter of the eleventh century, the history of painting on the subcontinent goes back at least to the third millennium B.C. The earliest extant evidence for painting occurs mostly on ceramics from the Harappan culture (c. 3000–1500 B.C.) discovered at several excavated sites stretching from Pakistan in the northwest to Maharashtra in the south.[2] Rendered both in monochrome and polychrome, they consist of depictions of fauna (FIG. 1) and flora, human figures as well as composite creatures, and a wide variety of geometrical and decorative patterns. Some of these motifs very likely had religious significance, while others may have been symbolic. For the most part the plants, animals, and human figures are executed both conceptually and minimally but not without a certain degree of naturalism. For instance, the artists took particular care in depicting the pipal tree and the bull, both of which have remained favorite motifs in Indian art. Even though most of the surviving examples of painted pottery are shards, there is no doubt that the prehistoric

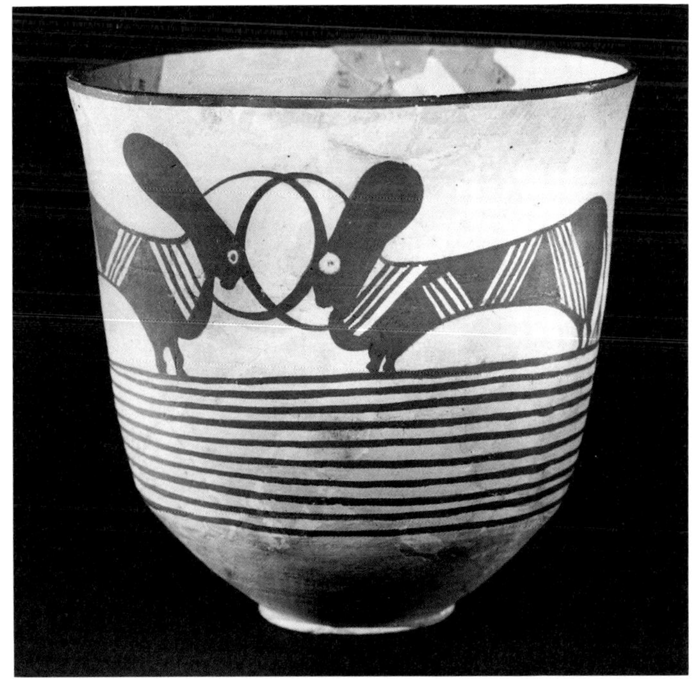

FIGURE 1
Pottery vessel with bull design, Damb Sadaat, Quettaq Valley, Pakistan, c. 2700–2300 B.C., height 14 in (35.5 cm), American Museum of Natural History, New York (photograph courtesy of Department of Library Services).

Indian artists drew with both imagination and graphic clarity in abstract as well as naturalistic modes. Some of the decorative motifs seen on these potsherds can be recognized in textile patterns through the ages.

The other early evidence of painting survives in caves and rock-shelters extending over a large area of the subcontinent.[3] The largest group has been discovered in Madhya Pradesh, but over the last few decades important centers have been found in other parts of the country as well. While not as old as the prehistoric painted potsherds, the rock-paintings do reveal similar interest in the animal world. Even though a wide variety of expressions may be discerned at different sites, there is a basic stylistic consistency among them, as there is between them and the earlier pictures on ceramics. An important thematic difference lies, however, in the preponderance of hunting scenes among the rock-paintings. While animals and humans are prominent in the prehistoric potsherds, they are not shown in combat. The palette is limited in both types of paintings, and by and large they bear little relationship to later pictorial traditions.

The story of Indian painting of the historical period really begins a century or so before the start of the Christian era in two Buddhist cave shrines at Ajanta in Maharashtra. The paintings are in caves 9 and 10, and although they are in very poor condition, one can discern their close stylistic kinship to the narrative reliefs in early Buddhist monuments such as those at Bharhut, Sanchi, and Amaravati.[4] The fragmentary paintings in the Jogimara caves at Sarguja in Madhya Pradesh also are contemporary to this early Ajanta phase. The paucity of material is somewhat compensated for by early literature, which abounds with references to painting. Such references are found particularly in the great Indian epics, the *Mahabharata* and the *Ramayana,* and in early Buddhist and Jain literature. A form of painting used frequently by storytellers was known as the *yamapaṭa.* Yama is the god of death, and the word *paṭa* means a picture on cloth. Apparently itinerant bards went around singing tales about the afterlife in Yama's realm and used scroll paintings to make their narration more graphic. This tradition of recitation with pictures still survives in village India, and in a sense, the great *Hamzanama* [46] pictures done for the Mughal Emperor Akbar served a similar narrative purpose.

Most surviving paintings from the historical period, except the rock-pictures, are religious in content. However, contemporary literature does inform us of the use of paintings to decorate both public and private buildings. A picture gallery and a portrait gallery were often integral parts of palaces, as may still be seen in surviving palaces of the Mughal period, and common folk decorated their doors and walls with divine images and auspicious symbols, as they still do in villages. Learning the art of painting was considered an essential part of every urbane and cultured person's education and was also a desirable accomplishment of the courtesan.

In addition to preserving the earliest remnants of painting of the historical period, the monastic complex at Ajanta also has the largest corpus of surviving murals from ancient India. Many of its finest paintings were executed during the Gupta period (c. 320–600). At the time Ajanta was part of the local Vakataka kingdom, whose rulers had matrimonial relations with the imperial Guptas. Murals of this period also survive in fragmentary condition at Bagh (Madhya Pradesh), at Badami and Pattadakal (Karnataka), and at Pithalkhora (Maharashtra).

It was during the Gupta period that technical books on art and iconography known as *śilpaśāstra* began to be compiled. One such important text known as the *Chitrasutra* (Aphorism about art), probably redacted in the seventh century but incorporating earlier material, is embedded in the encyclopedic religious text known as the *Vishnudharmottarapurana,* from which the verse used as the epigraph to this introduction has been quoted. Indeed, the focus of the treatise is on painting, which demonstrates how important and widespread this artistic form must have been in Gupta India. The text discusses at length the technical aspects of art as well as aesthetic issues. It is clear from this and other early theoretical works that line and color were regarded as the two most important elements of painting. Although one does find both shading and modeling with colors in the Ajanta murals as well as the use of a varied palette, by and large Indian artists preferred to use colors in bright, intense masses. In drawing, the emphasis is always on the expressive outline, which has remained the hallmark of Indian painting of all ages. Indeed, even after a strong influence was exerted by the European pictorial tradition in the sixteenth century, Indian artists continued to prefer their traditional mode, where a strongly linear definition of form and areas of unmodulated color remained the principal aesthetic concerns. The idea of the "suggestive outline" and manipulating colors to create effects of light and shade never did capture the Indian painter's imagination. Even at Ajanta, where volume is suggested through shading and by tonal gradations, the clarity of the outline remains paramount.

There is disagreement among scholars as to the exact date of the surviving paintings at Ajanta. One view is that all the murals were done in the second half of the fifth century in a burst of activity during the reign of the Vakataka monarch Harishena (r. c. 465–90).[5] The king himself was a Hindu and was not directly involved. However, some of his ministers and feudatory princes were ardent Buddhists and, along with rich merchants, were the major patrons at Ajanta. The site is situated not far from the trade route that crossed the plateau, linking the eastern regions with the important ports along the western coast. The inscriptions in the caves also mention resident monks as donors. With the loss of Vakataka political power soon after Harishena's death, the resources for the Buddhists appear to have dried up, and very likely the artists moved on. Other scholars, however, do not subscribe to this view and consider the caves to have been excavated and adorned over a longer time span, stretching from about 450 until 550 or even later.[6]

FIGURE 2
Ajanta, Maharashtra, cave 17, interior, detail of mural of the Buddha preaching before an audience, wall painting (photograph courtesy of American Institute of Indian Studies, Varanasi).

FIGURE 3
Ajanta, Maharashtra, cave 17, porch, detail of mural of Visvantara Jataka, wall painting (photograph courtesy of Asian Art Archives, University of Michigan, Ann Arbor).

FIGURE 4
Ajanta, Maharashtra, cave 17, porch, detail of floral decoration, ceiling painting (photograph courtesy of Asian Art Archives, University of Michigan, Ann Arbor).

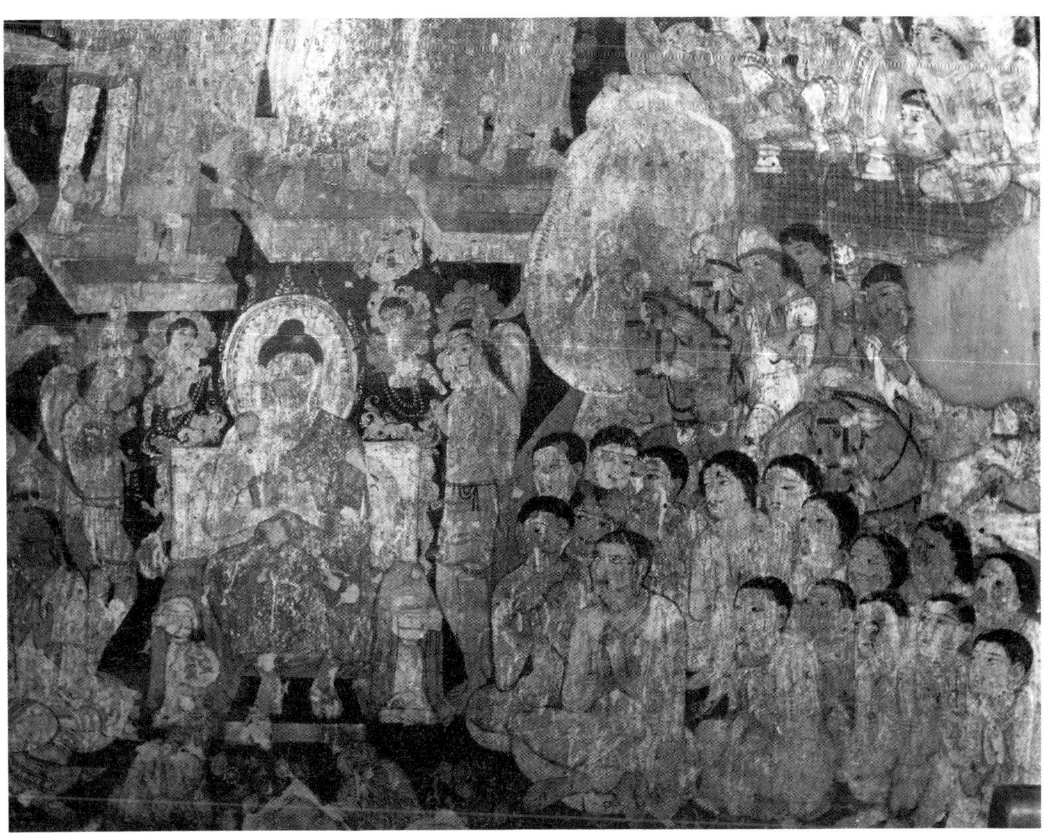

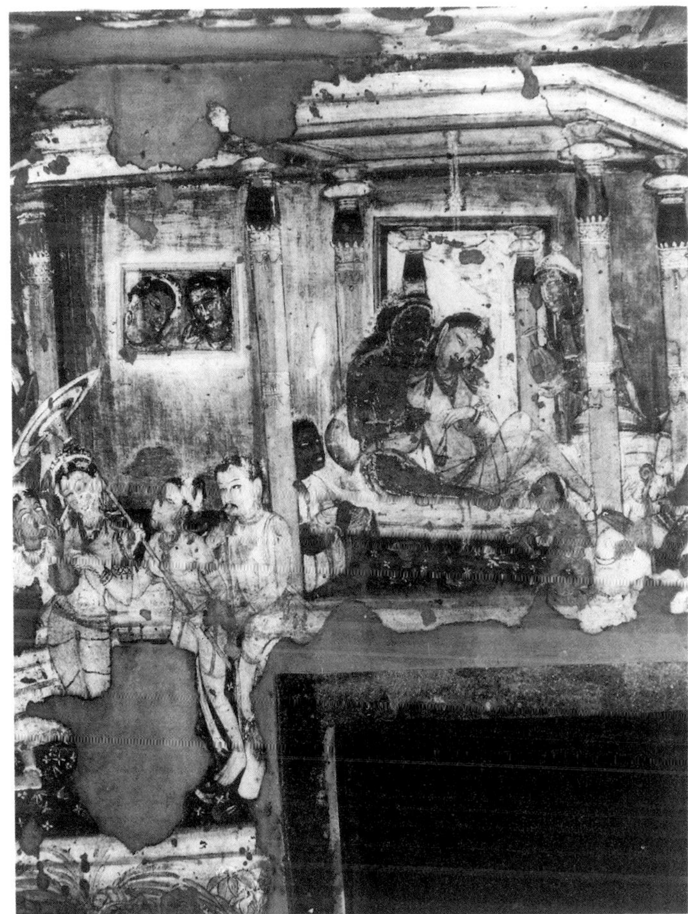

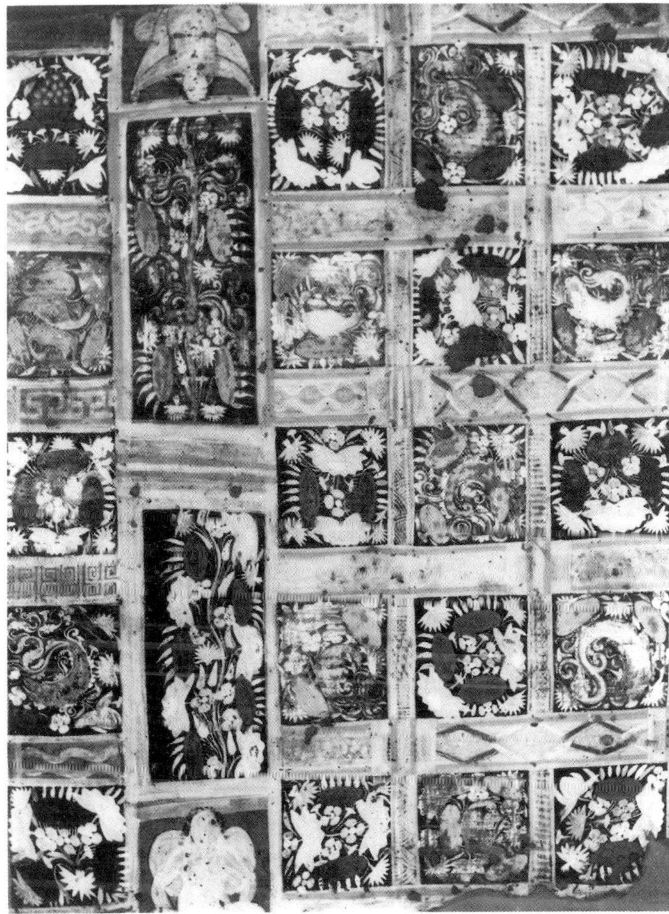

Most of the paintings of the Vakataka or Mahayana phase are now concentrated in caves 1, 2, 16, and 17 (FIGS. 2–5). The ceilings are beautifully decorated with a variety of designs consisting of lively floral and geometric motifs

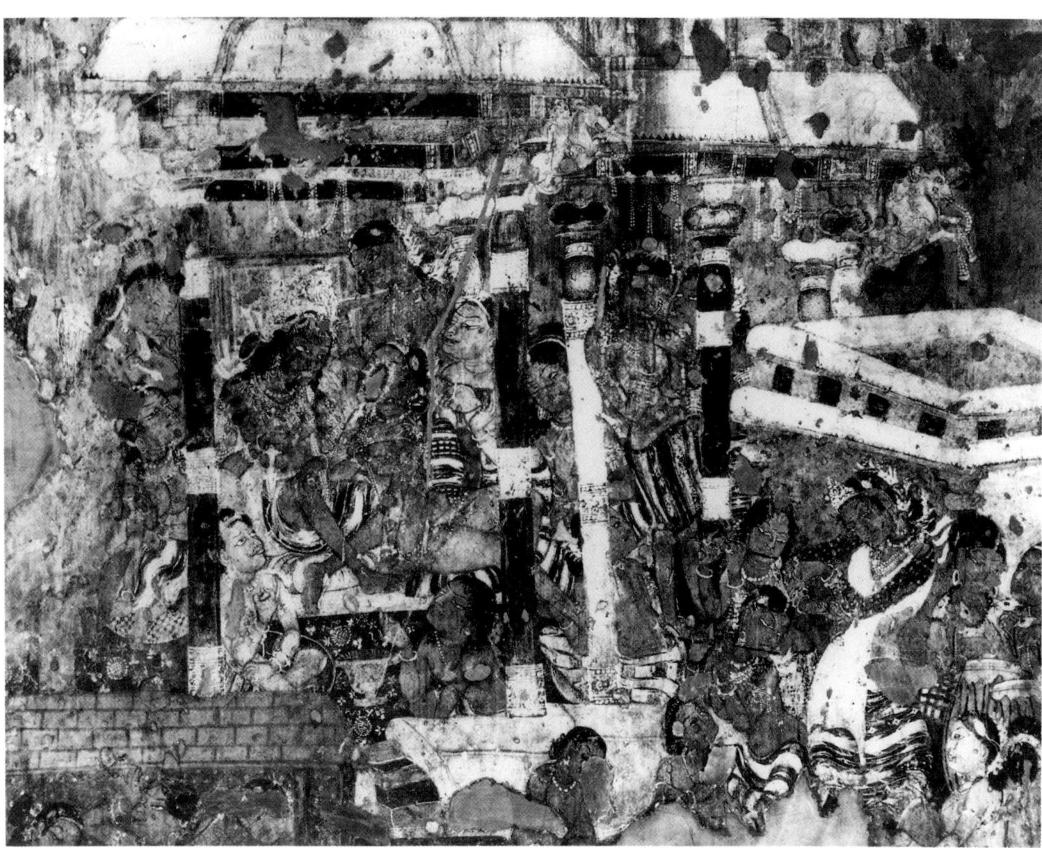

FIGURE 5
Ajanta, Maharashtra, cave 1, interior, detail of mural of Mahajanaka Jataka, wall painting (photograph courtesy of Asian Art Archives, University of Michigan, Ann Arbor).

as well as some animals, and the walls are covered with sprawling, overlapping compositions depicting legends of the Buddha's past lives known as *jataka.* At least two different styles can be discerned in the Mahayana paintings at Ajanta. The murals in caves 16 and 17 exude a sense of confidence in the draughtsmanship and assured handling of composition and coloring that are taken to indicate an early phase. In the murals of caves 1 and 2 one notes a greater nervous energy in the exaggerated posturing of the figures, a stronger penchant for ornamentation, a certain manneristic though sensuous grace, and the use of stronger highlights, especially with white, which is sparingly employed in the earlier murals. Some of the innovations and motifs that have a freshness in the murals of caves 16 and 17 have become clichés in caves 1 and 2.

The Ajanta murals clearly mirror the rich and sensuous life at the Vakataka court and of Gupta India generally. The city life described so eloquently by the greatest Sanskrit poet Kalidasa (fifth century) in the style of literature known as *kāvya* has been vividly transformed in brilliant line and color by the unknown master artists who painted the walls at Ajanta, ostensibly for the edification and pleasure of Buddhist monks and devotees. Significantly, one of the inscriptions proclaims that the caves will afford "enjoyment of well-known comforts in all seasons." The colorful and vibrant murals at Ajanta are admirable not only for the meticulously observed details of nature and the urban landscape—including architecture and furnishings, elegant attire, and alluring ornaments—but also for perceptive delineations of a variety of human characters, expressions, and moods. They are no less engaging for the intensity of their narrative clarity and power, for the sense of organic rhythm that moves like waves from one composition to another, and above all for their manifest spirituality.

The lyrical, sensuous, and elegant style of painting encountered at Ajanta appears to have prevailed with little change for about another two centuries.

It was employed in other parts of the country and for Hindu subjects as well. Unfortunately not much has survived, but what remains in the Buddhist caves at Bagh and Pithalkhora and the Hindu cave temples at Badami makes their stylistic kinship with Ajanta clear. There are differences in the figural proportions and types and in the expressiveness of the representations, but by and large the emphasis remains on the articulately defined outline despite the suggestion of modeling both by shading and by added highlights. The coloring is not as rich and varied as at Ajanta. For instance, lapis lazuli, applied abundantly in Ajanta, is conspicuously absent in these murals.

Remnants of mural painting belonging to the second half of the first millennium A.D. have survived mostly in southern India. There is little evidence that the numerous extant Hindu and Jain temples in the north were adorned with wall paintings. The Buddhists, however, made use of murals for both decorative and didactic purposes. Recent excavations at the monastic complex of Nalanda (Bihar) revealed traces of eleventh-century murals stylistically akin to the Buddhist manuscript illuminations in the collection [1–9].[7] A rich array of murals in a very distinct style that may be characterized as deriving from the ancient tradition prevailing in Kashmir has also survived in some of the monasteries in Ladakh (Jammu and Kashmir) and Himachal Pradesh. The most extensive series occur in the Alchi temple complex in Ladakh and in Tabo (Himachal Pradesh).[8] The murals at Tabo, particularly those that can be dated to the tenth and eleventh centuries, were probably rendered by Kashmiri artists (FIG. 6). The story of the murals at Alchi is more complicated. Executed mostly in the thirteenth century, they are rendered in a variety of modes deriving inspiration from styles that prevailed in both Kashmir and Bihar approximately two centuries earlier. Although these murals are generally regarded as examples of Tibetan painting, their importance for the history of Indian painting cannot be overemphasized. Apart from continuing the pictorial tradition of Ajanta, these murals constitute a significant body of surviving Buddhist paintings of northern India of the period.

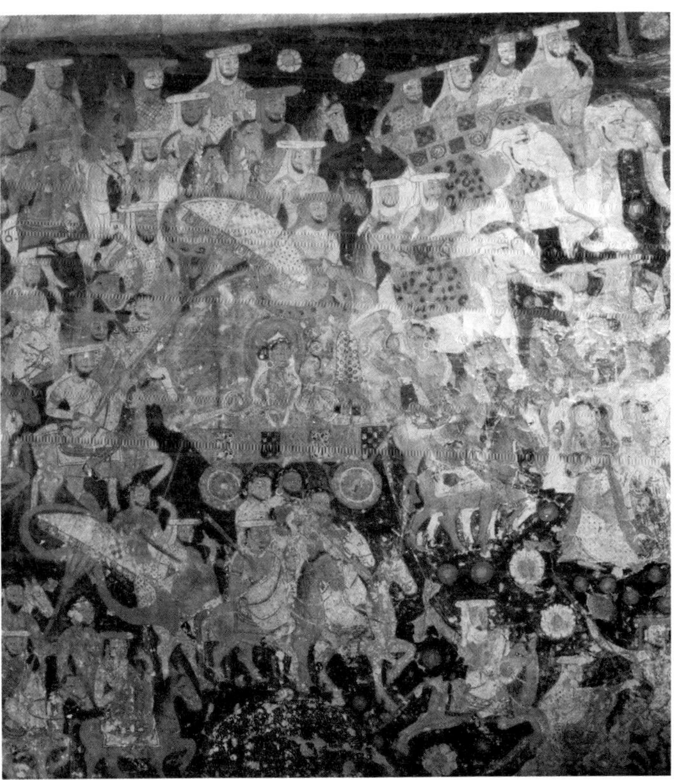

FIGURE 6
Tabo, Dukhang, detail of scene from the life of Sakyamuni Buddha, c. 1050, wall painting (photograph by Thomas Pritzker).

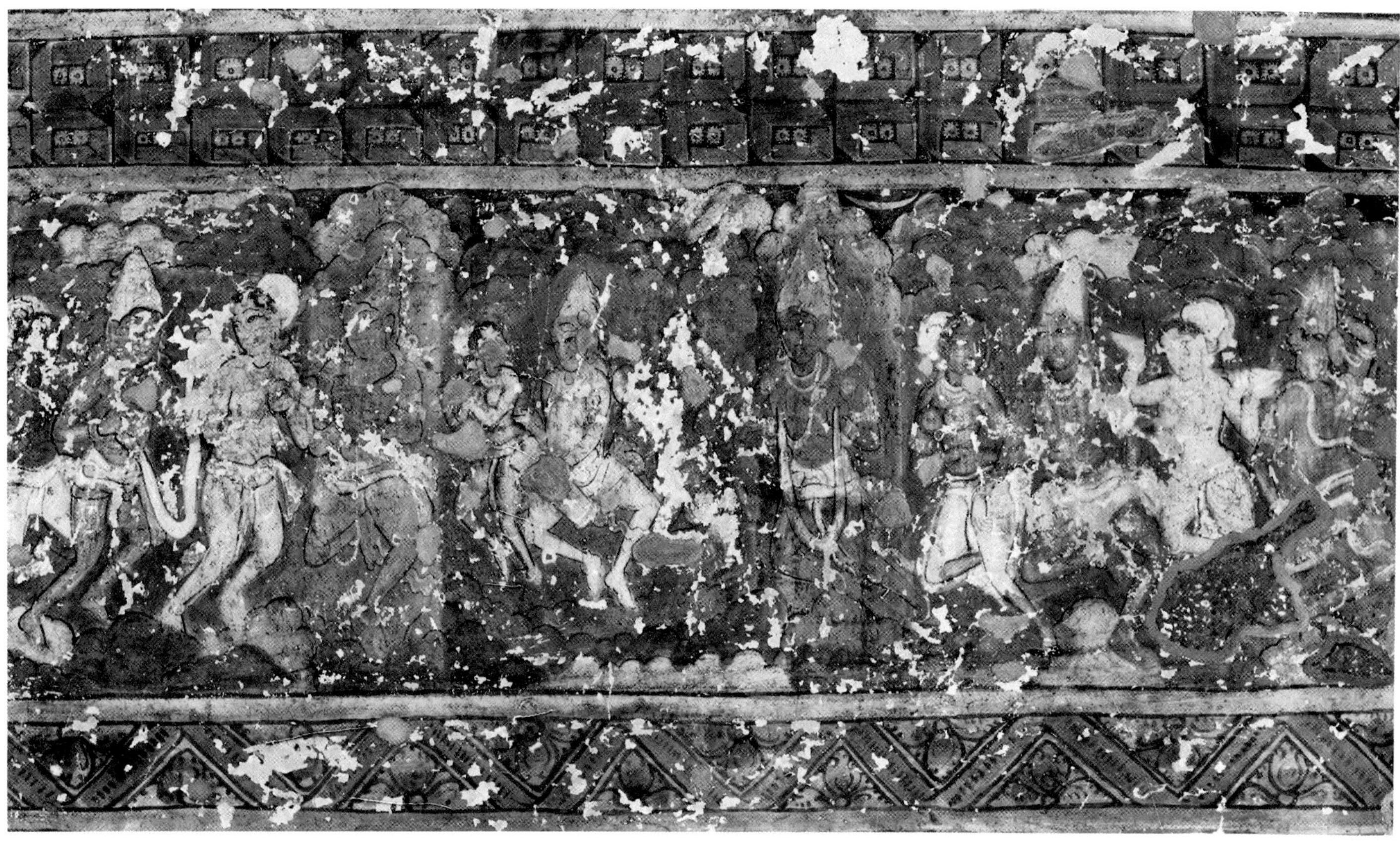

FIGURE 7
Ellora, Maharashtra, cave 1, frieze of celestial couples against clouds, late eighth century, wall painting (photograph courtesy of American Institute of Indian Studies, Varanasi).

Among the southern sites, several of the rock-cut temples at Ellora (Maharashtra) have fragmentary remains of three different dates, the earliest belonging to the eighth century (FIG. 7). Contemporary murals may also be seen in the small shrines in the courtyard of the Kailasanatha temple at Coonjeevaram or Kanchipuram (Tamilnadu). They have been cleaned and restored in recent years and are welcome additions to the history of painting on the subcontinent. Another early southern site is Sittanavasal (Tamilnadu), where some engaging murals have survived in Jain caves. Some of the murals at Sittanavasal are dated to the seventh and others to the ninth century. The earlier murals are stylistically related to the late Ajanta paintings, while the later specimens are akin to the Jain paintings at Ellora. Finally, mention should be made of murals in the impressive Chola temple called Brihadisvara at Tanjore or Thanjavur (Tamilnadu). Built by the great Chola monarch Rajaraja (r. 985–1014), the temple was begun in 1003 and completed in 1010. Hence the surviving murals are among the very few precisely dated documents of ancient Indian painting, although because of their situation they are not easily viewed. The earliest Buddhist manuscript illuminations in the collection [1] are roughly contemporaneous to the Tanjore temple murals but are far apart stylistically.

At most of these later sites there is a distinct change from Ajanta in the way murals are accommodated on the walls as well as in presentation. The emphasis on narrative is eschewed for more hieratic subjects with a stronger accent on the iconic. No longer does one encounter the expansive and panoramic compositions providing glimpses of contemporary life and culture. Instead, divine beings are portrayed either in iconic forms or in encapsulated myths. The compositions are limited since the scenes are divided into panels by means of borders decorated with geometric or floral patterns. This mode of representation remained unaltered for almost a millennium in murals, manuscript illuminations, and scroll paintings. A second noteworthy difference, visible in the murals at Ellora and elsewhere and in Jain manuscript illustrations, is that increasingly the style became even more linear, with limited modeling and little tonal variation of color. Volume is indicated more by the plasticity of outline than by modulated colors, as one notes in the Buddhist manuscript illuminations [1–3]. No source of light within the picture plane is indicated, and the colors are applied in flat, monochromatic areas bounded by the outlines. Emotion is suggested by gestures and postures rather than facial expressions. There is also a tendency to exaggerate the postures and resort to distortions of forms, while many of the earlier conventions continue to be used with a mannered elegance. This is clearly evident in the style adopted for Jain book illuminations, which is directly related to the Ellora paintings. In fact, even the unnatural convention of extending the further eye of a head seen in profile or three-quarter view, so characteristic of Jain painting, appears first at Ellora.

BUDDHIST, JAIN, AND HINDU MANUSCRIPT ILLUMINATIONS

By the eleventh century the Buddhists in the monasteries of eastern India and the Jains in the west and south had begun to illustrate some of their religious books. These books were made of loosely bound palm-leaf folios, usually about two feet long and about two inches high. In the northwest region of the subcontinent birch bark was preferred to palm leaves. Both palm-leaf and birch-bark books were provided with wood covers.

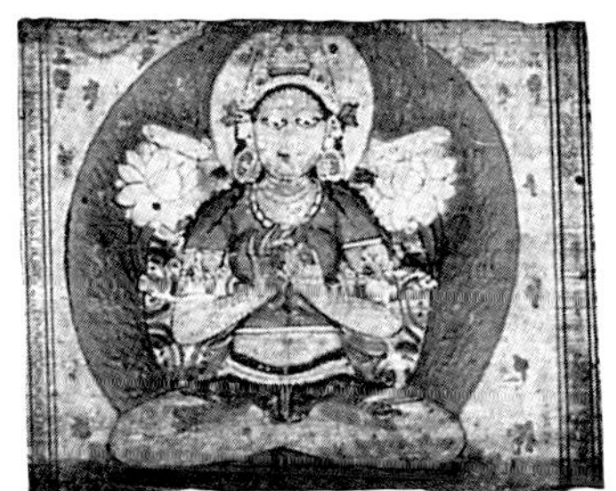

FIGURE 8
"Goddess Prajnaparamita," from a *Dharanisamgraha* manuscript, [3A].

The illuminated Buddhist manuscripts in the collection (FIG. 8) were produced for patrons associated with the monasteries of Bihar, West Bengal, and Bangladesh. Buddhism flourished in this region under the enlightened patronage of the Palas, some of whom may have been Buddhists, and other local Buddhist rulers. Donating books to monasteries was deemed an important act of piety. Other forms of painting executed during this period, such as murals and religious paintings on cloth, have not survived. Buddhist monasteries were targets of both Hindu and Muslim monarchs, and most were effectively destroyed or fell into disuse by the fourteenth century. Beyond surviving illuminated books on palm leaves and their wooden covers, like the splendid group in the museum, one can form an idea of what Buddhist murals and scroll paintings looked like from examples preserved in Nepal, Tibet, and Burma. The art of both Tibet and Burma was strongly influenced by that of the Pala empire.

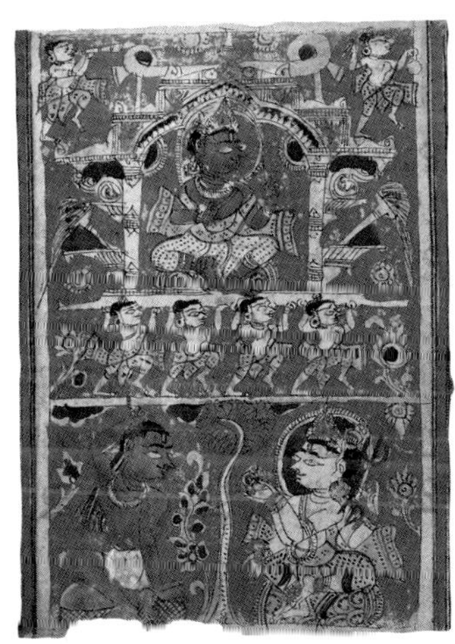

FIGURE 9
"Initiation and Haircutting of Parsvanatha," from a *Kalpasutra* manuscript, [12A].

Although surviving Indian books, primarily of the Buddhists, go back at least to the fifth century if not earlier, the tradition of illustrating them appears to have begun much later. The tradition in fact may have originated in Central Asia and subsequently been adopted in India. By the second century, when the Buddhists began composing such important Mahayana texts (sutras) as the *Prajnaparamita* and the *Lotus Sutra,* books themselves came to be considered as worthy of veneration.[9]

The Buddhists' reverence for their holy books appears to have spread also to the Jains and the Hindus. Like the Buddhists in eastern India, by the eleventh century the Jains in western India began to illustrate their books (FIG. 9). Illuminated Jain books, also made from palm leaves and with painted wooden covers, have been found both in western India and in the south. The existing early Jain palm-leaf manuscripts and their covers, produced between 1000 and 1300, show a less-varied repertoire than surviving Buddhist manuscripts, but the stylistic kinship between the two traditions is unmistakable. After 1300, while Buddhism faded out in India, the Jains appear to have become more prolific in commissioning religious books. There was a thematic expansion, and the style too changed notably.

Although Hindu religious texts called *purana* ("ancient tradition"), compiled mostly between the fourth and the ninth centuries, do recommend the practice of worshipping and donating books, few Hindu manuscripts, with or without illustrations, of any antiquity have survived in India. We know from Cambodian inscriptions that manuscripts of the *Mahabharata* and the *Ramayana* were being prepared as early as the sixth century, and Hindu manuscripts preserved in Nepal go back to the seventh. The earliest illustrated Hindu books have been preserved in Nepal, but none is earlier than the twelfth century.

Both the Buddhists and Jains generally deposited their manuscripts in libraries attached to their monasteries or temples. Although all Buddhist monasteries in India except some in Ladakh and the Chittagong hill tracts in Bangladesh were destroyed, a substantial corpus of books copied and illustrated in the monasteries of Bihar and undivided Bengal have been preserved in Nepal, Tibet, and as far away as Japan. A greater number of Jain books have been preserved in the libraries (*sastrabhandar*) attached to their temples, but again not too many are earlier than the eleventh century. Fewer Jain illustrated palm-leaf manuscripts exist than those of the Buddhists. However, whereas the Buddhist tradition died in India after the thirteenth century, the Jain tradition gathered momentum and flourished until the age of printing dawned in India early in the last century. The sudden spurt of interest in illustrated books among the Jains appears to coincide with the introduction of paper, which the Jains adopted with enthusiasm in the fourteenth century.

Hindus appear to have preferred donating books to individual brahmans rather than to institutions, which may have precipitated further the destruction of early Hindu books. That the tradition of illumination was not unknown among the Hindus is evident from manuscripts in Nepal as well as the continuity of the tradition in Orissa, although no surviving illustrated book there can be dated earlier than the seventeenth century. The conservative nature of the Hindu tradition is evident from the fact that even after paper became readily available in many parts of the country the Hindus continued to use palm leaves, particularly for their religious books. The use of illustrated books made from paper very likely gained currency among Hindus in northern India as late as the fifteenth century, after prolonged contacts with Muslims.

The substantial discussions in the sectional introductions to the Buddhist and Jain book illuminations in the collection may be supplemented here with a few general observations. Even a cursory comparison will demonstrate that both traditions were limited in the variety of books that were illustrated. Indian Buddhists seem to have preferred to illustrate primarily three texts: the *Prajnaparamita* (Perfection of wisdom), the *Pancharaksha* (Five protective charms), and the *Dharanisamgraha* (Collection of charms). None of the three has any narrative content. The first is a purely philosophical work, and the other two are compilations of charms and rites. All three manuscripts are generally adorned with images of deities, Buddhas, and bodhisattvas, whose presence is supposed to protect the books from coming to harm. In the case of the *Pancharaksha* [7] and the *Dharanisamgraha* [3], the pictures also help the devotee to visualize the divine forms described in the charms. In addition, it was customary to add eight major events, known as the Eight Great Miracles, from the life of Buddha Sakyamuni to the *Prajnaparamita* text or its covers (e.g., [1]). The exact purpose of this convention is not known, but very likely the scenes contributed to homologizing the words of the Buddha with his life. In any event, these and a few other incidents from his life, which are encountered occasionally [4], form the only narrative themes in Buddhist book illuminations. They are represented in a highly formulaic and stereotypical manner with the same iconographical and compositional elements throughout the three centuries when the tradition flourished.

The most popular Jain work was their canonical text known as the *Kalpasutra* (Book of sacred precepts; e.g., [10]), with or without the addendum known as the *Kalakacharyakatha* (Story of the teacher Kalaka; e.g., [15]). Two other texts were the *Trishashtisalakapurushacharita* (Lives of the sixty-three heroes; [11]) and the *Uttaradhyayanasutra,* a compilation of sermons by Mahavira, the systematizer of Jainism, with commentaries. A text that appears to have suddenly become popular with Jains in the sixteenth century is the *Samgrahanisutra* (Book of compilations), which is represented in the collection by several isolated folios [33, 34]. The first three works include a great deal of narrative material in the form of biographies of the Jinas and the saints as well as other legends, which provided the artists with their principal themes. However, once the compositions and iconographic conventions were established in the fourteenth century, it was not until the seventeenth century that the artists felt the urge to make any noteworthy alterations. Only occasionally, in such manuscripts as the Devasano Pado *Kalpasutra* [20], does one encounter an attempt to break the mold, and such variations as are found do not occur in the principal representations. Seldom in fact did an artist deviate in the selection of the events and incidents portrayed. In any event, the life of Mahavira is usually more extensively illustrated than that of any of the other Jinas. As in literature his life serves as a model for those of the others, so also in the illustrations of the various texts the same formulaic and iconographic pattern is repeated for lives of the other Jinas.

Narrative themes are more predominant in the Jain illustrations than they are in Buddhist manuscript illuminations, which are a rich source for the iconography of Buddhist deities. Nevertheless, the repertoire was limited in both, and since both were essentially a copyists' art, stylistic changes were slow to occur. Occasionally, in the hands of a gifted and innovative artist, the representations did deviate from the conventional norm.

The figures in the Buddhist manuscripts are more naturalistically delineated than those in the Jain illustrations. For instance, in the latter the physical distortions of the figures make the representations quite unrealistic and stylized. In that sense, the Buddhist illuminations are indeed closer to the Ajanta murals, but it is wrong to suggest that they are murals reduced to miniatures. Neither in the Jain nor the Buddhist narrative representations do we encounter the sprawling compositions teeming with masses of figures and wealth of architectural and natural forms that make the Ajanta murals so overpowering in their visual effect. Instead, each composition in the manuscripts is limited to a few figures with one or two props, such as a throne or a tree, to add topographical veracity. Even though colorful and lively, the representation is economical, graphic, and limited to a single plane.

The figural forms and proportions are quite distinct in the Jain and the Buddhist illuminations, as are the draughtmanship and the coloring. The artists working for Jain patrons employed a much richer palette that included the generous use of gold, which is seldom encountered in Buddhist works. The restraint and austerity and even geometrical severity of form that characterize much of Jain sculpture are also found in their paintings. The Buddhist illuminations are informed with more fluid rhythms and a sensuous charm. Furthermore, the two styles differ in the portrayal of natural forms such as trees and flowers—more stylized in Jain than in Buddhist pictures—as well as in the architectural forms, furnishings, jewelry, and textile patterns. Clearly in such details the artists of each region, the Jains in the west and Buddhists in the east, were reproducing what they observed around them. Although limited technically and in their pictorial language, given the paucity of surviving murals from the period, both the Jain and the Buddhist manuscript illuminations acquire an art-historical significance totally disproportionate to their diminutive size.

PAINTING DURING THE SULTANATE PERIOD (1200–1525)

Although the Muslims arrived on the subcontinent as early as the seventh century and established a small kingdom in Sind, not until the thirteenth century did they appear in sizable enough groups to make an impression culturally. One effect of the Muslim presence was the introduction of paper, which the Jains were the first to adopt. Initially they did not accept the codex format nor the artistic conventions of Islamic book illustration, however. Perhaps few Islamic books were accessible to non-Muslims, or even present in India, during the thirteenth and fourteenth centuries. By the fifteenth century Jain book illuminations show greater familiarity with Islamic books, particularly in the use of gold and the figurative form for the Sahi types in the Kalaka story [15C, 17]. By and large, however, the influence of illustrated Islamic books on both Hindu and Jain books remained limited until the seventeenth century.

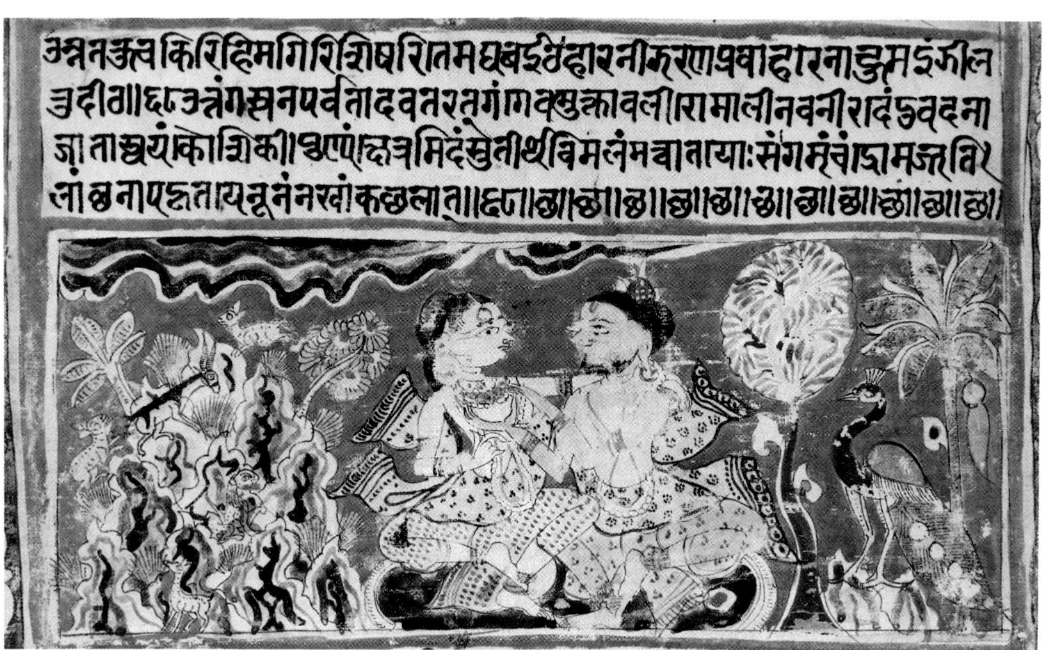

FIGURE 10
Section (scene 62) of the *Vasantavilasa* scroll, Ahmedabad, Gujarat, 1451, opaque watercolor on cloth, height 9 1/4 in (23.5 cm), Freer Gallery of Art, Smithsonian Institution, Washington, D.C., 32.24.

During the Sultanate period, illustrated books, both on cloth and paper, were also being produced for Hindu patrons, although less frequently than for the Jains and the Muslims, judging by the surviving examples. In fact, only one fifteenth-century document has survived that can be firmly dated. This is the 1451 *Vasantavilasa,* an erotic poem about spring, written and painted on cloth like a scroll (FIG. 10). There is nothing specifically Hindu about it, and its patron could have been a Jain bon vivant. Although its formal kinship with the Jain pictorial tradition is clear, it is not as formulaic, but more lyrical and more sensuously elegant. Stylized and decorative foliage is employed in a generalized landscape setting that is symbolic and expressive of the poem's mood rather than topographical.

Most illuminated Hindu manuscripts of the Sultanate period belong to the sixteenth century, in which there is also only one undisputed and dated anchor: a copy of the *Aranyakaparvan* (Book of the forest), a part of the epic *Mahabharata.*[10] It was rendered in 1516 at a place called Kacchauva (identified with present Kachaura on the river Yamuna) in the realm of the Lodis, the last of the Delhi sultans before the establishment of the Mughal empire. Although not as elegant, its style is derived ultimately from that of the *Vasantavilasa* and from the Jain style in general. A minor though noteworthy distinction is that the heads are always shown in proper profile and the protruding further eye is omitted, but the typically Jain distortion of the projecting chest is still continued. This style is now characterized by the expression *Chaurapanchasika,* from a richly illustrated copy of a poetical work of that name now in Ahmedabad. It is in the *Chaurapanchasika* manuscript that the style reaches its most refined and vivacious expression.[11]

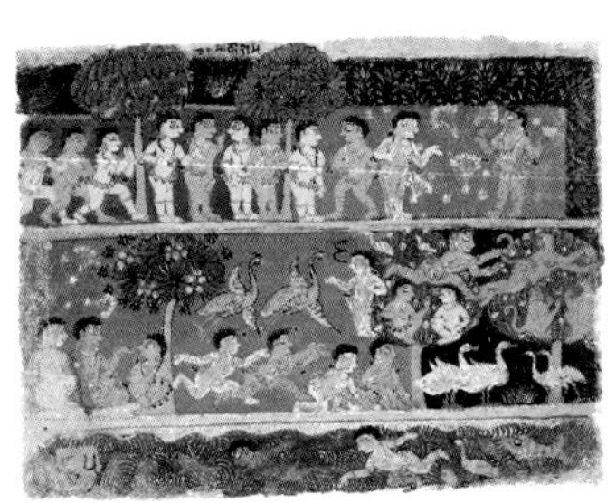

FIGURE 11
"Krishna and Balarama Play with Gopas," from a *Bhagavatapurana* manuscript, [36A].

The style is represented in the collection by five illustrated folios from two different manuscripts of the *Bhagavatapurana,* a Hindu religious text of encyclopedic nature extolling the Vaishnava deity Vasudeva-Krishna [36, 37] (FIG. 11). Subsequently it became one of the most popular texts to be illustrated for Hindu patrons. While rendered basically in the same style as *Aranyakaparvan* pictures, these illustrations differ in a significant way. In the *Aranyakaparvan* the illustrations and the text are accommodated on the same page, but in the *Bhagavatapurana* the pictures exist independent of the text, which is either banished to the back or confined as a caption in a narrow band above. The latter mode is first encountered in the *Vasantavilasa,* and it continued to be employed for books in which the text consisted only of couplets, such as the *Gitagovinda* [38]. Where exactly the other type of book—consisting of pictures on one side and the text on the other—originated is not known. The earliest example known is the earlier of the museum's two *Bhagavatapurana*s [36], provided its date in the first half of the sixteenth century is accepted. It should be noted, though, that the same arrangement of text and pictures is found also in the *Hamzanama,* the monumental book created about 1570 for the Mughal emperor Akbar [46]. There, however, the relevant text is on the facing page so that one could see the illustration as one read the story. In the *Bhagavatapurana* one has to turn over the picture to read the text.

Most surviving Hindu paintings of the period are from illustrated books that provide little or no information about their provenance or date. Thus it is not easy to determine where they were executed or who their patrons were. Some may have been done for powerful Hindu courts such as that of Mewar in Rajasthan, and others were probably rendered for rich merchants. Both the range of subject matter and style of the illustrated Hindu manuscripts are limited. No examples of Hindu portrait paintings of the period have survived. However, literary evidence as well as extant fragments make it clear that the temples and palaces were decorated with murals. The palaces were decorated largely with scenes from the *Mahabharata, Ramayana,* and the Krishna legends in public galleries and with erotic themes in the private apartments. Even though Sultanate period palaces are few, there can be little doubt that the mid-fifteenth-century murals would have been painted in the style of the *Vasantavilasa* and those of a century later in that of the *Chaurapanchasika* (cf. [36, 37]). The *Chaurapanchasika* style was a contributory factor to the formation of the Mughal style at Akbar's atelier.

The evidence for Islamic painting from the first two centuries of the Sultanate period is rather sketchy. Mausoleums remain in abundance, but no palaces or murals have survived. Literary evidence makes it clear, however, that certainly murals, both figurative as well as nonfigurative, did decorate the walls of palaces and public buildings, and some of the Muslim rulers must have been interested in owning illustrated books. At the beginning of the period books may have been imported from Iran and the Arab world, but by the early fourteenth century certainly local production must have begun. It is well known that scholars and literary figures from West Asia were attracted to Delhi as early as the thirteenth century. There seems no doubt that when the poet Amir Khusrau Dihlavi (1253–1325) was active there that books were not only being copied but also illustrated locally. The earliest surviving Islamic book that can be attributed securely to India is a Koran that was copied in Gwalior in 1399, a year after Timur, the conqueror from Iran, sacked Delhi. Timur probably looted what he found in the sultan's library

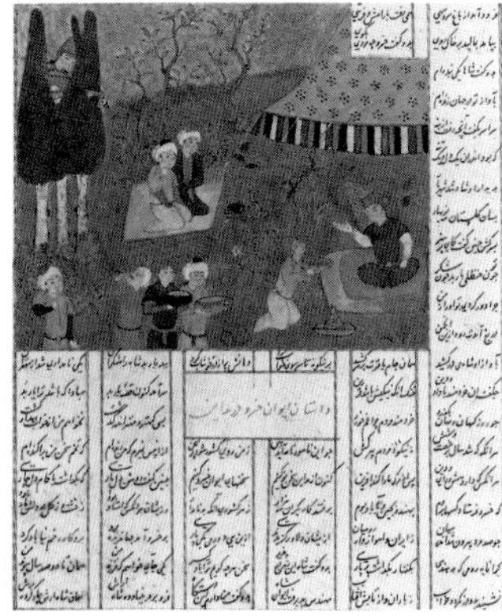

FIGURE 12
"King Khusrau and Barbad," from a *Shahnama* manuscript, [43D].

in Delhi, but this does not explain why books produced in other fourteenth-century sultanates have not survived.

Most Indian Islamic books of the Sultanate period belong to the fifteenth and the sixteenth centuries. A number of illustrated folios from copies of the great Iranian epic, Firdausi's *Shahnama* (Book of kings), in the collection [42–44] are rendered in so strong a Persian style that opinion is divided as to whether they were made in Iran or India (FIG. 12). If the books were produced in India, then very likely the artists simply copied imported models as desired by their patrons. This was not unusual and was, in fact, being done even as late as the 1570s [95]. However, the highly Persianized style of the Sultanate period appears to have had limited appeal and may also have had a restricted circulation. In most such works, including a *Khamsa* (Quintet) of Amir Khusrau [41], produced probably in the first half of the fifteenth century, Indian elements appear as occasional incursions and are not easy to discern.

Before the end of the century, however, the two pictorial traditions had mingled and several centers began producing books for Muslim patrons in which the style of the illustrations leaves no room to doubt their Indian origin. Mandu (Madhya Pradesh), the capital of the Malwa Sultanate, remained an important center for manuscript production throughout the fifteenth century. Several manuscripts produced at Mandu are illustrated in a more decorative and flattened version of the Persian Turkoman manner of Shiraz and with indisputably Indian features; the *Nimatnama* (Book of recipes) of about 1500 in the India Office Library, London, is probably the best known.[12]

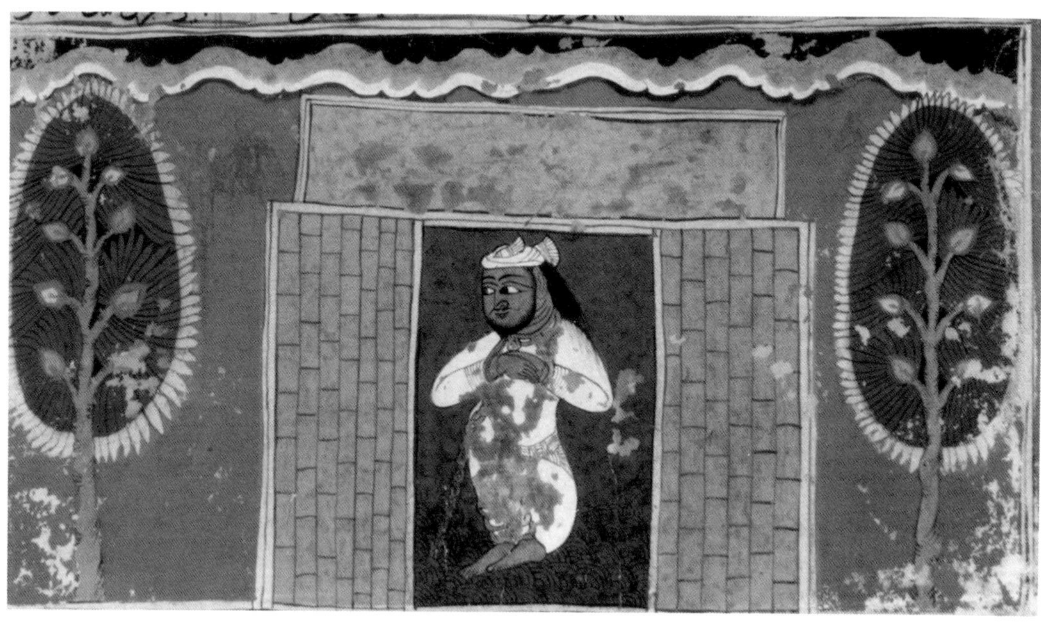

FIGURE 13
"Bizhan in the Dungeon," illustration from a *Shahnama* manuscript, Central India, c. 1450, ink and opaque watercolor on paper, 8 ⅛ x 4 ½ in (20.7 x 11.6 cm), collection of Dr. Alvin O. Bellak, Philadelphia.

There are other fifteenth-century illuminated Islamic books that are also unquestionably Indian, but their exact provenances are not known. Among them the most innovative is a recently dispersed mid-fifteenth-century *Shahnama* that clearly combines stylistic elements from the Jain and the Islamic pictorial traditions, as is evident from the illustration reproduced here (FIG. 13).[13] There can be little doubt that the artist—or artists—responsible for these illustrations was more than familiar with the Jain tradition and had a Muslim patron who was not an Iranophile. These highly original illustrations not only demonstrate the unknown artist's extraordinary self-assurance and complete mastery over his craft but also his innovative and open mind. Once begun, an Indo-Persian pictorial language evolved rapidly, and by the time Babur arrived in the third decade

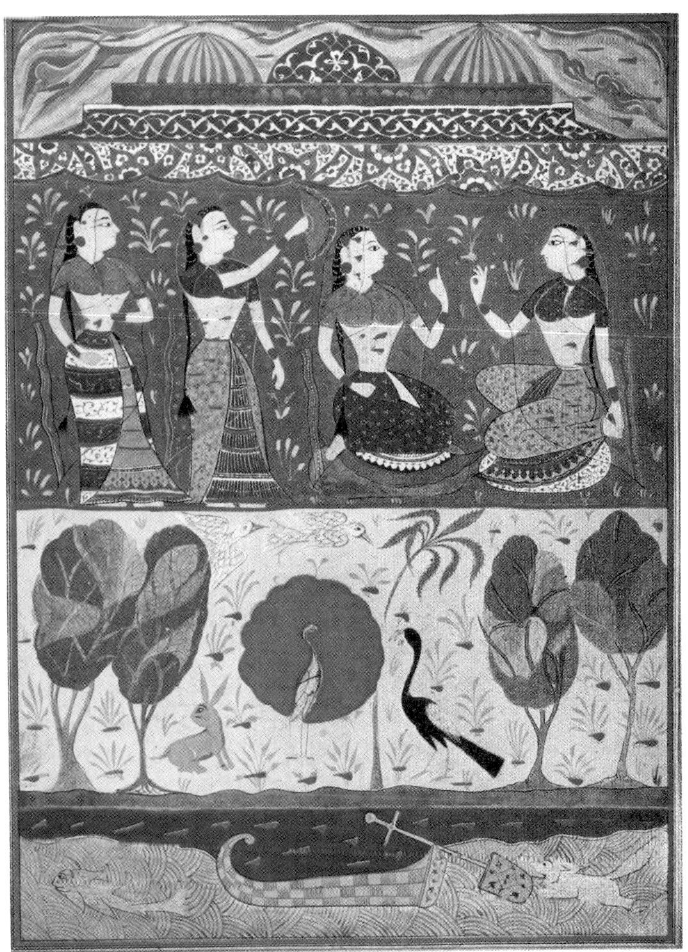

FIGURE 14
"Chanda in a Garden," from a *Laur Chanda* manuscript, provenance uncertain, c. 1550, opaque watercolor on paper, 10 ⅝ x 8 ¼ in (27.0 x 21.0 cm), Prince of Wales Museum, Bombay.

of the sixteenth century, a thorough synthesis of the Indian and Persian pictorial traditions had been achieved, as seen in such manuscripts as the Bombay *Laur Chanda* or *Chandayana* (Romance of Laurak and Chanda; FIG. 14). Although it was a felicitous marriage, there is little doubt that the Indian features and aesthetic predominate. Most of these manuscripts were illustrated by individual Indian artists, who, though familiar with Persian, particularly Shirazi, painting of about 1500, were very selective in what they borrowed. The exact provenance of the Bombay *Laur Chanda,* perhaps the finest of the Sultanate-period illustrated manuscripts, is uncertain. Some attribute it to Jaunpur (Uttar Pradesh), and others regard it as the product of the court workshop at Mandu. The pictures do demonstrate a close stylistic kinship with the earlier Mandu *Nimatnama.*

Summing up, in Sultanate-period painting one discerns at least four different manners. The conservative Jain style remained predominant with Jain patrons in western and central India well into the sixteenth century. A freer and more sensuous version of this style was apparently favored for other kinds of subjects at least in the mid-fifteenth century, as seen in the *Vasantavilasa.* Simultaneously in the fifteenth century, if not earlier, Islamic patrons were demonstrating a marked preference for books illustrated in strongly Persianized styles with few concessions to the pictorial tradition of their adopted home. A synthesis of the Persian and the Indian modes appears to have occurred sometime in the second half of the same century, mostly at Muslim courts apparently, as all the books illustrated in this style are written in the Arabic script. Hindu patrons continued to show a preference for a more Indian manner retaining the mannered elegance and lyrical flavor of the *Vasantavilasa* but by the early sixteenth century eschewing some of its distortions and adopting a few innovative features from what might be called the Sultanate Indo-Persian mode.

MUGHAL PAINTING

Radical changes took place in Indian painting in the second half of the sixteenth century in the court atelier of the Mughals. A master of the Turki language, Babur was interested in books and calligraphy as well as painting. There is no evidence, however, that he retained any artists. He certainly collected and appreciated illustrated books, and this interest was also evinced by his son Humayun. While in exile in Iran, Humayun took advantage of the Iranian monarch Shah Tahmasp's aversion to painting and recruited some of his artists. Although he did not live long enough to enjoy the creative talents of his recruits, fortunately his fourteen-year-old son, Akbar, who was not formally educated, was keenly interested in both books and pictures. Preoccupied though he was with expanding and administering his modest inheritance, he did not allow the talents of the Iranian masters, Mir Sayyid Ali and Abd as-Samad, to go to seed. Though the workshop may, in fact, have been established by his father, Akbar was behind its spectacular expansion in the 1560s. By the 1590s, when Abul Fazl, the court historian, wrote the official account of Akbar's reign, the workshop employed more than a hundred master painters and had already proved to be the most prolific center of book production in the Islamic world.

The century (1556–1658) spanned by the rule of the three great Mughals—Akbar, Jahangir, and Shah Jahan—may well be regarded as the most innovative and exciting period in the history of Indian painting. In fact, few periods or dynasties in the history of the world can match the creative output during the reigns of those three successive monarchs of the same dynasty in the visual arts and architecture. As in painting, so also in architecture, textiles and carpets, jewelry and decorative art: the century of the three early Mughals proved to be one of the most brilliant in the history of the Indian continent. Among Shah Jahan's sons, this passionate interest in the arts was inherited by the eldest, Dara Shikoh, but unfortunately, he lost the struggle for the throne and is life to the younger Aurangzeb (r. 1658–1707), whose response to the arts was lukewarm at best.

The majority of the Mughal pictures in the collection were rendered in the imperial workshop (*kitabkhana*) for either Akbar, Jahangir, or Shah Jahan. Only a few are from the Aurangzeb period, and there is no way to determine whether they were associated with the imperial workshop. Some paintings in the collection were executed for patrons other than the emperors, such as members of the nobility associated with the court as well as regional and local feudatory chiefs, known as maharajahs and nawabs. Production of Islamic books was both a costly and elaborate affair involving a large number of specialists, such as calligraphers, illuminators, painters, gilders, margin-makers, binders, and others. Only the very wealthy could afford to maintain such a production center, and usually only the ruler had one. During Akbar's reign, apart from the imperial workshop, there was at least one other, belonging to the courtier Abd ar-Rahim Khan Khanan, but several other courtiers did have large libraries. To satisfy the needs of those bibliophiles who did not have their own facilities, the artists attached to the limited number of workshops must have moonlighted. Those artists who did not qualify for the workshops probably set up shops in the bazaars and freelanced. A part of the imperial workshop always moved with the emperor whenever the court traveled, which was frequently. Otherwise the major centers of Mughal painting were Agra and Lahore. For a brief spell, when Prince Salim—later the emperor Jahangir—rebelled against his father, he set up his personal atelier in Allahabad, which served as his base camp. After Shah Jahan founded Shahjahanabad in Delhi, it too became a center of Mughal painting and remained so during the eighteenth and nineteenth centuries, until the eclipse of the empire.

There can be no doubt that the Mughals brought with them a kind of interest and connoisseurship previously unknown in India, even among the Muslim patrons. While we do have references in ancient Sanskrit literature to the appreciation of the visual arts among cultured gentlemen (*nāgaraka*), who were expected to learn the art of painting, and although we have descriptions of picture and portrait galleries in palaces, we know nothing specific about the patrons as we do about Akbar and Jahangir, who not only took a keen personal interest in painting but were directly involved in the origin and development of a style. In fact, though the world of art has known many famous patrons, none in any civilization has been so intimately and directly involved with the creation of a new style as was Akbar.

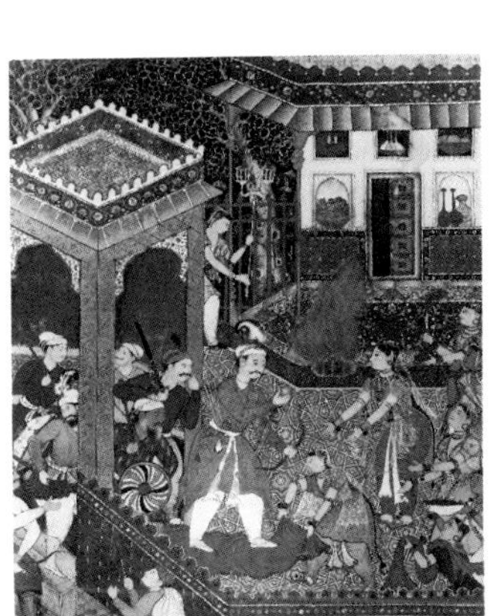

FIGURE 15
"Heroes Being Given Refuge," from a *Hamzanama* manuscript, [46].

Although a kind of stylistic amalgam between Persian and Indian painting had already been achieved during the late Sultanate period, it involved no radical technical leap or aesthetic innovation. This is self-evident if one compares the Sultanate Indo-Persian–style pictures (FIG. 13) with those of Akbar's *Hamzanama* [46] (FIG. 15). The *Hamzanama* is also notably different in form, composition, coloring, and draughtsmanship from the kind of pictures Mir Sayyid Ali and Abd as-Samad had been painting in Iran. Despite their heavy dependence on the Persian pictorial language and vocabulary, these masters were successful in creating a new style that is as different from the Persian manner as it is from the more purely Indian modes. It is generally admitted that the inspiring force behind the birth of this new style was the ever-inventive mind of Akbar. As Abul Fazl informs us, the emperor was deeply interested in the matter of raw materials and personally approved the quality of production, and he furthermore supervised the selection of incidents to be painted in the manuscripts. Besides, it was Akbar's rather than his artists' interest in and admiration for European works, introduced to the court by Portuguese visitors from Goa and other Europeans, that encouraged the adoption of European technical elements that contributed to the greater naturalism of the Mughal style. This concern for accurately recording what the eye sees constitutes a significant difference between the fifteenth-century Persianized pictures and the Mughal stylistic synthesis.

In addition to such traditional Persian literary works as the *Hamzanama* (Saga of Hamza), the *Shahnama,* the *Tutinama* (Tales of a parrot), Nizami's *Khamsa* (Quintet), the *Gulistan* (Rose garden) of Sadi, and others, the Mughals were also interested in histories, their ancestors' as well as their own. And so books such as the *Chingiznama* (Saga of Chingiz Khan), the *Timurnama* (Saga of Timur), the *Zafarnama* (Saga of conquest), the *Tarikh-i Alfi* (Millennial history), the *Baburnama,* the autobiography of Babur, and others of this genre were copied and illustrated. The *Baburnama* was especially admired, and several illustrated versions are known. In addition, Akbar had his own official history, the *Akbarnama,* written by Abul Fazl, and Jahangir's reign is recorded in the *Jahangirnama* and his own memoirs. A superbly and lavishly illustrated copy of the *Padshanama,* recounting the history of Shah Jahan's reign, is now in the British royal collection at Windsor.

It was one thing to illustrate the past but quite another to record contemporaneous events. The events in the *Chingiznama* or the *Tarikh-i Alfi,* or even in the *Baburnama,* were much more remote than those associated with Akbar. No other previous Indian ruler, either Muslim or Hindu, had had his own reign chronicled so thoroughly in his own lifetime. Notwithstanding the fact that all official histories were suitably embroidered, in the 1590s the hero of the drama was very much alive. Thus, the representations of the events in Akbar's chronicle had to have greater veracity than those described in works about the past. This meant keener observation and more accurate transcripts of the people, the incidents, and the topography. Undoubtedly the naturalistic representation of European paintings and engravings—even of biblical subjects—must have appeared particularly appropriate for the purpose.

Within their pictorial conventions, the Mughal artists seem to have worked in at least three different idioms depending on the subject matter of the book they were illustrating. Legendary and fictional subjects were treated with a more visionary and effusive style that allowed freer rein for the imagination. Historical works that required a greater degree of specificity, such as the *Timurnama,* were executed in a more Persianized style so that the flora, fauna, and topography, mostly of Iran and Central Asia, would provide a more authentic flavor of the locale where the incidents took place. Finally, the contemporary histories were illustrated in a more factual and partially realistic mode in which a genuine effort was made to add local color and topographical details and convey both the drama and the psychological concerns of the events. Moreover, the "selective realism" of the illustrations depended not only on the texts themselves, with their hyperbolic and stylized descriptions, and on the aesthetic conventions acquired by the artists but also on the patron's taste.[14] While Akbar did demand a certain degree of truthfulness, his interest in nature and observed phenomena was not as scientific and clinical as that of Jahangir, and Shah Jahan seems to have preferred a more refined, ordered, and idealized world in his paintings than did either of his predecessors.

Apart from manuscript illuminations, whose production declined after Akbar, the other type of Mughal pictures surviving from his reign is portraiture. Portraits were not unknown in earlier Indian art, but their use was limited and the representation was highly idealized. Realistic portraits of individuals were also not generally favored among the Muslims of West Asia. Although the Mughal artists may have begun executing portraits during the time of Humayun, who was familiar with Timurid portraits, it was Akbar who encouraged the art of realistic portraiture. As Abul Fazl has recorded, "At His Majesty's command portraits have been painted of all of His Majesty's servants and a huge album (*kitab*) has been made. Thus the dead have gained a new life, and the living an eternity."[15] The purpose of the portraits, however, was more practical. Not only was Akbar powerful enough to set aside the orthodox Islamic objections to figurative painting that discouraged the art of portraiture, but he was astute enough to realize the advantages of being personally familiar with every important officer of his reign. His son Jahangir too was very aware of the necessity to know intimately both one's friend and foe, if not in person, at least through portraits. Hence when he dispatched an embassy to Iran in 1619, he sent along the artist Bishandas to draw likenesses of the Iranian monarch Shah Abbas II, whom he never forgave for having snatched Qandahar.

That the Mughal portraits were drawn from life is known both from surviving pictures where we see artists directly sketching the subject and also from such perceptive and unglamourized drawings as that of Jahangir in the collection [73]. Although Mughal portraiture under both Akbar and Jahangir was strongly influenced by realistic European portraits encountered in miniatures and engravings, the technical limitations of the genre are clear. The paintings are of diminutive size and the figures are generally portrayed full length, which considerably reduces the potential for rendering highly detailed and expressive faces capable of projecting the subject's personality, as was done in the much larger busts in oil favored in contemporary Europe. Moreover, the Mughal representation is generally in profile, which imposed certain limitations on the expressiveness of the depiction. While not as idealized and generalized as earlier Indian portraits, Mughal portraits, like the landscapes in historical pictures, are combinations of both realism and stylization. The character of the portrait, especially of his own, changed under Shah Jahan. Unlike Akbar and Jahangir, who were interested in both the spirit and the form, Shah Jahan was more concerned with style than substance. His own portraits therefore lack the psychological depth of earlier Mughal portraits and present the emperor in highly cosmetized and flattering images. Other portraits from his reign, such as those by such accomplished artists as Hashim [76], are technically flawless but less expressive than those done under Jahangir.

Portraiture was only one aspect of the general humanistic interest and the insatiable curiosity of the early Mughals, which resulted in paintings that present both the human and physical worlds with a veracity and an empathy rarely encountered in earlier Indian art. Only in the murals of Ajanta is contemporary court life recorded in such lively detail and rich variety as Mughal India is in its paintings. The Mughals also adopted the Persian idea of the album in which examples of calligraphy and pictures of a wide variety of genres alternated and were savored in a relaxed atmosphere.

The museum's collection has a number of Mughal pictures that were painted for both Muslim and Hindu patrons who were probably influenced by Mughal taste. Apart from the imperial circle—which included members of the royal family as well as courtiers—Rajput princes, especially those closely allied to the Mughal court, also admired Mughal paintings. Some of the artists trained in the Mughal tradition worked for Rajput courts, just as in the nineteenth century their descendants would do for the British in Calcutta, Delhi, and elsewhere. Moreover, a certain number of paintings of more popular subjects, such as *Ragamala* (collections of poems describing the various musical modes known as *raga* and *ragini*), were painted in the bazaars of Agra, Lahore, or Delhi for general consumption. Most of these have Hindi texts and may have been done for either Hindu or Muslim patrons who also loved music. These provincial and popular Mughal pictures vary in their aesthetic richness or quality depending on the skill of the artist and the pocketbook and the taste of the patron. Although less refined and more summarily rendered than the imperial paintings, they were of seminal importance for the development of the Rajput tradition.

DECCANI PAINTING

Apart from the Mughal school, centers of painting developed in the sixteenth century at the three southern Islamic kingdoms of Ahmadnagar, Bijapur, and Golconda and by the seventeenth century at some of the Hindu courts that had come under Mughal hegemony. Paintings for Hindu patrons from the seventeenth century and later will be the subject of the next volume of the catalogue, but pictures produced for the three Islamic kingdoms of the Deccan until about 1700 will be discussed here.

All three kingdoms were situated on the Deccan plateau in parts of the three states known today as Andhra Pradesh, Maharashtra, and Karnataka. Collectively the style of painting that developed at the three courts is known as Deccani.[16] At the time of Babur's conquest the three kingdoms flourished as independent entities, but before the end of the seventeenth century all three had been incorporated into the Mughal empire. The Deccani rulers maintained even closer ties than the Mughal court with the various Islamic kingdoms of West Asia, and Iranian culture and tastes were the most influential. Fewer Deccani than Mughal pictures have survived, and most of them are undocumented, which creates problems in determining both provenance and date. Although the Deccani tradition did develop a distinct character of its own, one also finds paintings done in strongly Persianized styles or even in close imitation of foreign works [95, 98]. Notwithstanding a common Deccani flavor or aesthetic, there are subtle differences of style perceptible in the pictures executed for the three courts.

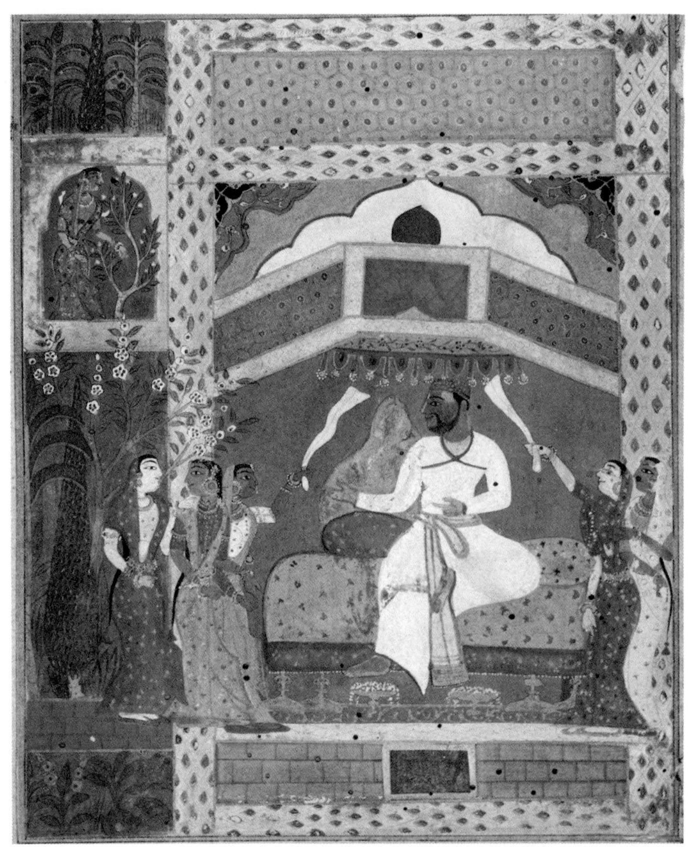

FIGURE 16
"Sultan Husayn Nizam Shah in the Zenana," from a *Tarif-i Husayn Shahi* manuscript, Ahmadnagar, Maharashtra, 1565, opaque watercolor on paper, 6⅝ x 5 in (16.9 x 12.7 cm), Bharat Itihasa Samshodhana Mandala, Poona.

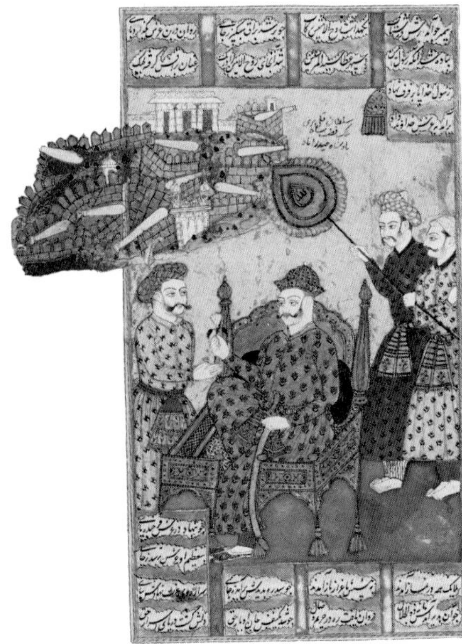

FIGURE 17
"Sultan Quli Qutb Shah (?)," from a *History of the Qutb Shahi Sultans of Golconda* manuscript, [103D].

With one exception, a rare *Ragamala* picture probably from Ahmadnagar [112], all the Deccani paintings in the museum's collection are either from Bijapur or Golconda. Fewer Ahmadnagar pictures appear to have survived and most are of uncertain provenance. Moreover, Ahmadnagar lost its independence by 1636, whereas Bijapur was absorbed into the Mughal empire in 1686 and Golconda the following year. Fortunately the earliest surviving Deccani work has an unambiguous Ahmadnagar provenance and is also dated. It is an illustrated manuscript of a historical book called the *Tarif-i Husayn Shahi* copied for the court in 1565. The style of the illustrations (FIG. 16) is clearly related to the *Ragamala* painting in the collection and is also reminiscent of the Bombay *Laur Chanda* (FIG. 14).

In all three centers, despite the emergence of local modes, a Persianized manner continued to exist simultaneously. Although the Deccani courts had become familiar with the Mughal tradition, possibly as early as the last quarter of the sixteenth century, both the artists and the patrons seem not to have been impressed with the Mughal concerns for naturalism and psychological acuity and their interest in history and the world around them. Rather, the pictures of all three Deccani centers, including portraits, reveal a penchant for idealization and fantasy; a mystical, otherworldly mood; brilliantly luxuriant colors; and audacious distortions of form (FIG. 17). As M. Zebrowski has summed up elegantly:

Few Deccani paintings record historical events or realistically portray their subjects, as Mughal art does. Nor was there much interest in the thrills of the hunt, court ceremonial or Hindu ritual, favourite Rajasthani themes. Instead, princely portraits predominate which aim to establish a gently lyrical atmosphere, often one of quiet abandon to the joys of love, music, poetry or just the perfume of a flower. Although figures are conventional types, moods are brilliantly established through fantastic colours and unconventional poses. We are admitted into a private world of feeling, inhabited by pages, princes, dervishes and mullahs. . . .

The delicate rhythms of Persia, the lush sensuality of southern India, the restraint of European and Ottoman Turkish portraiture all contributed to its uniqueness.[17]

Unlike those in the Mughal atelier, very little is known about the artists who worked for the Deccani courts. Since calligraphers, poets, and scholars thronged to the Deccan from West Asia, it is likely that artists too were attracted by generous patrons. Some of the artists who worked for the Vijaynagar empire, on whose ruins the three Muslim kingdoms had been founded, must also have worked for the new courts. Certainly the robust female forms and the glowing colors of the *Tarif-i Husayn Shahi* pictures (FIG. 16) are reminiscent of murals in monuments of the Vijaynagar empire. It should be noted further that artists and pictures must have moved about from one court to the other, as is clear from the paintings themselves. It would be difficult to explain otherwise the common aesthetic norms and stylistic features that the three centers shared.

The principal effect of the Mughal conquest in the late 1680s was to alter the nature of patronage. With the abolition of the monarchies in Bijapur and Golconda, the task of extending patronage to artists passed on to the provincial Mughal governor and the local nobility, at least until Hyderabad became an independent kingdom in 1724. Although Mughal influence is perceptible in portraits of the last quarter of the seventeenth century, by and large the Deccani artists continued to paint in their own romantic, lyrical, and intensely colorful manner.

CALLIGRAPHY

The early Buddhist and Jain books are written in two different forms of Brahmi, the script used to write most Indic languages during the historical period. It was expected of the scribes to write diligently and with a fine hand. Some of the writing, especially in Jain manuscripts, even achieved a calligraphic quality. By and large, however, calligraphy did not develop into as important an art form or aesthetic pursuit as it did in the Islamic world or in East Asian civilizations. While a uniform size of lettering and legibility were the prime concerns in Buddhist palm-leaf manuscripts, in Jain palm-leaf manuscripts one does find several different types of lettering, though it is always in ink. In the later paper manuscripts of the Jains we encounter attempts to beautify the lettering both in form and coloring and to adorn the page with ornamental designs. Often the paper was dyed and silver and gold lettering was used to make the manuscript sumptuous [20, 22]. This desire on the part of the Jains to adopt more calligraphic writing and to decorate the pages more richly may be due to Islamic influence.

In the Islamic world calligraphy not only has primacy over painting but is also accorded a sanctity unlike in any other civilization. In the words of Abul Fazl:

I shall first say something about the art of writing as it is the more important of the two arts [the other being painting]. . . . And indeed, in the eyes of the friends of true beauty, a letter is the source from which the light confined within it beams forth; and in the opinion of the far-sighted, it is the world-reflecting cup in the abstract. The letter, a magical power, is spiritual geometry emanating from the pen of invention; a heavenly writ from the hand of fate, it contains the secret word, and is the tongue of the hand.[18]

It is therefore understandable why the calligrapher ranks higher than the painter in Islamic society. It is the calligrapher who copies the word of God as contained in the Koran. This attitude ensured an exalted status for calligraphy that was never attained by painting. Calligraphy and the arabesque formed the twin pillars of Islamic art and architectural decoration and provided the preeminent decorative motifs in a way unknown in other cultures. Moreover, since Arabic is the language of the Koran, its script was adopted by many peoples who adopted Islam but spoke a different language. The most eminent among these were the Persians, who write their language in the Arabic script.

In addition to owning beautifully written Korans and other books, the Muslim patrons also admired individual pages of calligraphed didactic and poetical passages and verses expressing a wide variety of emotions and sentiments. Calligraphy was, in fact, not confined to paper but from early times was employed extensively on buildings, textiles, ceramics, metalwork, and other artistic forms. There is no doubt that the use of calligraphy on these forms preceded the custom of collecting examples of calligraphy on paper and assembling them in albums for more intimate viewing. Most examples of aesthetically mounted calligraphy in the collection are from Mughal or Deccani albums. The earliest specimens, belonging to the Sultanate period, consist of two folios from a Koran of about 1400 [39]. Several other leaves from various Islamic books of the Sultanate period provide less ornamental and more prosaic examples of Arabic writing from either Iran or India. Most of these are written in the popular *naski* or *nastaliq* scripts. However, fine examples of such other Arabic scripts as *raihani* or *muhaqqaq, thuluth,* and *behari,* a local variation developed in India, are also included in the collection.

Indian patrons were fond of acquiring calligraphic specimens of noteworthy local scribes as well as those of eminent calligraphers of West Asia. The best-known Indian calligrapher of the Mughal period was Muhammad Husayn of Kashmir, who received the title of *zarin qalam,* "the golden pen," from Akbar. But the calligrapher who was admired most by the Mughals was Mir Ali of Herat [77A, 78A]. A pupil of the famous Sultan Ali of Mashhad, he is credited with a new and elegant style of *nastaliq.*

While on public buildings calligraphy assumed monumental proportions but remained rather conservative, in books and pages meant for private use the calligraphers were much more inventive and playful. Apart from the diverse individual styles of the calligraphers, careful attention was given to the aesthetic placement and elegant ornamentation of the writing as well as the background. For instance, the text may be written at an angle across the page or in more complex formations, the letters may be surrounded by cloud patterns and the background encircled with floral and arabesque patterns in gold or with marbled designs. Then again the central panel may be surrounded by smaller cartouches with other examples of calligraphy in varying sizes and with different forms of decoration. Further elaboration was achieved, especially under Jahangir and Shah Jahan, when these arrangements of calligraphic panels were surrounded by sumptuous outer borders richly illuminated with flowers, animals, and human figures [55, 77–79].

ARTISTS AND PATRONS

No names of painters are known until the Mughal period. Names of patrons occur in both Buddhist and Jain manuscripts in the collection but on none of the Sultanate-period paintings. The names appearing on the sixteenth-century *Bhagavatapurana* pictures [36] may have been later additions. Both Buddhist and Jain manuscripts were generally copied by professional scribes, some of whom are named, but artists are not. It is of course possible that the scribes also painted the pictures, but one cannot be certain.[19] If they did, it is strange that they mention copying the manuscripts but not illustrating them. Professional scribes often filled administrative posts and enjoyed a higher social status than artists in traditional, non-Muslim Indian society. Generally the professional artists in India ranked rather low in the caste hierarchy, as in fact they still do. For instance, it is unlikely that any of the Hindu artists recruited by Akbar would have been from the higher castes. Many, in fact, belonged to the lower subcastes of palanquin bearers or carpenters. However, like many other occupational groups, the artists did form themselves into guilds, as was done in medieval Europe.

The few names that occur in the Buddhist manuscripts in the museum's collection indicate that monks and merchants were the principal patrons who commissioned the books (see colophons in the Appendix). Although the manuscripts were copied and illustrated largely in the east, the patrons came from different regions of the country (e.g., [3]). Merchants were enthusiastic patrons in the Jain communities as well, but monks appear to have been recipients rather than patrons. Several of the manuscripts in the collection were commissioned by court officials in Gujarat. Generally the Jain patron belonged to the local temple where the manuscript was deposited. Often several members of a Jain family are named as joint patrons in a dedication. In Buddhist manuscripts usually a sole donor is named, but sometimes a couple is. It was expected, however, that the merit of the act would benefit all members of the donor's family and humankind in general. Both the Buddhists and the Jains, as well as the Hindus, dedicated religious books as acts of piety and not for personal use. Therefore they had little to do with the selection of the subject matter or how the books should be illustrated, and only a very limited number of texts were illuminated. These are some of the reasons why the artists did not have the incentive to be highly inventive with the illustrations. Neither the donors nor the artists were interested in deviating from established norms. There is no evidence at all that before the Sultanate period works of secular literature were illustrated for Hindu, Jain, or Buddhist patrons.

The arrival of the Muslims with their interest in illustrated books may have engendered among native Indians a desire to illustrate their own texts, especially after the adoption of paper. During the Sultanate period both calligraphers and artists must have

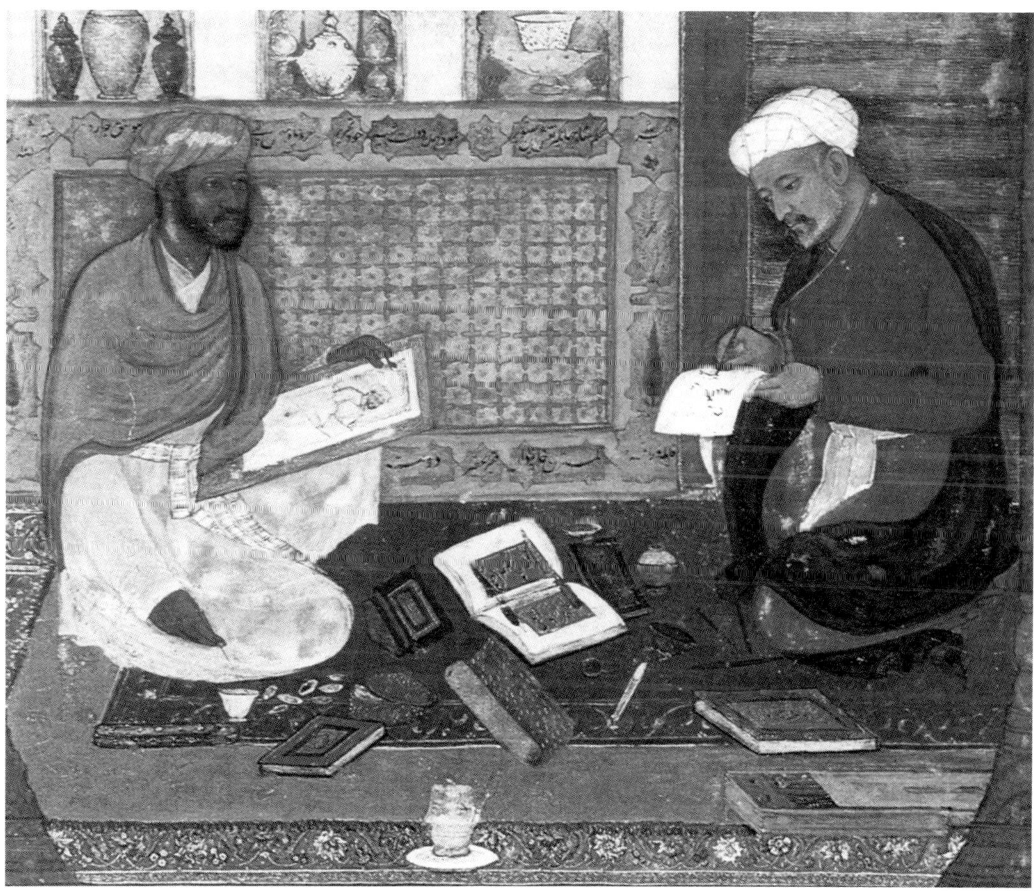

FIGURE 18
Detail of a painting by Daulat showing himself and the calligrapher Abd ar-Rahim, the "Amber Pen," at work, illustration from a *Khamsa* of Nizami, Mughal, c. 1610, opaque watercolor on paper, 11 7/8 x 7 3/4 in (30.0 x 19.5 cm), British Library, London.

come to the subcontinent from Iran and the Arab world, but very little information is available about them or their patrons. However, judging by the norms in Muslim society, which does not have a caste system, artists and calligraphers not only enjoyed a certain amount of status but were particularly admired for their skills. None of this seems to have had any effect on improving the social position of the Indian artist in his society.

Dramatic changes took place in the relationship between the patron and the artist in the Mughal court (FIG. 18). Artists employed by the imperial workshop not only enjoyed a certain degree of economic security, they may have wielded some political clout as well because of their proximity to the emperors. Certainly the facts that Mughal artists signed their pictures, librarians took care to inscribe artists' names, and even the rulers remarked on the individual talents of the painters indicate a shift in the importance of the artist under Mughal patronage. There is no doubt that the Muslim artists in the court enjoyed a more exalted position than their Hindu counterparts. The Iranian master Abd as-Samad was honored with a title and was appointed to a high administrative position. His son Muhammad Sharif remained a lifelong personal friend of Jahangir. Abul Hasan and Mansur, two of Jahangir's favorite painters, were also honored with titles. Jahangir once rewarded Bishandas with an elephant upon his return from Iran; ownership of an elephant in India implied both social and financial status. On the other hand, there are portraits of Mughal artists that do indicate their humble social and economic condition. According to a seventeenth-century European visitor, fortune did not exactly smile on an artist unless he was employed by the court.[20]

Both Akbar and Jahangir worked closely with their artists. Indeed rarely in the history of mankind have so many artists been so strongly influenced by their patrons. Abul Fazl describes Akbar's direct and deep involvement with his artists both in the selection of the subject matter and in technical matters such as the manner of coloring. In fact, without Akbar there would have been no Mughal style. The interaction between Jahangir and his artists was more fluid, and the artists working for him were encouraged to demonstrate their individuality with unprecedented freedom. Although Shah Jahan's primary passion was architecture, he too impressed his personality and aesthetic tastes on his artists. No other period in Indian history offers such insight into the relationship between the artist and the patron as does the first century of Mughal rule.

NOTES

1. On the techniques used in Indian painting, see Johnson 1972.

2. No single volume or article is devoted to the study of prehistoric Indian painting. For brief discussions and illustrations, see B. Allchin and R. Allchin, *The Rise of Civilization in India and Pakistan* (Cambridge: Cambridge University Press, 1982).

3. See R. R. R. Brooks and V. S. Wakankar, *Stone Age Painting in India* (New Haven: Yale University Press, 1976).

4. See A. Ghosh, ed., *Ajanta Murals* (New Delhi: Archeological Survey of India, 1967) for an overall description and color illustrations of Ajanta. For an iconographic study of Ajanta murals, see D. Schingloff, *Studies in the Ajanta Paintings* (Delhi: Ajanta Publications, 1988).

5. See W. Spink, "Ajanta: A Brief History," in P. Pal 1972; see also Spink 1990.

6. Khandalavala 1990. See also K. Khandalavala, ed., *The Golden Age* (Bombay: Marg Publications, 1991), pp. 93–102, for a discussion of both the Bagh and Ajanta murals.

7. See G. Bhattacharya, "The Newly Discovered Buddhist Temple at Nālandā," in *South Asian Archaeology 1983*, eds. J. Schotsmans and M. Taddei (Naples: Istituto Universitario Orientale, 1985), 1: 719–40, figs. 5–8; and B. Nath, *Nalanda Murals* (New Delhi: Cosmo, 1983).

8. See P. Pal and L. Fournier, *A Buddhist Paradise: The Murals of Alchi, Western Himalayas* (Basel: Ravi Kumar, 1982); and T. J. Pritzker, "The Wall Paintings of Tabo," *Orientations* 20, no. 2 (February 1989): 38–47.

9. See Pal & Meech-Pekarik 1988.

10. For overviews of Sultanate-period painting, see Khandalavala & Chandra 1969; and Losty 1982. For the *Aranyakaparvan* manuscript, see Khandalavala & Chandra 1974.

11. See Shiveshwarkar 1967.

12. See Khandalavala & Chandra 1969, pp. 58–63, figs. 131–39, pls. 11–12.

13. See Goswamy 1988 for an extensive discussion of this important document.

14. See Converse 1986 for an interesting discussion of "selective realism" in Mughal art.

15. Quoted in P. Chandra 1976, p. 184.

16. See Zebrowski 1983 for a discussion of the Deccani schools.

17. Ibid., p. 10.

18. Blochmann [1927] 1939, p. 103.

19. From surviving seventeenth-century manuscripts in Orissa we learn that often the scribe was also the illuminator. See J. P. Das, *Chitra-Pothi Illustrated Palm-Leaf Manuscripts from Orissa* (New Delhi: Arnold-Heinemann 1985), pp. 34–44.

20. Bernier [1891] 1972, p. 254.

Note on the Catalogue

CATALOGUE NUMBERS
Entries are numbered continuously throughout. Small capital letters, such as A, B, or D, refer to reproductions, not necessarily to folios within a manuscript (nor to sides of a folio), an accession number, or an entry.

PLACE NAMES
In the captions, modern states and cities are given. In the text, modern states are given in parentheses, as in "at Bagh (Madhya Pradesh), Badami and Pattadakal (Karnataka), and Pithalkhora (Maharashtra)."

MEDIUMS
Since within sections most works are of the same mediums and on the same support, consult the note at the beginning of the section if the materials of a work are not specified in the caption. "Watercolors" have a binder added, usually gum arabic.

DIMENSIONS
The dimensions for "folio" and "illustration" are stated when a folio is presently complete, even if, as in some Mughal examples, an outer border is from a later remounting (which is mentioned in the text when known); "overall" indicates that a folio has been cropped (most often to an illustration's inner border); and dimensions alone indicate the lack of borders around the entire image area or page. When folios and/or illustrations from a manuscript or album in an entry vary only slightly, a single set of approximate dimensions is stated.

ACCESSION NUMBERS
In multiple item entries, the accession numbers are stated in the order items are catalogued, e.g., in the "M.82.6.6,.5" of [83], M.82.6.6 is A and M.82.6.5 is B. The same is true for accession numbers ending in letters; for instance, in [1] "M.86.185a–d." In the case of complete manuscripts, individual accession numbers for the parts catalogued are not stated.

FOLIO NUMBERS AND SIDES
Folio numbers that appear on a folio itself are given after the title or in the text of an entry. Sides are stated when discernable: "recto" (abbr. "r") refers to the first side of a folio as encountered in a book and "verso" (abbr. "v") the second. Hence, for example, for Jain manuscripts, which are stacked like Venetian blinds, the recto is the top of the folio and the verso the underside; for bound Islamic books, the recto is on the left side when looking at an open book, as Persian and Arabic are read from right to left, in the opposite direction of books in European languages.

COMPLETE MANUSCRIPTS
A full physical description is provided at the beginning of the entries for complete manuscripts, e.g., [15].

CAPTIONS
Captions identified as details indicate that the full folio is not shown, even if the entire painting (without borders) is illustrated.

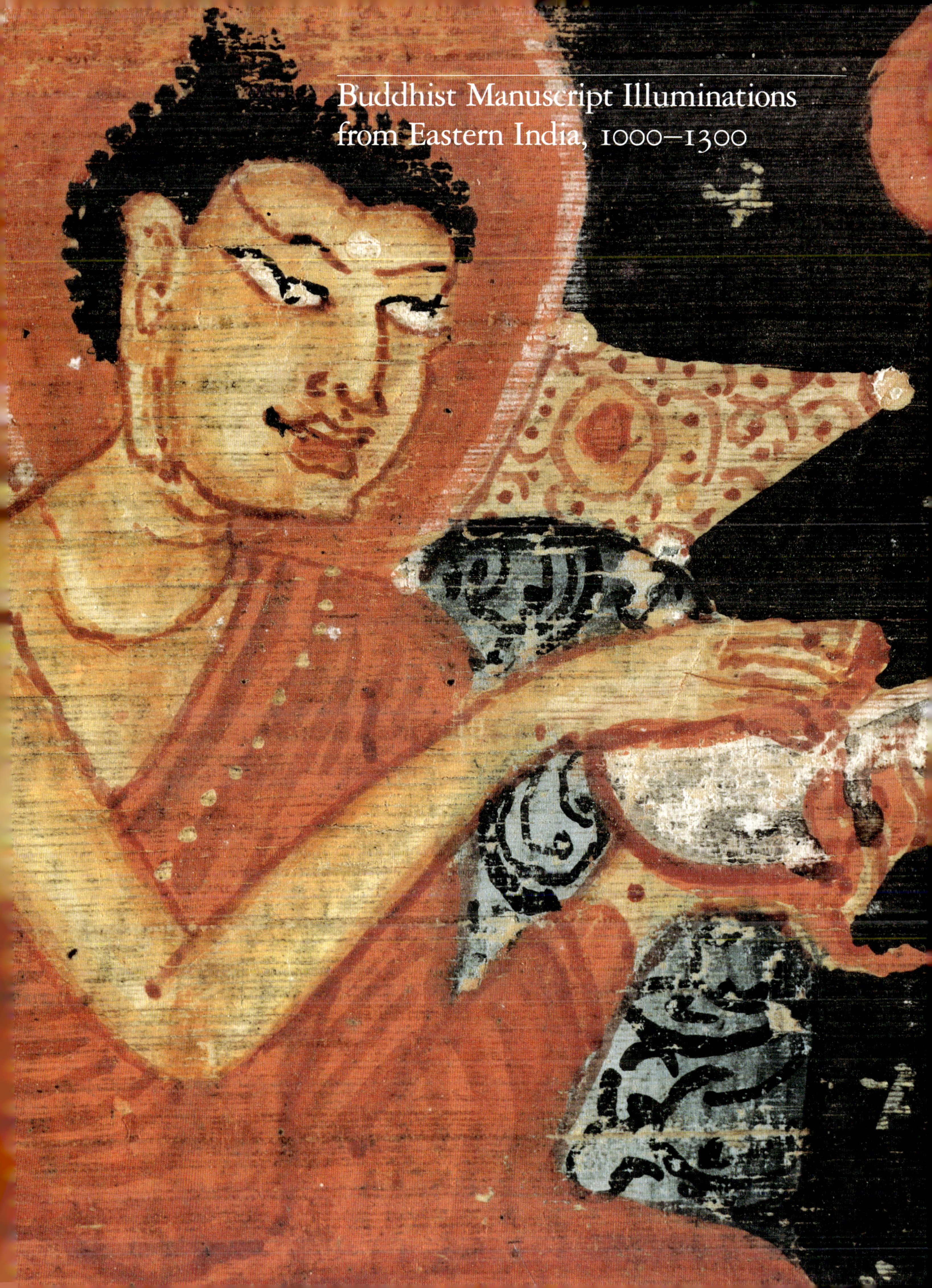

Buddhist Manuscript Illuminations from Eastern India, 1000–1300

Moreover, Kauśika {Indra}, among the Gods

of the Four Great Kings those Gods who have set out

for full enlightenment will make up their minds

to come to the place where someone has put

a copy of the perfection of wisdom, and worship it.

They will come, look upon the copy of this

perfection of wisdom, salute it respectfully,

pay homage to it, learn, study and repeat it.[1]

Introduction

The words opposite are uttered by the Buddha in the well-known Mahayana sutra known as the *Prajnaparamita* (Perfection of wisdom), which was composed no later than the second century A.D. One can therefore infer that by that date the Buddhists had not only begun to write down their sacred texts but had also started to worship the books literally. The earliest Buddhist books that have survived are from a slightly later period, and the earliest illustrated examples prepared on the Indian subcontinent belong to the ninth century.[2] Yet the tradition of illuminating books with images and symbols was known among the Chinese and Central Asian Buddhists as early as the seventh century. Why the Indian Buddhists were slow to adopt the practice is somewhat mysterious.

The bulk of the surviving illuminated Buddhist books of Indian origin were produced in Bihar and Bengal during the Pala period (800–1200), but none was discovered in India proper. Almost all such manuscripts now preserved in libraries and museums in Asia, Europe, or North America emerged from monasteries in Nepal and Tibet, where they were reverently preserved for centuries. They were taken by monks to those Himalayan sanctuaries in the twelfth and thirteenth centuries to save them from destruction from Muslim attacks. Curiously, neither country has yielded a single manuscript, whether illustrated or not, that was prepared in Orissa or Kashmir, two other regions where Buddhism still flourished as late as the twelfth century if not after. In northeastern and southern India books were written on palm leaves, a material that is especially vulnerable to the Indian climate. In the Himalayan regions of Nepal and Tibet, however, the climate is more congenial to the manuscripts' preservation. This is also true of Kashmir, where books were written on birch bark, although no books have survived there: after the fourteenth century Islam became the predominant faith in Kashmir, and presumably the Buddhist libraries were systematically destroyed. What is also curious is that no Kashmiri books have been discovered so far in the monasteries of Ladakh, Spiti, and western Tibet, where one might have expected Kashmiri manuscripts to have survived. Books on birch bark with illustrated covers going back to the seventh century have been found deposited in stupas in Gilgit (Pakistan).

According to the information provided by the colophons of the manuscripts, the patrons were all followers of Mahayana Buddhism. The expression *Mahayana* literally means the "Great Path" and is used to denote later developments in the history of the religion. The early form of the faith, based directly on the teachings of Buddha Sakyamuni (c. 563–483 B.C.), is generally known by the expressions *Hinayana* (Lesser Path) or *Theravada* (Way of the Elders). The early sacred books of the Buddhists are in the Pali language, whereas the Mahayana scriptures are written in Sanskrit. While accepting the early teachings as valid, the followers of the Mahayana created new scriptures but attributed them to the Buddha himself. Two of the most important of these are the *Lotus Sutra* and the *Perfection of Wisdom Sutra.*

While the early forms of Buddhism emphasized that attaining nirvana was an individual effort, Mahayana is a more altruistic and salvific faith that believes in the intervention of divine grace. It is also more devotionally oriented and recommends the worship of transcendental and cosmic Buddhas as well as a host of bodhisattvas. A bodhisattva is a being who is capable of attaining nirvana or *bodhichitta* but postpones it to help others. Apart from Buddhas and bodhisattvas, the pantheon also includes diverse gods and goddesses who are basically similar to their Hindu counterparts and who are invoked at the elemental level of religious praxis. The religious system that stresses the role of gods and goddesses, mandalas and mantras, and various esoteric and mystico-yogic rites and practices came to be known by the name *Vajrayana* (Diamond or Adamantine Path). This is the final phase of the development of Buddhism. Mahayana coalesced around the time of the birth of Christ, and Vajrayana flourished in Kashmir and eastern India between roughly 700 and 1200.

Between the eleventh and the thirteenth centuries Buddhists in the monasteries of Bihar and Bengal, and to a lesser extent in Orissa, were highly active in the production of palm-leaf manuscripts of their sacred texts. Apart from monks themselves, for whom to copy and illustrate sacred books was an act of piety, the major monasteries such as Nalanda, Vikramsila, Apanaka, Somapuri, and others must have had their own production centers that retained professional scribes as well as artists. While names of scribes are often included in colophon statements, not a single artist's name is known. It is not improbable that some of the scribes themselves were also illuminators.

Although countless different religious texts were copied by the Buddhists in Bihar and Bengal, it seems only a few were selected for illustration. Principal among these are manuscripts of the *Ashtasahasrika Prajnaparamita* (Perfection of wisdom in eight thousand verses), the *Pancharaksha* (Five protective charms), and the *Dharanisamgraha* (Collection of charms), which are the three texts represented in the collection. The *Prajnaparamita,* the title of which refers to the wisdom that takes one to the other shore, is a basic text of Mahayana philosophy. Unquestionably this was the text most often copied, though not always illustrated, by the Buddhists in eastern India and also in Nepal. As is clear from the passage quoted as the epigraph to this introduction as well as from other similar passages, the text itself highly recommends the practice of copying this book. It was considered even more meritorious to donate a copy to someone else, which is why most manuscripts were given to monasteries rather than retained for personal use. The next most important book was the *Pancharaksha.* The five charms were considered particularly propitious for averting evil influences and physical afflictions of all kinds. A *Dharanisamgraha* text served the same purpose, although it was not as popular or potent as the *Pancharaksha.* The museum's collection contains leaves from five different *Prajnaparamita* manuscripts and two each from a manuscript of the *Pancharaksha* and of the *Dharanisamgraha.*

The principal reason the books were illuminated with pictures was to enhance their spiritual potency, as well as to protect them from physical and supernatural harm. All three texts were typically illuminated with hieratic images of the various

Buddhas and Vajrayana divinities, and the *Prajnaparamita* was additionally adorned with eight stereotyped incidents from the life of the Buddha Sakyamuni. Whereas the divinities adorning the *Pancharaksha* and the *Dharanisamgraha* are described in the texts, the *Prajnaparamita* illuminations have little relation to the text. A few of the divine figures are relevant, but others seem to have no particular textual association. Some of the Buddhist manuscripts may, in fact, have been adorned with figures constituting a mandala.

The eight scenes from the life of the Buddha shown in the *Prajnaparamita* are the only narrative subjects represented in these three books. Known as the Eight Great Miracles, they include the Four Principal Events: his birth at Lumbini, his enlightenment at Bodhgaya, his preaching of the first sermon at Sarnath, and his final extinction (*mahaparinirvana*) at Kusinagara. The other four miracles are his descent at Sankisya after preaching to his mother in heaven, the occasion in Vaisali when a monkey offered him honey, his conversion of the heretics at Sravasti by multiplying himself, and his taming of the mad elephant Nalagiri, which was sent by his envious cousin Devadatta to kill him. The formula for several of the principal miracles had already become stereotyped by the Gupta period (320–600), as is known from sculptural depictions, and the Pala artists did not alter the mode fundamentally. Even from the few manuscripts in the collection, however, it is evident that there are minor differences in emphasis and minutiae.

A *Dharanisamgraha* manuscript is usually illuminated with formal representatives of divine figures only. Two folios of a *Dharanisamgraha* in the collection [3], however, include some of the Eight Great Miracles. The *Pancharaksha* is generally adorned with images of the five goddesses who are the personifications of the five charms of the title and with representations of the five transcendental Buddhas. As there are several textual traditions for the iconography of the five goddesses, their representations vary considerably from one manuscript to another.

Whether the subject is narrative or hieratic, the number of figures in a panel is kept to a minimum, although often these diminutive compositions are more elaborate than those in contemporary, or earlier, sculptural representations. Since a palm leaf usually is only about twenty inches wide and between two and three inches high, a single panel is limited to the height of the leaf, and the width varies between three and four inches. Each composition is usually dominated by the principal actor, whose prominence is further emphasized by a reduction of the scale of the others. Nevertheless, there is sufficient interaction among the figures to make each composition animated and sometimes vivacious. Occasionally the artists introduced unusual or whimsical details in the narrative scenes, which further enliven the representations.

In addition to figurative subjects, a manuscript page containing illustrations is often adorned with decorative bands or panels around the string holes and at the ends. Sometimes these bands are filled with stupas or images of divinities. Occasionally a page may be embellished further with floral designs or roundels. Interestingly, no such decorations are employed on unillustrated pages.

In addition to the leaves themselves, the wood covers of a book may also be illustrated. Generally only the insides of the covers are painted. The collection contains two pairs of covers, and although it cannot now be determined to which books they belonged, they are of exceptional quality and art-historical interest. Because covers are often separated from the original manuscripts, they cannot always be precisely dated. Whereas some standard iconographic conventions were followed for the subject matter of paintings in the books, no such set pattern is discernible for book covers. For instance, one set of covers in the collection [4] is adorned with scenes from the Buddha Sakyamuni's life other than the Eight Great Miracles and with Buddhas and a bodhisattva. While the latter are present on other known covers, no other Indian book cover has yet been found with these same incidents from the Buddha's life. The second pair [9] depicts individual deities of the Vajrayana pantheon, each within a shrine. Once again, while it is not uncommon to encounter such hieratic images on covers, this set not only reveals a particular iconographic program not entirely understood today, but many of the depictions are quite unconventional, as much for their iconography as for their lively compositions.

The aesthetic effect of the pictures on the covers is also quite different from those on manuscript leaves. While the latter include small painted panels with the writing, the entire length of a cover is filled with pictures. And even though a cover is divided into individual panels or compositions for both narrative and hieratic themes, because of the absence of writing the total picture creates a stronger visual impact. Compared with the miniature vignettes on the folios, the paintings on the covers are often livelier, conveying a stronger rhythmic sense of movement, and have more complex compositions. Moreover, the representations on the covers seem to be bolder, brighter, and more vivacious. Certainly the vitality that is exuded by the figures in the mid-twelfth-century book covers [9] is unmatched by even the narrative themes on the other covers or on the leaves themselves.

By and large, the illuminations on Buddhist manuscripts and their covers are figurative and strongly linear. Although in some instances attempts were made to suggest volume through tonal gradations of color, generally plastic effects are achieved through the skillful manipulation of the outline and the garments, through contrasting colors, and by placing the figures within architectural settings that impart an illusion of depth. The outlines of the figures are often drawn in bolder hues to emphasize the contours of the form. Generally a red aureole serves as the immediate background of the figures. Sometimes a stylized tree is added behind an architectural element to create a sense of space within the composition. At other times a patterned cushion of a different color is added behind a seated Buddha or deity to suggest more than one plane. Small areas at the top of the panel are occasionally painted in indigo blue speckled with tiny flowers, perhaps to suggest a deep blue sky. These starlike floral specks also represent the belief that the divine presence is always indicated by a shower of flowers.

At times the ground around the aureole is treated in an unusual fashion. On one leaf [2A] there are tiny red dots on red, and on the other two [5A,B] tiny dark blue dots fill a ground of lighter blue that has delicate washes of white. In the taming of the mad elephant scene [5A] the Buddha's aureole is an effulgent light blue with a darker blue border, while the ground around it is red with faintly visible burgundy dots. These dots create a pointillist effect, which is, however, more impressive in blue than it is in red. This treatment of the background is rarely encountered in other Pala manuscripts but is a prominent feature of a twelfth-century *Gandavyuha* manuscript from Nepal.[3] It may be noted that ancient Indian theoretical texts on painting do speak of a form of shading with tiny dots, but clearly that is not the artist's goal here. Since it is combined with the white highlights in the blue panels, perhaps the interest was to provide a greater sense of depth to the picture.

The illuminators had little choice in the colors of the deities, whose complexions were restricted to yellow, red, green, blue, or white by iconographic rules. The golden complexion of the Buddha is usually suggested by yellow, but on occasion (as in [5]) he is given a more naturalistic flesh color that seems to be a combination of brown and white with pink highlights. Human attendants are painted in diverse colors, including brown. The Buddhas invariably wear red robes, but one notices considerable variation in the colors and patterns of the other figures' textiles. The artists were probably quite free to render the garments as well as tiaras and ornaments as they wished, but hair is painted in black for everyone.

The tradition of illuminating manuscripts among Buddhists in Bihar and Bengal was shortlived, stretching roughly over only two centuries.[4] As it was a rather conservative tradition, only minor stylistic changes are perceptible. As is apparent in the early eleventh-century pictures in the collection [1], the compositions of the scenes of the Buddha's life are less elaborate than those seen in later manuscript representations. The figures seem more fully modeled, their plasticity more clearly defined than in later examples. The carefully delineated outlines are smooth and rounded, while in later illuminations [4–9] they become increasingly more agitated and distorted. Flowing and sensuous in the early eleventh-century manuscript, the line becomes palpably brittle and desiccated with time, as if displaying a nervous energy. The postures and gestures are elegantly restrained in the earlier paintings, but they become more exaggerated and contrived in later pictures. The same distortions occur in the proportions of the figures, which are more naturalistic in the earlier representations. A minor detail that distinguishes the figure of the Buddha in the early illuminations is the fact that his garment is plain and transparent, but by the mid-eleventh century it became the norm to add striations to it to impart a sense of volume [3–5]. Later illuminations also make more extensive use of trees and architectural forms and reveal a greater penchant among the artists for enlivening the figures by both exaggerating their stances and diversifying their apparel.

All but one of the illuminated manuscripts and the covers in the collection date after the mid-eleventh century. Apart from differing substantially from the early eleventh-century manuscript, they also differ from one another in minutiae depending on their subject matter and the talent of the artists. Some artists were clearly more inventive than others, as is visible in the two pairs of richly illuminated covers in the collection [4, 9]. By and large, however, the majority of the artists remained tradition-bound and had little scope or interest in deviating in either the themes or mode of representation.

Although the number of illuminated Buddhist manuscripts in the collection is small, fortunately several include colophon pages. Some of the colophons provide information that is significant for the broader cultural history of the period.

The colophons in Buddhist manuscripts are generally presented in a standard formula. They begin with the declaration that the book is the pious gift of so-and-so, who is a steadfast follower of the Mahayana form of Buddhism. Occasionally a word may be added about his or her profession or social status. The second sentence invariably consists of the following universal supplication that is a part of all Mahayana dedications: by this act the donor seeks enlightenment for his or her teachers, parents, ancestors, and for all sentient beings. This is generally followed by the name and regnal year of the king and sometimes by the place where the manuscript was copied and the name of the scribe. The inclusion of the names of ruling monarchs and dates in such statements increases the historical importance of the manuscripts but does not necessarily help us to date the paintings precisely. The chronology of the Pala rulers is uncertain at best. Occasionally the scribes provided additional information of a personal nature, generally referring to themselves simply as a *kayastha,* meaning "scribe" (today regarded as a subcaste), or a *lekhaka,* which means "a writer." Sometimes a specific monastery is also named, as is the case with two of the works in the museum's collection.

The earliest manuscript in the collection [1] was dedicated by a woman named Tejoka, who was the wife of one Srikumara, who describes himself as a *kayastha.*

Usually scribes, some *kayastha*s were also officials of either state or local administrations. Since commissioning an illustrated manuscript involved a considerable expenditure, very likely Srikumara was a man of means and perhaps a government official. Or he could have been a prosperous scribe and may have copied the manuscript to earn religious merit for himself and his wife. It may be noted that the scribe of another manuscript, Jayakumara, also has a name ending in *-kumara* [5].

Jayakumara was a resident of the Apanaka monastery and describes himself as a *vamatanaka* rather than a *kayastha* or a *lekhaka*. Unfortunately, the meaning of the expression *vamatanaka* remains elusive. Most likely it was a designation of a lay functionary in a monastery. Apanaka was the most important monastery in Kurkihar (Bihar), not far from Bodhgaya. This is the only known manuscript to have been copied in this obscure monastery. No less interesting is the fact that the book was dedicated at the monastery by a monk who had come from the Malaya country, which is the ancient name of the Malabar region on the coast of Maharashtra. This confirms evidence from other sources that the Apanaka monastery in Kurkihar was especially patronized by monks from southern India.

A second instance of a monk from a different region visiting a monastery in Bihar is provided by another manuscript in the collection [3]. It was commissioned by a Ramajiva from Nepal at the famous Nalanda monastery, which must have had the largest library in the region. Although nothing is known about Ramajiva except that he was a pious follower of the Mahayana, he could have been a merchant or a monk. What this manuscript does prove is the international character of Nalanda, which was the most important seat of Buddhist learning in India at the time.

The final colophon [7] is in some ways the most important, as it sheds some light on the political history of Bihar in the second half of the twelfth century. The manuscript was donated by Prince Vikramamana, the son of Rudramana, whose name is known from only one inscription.[5] In it Rudramana is described as the ruler of Magadha, which was the general designation for southern Bihar. The epithets used to describe him in the inscription clearly indicate that Rudramana owed only nominal allegiance to the Pala ruler, Madanapala, and was for all practical purposes independent. Not only does the manuscript's colophon corroborate the epigraphical evidence for this ruling family of Magadha, it also furnishes us for the first time with the name of a third member of the family. The colophon further informs us that the family was Buddhist.

Thus, of the four manuscripts in the collection with colophons only one was certainly dedicated by a monk and two by lay devotees, one of whom was the wife of a scribe and the other a prince. The vocation of the donor from Nepal is unknown. The royal dedication is the third such instance that has come to light among Pala-period manuscripts.[6] From this scanty evidence, as well as from other surviving manuscripts, it would appear that the commoner was more interested in commissioning and dedicating sacred books than the royalty.

NOTES

1. E. Conze, trans., *Aṣṭasāhasrikā Prajñāpāramitā* (Calcutta: Asiatic Society, [1958] 1972), p. 32.

2. These consist of book covers discovered in a stupa at Gilgit in Pakistan. See Pal & Meech-Pekarik 1988, pp. 41–44, pls. 1–3.

3. For the Nepali manuscript, see Pal & Meech-Pekarik 1988, pl. 25. For a limited, slightly different use of this technique in an Indian manuscript, see Losty 1982, p. 33, no. 9.

4. See Pal & Meech-Pekarik 1988, pp. 77–94, for a discussion of manuscripts painted in Bengal.

5. R. C. Majumdar, ed., *The History of Bengal* (Dacca: University of Dacca, [1943] 1963), 1: 583.

6. Pal & Meech-Pekarik 1988, p. 36.

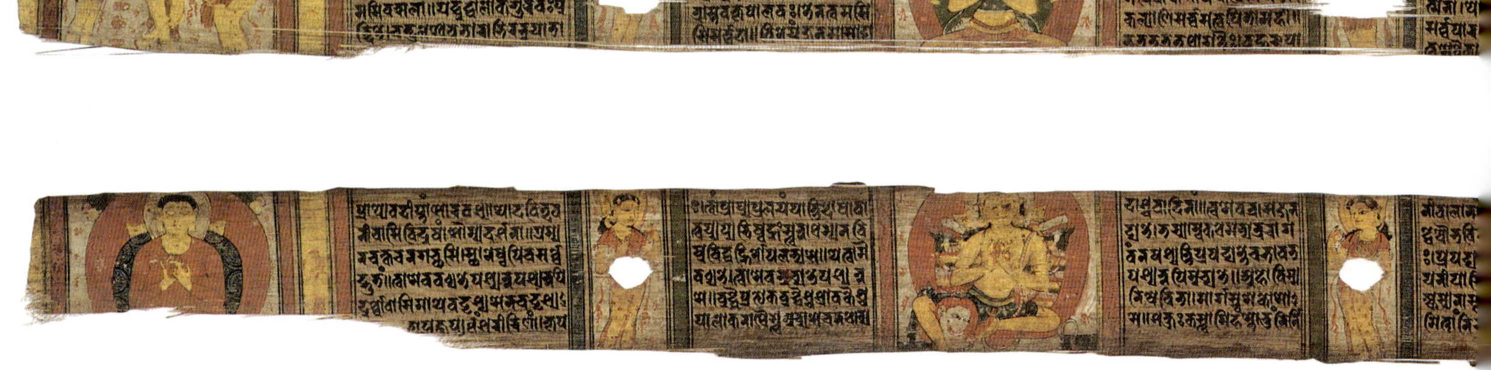

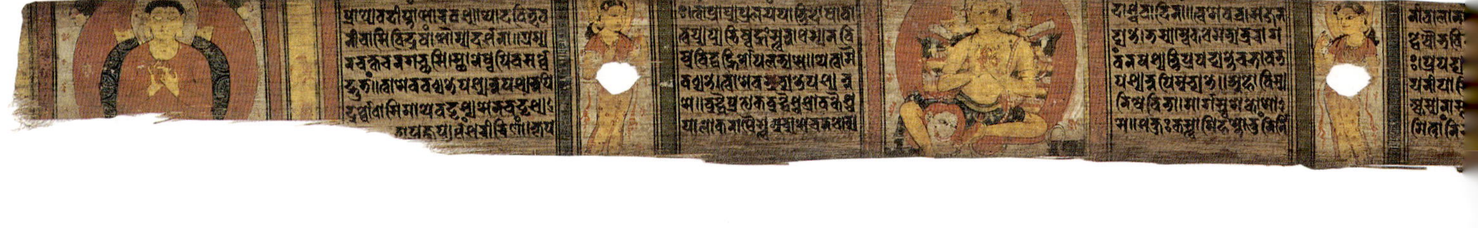

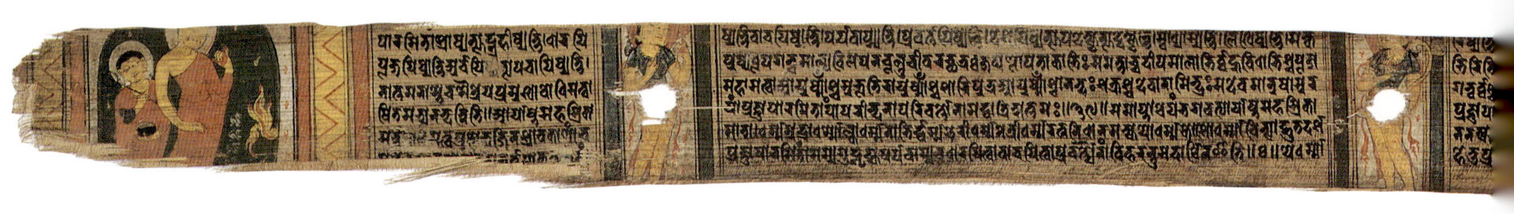

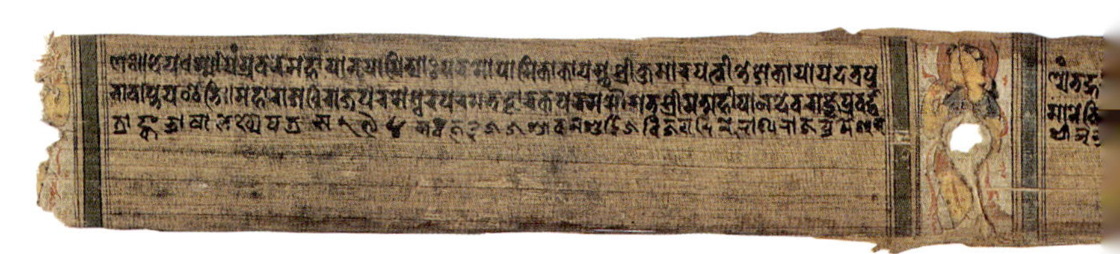

Catalogue

All texts are written in ink and all pictures painted in opaque watercolor on palm leaf. All manuscript covers are opaque watercolor on wood.

I FOUR FOLIOS FROM A *PRAJNAPARAMITA* MANUSCRIPT

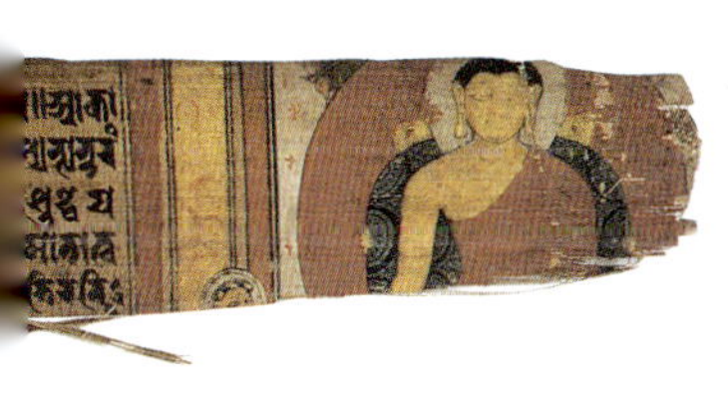

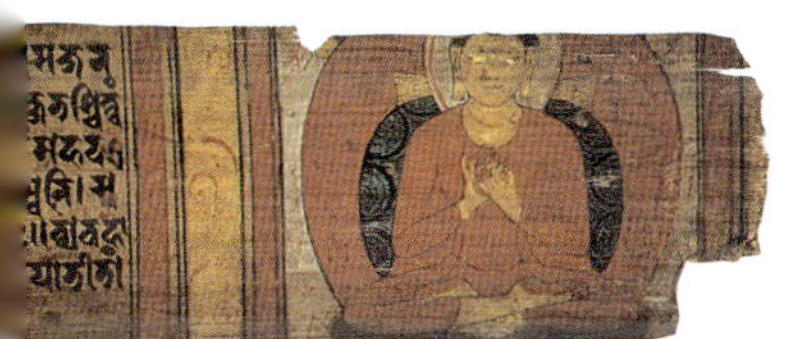

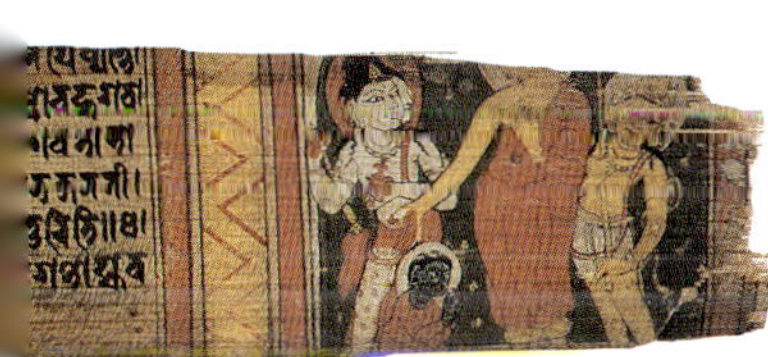

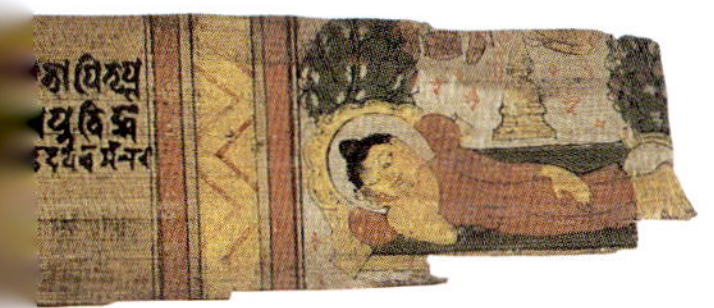

Bihar; c. 1025
Folios, approx. 1¾ x 20½ in (4.4 x 51.9 cm)
Illustrations, approx. 1¾ x 2⅛ in (4.4 x 5.4 cm)
Purchased with funds provided by
Mr. and Mrs. Paul E. Mannheim and
Dr. and Mrs. Pratapaditya Pal
M.86.185a–d
Literature: Pal & Meech-Pekarik 1988, pp. 58–61, figs. 10, 11, pl. 4.

A *Prajnaparamita and Scenes from the Buddha's Life*
B *Manjusri and Scenes from the Buddha's Life*
C *Scenes from the Buddha's Life*
D *The Death of the Buddha*

These four illuminated leaves are from a *Prajnaparamita* manuscript. Fortunately, one of them (D) includes the colophon (see Appendix), and despite its damaged condition, the following relevant information can be gleaned.

The manuscript was dedicated in the twenty-seventh regnal year of King Mahipala by Tejoka, who was the wife of the scribe Srikumara and a pious Buddhist. Unfortunately no information is available as to where it was copied and dedicated, but Nalanda remains a strong possibility (see [3]). As Tejoka's husband Srikumara was a scribe, he may have copied the manuscript himself. The king mentioned would be Mahipala I of the Pala dynasty, since the second Mahipala had a short reign of a few years. The exact date that Mahipala I began to rule is uncertain, but the most likely date is sometime in the last decade of the tenth century. Thus this manuscript was dedicated sometime about 1025.

A shorter and later inscription provides two dates and two names. The dates are in the Newari era of Nepal, 194 and 355, which correspond to 1074 and 1235 of the Christian era. One of the names mentioned is Abhaya, which is very likely the name of King Abhayamalla of Nepal (r. c. 1216–55). The second name, Udayavarman, which is also associated with the second date, is unfamiliar. The reason why the dates are mentioned cannot be determined from the incomplete inscription, but it seems clear that the manuscript was taken to Nepal before 1074.

Altogether there are nine panels and eight narrow bands around the string holes; the paintings on them are in various states of preservation. Each of the bands is filled with a figure with a halo behind her or his head indicating divine status. All of them represent serpent deities. The two in A are male, while the others are female. Each painted panel was once framed by borders with red and yellow curlicue or zig-zag patterns, those on the inside still being preserved. The two central panels depict the goddess Prajnaparamita (A) and the bodhisattva Manjusri (D). Each of the side panels represents one of the Eight Great Miracles from the Buddha's life. The two scenes on leaf A depict his birth at Lumbini and the enlightenment at Bodhgaya. In the birth scene Maya stands holding the *sala* tree, with her sister behind her. The infant is seen emerging from his mother's hip and is watched by a male deity waiting to receive him. Below the newborn (who looks more like a boy than an infant) are four

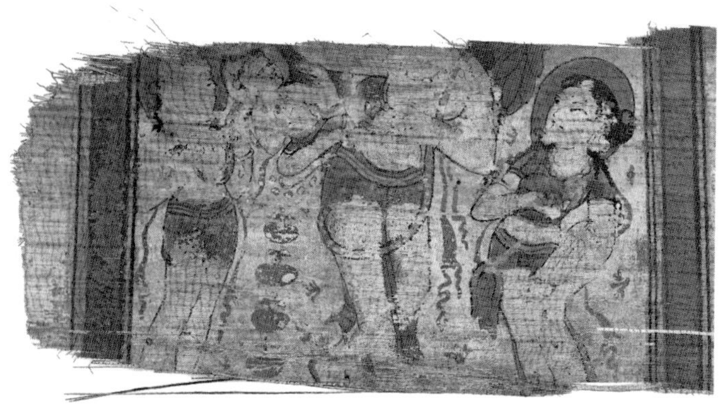
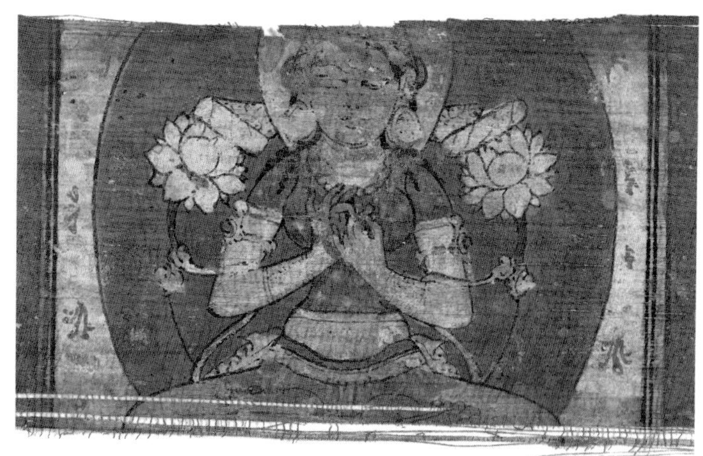
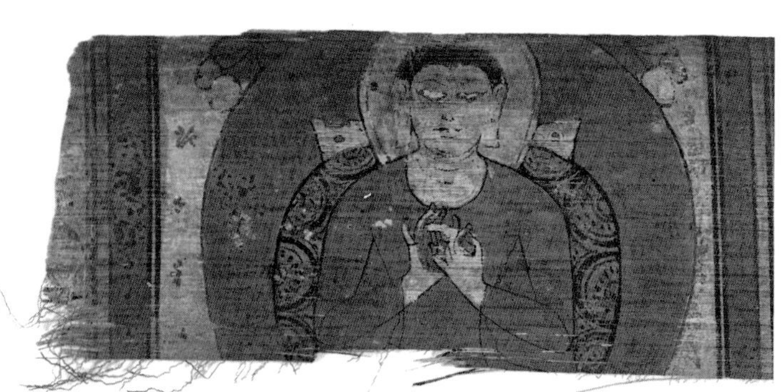
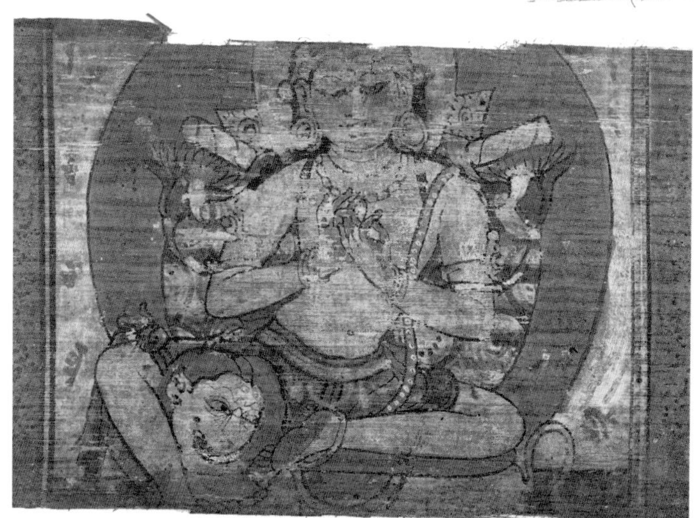
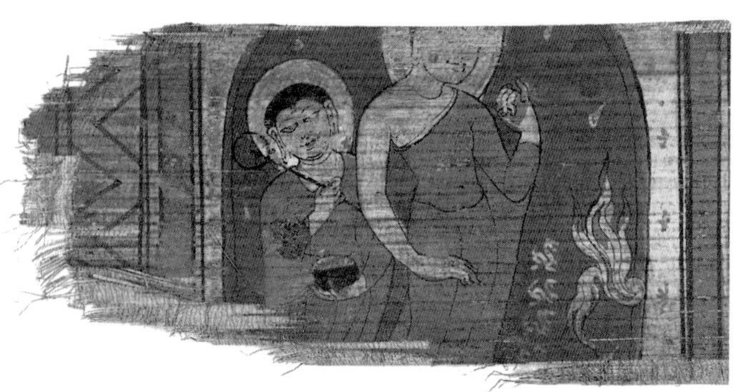

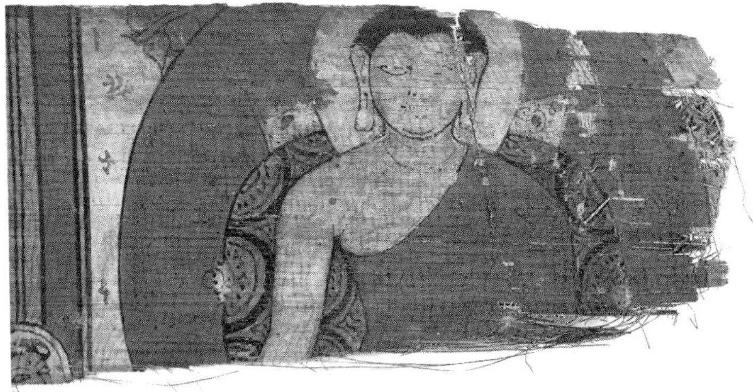

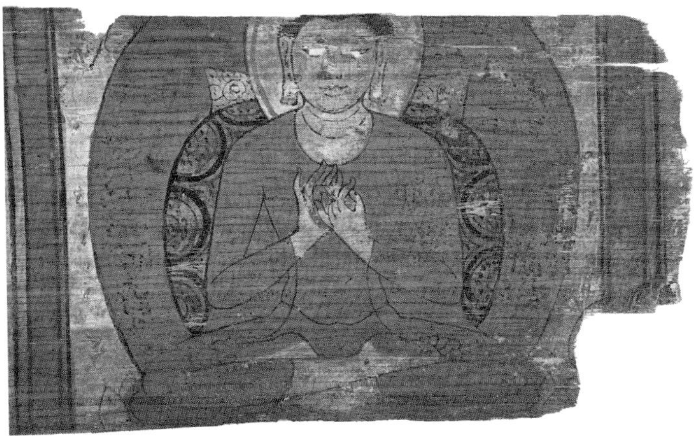

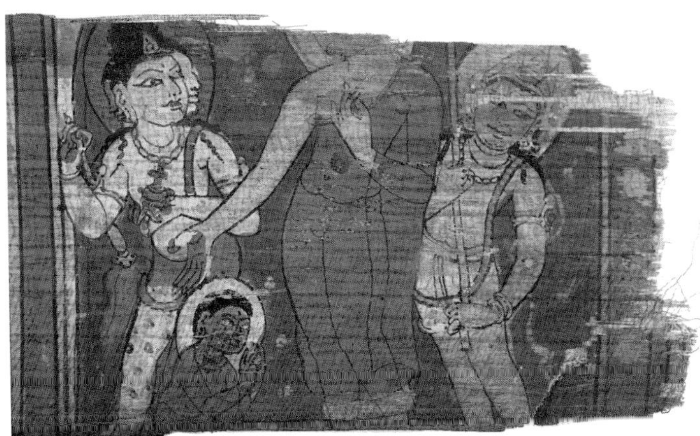

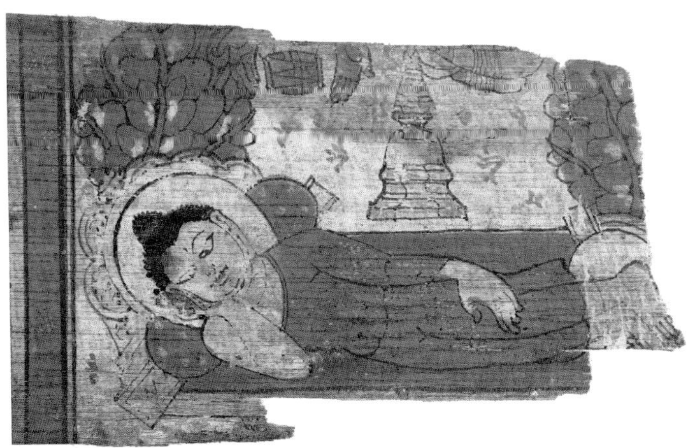

pots, no doubt filled with water for the first bath. The scene of enlightenment is represented by remnants of figures of the Buddha and the earth goddess. On leaf B are two preaching Buddhas, symbolizing the first sermon at Sarnath and very likely the multiplication miracle at Sravasti, distinguished by the mango tree above. On leaf C the scene on the left depicts the occasion when the Buddha tamed the mad elephant Nalagiri (cf. [5A]). A nimbate monk watches the miracle from behind the Buddha. The elephant cannot be seen but the artist has included four lions and a stylized flame looking like a floating scarf. The flame-issuing lions, released by the Buddha's palm, are said to be a metaphor for the Buddha's dharma-roar. At the other end is portrayed the miracle at Sankisya, where the Buddha, accompanied by the gods Brahma and Indra, returned to earth after preaching to his mother in heaven (cf. [5A, 6]). The four-headed Brahma (the fourth head is not shown) holds a flywhisk and Indra the parasol. The nimbate kneeling figure is very likely the nun Utpalavarna welcoming him. The death of the Buddha (*mahaparinirvana*) is represented on the remaining leaf. The Buddha is stretched out on a couch below the twin *sala* trees, and a stupa appears in the sky; flanking the stupa are a pair of divine hands playing a drum and another pair apparently holding symbols.

Although it is not known where exactly this manuscript was copied, it most likely was an important monastery in Bihar, such as Nalanda or Vikramasila. As I have discussed elsewhere (Pal and Meech-Pekarik 1988, p. 60), the style of the script is very close to that engraved on a pedestal of a sculpture dedicated in Sarnath during the reign of Mahipala I. Moreover, female figures similar to those in the narrow bands on these pages occur also on a door frame carved in the eleventh regnal year of Mahipala I and found at Nalanda (Huntington 1984, pl. 56).

Not only do these illuminations constitute the earliest surviving examples of Buddhist paintings from Bihar, with their emphasis on modeled forms and elegantly proportioned figures they are of outstanding quality as well. The controlled and firm drawing of the articulate outlines, the subtle manipulation of the transparent garments to reveal the body underneath, and the graceful postures and gestures are reminiscent of the classical style of Ajanta.

CAT. 1A details
CAT. 1B details
CAT. 1C details
CAT. 1D detail

Bihar; c. 1050
Folios, A, 1 5/8 x 20 1/8 in (4.1 x 51.1 cm);
B, 2 x 21 3/4 in (5.1 x 55.2 cm)
Center illustrations, A, 1 5/8 x 2 in (4.1 x 5.1 cm);
B, 2 x 2 in (5.1 x 5.1 cm)
From the Nasli and Alice Heeramaneck
Collection, Museum Associates Purchase
A, M.71.1.43; B, M.72.1.21
Literature: Tucci 1949, pl. A; *Heeramaneck* 1966,
p. 106, no. 113 (not illustrated).

A *Three Deities*
B *Bodhisattva Manjusri*

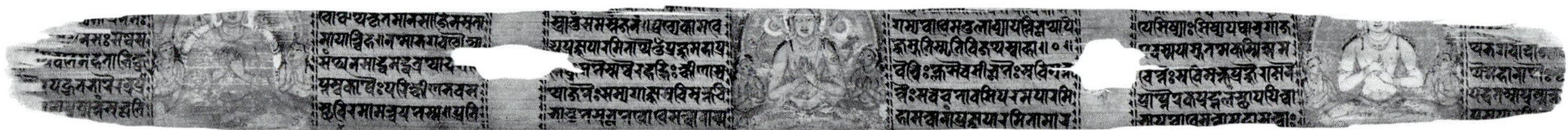

CAT. 2A
CAT. 2B detail

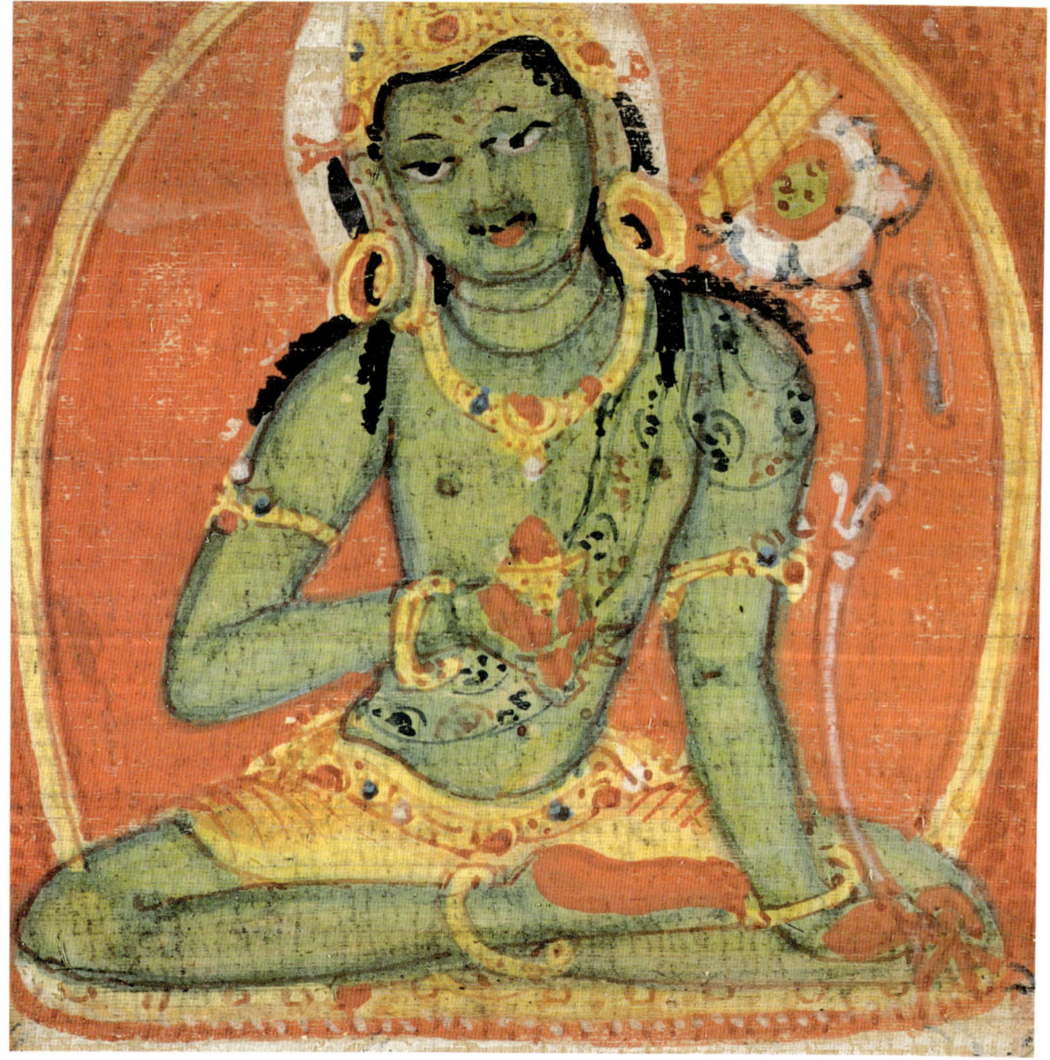

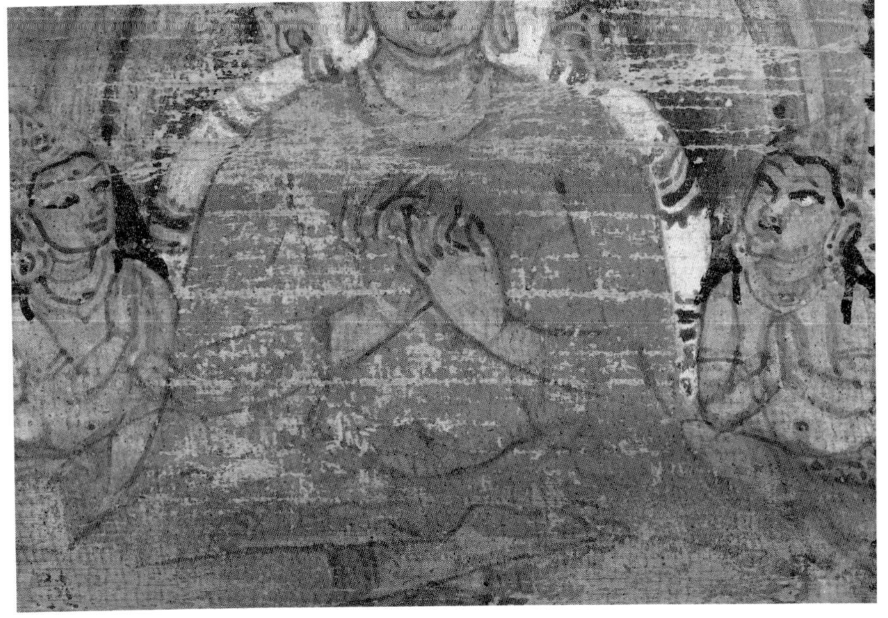

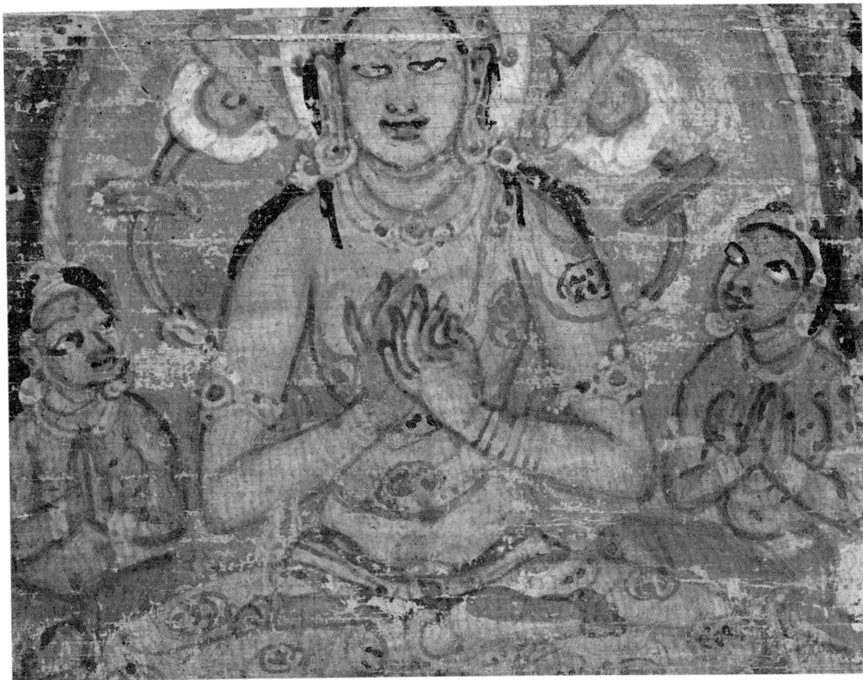

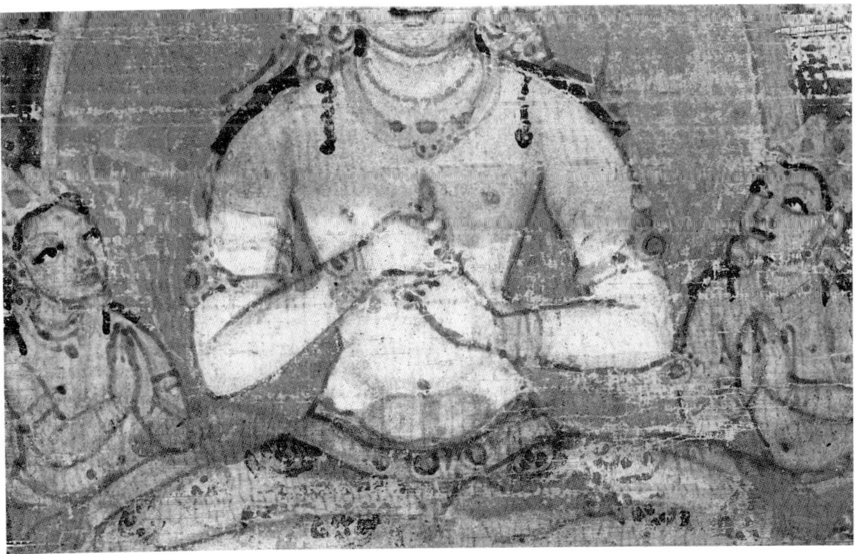

Although only a portion of the text on A is legible, it is very likely that A is the first folio of the manuscript for several reasons: the preaching Buddha is the first image on the left, the goddess Prajnaparamita is in the center, and the folio has no writing on the reverse. The styles of both the illustrations and the writing identify it certainly as a manuscript of the eleventh century copied somewhere in Bihar. The writing is closer to that of early eleventh-century manuscripts, and the pictures, though not as elegant, are stylistically closer to those in the Mahipala I manuscript [1] than to those of the late eleventh or twelfth centuries, e.g., [5, 6]. Thus a mid-eleventh-century date for these two folios is not improbable.

In the first illumination on leaf A the Buddha is shown preaching and is flanked by two identical crowned and adoring bodhisattvas. Noteworthy is the fact that no striations are indicated on the Buddha's red robe, a characteristic of the earlier illuminations. In the center of the leaf the goddess Prajnaparamita is also engaged in preaching. On either side of her head is a lotus, each supporting a book symbolizing wisdom. Her companions are two green, adoring females, both looking up at the goddess. In the third composition unfortunately the deity's head has been badly damaged. Nevertheless, his white complexion and bare torso as well as ornamentation indicate that he is very likely a bodhisattva rather than a Buddha. The gesture of his two hands is rather rare. Known as *bodhyaṅgi* (limb of enlightenment), it may be displayed by either the transcendental Buddha Vairochana or a form of the bodhisattva Manjusri known as Siddhaikavira, "the sole perfected hero," who is probably intended here. He too is accompanied by two crowned attendants, these of yellow complexion, as is the Buddha at the other end.

The second leaf has only one panel in the center, representing the more conventional form of the bodhisattva Manjusri. Here he holds a lotus stalk with his left hand, the flower supporting a book. The emblem in his right hand may be a jewel. His complexion is green, and he too has an elaborate crown and is bejeweled, as are the other deities.

The Buddha is represented against cushions and with a blue aureole; the three others are provided with red aureoles. While the principal figures are outlined carefully, the attendants are more freely rendered.

CAT. 2A details

Bihar, Nalanda; c. 1075
Folios, 1 15/16 x 20 3/4 in (4.9 x 52.7 cm)
Illustrations, A, 1 15/16 x 2 in (4.9 x 5.1 cm);
B, 1 15/16 x 2 1/8 in (4.9 x 5.4 cm)
From the Nasli and Alice Heeramaneck Collection, Museum Associates Purchase
M.72.1.20a,b
Literature: *Heeramaneck* 1966, p. 105, no. 111 (not illustrated); Saraswati 1978, pp. 40–42 (colophon only).

A *Prajnaparamita and Scenes from the Buddha's Life*
B *Manjusri (?) and Scenes from the Buddha's Life*

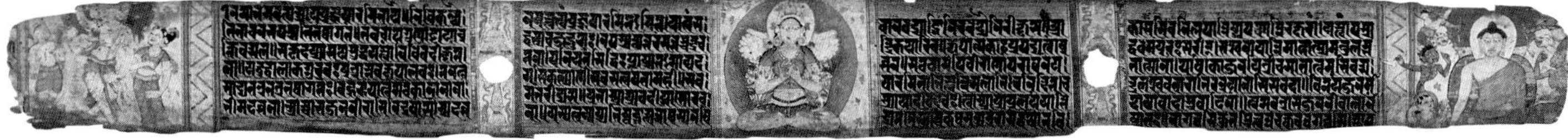

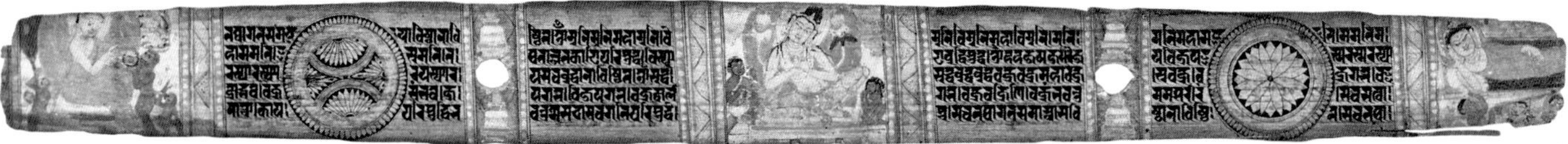

According to the colophon (see Appendix) this manuscript was dedicated by the pious Ramajiva, who was from Nepal, on the thirteenth day of Phalguna (February-March) in the fourteenth regnal year of King Nayapala. It was copied in Nalanda by the scribe Svamesvara.

Although there is disagreement as to the exact reign of Nayapala, he is known to have ruled for at least fifteen years sometime in the third quarter of the eleventh century. Thus this manuscript of the *Dharanisamgraha* was very likely commissioned and dedicated by the Nepali Ramajiva at the great Nalanda monastery sometime about 1075. Another manuscript has survived that was also prepared in the fourteenth regnal year of Nayapala (Pal and Meech-Pekarik 1988, pp. 70, 72).

The scene at the left extremity of the first leaf depicts the Buddha's birth. Compositionally and iconographically the scene is very close to that in the earlier manuscript [1A]. Here also one can discern the waterpots below the emerging infant. In the central composition is the goddess Prajnaparamita. Her hands form the gesture of turning the wheel of law, and on either side is a lotus supporting a book. The third scene on this leaf depicts the enlightenment of the Buddha at Bodhgaya. The Buddha is being attacked by a lively group of Mara's companions as the earth goddess looks on.

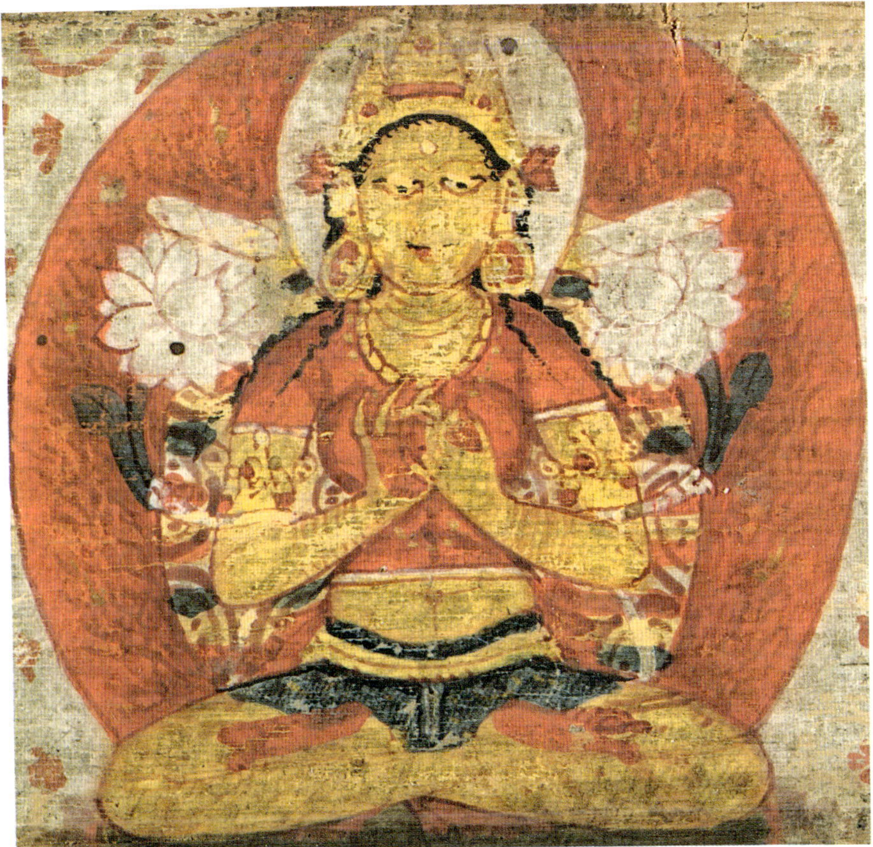

CAT. 3A detail

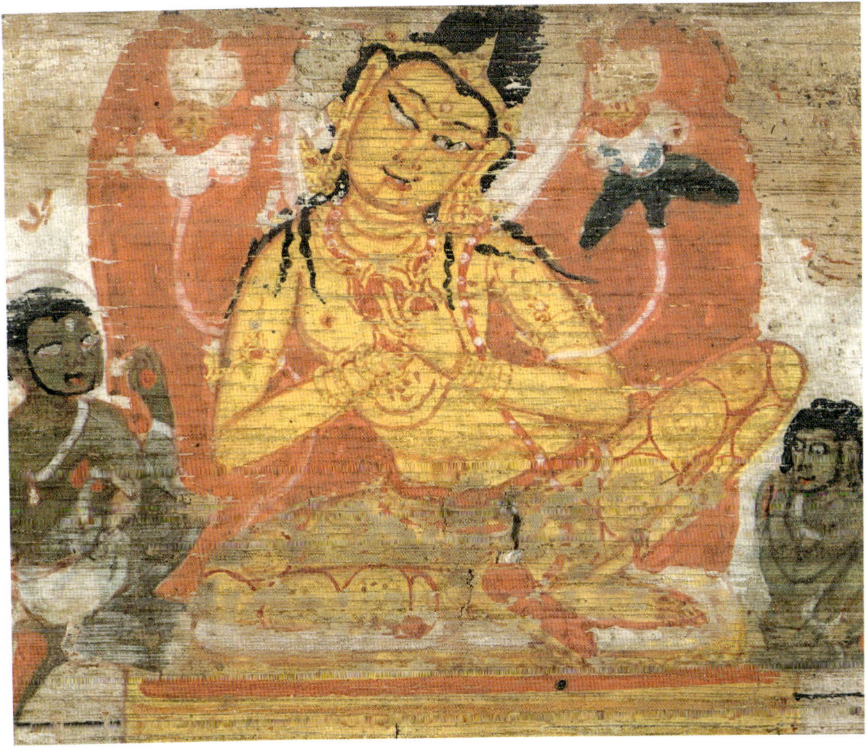

CAT. 3B detail

The panel on the left of the second leaf depicts the miracle of the monkey. The monkey behind the Buddha is approaching the master with the pot of honey; he then offers the pot, after which he ascends to heaven as a bodhisattva (see [5]). In the middle panel is an image of a bodhisattva whose exact identification is difficult. Of yellow complexion, he is seated in the posture of royal ease (*maharajalila*) with worshippers on either side. His hands make the same gesture as Prajnaparamita's, but it is not clear if the flowers beside him support books. However, the gesture and the complexion indicate that the figure probably represents the bodhisattva Manjusri. The remaining scene illustrates the death of the Buddha and includes three grieving monks in front. Stupas adorn the bands around all the string holes. In addition, two large roundels of lotus designs embellish the second leaf.

Leaf A is certainly the first page of the book; it begins with incantations addressed to Prajnaparamita. The second leaf (B) has the colophon on the reverse, and it is unambiguous about the manuscript being a collection of *dharani*s. Yet the inclusion of the scenes from the Buddha's life is most unusual: such scenes are generally included only in *Prajnaparamita* manuscripts. *Dharani* manuscripts are usually adorned solely with hieratic images of gods and goddesses. There is no apparent explanation for this departure from the norm. That the folios are from the same manuscript is certain.

This is the only known example of an illuminated manuscript dedicated by a Buddhist from Nepal on a visit to the Nalanda monastery. After being copied by Svamesvara at Nalanda, it must also have been illustrated locally. The style of the pictures still echoes the suave modeling and refined elegance of the *Prajnaparamita* illustrations of the early part of the century [1], however, the striations of the Buddha's robes indicate a later date. Although the compositions are somewhat more elaborate, they are not quite as exuberant as those encountered in illuminations of the latter part of the century. As a matter of fact, the remarkable similarities between the nativity panels in this and the earlier manuscript are probably not fortuitous, and Ramajiva's illustrator may well have been familiar with the earlier work. Some of the missing portions in the panels in the earlier manuscript can be reconstructed from surviving details here.

Bihar; 1075–1100
Each, 2⅛ x 22¼ in (5.4 x 56.5 cm)
From the Nasli and Alice Heeramaneck Collection, Museum Associates Purchase
M.72.1.20c,d
Literature: Pal 1984, p. 59; Pal & Meech-Pekarik 1988, pp. 34, 73–74, pl. 14.

A *Scenes from the Buddha's Life*
B *Buddhas with a Bodhisattva*

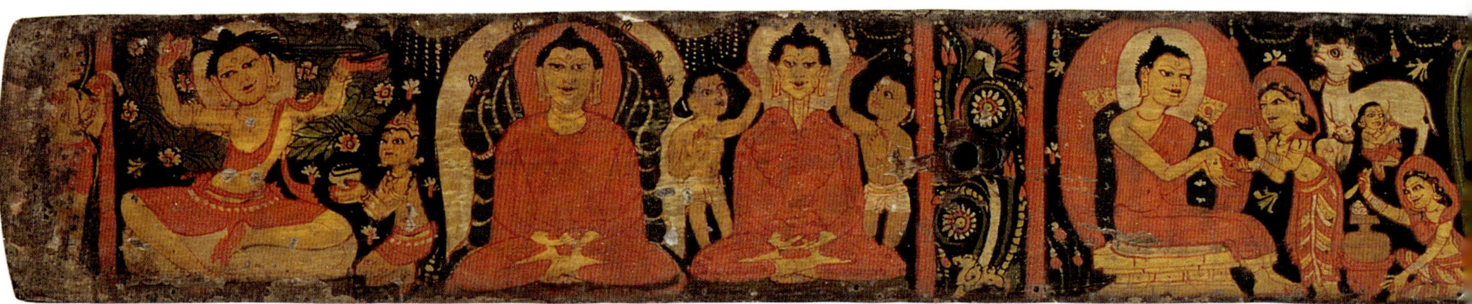

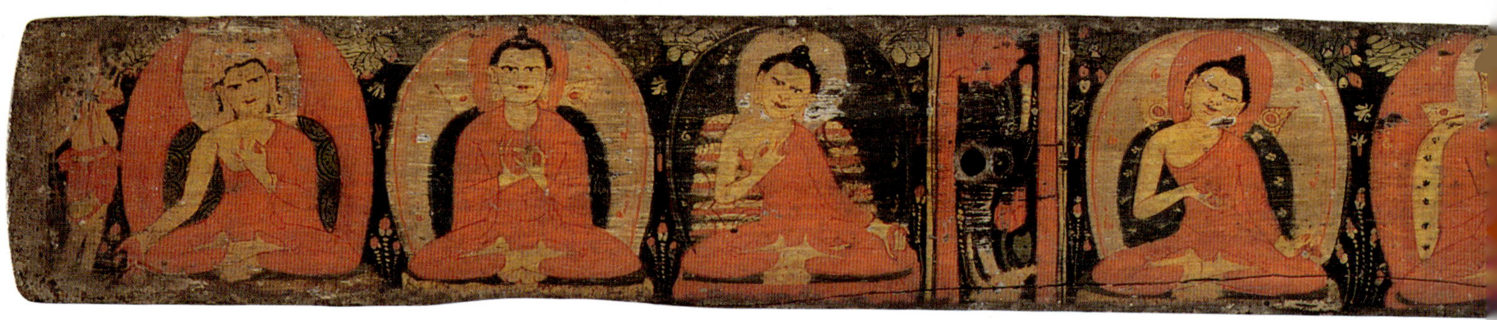

Because of their unusual subject matter, it is not clear to which book this pair of covers belonged. When they entered the collection, it was believed that they were covers of the preceding *Dharanisamgraha* manuscript [3], but this is unlikely; the sizes of those folios and the covers do not match, nor do the positions of the string holes. The inclusion of several scenes from the life of the Buddha on one of the covers may indicate that they protected a *Prajnaparamita* manuscript. However, it must be emphasized that the scenes represented here are not the conventional Eight Great Miracles but rather depict incidents not encountered on any other book cover, whether from India or Nepal.

The scenes from the Buddha's life on A may be identified as follows (left to right):

1 Indra waits eagerly with a bowl to collect the hair of the Buddha, which he himself is shearing.

2 An occasion from the Enlightenment Cycle, when during a storm the Buddha was sheltered by the serpent king Muchalinda.

3 Two youths try to distract the meditating Buddha, who has become emaciated from prolonged starvation.

4 The Buddha accepts rice cooked in milk from Sujata, the cowgirl.

5 The Buddha is shown walking.

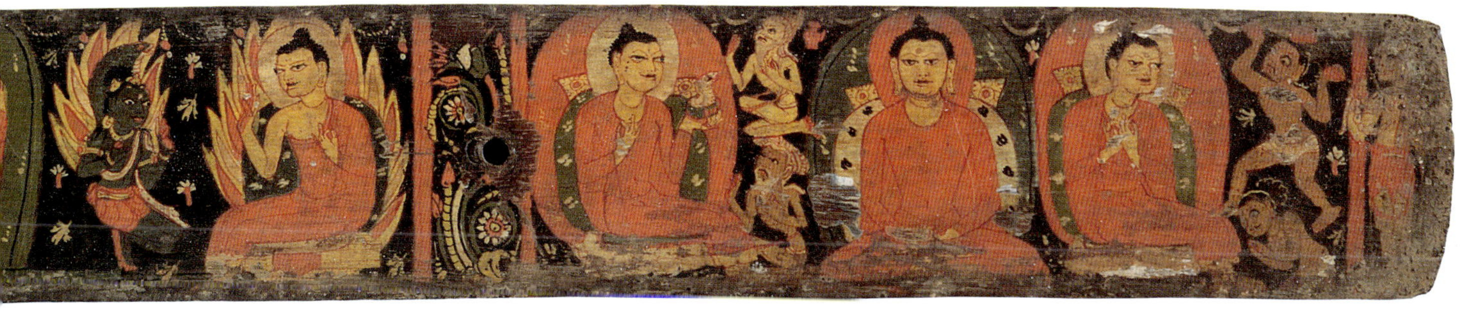

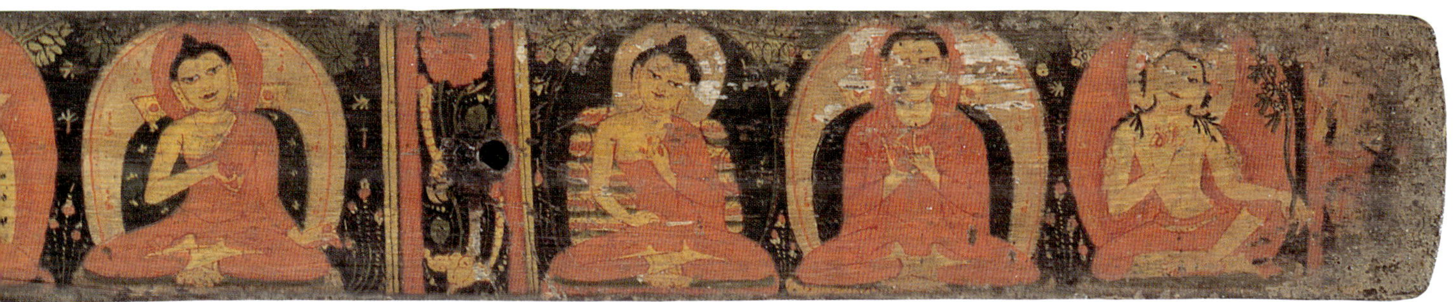

6 The Buddha confronts the serpent in Kasyapa's fire temple at Uruvila, near Bodhgaya.

7 The Buddha holds a tamed serpent in his hand as two ascetics look on.

8 The Buddha is shown meditating, but the occasion remains elusive.

9 The Buddha receives homage from an unidentified couple.

More intriguing is the iconographic program of the second cover (B). With the exception of the figure at the right edge, each represents a Buddha. All eight figures have yellow complexions, exhibit the teaching gesture with one or both hands, and have canopies of foliage above their heads. The foliage, however, is not articulated precisely enough to identify the individual trees associated with each Buddha. The bodhisattva holds a *nagakesara* flower, which is a distinctive attribute of Maitreya, the future Buddha. Seven of the eight Buddhas represent the seven Buddhas of the past. Usually the seven, including Sakyamuni, are shown together with Maitreya, making a group of eight. The ninth representation here—that of the crowned figure—very likely also depicts Maitreya, but as a Buddha. Maitreya is generally portrayed either as a bodhisattva or a Buddha. Such a grouping of the seven Buddhas of the past with two Maitreyas is not common.

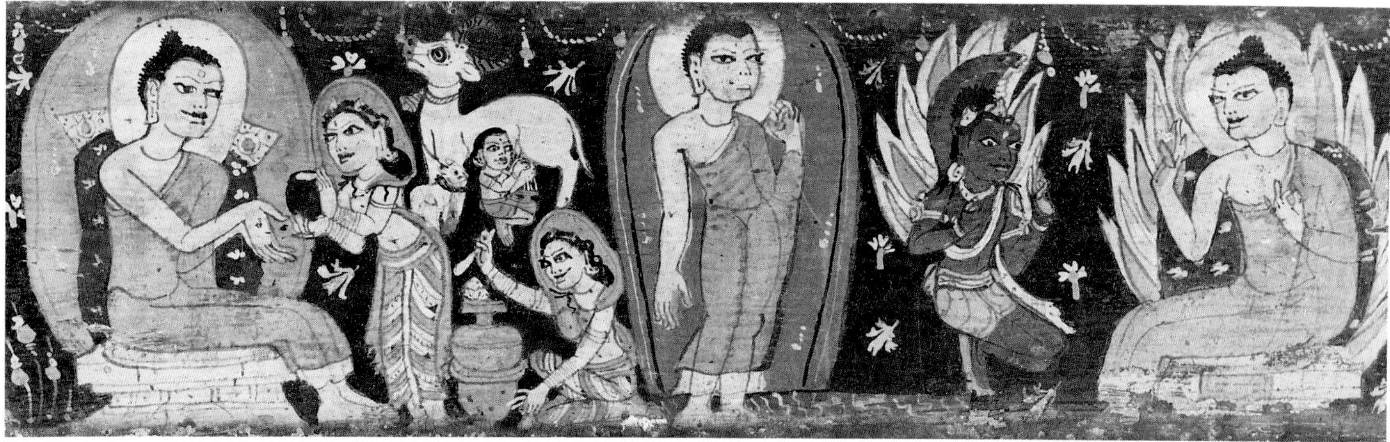

CAT. 4A detail

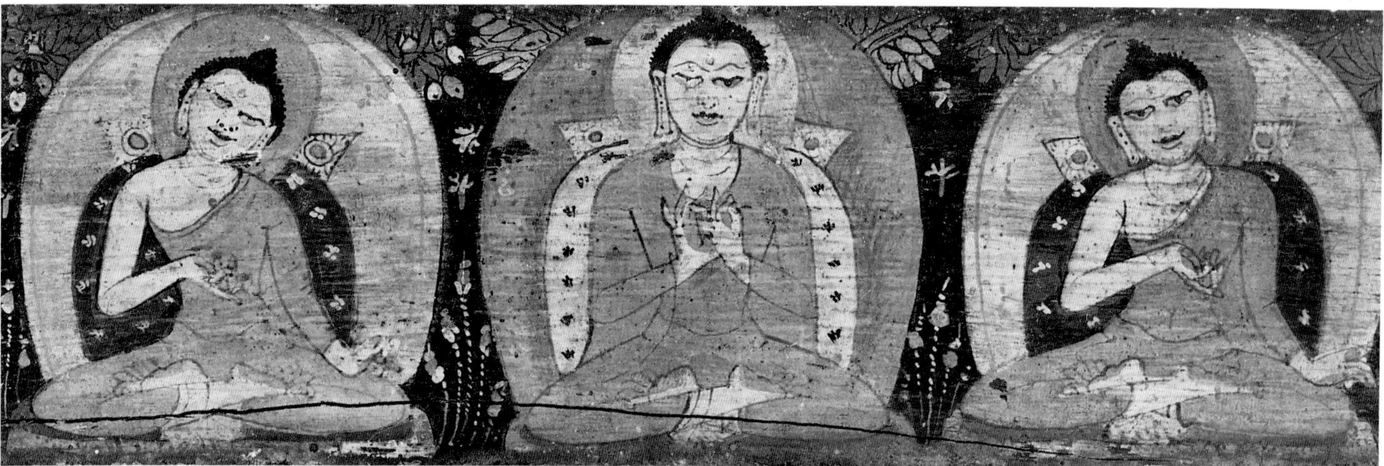

CAT. 4B detail

At each end of both covers is a standing figure holding garlands, presumably a devotee. The bands around the string holes are adorned with a distinctive and attractive floral design. The cushions behind the seated Buddhas on both covers are covered in fabrics of various designs.

Above and beyond the unusual themes, the covers are interesting for their varied compositions as well. Even the three panels with the Buddhas (B) reveal some originality in the manner in which the somewhat immobile central Buddha is contrasted with the more lively flanking figures, their bodies swaying in different directions. Especially engaging are the narrative panels (A), where with two exceptions each incident is represented with utmost brevity and vivaciousness. The exceptions are the incident with Sujata and the miracle at Uruvila. Why these two occasions were represented in greater detail cannot be ascertained, but perhaps they were favorite stories of the person who commissioned the book.

Stylistically these covers are closer to several others (Pal and Meech-Pekarik 1988, p. 56, figs. 12, 13) painted during the reign of Mahipala II, who had a reign of less than a decade in the last quarter of the eleventh century, or during the reign of Ramapala (see [5]) than they are to earlier illuminations such as those rendered in the first half of the century [1–2]. The representations of the life scenes are particularly animated, with the figures in each composition interacting with greater expressiveness than is seen on the conventional representation of the miracles on the folios. Considering their age, the covers are in remarkably good condition, with the colors still bright and glowing.

Bihar, Kurkihar; c. 1100–1125
Folios, A, 2 1/8 x 22 1/8 in (5.4 x 56.2 cm);
B, 2 1/8 x 21 3/4 in (5.4 x 55.2 cm)
Center illustrations, approx. 2 1/8 x 2 5/8 in (5.4 x 6.7 cm)
From the Nasli and Alice Heeramaneck Collection, Museum Associates Purchase
M.72.1.19a,b
Literature: *Heeramaneck* 1966, p. 106, no. 112 (not illustrated); Trabold 1975, pp. 27–28, no. 33 (not illustrated); Pal 1988, pp. 83–84, fig. 1; Huntington & Huntington 1990, pp. 182–85, no. 57 (B only).

A *Avalokitesvara and Scenes from the Buddha's Life*
B *Maitreya and Scenes from the Buddha's Life*

According to the colophon (see Appendix) this manuscript was dedicated by the elder monk Trailokyachandra, who was from the Malaya region and a disciple of the elder monk Purnacandra. The book was copied by Jayakumara, who was a *vamatanaka* and a resident of the great Apanaka monastery in the eighteenth regnal year of King Ramapala.

The date of this manuscript would fall somewhere in the first quarter of the twelfth century, depending on the monarch's accession date. Ramapala attained the throne probably in the last decade of the eleventh century and ruled for almost half a century. Although a relatively large number of illustrated manuscripts from Ramapala's long reign have survived, this manuscript is unique in that it was dedicated in a monastery from which no other example has yet come to notice.

The middle of each page is decorated with an image of a bodhisattva, Avalokitesvara on leaf A and Maitreya on leaf B. The other four panels represent four miracles from the life of the Buddha. The scene on the left of A depicts the miracle of taming the mad elephant Nalagiri. As the Buddha calms him down, the white and pink elephant is shown twice, once with a raised trunk and then kneeling in submission. A monk with his bowl and staff stands behind the Buddha, while in the upper right corner of the aureole is the floating flame. The row of lions (cf. [1C]), drawn summarily in white, are clustered together on the Buddha's garment near his left elbow. It may be recalled that the Buddha is often characterized as the lion of the Sakyas, and his voice is compared with the roar of a lion.

The panel on the right of this page illustrates the Buddha's miraculous descent at Sankisya after having preached to his mother in heaven. The nun Utpalavarna kneels at his feet. Behind him stands Indra, the king of gods, holding the parasol. He is distinguished by additional eyes on his body, which symbolize his superhuman nature. Brahma is shown as a white ascetic figure and holds the flywhisk with his right hand.

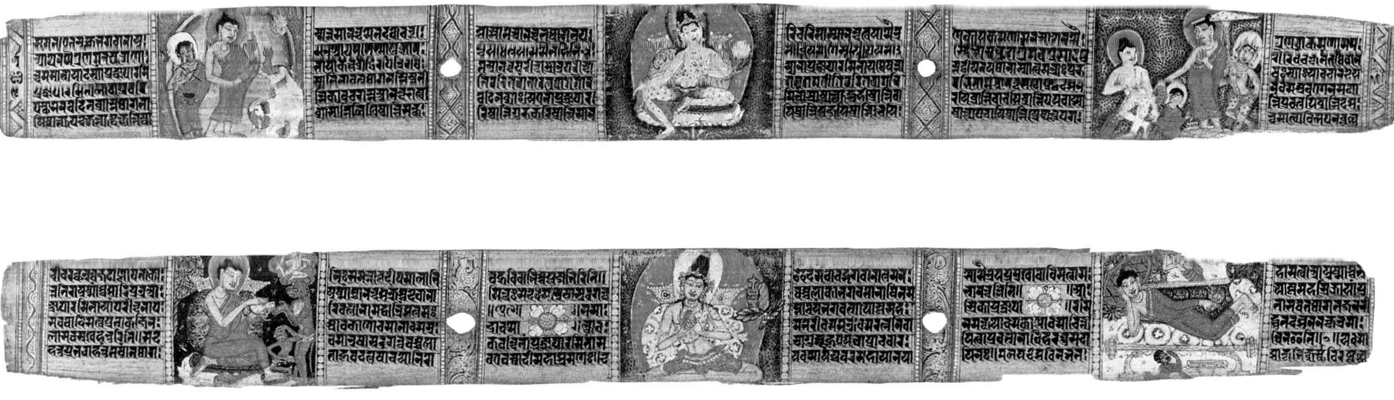

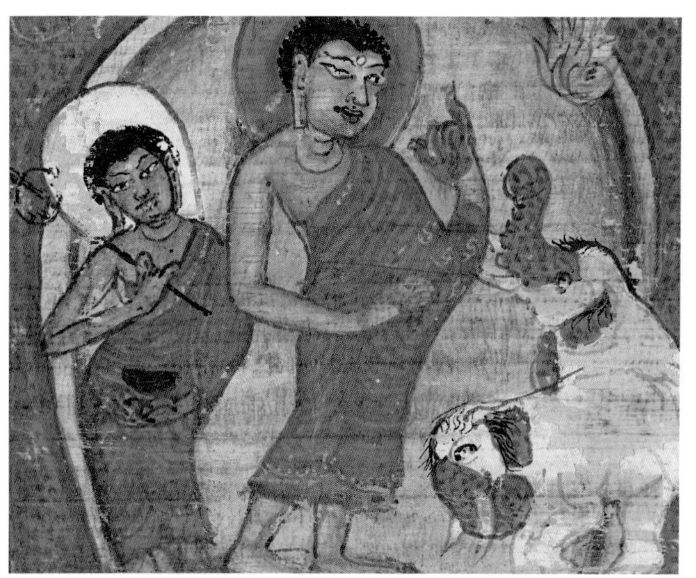

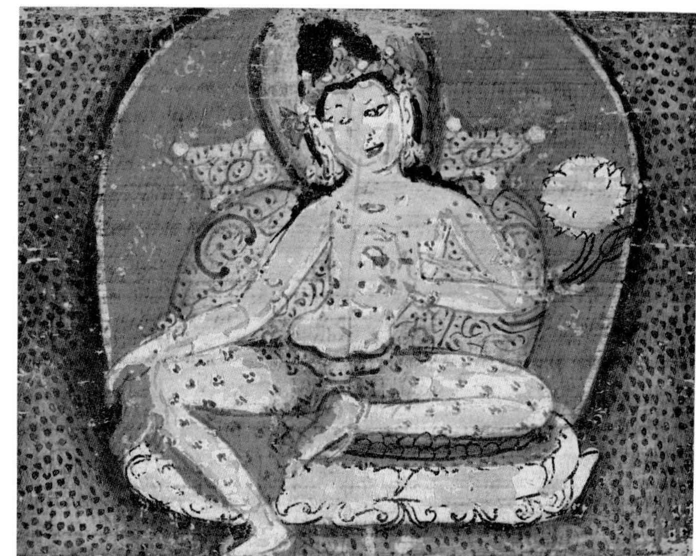

CAT. 5A details

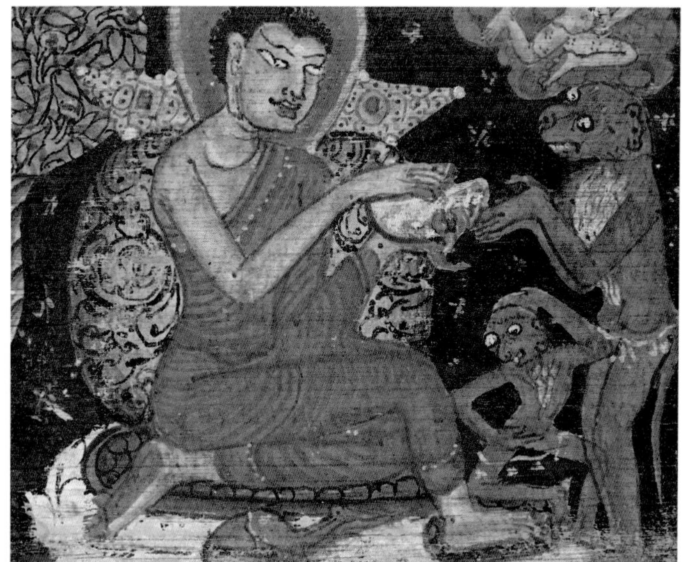

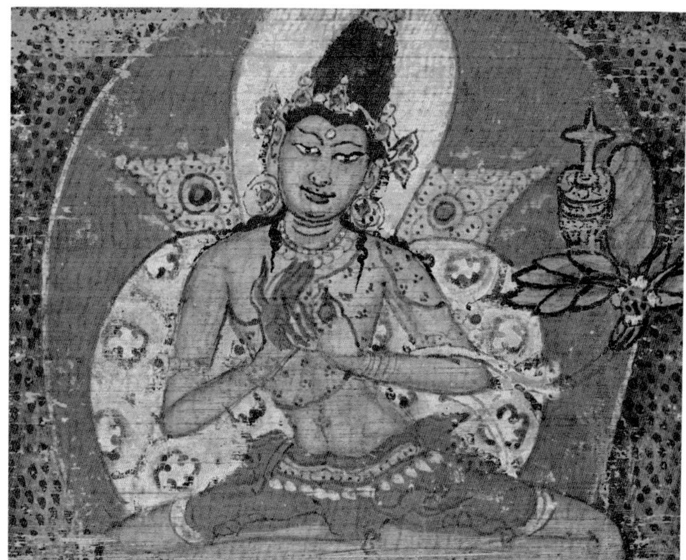

CAT. 5B details

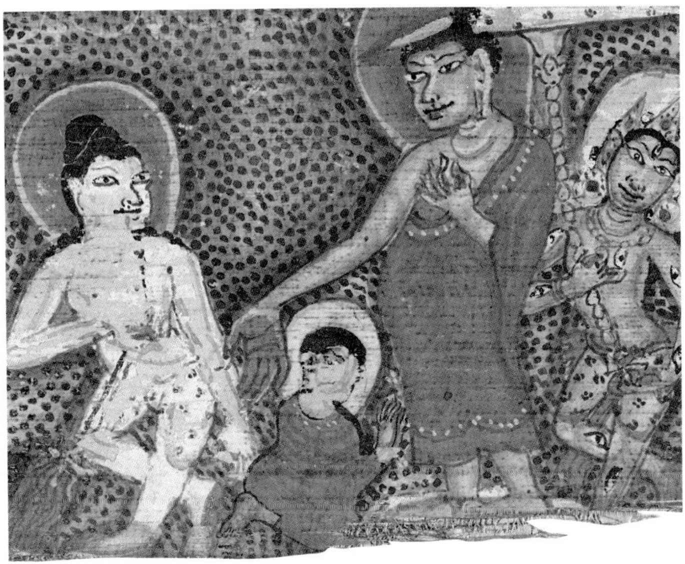

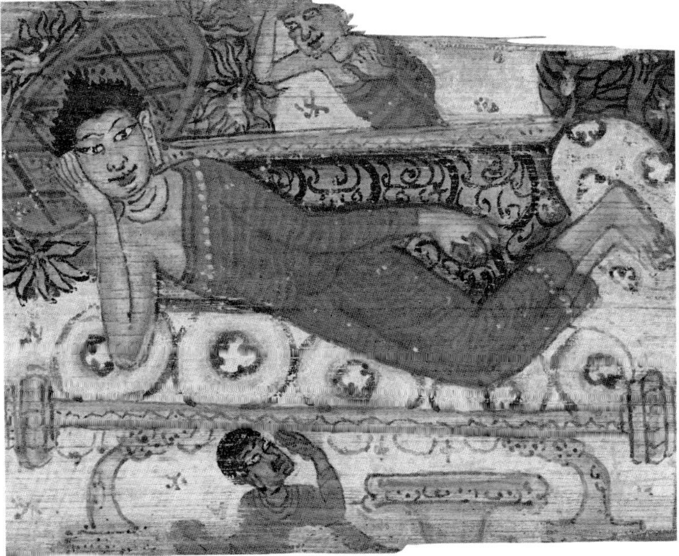

The panel on the left of the second leaf (B) depicts the occasion when a monkey offered the Buddha some honey. In the composition the monkey is first shown offering honey to the enthroned Buddha and then dancing joyfully because his gift has been accepted. We see him a third time diving into a hole or well in the foreground between the Buddha's legs. In the most elaborate textual description of the incident the monkey dies accidentally, but from about the Gupta period on there developed a convention, followed by the Pala manuscript illustrators, of showing him as taking his own life by diving into a well. This is rather strange, considering that Buddhism generally does not condone suicide. The fair figure with a sword floating in the clouds in the upper right corner is said to be the monkey reborn in paradise.

The panel on the right of B represents the death of the Buddha. The scene is somewhat different from the composition in the earlier representation [1D] in that two monks, one below and one above the recumbent Buddha, are shown expressing their grief, and the stupa and the musicians' hands are not present here. The bed here is more elaborate, with several cushions to make the Buddha more comfortable even though he stretches in an awkward posture.

Narrow bands of decorative designs adorn the string holes and the edges of each leaf on both ends. In addition, floral motifs signal the end of a chapter and the beginning of the next on page B.

Bihar; c. 1150
Folio, 2½ x 21⅝ in (6.4 x 54.9 cm)
Center illustration, 2½ x 2⅜ in (6.4 x 6.0 cm)
From the Nasli and Alice Heeramaneck Collection, Museum Associates Purchase
M.72.1.23
Literature: Tucci 1949, pl. A; *Heeramaneck* 1966, pp. 106, 107, no. 115 (detail illustrated); Larson et al. 1980, p. 53, no. 18; Huntington 1985, pp. 406–7, pls. 28, 29; Pal & Meech-Pekarik 1988, p. 67, fig. 20; Huntington & Huntington 1990, pp. 190–91, no. 59.

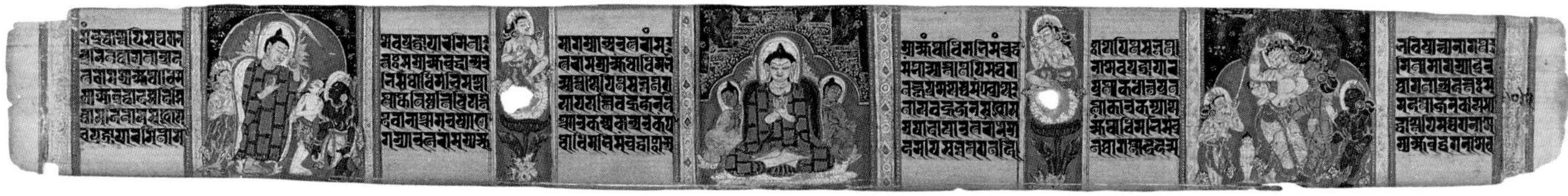

This isolated folio from a *Prajnaparamita* manuscript was evidently acquired by Giuseppe Tucci in Tibet. Unfortunately the whereabouts of the bulk of the manuscript is not known, but from this folio it is clear that both the writing and the paintings are of extremely fine quality. Both in style and expressiveness the pictures compare closely with an illustrated manuscript in Boston that can be dated with some certainty to about 1140 (Coomaraswamy 1921). As in the Boston manuscript, the band around the string holes is filled with the figure of a celestial male seated precariously on a lotus. In addition, the three scenes from the Buddha's life are each framed by narrow bands with decorative designs. The edges of the leaf are also adorned with similar bands, as is usually the case in Pala manuscripts. It should be noted, however, that the bands on the reverse are left unadorned.

The birth of the Buddha is represented in the panel on the right. Clutching the branch of a tree, his generously endowed mother stands in pronounced *contrapposto* supported by her sister. In keeping with the convention, Maya's complexion is yellow and her sister's green. Beside them stand Indra, holding the parasol, and a dark blue female deity whose identification is uncertain but who has replaced the customary Brahma. The infant Buddha is shown twice, first emerging from his mother's right hip with his hands clasped in adoration, as if thanking her for delivering him safely, and then standing like a statue between her and Indra. This second representation probably symbolizes the seven steps that the infant took immediately after his first bath to announce his spiritual sovereignty over the earth.

The scene in the middle shows the great miracle of Sravasti when the Buddha multiplied himself before a congregation to establish his superior magical abilities. This too is depicted in the conventional manner, with a larger preaching Buddha in the middle flanked by two identical smaller figures who represent the Buddha but wear different garments and sit in a different posture from the central figure. The Buddha on the right is green and wears a yellow robe, and the other is brown and wears a purple robe. The three figures are enclosed in a shrine with an elaborate superstructure minutely decorated with birds and flowers and red flames along the edge of the arch.

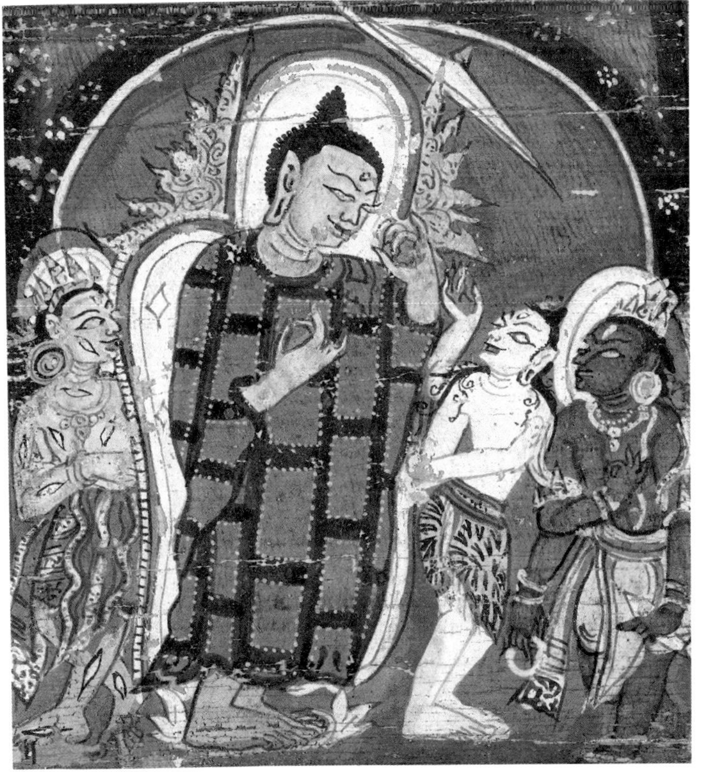
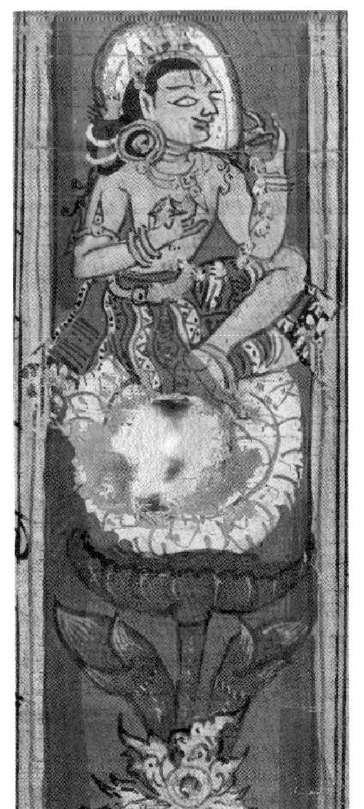
CAT. 6 details
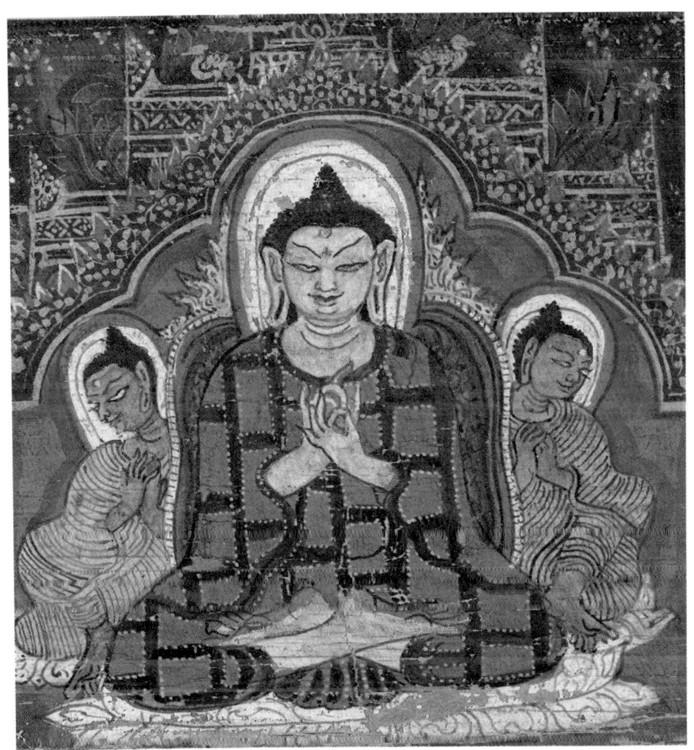
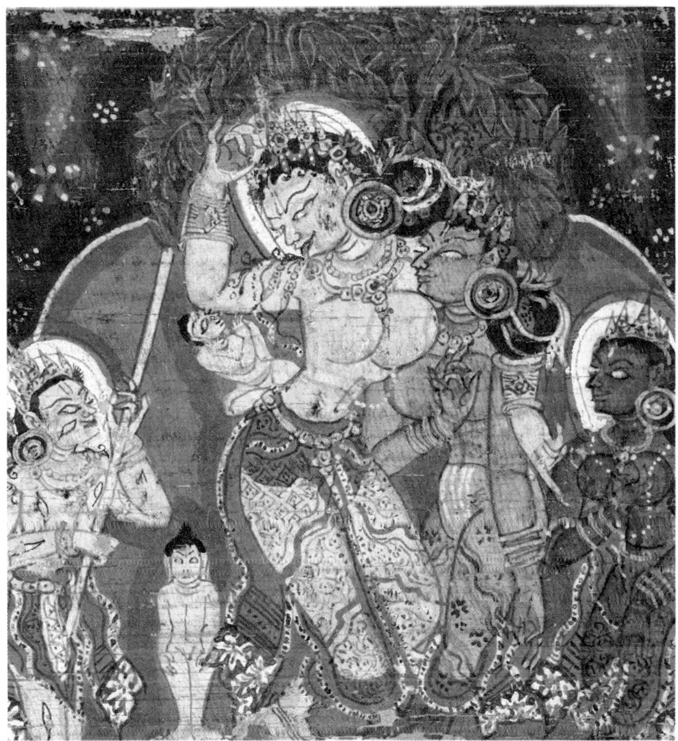

The remaining scene depicts the miracle of the descent from the heavens at Sankisya. In comparison with the earlier representation in the Ramapala-period manuscript [5A], one or two interesting variations may be noted. Here the Buddha is accompanied by three instead of two divinities. Behind him stands Indra holding the parasol. In front, however, the white figure with a third eye who wears a tiger-skin is Siva rather than Brahma, and the four-armed, dark figure is Vishnu.

Another minor difference between these representations and the others in the collection is the distinctive design of the Buddha's garment. The boldly delineated rectangular pattern indicates that he is wearing a garment sewn from discarded rags. The Buddha himself is said to have advised his disciples that as a symbol of their vow of poverty as well as a mark of humility monks should gather rags from the householders and sew them into patchwork garments resembling the rice fields of Magadha (Bihar). Seldom was this instruction followed, however, and only occasionally in art do we encounter such a garment on Buddha images.

Not only are these illuminations remarkably well preserved, the figural representations are both lively and engaging. The drawing is highly refined and the vivacious colors retain much of their original brilliance. In the scenes of the birth and the descent there is an unusual degree of interaction among the various personalities. The iconographic variations also make these depictions interesting.

S. L. Huntington (1985, pp. 406–7) infers that "on stylistic grounds" the manuscript "was executed in Bengal during the twelfth century." What stylistic grounds are not specified, however. She does remark that "the high quality of craftsmanship seen in both stone and metal images in Bihār and Bengal is also apparent in the remarkable craftsmanship of these miniature paintings." Apart from the inconsistencies in such statements, there seems no particular grounds for attributing this isolated folio to Bengal. The paintings rather correspond to the style that was prevalent in Bihar, as is seen in two dated manuscripts dedicated during the reign of Gopala III (r. c. mid-twelfth century), one of which was certainly painted in Bihar (Coomaraswamy 1921; Losty 1982, p. 32, no. 7, pl. III).

7 TWO FOLIOS FROM A *PANCHARAKSHA* MANUSCRIPT

Bihar; 1160/61
Folios, 2½ x 21⅞ in (6.4 x 55.6 cm)
Illustrations, 2½ x 2 in (6.4 x 5.1 cm)
From the Nasli and Alice Heeramaneck Collection, Museum Associates Purchase
M.79.9.9a,b
Literature: Tucci 1949, pl. A; *Heeramaneck* 1966, p. 106, no. 116 (not illustrated); Saraswati 1978, p. 48 (colophon only).

A *Goddess*
B *Goddess Mahapratisara*

This manuscript was dedicated in the seventeenth regnal year of King Madanapala by Prince Vikramamana, son of Rudramana, who is characterized as the chief of all the feudal lords, a provincial governor, and also a king of kings. From a solitary inscription found in Bihar it seems that Rudramana was the ruler of Magadha (southern Bihar) at this time. It is clear from the donation that the family was Buddhist. As Madanapala's regnal dates are relatively certain, this manuscript can be dated to 1160/61, soon before his death.

One of the five Pancharaksha goddesses is represented on each leaf. Each illustrated page is also adorned with decorative bands over the string holes and at the extremities. No such ornamental bands occur on the leaves' other sides. Red and yellow with touches of blue are the principal colors used for the geometric and floral motifs that constitute the decorative designs. The goddess on leaf A is represented against a fiery aureole, and the one on B against a red background within a shrine. Some foliage is visible behind each shrine. The arch of the shrine contains roundels enclosing floral motifs and geese rendered so minutely and delicately as to be scarcely visible to the naked eye.

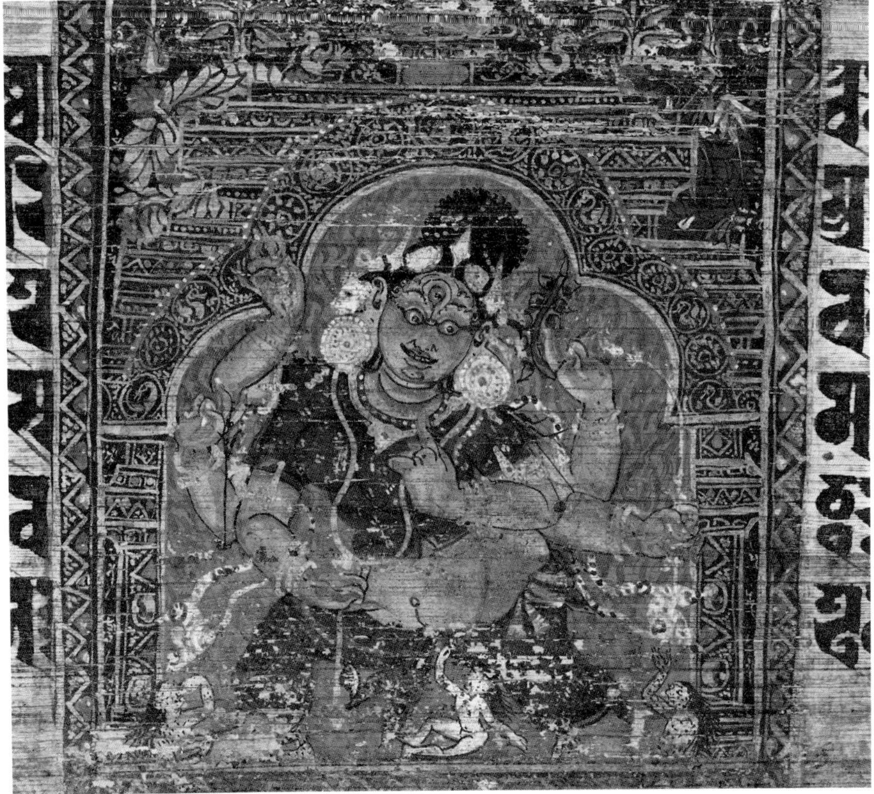

CAT. 7A detail

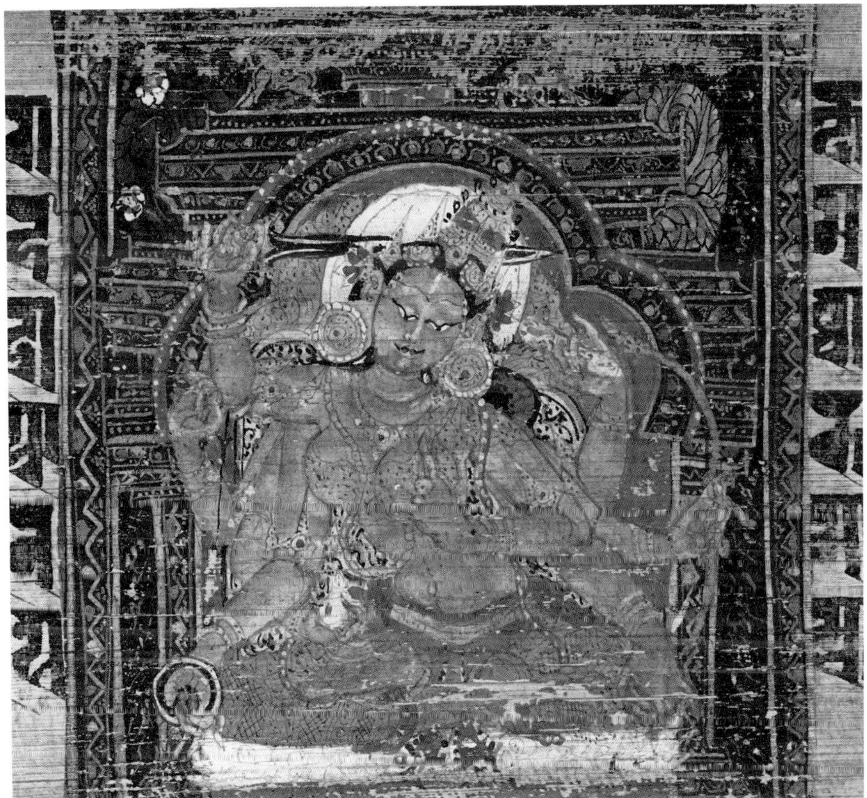

CAT. 7B detail

The goddess on A (which leaf includes the colophon on the reverse) is awesome, with a large overhanging belly, a ferocious face, and a green complexion. With her six arms she seems to exhibit (clockwise from lowest proper right) a battle-ax, an arrow, a thunderbolt, a sprig of leaves, the gesture of admonition (*tarjanī-mudrā*), and a noose. The attributes agree with those prescribed for Mahamantranusarini, although the green complexion does not (see Mevissen 1989). However, there appears to have been little consistency in the descriptions of the Pancharaksha goddesses. The identification would seem to be reinforced by the fact that the text ends on the other side with the statement that "here ends the charm describing the Raksha goddess Mahamantranusarini." It should be noted though that her complexion, all six emblems, and her posture are identical with textual descriptions and images of a goddess called Parnasavari (Bhattasali 1929, p. 59, pl. XXIII). It is also written that Parnasavari "treads down under her feet countless diseases and epidemics," which might be represented here by three witchlike figures at the bottom shying away from the goddess. However, Parnasavari is supposed to have three heads, which are not clearly delineated here. Nor is this figure attired in leaves as Parnasavari is supposed to be. It is not unlikely that Parnasavari and Mahamantranusarini are being identified here.

The second goddess, who is of yellow complexion and has eight arms, is less difficult to identify, even though all her emblems cannot be clearly recognized. She brandishes a sword with her uppermost right hand, and two of the other attributes are the bow and the arrow. The left hand against her chest exhibits the gesture of admonition. This goddess is Mahapratisara, and as is usual, she is represented as a placid figure. This goddess protects women during their pregnancies and ensures safe deliveries.

Not only is the colophon (see Appendix) important for the political history of Bihar, but the fairly precise date makes this an anchor for securely ascribing dates to other twelfth-century paintings. Although when this manuscript was created, the major monasteries in Bihar had already been destroyed, it does demonstrate that competent scribes and artists were still available and manuscripts were being commissioned by individuals in some areas.

Bihar; 1150–1200
Folios, 2½ x 17¼ in (6.4 x 43.8 cm)
Center illustrations, 2½ x 1⅞ in (6.4 x 4.8 cm)
From the Nasli and Alice Heeramaneck
Collection, Museum Associates Purchase
M.72.1.24a–c
Literature: *Heeramaneck* 1966, pp. 106, 108,
no. 117 (not illustrated).

A *Goddess Tara*
B *Vajrayana Deities*
C *Vajrayana Deities*

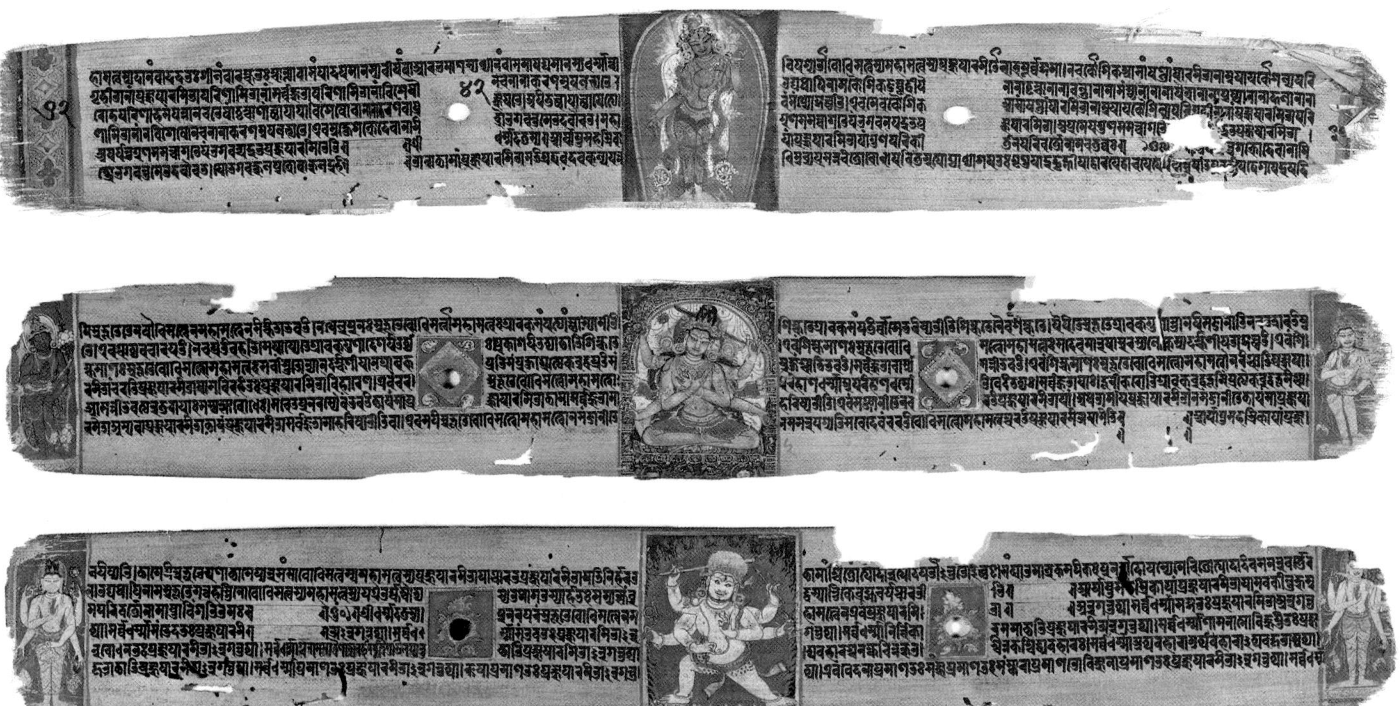

These three leaves are from a profusely illuminated manuscript, the bulk of which is in the R. H. Ellsworth Collection, New York. Five folios are in the J. D. Rockefeller 3d Collection at the Asia Society, New York (see Pal and Meech-Pekarik 1988, pp. 69, 72, fig. 21, pl. 10), and six more in the Virginia Museum in Richmond (Huntington and Huntington 1990, pp. 191–94, no. 60). While there is no colophon on the last page of the manuscript, now in the Ellsworth collection, there is a later Newari inscription recording the reading of the book with a date corresponding to 1234. Hence the book had to have been prepared sometime before this date and taken to Nepal.

The iconographic program for this manuscript is much more elaborate than that of the other *Prajnaparamita* manuscripts in the collection. The eight standard miracles from the Buddha's life seem to have had less importance for the illustrator and have been pushed to the margins. Instead, the book is generously illustrated with images of Vajrayana deities, making it a rich iconographic source. In addition, the bands along the edges are illuminated with decorative designs, stupas, or more figures of divinities, as may be seen on two of the three leaves in the museum's collection. In other manuscripts such marginal figures are limited to a few pages. What precise iconographic scheme was followed by the artist cannot, however, be determined without bringing all the leaves together. It is not improbable that together the deities constitute some sort of a mandala.

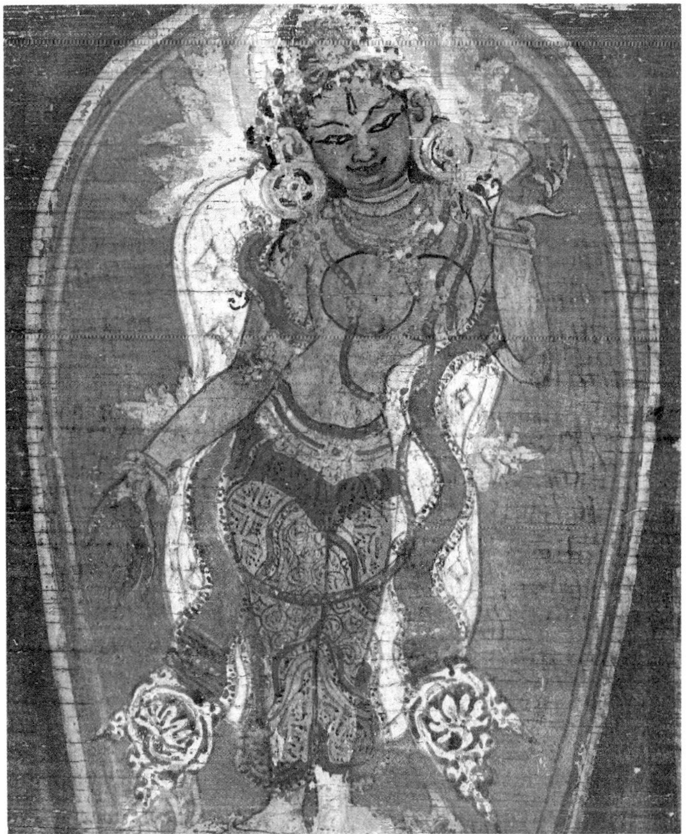

CAT. 8A detail

The divine figures represented on these three leaves can be identified as follows. Leaf A includes only a single figure of green Tara in the middle, the side bands being adorned with a decorative design. The enshrined deity in the middle of the second leaf is an esoteric form of the bodhisattva Manjusri known as Guhya-Manjuvajra. The red figure at the left edge is probably the bodhisattva Khadagapani, and the figure at the other end is the bodhisattva Avalokitesvara. The central figure on C represents one of the angry deities. White in complexion, his emblems are (clockwise from his lowest proper right hand): a thunderbolt, a noose, a cot's leg, an elephant goad, and a bell. He may be a form of Vajrapani or an angry emanation of Manjusri. Being an angry deity, he is represented with a bright red-and-orange fiery aureole. He is flanked at either end of the leaf by two figures of Avalokitesvara or Lokesvara that are identical except that they seem to hold different flowers in their upper left hands.

Although the style of writing on these pages seems closer to that in a manuscript that can be attributed with greater certainty to undivided Bengal rather than Bihar (Pal and Meech-Pekarik 1988, pls. 17, 18, fig. 29), the illustrations are stylistically akin to those seen in Prince Vikramamana's manuscript [7]. Both share the same penchant for rich detailing and energetic portrayal of the militant figures. The shrine around Guhya-Manjuvajra (B) not only exhibits a more elaborate design than those seen in earlier illustrations but is enlivened with a large number of animals and figures cursorily rendered within medallions as in [7].

The representations of angry deities are animated by the vigorous postures of the figures as well as by the red-orange flame design of the background with leaping tongues. The larger number of deities with varied complexions, multiple limbs, and diverse garments add to the visual appeal of these illustrations.

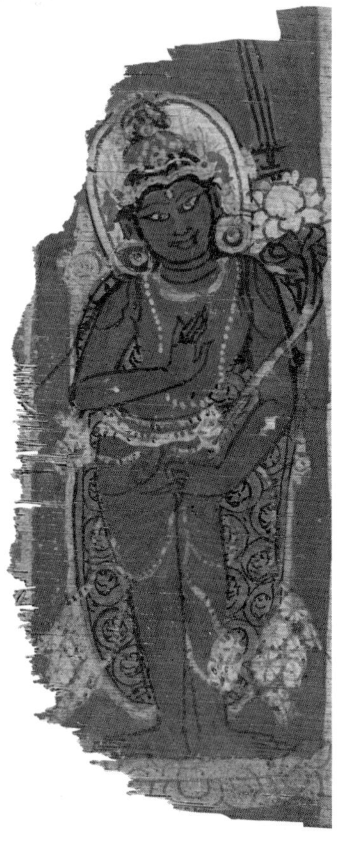
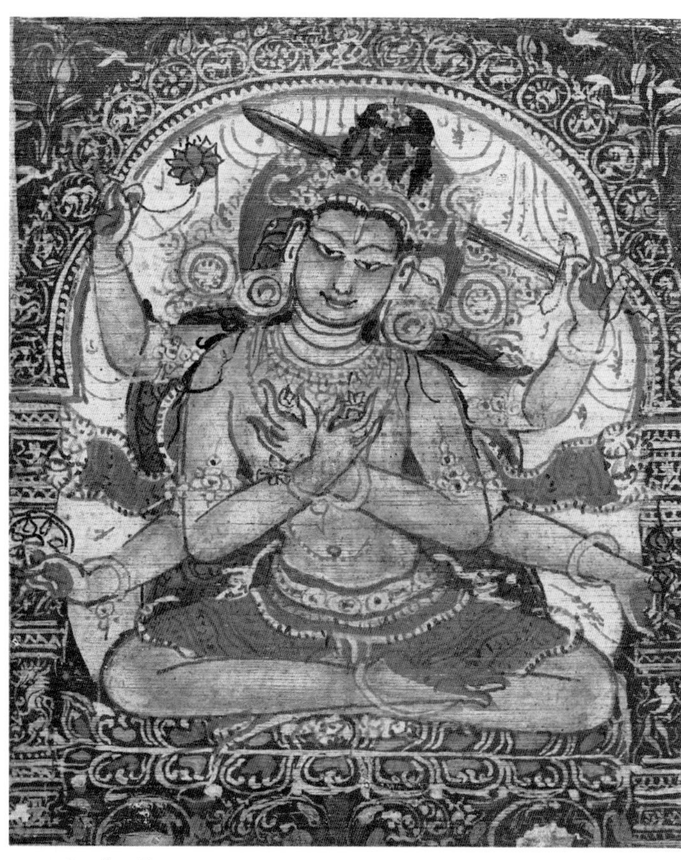
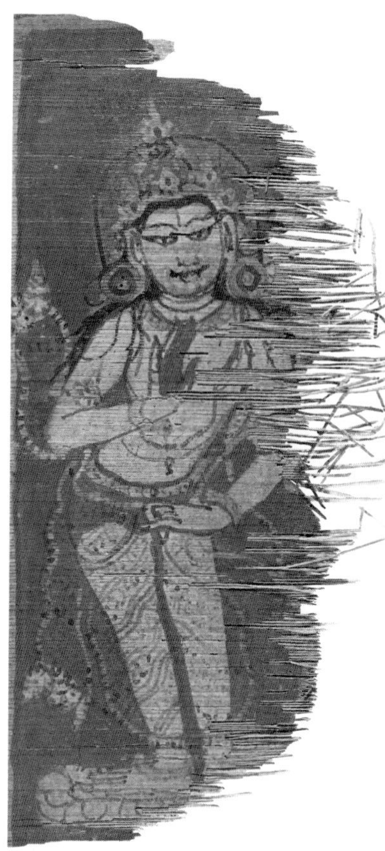

CAT. 8B details

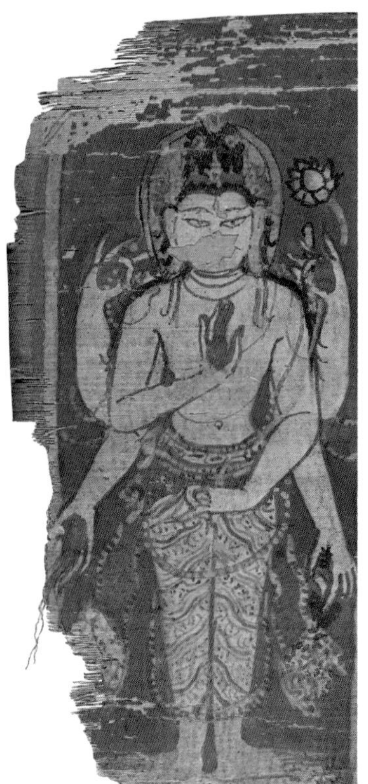
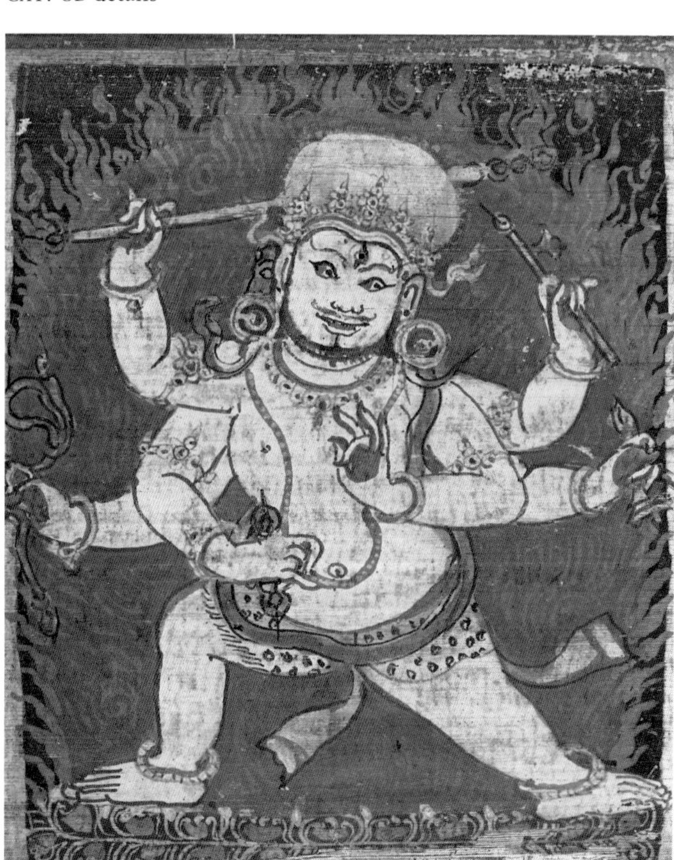
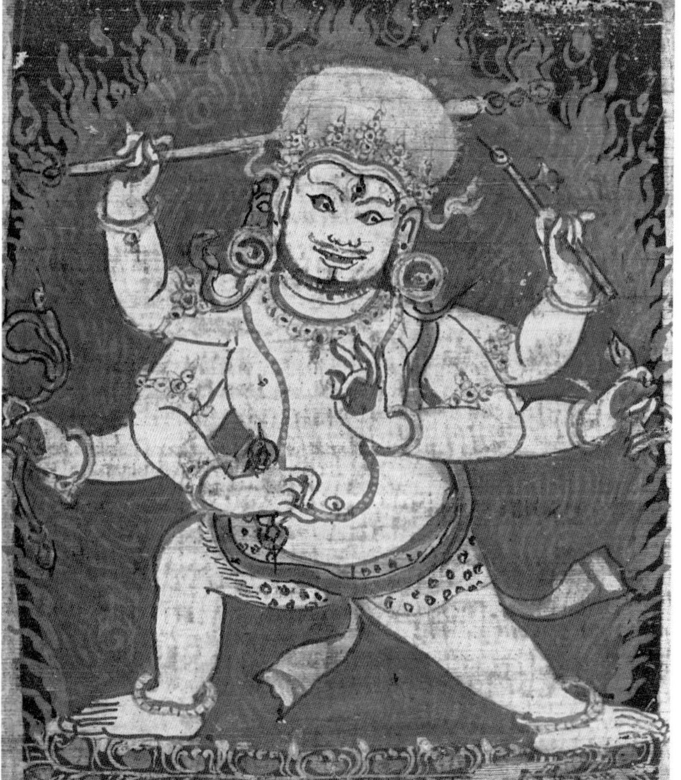
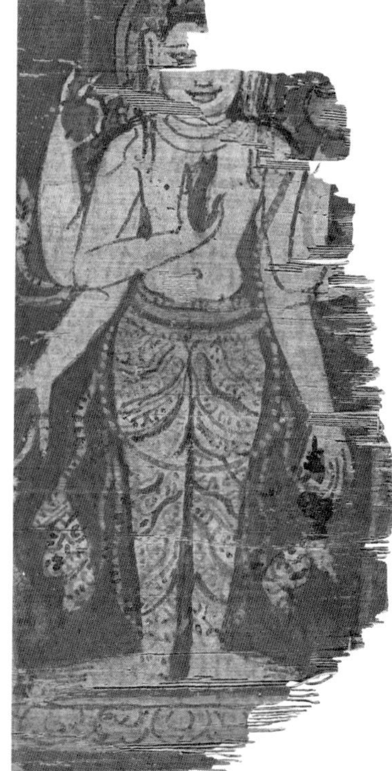

CAT. 8C details

Bihar; 1150–1200
Each, 2½ x 22⁹⁄₁₆ in (6.4 x 57.3 cm)
From the Nasli and Alice Heeramaneck Collection, Museum Associates Purchase
M.77.19.2a,b
Literature: *Heeramaneck* 1966, p. 108, no. 120 (not illustrated); Pal & Meech-Pekarik 1988, pp. 74–75, fig. 23a–b.

A *Vajrayana Deities*
B *Vajrayana Deities*

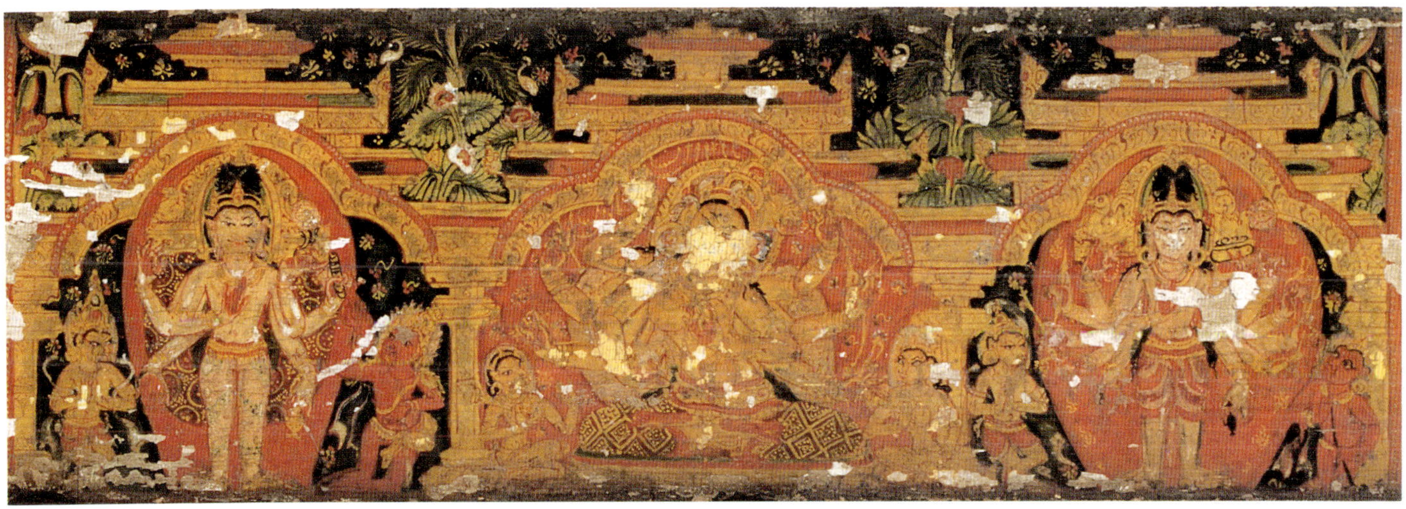

CAT. 9A detail

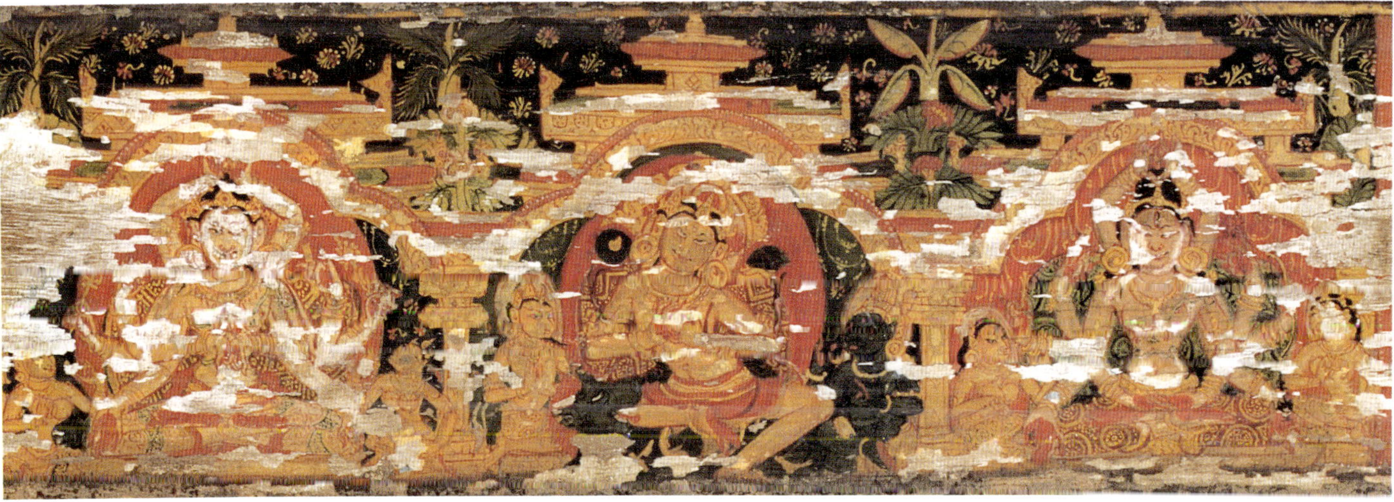

CAT. 9B detail

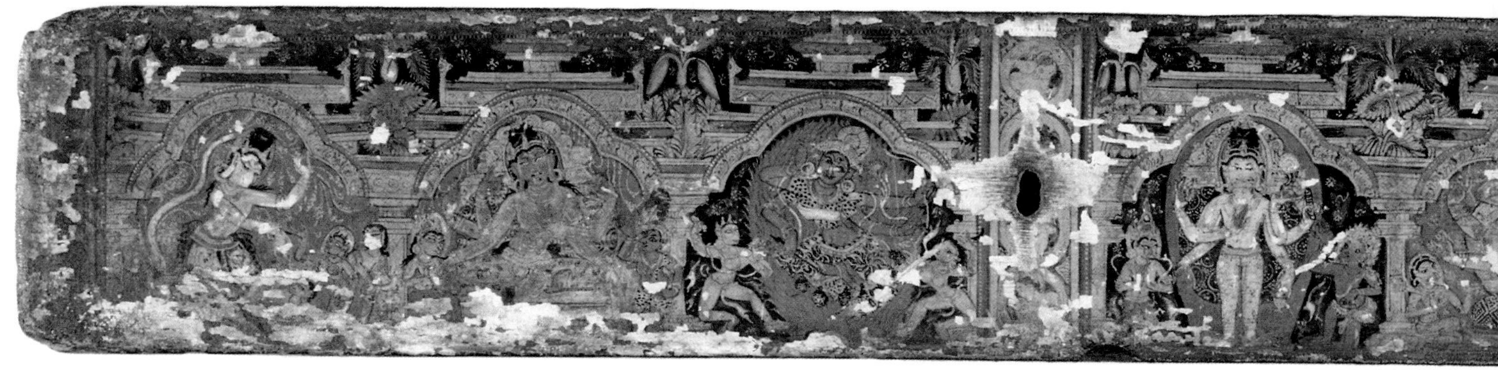

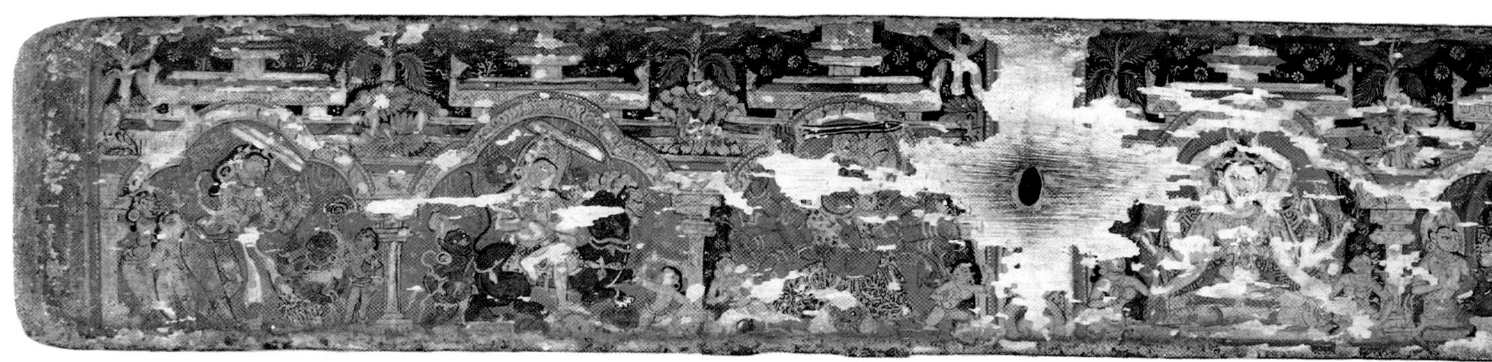

Although somewhat damaged, these two covers of an unknown manuscript are among the most sumptuous known. Because of the predominance of Vajrayana deities, the manuscript may well have been a *Dharanisamgraha.* There is a rich variety of divinities, in many instances represented in unusual compositions. Because the pigments have peeled off in places and also because of the indistinctness of the emblems in their hands, it is not possible to identify all the figures nor to describe them in detail. The following deities may be identified, beginning from the left:

A Bodhisattva Avalokitesvara; a bodhisattva; goddess Kurukulla; bodhisattva Sugatisandarsana Lokesvara; a goddess; Twelve-Armed Avalokitesvara; goddess Nairatma; a bodhisattva; goddess Tara.

B Goddess Tara; bodhisattva Manjusri; a red, angry goddess; Namasangiti Manjusri; another form of Manjusri (?); goddess Chunda (?); a green, angry goddess; bodhisattva Simhanada Avalokitesvara (?); Tara (?).

The eighteen deities appear to have been represented in groups of three, but the groupings may only be apparent, suggested by the interruptions of the decorative bands around the string holes. Each figure is depicted in an identical shrine. Behind the columns supporting the arches are domes of foliage and either a coconut or a banana tree. The dark blue background is speckled with flowers, giving the impression of a starry night sky. Interestingly, not a single deity is depicted alone. Each is accompanied by two or more figures engaged in various activities. Unusual also is the fact that several of the divinities are shown in unconventional postures or are riding animals in distinctive ways.

Indeed, few manuscript covers of this period are filled with such vivacious and unusual compositions as these. The four deities at the ends of the covers stand in relaxed, graceful postures and are shown interacting with their diminutive companions. The first figure of Avalokitesvara on cover A clutches the branch of a curving tree as he feeds ambrosia to the denizens of hell. The other three figures are female and very likely represent three different forms of the goddess Tara. On the right end of A she holds the branch of a tree and is apparently blessing two devotees. Behind her is Tara's

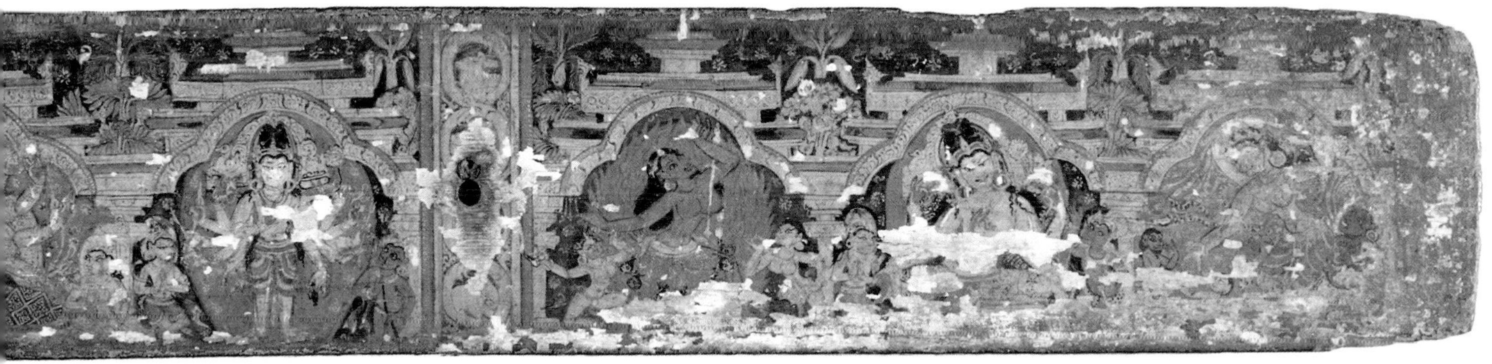

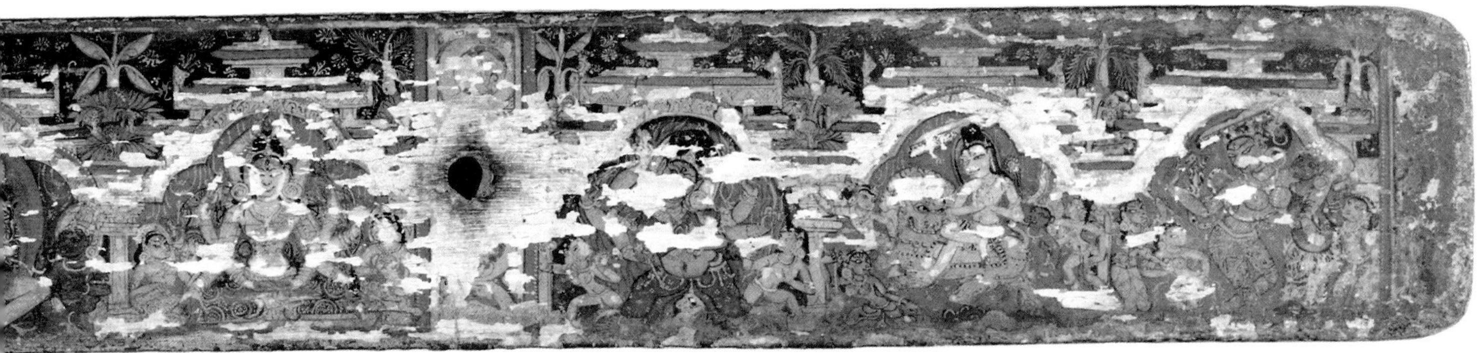

companion, the blue Ekajata, wearing a tiger skin. Ekajata accompanies her mistress in the two compositions on the other cover (B) as well. On the extreme left Tara seems to be engaged in a conversation with her attendant while holding a lotus flower with her left hand. At the other end she stands supporting herself on the shoulders of Ekajata exactly as does Maya when giving birth to the Buddha (cf. [6]). A second female stands behind Ekajata and holds a parasol, while two others are in front of Tara. What exactly these three different representations of Tara signify is a mystery. Unlike the other compositions, these seem to have a narrative intent.

All the attendant figures in front of the shrines seem to interact with the deities, some more energetically than others. For instance, the attendants of the two dancing goddesses on cover A are also shown dancing in rather wild postures. Their nakedness suggests that they are *dakinis*, a class of female semidivine beings who play an important role in Vajrayana Buddhist ritual and esoteric praxis. On the other cover the attendants of the two angry deities seem to be recoiling in fear, while the companions of the lion-riders appear to be cheering their masters as they move toward the center. Such spirited and varied delineation of gods and goddesses is indeed rare in illuminated manuscripts of the region. Clearly in these two book covers we are witnessing the work of an accomplished and imaginative artist.

The exuberant and lively rendering of these pictures with their elaborate compositions is akin to the manner encountered in the illustrations on some covers in the Museum of Fine Arts, Boston, that can be dated to the mid-twelfth century (see Pal and Meech-Pekarik 1988, p. 71, fig. 22; and Coomaraswamy 1921) as well as to that in the 1160/61 *Pamcharaksha* manuscript illuminations in the collection [7]. The compositions in the Boston covers are even more complex and busy, but the drawing and the coloring are similarly vibrant in both.

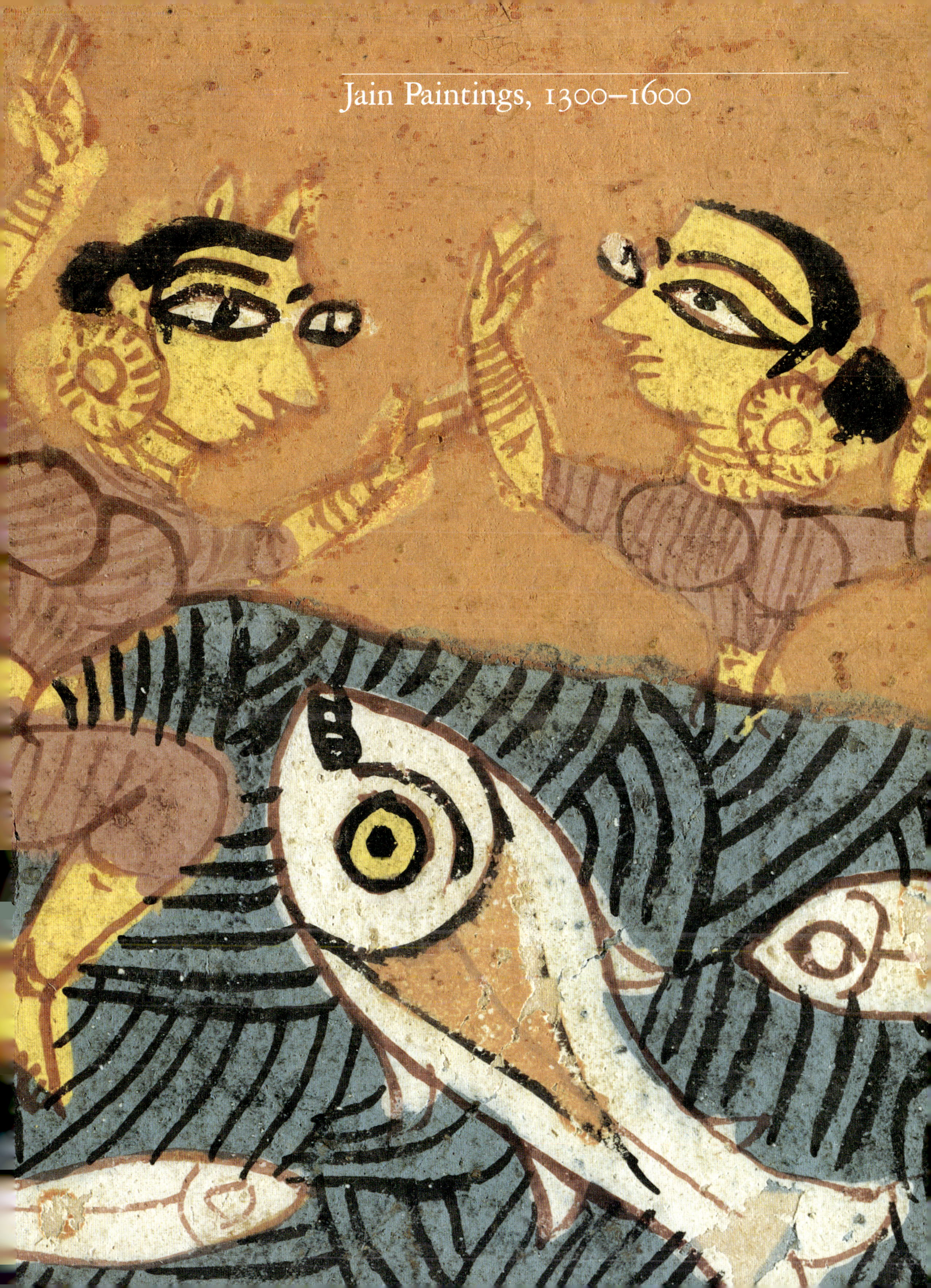

Jain Paintings, 1300–1600

The art is one of pure draughtsmanship; the pictures are brilliant statements of the facts of the epic . . . where every event is seen in the light of eternity. . . . There is no preoccupation with pattern, color, or texture for their own sake; but these are achieved with inevitable assurance in a way that could not have been the case had they been directly sought. The drawing has in fact the perfect equilibrium of a mathematical equation, or a page of a composer's score. Theme and formula compose an inseparable unity, text and pictures form a continuous relation of the same dogma in the same key.[1]

Introduction

The Jain paintings in the museum's collection are mostly from Gujarat in western India. All but two are in the form of book illustrations; the exceptions are religious paintings on cloth representing mystical diagrams known as *yantra* [13, 16]. Like the Buddhists, the Jains encouraged copying and illustrating books, which were made of palm leaves before paper became popular from the fourteenth century.

A living religion in India, the Jain faith, like Buddhism, is regarded by the Hindus as a heretical tradition. Unlike Buddhism, however, Jainism survived the antagonism of both Hinduism and Islam. The name of the religion derives from the word *Jina*, meaning "conqueror." Obviously the conquest is spiritual rather than temporal. The final aim of a Jain—like that of a Hindu or Buddhist—is to snap the chain of rebirth and attain complete freedom, which is known as *kaivalya* or *moksha*. Jains believe in a group of twenty-four such liberated beings who were human teachers. They are known as *Jinas* or *Tirthankaras* (literally, "forder"). Jainism developed into a religion with an elaborate pantheon and is no less ritualistic than Hinduism and Buddhism. It is, in fact, possible that the Jains may have made use of images and art to propagate their faith and doctrine even earlier than the Hindus or the Buddhists.

There are two principal sects or divisions of the Jains, known as Svetambara, "clad in white," concentrated mostly in the north, and Digambara, "sky clad" (naked), confined largely to the south. The split probably occurred as early as the first century after Christ, largely due to disagreements on matters of conduct, such as whether or not to possess material things, including clothes. A more fundamental difference between the two sects concerns the nature of the Jina rather than the body of doctrine. Svetambara Jains contend that the Jina is capable of communicating at a normal human level even after achieving the omniscient state and must obey bodily laws while engaging in various human and physical functions. Digambaras conversely insist that the omniscient Jina is completely free from all biological processes and is incapable of participating in worldly activities or performing any bodily functions. Thus Svetambaras make greater use of images and temples, and almost all illustrated manuscripts in the museum's collection were used by them rather than the Digambaras.

Like the Buddhists, and to a lesser extent the Hindus, the Jains believe that donating a sculpted or painted image or a religious book to a monk or temple constitutes an act of piety. Lay followers have been particularly encouraged to do so. As were those of the Buddhists, the books were generally donated to religious establishments rather than retained for individual use. Most Jain temples have a depository or library attached; these *sastrabhandars* (or *bhandars*) are rich resources for Jain art and literature.

The Jain religious year consists of a number of festivals, all of which involve special morning sermons by members of the mendicant community, or the *sadhus,* and reading from sacred texts. As J. E. Cort has noted, "The paradigmatic event behind the Jain understanding of a festival is almost invariably from the life of one of the 24 Jinas,"[2] and so texts such as the *Kalpasutra,* which contains biographies of four of the Jinas, are of fundamental importance. Various sections are read on different occasions. For instance, the reading of the third section of the text, which includes a description of the ancient Paryushan festival—an eight-day festival held in the month of Bhadrapada (August-September) to usher in the rainy season retreat—is obligatory during that festival.

Manuscripts of the text are used in other ways too, especially by Svetambara Jains. During the Paryushan festival the *Kalpasutra* is recited for four days, and in some communities a copy of the manuscript is taken out in procession and worshipped as a symbol of knowledge (*jñāna*). As described by Cort:

A young girl dressed in pure pūjā *clothes carries the book in a tray atop her head, while water from the morning* pūjā *at the temple is sprinkled before her to purify the ground. The book is taken to the house of a man who won the public auction for presenting the book the next day. It is kept at his house overnight, and worshipped with devotional songs. . . . The next morning the book is taken, again in a small procession, to the* upāśray [a hall where mendicants reside that is used by the laity for special rituals].[3]

At the *upāśray* the book is placed before a *sadhu* along with a table carrying an auspicious symbol made with rice, a coconut, and a coin. Following devotional songs and *puja* with sandalwood and saffron the book is presented to the holy man.

Of interest regarding the illustrations are Cort's observations about the reading aloud of the Prakrit root-text of the *Kalpasutra* on the morning of the eighth and final day:

As the sādhu *recited the Prakrit text, a young boy (ideally dressed in* pūjā-*clothes; at a minimum covering his mouth with* muhpattī *[mouth cloth]) held aloft for all to see an illustration of the portion of the text being recited. Another* sādhu *clued the boy as to which picture to hold aloft. Most of the people bowed their heads to each picture as it was shown.*[4]

It is clear that the books are not read by individuals as a Christian reads the Bible or a Muslim the Koran. Moreover, the pictures are not viewed closely, since the audience would be at some distance from them. They are merely glimpsed and venerated as icons. That no aesthetic appreciation is involved may explain why the mode of representation hardly changed over the years.

The earliest Jain illuminated leaves in the collection are from two palm-leaf manuscripts of the fourteenth century [10, 11]. As is the case with the Buddhist manuscripts of eastern India, no Jain illuminated book has been found so far that can be dated earlier than the eleventh century. This is rather surprising, since the Jains are very diligent about preserving their heritage. The museum's palm-leaf folios indicate that even after paper had been adopted by some Jains, palm-leaf manuscripts continued to be produced, perhaps in places remote from major centers of manuscript production such as Patan or Ahmedabad in Gujarat.

After the introduction of paper, the two texts that proved to be more popular than others were the *Kalpasutra* and the *Kalakacharyakatha.* The *Kalpasutra* is the most important canonical work of the Jains, which is why it is the choice text for dedication. The word *kalpa* generally means a "sacred precept, law, rule, or ordinance," and a sutra is a short aphorism. In point of fact, however, the *Kalpasutra* contains more than the sacred precepts or monastic rules.

Believed to have been written in the Prakrit language by Bhadrabahu (d. c. 385 B.C.), the *Kalpasutra* is divided into three sections. The first is called the *Jinacharita* (Biographies of the Jinas) and consists of the lives of Mahavira, Parsvanatha, Neminatha, and Rishabhanatha, four of the twenty-four Jinas. Of the four, Mahavira (sixth century B.C.), the last of the twenty-four but often regarded as the systematizer of Jainism, is the most important, and his life is narrated in far greater detail than those of the others. The second book is known as the *Sthavirāvalī* (Genealogies of the elders). Apart from lists of names, this book includes brief biographies of some of the Jain pontiffs. The third, known as the *Samāchārī*, contains the rules and ordinances to be observed by the monks. Usually only the first two books are illustrated.

The *Kalakacharyakatha* (Story of the teacher Kalaka) consists of four edificatory tales woven around an extraordinary monk named Kalaka. Associated with the Svetambara Jains, the *Kalakacharyakatha* is not a canonical text but has almost acquired that status and is frequently appended to the *Kalpasutra*. Both the *Kalpasutra* and the *Kalakacharyakatha* are recited during the Paryushan festival. A number of versions of the Kalaka compendium exist in Sanskrit, Prakrit, and other languages. One of the manuscripts in the collection, copied in 1442 [15], includes one of the shorter versions of the Kalaka story composed by one Dharmaprabhasuri in 1389.

The most frequently illustrated of the Kalaka stories is the one that recounts the struggle between Kalaka and King Gardabhilla of Malava. Briefly, the story runs as follows. Originally a prince, Kalaka renounced the life of a householder and became a monk. His beautiful sister Sarasvati followed suit and joined a nunnery. One day she was spotted by King Gardabhilla, who abducted her. Upon failing to persuade the monarch to release her, Kalaka gathered together a number of Saka or Scythian chiefs known as Sahi, ninety-six of whom were dissatisfied with their harsh overlord. Kalaka led them south to conquer Ujjaini, Gardabhilla's capital. As they did not have sufficient financial resources to launch the attack, Kalaka used his magical powers to transform clay bricks into gold. But Gardabhilla also had a trick or two. He owned a she-ass with magical powers. If on the eighth day of a fortnight the sound of this she-ass's braying reached the ears of Gardabhilla's enemies, they would immediately die. Kalaka devised a stratagem to forestall the braying. Since Jains are enjoined to refrain from killing, he collected the best archers and asked them to fill the mouth of the she-ass with arrows before she could utter a sound. This they did, and so Gardabhilla was captured and Kalaka's sister released. Gardabhilla was sent into exile, and Kalaka atoned for the sins he had committed, even though they were for a good cause. Ujjaini then became the capital of a Saka kingdom.

Three other works represented in the collection by isolated illustrated leaves are the *Trishashtisalakapurushacharita,* the *Samgrahanisutra,* and the *Yasodharacharita*. The first is represented by two palm leaves [11] with one illustration, the second by four illustrated folios from two different manuscripts [33, 34], and the third by a solitary illustrated leaf [19].

The *Trishashtisalakapurushacharita* (Lives of the sixty-three heroes) was composed from earlier sources by Hemachandra Suri (1089–1172). One of the greatest of Jain teachers, Hemachandra was a polymath with encyclopedic knowledge. He was prolific as a poet as well as a writer of scholarly works. *The Lives of the Sixty-three Heroes* comprises hagiographies of the twenty-four Jinas and their contemporaries the twelve *chakravartins* (world rulers) and the twenty-seven heroes of antiquity, including, for example, Rama of the Hindu epic *Ramayana*. Indeed, the *Lives* may well be regarded as the epic of the Jains.

The *Samgrahanisutra* (Book of compilations) is a summary of Jain doctrine on cosmology and provides a great deal of information about the various universes and their continents and oceans, their inhabitants, and so on. It also describes all the different heavens and hells and who goes where for what actions. Additionally, it discusses the forms and nature of the various gods and their symbols, the theory of the fourteen jewels of a universal monarch, and the doctrine of *lesya* (thought-colors). Although the text is concerned with a wide variety of cosmological and iconographical subjects, judging by the known illustrated manuscripts, they do not appear to have inspired any of the artists to create exciting pictures. This is why the illustrated *Samgrahanisutra* manuscripts have received little attention from modern scholars. Various versions of the text exist, but the most popular are those composed by Jinabhadragani Kshamasramana in the sixth century and by Trichandra Suri in 1136. Despite the antiquity of the text, most known illustrated manuscripts belong to the last quarter of the sixteenth century or later. It is not clear why illustrated copies were in demand in the sixteenth century and apparently not before.

The majority of the Jain manuscripts in the collection are of the *Kalpasutra*. It need hardly be emphasized that usually only the first two parts of the *Kalpasutra,* the lives of the Jinas and the genealogies of the elders, are illustrated. Moreover, since these sections are concerned with biographies, most illustrations are narrative in character and are closely related to the text, in contrast to the illustrations in Buddhist books, which are hieratic pictures of deities, except for the Eight Great Miracles from the Buddha's life, which illustrate a non-narrative philosophical text. As is the case with the scenes of the Buddha's life, those of the Jinas' too are represented in a cryptic manner. Once the iconography was established, no artist dared, or perhaps cared, to deviate even in matters of composition except in minor details. The scenes were repeated with monotonous regularity for centuries without any artistic innovations. This is also true of the illustrations to the story of Kalaka. Here again the artists neither departed from the norm nor selected different incidents. As A. K. Coomaraswamy put it so poetically in the epigraph to this chapter, their task was to see the events in the light of eternity. Not all manuscripts are adorned with the same number of illustrations, but the principal events are always included. There was no strict rule regarding the placement of the illustrations, which are found on both sides of a folio.

When the switch was made from palm leaves to paper in the fourteenth century, the basic shape of a folio did not change but the size did. The paper folios are not as wide as the palm-leaf folios and are a good deal higher. This meant that the size of each illustration also increased, but the form of the picture was not altered significantly. Some compositions became more elaborate, and often two different incidents came to be included within one illustration, continuing the ancient Indian practice of continuous narration. Although the painters of the Jain texts were by then familiar with illustrated Islamic books and their more painterly representations, they chose not to adopt their aesthetic and styles except in minor details, nor did they adopt the bound codex or the vertical orientation of the Islamic book. The Jain book remained a collection of loose horizontal folios within two covers. Whereas the early palm-leaf books and their wood covers were loosely bound together with strings, the paper manuscripts were not bound at all. The string holes were replaced by small red or gold circles that became a vestigial decorative motif, and the wood covers were replaced by ones made with board and wrapped in cloth. As was the case with Buddhist books, the covers of the palm-leaf manuscripts of the Jains were often richly illustrated with sprawling compositions imitating a long scroll painting or a mural, but the practice was discarded with the adoption of paper and the cloth-wrapped cover.

Already in the early palm-leaf manuscripts the western Indian artists had developed distinctive figural forms that remained in use through most of the sixteenth century, until their contacts with the Mughal style. Indeed, even a cursory comparison with eastern Indian Buddhist manuscript illumination will make it clear how distinct the figurative forms are in the two traditions. The western Indian figures are proportionately shorter and stockier, while those in the Buddhist illustrations are more elegantly formed. Most distinctive are the figures' faces, with characteristically looped chin, long, pointed nose, and, of course, the protruding further eye when the face is shown in three-quarter view. This idiosyncracy is occasionally encountered in the palm-leaf manuscripts of eastern India but in a restrained manner. Generally in palm-leaf manuscripts of both traditions the figures are so small that the extension is not prominent. In Jain paper manuscripts, however, because of the larger folio and painted compositions, not only is the distortion more pronounced, but it appears as if the fourteenth-century western Indian artists deliberately made this into a hallmark of their style. J. P. Losty has explained this unusual feature as a technical difficulty on the part of the artist when moving from the three-quarter view of earlier pictures to the strict profile of the late sixteenth century.[5] There may have been other reasons as well. In religious art an idiosyncracy can easily become a convention and may have no rational meaning. The cliché was not finally abandoned in western Indian paintings until the end of the sixteenth century. The only exception is the figural type employed in the illustrations of the Kalaka story to represent the Saka kings [15C]. Unquestionably adopted from Islamic art, this figural type—commonly known in the literature as the Sahi type—is rarely shown with the protruding further eye.

The illustrations of the paper manuscripts show stronger stylization and distortion of the figures than do earlier illuminations, where greater naturalism prevails. Although the emphasis is on the narrative, within a given composition the figures interact with one another through formal, ritual gestures and display little emotion. As in the palm-leaf illustrations, no effort is made to indicate a source of light within a composition or represent illusionary depth in the picture. Flowers and plants are introduced either as symbols or for decorative purposes and are seldom depicted naturalistically. The trees are often golden, like the figures, and bear imaginary flowers of variegated hues. Although the species of animals and birds are generally recognizable, their coloring is more fanciful than realistic.

There is a much keener interest in the designs of the garments and textiles in the paper manuscripts than in the earlier palm-leaf books. This is apparent both in the dhotis and saris worn by lay figures as well as in the cushions, bedspreads, and canopies. Unlike those in the eastern Indian Buddhist illustrations, where they rarely don blouses except in the birth scene of the Buddha, women in Jain illuminations always wear a blouse made from colorful material. In fact, these Jain paintings are a rich source for the study of contemporary textile designs, for which Gujarat was famous all over India and beyond. While few early textiles have been preserved in the destructive Indian climate, these pictures do demonstrate that both the tie-dye and block-printing techniques were popular and that the international reputation of Gujarat as a major center of fine cottons was truly justified.

Perhaps the most significant difference between the illustrations on palm-leaf and paper manuscripts is in the coloring. The coloring in palm-leaf manuscript illustrations—both on the folios and covers—was restricted to the primary hues of blue, yellow, and red and a few others, such as green, white, and black, with particular emphasis being given to the red, which was the preferred background color. Occasionally indigo-blue was used for the background. The favorite for the complexion of the figures was yellow, with black for the hair. One does, however, encounter some modulation of the body hues with occasional highlights to indicate volume.

Rarely in a paper manuscript does one find any interest in modeling with colors, and there is greater emphasis on the linear definition of form. Whatever plasticity is achieved is due entirely to the brittle outline. As if in compensation for the lack of modeling, the artists used a richer palette with gold, ultramarine, brilliant crimsons, and purples to create, in the best examples, sumptuously bright and glossy surfaces. Undoubtedly the use of gold, occasionally also silver, and the rich ultramarine blue is due to a familiarity with Persian illuminated manuscripts as well as Korans and perhaps even Christian books. Gujarat had been a commercial entrepôt from ancient times and had always attracted mariners and merchants from distant lands to its ports. Besides, by the time paper was adopted enthusiastically, Gujarat had come under the political aegis of the Muslims. Arabs, Iranians, Armenians, and Jews were certainly among the visitors to the port cities, so Korans and Bibles would not have been unfamiliar to the local scribes and illuminators. While the typical Jain book is written in black ink with red punctuation marks on buff paper, some of the more sumptuous books have colored pages and gold lettering or highly decorated margins and borders and reflect the work of imaginative and talented artists who did not hesitate to borrow ideas from other traditions.

It is generally believed that gold was introduced sometime early in the fifteenth century and blue, both ultramarine and lapis lazuli, about 1450. Thereafter these two colors became the favorites and red lost ground. Both gold leaf and gold paint were employed. In the case of the former, the entire area to be painted was covered in gold leaf before the outlines were drawn in black. Clearly the dazzling effect of gold and blue, which must have cost more, satisfied the egos of the donors as much as it appealed to their aesthetic sensibilities.

Within the conventional framework the later illuminations differ in their technical quality as well as their opulence. A few manuscripts are much more sumptuously adorned with elaborate marginal decorations than others. Whether this was because the patrons were willing to spend more money or whether the artists involved were specially gifted and desirous of showing off, or a combination of both, is not known. But certainly a manuscript like the Devasano Pado *Kalpasutra* [20] must have required considerable planning and cooperation between the scribe and the artist or artists. The unknown artist was certainly daringly innovative to assimilate so many new motifs and ideas from various sources. One such source was Timurid art, perhaps illustrated books, ceramics, as well as carpets and textiles, all of which may have contributed to the decorative scheme and the rich repertoire of varied motifs of this unusual manuscript. Nowhere is Persian influence more evident than in the landscapes in the border decorations, even though the individual motifs, such as the stylized trees, lotus pools, and the basket pattern to indicate water are of Indian origin. As K. Khandalavala and M. Chandra have perceptively observed, "it is in the border decoration of the Devsano Pāḍo manuscript that the illustrator found the fullest expression of his decorative genius. His inventive skill imbues the landscape, which is one of the important elements of the border panels, with sympathy and understanding hitherto unknown in Jain illustrated manuscripts."[6] Indeed, this manuscript remains the most lavishly illuminated of all Jain books to come to light, although technically it is not as accomplished as the Mandu *Kalpasutra* (see [14]).

The highly conventional style of painting developed in western India during the fourteenth century remained unchanged well into the sixteenth century, as is evident from several examples in the collection [24–29]. It is also clear that more than two centuries of continuous reiteration with negligible innovations led to the ossification of the style. Occasionally, as in a solitary leaf in the collection [29], we come across the work of an artist who succeeded in creating a personal style within the rigid pictorial tradition he had inherited. Such instances are rare, however, and clearly during two centuries of continuity the style had acquired a religious rigidity that discouraged innovations even though other modes of expression were available.

Changes were effected in the second half of the sixteenth century when several additional texts were taken up for illustration. One of these is the *Samgrahanisutra,* represented in the collection by four leaves from two different manuscripts [33, 34]. These illustrations are rendered in a completely different style, more akin to that in which the Hindu *Bhagavatapurana* [36] or *Gitagovinda* [38] pictures are executed, though with less sophistication and complexity. Nevertheless, before the end of the sixteenth century the Jains seem to have abandoned their obsession with the protruding further eye, and the faces are shown in complete profile. Thereafter the figurative types, their costumes as well as coloring, reveal dramatic changes from the conventional mode that still held its appeal even in mid-sixteenth century. As a matter of fact, the stylistic changes seem to have coincided with the sudden loss of interest in having the *Kalpasutra* copied and illustrated. The reason for this shift in taste is yet to be explained.

Several of the Jain books contain colophons that provide information about the donors and their gifts. Apart from containing dates, the colophons include names of several members of the donor's family and sometimes the place where the manuscript was dedicated. A colophon may also contain the name of the donee and of the scribe but almost never any information about the artist. Clearly the act of writing was more important than the art of illustrating. In some instances a later hand has added a date when a particular volume was used for recitation by a teacher (see colophon of [18] in Appendix).

Three of the *Kalpasutra* manuscripts in the collection were dedicated by influential families. The donor of one [28] was Puti, who was the wife of Madhava. His father is described as "the lord of ministers," but the court or state is not mentioned. Apparently she was advised by her guru, Somaratna, that worshipping the holy scripture constituted an act of merit, and so she had a manuscript copied and illustrated.

Another *Kalpasutra* manuscript [15] was dedicated in 1442 by members of the Ukesa family of Satyapura. The collection also includes a manuscript commissioned in 1510 by Kadua, who belonged to the Ukesa family [27]. Kadua is described as "lord of the ministers," as is his father, Javada, but we are not told where. A later inscription states that the manuscript was read in 1811 in the city of Anahillapura. Very likely this is Anahilwara Patan, which was the capital of Gujarat. It is not improbable that the manuscript was dedicated in that city and that members of the Ukesa family served the Muslim sultans of Gujarat. A third *Kalpasutra* manuscript dedicated by a member of the Ukesa family is in the collection of the Museum of Fine Arts, Boston. In his catalogue Coomaraswamy commented, "The Ūkeśa (Oswāl) family is well known," but provided no further information nor any references.[7]

In addition to illuminated manuscripts the collection includes two paintings on cloth that represent *yantras* [13, 16]. Like the mandala, a *yantra* is primarily a

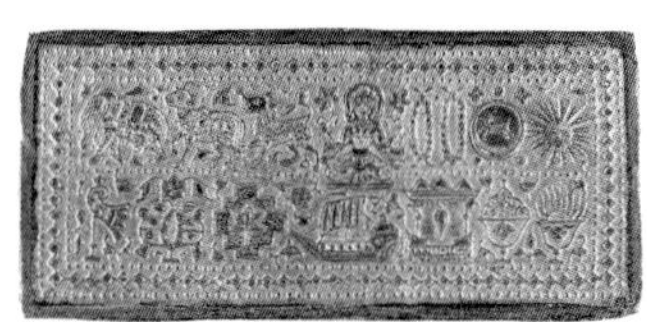

FIGURE 19
Cover for Jain manuscript, with fourteen auspicious symbols, Western India, sixteenth century, lacquered and gilded cloth over cardboard, 11 11/16 x 5 1/2 in (29.8 x 14.0 cm), Los Angeles County Museum of Art, from the Nasli and Alice Heeramaneck Collection, Museum Associates Purchase, M.72.53.22.

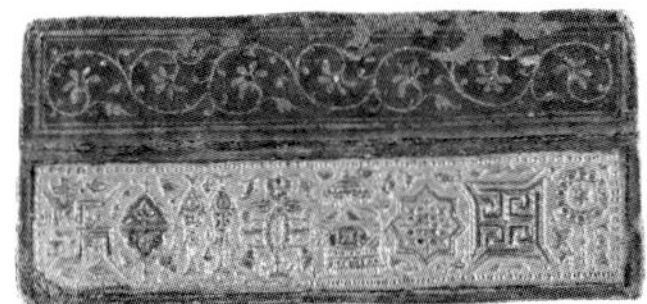

FIGURE 20
Inside of the cover shown in FIG. 19, with vine and eight auspicious symbols.

geometrical configuration based on the square and circle. It is an abstract diagram of cosmic power and is also regarded as a divine citadel. It is used as an aid in meditation in tantric praxis. While many painted *yantras* of the eighteenth and nineteenth centuries have survived, ones from the fifteenth century are rare. As is evident from a comparison of the museum's *yantras* with contemporary manuscript illuminations, the same style was employed for both forms of art. However, the *yantras* are not as sumptuously colored. Seldom is gold or lapis lazuli employed, and generally the *yantras* tend to be even flatter and more linear than the manuscript illuminations. Conventional as the narrative tradition in Jain manuscript illuminations is, the subject matter of the *yantras*, which include both letters in the form of mantras as well as figural forms and symbols, is limited by ritualistic and iconographic injunctions. The *yantras* are rendered on a much larger scale, though, and provide us with some idea of what Jain paintings on cloth look like.

Finally, a few words should be said about the Jain book covers in the collection. They have not been included in this catalogue because none is painted. When Jain books were written on palm leaves prior to the fourteenth century, the covers were painted, as was the case with Buddhist book covers. All the covers in the collection are later than the manuscripts—most date from the late nineteenth to early twentieth centuries—and are made from cardboard, which is then wrapped in cloth. One or two, such as the one illustrated here, are covered with gilded and lacquered cloth and are quite richly adorned with various symbols. On the top of the one shown (FIG. 19) are the fourteen auspicious symbols that Trisala dreamed when Mahavira entered her womb. The bottom (FIG. 20) is decorated with a painted floral vine in one register and the eight auspicious symbols in the other.

NOTES

1. Coomaraswamy 1924, 4: 33.
2. Cort 1989, p. 151–52.
3. Ibid., pp. 170–71.
4. Ibid., pp. 177–78.
5. Losty 1982, p. 44.
6. Khandalavala & Chandra 1969, p. 32.
7. Coomaraswamy 1924, 4: 41.

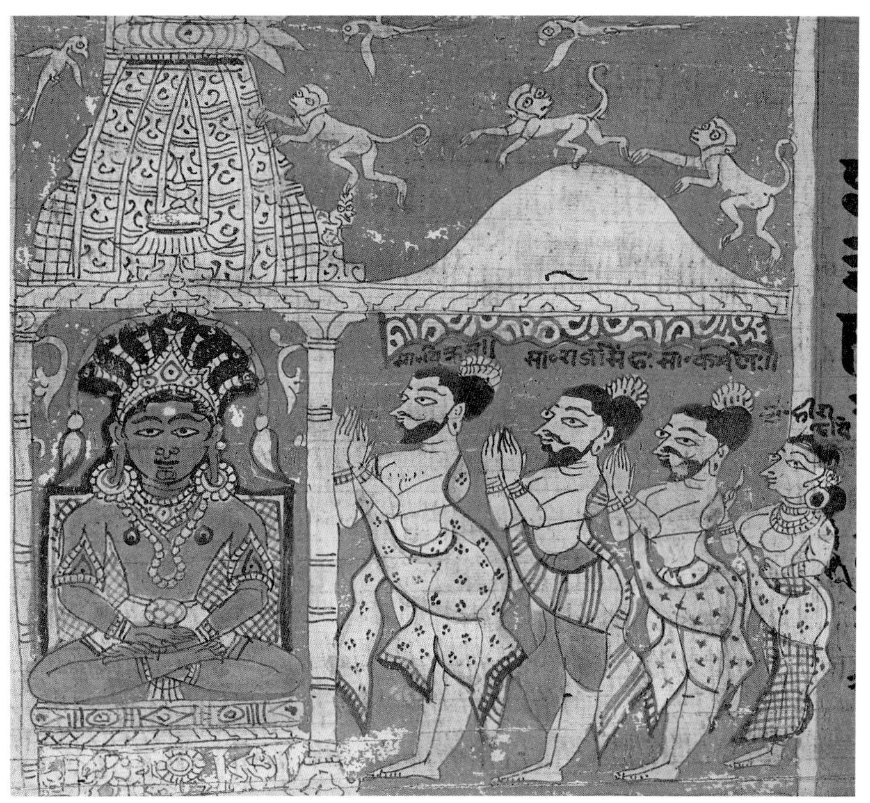

CAT. 10A detail

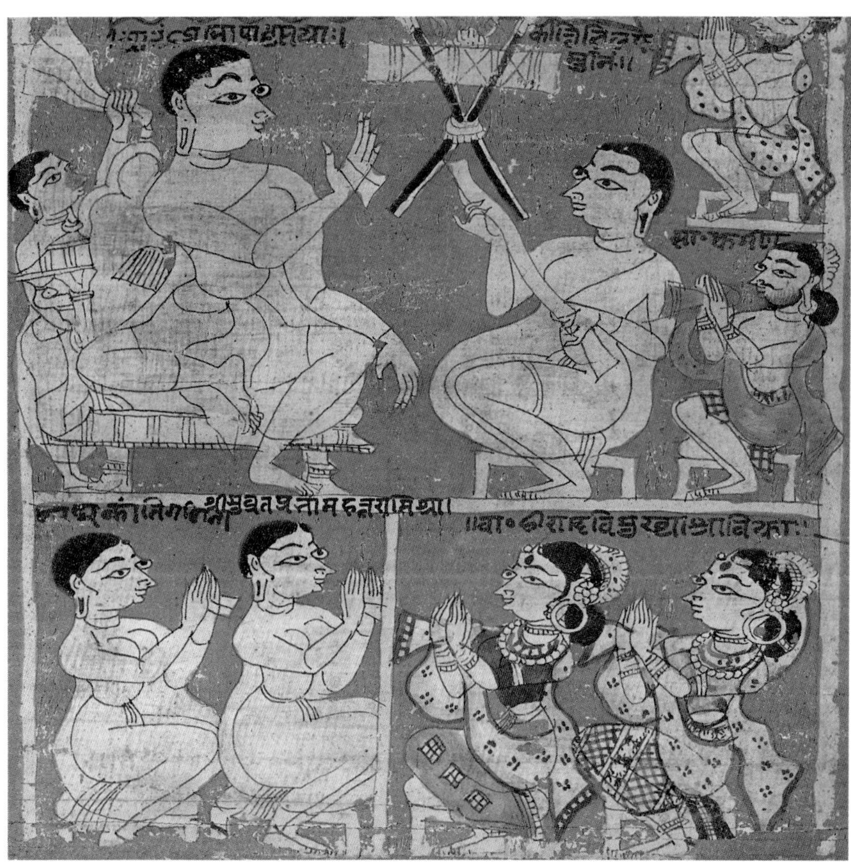

CAT. 10B detail

Catalogue

Unless otherwise noted, all texts are written in ink and all pictures painted in opaque watercolor and gold on paper. For numbered folios, the number and sides are given after the illustration titles.

10 TWO FOLIOS FROM A *KALPASUTRA* MANUSCRIPT

Gujarat; c. 1350
Ink and opaque watercolor on palm leaf
Folios, 2½ x 9¼ in (6.4 x 23.5 cm)
Illustrations, 2½ x 2¼ in (6.4 x 5.7 cm)
Purchased with funds provided by the Indian Art Special Purpose Fund, Mrs. Wilbur Archer Beckett, Gerald Stockton and S. Louis Gaines, the Christian Humann Fund, Jo Ann and Julian Ganz, Jr., and Dr. and Mrs. Peter S. Bing
M.88.62.1,.2

A *Worship of Parsvanatha*
B *Instruction by Monks*

A On the left is an enthroned figure of Jina Parsvanatha, identified by his snake hood, seated within a temple. On the right under a canopy stand four worshippers who are identified by inscriptions above their heads. The three males are Vikrama, Rajasimha, and Karmana. The female at the rear is Hiradevi. The name of each male is preceded by the letter *sa,* which is usually an abbreviation of the word *sarthavaha* or *sahu,* meaning "merchant." The progressively decreasing size of the figures indicates their relative importance. Above, three monkeys jump across the roofs and three parrots fly in the sky.

B This illustration is divided into three sections. In the larger, upper register the principal monk is seated on an elaborate chair with his right arm extended in the gesture symbolizing a discourse. The legend above his head is not clearly legible, but his name appears to be Anandaprabhapadhyaya. Behind the eminent teacher stands a lesser monk fanning him with a piece of cloth. A third monk sits on a stool in front and holds a folio from a manuscript that is placed in between them on a stand. He is identified as Kirtitilakamuni. Of the two lay figures behind him, the one at the bottom is Karmana, who is also included in illustration A. The figure above is perhaps either Rajasimha or Vikrama.

The lower register is divided into two sections with two nuns clearly separated from two ladies. The nuns on the left are identified as Dharama(?)kantiganini and Sri Subrataprabhamahattara, who is described as *sishyā,* or "disciple." Of the two lay women on the right only the one in front is identified, as Hiradevi, who is described as the chief hearer (*mukhyā śrāvikā*).

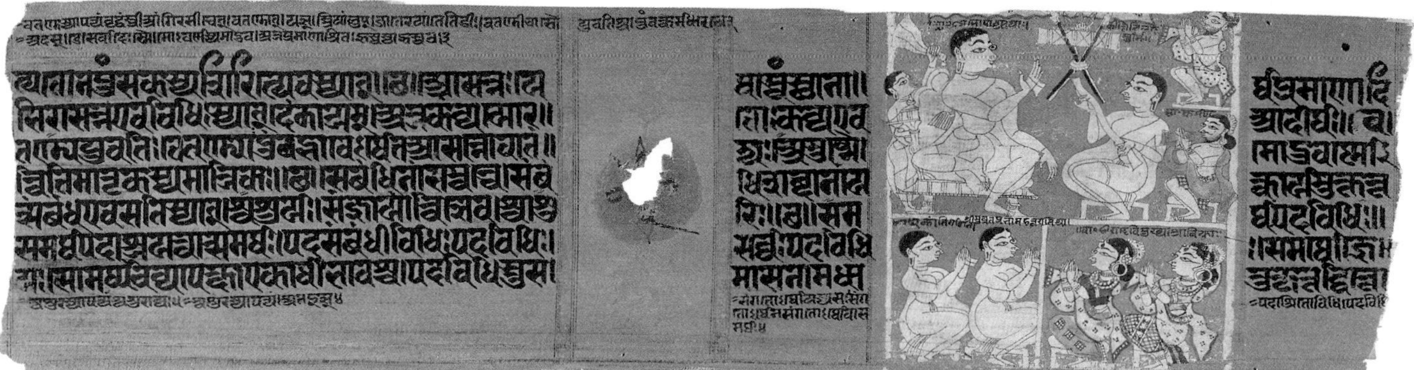

CAT. 10B

The two folios are from the section of the *Kalpasutra* recounting the life of Parsvanatha. The scene with the merchants is simply a more elaborate composition than that encountered in an earlier palm-leaf manuscript of the text (Doshi 1985, p. 40, fig. 19 [left]). Noteworthy in this illustration is the shrine in which Parsva is seated. It is a precise rendering of a northern Indian *sikhara*-type of temple of the period. Interesting also is the depiction of monkeys and parrots, which not only add a realistic touch but offer a lively contrast to the conventional postures of the figures. While the figures and their garments are articulately rendered, the design of the temple's superstructure and the details of the throne, as well as the animals and birds, are more freely and cursorily sketched.

In each illustration the color red is used as a background, and each composition is bounded by a yellow border. Except for Parsva, whose complexion is green, all the figures are white with a yellowish tinge. The monks and nuns wear white robes, but the laypersons are elegantly dressed in costumes of mauve, green, and red. The hair of both sexes is arranged in a bun and adorned with comblike floral decorations. The women are more sumptuously ornamented, and the men wear substantial beards.

Both the style of writing and the pictures indicate a date not much later than the mid-fourteenth century for these folios. The style of writing is in fact closer to that in thirteenth-century manuscripts than those from the last quarter of the fourteenth century such as the *Kalpasutra* of about 1375 in the Prince of Wales Museum, Bombay (Khandalavala and Chandra 1969, pl. 1). The illustrations on the museum's palm-leaf folios are not as sophisticated or sumptuous as that *Kalpasutra* but are stylistically more akin to those seen in late thirteenth-century palm-leaf manuscripts (Doshi 1985, pp. 40–41, no. 19, and p. 44, nos. 22, 23). Thus a date about 1350 or earlier still for these two illustrated folios seems reasonable. This date is reinforced by the design of the temple, which is rarely encountered in post-1350 paper manuscripts.

Northern India; c. 1375
Ink and opaque watercolor on palm leaf
Folios, A, 2 x 7¼ in (5.1 x 18.4 cm); B, 1½ x 6 in (3.8 x 15.2 cm)
Illustration, 2 x 2⅞ in (5.1 x 7.3 cm)
Purchased with funds provided by the Indian Art Special Purpose Fund, Mrs. Wilbur Archer Beckett, Gerald Stockton and S. Louis Gaines, the Christian Humann Fund, Jo Ann and Julian Ganz, Jr., and Dr. and Mrs. Peter S. Bing
M.88.62.3,.4

Enthroned Mahavira

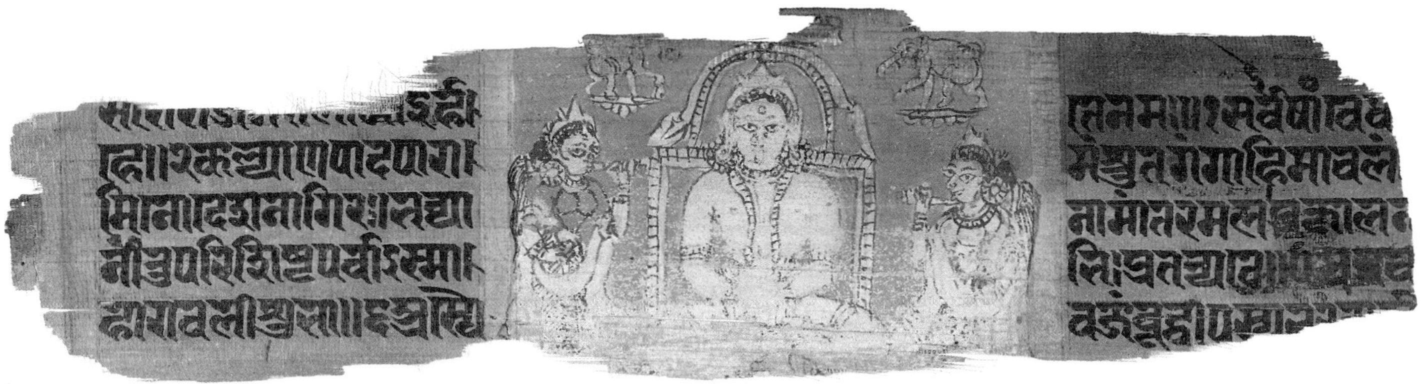

These two folios, only one of which is illustrated, once belonged to a manuscript of the *Trishashtisalakapurushacharita* (Lives of the sixty-three heroes). Both folios are badly damaged but the text can be identified as portions of the tenth chapter of the life of Mahavira (*Mahaviracharita*). The solitary illustration shows a pale yellow Jina, presumably Mahavira, seated in meditation within a simple shrine. Two women stand on either side and fan the Jina with flywhisks, and two elephants are placed above. The jewelry of all three figures is rendered in black. The shrine and the elephants are drawn in black and tinted in light purple. The woman on the left wears a green blouse and the other a purple blouse. The background is red.

The script is generally comparable to several manuscripts of the thirteenth and fourteenth centuries (see Shah 1978, figs. 4, 6–9), but the picture is more difficult to place. The quality of the script is on the whole far superior to that of the illustration. It is not improbable that the manuscript was copied somewhere in north-central India rather than in Gujarat or Rajasthan. Both the script and the drawing share features with illustrated manuscripts done between Gwalior and the Delhi region (Doshi 1985, p. 59, figs. 19–21). Similarly cursive, simple, and somewhat folksy paintings may also be seen in a few surviving Buddhist manuscripts of the early fifteenth century (Pal 1965). However, by the fifteenth century paper had virtually replaced palm leaves in northern and central India, which makes it unlikely that this manuscript was painted after 1400. Moreover, the style of writing indicates a date in the fourteenth rather than the fifteenth century.

Western India; c. 1425
A, with silver
Folios, 4½ x 10¼ in (11.4 x 26.0 cm)
Illustrations, 4½ x 3⅛ in (11.4 x 7.9 cm)
From the Nasli and Alice Heeramaneck Collection, Museum Associates Purchase
M.71.1.6a,b
Literature: *Heeramaneck* 1966, p. 120, no. 143 (not illustrated); Trabold 1975, p. 28, no. 34 (B only illustrated).

A *Initiation and Haircutting of Parsvanatha*
B *Liberation of Mahavira*

CAT. 12A detail

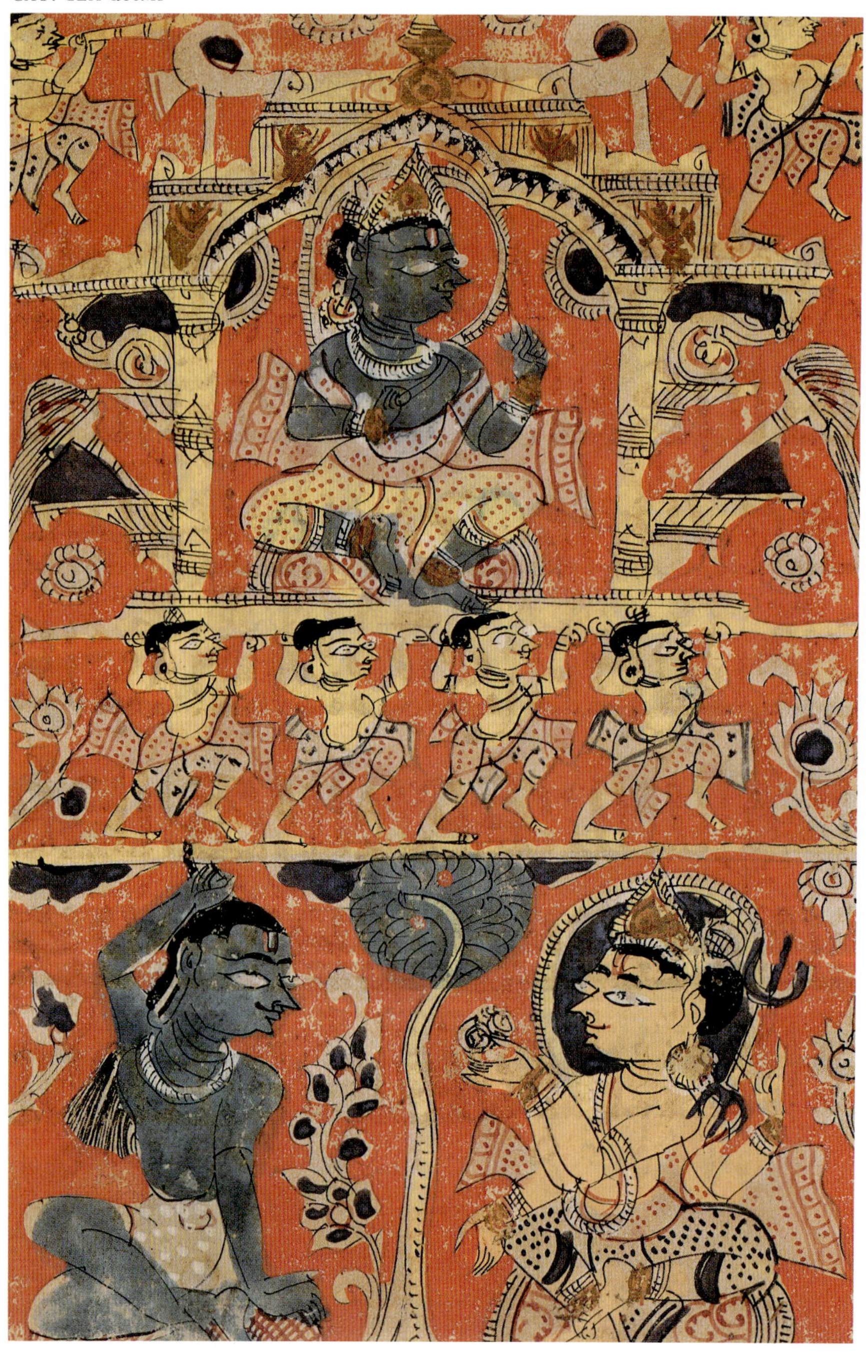

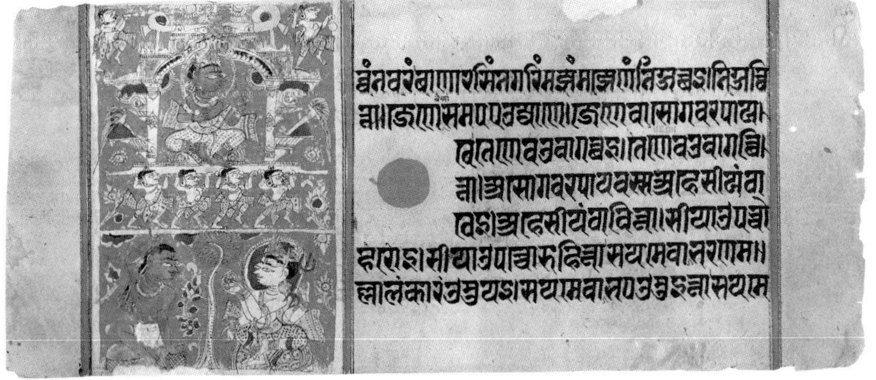

CAT. 12A

CAT. 12B detail

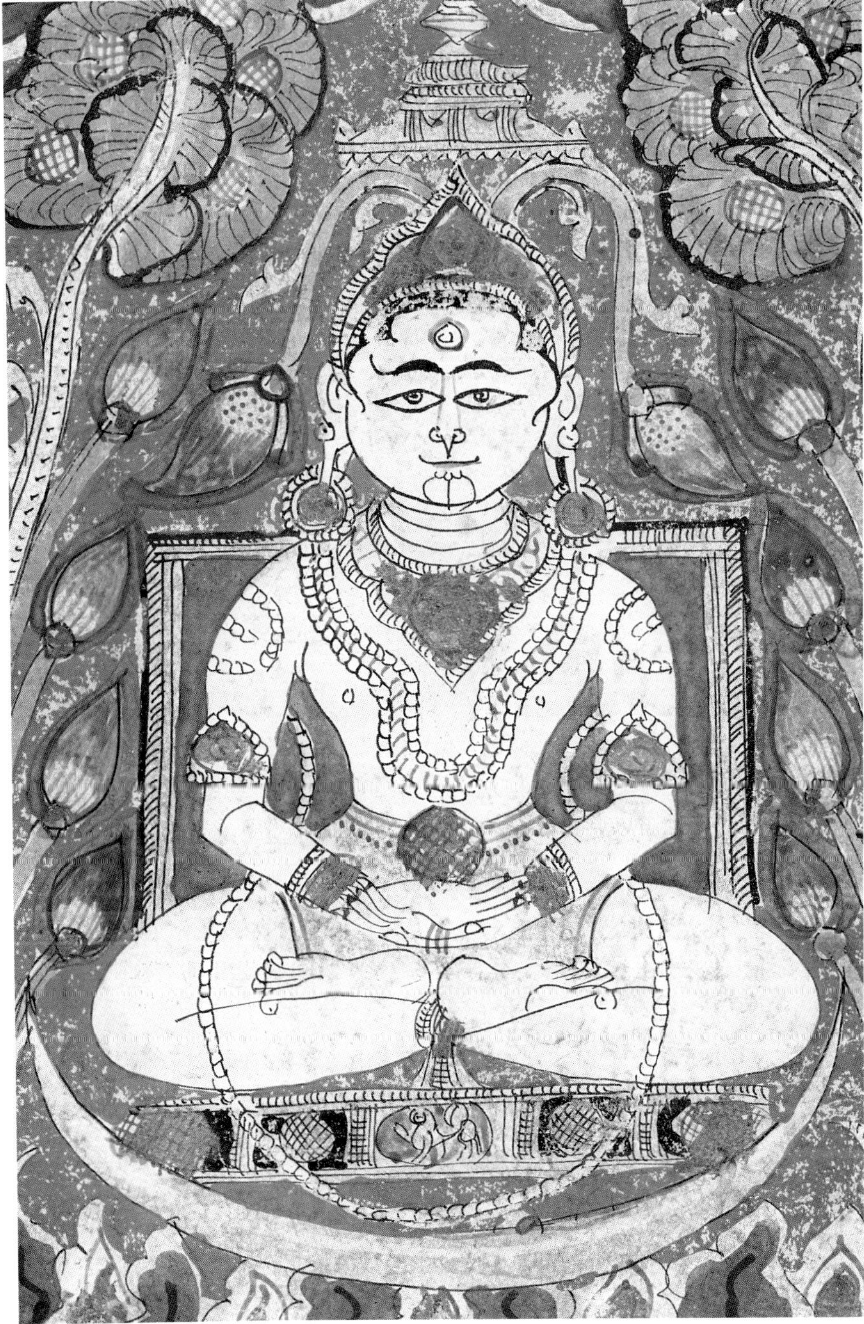

A In the upper half of the composition a Jina is being carried in a palanquin supported by four bearers. Two more attendants above play musical instruments. The princely figure is being taken to his spiritual initiation ceremony. In the lower half, in preparation for a monk's life, the Jina is seen cutting off his hair, which is being received by the god Sakra (Indra). The Jina here is blue, leading to his identification as Parsvanatha. It may be noted that Sakra is here given four arms, one of which clearly holds the thunderbolt (*vajra*), his principal emblem.

B This scene represents the liberation of Mahavira, who is given a pale yellow complexion. Usually in such liberation scenes the Jina sits in meditation above a crescent that is supported by a highly stylized rock formation. These rocks represent the cosmic Mount Meru, and the crescent is in fact an inverted white parasol made of silver rather than a lunar crescent. This inverted parasol symbolizes Siddhasila, which is at the top of the universe. The expression *Siddhasila* literally means "stone of perfection" or "liberation," although why an inverted parasol was used to symbolize it is a mystery. A small conventional parasol is above Mahavira's crowned head. Interestingly, Mahavira is here shown as richly adorned, just as in some forms a Buddha is depicted as crowned and ornamented [4]. That this figure is Mahavira is clear not only from the accompanying text but also from the little effigy of a lion in the middle of his seat. Lotus buds and two identical trees sway toward him in adoration. Two lotuses are also seen to emerge from Mahavira's head, as is typical. In all such scenes Mahavira holds an object in his hands, the exact significance of which is not clear. In form it looks like the fruit on the stylized trees above.

Both the style of writing and of the illuminations suggest a date early in the fifteenth century. The illustrations are stylistically very similar to those in a *Kalpasutra* manuscript in the Freer Gallery of Art, Washington, D.C., generally considered to be of the fifteenth century (W. N. Brown 1934, fig. 81) and to several others that are dated to the first half of the fifteenth century (Shah 1978, figs. 37, 38).

Rajasthan, Dilwara (?); c. 1425
Opaque watercolor, ink, and gold on cotton
9 x 8⅛ in (22.9 x 20.6 cm)
Gift of Navin Kumar in memory of his mother, Mrs. Prakash Wati Jain
M.82.164

There are two inscriptions on the back of this painting. The shorter one, in the Devanagari script, is a tantric invocatory formula in Sanskrit. The longer one is in Gujarati and has been read and translated as follows by M. A. Dhaky:

pañchāṅguli devī sādhaka 5 śri mandirasvāmī adhishṭhātri devī
Pañchāṅguli devī {and} five adorers. The presiding goddess {of the religious domain of} Śri Mandirasvāmī.

Commenting on the inscription, Dhaky wrote (personal communication): "Śri Mandirasvāmī is a Gujarati rendering of [Jina] Simandhara, the first of twenty Tirthankaras of the mythical Mahavideha land of the Jaina cosmographical geography, whose religious ordinance is currently prevailing in that land; and Pañchāṅguli devī is the *sāsana-devatā,* i.e., the presiding and protecting female attendant-divinity in that Jina's religious domain. The central deity portrayed in the mandala is seemingly Pañchāṅguli devī."

Panchanguli is depicted as a golden-colored goddess with eighteen arms seated in the lotus posture within two intersecting triangles. Of her two principal arms, that on the right displays the teaching gesture; the other is placed in her lap in the gesture of meditation. Not all of the attributes and gestures of the remaining hands can be recognized. Some of them, clockwise from the uppermost proper right hand, are a sword, shield, banner, trident, elephant-goad, bow and arrow, perhaps a conch, and lotus. Below the goddess's knees are two elephants, presumably supporting her seat. In the six apexes of the triangles are six sacred syllables. The triangles are enclosed by three rings with a spout directly above the goddess's head. The next circle contains a long mantra beginning with the expression *om pañchāṅguli.* This is followed by a wider circle of a continuous scroll with medallions enclosing the syllable *hrim* written in gold against blue sixteen times. The circle beyond is filled with mantras of several verses. The golden syllable *hrim* is contained within the lip or spout formed by the next three rings at the top and flanked by two eyes and shielded by a blue canopy.

At the four corners are four protective deities, three of whom have four arms and the same attributes—including a sword, a cup, a shield, and a small drum—and who are accompanied by an animal that looks like a dog. Of the three, the figure in the upper right corner is blue and the other two are white. The fourth figure, in the lower left corner, is blue and has only two arms. His left hand carries a cup, and he stands astride a black-and-white snake. The smallest of the three figures at the bottom right represents a monk during *puja;* his white robes indicate that he is a Svetambara Jain. The remaining nine figures outside the circle depict the planetary deities (Navagraha), some of whom can be more easily recognized than others. The two figures on either side of the eyes at the top are the Sun god (left, red) and the Moon god (right, white). Rahu, who causes eclipses, is represented along the left margin as a head facing a crescent moon. The figure below him with a serpentine lower part is Ketu, the meteor deity.

The closest iconographic and stylistic parallel for the central deity is offered by an image in a manuscript recounting the life of the seventh Jina, Suparsvanatha (*Supāsanāhacharita*), published by U. P. Shah (1978, fig. 37). Shah, an authority on Jain iconography, has identified that figure, who is twenty-armed, as Kali, the female tutelary deity of Suparsvanatha. Both figures share the same emblems and gestures, although they are not disposed in identical fashion. Thus the same basic form appears to have served for two different deities. It should be noted further that the mantra beginning with *om pañchāṅguli* includes the words *Maheśvara* (Siva) and *Maheśvarī* (Durga or Kali). Other features of the mantra too indicate Panchanguli's conceptual relationship with the Hindu Kali, although the Jain goddess is not at all terrifying. The combination of the mantras and the images would make this a very potent *yantra.* The mantras constitute the charm, whose title *Pañchāṅguli* means "five fingers," which apparently was recited to ward off evil influences and to cure diseases, and is reminiscent of the Buddhist Pancharaksha charm (see [7]).

So similar are the two Jain representations that one must conclude that they were painted at about the same time and in the same locality. Fortunately we know where and when the manuscript of Suparsvanatha's life was copied and illustrated. The place was Dilwara in Rajasthan and the year 1423. Very likely the same workshop or artist was responsible for illustrating the manuscript and the museum's painting. No matter where or when it was executed, it remains an important document of tantric rite and art among the Jains.

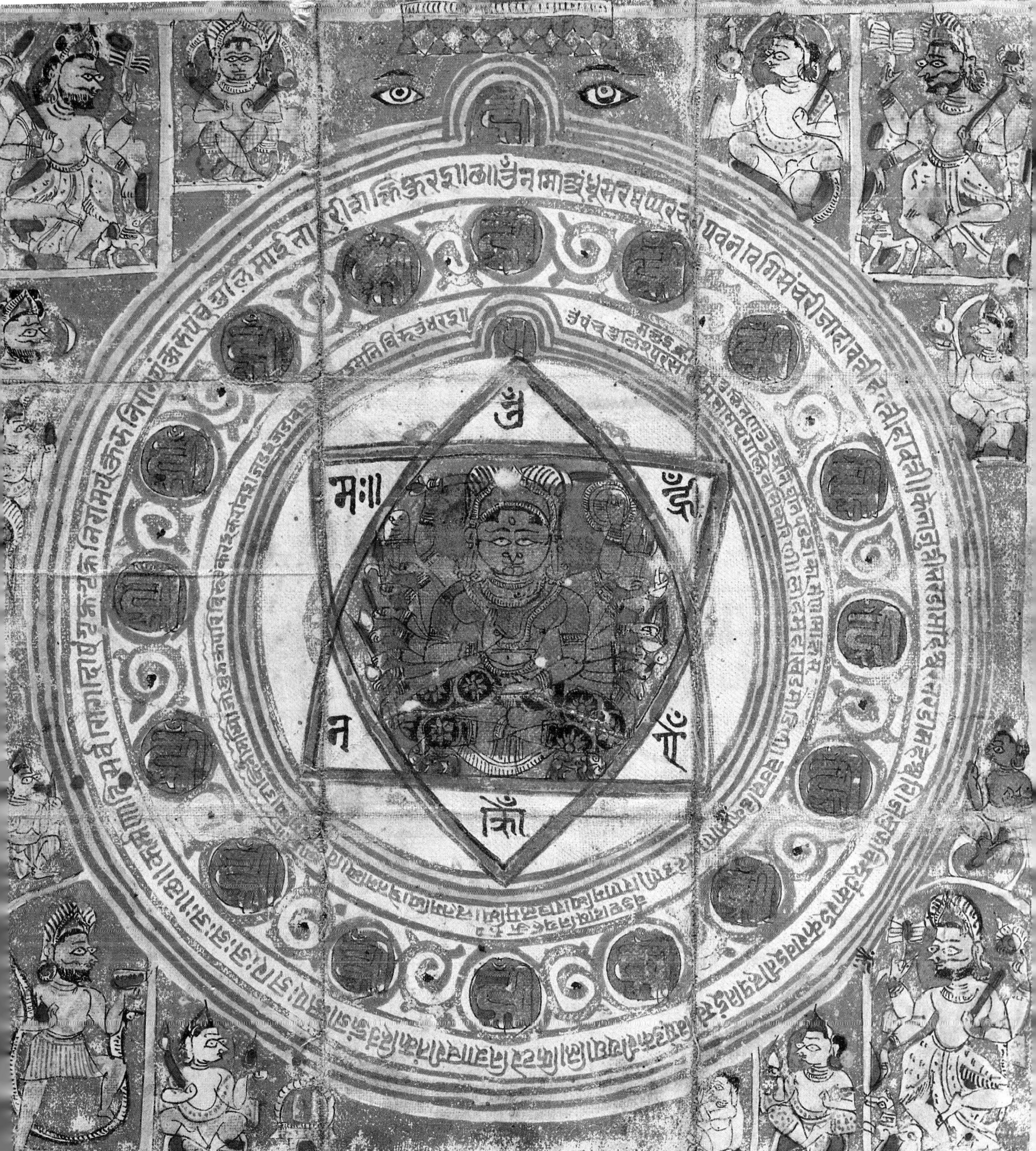

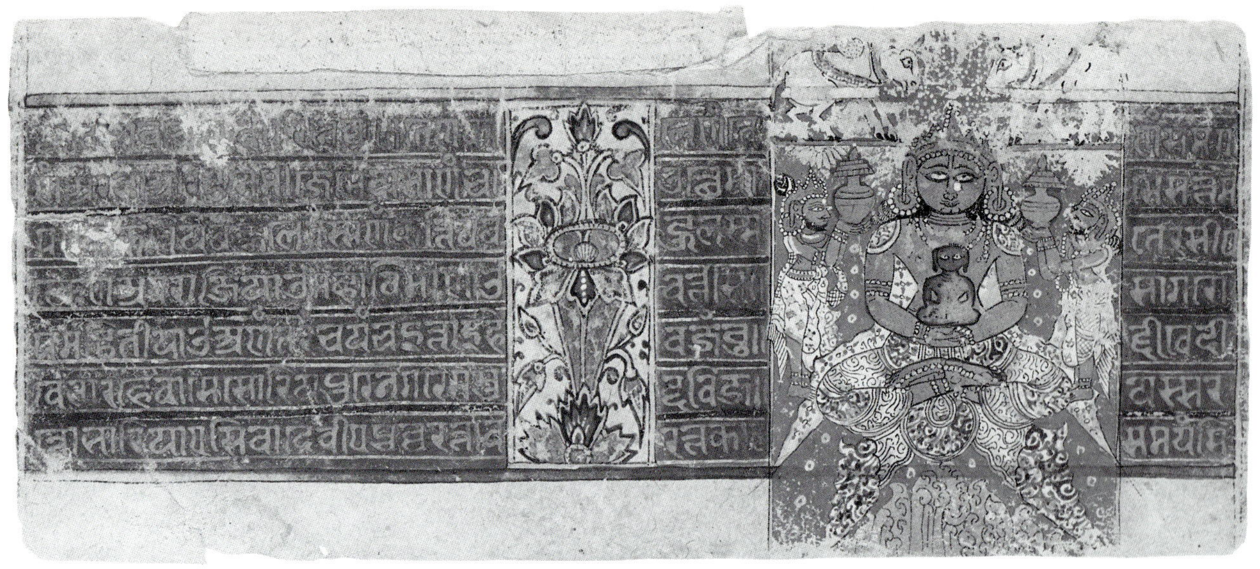

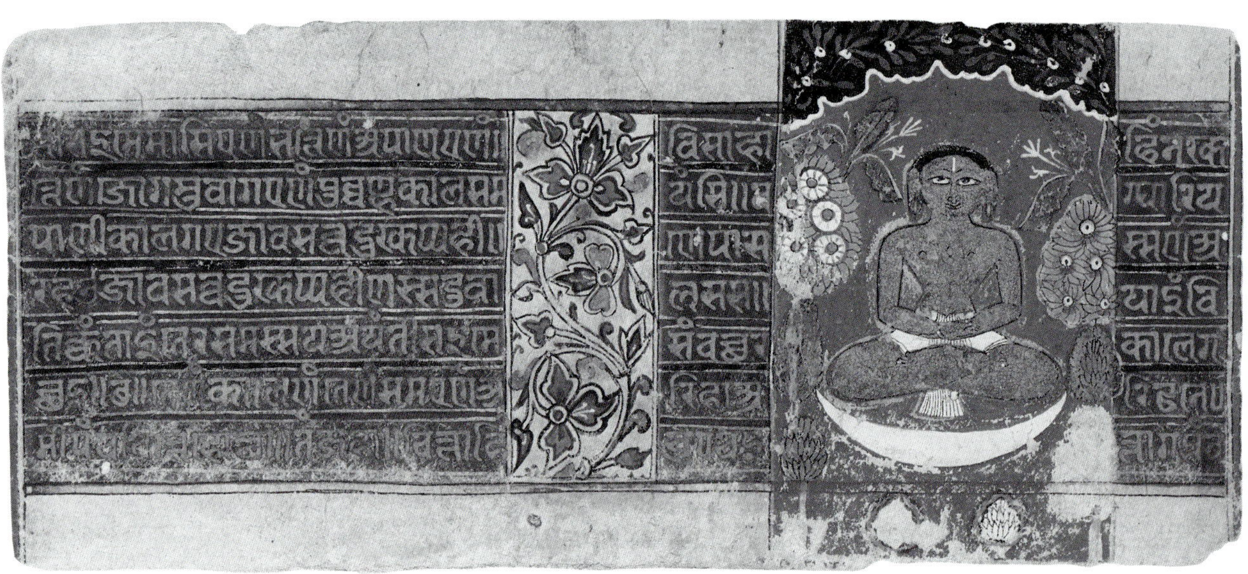

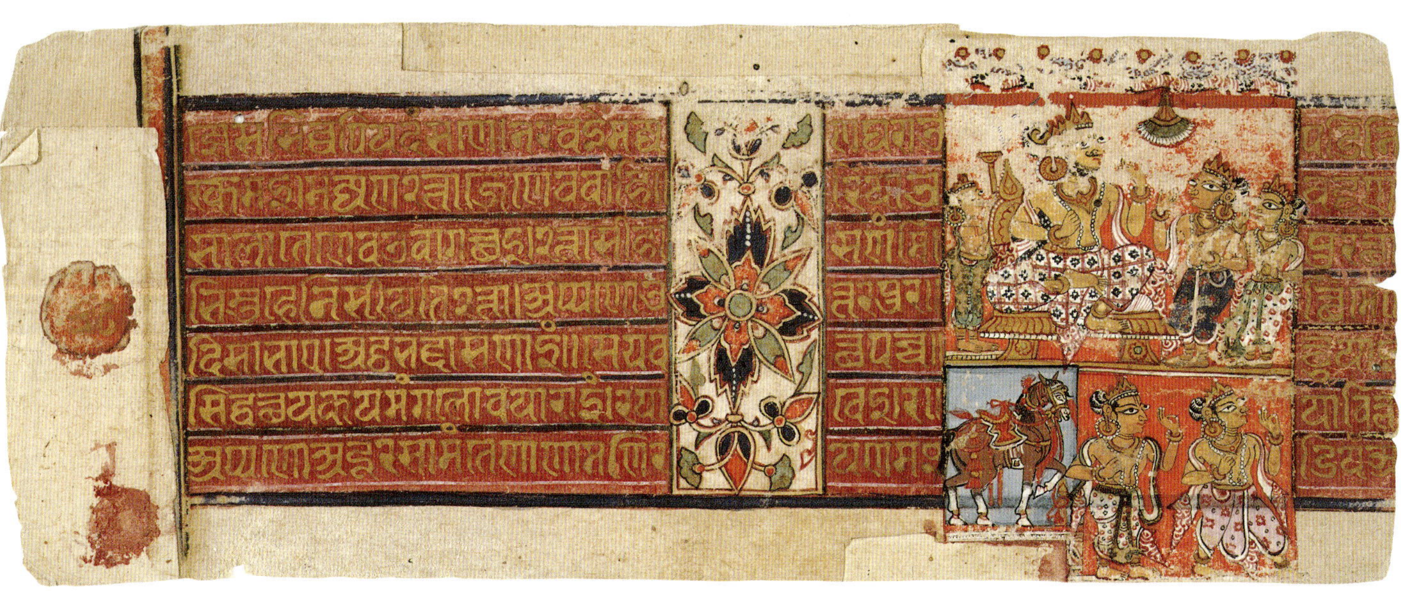

Madhya Pradesh, Mandu; 1439
Text in gold
Folios, A, B, 4 x 9⅛ in (10.2 x 23.2 cm);
C, 4 x 10⅛ in (10.2 x 25.7 cm)
Illustrations, A, B, 4 x 2½ in (10.2 x 6.4 cm);
C, 3⅞ x 2½ in (9.8 x 6.4 cm)
From the Nasli and Alice Heeramaneck Collection, Museum Associates Purchase
A, B, M.71.1.4a,b; C, M.71.1.5
Literature: *Heeramaneck* 1966, p. 120, nos. 141, 142 (not illustrated); Goswamy 1988, p. 30, no. 48 (A only).

A *Lustration of a Jina*
B *Liberation of a Jina*
C *Unidentified Scene*

Although the leaves vary slightly in length, all three belong to the same *Kalpasutra* manuscript. It is possible that the folios are from the well-known Mandu *Kalpasutra,* the bulk of which is in the National Museum, New Delhi (see Khandalavala and Chandra 1969, pp. 17–21; and Losty 1982, p. 60, no. 28, where he notes that four folios are missing). The fourth missing folio is probably in the Brooklyn Museum. The colophon statement in the Mandu manuscript informs us that it was commissioned by Kshemahamsagani for his use at Mandapagarh (Mandu) in the Vikrama year 1496 (A.D. 1439). We are further told that the donor was a disciple of the master reciter Kshemakirtigani. Almost certainly Kshemahamsagani was also a reciter as well as a Svetambara monk.

On each page seven lines of text are written in gold letters against a purplish-red background. The area of writing is contained within blue borders; similar but thinner borders separate each line. Another peculiarity of this manuscript is that each page is divided into halves by a wide band of floral design placed slightly off center. The floral element differs from page to page, thereby offering an enormous variety of designs. There is an illustration on only one side of each leaf. Whereas the scribe left a wide margin at the top and the bottom of each page, the artist extended his compositions to both edges. All three folios are slightly damaged in places.

A This scene represents the lustration of an infant Jina immediately after his birth. The small blue figure of a Jina is seated in the lap of Sakra, the king of the gods, who has a golden complexion. Below him are the peaks of the cosmic Mount Meru, which are said to bend down before a Jina. The two figures holding waterpots are also Sakras; altogether sixty-four Sakras are said to have participated in the ceremony. The two bulls above represent two of the four crystal bulls that Sakra had created for the four directions for the occasion. Interestingly, in these Jain representations, although Sakra is dressed and adorned as befitting a god, he is not given his distinctive horizontal third eye as he is in Hindu and Buddhist depictions.

Usually in *Kalpasutras* this incident is described in the lives of Mahavira, Parsvanatha, and Rishabhanatha. In the Svetambara tradition both Parsvanatha and Mallinatha may be shown with a blue or green complexion, and so the infant here may represent Parsvanatha since Mallinatha's biography is not included in the text.

B A green Jina is seated in meditation above the white crescent of an inverted parasol. He is flanked by stylized trees standing one above another. Above him is a leafy arch against a blue background. Although the Jina cannot be precisely identified, the scene represents him after death when as a liberated soul (*siddha*) he goes to Siddhasila, which is at the summit of the universe.

C This illustration cannot be identified exactly, but it may represent an incident from the story of Neminatha. The composition is divided into two segments. Above is a court scene with an enthroned figure—attended by a parasol bearer—who is engaged in conversation with two male visitors. Below are two other men and a caparisoned horse. The men may represent Neminatha's cousins Krishna and Balarama.

In addition to being one of the most important documents of Jain painting because it is dated and can be placed precisely, the Mandu *Kalpasutra* is considered to be one of the finest examples of an illuminated Jain manuscript to have survived from the fifteenth century. Although not as sumptuous as the somewhat later Devasano Pado manuscript [20], it is certainly one of the most ornate in its generous use of gold and the flamboyant floral motifs. Unlike an average manuscript, here one encounters a conscious attempt to truly illuminate the pages with gold writing on a purple background. Very likely the margins on top and bottom were left blank to be adorned as richly as the Devasano Pado folios but could not be done because of a shortage of time or money. The figures are well drawn, the colors are luminous, and the garments are delightfully varied, making these illuminations particularly rich for students interested in textile design. It is also a valuable source for the study of contemporary furniture design.

Gujarat, Satyapur; 1442
Folios, $4\frac{1}{2}$ x $10\frac{7}{16}$ in (11.4 x 26.5 cm)
Illustrations, $4\frac{1}{2}$ x $2\frac{3}{4}$ in (11.4 x 7.0 cm)
Covers, $5\frac{1}{4}$ x $11\frac{1}{4}$ x in (13.3 x 28.6 cm)
From the Nasli and Alice Heeramaneck Collection, Museum Associates Purchase
M.72.53.18

A *Image of Rishabhanatha* (67v)
B *Scenes from Nemi's Life* (61v)
C *Kalaka and Sahi Chief in Conversation* (99v)

Complete manuscript with 105 folios and 36 illustrations. Nine lines of text per page, written in black ink on buff paper. Text on each page usually divided into two panels with narrow vertical columns in red. Three red circles, some decorated, per page. Short descriptive captions accompany the illuminations. Apart from ink and gold, the colors employed are red, black, blue, white, and green. Covers wrapped in light blue silk brocade adorned with red pomegranates.

In addition to the dedicatory inscription following the colophon of the *Kalpasutra* on page 97, the manuscript also provides interesting information as to the version of the Kalaka story copied (see Appendix). The dedicatory statement informs us that the manuscript was commissioned at Satyapura in the Vikrama year 1499 (A.D. 1442) by the noble lady Meghadevi and other members of the Ukesa family on the advice of the teacher Jayakirti Suri, the chief of the Anchalagaccha. The colophon of the Kalaka story, on page 103, gives us the interesting information that the short *Kalakacharyakatha* was composed by Dharmaprabhasuri in the Vikrama year 1389 (A.D. 1332). (See W. N. Brown 1934, pp. 32, 92–97 for an edited version of the entire text.) In the middle column of the same page there are two later inscriptions in cursive handwriting providing the names of two subsequent owners of the manuscript, Hemasagara and Nandaraja.

A The accompanying caption identifies this representation as the image of Rishabhanatha (*Rishabhanathamurti*). Known also as Adinatha, Rishabhanatha is the first of the twenty-four Jinas and is regarded as founder of the faith. Crowned and regally adorned, Rishabhanatha is seated in meditation within a shrine. His throne is supported by elephants and lions, and he is accompanied by six attendant figures who cannot be precisely identified. Above, two elephants salute the Jina. The scene very likely represents Rishabhanatha in his heaven before his descent to earth. Curiously, the black pupils of his eyes are missing. Whether this was an accident or deliberate on the artist's part is not clear.

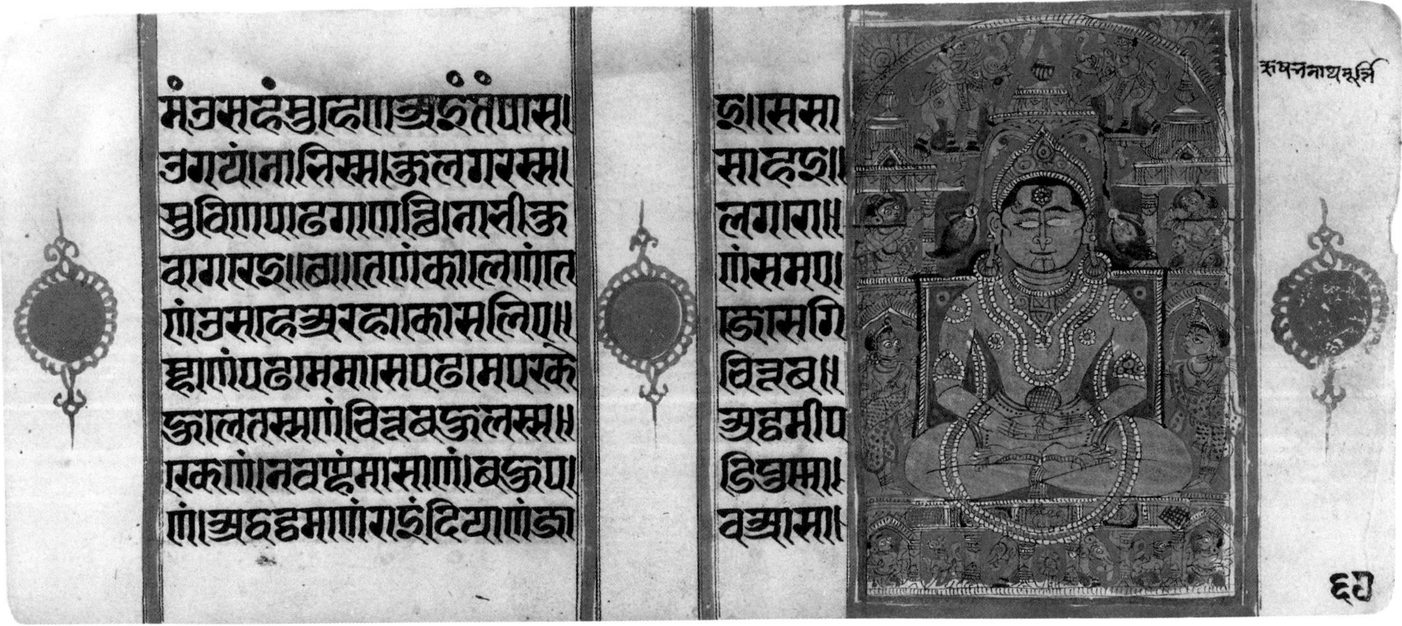

CAT. 15A

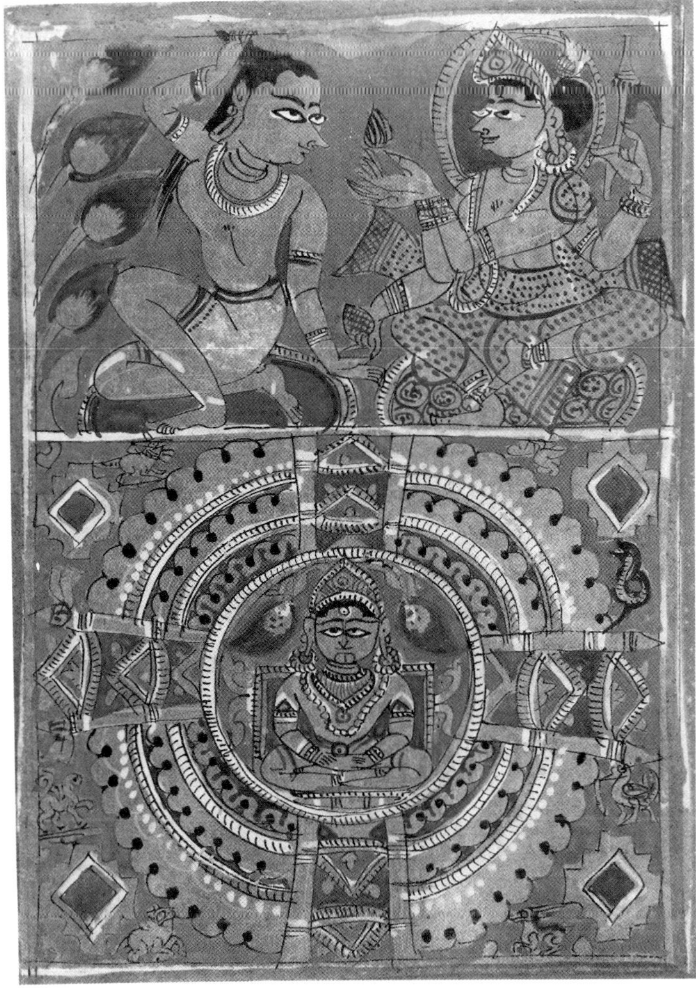

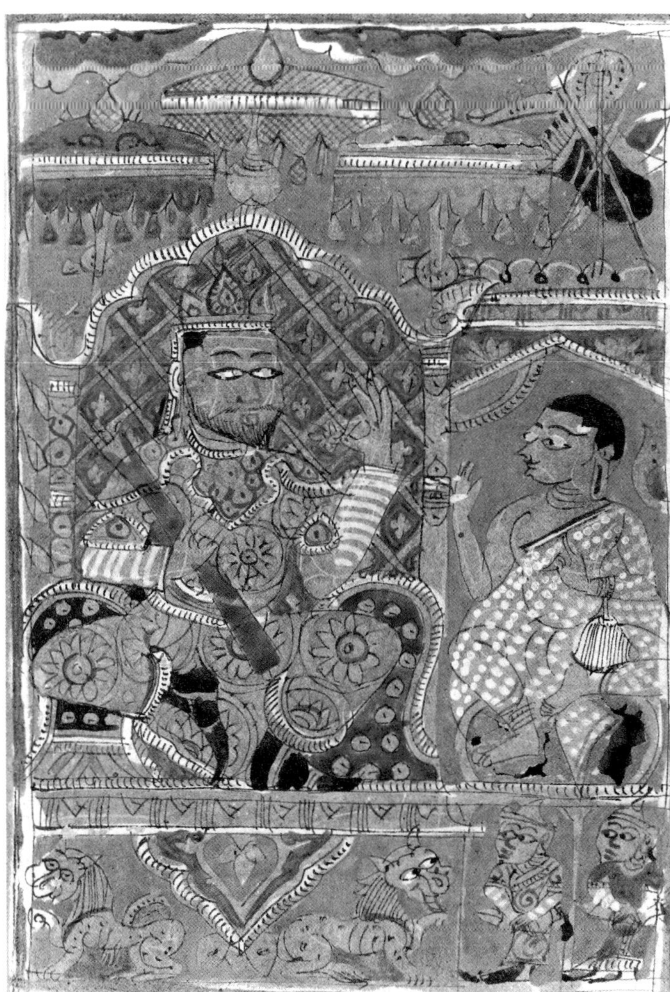

CAT. 15B detail *(left)*
CAT. 15C detail *(right)*

B This illustration depicts two different incidents from the life of Neminatha. In the upper section is the scene of Nemi's renunciation (the caption says *Nemidikshā*). Nemi is about to cut off his hair, which Sakra will receive. The scene below shows Nemi's enlightenment (*Nemisamavasarana*). It is customary to represent this scene as a *yantra* or a mandala. "When a jina obtains perfect knowledge, the gods prepare his *samavasarana*. The earth is cleansed for a space of a *yojana* (two miles) around, scented and ornamented. Three walls are erected, the innermost of jewels, the middle of gold, and the outermost of silver. There are four jewelled gates to each wall" (W. N. Brown 1934, p. 38). The Jina sits on a lion throne below a tree (missing here), and preaches to the gods, men, and animals. At the four corners but outside the consecrated area are four diamond-shaped water tanks—beside which are various animals, such as a snake, a peacock, a lion, a bull, and a deer. These animals are usually represented as confronting pairs, as may be seen in a *yantra* in the collection [16]. Here the pairing is unclear.

C This illustration is from the story of Kalaka. Kalaka is the figure on the right in a monk's garb with white polka dots, and the regal, enshrined figure is a Sahi chief. He wears a Muslim beard and is dressed in Central Asian attire with a "cloud collar" cape around his shoulders. Compare the figural form, dress, posture, and the facial expressions of both the chief and the diminutive attendants below with those in the fifteenth-century *Khamsa* illustration in the collection [41]. There seems little doubt that manuscripts such as this *Khamsa* were available to artists working for Jain patrons. As they did not have a type for the Sahis in their traditional repertoire, it was simple for them to adopt the conventional Muslim male figure from Islamic manuscript illuminations.

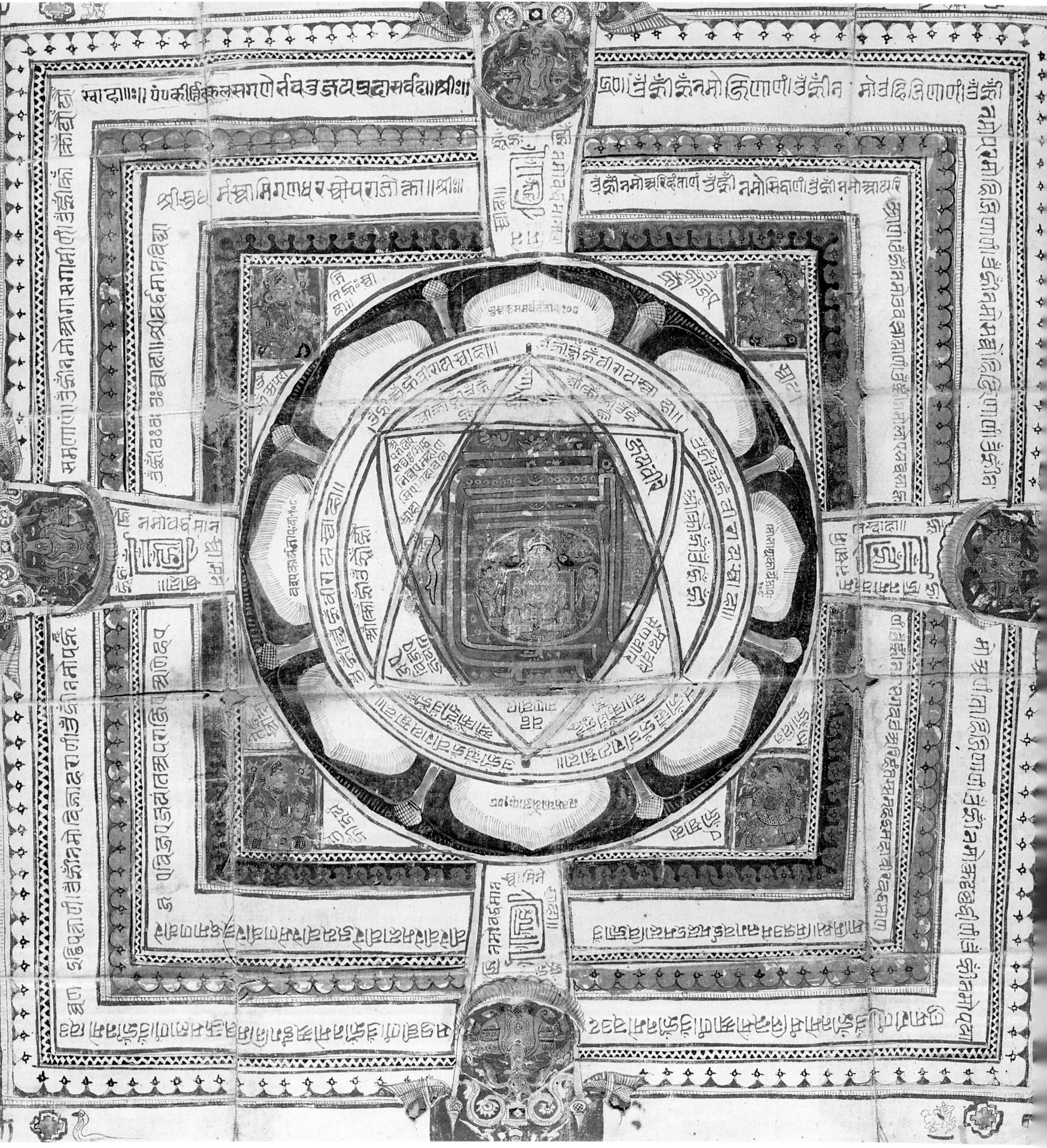

Gujarat or Rajasthan; 1425–50
Opaque watercolor and gold on cotton
19 x 18½ in (48.3 x 47.0 cm)
Purchased with funds provided by Paul F. Walter
M.89.92

In the center of the *yantra* a scene of the lustration of a golden Jina is superimposed on a design formed with the two syllables *om* and *hrim* boldly delineated in gold against blue. The Jina is, in fact, seated in meditation on the lower loop of the letter *om,* as if on a crescent. He is flanked by two yaksha attendants, and two elephants above are engaged in lustrating him. This elaborate central configuration is placed within a star formed by two intersecting triangles, as in the other *yantra* [13]. Mantras and invocations of the hero Varddhamana, the given name of Jina Mahavira, fill the surrounding circle, which is followed by an eight-petaled lotus. Then follow several concentric squares. At the four corners of the innermost square are four goddesses identified as Jayanti, Jaya, Aparajita, and Vijaya.

At least two of the squares, if not three, are decorated with motifs that are suggestive of ramparts of a citadel (cf. [17B]). In the middle of each side and cutting across these squares is a band that may represent a passageway or a stairway. The outer end of each terminates in a beautifully adorned auspicious waterpot. Leaves emerge from the necks of these golden pots, which sit between crescents and elaborate arches with festoons and parrots. Two eyes have been added on either side of each waterpot to suggest its anthropomorphic character. The boundary lines of the outermost square have been extended at each end to form tridents, each of which has beside it a tank of blue water and an animal, a bird, or a snake. These animals in fact are traditional enemies who are paired at each corner to symbolize their peaceful coexistence. Thus, the lion is represented twice, once with a bull and again with an antelope. The snake is similarly paired with a mongoose and a peacock.

The diagram of the double triangles best known in the West as the Star of David is more commonly used in the *yantra* of a goddess in Hindu and Buddhist rituals, whereas among the Jains it is employed for both sexes, as is apparent from the two examples in the collection. Generally in Hindu and Buddhist tantric rituals the upward-pointing triangle represents the male and the downward-pointing the female. An interesting feature of this particular *yantra* is the placing of the syllables *om* and *hrim* at the center. While both are familiar in tantric worship, the significance of these two syllables in Jain religion is explained as follows according to the esoteric text known as *Rishimandala.* "Between the first letter 'a' and the last letter 'h' come all the letters. By adding a dot and a 'mi'-sign to the last letter which is 'sound' and is like a flame, the word 'arham' is made. The word thus made is like the flame and washer of the dirt of the mind and is very pure. Having installed it in the Lotus of my heart I salute it, 'arham' is the syllable . . . indicative of the five great beings, the essence of *Siddhachakra* and is worshipped on all occasions" (Jain and Fischer 1978, pt. 2, p. 4).

The presence of Mahavira in the center of this *yantra* and of the four protective goddesses as well as the mantras make it clear that this diagram was used for the esoteric rite known as Varddhamana Vidya. *Varddhamana,* "one who expands," was the given name of Mahavira, and *vidya* literally means "knowledge." In tantric parlance *vidya* further denotes a charm. The inclusion of the four goddesses as guardians of the *yantra* is unusual, for in Hindu iconography all four are generally attendants of the Goddess Durga rather than a male deity.

Two other published examples of fifteenth-century Varddhamana Vidya *yantras* are known. One of them (U. P. Shah 1941) is largely figurative, but the other (Calliat and Kumar 1981, pp. 36–37), like the museum's example, incorporates much of the mantra within the *yantra.* Stylistically, all three paintings are closely related.

Gujarat; c. 1450
Folios, 4¼ x 10 in (10.8 x 25.4 cm)
Illustrations, 4¼ x 2⅞ in (10.8 x 7.3 cm)
From the Nasli and Alice Heeramaneck Collection, Museum Associates Purchase
M.72.53.21a–d
Literature: Pal 1987, p. 114, fig. 70 (C only).

A *Kalaka Converts Bricks to Gold* (5v)
B *Destruction of the She-ass* (5r)
C *King Gardabhilla Brought Captive to Kalaka* (7r)

The four surviving folios have five illustrations altogether. The folios are numbered 1, 5, 7, 10 (*10* in red), with 10 being the last folio of the manuscript. It contains a colophon statement that provides only a formulaic supplication for the longevity and safety of the manuscript. The text is written in black ink, nine lines to a page, the punctuation and verse numbers in red. There are red circles roughly in the middle of each page. Red, gold, and lapis lazuli blue are the principal colors, with some black, white, and magenta.

A The incident depicted here is the occasion when Kalaka transforms bricks into gold in order to raise money for the campaign against King Gardabhilla. The scene is divided into two registers. In the upper one Kalaka, robed in a transparent garment with white polka dots, sprinkles magic powder on a pile of bricks in the potter's kiln on the left, while behind him a Sahi carries the golden bricks away. In the bottom register a Sahi walks away with bricks on his head and is followed by a second Sahi on a horse.

B This spirited scene depicts the silencing of the braying she-ass. Within the fort indicated by a semicircular rampart King Gardabhilla is offering oblations into the fire as part of his magical practice. The figure above him is probably the confined nun Sarasvati. From outside the fort Sahi marksmen, as well as Kalaka on a horse, are shooting arrows at the she-ass, which is in the middle of the composition.

C In this picture a Sahi holds King Gardabhilla, a rope around his wrists, by his hair. Behind, a Sahi rides his horse. Below, the captive Gardabhilla is being presented to Kalaka.

The two pictures not illustrated here may be described as follows. On page 1 two different incidents are included in one picture divided into two segments. In the lower register Kalaka exercises a horse, while in the upper segment he hears Gunaprabha preach. In the illustration on the other page Kalaka is seated in conversation with Sakra.

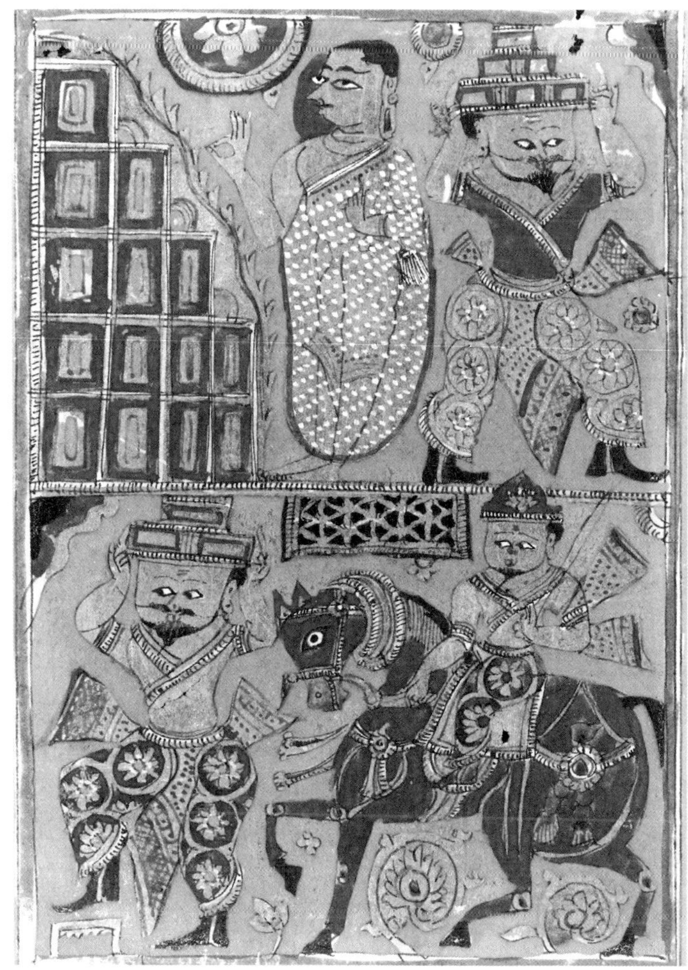

CAT. 17A detail *(top)*
CAT. 17B detail *(bottom left)*
CAT. 17C detail *(bottom right)*

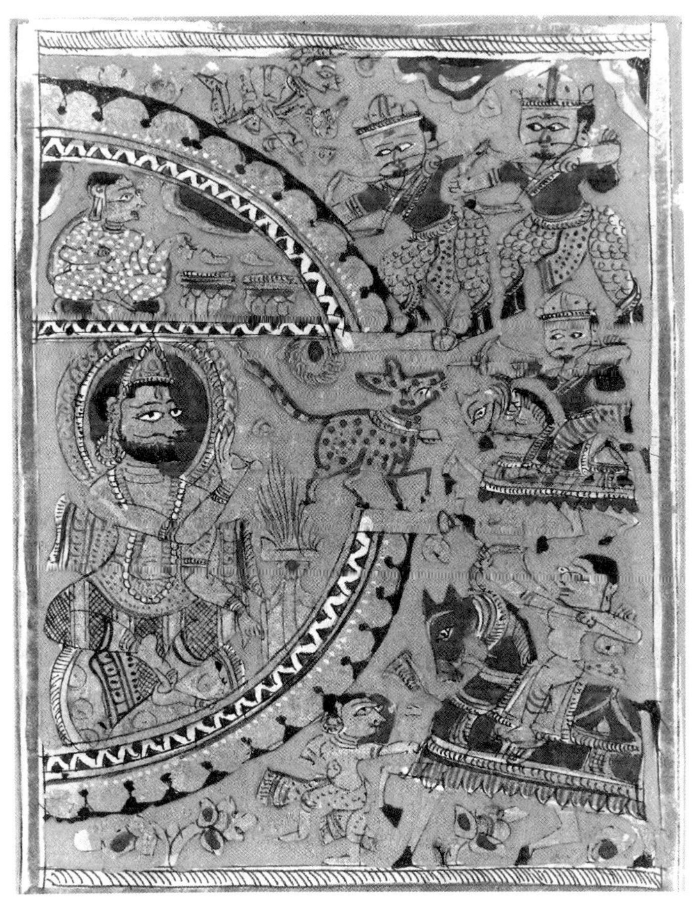

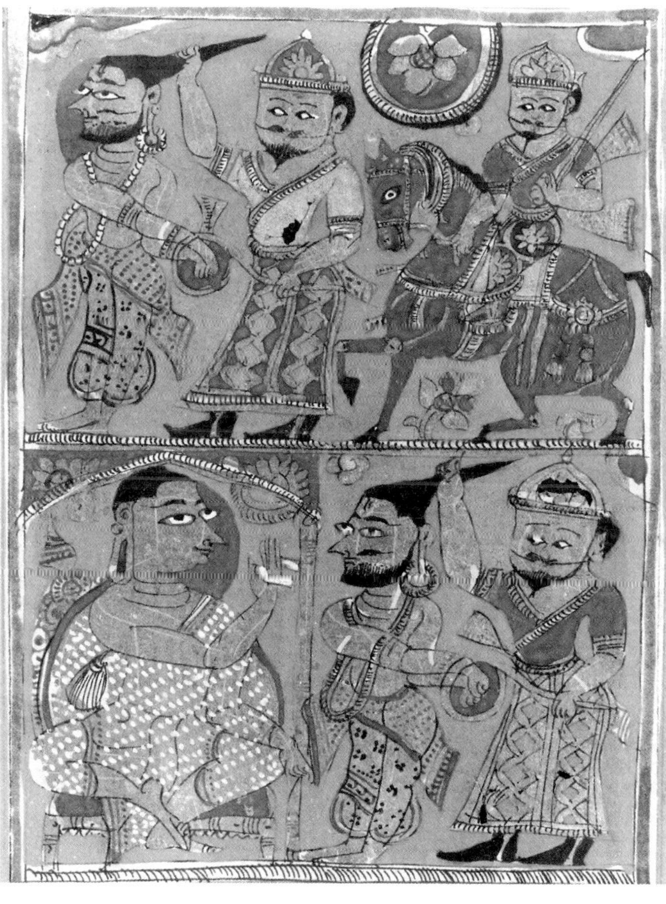

Gujarat or Rajasthan; c. 1450
Folios, 4½ x 10½ in (11.4 x 26.7 cm)
Illustrations, 4½ x 2⅞ in (11.4 x 7.3 cm)
Covers, 4⅞ x 10 7/16 in (12.4 x 26.5 cm)
From the Nasli and Alice Heeramaneck Collection, Museum Associates Purchase
M.72.53.20
Literature: Larson et al. 1980, p. 52, no. 17a; Canby 1983, no. 1 (not illustrated).

A *Sakra Instructing Harinaigamesha* (10r)
B *Transfer of the Embryo* (26v)

Incomplete manuscript with 98 of original 103 folios and 29 illustrations. Seven lines of text per page, written in black ink on beige paper. Writing highlighted in places with patches of red. Each page divided into two sections by a vertical column with red borders. Three red circles on the rectos and one on the versos. Illustrations in red, blue, green, yellow, white, black, purple, and gold. Covers wrapped in yellow silk brocade with floral design in red, white, and blue.

The last page of the manuscript contains a florid eulogy of the *Kalpasutra* but no colophon. An inscription in a much later, cursive hand (see Appendix) informs us that the text was recited by Vijayasimha Suri and others in the month of Pausha (December-January) in the year corresponding to A.D. 1644.

CAT. 18A detail

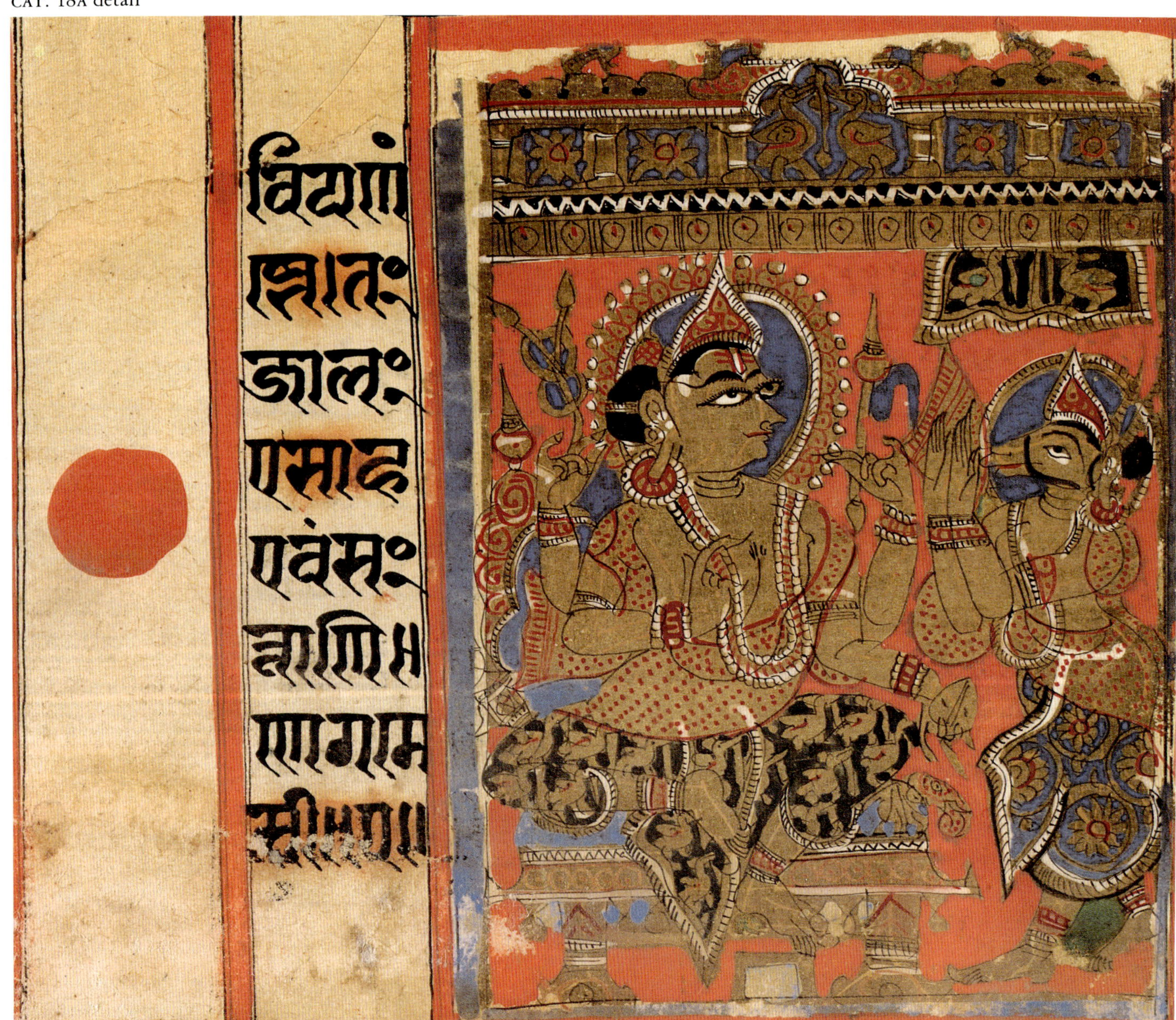

A The enthroned four-armed figure on the left is the king of the gods, Sakra, and the goat-headed figure on the right is Harinaigamesha. The story goes that Mahavira was first conceived by Devananda, a brahman woman. However, as all Jinas were to be born in the ruling or warrior caste (*kshatriya*) rather than that of the brahman or priestly caste, Sakra decided to have the embryo transferred from Devananda's womb to that of Trisala, the spouse of King Siddhartha. The actual transfer was accomplished by Harinaigamesha, in Jain mythology the goat-headed commander of Sakra's infantry. Here, with his hands in the gesture of obedience and respect, Harinaigamesha receives his instructions.

B Harinaigamesha is here engaged in transplanting the embryo to the womb of Queen Trisala, who, as does Sakra, wears a garment adorned with gander pattern. He subsequently returns to transplant Queen Trisala's embryo in Devananda's womb. Sakra's envoy had to cast the queen and her companions into a deep sleep in order to accomplish his task.

In the illustrations in this manuscript all the figures are in gold and the background is either in red or blue. The coloring is of uniformly high quality, but that of the drawing is uneven. The illustrations may be regarded as typical of the Jain pictorial mode that continued to be used with little innovation from the mid-fifteenth to mid-sixteenth century.

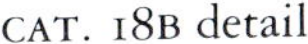

CAT. 18B detail

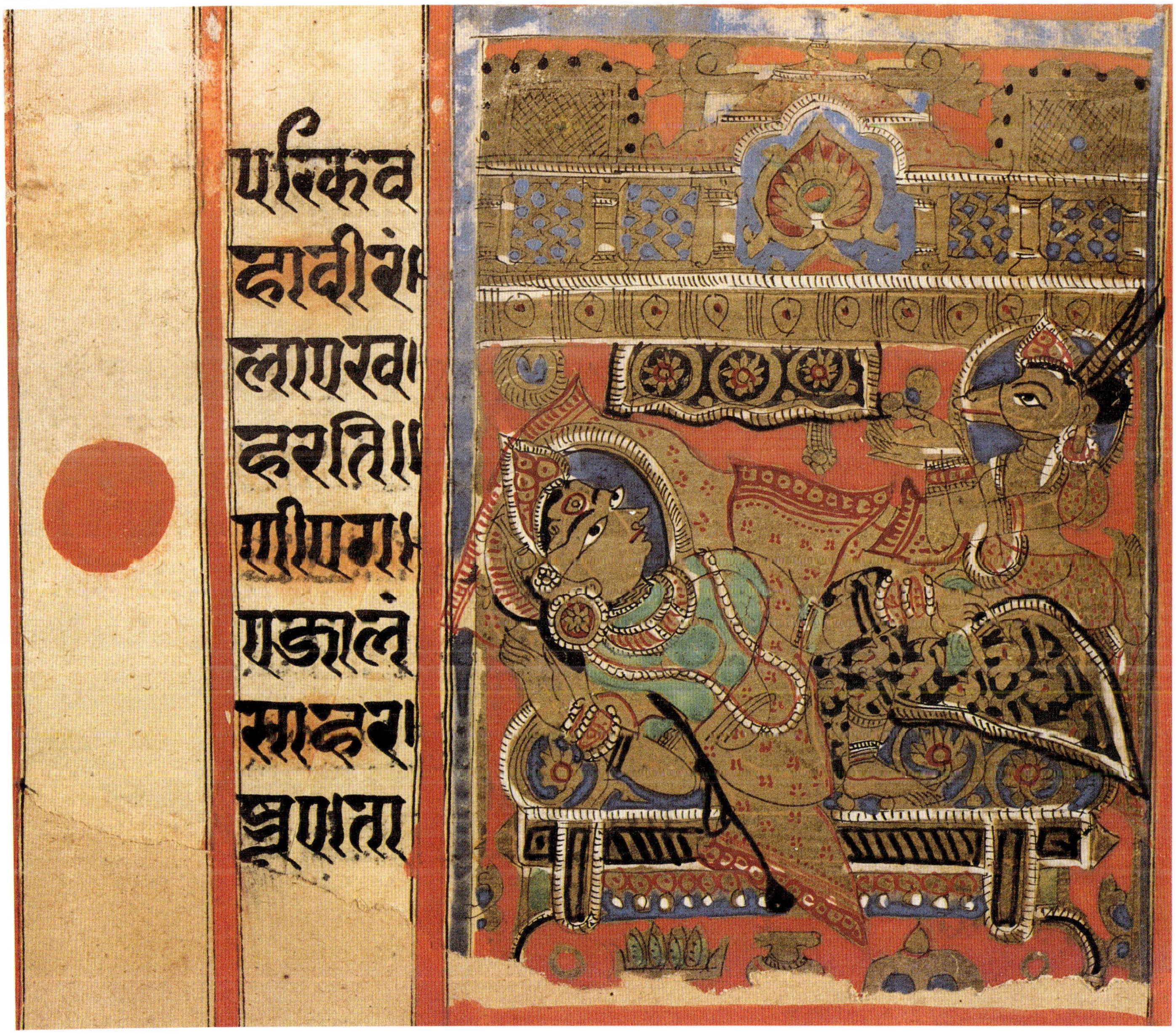

19 FOLIO FROM A *YASODHARACHARITA* MANUSCRIPT: A DOLPHIN *(SISUMARA)* ATTACKS A WOMAN

Madhya Pradesh (?); 1454
Ink and opaque watercolor on paper
Folio, 4¾ x 10⅝ in (12.1 x 27.0 cm)
Illustration, 2⅜ x 4 in (6.0 x 10.2 cm)
Purchased with funds provided by Paul F. Walter
M.90.86.1

This folio is from a manuscript of the *Yasodharacharita* (Life of Yasodhara), a noncanonical Jain text extolling the virtues of nonviolence, the first tenet of the faith. Popular with both sects of Jainism, the text was illustrated only for the Digambaras. Written in a colloquial form of Prakrit known as Jain Apabhramsa, there are several versions of the text composed at different times by various authors. The colophon of this manuscript unfortunately does not include the author's name.

The story is about a king named Yasodhara and his queen, Amritamati, who is discovered by her husband with her lover. Along with his mother, Chandramati, Yasodhara goes to the temple of the goddess Chandamari and sacrifices a rooster made with flour. A few days later both the king and Chandramati are killed by Amritamati. Because they had committed a sin by sacrificing a bird, even though made with flour, they had to undergo several rebirths. The picture represented on this folio illustrates their third rebirth, when Yasodhara was reborn as a fish and Chandramati as a dolphin (*sisumara*) in the river Sipra. One day when some palace maids came to bathe, the dolphin caught one of them by the leg and dragged her down. This infuriated her royal master, who ordered the animal destroyed. A net was cast and both the dolphin and the fish were caught. The dolphin was killed and the fish was taken to the royal kitchen and served to the king for his supper.

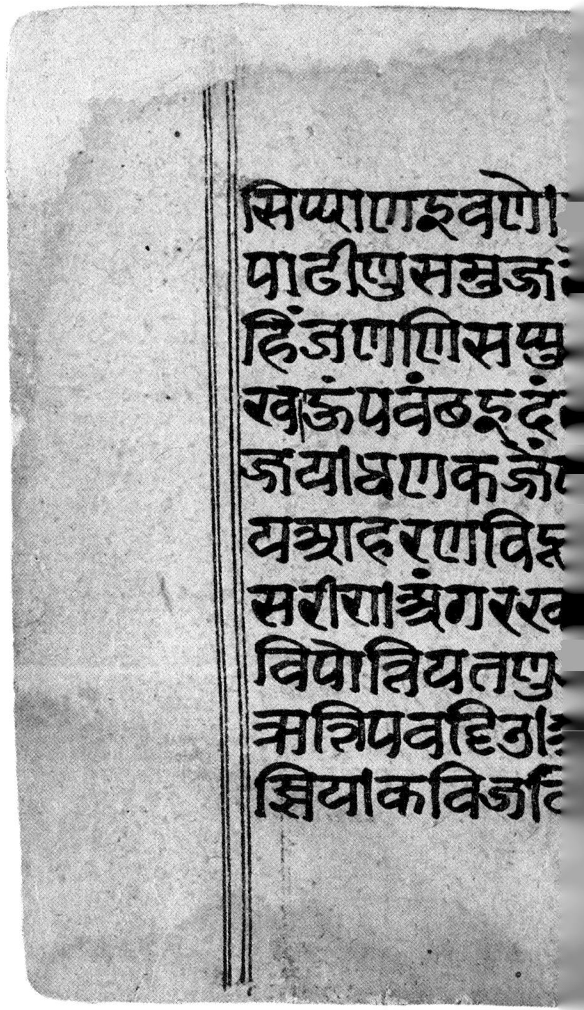

According to Doshi (1985, p. 146, fig. 23), who has published another illustrated page from this manuscript, it was copied and illustrated in the Delhi-Gwalior region. This is certainly a strong probability, for both the script and the picture are noticeably different from manuscripts copied and illustrated in Gujarat. Moreover, the style of this illumination is closely related to paintings in other Jain manuscripts of the period copied in the Delhi-Gwalior region (Doshi 1985, pp. 59–61, figs. 20–29). Both in coloring and composition, these illustrations are more naïve and restricted than one encounters in contemporary western Indian paintings. The artists responsible for these northern Indian Jain texts seem to have had little or no acquaintance with the more sophisticated illustrated manuscripts that were being produced for Jain patrons in Gujarat and western Rajasthan at this time.

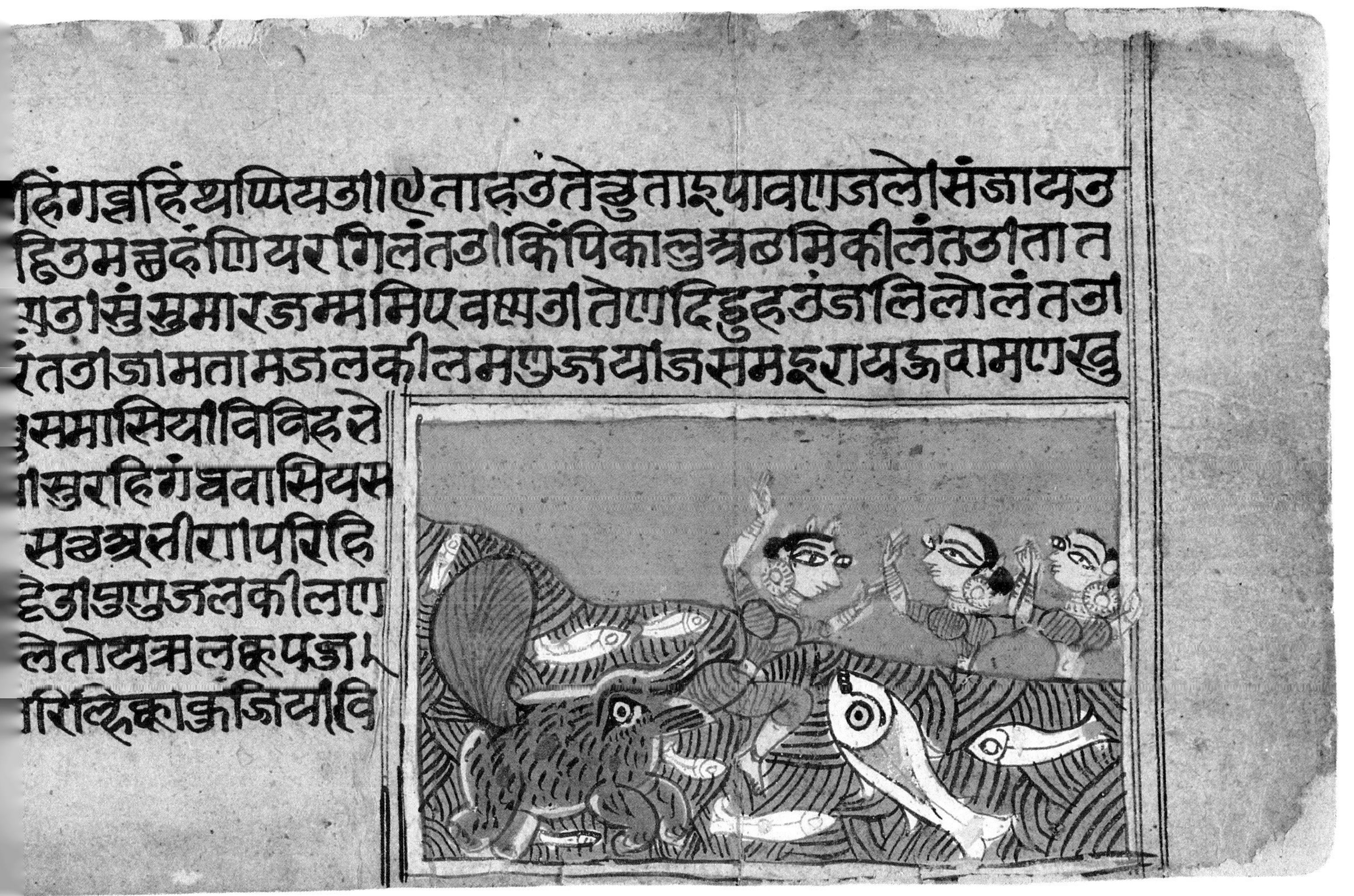

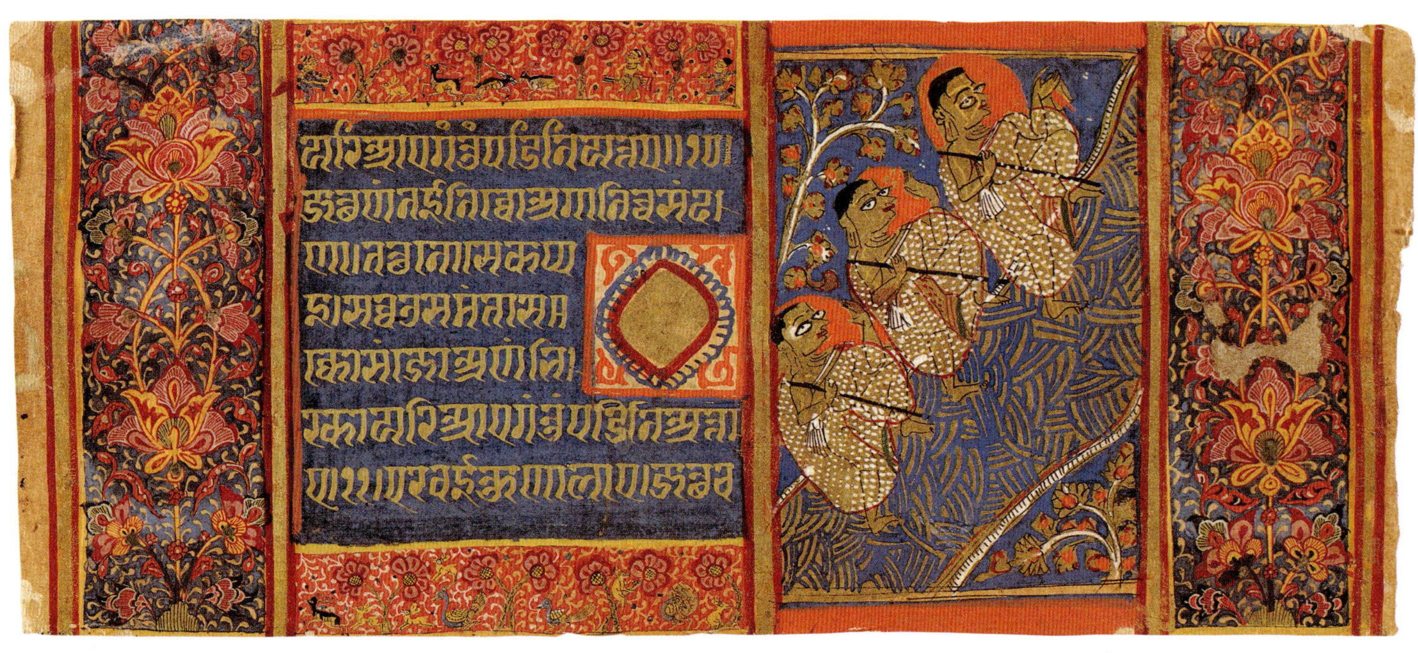

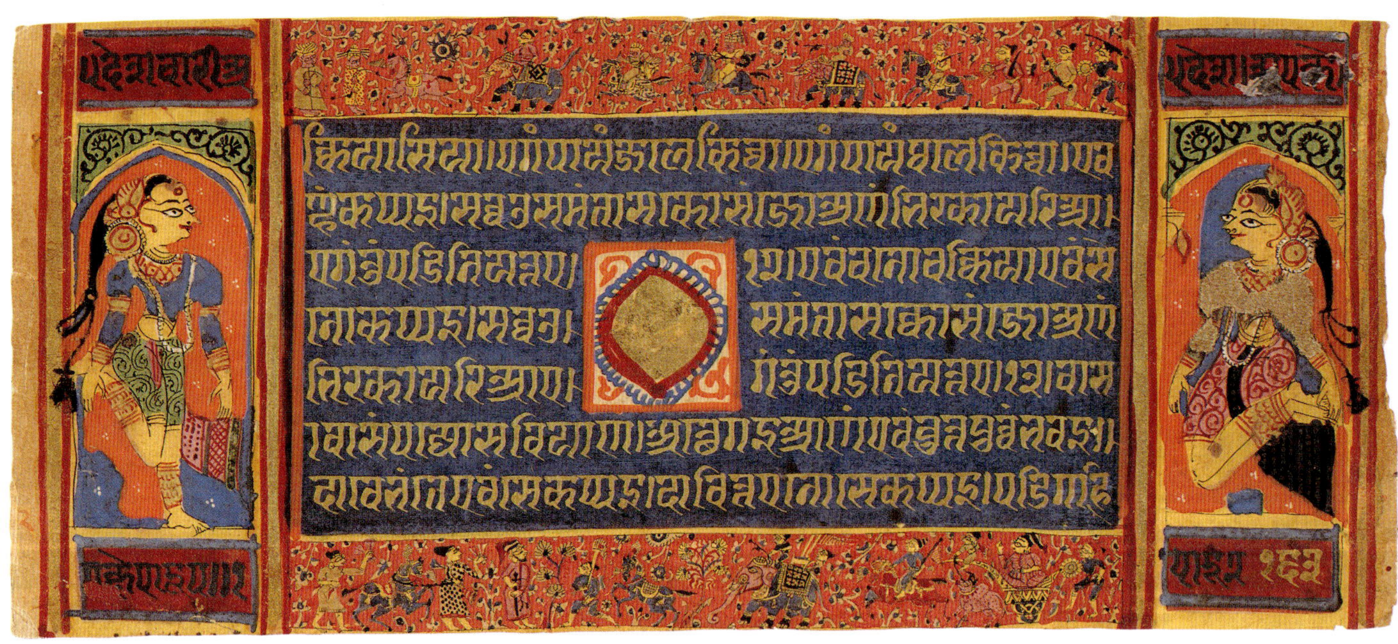

Gujarat; c. 1475
Text in gold
Folio, 4½ x 10¼ in (11.4 x 26.0 cm)
Gift of Dr. and Mrs. Pratapaditya Pal
M.87.275.3

A *Three Monks* (r)
4½ x 2¾ in (11.4 x 7.0 cm)
B *Two Celestial Nymphs* (v)
Each, 2⅞ x 1 13/16 in (7.3 x 4.6 cm)

This leaf, numbered 163, is from the most sumptuously illuminated Jain manuscript to have survived. The bulk of the manuscript is in a Jain library known as the Devasano Pado Bhandar in Ahmedabad, Gujarat, which is why it is generally known as the Devasano Pado *Kalpasutra*. In point of fact, however, the manuscript also includes the *Kalakacharyakatha*, and this leaf probably relates to that text. As is clear from the reproductions, the leaves in this manuscript are generously painted on both sides compared with the standard *Kalpasutra* manuscript. The text is written in clear, bold letters of gold against a bright blue background. A small, rectangular panel—perhaps a vestigial string hole decoration—is placed slightly left of center on each page; the panel encloses an oval patch of gold. Otherwise these two pages are quite differently adorned. The profusion of ornamental patterns and the variety in the borders and margins, which are filled with humans, animals, and flowers, clearly indicates the originality of the artists, who appear to have been familiar with Islamic manuscripts. The style here is much more sensuous and vivacious than the more austere mode encountered in most Jain illustrations of the period.

A The greater part of this page is filled with pictures, the text panel being smaller than that on the other page. At either end are broad, vertical panels containing flowering plants of variegated colors. The rather small text panel on the left has borders on the top and the bottom. The upper border shows a hunting scene in a forest represented by decorative trees with daisylike flowers. Three hunters have trapped three black bucks and a hare. Running hares, birds, and a black buck share the border below with the flowering plants. The illustration shows three monks walking on the water of a river placed diagonally across the composition. It is not clear whether the monks are crossing the river miraculously on foot or whether they are supposed to be walking along the bank. Nor has it been possible from the accompanying text to identify the scene.

B On this page the rectangular text panel is framed with borders on all sides. The bands on the sides are wider than those above and below, and both contain a celestial nymph; the one on the left stands with one leg raised and bent, while the other has both legs raised and bent as if she is seated on her haunches. Each is framed above by a decorated arch. They probably represent celestial beauties (*surasundari*). The upper and lower borders are longer and narrower and are adorned in a more lively fashion. Stylized flowers and miniature figures of foot soldiers as well as horse and elephant riders are interestingly juxtaposed against a red background. On top all the figures move from right to left, and in the lower border three men and a horse confront a procession approaching from the other direction. The procession includes a bull-drawn chariot, the figure seated in which may be a king. Whether these scenes on the borders have any relevance to the narrative is not clear, although it remains a probability. They may represent the march of the Sahis' army.

Unfortunately the part of the colophon page of this manuscript containing the date is missing, but the names of the owners have survived. This lavishly illustrated manuscript was prepared for Sana and Jutha, two bankers who lived in Gandhar Bandar near Broach. There is a minor disagreement among scholars about when this manuscript was executed. While some date it to about 1475, others prefer a date of circa 1500. For an extensive discussion of this illuminated manuscript, see Khandalavala and Chandra 1969, pp. 29–40.

CAT. 20A
CAT. 20B
CAT. 20A, B details *(overleaf)*

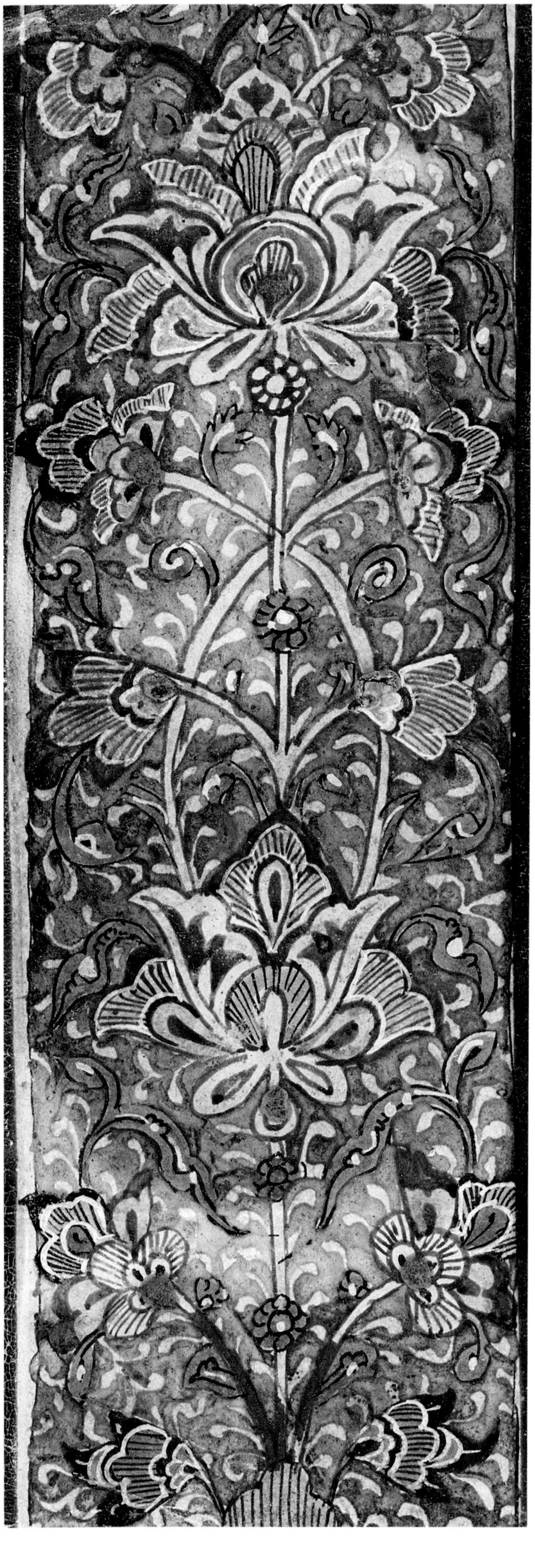

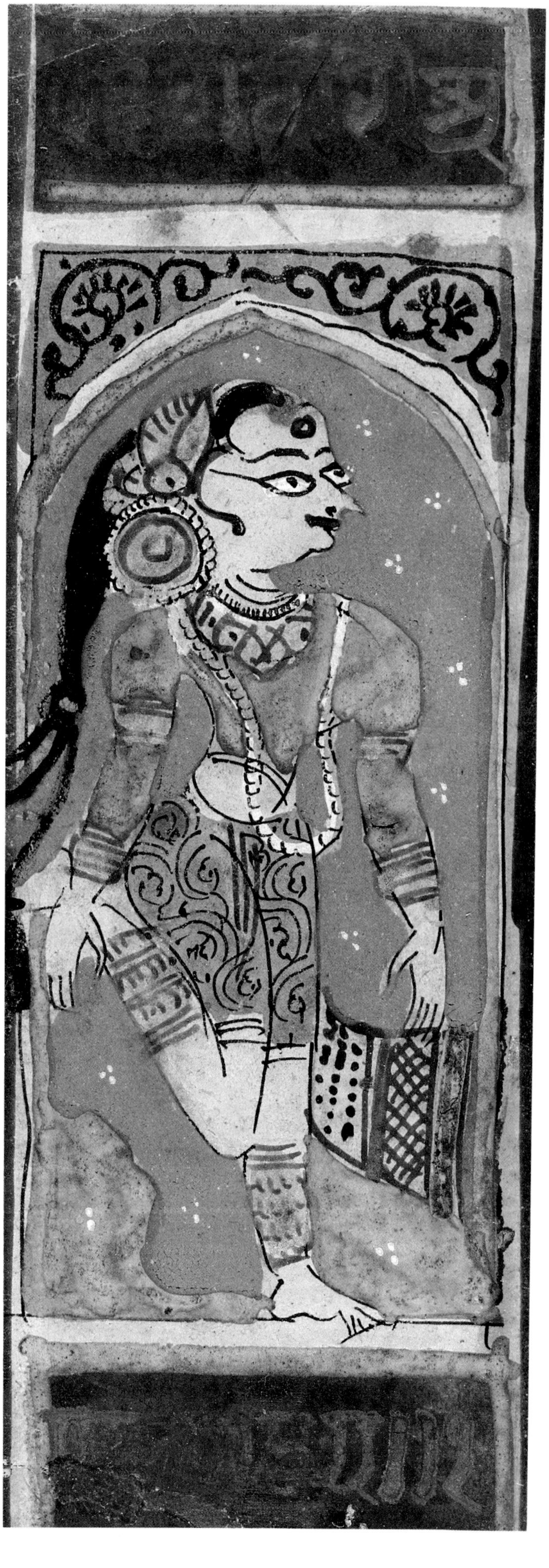

Gujarat; 1475–1500
Folio, 4 3/8 x 10 1/4 in (11.1 x 26.0 cm)
Illustration, 4 1/4 x 3 1/8 in (10.8 x 7.9 cm)
Gift of Navin Kumar
M.88.28.1

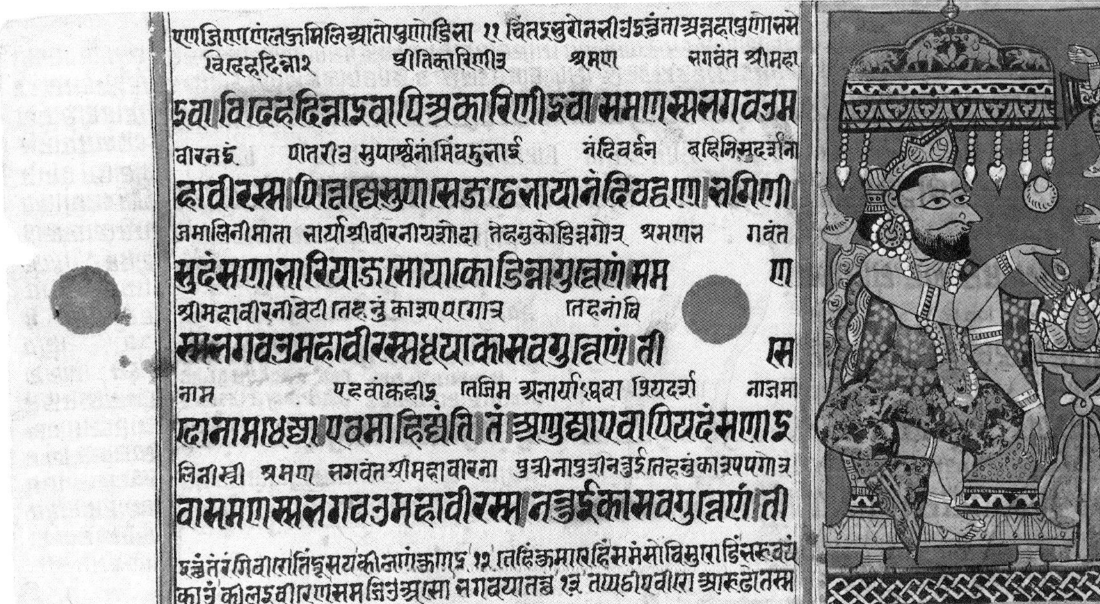

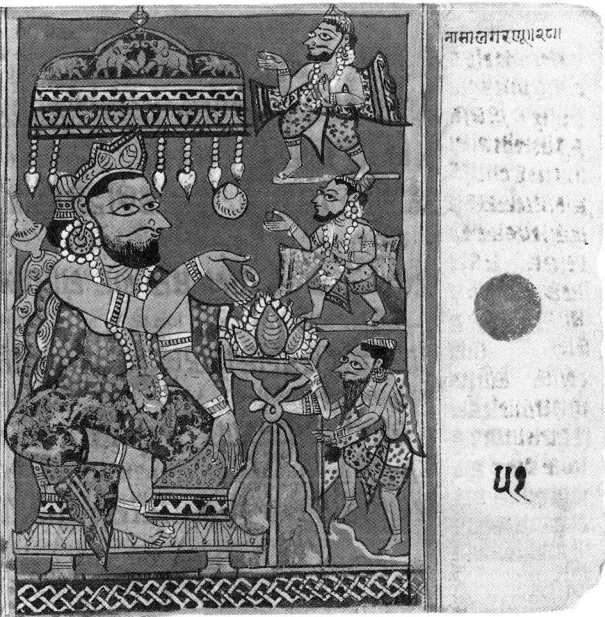

This leaf from a *Kalpasutra* manuscript is numbered 51 and is illustrated only on one side. Noteworthy is the fact that the lettering is in two different sizes. The text is written in larger and bolder letters, while the interlinear commentary is in smaller letters, as one finds in manuscripts of Koran with Persian translations (e.g., [39]).

The illustration depicts the occasion when Mahavira gave away all his personal property before renouncing the world and adopting the life of an ascetic. In the picture Mahavira is seated on a throne with a gem-filled container on a stand before him. He has picked a piece of jewelry to give to an emaciated figure with a long beard, representing a brahman. Curiously, the brahman is as well dressed and adorned as the two figures above him. Obviously the recipients of the gifts were not indigent.

The illustration is closely related in style to those in a *Kalpasutra* and *Kalakacharyakatha* manuscript now in the Prince of Wales Museum, Bombay (see M. Chandra 1953–54; and Doshi 1985, p. 49, fig. 4). That manuscript is generally considered to have been prepared between 1375 and 1400. Apart from the broader aspects of style, the illustrations in both the Bombay manuscript and the museum's page share many identical details, such as designs of textiles. However, the style of the script is different in the two manuscripts, and because of the presence of the commentary, which generally began to be added in the second half of the fifteenth century and more frequently thereafter, this leaf is probably not as early as the Bombay manuscript. The artist who illustrated the manuscript to which this folio belonged may well have been familiar with the Bombay manuscript.

A curious feature of this illustration is the fact that the artist has rendered both eyes of Mahavira on the nearer side of the face. The further eye should have protruded from the other side of the nose. Whether this abnormality, not encountered elsewhere, was deliberate or accidental is difficult to determine without examining the other illustrations of this manuscript. It should also be noted that the figures in this illustration are less naturalistic and the drawing is not as elegant as those in the Bombay manuscript. This is particularly noticeable in the rendering of the hands with their inarticulate and stiff fingers.

Gujarat or Rajasthan; 1475–1500
Text in gold
Folio, 4½ x 10⅝ in (11.4 x 27 cm)
Illustration, 4½ x 3¼ in (11.4 x 8.3 cm)
From the Nasli and Alice Heeramaneck Collection, Museum Associates Purchase
M.71.1.3
Literature: *Heeramaneck* 1966, p. 120, no. 140 (not illustrated).

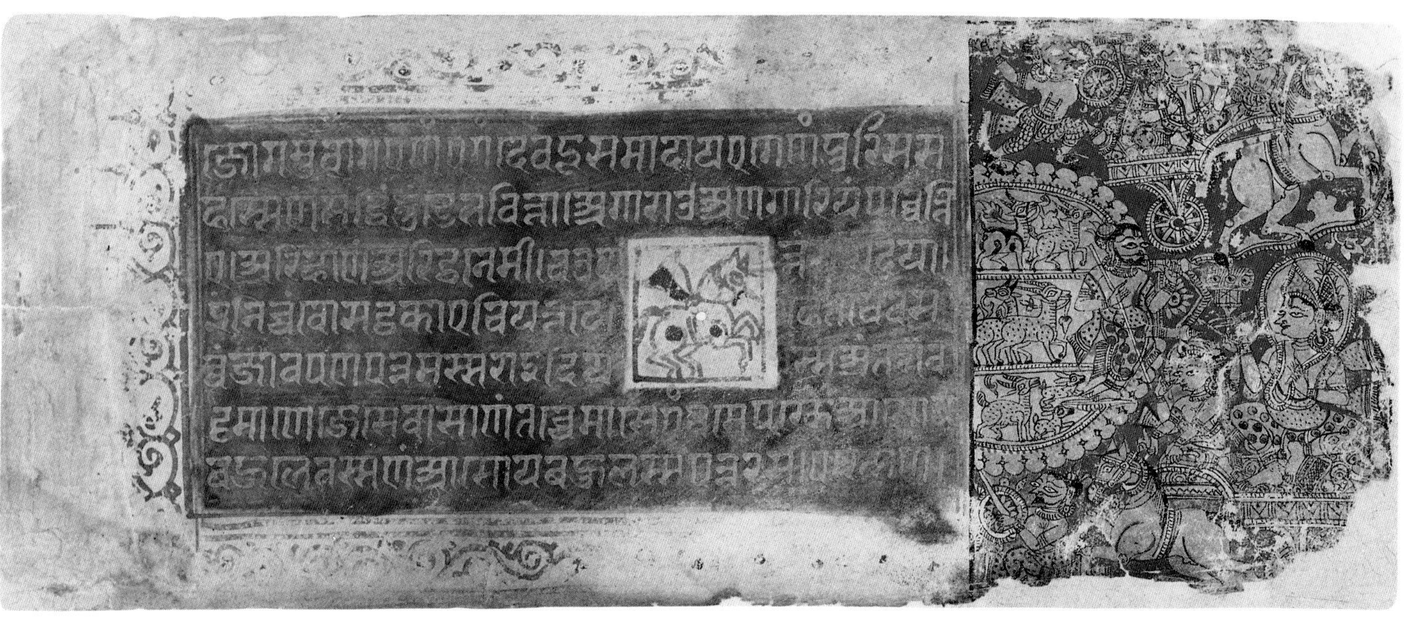

The text is written in gold letters on a purple-red background. On each page the text panel is surrounded by a scroll design in blue with red specks. Small, square panels are placed slightly off-center on both sides, adorned with a rearing horse in blue on one side and a floral design on the other. There is only one illustration, extending from top to bottom of the page.

The picture depicts Neminatha's renunciation of a householder's life. The legend goes that Nemi was on his way to his wedding when he heard the sad wailing of animals. Upon enquiry he learned from his charioteer that the distressful cries emanated from animals waiting to be slaughtered for the wedding feast. Nemi was disgusted at the thought of such slaughter and decided to abandon his bride and the world to become a homeless wanderer in search of salvation.

In the composition Neminatha is shown twice in his chariot, presumably once on his way to his bride and the second time after turning his chariot around and driving away. The slaughterhouse with animals—five antelopes and a couple of hares—is a circular enclosure with a single guard. Everything is painted in black and gold against a red background. Other colors used sparingly are red, purple, and blue.

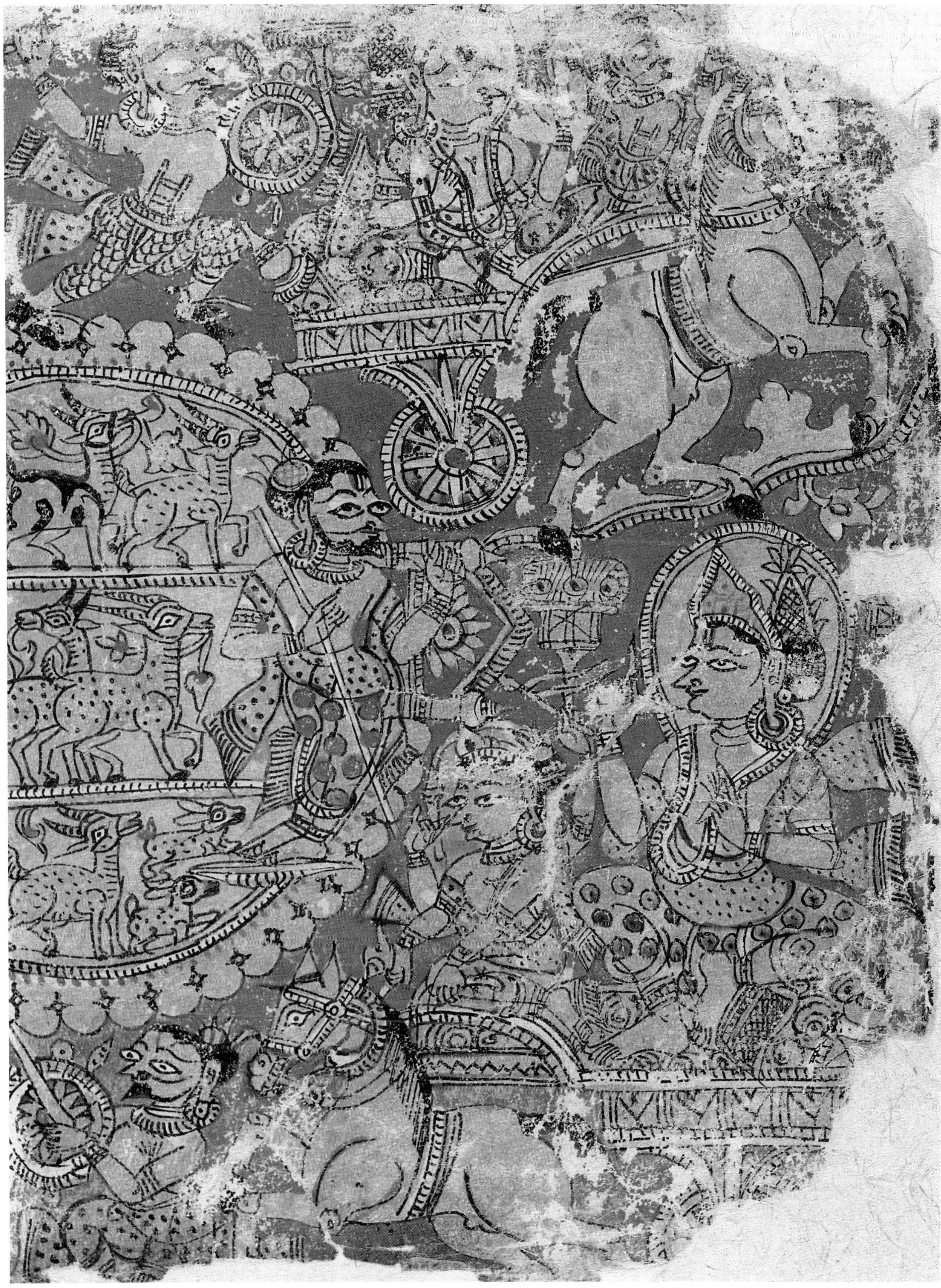

CAT. 22 detail

Gujarat or Rajasthan; 1475–1500
Folios, 4½ x 11 in (11.4 x 27.9 cm)
Illustrations, 4½ x 3¼ in (11.4 x 8.3 cm)
Covers, 4½ x 12³⁄₁₆ in (11.4 x 30.9 cm)
From the Nasli and Alice Heeramaneck Collection, Museum Associates Purchase
M.72.53.16

A *Scene with Wrestlers* (23v)
B *Kosha Dances before the Royal Archer* (66v)

Incomplete manuscript with 81 folios and 24 illustrations. Seven lines of text per page, written in black ink with red punctuation marks on buff paper. Text framed by red and black lines. Additional ornaments either of oval or square shapes in gold, red, and blue. Illustrations accompanied by brief captions. Predominant colors in illustrations are red, blue, and gold, with some white and black and occasional green. A few illustrations are damaged. Covers wrapped with red silk brocade with silver paisley (*būṭā*) pattern.

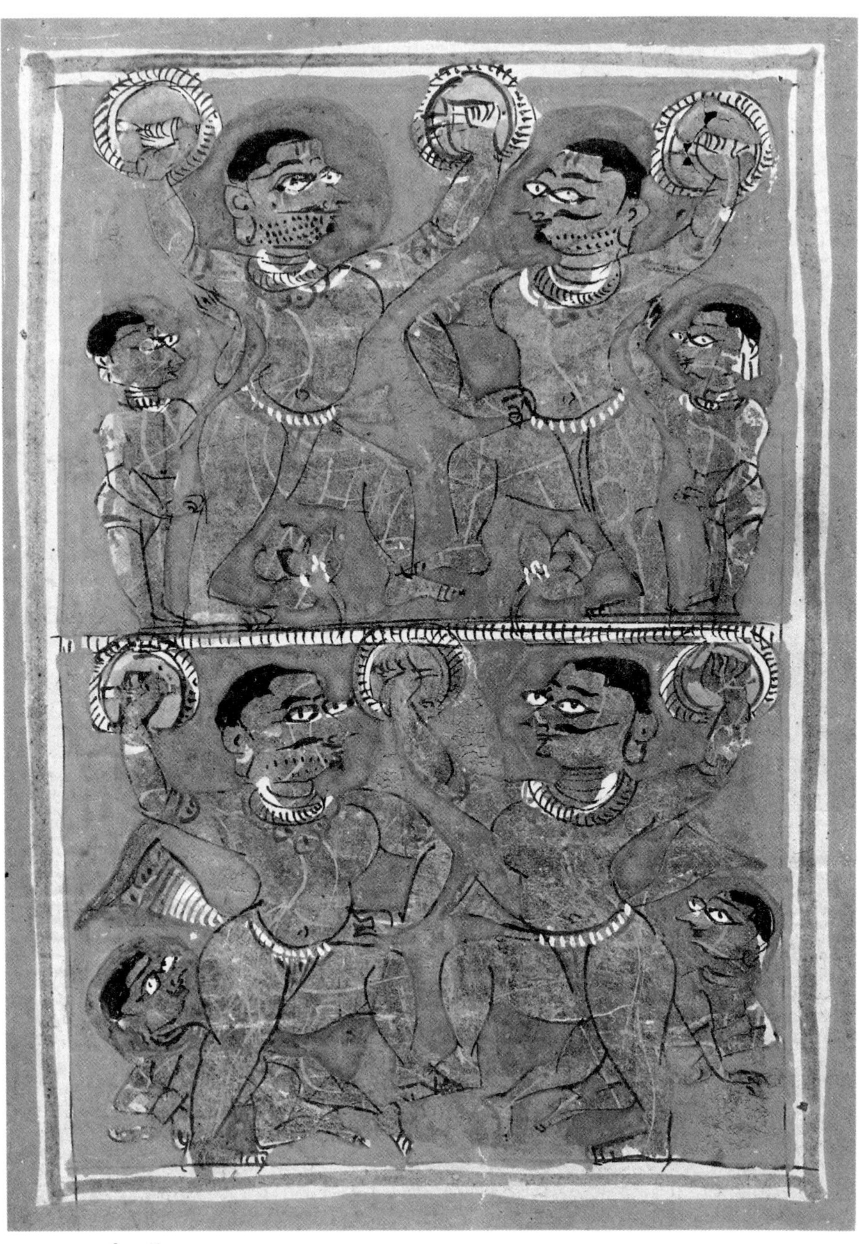

CAT. 23A detail

The majority of the illustrations occur in the first part of the book and depict Mahavira's life in considerable detail. Other biographies, however, are represented by one or two pictures only. Although not as sumptuous as some of the other fifteenth-century manuscripts in the collection, both the coloring and drawing are of good quality.

A The caption identifies this picture as a wrestling match (*mallayuddha*). According to the story, Mahavira's father, King Siddhartha, would go to the gymnasium every morning and exercise by wrestling, which is what he is doing here. There is no way to tell, however, who is the king, nor can we identify the two smaller figures who in the lower picture are on the ground, as if overwhelmed by the ferocity of the duel.

B This is an incident from the life of Sthulabhadra, one of the Jain pontiffs whose hagiographies form the subject matter of the second book of the *Kalpasutra*. The animated and graceful dancer wearing a green blouse is the courtesan Kosha, who was Sthulabhadra's mistress for twelve years before his conversion. Thereafter, the local king bestowed Kosha upon his charioteer, who tried to impress her with his skill in archery. Not to be outperformed, Kosha demonstrated her own ability by placing a needle vertically upon a heap of mustard seeds, covering it with flower petals and dancing on top. The charioteer was most impressed and offered her a reward. Kosha, however, replied that while her skill was acquired by practice, Sthulabhadra's achievement was of a much higher order, for he had succeeded in subduing the passions. The charioteer then converted to the Jain faith and Kosha became a nun.

In the illustration the charioteer stands below a panel of ganders, perhaps representing a canopy. He is shooting his arrow at a mango tree, which is rendered in gold and red but has no fruit. Below the tree is the elegant figure of Kosha, striking a typical dancing posture. The flower-covered needle and heap of mustard seeds are indicated by a small, white bulge below her right foot.

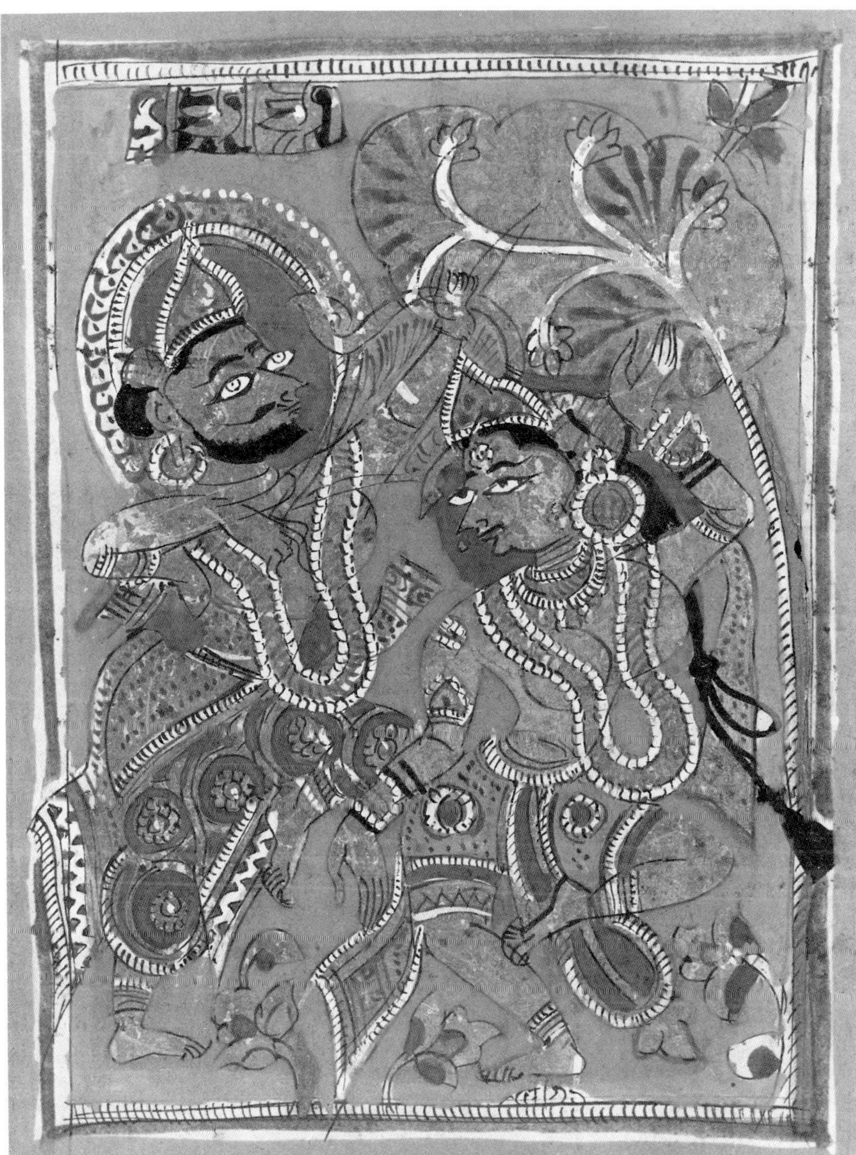

CAT. 23B detail

Gujarat or Rajasthan; various dates, fifteenth–eighteenth centuries
Folios, various dimensions, average, 4½ x 10½ in (11.4 x 26.7 cm)
Illustrations, 4½ x 2⅝ in (11.4 x 6.7 cm)
Covers, 5⅜ x 10⅞ in (13.7 x 27.6 cm)
From the Nasli and Alice Heeramaneck Collection, Museum Associates Purchase
M.72.53.15

A *Parsvanatha's Austerities or Dangers* (cat. Avii)
B *The Infant Vajra* (cat. E)

Although accessioned as one manuscript, in fact the eleven folios belong to several different manuscripts from different periods. All except two leaves are from *Kalpasutra* and *Kalakacharya-katha* manuscripts. Apart from their various sizes, the leaves differ considerably in their style of writing, decorative themes, and in their representational styles. Some of the pages and illuminations are better preserved than others.

A Five folios from a *Kalpasutra* manuscript with seven illustrations, of which one is heavily damaged. The leaves have been either completely or partially backed with plain paper on the side without an illustration. The text is written in ink in bold letters with copious commentary added on some pages. A distinguishing feature of this manuscript is that on each page the text is arranged around a centrally placed red circle to make a cruciform shape imitating the conventional design of a water tank in the corner of *yantras* (see [16]). Some of the illustrations are identified by captions along the margins. The themes illustrated are:

- i Sakra worshiping Mahavira's embryo
- ii Fourteen auspicious symbols
- iii, iv Substitution of the embryos by Harinaigamesha
- v Birth of Mahavira
- vi First bath of Mahavira
- vii Parsvanatha's austerities or dangers

In the last (illustration A) Parsvanatha stands immobile in the body-abandonment (*kayotsarga*) posture before what appears to be water, shown in a highly stylized fashion by a crisscrossed design in blue. This water represents the floods that resulted when the demon Meghamalin unleashed a storm to distract the Jina. Parsva was protected by his *yaksha,* or tutelary deity, Dharana, who is also the king of serpents. The Jina, however, is concerned neither with the attack nor with Dharana's help. The Buddha too had a similar experience where he was protected by the serpent Muchalinda (see [4A]). The style of writing as well as the pictures indicates a date toward the end of the fifteenth century.

B Folio 1 of a *Kalpasutra* manuscript. The damaged illustration is pasted onto the page. The writing is certainly not of the same age as the picture, which is of the fifteenth century.

C Folio 121 of a *Kalakacharyakatha* manuscript, probably of the early sixteenth century, with a rather abraded illustration showing Sakra's visit to Kalaka.

D Folio 4 from a *Kalakacharyakatha* manuscript depicting the abduction of Sarasvati. Both the style of writing as well as the illustration rendered in dazzling gold against a bright blue indicates a date in the late fifteenth or early sixteenth century.

E This folio, number 114 from a *Kalpasutra* manuscript, is one of the most puzzling in the group. Except for two pictures the pages are completely unadorned, and the distinctive script is certainly quite different from the usual style of writing in western Indian manuscripts. The illustrations, however, are in the conventional western Indian style.

The picture illustrated as B is interesting in that it shows a story from book two of the *Kalpasutra,* which contains lives of the successive Jain pontiffs. One of these was Vajra, whose father became a monk soon after his son's birth. Vajra wanted to follow his father, but his mother disagreed, and so he became a nuisance at home. One day when the father returned on a visit, the mother handed the difficult child over to the father, who took him to a convent. In this representation we see first the father handing Vajra to a nun and in the second part a nun swinging Vajra in a swing. Needless to say, with the nuns Vajra had a changed personality. In the upper panel Vajra is seen in a basket on the outspread arm of the nun. In this instance the nun's right shoulder is bare while usually, as in the other panel, nuns are fully clothed.

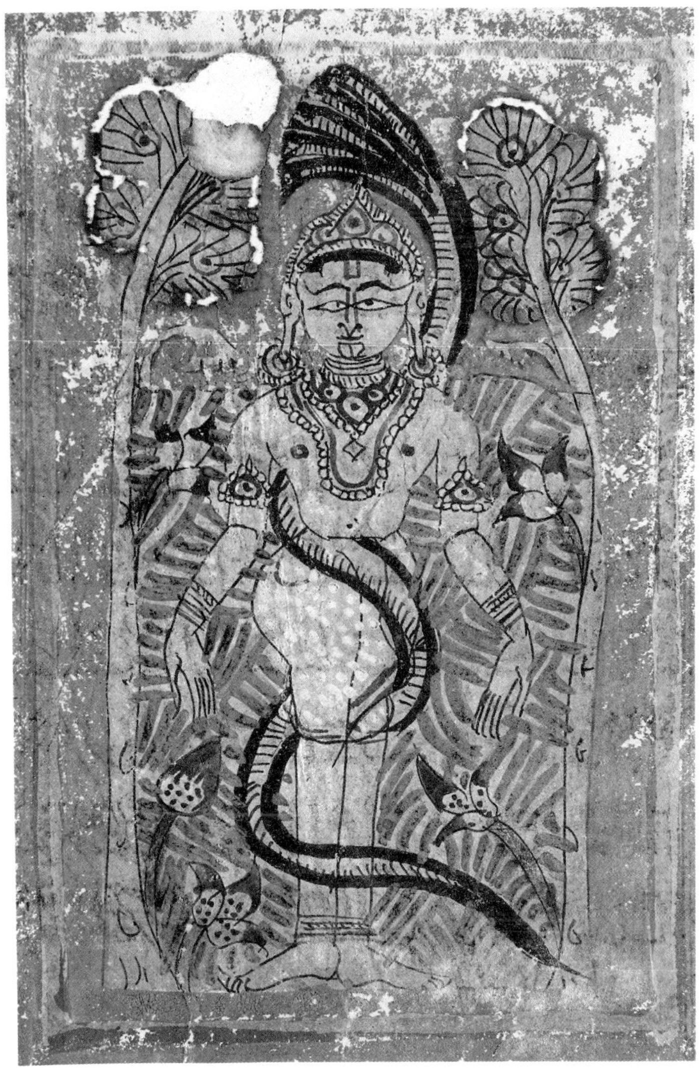

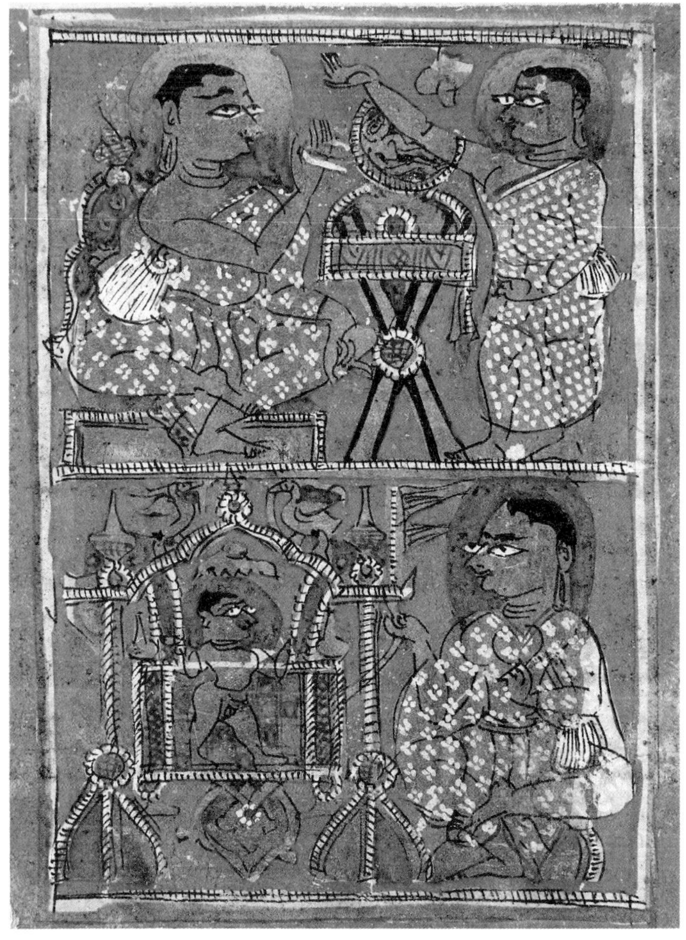

CAT. 24A detail *(left)*
CAT. 24B detail *(right)*

F These are the first and last folios of *Śrīpāla Chatuḥpadī*. There is text on only one side of each folio, the reverse being adorned with floral designs; the text is written in black ink with verse numbers, period signs, chapter endings, and colophon in red. According to the colophon the manuscript was written in 1716 for the female disciple Kesi, who lived in Vikramapura. The writer lived in Sophitanagara. Neither of these two places can be identified. The text comprises 83 verses eulogizing the very esoteric but important tantric rite known as *Siddhachakra*, "circle of perfection."

G These two covers are probably from two different manuscripts. The silk cloths covering both are embroidered with various symbols. On one, the fourteen auspicious dreams along with the eight auspicious symbols are depicted against a red background, and on the other are the fourteen dreams and a monk against a blue ground.

Gujarat or Rajasthan; c. 1500
Folios, 4½ x 10⅛ in (11.4 x 25.7 cm)
Illustrations, except B, 3¾ x 2$^{11}/_{16}$ in (9.5 x 6.8 cm)
Covers, 5⅛ x 11⅛ in (13.0 x 28.3 cm)
From the Nasli and Alice Heeramaneck Collection, Museum Associates Purchase
M.72.53.12
Literature: W. N. Brown 1934, p. 3, figs., 17, 43, 91, 99, 110, 121.

A *Birth of Mahavira* (55r)
B *Renunciation of Neminatha* (88r)
4 x 7⅞ in (10.2 x 9.9 cm)

Complete manuscript with 139 folios and 43 illustrations; folio 2 is a later replacement. Seven lines of text per page, written in black ink with red punctuation marks on buff paper. Marginal columns of gold and red frame the text as well as the pictures. Oval- and diamond-shaped lozenges in gold, red, and blue. Paintings in gold, red, blue, white, and black. Covers wrapped in blue silk brocade with flowers with leaves in two shades of green.

The paintings are closely related in style to those in the manuscript of 1502 in the collection [26]. A noteworthy feature of this manuscript is that one whole page is devoted to an illustration without any text (B). While this is more common in manuscripts of the seventeenth century and later, it is unusual in manuscripts of the pre-Mughal period (for two other examples see Khandalavala and Chandra 1969, pl. 5; and Doshi 1985, pp. 50–51, fig. 9).

A Queen Trisala is stretched out on a couch with the infant Mahavira, who is simply a miniature version of the adult figures, placed like a doll in her lap. As does a grown-up Jina, the infant makes the gesture of reassurance with his right hand. A maid attends upon the queen, and above them two females flank an auspicious waterpot.

B The story represented here has been recounted elsewhere [22]. A comparison of the two depictions as well as a third in the collection [26A] will demonstrate how much more detailed and elaborate this composition is. The sprawling composition also looks more monumental and is reminiscent of wall paintings. Among additional elements, mention should be made of the god Krishna following Neminatha as he approaches his expectant bride, Rajmati. Nemi rides a gaily caparisoned elephant with two companions, and Krishna rides in a chariot. In front of the bride a lady waits to welcome the groom; above, a peacock watches the scene. Below them the animals and birds for the slaughter are represented within pigeonholes. It should be noted that birds are not mentioned in the text nor generally included in other representations. We then see a disillusioned Nemi riding away in a chariot escorted by a retinue. It is rather curious that Nemi arrives on an elephant but departs in a chariot, since he is supposed to have turned away from the palace gates without alighting. Moreover, Krishna does not return with him.

In describing this illustration, W. N. Brown (1934, p. 48) remarked, "The full page illustration gives an idea of the importance the scene holds for the Jains; it is one of the best-loved episodes in all Jain hagiography." However, he did not cite any other example of a similar full-page illustration of this episode, and I am not familiar with any. What can be inferred from this example is that this particular episode must have had a special significance for the patron of this manuscript.

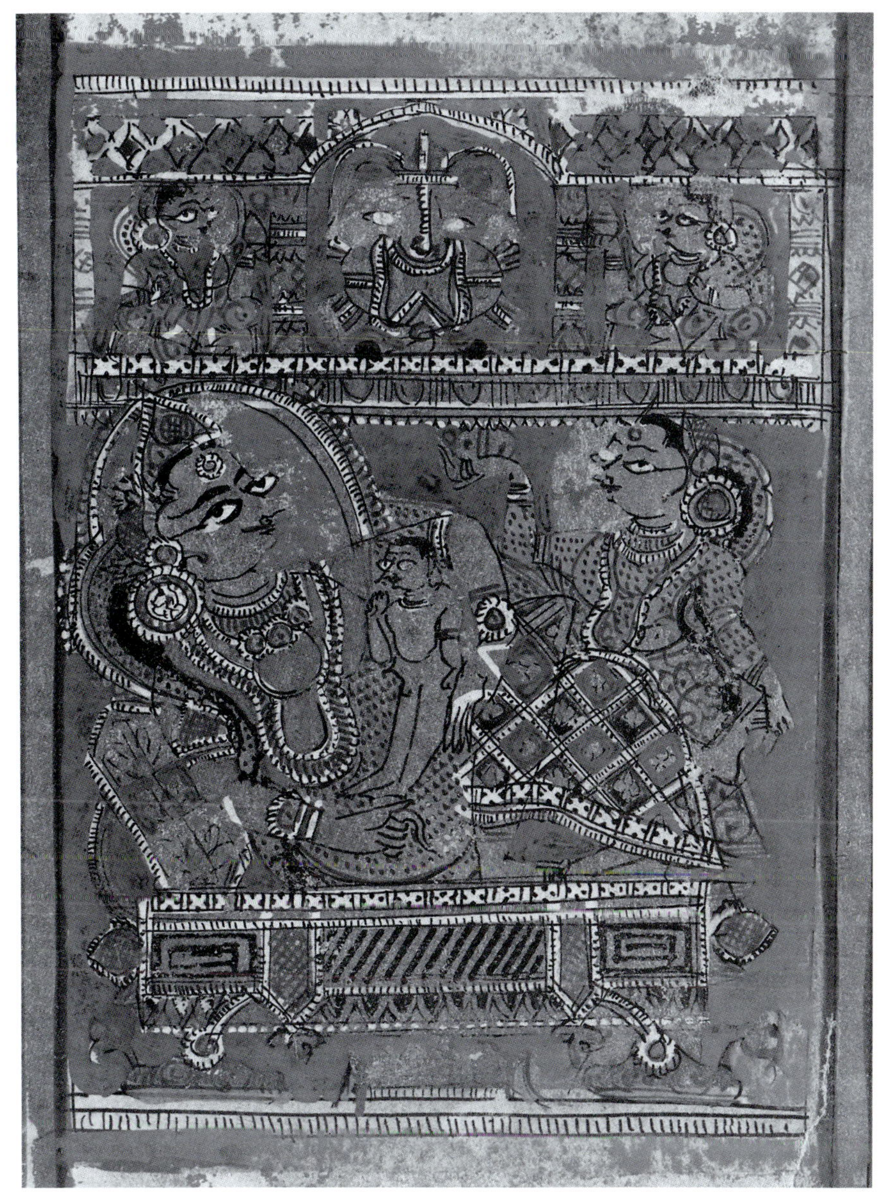

CAT. 25A detail
CAT. 25B

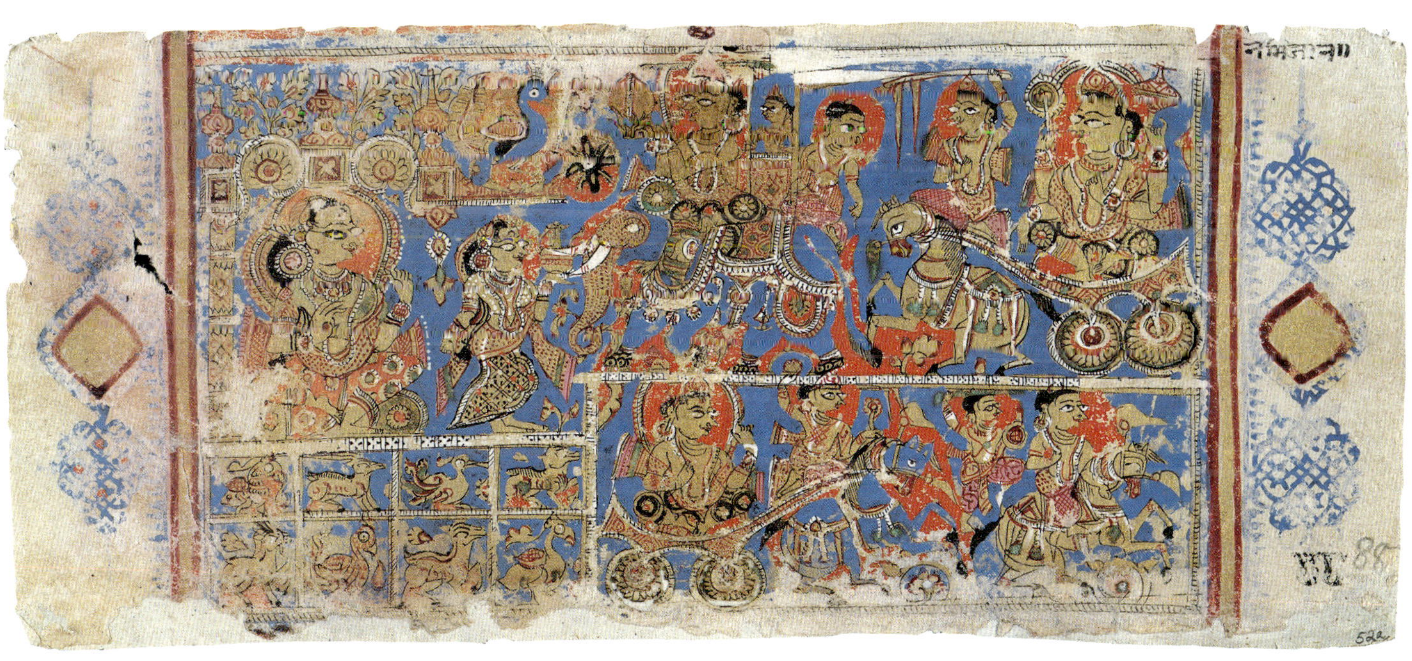

Gujarat or Rajasthan; 1502
Folios, 4 3/8 x 10 in (11.1 x 25.4 cm)
Illustrations, 4 3/8 x 3 1/8 in (11.1 x 7.9 cm)
Covers, 4 3/4 x 10 1/2 in (12.1 x 26.7 cm)
From the Nasli and Alice Heeramaneck Collection, Museum Associates Purchase
M.72.53.11
Literature: W. N. Brown 1934, p. 3, figs. 40, 142.

A *Neminatha's Birth,* left;
Neminatha's Renunciation, right (47r)
B *Scenes from the Life of Sthulabhadra* (59v)

Incomplete manuscript with 74 folios and 19 illustrations; when published in 1934, W. N. Brown noted 75 folios and 20 illustrations. Eight or nine lines of text per page with copious commentaries in smaller lettering along margins; written in black ink with red punctuation marks on buff paper. Colors used are two shades of red, blue, gold, green, white, and black. Covers wrapped with black silk brocade with rows of red and gold flowers.

It appears that the last page was damaged at some point and the text was copied onto another sheet and pasted over the original. The date given at the end therefore must refer to the day when the writing of the manuscript was completed (see Appendix).

A The scene on the left depicts a rather elaborate version of Neminatha's birth. His mother is stretched out on a bed in a pavilion with the infant in the crook of her right arm. A female companion stands in front holding what may be a fan, even if it looks like a scarf. The scene on the right is divided into two sections. On top Nemi rides on a horse toward his bride, but below he turns back from the palace in a chariot after hearing the cries of the animals waiting to be slaughtered for the wedding feast (cf. [22, 26]).

B This illustration depicts incidents from the life of Sthulabhadra, one of the later pontiffs whose biographies constitute the second book of the *Kalpasutra.* In the upper register Sthulabhadra in the form of a lion is being greeted by two of his seven sisters, all of whom are nuns. In an identical composition in the lower segment the lion has been replaced by a monk, perhaps representing Sthulabhadra or Bhadrabahu, who is generally regarded as the author of the first part of the *Kalpasutra.* The lion is supposed to be in a cave, but as is characteristic of *Kalpasutra* paintings of the later fifteenth or sixteenth century, the animal is placed below an arch.

While stylistically the pictures continue the well-established mode, two features should be noted. At least three of the folios in this manuscript have two illustrations on the same page, as does leaf A reproduced here. Usually most illustrated *Kalpasutra* manuscripts have only one picture per page. Another curious feature is that several panels of different sizes meant to be filled with illustrations have been left empty, although not in any recognizable pattern.

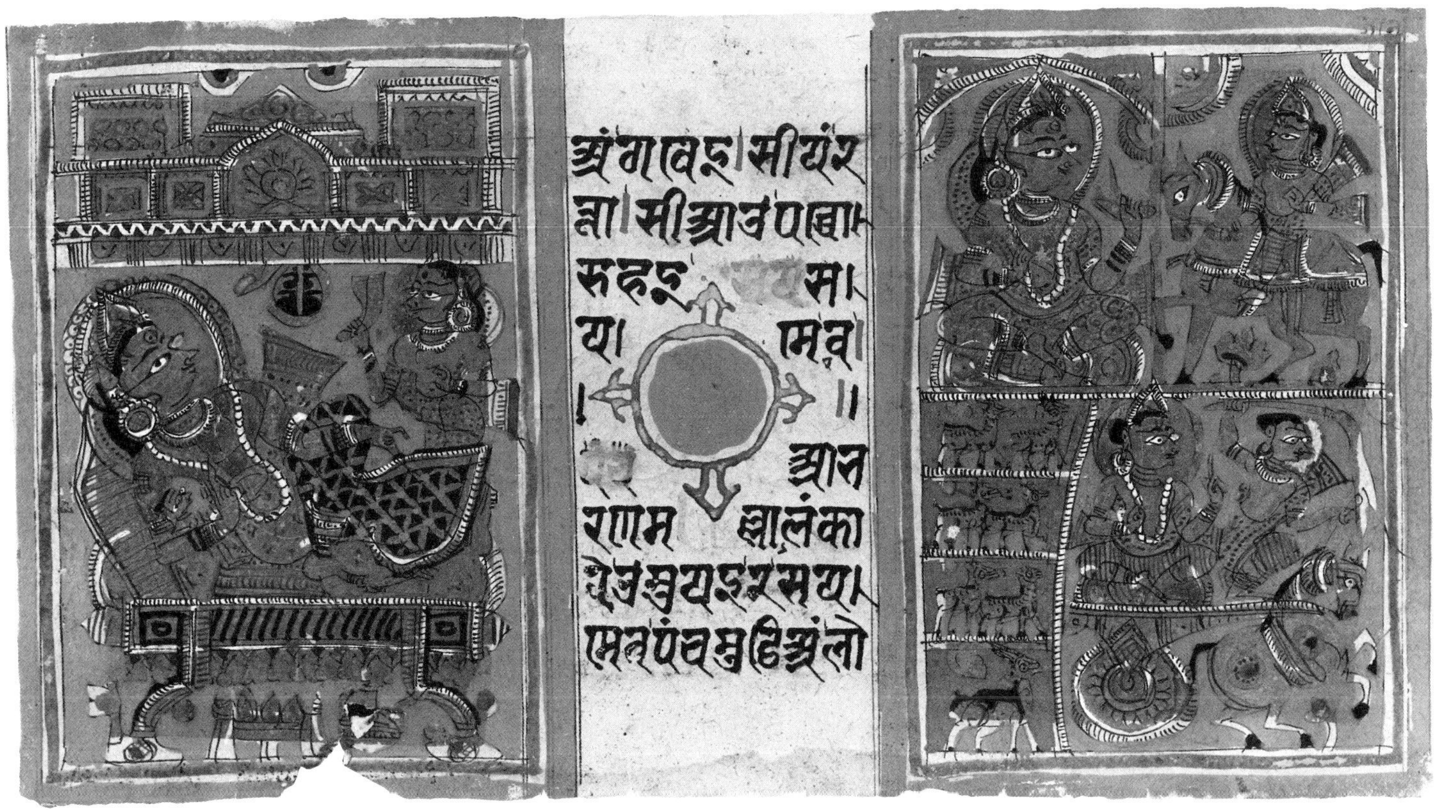

CAT. 26A

CAT. 26B detail

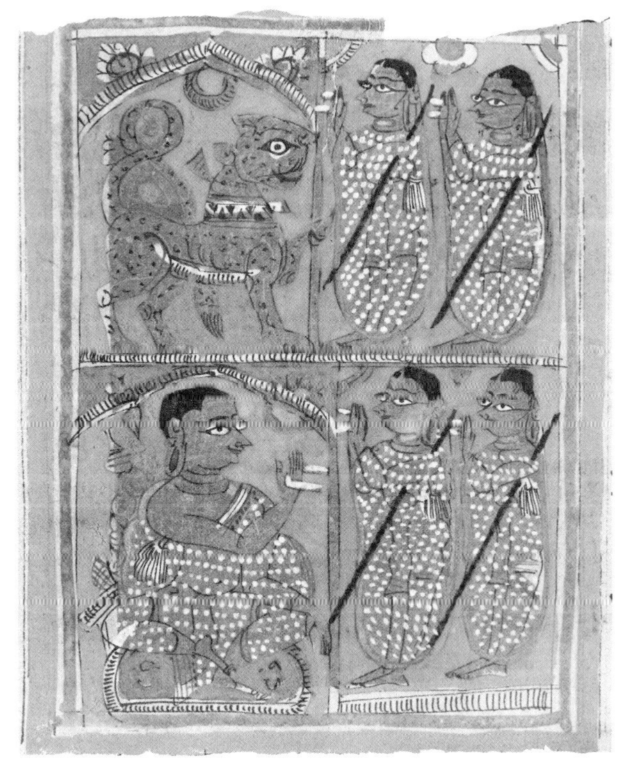

Gujarat; 1510
Folios, 4 7/16 x 10 1/4 in (11.3 x 26.0 cm)
Illustrations, 4 7/16 x 2 3/4 in (11.3 x 7.0 cm)
Covers, 4 5/8 x 10 3/4 in (11.7 x 27.3 cm)
From the Nasli and Alice Heeramaneck Collection, Museum Associates Purchase
M.72.53.17
Literature: W. N. Brown 1934, p. 3, figs. 95, 105, 107.

A *Adoration of the Conch* (89v)
B *Krishna and Neminatha* (90v)

Complete manuscript with 147 folios and 49 illustrations. Seven lines of text per page, written in black ink with red punctuation marks on thin, buff paper. Vertical dividing columns in red and black. Three red circles on each recto page and one in the middle of each verso page. Captions in margins of illustrations. Illustration colors are blue, gold, red, white, black, and occasionally purple. Covers wrapped with blue silk brocade with red and green floral motifs, with band of red and silver glued across one cover.

According to the colophon (see Appendix) this manuscript was copied and recited in an assembly of monks in Vikrama year 1567 (A.D. 1510) (exact day not provided), at the request of Kadua. Born in the Ukesa family, he is styled as the lord of the ministers. His parents were Javada and Rati, and he had a brother named Bhima. Kadua's wife was the "famous Kamaladevi,"

CAT. 27A detail

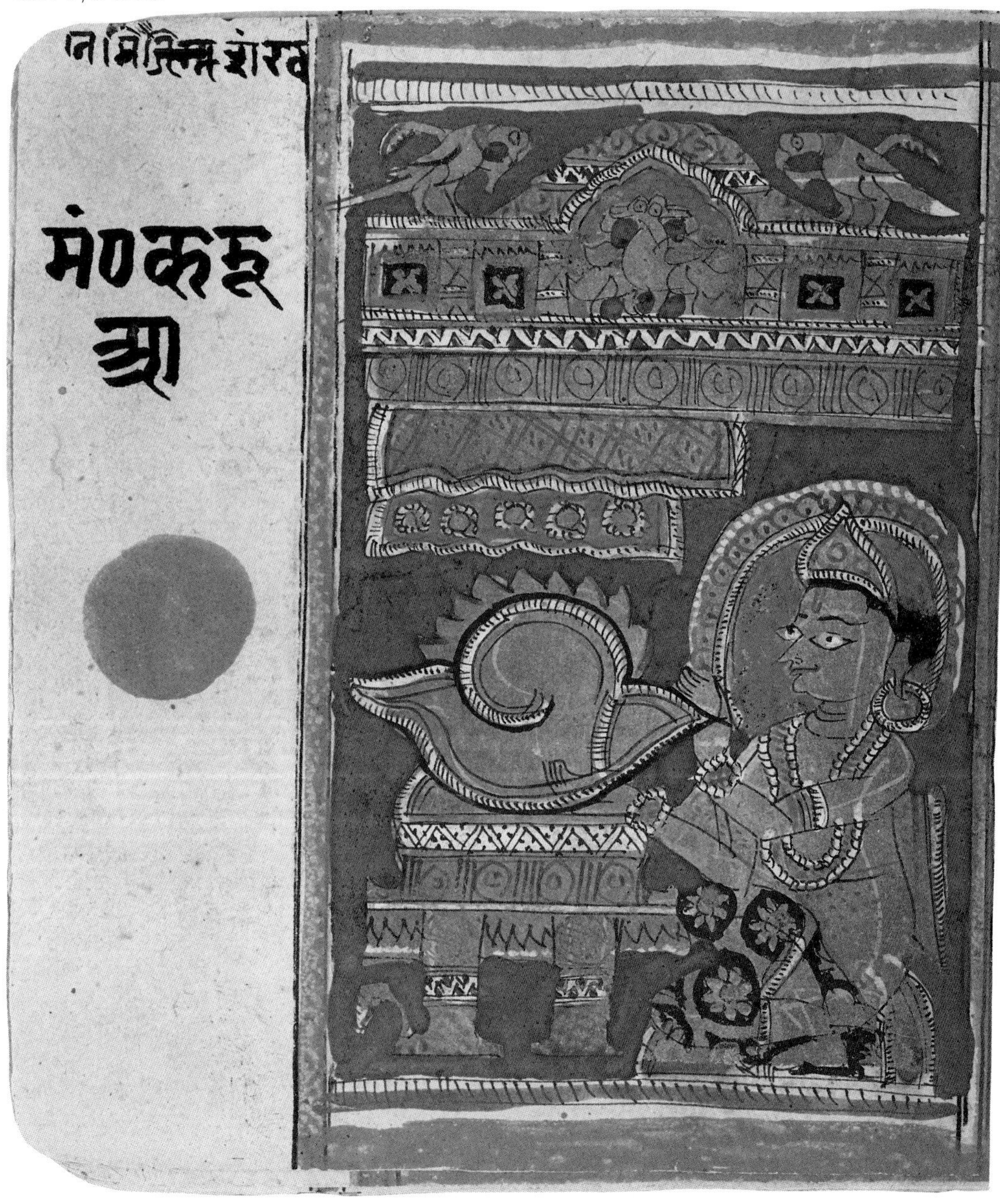

while Bhima's wife was known as Bhimadevi. Kadua's son Varddhamana was obviously named after Mahavira. Unfortunately, the inscription says nothing about where they lived and which royal family they worked for.

A The caption identifies the scene as the conch of Nemi (*Nemisankho*). Below a canopy of various cloths that is surmounted by two parrots, a seated man is adoring Neminatha's conch in the Aparajita heaven. The conch is the distinctive emblem of Nemi but is also an important attribute of the Hindu god Vishnu. The worshipper wears a dhoti of black and gold design.

B In this illustration Krishna is trying to persuade Neminatha to marry. Krishna is on the left and distinguished by two additional arms. He is not given a dark complexion as is the case in Hindu art, nor does he hold the usual attributes. In fact, appropriate to the occasion, his lower hands make gestures expressive of conversation; the objects in the two upper hands cannot be identified. Nemi's left arm is similarly raised. The gestures of these hands clearly convey the impression of two arguing Indians. Krishna wears a black-and-gold dhoti, while Nemi is clad in a red dhoti with blue flowers.

The paintings in this book are well preserved, and the colors have retained much of their original freshness. One assumes that the influential donor would have hired the best available artist in his hometown to illustrate the manuscript. As it happens, the artist was competent rather than brilliant or innovative.

CAT. 27B detail

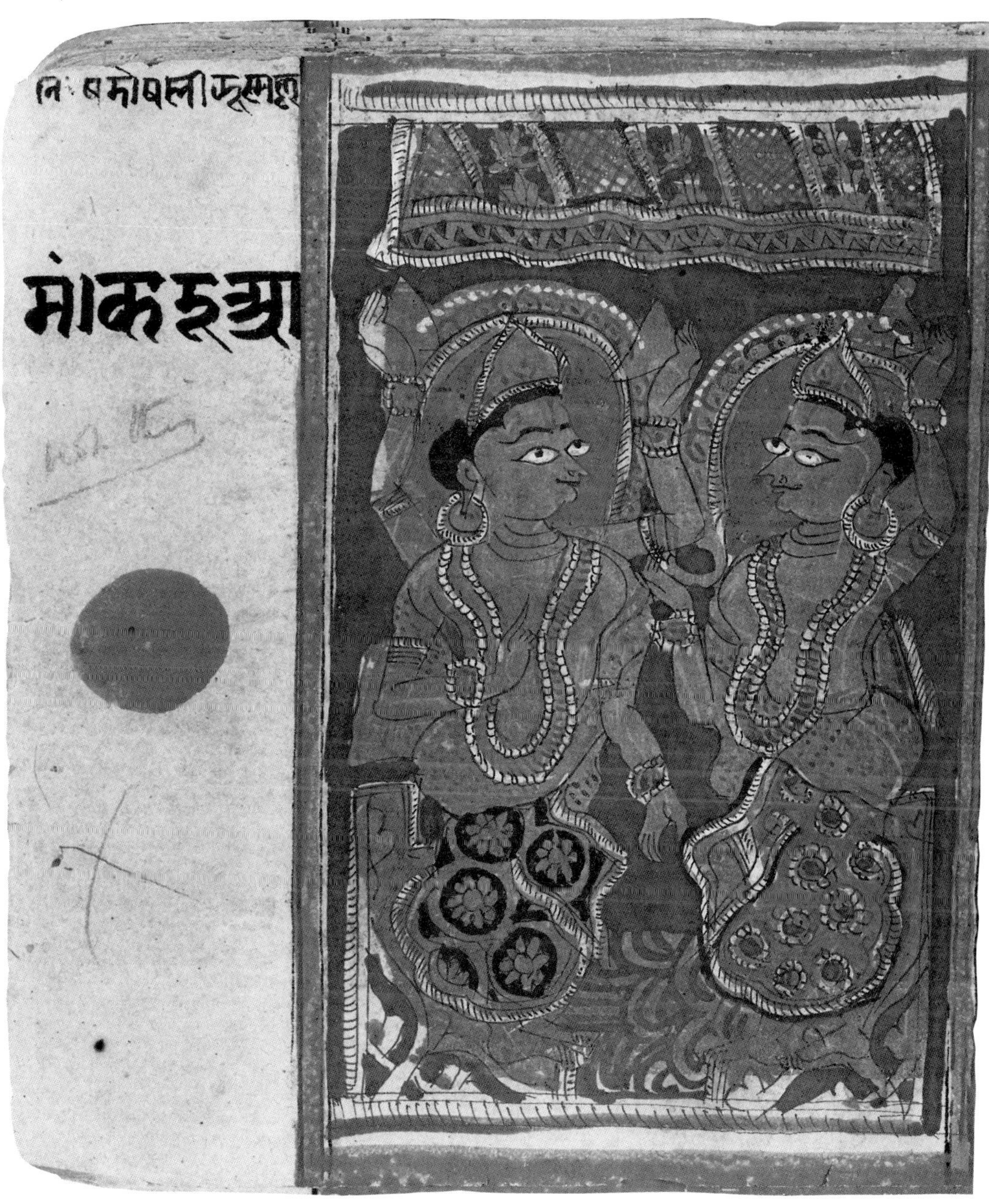

Gujarat; 1520
Folios, 4½ x 11 in (11.4 x 27.9 cm)
Illustrations, 4½ x 3 in (11.4 x 7.6 cm)
Covers, 4¾ x 10¾ in (12.1 x 27.3 cm)
From the Nasli and Alice Heeramaneck Collection, Museum Associates Purchase
M.72.53.13
Literature: W. N. Brown 1934, p. 30, figs. 15, 104; Larson et al. 1980, p. 52, no. 17b; Canby 1983, no. 2, fig. 2.

A *Vigil on the Sixth Night* (52r)
B *Scenes from Parsvanatha's Life* (72v)

Complete manuscript with 129 folios and 51 illustrations. Seven lines of text per page, written in black ink on buff paper. Margins as well as central columns in red and gold. Marginal decorations of circles and squares in gold, red, and blue. Some pictures identified by short captions. Predominant colors of pictures are blue, gold, and red, with some black and white. Covers wrapped with variegated silk brocade with striped geometric designs.

According to the colophon (see Appendix) this "beautiful Kalpa manuscript" was commissioned by Puti, the wife of minister Madhava, in the year 1520. Although the manuscript is quite generously illustrated, the pictures are painted in the conventional style. Despite the fact that it was commissioned by the wife of a minister, the illustrations are not unusually lavish.

CAT. 28A detail

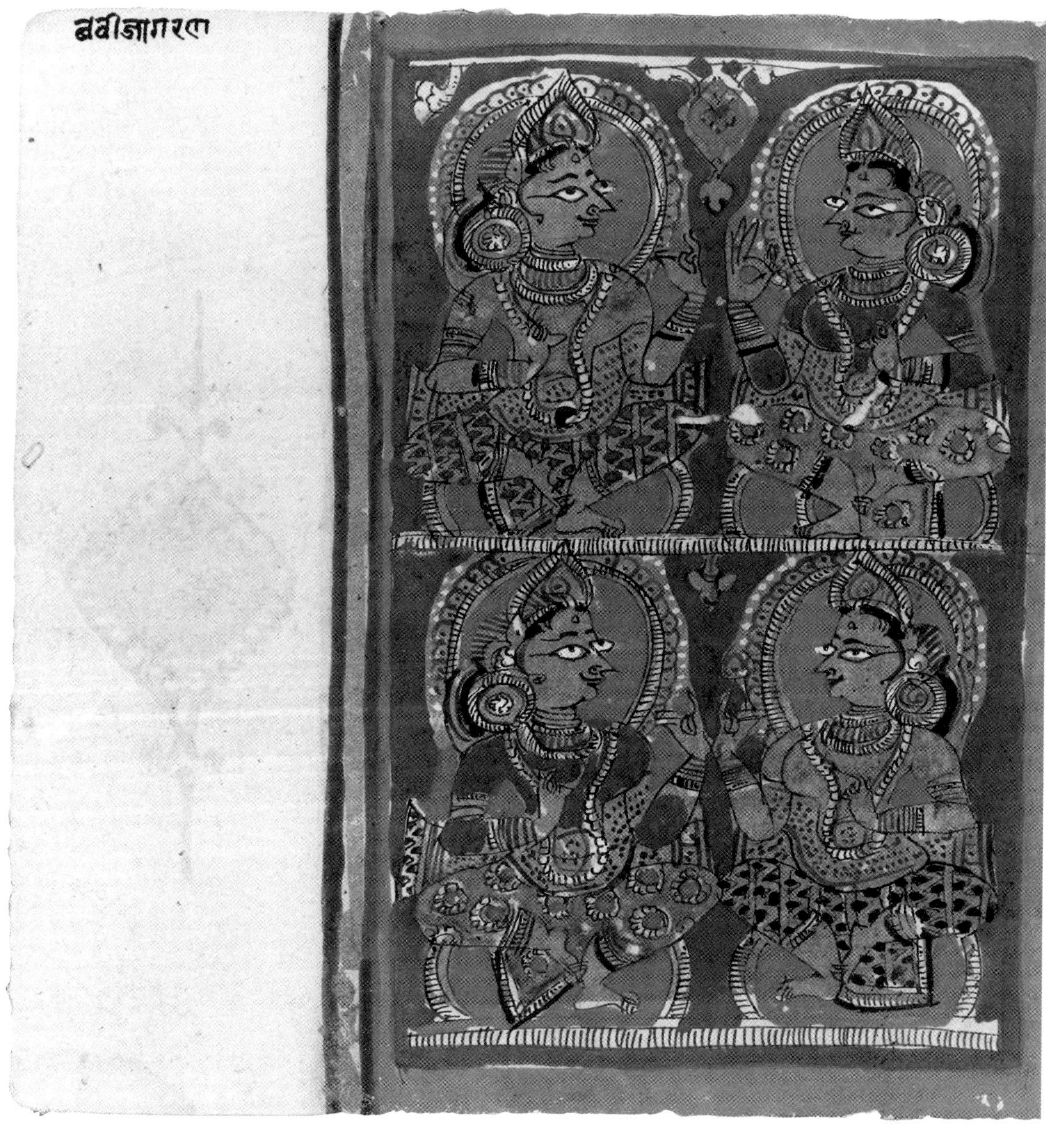

A The customary vigil that was held on the sixth day after the birth of Mahavira is represented by four seated women, each pair engaged in conversation, perhaps to stay awake.

B This illustrates an event from the life of Parsvanatha involving the heretical ascetic Kamatha, who was the Jina's arch-antagonist. One day Parsva approached Kamatha while he was engaged in performing the fire austerities. In the upper register of the illustration Kamatha sits among five fires (*pañchāgni tapa*). Four of them are terrestrial and are burning in the four corners; the fire of the sun shown partially above Kamatha's forehead is the fifth. Through his clairvoyance Parsva perceived a family of snakes within a hollow log burning in one of the fires beside Kamatha and saved them. Below, Parsva releases a snake from a log. Kamatha was both angered and humiliated. It was one of these snakes, reborn as Dharana, who later sheltered Parsva from a violent storm (see [24A]). It is not clear who the elephant rider is. Perhaps he is Sakra witnessing the miracle.

CAT. 28B detail

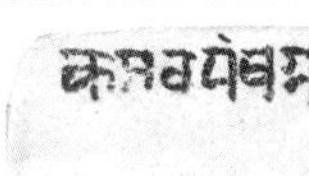

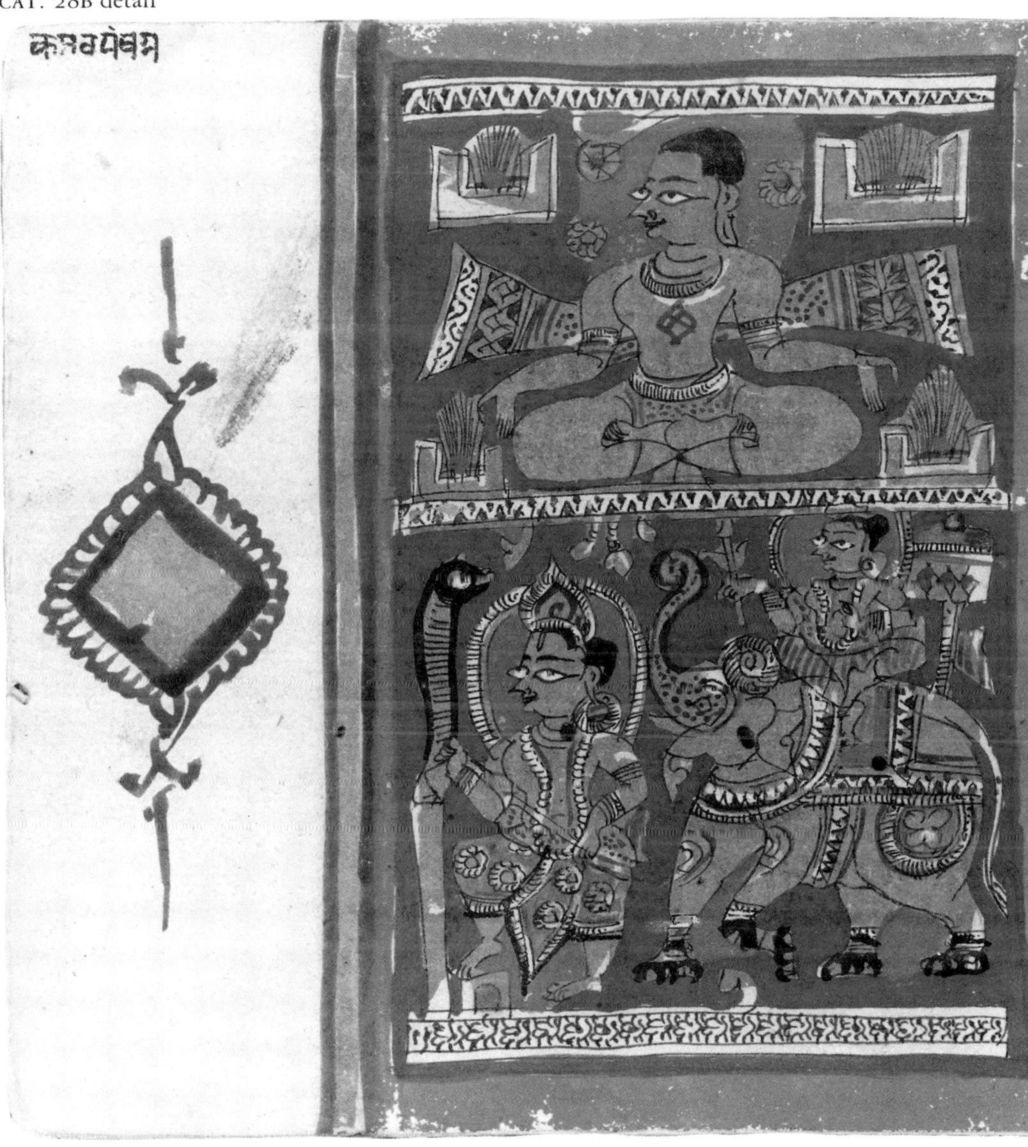

29 FOLIO FROM A *KALAKACHARYAKATHA* MANUSCRIPT

Gujarat or Rajasthan; 1500–1525
Folio, 4 7/16 x 10 7/8 in (11.3 x 27.6 cm)
Illustrations, 4 7/16 x 2 7/8 in (11.3 x 7.3 cm)
From the Nasli and Alice Heeramaneck Collection, Museum Associates Purchase
M.71.1.2
Literature: *Heeramaneck* 1966, p. 120, no. 139 (not illustrated).

A *Kalaka Conversing with Two Monks* (r)
B *Abduction of Sarasvati* (v)

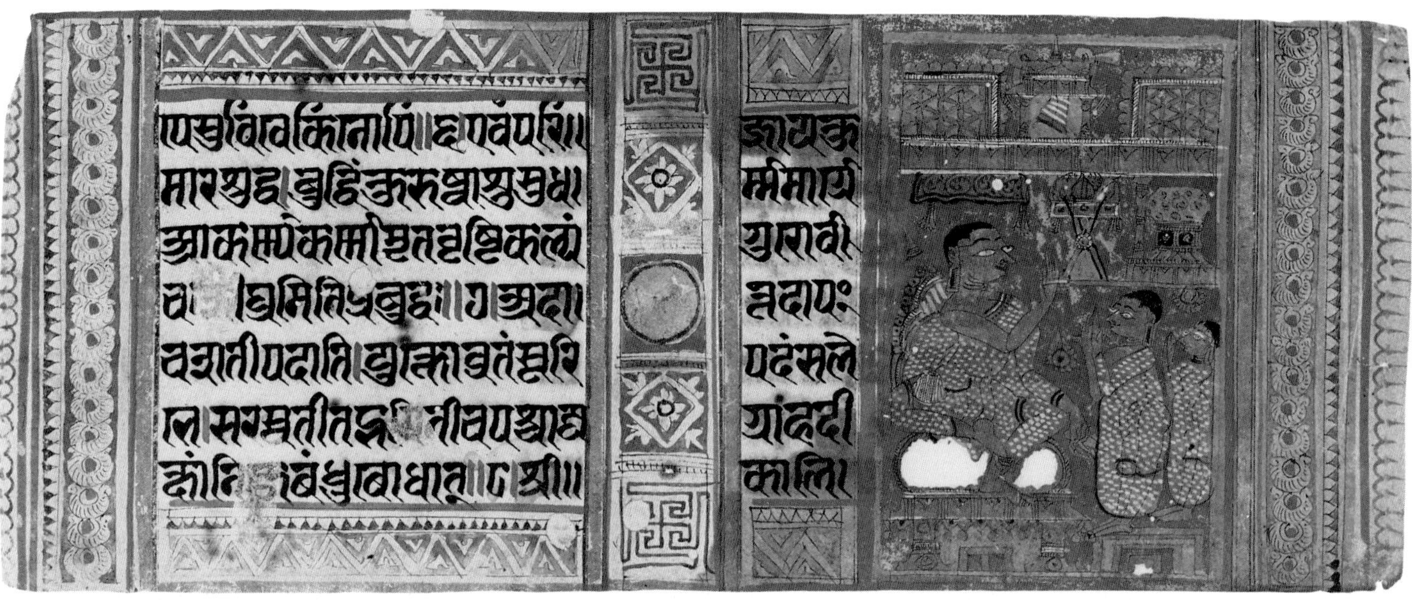

CAT. 29A
CAT. 29B detail *(opposite)*

This richly decorated leaf, folio 2 from a *Kalakacharyakatha,* is illustrated on both sides. In addition to the pictures, each page is adorned with several decorative borders that leave a rather small area for the text, which is written in black ink, seven lines per page. The predominant colors are blue, red, and some yellow. The figures in the illustrations, including the horses, are painted in brown with touches of gold. The monks and nuns wear transparent garments with white polka dots and red outlines.

A The scene here depicts Kalaka conversing with two monks, who stand before him with their hands forming the gesture of obeisance. The scene takes place within a pavilion. At the level of Kalaka's head is a book on a book stand.

B In the upper half of this illustration King Gardabhilla, riding his horse, meets Sarasvati and her companion. Sarasvati was Kalaka's sister and was ordained as a nun. Gardabhilla was at once smitten by Sarasvati and abducted her, which is depicted in the lower section. Rather than being carried on his horse, she is on the shoulders of one of his attendants.

Although the nuns are fully robed, beneath the transparent material the artist has prominently delineated their breasts, thereby clearly indicating their sex. Such direct exposure of nuns' bodies is not commonly encountered in Jain book illuminations. The artist was fairly good at rendering horses, which are much better drawn here than they usually are in such illustrations.

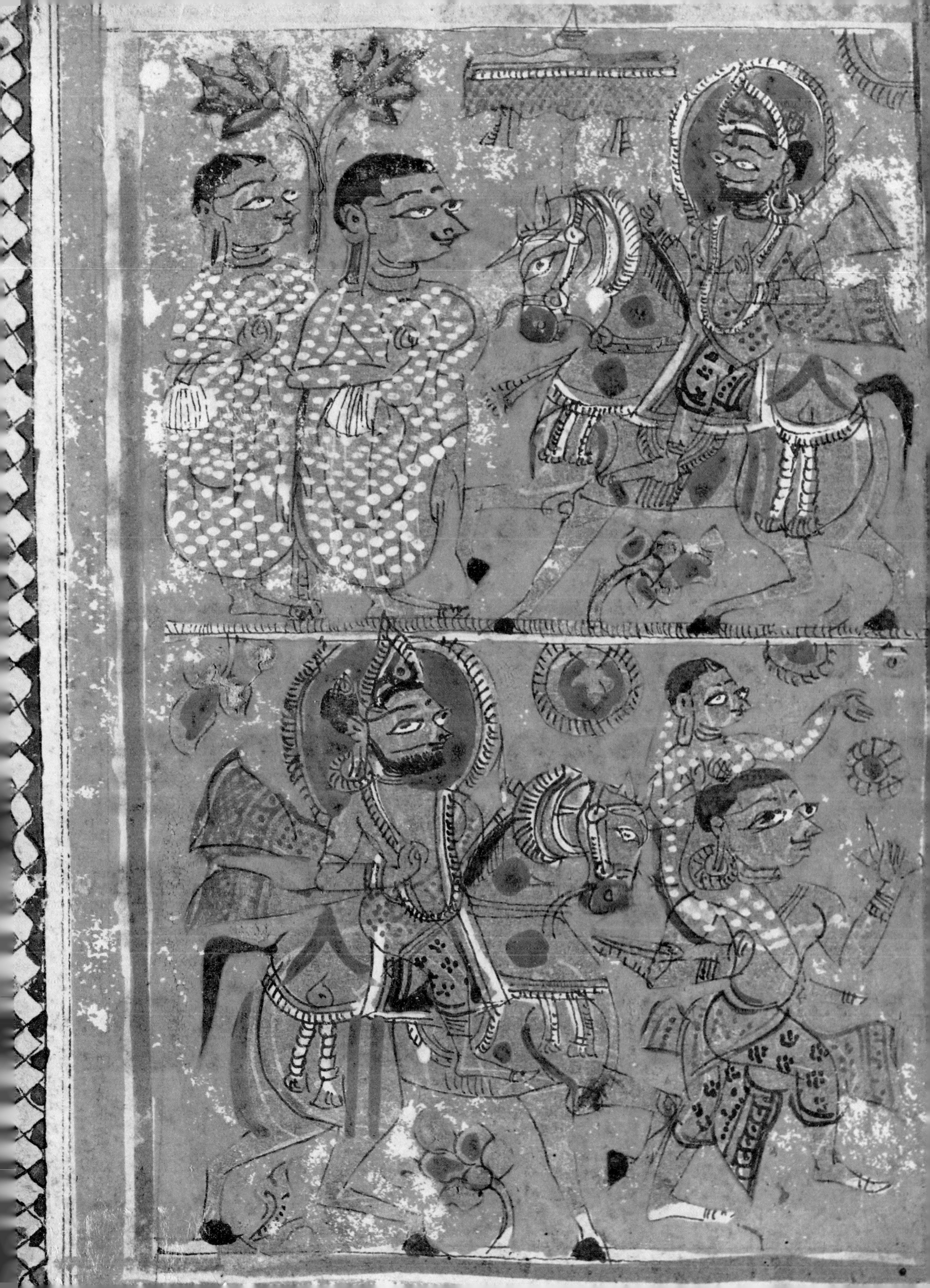

Gujarat or Rajasthan; 1500–1550
Text in gold
Folio, 4½ x 11½ in (11.4 x 29.2 cm)
Illustrations, 4½ x 1⅛ in (11.4 x 2.9 cm)
Indian Art Special Purpose Fund
M.77.35

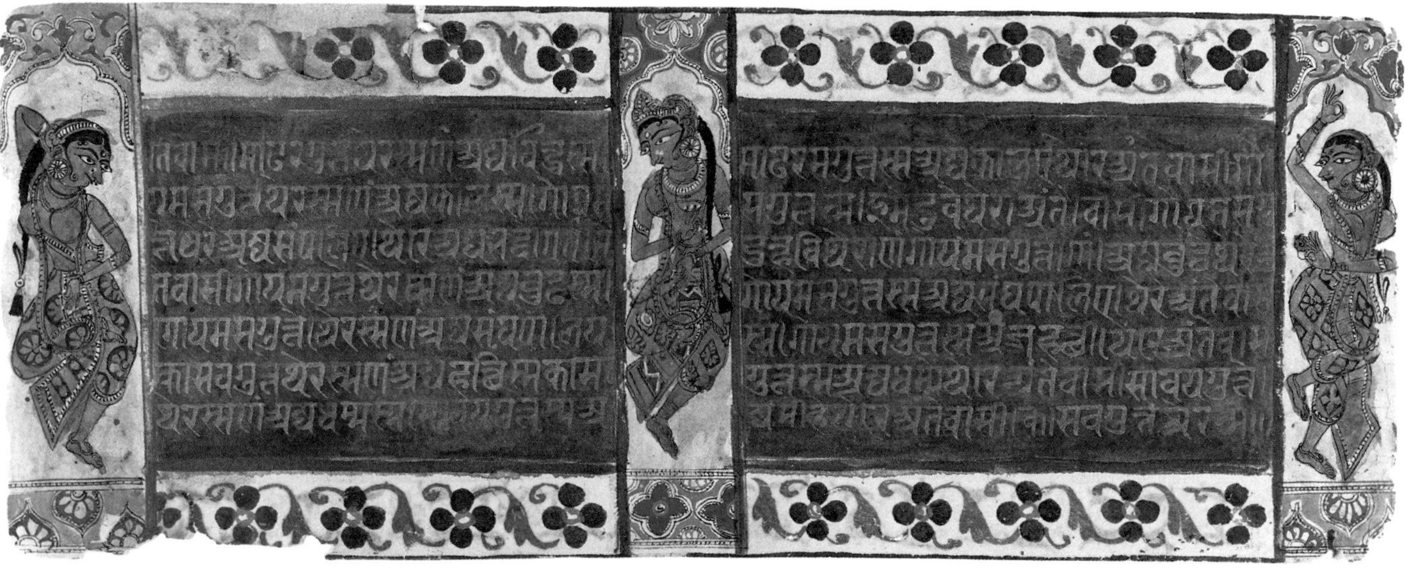

The exact identification of the text of this unnumbered folio is difficult, but as dancers usually decorate *Kalakacharyakatha* manuscripts, very likely this leaf is from a manuscript of that text. The text is written in gold letters on a purplish-red ground, as is seen in some earlier manuscript pages in the collection [14]. The decorative design is quite different, however.

On each page three narrow vertical columns divide the text into two panels. Both pages are further embellished at the top and bottom with borders containing vegetal motifs consisting of gold leaves with blue and red flowers. The columns, however, are adorned with different designs on the two sides. On the recto the columns are decorated with geometric and floral motifs, but on the verso with three lively female dancers (illustrated). Each strikes a different pose under an arch. They and their garments are painted gold, but the patterns on their attire are different. Noteworthy are the long braids of their luxuriant hair. The forms of all three dancers are well drawn, with full breasts and slender waists. Their postures as well as their gestures reveal the artist's familiarity with the repertoire of classical Indian dance.

A similarly adorned folio from the same manuscript is in the Cleveland Museum of Art (Leach 1986, p. 15, no. 5), and a third is in the Brooklyn Museum.

Gujarat or Rajasthan; c. 1550
Folios, 4½ x 12³⁄₁₆ in (11.4 x 30.9 cm)
Illustrations, 4½ x 3¾ in (11.4 x 9.5 cm)
Covers, 4⅝ x 12½ in (11.7 x 31.8 cm)
From the Nasli and Alice Heeramaneck Collection, Museum Associates Purchase
M.72.53.14

A *Mahavira in the Initiation Palanquin* (35r)
B *Enshrined Parsvanatha* (43r)

Complete manuscript with 72 folios and 21 illustrations. Nine lines of text per page with copious commentaries in the margins, written in black ink on buff paper. Marginal columns in red and black; red circles and rimless wheels as additional decorations. Colors in illustrations are gold, red, blue, green, white, and black. Some illustrations are damaged, especially along the top. Covers wrapped with beige silk brocade with colorful *būṭās*.

A Mahavira is being carried in a palanquin through the city to a park, where he will renounce the world by cutting his hair (cf. [12A, 15B]). The celestial palanquin was provided by Sakra. Four divine bearers support the palanquin, and two celestial nymphs fan the prince with flywhisks. The peacocks above carry garlands in their beaks.

B The exact identification of this illustration is difficult, although there is no doubt that the central figure is Parsvanatha. He can be recognized by both the multiple snakes above his head and the small snake in the middle of the top register of his throne. Various other figures are in attendance upon the Jina. The scene may represent Parsva in his heaven before his birth. In another manuscript the Jina Neminatha is shown in an identical manner enthroned in the Aparajita heaven (W. N. Brown 1934, p. 45, fig. 101). The other possibility is Parsva's passing, when he became a *siddha,* but this is less likely since in such scenes the Jina is usually seated on an inverted parasol over Mount Meru (cf. [12B]). In any event, this is the only picture illustrating Parsva's life in this manuscript. The majority of the pictures depict scenes from Mahavira's life.

The drawing in these pictures is very perfunctory, and both figures and objects seem to have been rendered almost impressionistically. Nevertheless, some of the figures, such as the dancers and the palanquin bearers, are vivacious and energetic despite their crude outlines.

CAT. 31A detail *(left)*
CAT. 31B detail *(right)*

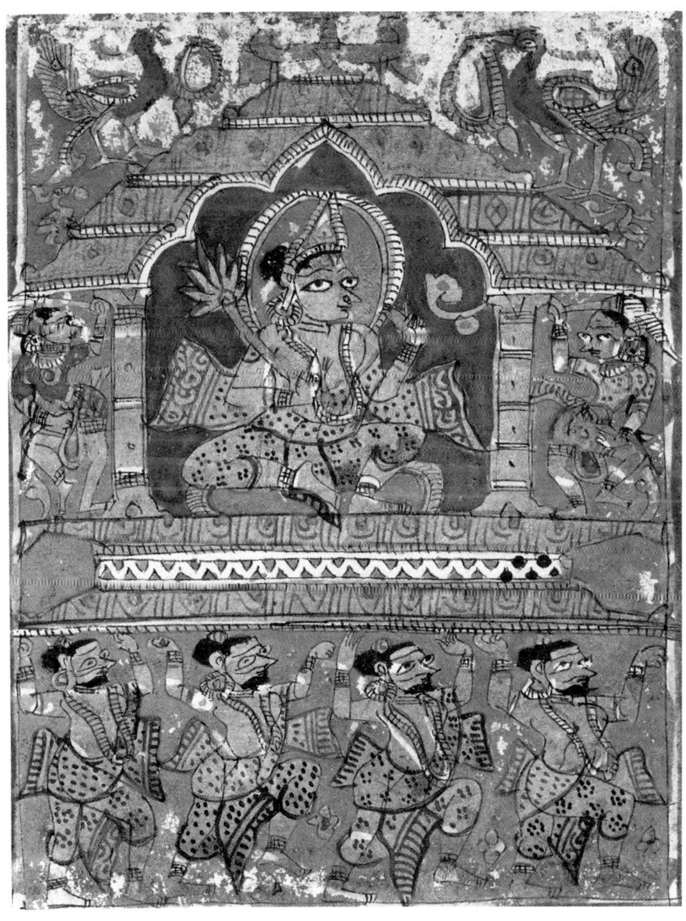

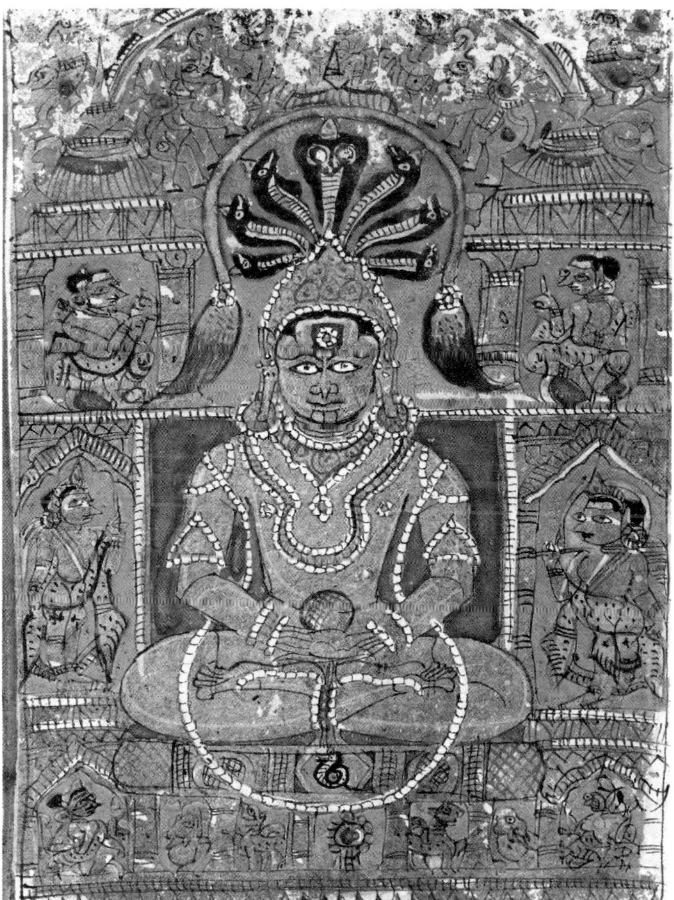

Gujarat; c. 1575
Opaque watercolor and ink on paper
10⅝ x 5⅛ in (27.0 x 13.0 cm)
Gift of Anna Bing Arnold
M.87.159.2

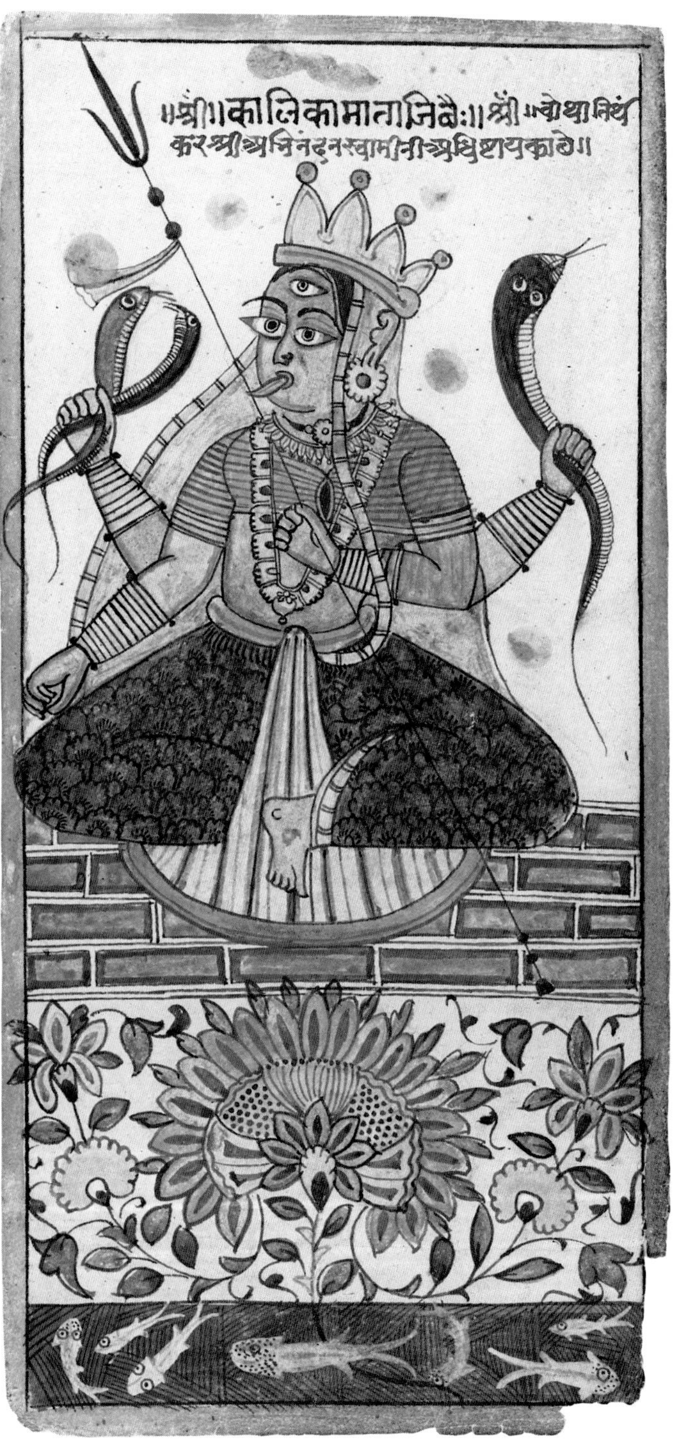

The inscription above invokes the goddess, who is addressed as Mother Kalika, and informs us that she was attained by the fourth Tirthankara or Jina, Abhinandanasvami, also known as Abhinandanatha. In the Jain pantheon, Siva is the yaksha and Kali or Kalika the yakshi of Abhinandanatha. Yakshas and yakshis form a class of deities who were universally worshipped in ancient India. Some of them were adopted into the Jain pantheon as tutelary deities of the Jinas.

The language of the inscription is Gujarati, which, along with the style, makes a Gujarati provenance very likely. Moreover, the leaf clearly has the same proportions as a typical Jain manuscript folio, although the representation is vertically oriented.

The blue goddess wears a green sari and a red blouse. The crown and ornaments are all in yellow, no doubt imitating gold, with touches of black and pink. She is seated on a brick platform. With two of her hands she carries cobras, and a third holds a trident. The fourth hand shows a clenched fist. She sticks out her tongue, and the third eye is placed horizontally across her forehead. Below the brick platform are beautifully rendered flowers, presented to the goddess as a bouquet. The stem of the large flower emerges from a stream below, where fishes are swimming. The smaller flowers are in two shades of purple and the leaves are all green, but the larger flower is more richly painted in blue, purples, yellow, orange, and red. Although it emerges from the water, it is not a lotus but an imaginary flower.

While the shape of the folio continues the Jain tradition, the vertical orientation of the picture is a novelty and probably resulted from the influence of Islamic books. The painter of this picture does not, however, seem to have been aware of the Mughal tradition, as is clear from the conceptualization of water rendered as a basket pattern as well as the extension of the further eye. Interestingly, although her body is shown almost frontally, Kalika's head is depicted in a three-quarter view. The bold floral design is not unlike similarly exuberant floral decorations in an Islamic manuscript attributed to mid-sixteenth-century Gujarat (S. C. Welch 1985 p. 137, no. 81).

33 FOLIO FROM A *SAMGRAHANISUTRA* MANUSCRIPT: VARIOUS HEAVENS

Gujarat or Rajasthan; 1575 1600
Opaque watercolor and ink on paper
Folio, 4 3/8 x 9 7/8 in (11.1 x 25.1 cm)
Illustration, 4 x 9 5/8 in (10.2 x 24.4 cm)
From the Nasli and Alice Heeramaneck
Collection, Museum Associates Purchase
M.71.1.7
Literature: *Heeramaneck* 1966, p. 120, no. 144
(not illustrated).

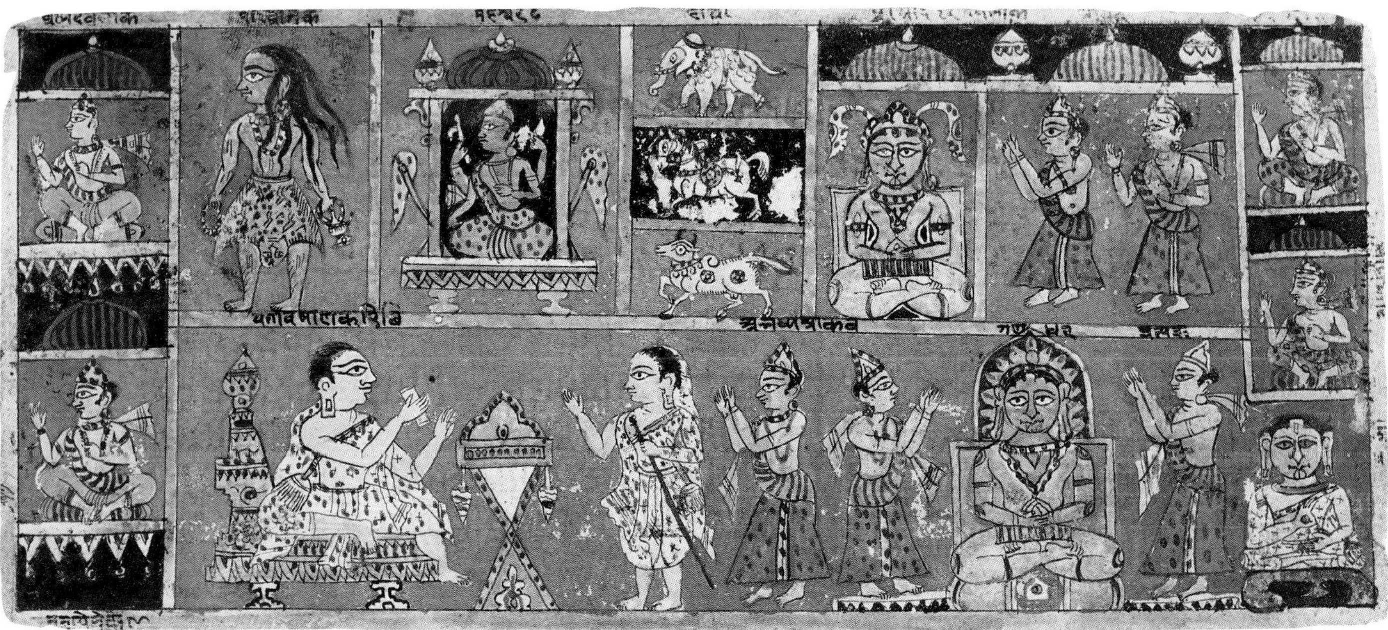

This is folio 12 from a manuscript of the *Samgrahanisutra,* whose whereabouts are otherwise not known. One side of the leaf has text with marginal decorations, and the other side is given entirely to illustration. The composition consists of several panels of different sizes and shapes containing one or more figures or animals. Small inscriptions, some of which are quite indistinct, help in identifying some of the figures.

The illustrations depict various heavens populated by certain classes of creatures after death. Even animals who die with good intention may attain a particular heaven. The animal world is represented here by an elephant, a horse, and a bull. Along the left edge are two divinities in their pavilions. The standing figure with long unkempt hair in the second panel in the upper register is identified as a *parivrajaka,* or wandering ascetic. Next is Mahesvara (Siva) seated in a pavilion. Also included are three Jinas, who will attain a heaven called Graiveyaka; their lay worshippers, whose heaven is Achyutadevaloka; and a teaching monk called a *ganadhara* (a leader of a group), who will reside in the Sarvarthasiddivimana, the highest heaven in Jain cosmology.

The form of the writing on the text page as well as its marginal decorations suggest that this manuscript was copied in Gujarat. Stylistically comparable manuscripts are a 1583 *Samgrahanisutra* in India (M. Chandra and Shah 1975, pp. 63–69, figs. 41–52, pls. VIII–X) and the 1604 manuscript in the Spencer Collection in the New York Public Library (Doshi 1985, pp. 72–75, figs. 10–13). However, the figural forms here differ from those in both manuscripts as well as in the other *Samgrahanisutra* illustrations in the collection [34]. The background is generally red with a few areas painted in dark blue. Other colors used are yellow, white, pink, lavender, mauve, sky blue, green, and black. Indeed, the palette here is more varied than that employed in *Kalpasutra* manuscripts. Noteworthy also is the fact that the partial representation of the further eye is absent in these illustrations and in those in the next entry.

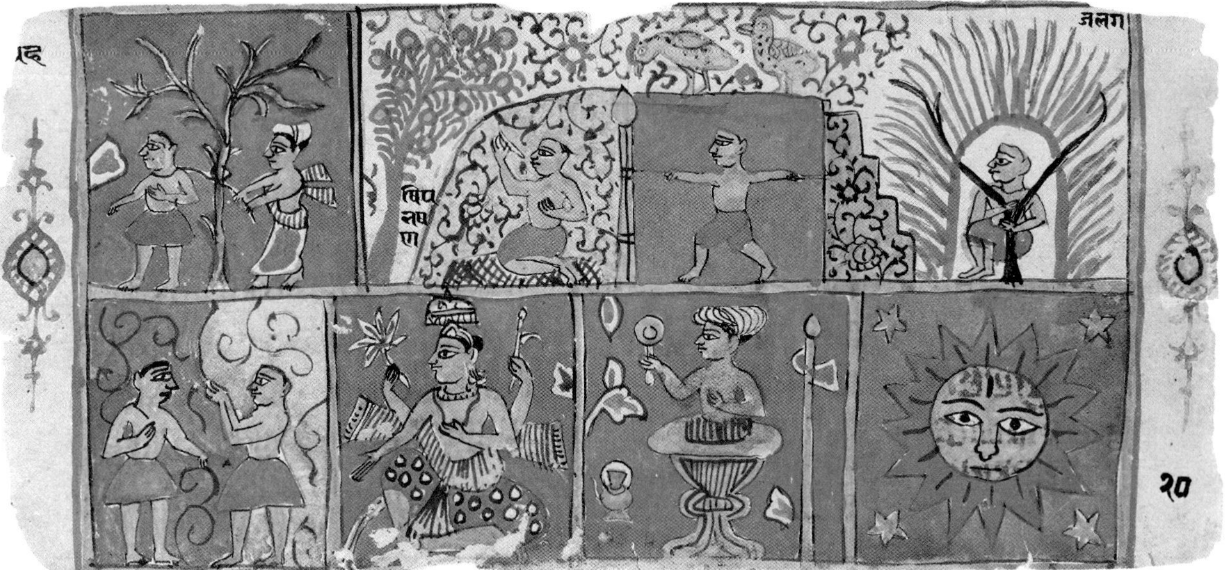

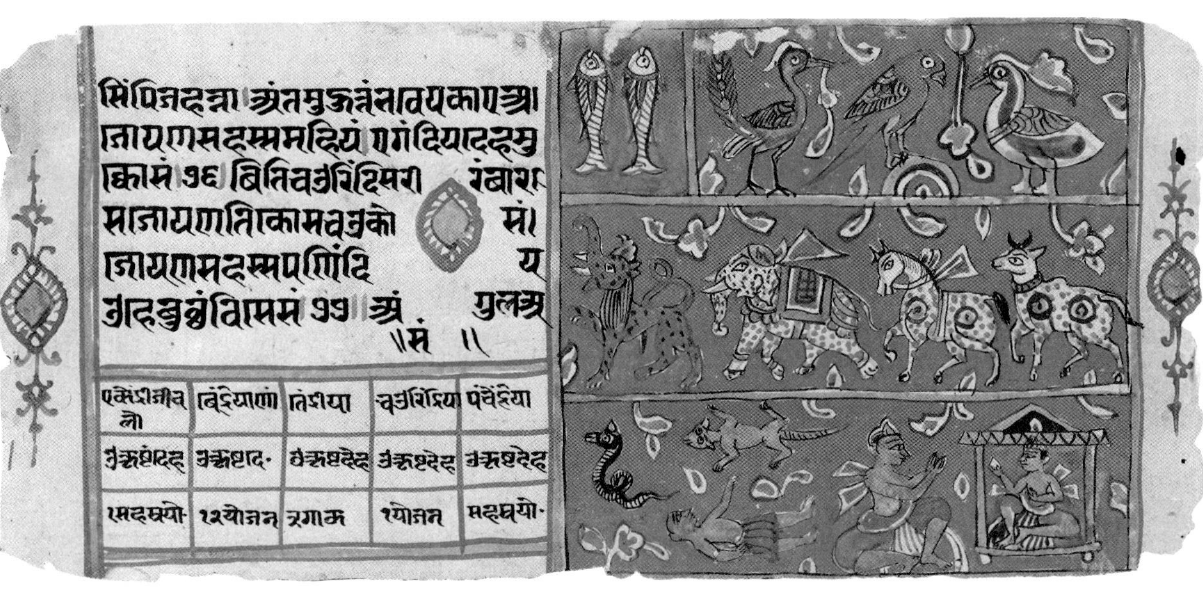

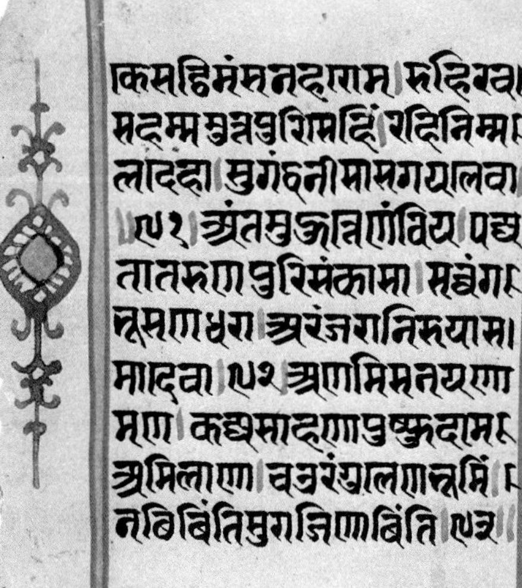

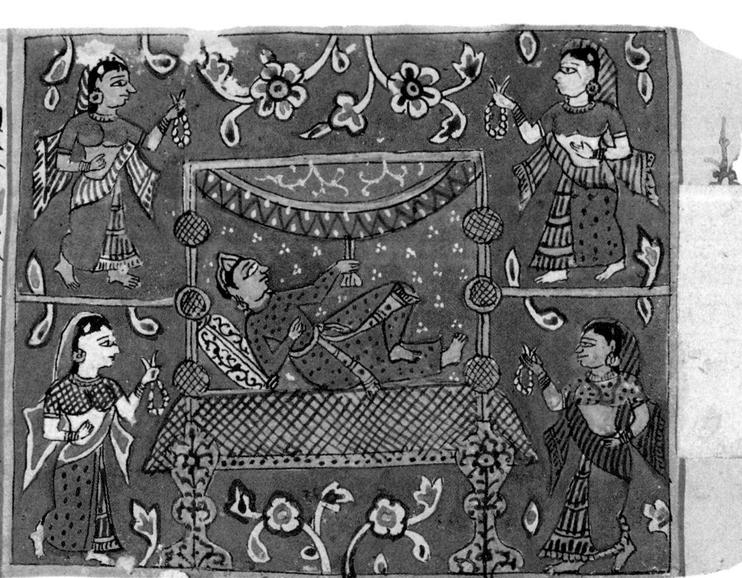

Gujarat; 1575–1600
Opaque watercolor and ink on paper

A *Consequences of Certain Actions* (20v)
Folio, 4⅛ x 10 in (10.5 x 25.4 cm)
Illustration, 4⅛ x 8½ in (10.5 x 21.6 cm)
Gift of Navin Kumar
M.88.28.2

B *Symbolic Animals* (38r)
Folio, 4⅝ x 10¼ in (11.7 x 26.0 cm)
Illustration, 4⅝ x 4¾ in (11.7 x 12.1 cm)
Purchased with funds provided by Dorothy and Richard M. Sherwood
M.89.120.1

C *Reclining God with Attendants* (26r)
Folio, 4½ x 10¼ in (11.4 x 26.0 cm)
Illustration, 4½ x 5½ in (11.4 x 14.0 cm)
Purchased with funds provided by Dorothy and Richard M. Sherwood
M.89.120.2

The sizes of the illustrations vary on the three leaves, and marginal decorations are included on both sides. These patterns as well as the style of writing indicate a Gujarati origin for the manuscript. The figural forms, however, are quite distinct from those in the dated Gujarati manuscripts of this period, which are far more loosely and freely drawn (cf. Chandra and Shah 1975, pp. 63–69, figs. 41–52, pls. VIII–X). Also, the attire is less sumptuously rendered and the coloring less intense. The coloring in these illustrations is also less varied than that seen in the other leaf from another *Samgrahanisutra* manuscript in the collection [33]. Missing are the pinks, the mauve, and the light blue. Instead, this artist preferred to use silvery gray and magenta rather liberally. He was also fonder of flowers and arabesques, which he employed freely to enliven the red background.

A According to the *Samgrahanisutra,* those who commit suicide by various methods but with good intention are reborn in the heaven known as Vyantara devaloka. In the first panel of the upper register a man is about to be hanged. In the next panel a man is taking poison. The third panel shows a man drowning in a water tank, which has aquatic birds on top. In the fourth panel a man is burning himself alive. The subject of the first panel in the lower register remains unidentified. Next is the representation of a four-armed god, followed by that of a wandering ascetic known as a *charaka-parivrajaka.* He can be identified by the waterpot and the staff on either side. The last panel shows a conventional representation of the sun.

Noteworthy are the arabesquelike scrolling and the highly abstract treatment of the trees. The water in the tank below the drowning man's arms is blue, and the fire is painted in red and green.

B It seems the artist did not want to leave out any of the animated creatures in the world while representing various fauna as auspicious symbols. In addition to the conventional pair of fish, there are a peacock, a parrot, and a gander representing the avian realm; a mythical lion-cum-makara, an elephant, a horse, and a bull symbolizing the animal world; two reptiles, a snake and an iguana or alligator; and three human beings.

C This composition is a typical representation of a god, obviously modeled after an indolent mortal ruler. The handsome, youthful figure, well attired and ornamented, is stretched out on a couch and is attended by four women, who approach him with garlands. This illustration's purple, gray, red, white, black, yellow, and green show the full range of the artist's palette.

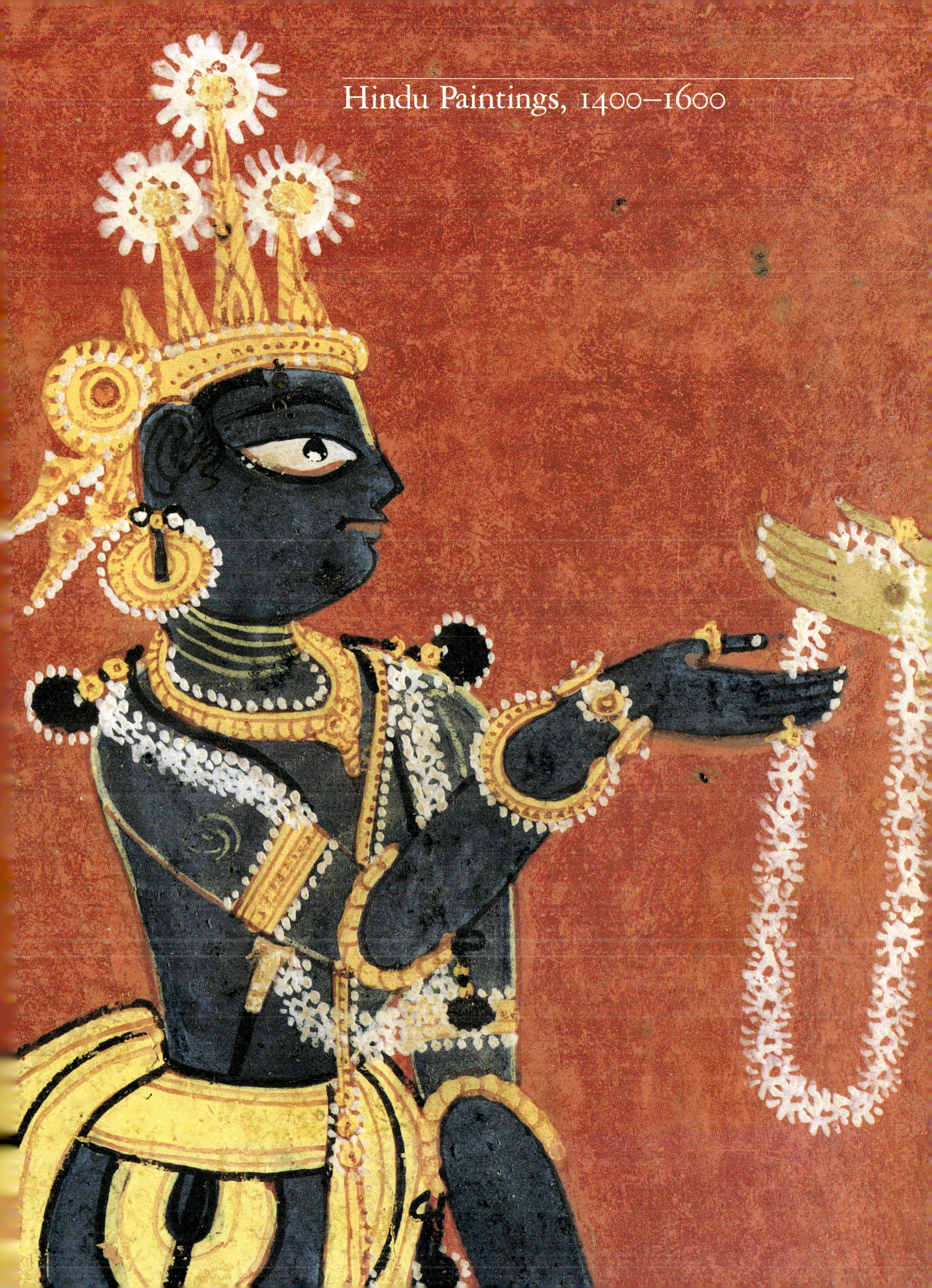

Hindu Paintings, 1400–1600

When the palace was ready the painter approached the ruler, obtained the five basic colours from him and started to work. After invoking Gaṇapati he held the brush in correct position {and} then painted the figure of Sarasvatī, the meeting and separation of Nala and Damayantī, scenes from the Rāmāyaṇa *and* Mahābhārata *and also hunting scenes. . . . The reputation of this art gallery spread.*[1]

Introduction

The epigraph from the *Chiltai-Varta* (Story of Chiltai), a fifteenth-century romance, provides a brief but interesting account of an art gallery in a Hindu palace. Although no murals of the period have survived, other literary references as well as wall paintings in later palaces amply confirm this evidence. As in earlier ages, most Hindus preferred religious themes not only for their temples but also for decorating their palaces. This is also true of the books that were written and illustrated for Hindu patrons in this period.

Compared with the Buddhist and Jain paintings in the collection, pictures from the pre-Mughal period depicting Hindu subject matter constitute a modest group. They are all executed on paper and are detached folios from manuscripts or what may be termed "picture books."

All the illustrations belong to Vaishnava texts. A Vaishnava is a Hindu who believes in the supremacy of Vishnu or his emanation Krishna, one of the three aspects of the supreme being of the Hindus. The other two are Brahma, the creator, and Siva, the destroyer. Vishnu is considered to be the preserver. During the period when these manuscripts were copied and illustrated, the focus of Vaishnava devotionalism was Krishna. Texts describing his myths and legends became popular, and following the earlier Buddhist and the contemporary Jain practice, the Vaishnava too began to commission copies of these books, some with illustrations, for their personal use or for giving to brahmins to earn merit. Listening to recitations of texts such as the *Bhagavatapurana,* one of the most important Vaishnava religious works, or the more ancient epics such as the *Mahabharata* and *Ramayana* became an essential feature in the life of a pious Vaishnava. The *Bhagavatapurana* is an encyclopedic text, and the section that seems to have been particularly selected for illustration is the tenth book, which recounts the myths and legends of Krishna.

Two other Vaishnava works are the *Balagopalastuti* (Eulogy of the child cowherder) and the *Gitagovinda* (Song of the cowherd god), poetical works praising Krishna. As the title suggests, the former eulogizes the child Krishna; the latter is an ecstatic lyrical composition extolling the mythical love of Krishna and Radha. The author of the *Balagopalastuti* was Bilvamangala, who may have lived in the Malabar region of the southwestern coast of the subcontinent between 1250 and 1350. The *Gitagovinda* was composed by the poet Jayadeva, who is considered to have been the court poet of King Lakshmanasena of Gaur (West Bengal; r. c. 1180–1200/2). Although the *Gitagovinda* was composed as a love poem, it has attained the status of a religious devotional work and is sung daily in the famous temple of Jagannatha (= Krishna) in Puri (Orissa).

The other literary compositions that will be mentioned in this brief introduction are the *Vasantavilasa* and *Chaurapanchasika,* both of which are love poems. Unlike the *Gitagovinda,* however, they retained their strictly secular character. Such literary compositions could have been appreciated by either Hindu or Jain patrons. Other illustrated books concerned with secular themes, such as music (*Ragamala*), have also survived from the period, and very likely texts dealing with rhetorical subjects were illustrated as well. Hindu palaces were adorned profusely with murals, most of which no longer exist. In any event, in the style of painting there was no distinction between the sacred and the secular.

Hindu manuscripts copied in Gujarat and Rajasthan generally followed both the format and the style of the Jain illustrated manuscripts (e.g., [35]). However, Hindu books occur in at least two other formats that are quite different from Jain books. In one of these the text is usually placed along the top of the page in a narrow band and the rest is given over to the illustration. Clearly this arrangement derives neither from the Jain or the Buddhist manuscript tradition nor from the Islamic book. Nothing is known about when and where this type of illustrated book was invented. The earliest example is the 1451 *Vasantavilasa* (Manifestation of spring) now in the Freer Gallery of Art in Washington, D.C. (FIG. 10, page 26). There are important differences, however, in that this work is on cloth and the text and illustrations are presented continuously as a scroll rather than on loose folios. Nevertheless, the relationship between the panel of text and the illustration is similar to that seen in the *Gitagovinda* in the collection [38]. While no surviving illustrated Hindu book on paper is contemporaneous with the Freer *Vasantavilasa* (a rare example of secular painting from pre-Mughal India), by the sixteenth century illustrated books in this format seem to have become popular among the Hindus. Among the better known examples are a *Gitagovinda* in the Prince of Wales Museum, Bombay, and a *Chaurapanchasika* in the Lalbhai Dalpatbai Institute Museum, Ahmedabad.[2] This mode may have been favored for works where the text is in short verses, which made it possible to accommodate the relevant text and picture on the same page.

The other type of illustrated manuscript that became popular, also in the sixteenth century, is exemplified in the collection by the four folios from a manuscript of the *Bhagavatapurana* [36]. Here the text and the illustration are separated completely, the former being accommodated on the verso and the latter on the recto. Moreover, the shape and size of these folios are quite different from those in the earlier Jain manuscripts as well as the other contemporary Hindu illustrated books [35, 38]. Not only is the folio larger, it is more or less square in shape. Clearly, the patrons of such manuscripts deemed the pictures no less important than the text and perhaps even more so. The Sanskrit term *kalapustaka,* "picture book," probably refers to such books. This type of arrangement appears to have been preferred for narrative works where the text for the incident illustrated can run into several verses. No doubt this is why the text and the pictures were presented back-to-back: the text did not intrude upon the picture, which allowed the artist greater freedom to organize his compositions.

In a second *Bhagavatapurana* series [37] there is no text at all on the verso, and captions or labels have been added above the picture for simple identification. Once again it is uncertain where and when this type of picture book originated. It is unlikely to have been done where the Jain tradition was strong, such as Gujarat or the contiguous areas of Rajasthan. The format of the books, the style of writing, and the pictorial modes differ greatly from Jain illustrated manuscripts. This seems to indicate that these manuscripts were prepared for Hindu patrons somewhere in a wide area stretching from the Panjab to Bihar, including the northern parts of Rajasthan. The uncertainty of their provenance is evident from the fact that scholars are divided as to whether the earlier *Bhagavatapurana* was prepared in Rajasthan or Uttar Pradesh. As to the time, no picture book of this type has so far surfaced that can be dated earlier than the sixteenth century. It should be noted that the idea of separating the picture and the text on different pages and giving greater prominence to the picture is characteristic of the Mughal *Hamzanama* (c. 1570) and later books.

The earliest example of a Hindu painting in the collection, probably from Gujarat or Rajasthan and belonging to the mid-fifteenth century, is a folio from a *Balagopalastuti* [35]. The picture is painted in a style not unrelated to Jain manuscript illuminations but is less formulaic. There is greater freedom both in the composition and the disposition of the figures. Even though perfunctory, some attempts have been made to represent a landscape with trees in the background and a cloud-laden sky above. These details or elements are stylistically akin to the Freer *Vasantavilasa,* but the execution is less accomplished. While many characteristics are similar to Jain manuscript illuminations, the representation generally is more spontaneous and spirited.

The earlier of the two *Bhagavatapurana* series in the collection [36] is generally regarded as one of the most important documents of Indian painting of the pre-Mughal period. The pictures are typical of a style that has come to be characterized as "Chaurapanchasika" following the name of the richly illustrated sixteenth-century manuscript of this poetical work now in Ahmedabad. Although there is no agreement about either its provenance or its date, most scholars believe that the *Bhagavatapurana* series was painted sometime in the first half of the sixteenth century, more precisely around 1540.

Since 1969 K. Khandalavala has consistently asserted that the *Bhagavatapurana* pictures in particular and the Chaurapanchasika style in general cannot be dated earlier than 1556, the date Akbar ascended the throne, because of the cut of a shirt worn by some of the figures in these paintings. According to Khandalavala this particular type of tunic, the *chākdār jāmā,* with four or six pointed ends, was invented in Akbar's court.[3] Most scholars, however, disagree with this view.[4] It must be stressed that except for early Mughal paintings, this type of *jama* with extended points occurs only in some of the Chaurapanchasika-style pictures and in a solitary portrait painted around 1575 in Ahmadnagar in the Deccan.[5] Unfortunately none of these pictures is dated, and the garment does not appear in any of the dated manuscripts of the late fifteenth or early sixteenth century.

This sartorial issue aside, as it cannot be satisfactorily resolved in the present state of knowledge, all stylistic characteristics indicate a date in the first half of the sixteenth century for the earlier of the museum's *Bhagavatapurana* series. If indeed it was painted, as Khandalavala believes, as late as 1570 at Palam (where the Delhi airport is now located), then it is difficult to explain the complete absence of Mughal influence other than the adoption of a shirt design, if indeed that was invented at Akbar's court. In fact, the particular turban worn by some of the men in this series, known by the term *kulahdar,* is pre-Mughal and was popular in the Lodi kingdom. Thus it seems strange that an artist painting this series at Palam around 1570 would adopt the design of a shirt from the contemporary court at Agra but retain an earlier form of turban and yet exhibit little or no awareness of the dramatic innovations of the newly formed pictorial tradition. In fact, the Isarda *Bhagavatapurana* [37] is dated somewhat later precisely because some of its pictures show some Mughal stylistic elements.

Another enigmatic feature of the museum's earlier *Bhagavatapurana* series [36] is the inclusion of one of two names, either Nana or Mitharam, on top of the majority of the pictures. Both names are preceded by the syllable *sa.* On several of the paintings a third name, Hira or Hirabai, which is that of a woman, is added in a different and cursive writing, probably at a later date. There are two schools of thought on the significance of these names, particularly the names Nana and Mitharam. One school believes them to be those of two artists responsible for the paintings. However, there are no other instances known of artists' names being attached to their work in pre-Mughal India, either by them or posthumously; awareness of the name and personality of an artist is first encountered at the Mughal court. The other school of thought holds that the names belong to two different owners of the series, perhaps two brothers between whom the manuscript was divided upon inheritance. Such a division of possessions in an Indian joint family is not uncommon, even though no other evidence of it has survived on paintings.

A clue that may help solve the mystery of both names is the syllable *sa,* which seems to have received little attention from scholars. So far the prefix *sa* has been interpreted as having a possessive connotation. However, the same prefix occurs clearly as an abbreviation of an honorific or descriptive term in an earlier Jain manuscript illumination in the collection [10]. In the context of Jain painting, the prefix *sa* is very likely an abbreviation of the word *sarthavaha* or *sahu,* meaning "merchant." This would throw doubts on the theory that Nana and Mitharam are names of painters and would strengthen the alternative opinion that they were joint owners of the series. It does not, however, necessarily mean that they were the patrons who commissioned it. They could have been later owners. Similarly, Hirabai may have been a still later owner of some of the paintings. Even though the series may have been divided, it apparently remained in one family until the middle of this century, when it was dispersed.

So far as is known, the series consists of more than two hundred pictures, and very likely more than one artist was involved. Given the frequency of the practice in India, the series may well have been painted by a family of artists. Khandalavala feels strongly that it could not have been executed in Rajasthan, specifically Mewar, as suggested by some, because the Rajputs hated the Lodis and would never have adopted the Muslim *kulahdar* turban for divine figures in a Hindu religious text.[6] This seems an even less persuasive argument than the matter of the shirt. In any event, he firmly attributes the series to Palam on the strength of an inscription that he noted on one of the now-lost folios stating *sa Mitharam Palam nagar madhye,* "*sa* Mitharam in the city of Palam." Even if such an inscription were present, all it proves is that Mitharam, probably one of the owners, lived in Palam, where the series could have been brought from somewhere else. While Palam is not an improbable provenance, the claim for Rajasthan or Uttar Pradesh cannot be entirely dismissed.

Judging from differences in their compositions and dramatic expressiveness, the four pictures in the collection may have been painted by at least two different hands. *Krishna Uproots the Parijata Tree* [36C] is so much more sophisticated and elegantly rendered than the other three pictures that one must consider the likelihood that at least two, if not more, artists worked on this profusely illustrated manuscript. All scholars agree that the pictures are rendered in the same basic style as a 1516 *Aranyakaparvan* (a section of the *Mahabharata*) prepared at Kacchauva (Uttar Pradesh) and a 1540 *Mahapurana* (a Jain text) manuscript rendered in Palam.[7] However, the *Bhagavatapurana* pictures are much more vivacious and more refined technically than either of the two dated manuscripts. Other stylistically similar manuscripts are the Bombay *Gitagovinda,* the Ahmedabad *Chaurapanchasika,* and the Isarda *Bhagavatapurana* [37], none of which is dated.[8] Although there are differences in quality and vitality among these paintings, they are all rendered in a basically uniform style that is distinctly different from the austere and rigid Jain-manuscript style of western India. Among major differences between the Jain and the Chaurapanchasika styles are more complex compositions, livelier figural forms, more naturalistic interaction among the figures, the strict profile representation of the face, and the omission of the protruding further eye.

J. P. Losty has given a coherent account of the development of this style and its relation to earlier paintings.[9] He has also demonstrated that the device of the protruding eye was dropped as early as 1499, which is one reason why he dates the earlier of the museum's *Bhagavatapurana* series [36] to around 1500. This, however, may be too early a date for the pictures. What does seem certain is that both the museum's *Bhagavatapurana*s are pictorially much more sophisticated and complex than either the 1516 *Aranyakaparvan* or the 1540 *Mahapurana,* a difference that could be attributed to the varied capabilities of the artists as well as to the tastes of the patrons. Moreover, the *Bhagavatapurana*s are essentially picture books in which the illustrations exist somewhat independently of the text; in the *Aranyakaparvan* and the *Mahapurana* the texts retain their primacy despite the profusion of illustrations. The Chaurapanchasika-style picture books are derived from the 1451 *Vasantavilasa* type of book, the earliest surviving secular work of the pre-Mughal period in which the pictures are clearly more prominent than the text. Until more firmly dated examples of the Chaurapanchasika style emerge, it may be safer to date the style closer to 1550 than 1500.

By 1570, when manuscripts were being prepared for the imperial Mughal atelier, some of the artists recruited for the court were, in fact, painting in this vibrant, unpretentious, and lyrical style that was preferred by Hindu patrons. As is evident from the museum's folio from a *Gitagovinda* manuscript of the 1580s [38], many Hindus continued to prefer this style even after the Mughal style had flourished for several decades.

What does seem clear from the available evidence is that western Indian paintings rendered for the Hindus generally were painted in the same style as that encountered in Jain works. In the central part of the country, particularly in Uttar Pradesh, including the Delhi region, and the northern part of Madhya Pradesh, two versions of the same style were familiar. The 1516 *Aranyakaparvan* and the 1540 *Mahapurana* represent a naïve folk version of the style, while the *Bhagavatapurana* and other similar manuscripts were painted in a more elegant and sophisticated manner in which the artists attempt to express themselves in pictorial rather than illustrative terms. Neither mode, however, reveals much influence of the Islamic or early Mughal traditions.

NOTES

1. Khandalavala & Chandra 1969, p. 8.

2. See Khandalavala & Chandra 1969 for a discussion of these two and other examples of Hindu book illustrations of the Sultanate period; see also Losty 1982.

3. Khandalavala & Chandra 1969, pp. 75–78; and Khandalavala 1987, p. 92.

4. See Losty 1982, pp. 48–53, for an extensive discussion of the *Chaurapanchasika* in the context of the Chaurapanchasika group. B. N. Goswamy (1988, p. 22, no. 32) dates the series to the mid-sixteenth century.

5. Zebrowski 1983, pl. II.

6. Khandalavala 1987, p. 91.

7. For the *Aranyakaparvan,* see Khandalavala & Chandra 1974; for an extensive discussion of the *Mahapurana,* see Khandalavala & Chandra 1969. See Losty 1982 for both.

8. These also are thoroughly discussed in the three publications cited in the previous note.

9. Losty 1982.

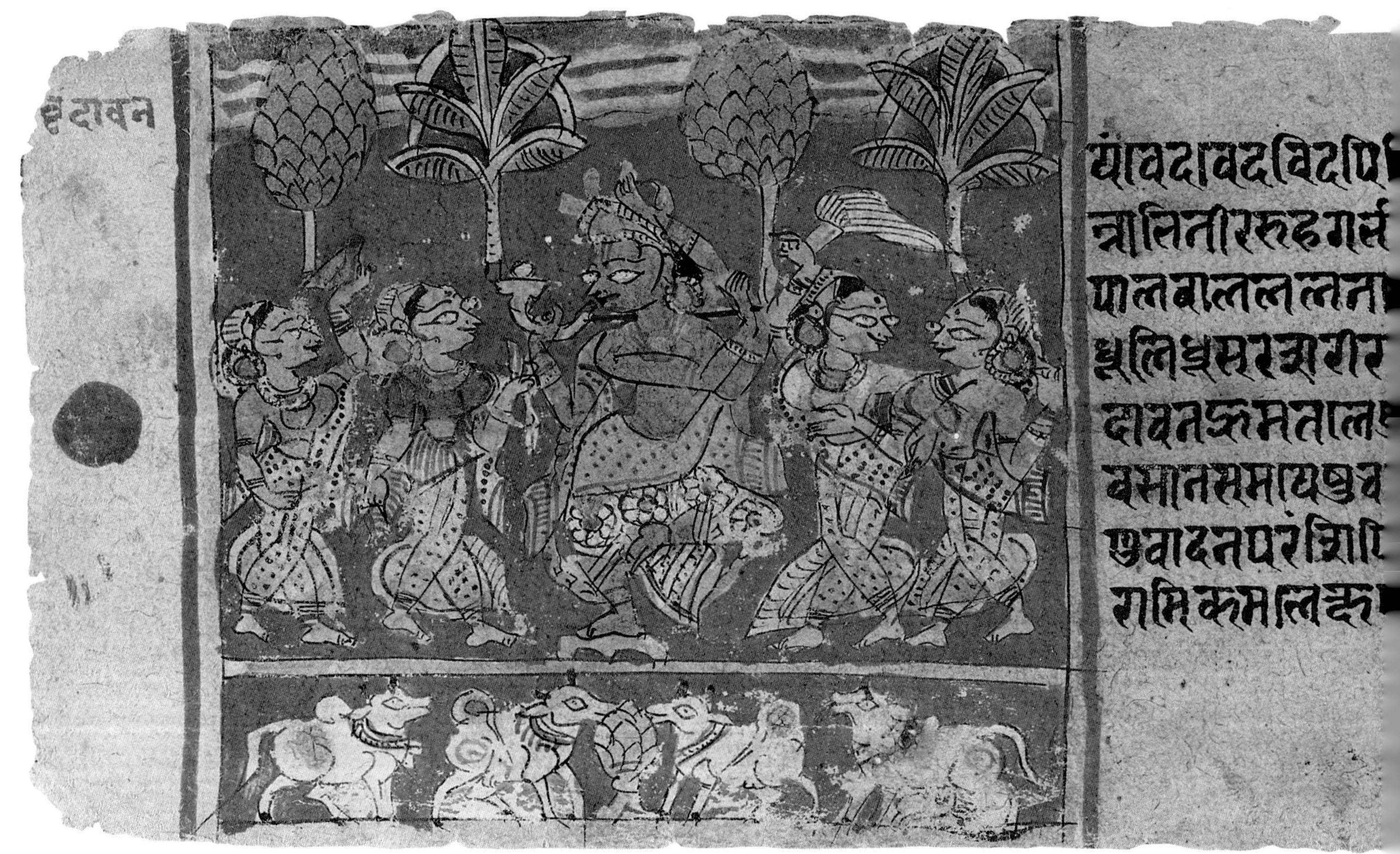

Catalogue

Unless otherwise noted, all texts are written in ink and all pictures painted in opaque watercolor on paper.

35 FOLIO FROM A *BALAGOPALASTUTI* MANUSCRIPT: KRISHNA DANCING WITH GOPIS IN VRINDAVAN

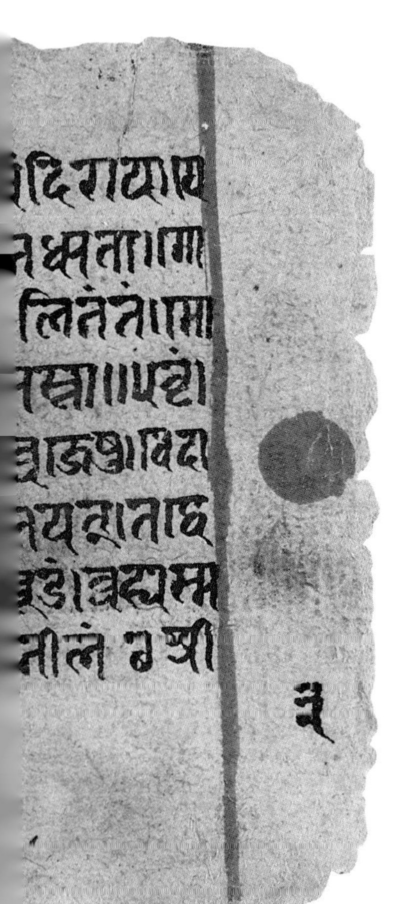

Gujarat or Rajasthan; c. 1450
Opaque watercolor and ink with touches of gold and silver on paper
Folio, 4⅛ x 9⅛ in (10.5 x 23.2 cm)
Illustration, 4⅛ x 4¼ in (10.5 x 10.8 cm)
Purchased with funds provided by Lizabeth Scott
M.88.49

The *Balagopalastuti* (Eulogy of the child cowherder [Gopala Krishna]) is a Vaishnava devotional text composed by a poet named Bilvamangala. Very little is known about the poet except that he was an ardent devotee of Krishna and wrote several other poetical works in praise of the god. Very likely he lived in the thirteenth century somewhere on the western coast of India, perhaps in the Malabar region.

An incomplete but richly illustrated manuscript of the *Balagopalastuti* in the Museum of Fine Arts, Boston, has been discussed extensively by W. N. Brown (1930). Although the style of the illustration on this page is very similar to that of the Boston manuscript, the mode of writing is somewhat different. Moreover, the scene depicted on this page is identified by a caption in the margin; no such caption occurs beside any of the forty illustrations in the Boston manuscript. Thus, this folio (numbered 3) is from a different manuscript, which, however, must have been written and illustrated at about the same time and in the same general region as the Boston example. Most scholars concur that the Boston manuscript was copied and illustrated somewhere in Gujarat or western Rajasthan about 1450.

The caption in the left margin states that the dance illustrated here takes place in Vrindavan, near Mathura. Vrindavan is where Krishna was brought up in the family of a cowherd. The youthful god is portrayed here as a gray-blue figure with four arms, thereby clearly establishing his divine status. Two of his hands hold a stick, perhaps representing a flute, behind his neck. The second right hand holds a horn, while the fourth arm is raised above his head in a dancing gesture. Of the four *gopis* (cowherdesses) flanking him, one holds up a pot or dish and another swings a flywhisk. In the lower panel are four cows. The background is uniformly red except for the sky, indicated by a narrow gray band that is followed by alternating, uneven bands of white and purple. Purple is used also for nimbuses provided for the two banana trees, but the other two trees pierce the sky directly. The ladies all have yellow complexions and wear identical saris and scarfs, but their blouses are of different hues. Although the depiction is flat and the composition simple, the freely drawn figures are remarkably animated. Especially noteworthy are the *gopis*, whose postures are made more lively by the elegant swirling of their garments around their legs.

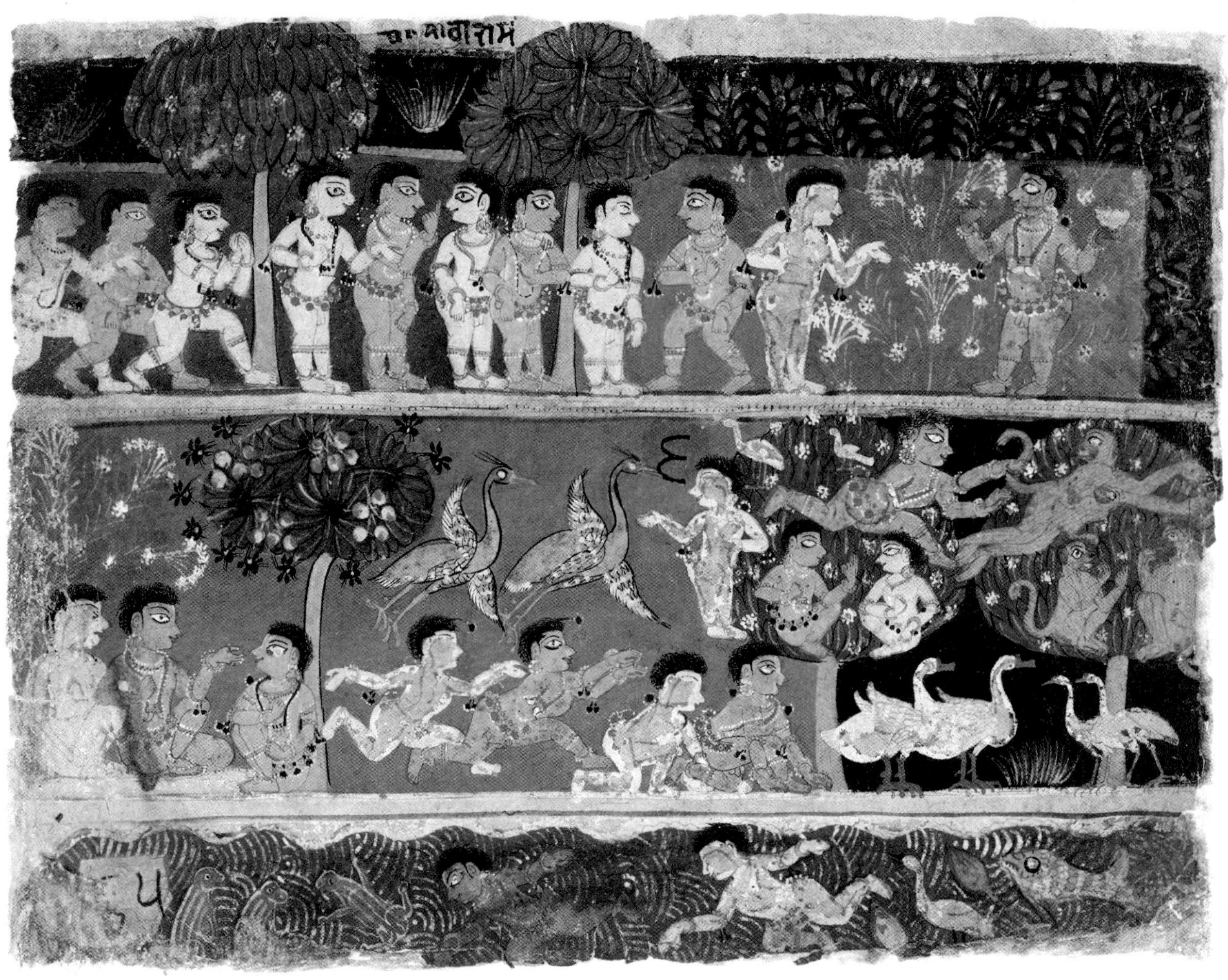

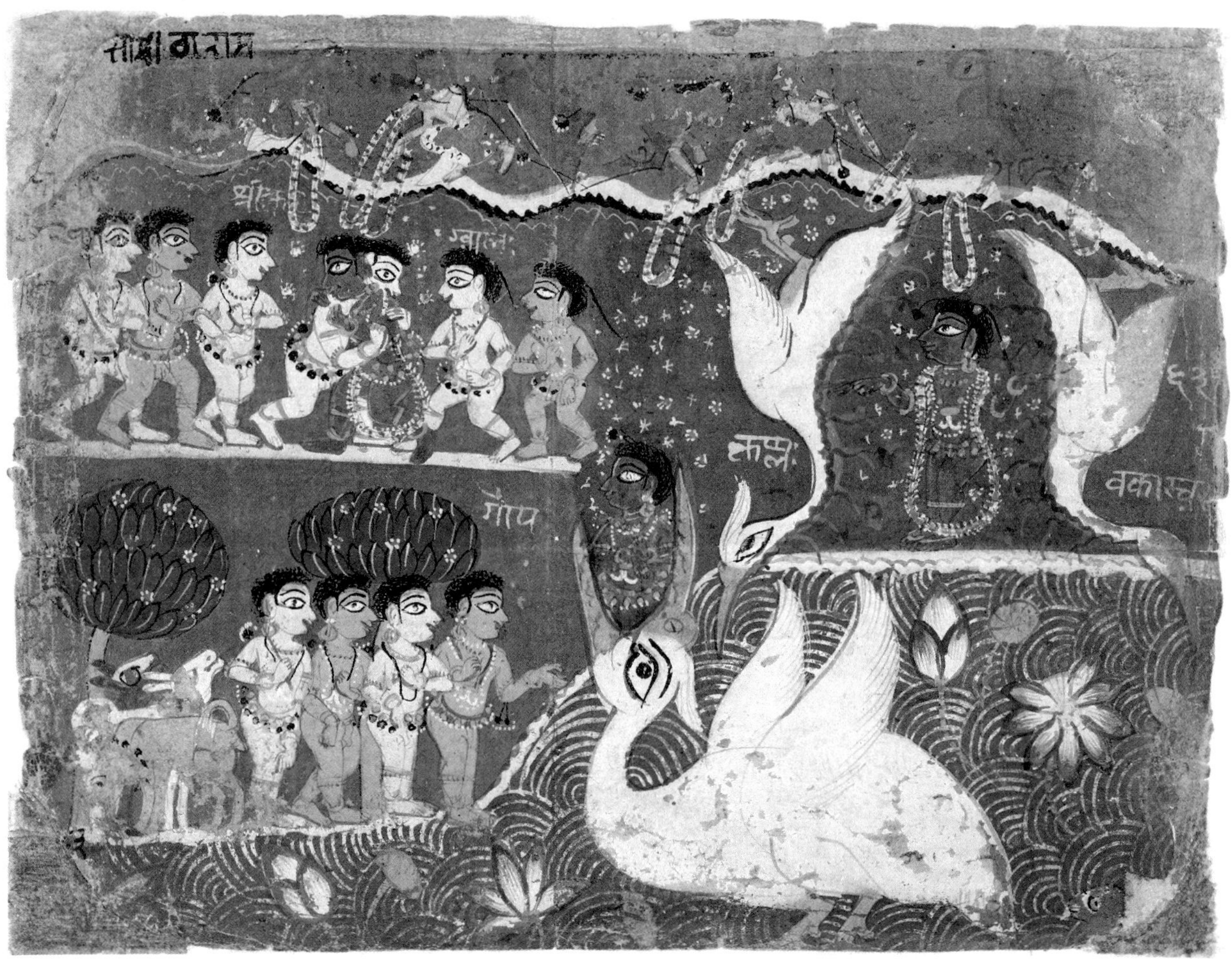

Northern India; 1525–50
Folios, approx. 7¼ x 9½ in (18.4 x 24.1 cm)
Illustrations, approx. 7 x 9½ in (17.8 x 24.1 cm)
A–C, From the Nasli and Alice Heeramaneck Collection, Museum Associates Purchase;
D, Gift of Cynthia Hazen Polsky
A, M.71.1.9; B, M.71.1.8; C, M.72.1.26;
D, M.91.69
Literature: A–C, *Heeramaneck* 1966, p. 122, no. 146 (B only illustrated); Sanford 1970, pp. 42–43, pl. 1 (C only); Trabold 1975, pp. 29–30, no. 36 (C only).

A *Krishna and Balarama Play with Gopas; text on verso*
B *Krishna Kills the Crane Demon*
C *Krishna Uproots the Parijata Tree*
D *Brahma Salutes Krishna*

These four folios are from a very large, dispersed manuscript of the tenth book of the *Bhagavatapurana*. On each folio the Sanskrit text is written on one side and a painting is on the other. In the case of A, B, and D the complete text is provided; C has only one line of text. Only on B is there a legible chapter number and the title. The chapter number on D is indistinct. The following short inscriptions occur at the top or bottom of the paintings: (A) *sa mitharam;* (B) *sa mitharam* as well as identifying labels for some of the figures and the number *63*; (C) *sa nana* followed by *hira* and in the lower left-hand corner the number *136; (D) mitharam(?)* on top and *hirabai* at the bottom.

A This painting is divided into three horizontal registers. Along the top the white Balarama and the blue Krishna are shown frolicking with a group of other *gopa*s (cowherds) who are given either yellow or pink complexions. On the far right of the top register Krishna and Balarama are plucking flowers. In the middle register they chase birds and monkeys on trees; the ripe fruit of the mango tree on the left has attracted a swarm of black bees. In the bottom register the two swim in the water along with a fish. A crane and some monkeys, seemingly under water, are probably on shore but the ground plane does not show.

B This picture illustrates the destruction of the crane demon, one of the many heroic feats of the child Krishna. The story begins in the lower register, where Krishna is being swallowed by the giant crane while the other boys, along with their cows, watch helplessly. The narrative continues above, where Krishna is first shown emerging from the stomach of the bird after splitting it in half and then being congratulated by his companions. Balarama and Krishna enthusiastically embrace while angels from the sky above shower garlands over the hero.

C Here Krishna is an adult, and the incident depicted is one of the most significant among the Krishna myths. It tells the story of the conflict between the god Indra and Krishna. Egged on by Satyabhama, his favorite wife, Krishna goes to Indra's heaven and brings back the *parijata* tree, which is obviously the heavenly Tree of Wisdom or of Life as well as the wish-fulfilling tree. The myth may further disguise the hostility between the growing cult of Krishna and that of the more ancient Vedic form of religion in which Indra is a leading divinity. In the picture a celestial who cannot be identified is seated on the left in a pavilion that is crowned with Siva's trident. In the pavilion on the right Indra, distinguished by the multiple eyes on his body and holding a lotus, is seen greeting Krishna. In the middle Krishna first uproots the tree and then is carried by Garuda along with Satyabhama, the troublemaker. Curiously, Garuda carries two trees instead of one. Moreover, by having them ride Garuda and by providing Krishna with four arms and the emblems of the conch shell, wheel, and club, the artist is clearly identifying him with Vishnu.

D This picture seems to be divided into two portions. The upper one consists of two registers separated by a white wavy line denoting the horizon. Above, against a light blue sky, are several celestial females with garlands and two drummers. The scene below represents Vrindavan, where Krishna and Balarama tend to their herd and a pair of deer move away in the panel on the far right. The next two registers are divided into eight panels by lines or changes in the background color. In five of them a four-armed Krishna/Vasudeva is being greeted by the four-headed god Brahma and his spouse. The other three panels are occupied by an empty shrine, a canopied bed with bolsters, and Brahma seated on his gander. Four different colors—green, blue-black, red, and yellow—have been used as background in the different panels, with red predominating.

The picture very likely illustrates Brahma's experience with the child Krishna after the latter destroyed the demon Aghasura. Earlier Brahma had made the cows in Krishna's herd disappear, but Krishna was aware of Brahma's trick. In order to impress Brahma, Krishna transformed every cowherd into another Krishna. Following the practice of continuous narration, Brahma is here shown saluting five Krishnas.

CAT. 36A
CAT. 36B

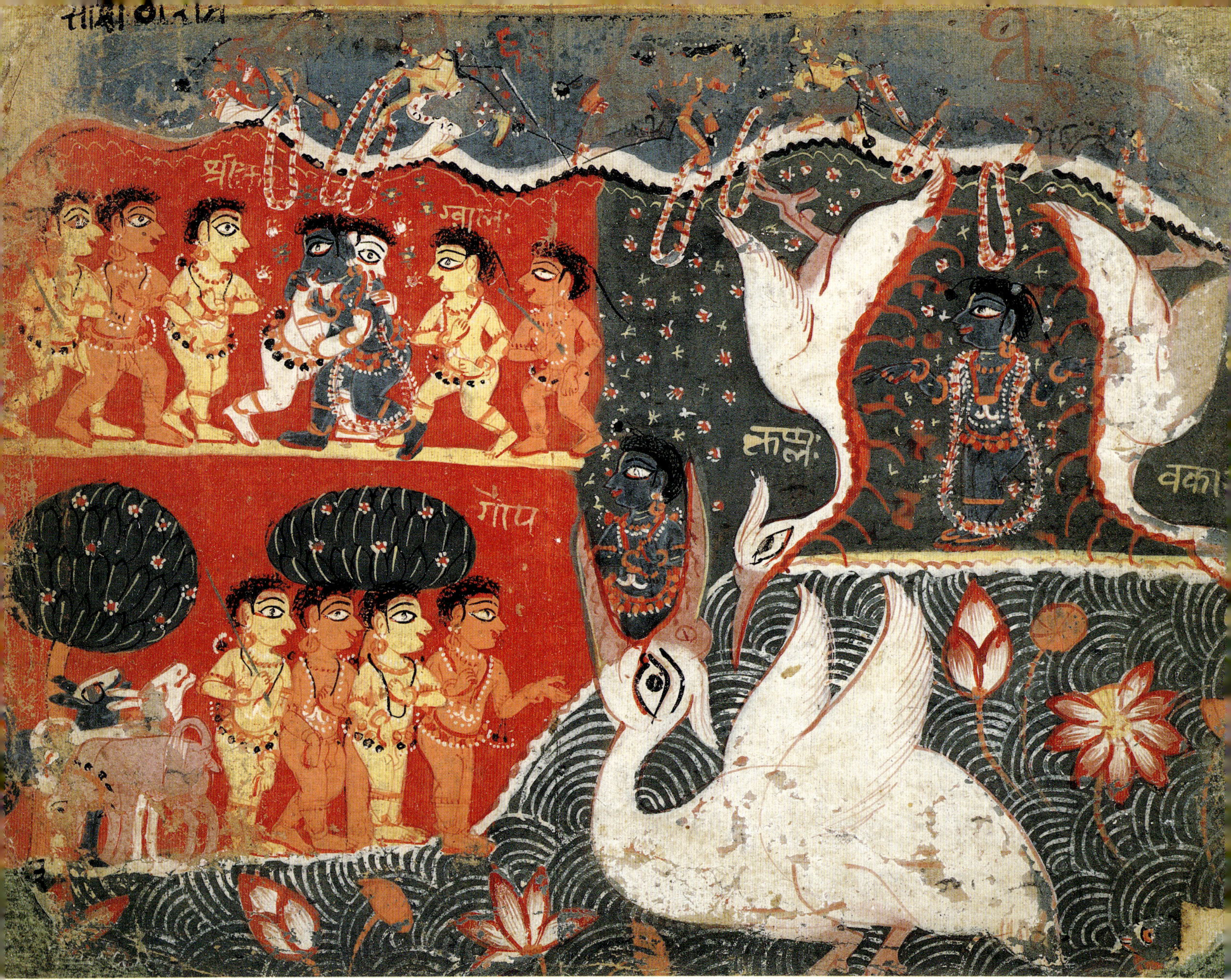

CAT. 36B detail *(top)*
CAT. 36B verso, detail *(bottom)*
CAT. 36C *(opposite top)*
CAT. 36D *(opposite bottom)*

A number of scholars have written eloquently about this series of pictures, admiring the animated compositions, the vigorous drawing, and the intense and warm coloring (even if dominated by blue and red). Although the figures conform to types, they are a vivacious group and act their roles with unaffected spontaneity. Even though the faces register no variations in feeling, the scenes are charged with appropriate emotions through lively postures and gestures as well as the interactions of the actors, thereby emphasizing the drama of the occasion. Especially engaging are the animals, which express the tender and joyous atmosphere of the idyllic world of Vrindavan with gentle eloquence.

While A and B represent incidents from Krishna's childhood in Vrindavan, in C and D we encounter the adult hero. The mood expressed in A and B is clearly that of a pastoral setting. In C and D we encounter both figural and architectural forms more typical of the Chaurapanchasika style. Of the four pictures, the representation in C is unquestionably the most sophisticated pictorially and may well be the work of a different artist than the one, or ones, responsible for the other three. The floral design below Garuda is reminiscent of a carpet with arabesques. Similar but simpler arabesquelike patterns are visible on the architectural elements in the picture, suggesting that the artist responsible may have been aware of Islamic works.

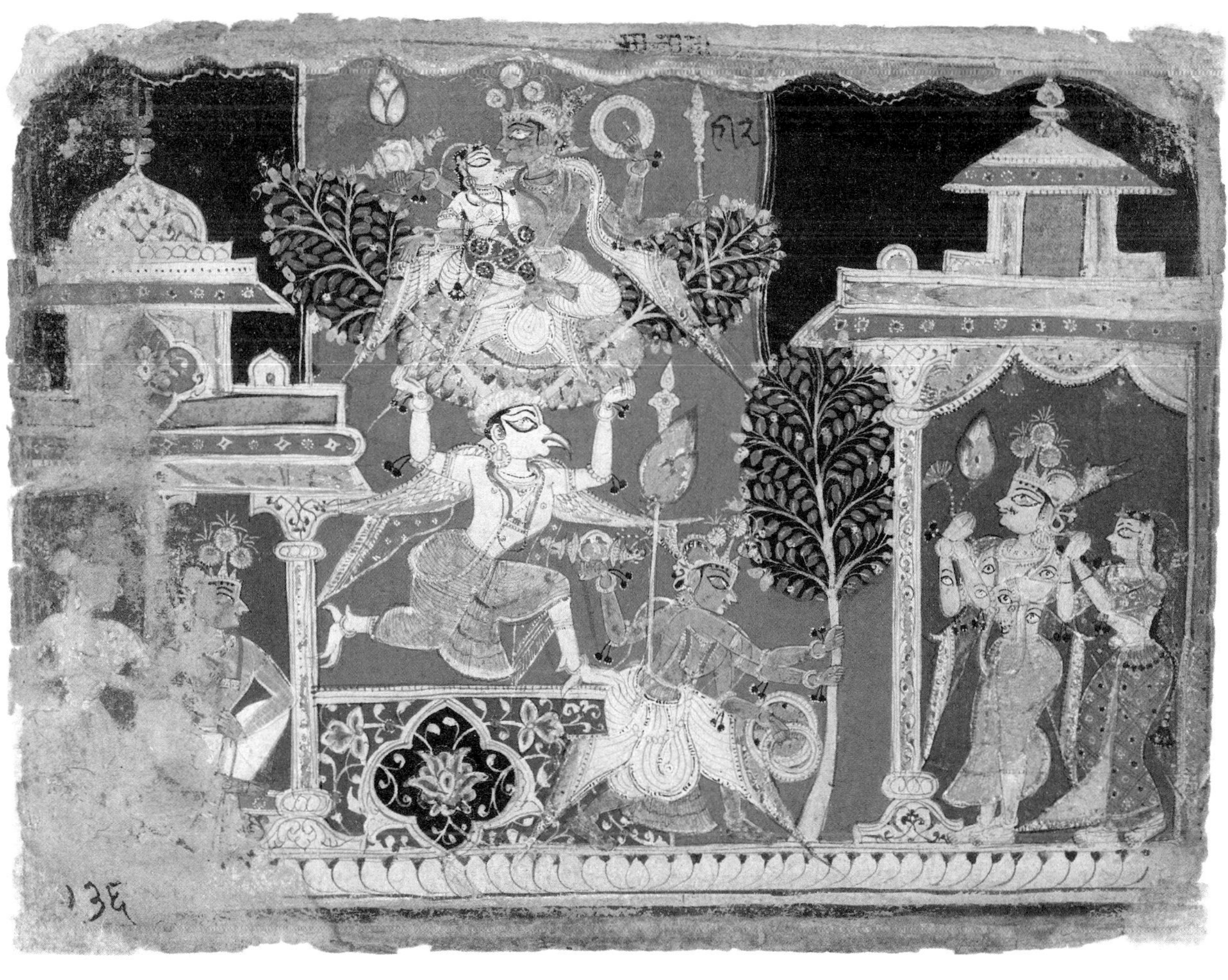

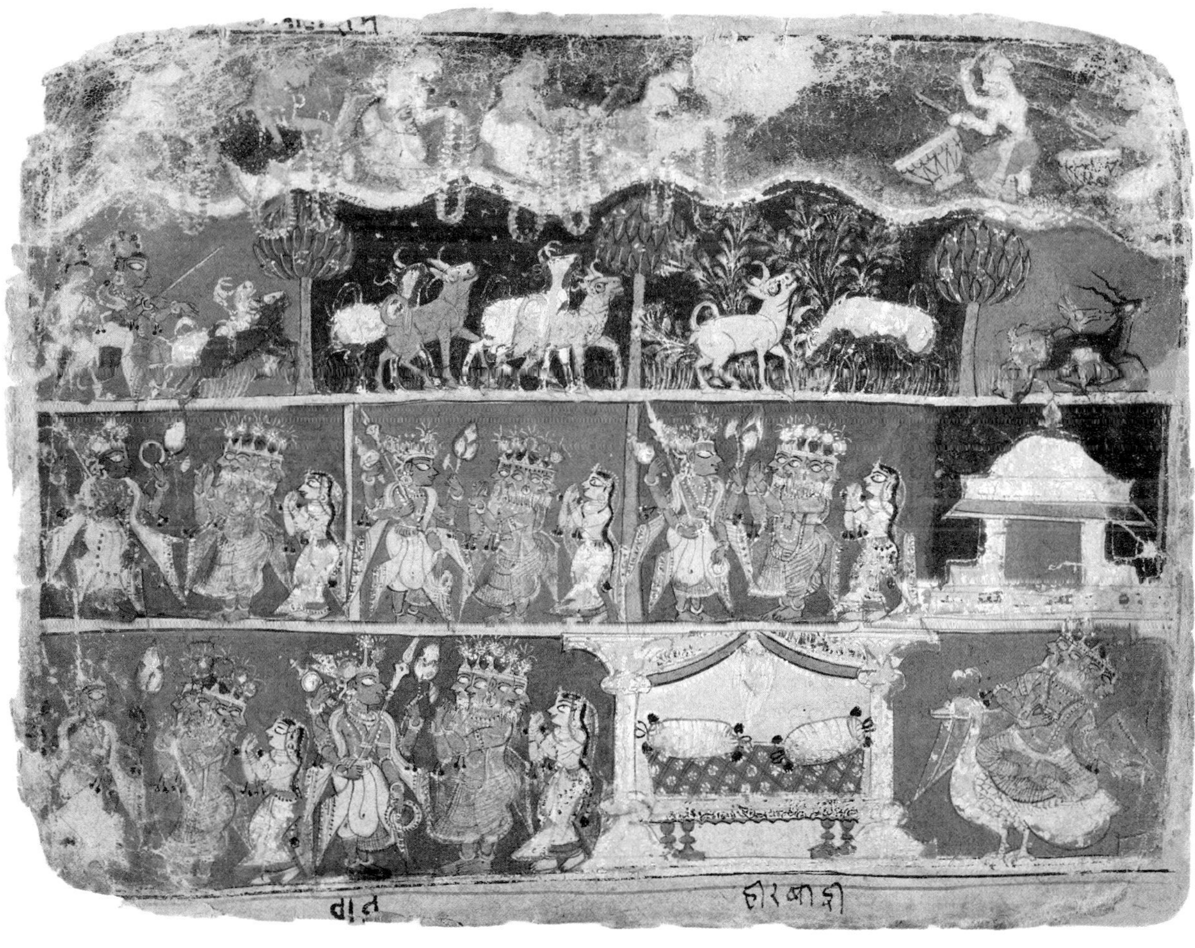

Northern India; 1550–75
Folio, $7\frac{3}{8}$ x $9\frac{7}{8}$ in (18.7 x 25.1 cm)
Illustration, $5\frac{3}{8}$ x 9 in (13.7 x 22.9 cm)
Gift of Paul F. Walter
M.83.219.3
Literature: Pal 1978, pp. 52–53, no. 3.

Because the manuscript from which this folio comes was found in Isarda in Rajasthan, it is generally referred to as the Isarda *Bhagavatapurana*. Unlike the folios from the earlier manuscript of the same text [36], there is no writing on the back of this folio, making this an album of pictures with captions rather than a manuscript proper. The inscriptions above the painting appear to be in three different hands, but all refer to the gardener Sudama, who is shown presenting a garland made of fragrant flowers to Krishna, immediately behind whom stands Balarama. The four other figures represent the cowherd companions of the two heroes.

While Sudama and the companions are represented against a blue-black background, the two divine figures—the blue-black Krishna and the white Balarama—are backed by a rectangular panel of red, which also serves as a sort of aureole. Krishna and Balarama are further distinguished by elaborate tiaras crowned with blossoms, while the others wear turbans. Noteworthy are the short dhotis, almost like loincloths, worn by the heroes and the *gopas*. The long, flaring ends and the loops of the sashlike garment are unusual. Sudama, however, wears a longer dhoti in the more conventional mode. The well-lit sky is indicated by thick white paint immediately above the horizon surmounted by a wider area tinted in purple.

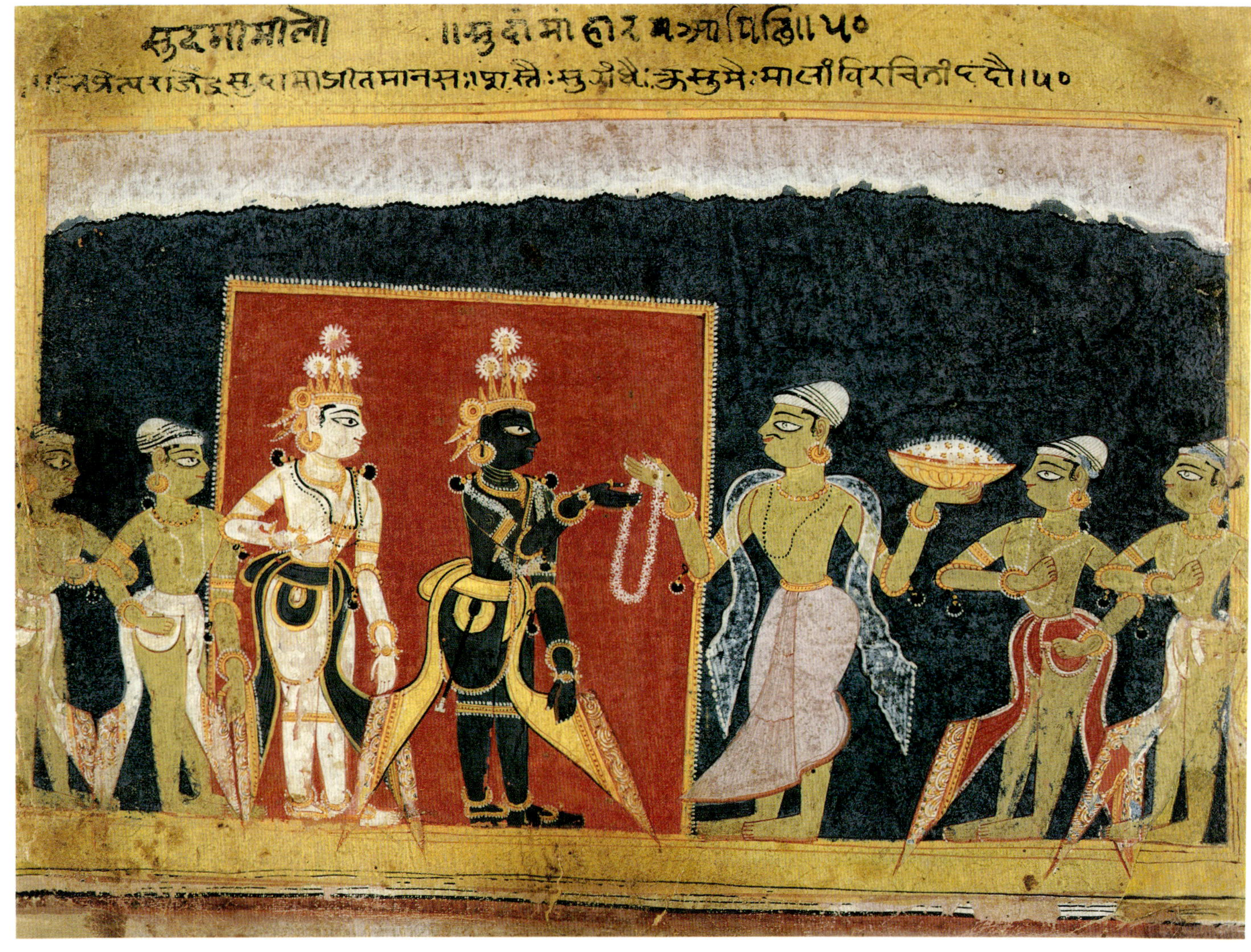

Although this picture is rendered in the same basic style as the earlier *Bhagavatapurana* [36], the Isarda series is considered to be later because of certain stylistic features that are said to show influences of the Mughal tradition as seen in the *Hamzanama* [46]. The impact of the Mughal style is marginal, however, and may only be reflected in the adoption of some minor motifs, more elaborate brushwork, and the lightly burnished surface of these paintings. The artists responsible show very little awareness of the more subtle pictorial elements that characterize even the earliest Mughal pictures. Their greater refinement notwithstanding, the Isarda *Bhagavatapurana* pictures are not quite as vivacious and artless as the earlier renderings of the subject.

38 FOLIO FROM A *GITAGOVINDA* MANUSCRIPT

Attributed to Govinda, fl. c. 1583
Gujarat; c. 1585
Folio, 4⅝ x 9¾ in (11.7 x 24.8 cm)
Illustrations, 4 x 8⅝ in (10.2 x 21.9 cm)
Gift of Mr. and Mrs. Ramesh Kapoor
M.88.225

A *Krishna and Gopis* (r)
B *Kamadeva Attacking Krishna* (v)

This folio from an illustrated *Gitagovinda* (Song of the cowherd god) manuscript is numbered 15. The two verses correspond to verses 33 and 34 of the first part of the poem, describing a joyful Krishna with the coming of spring in Vrindavan, the setting for the poem. The following translations of the verses are by B. S. Miller (1977, p. 75):

A

Budding mango trees tremble from the embrace of
rising vines.
Brindaban forest is washed by meandering Jumna
river waters.
When spring's mood is rich, Hari roams here
To dance with young women, friend—
A cruel time for deserted lovers.

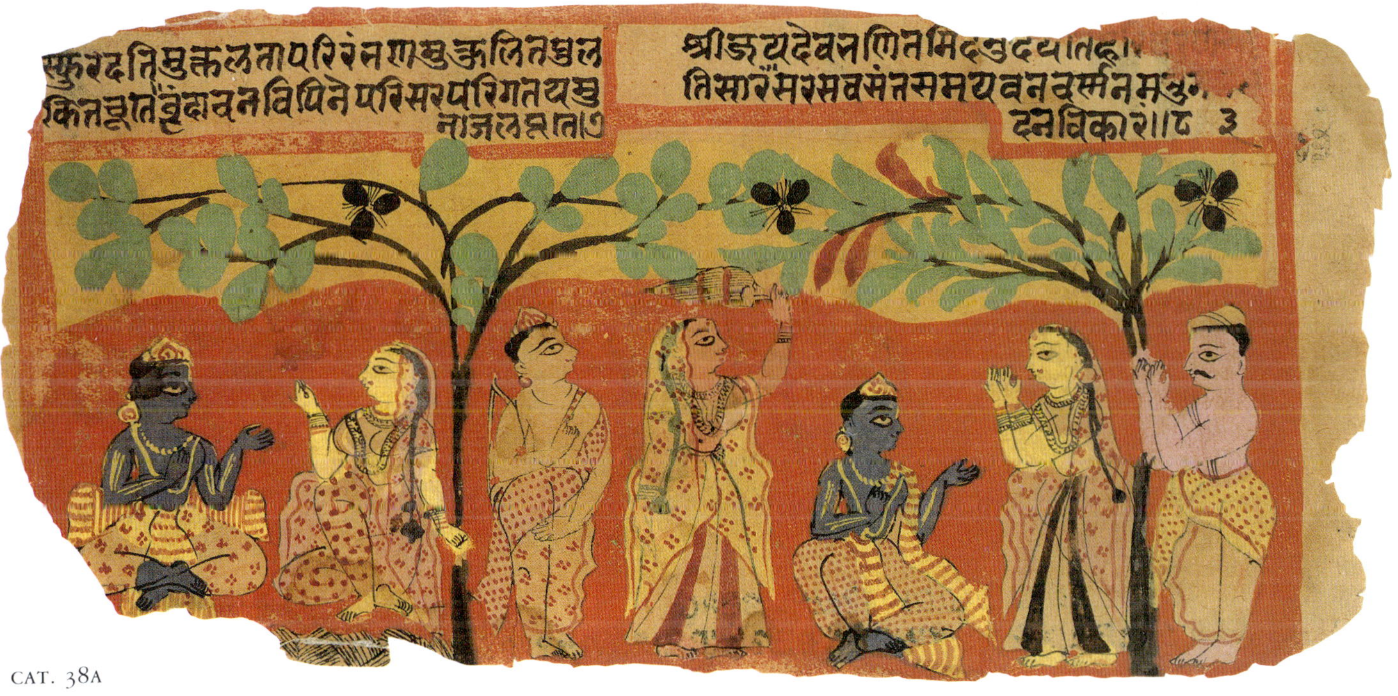

CAT. 38A

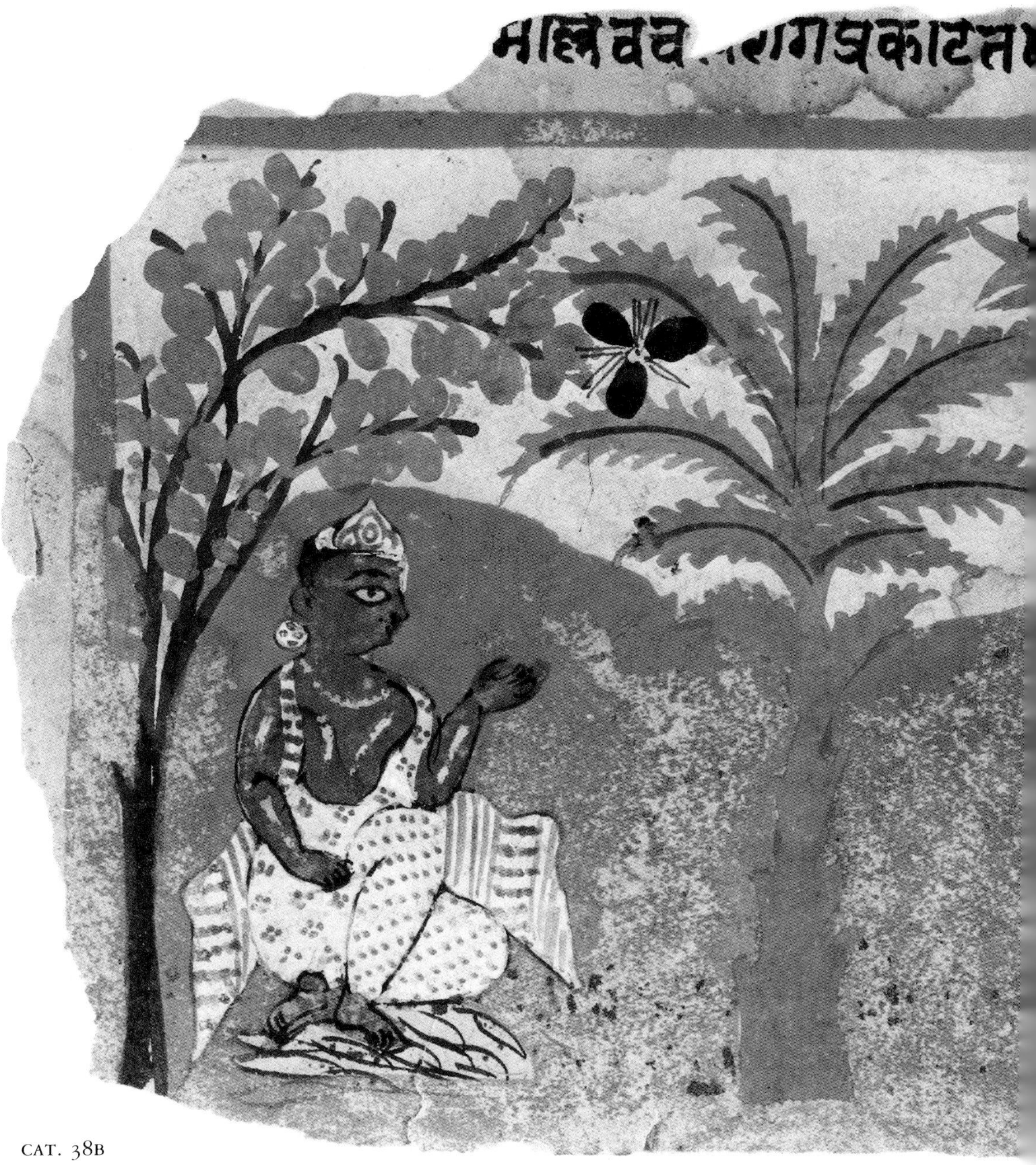

CAT. 38B

B

Jayadeva's song evokes the potent memory of
Hari's feet,
Coloring the forest in springtime mood heightened by
Love's presence.
When spring's mood is rich, Hari roams here
To dance with young women, friend—
A cruel time for deserted lovers.

The paintings occupy the greater part of the pages, and the text is confined to narrow, irregularly shaped panels above. In neither instance has the artist interpreted the verses literally, as is clear from a comparison of the texts and the pictures. For instance, there are no "budding mango" trees nor entwining vines in A. (The trees are mostly imaginary except for the stylized palm tree in B.) Although in A the characters stand or sit beside the river, indicated by the basket pattern on the left, the activities they engage in are not those given in the verse. On the left Krishna converses with a *gopi,* and on the right he is venerated by a couple in front while behind him stands a *gopi* with a flywhisk and a man with a bow, who is not mentioned in this

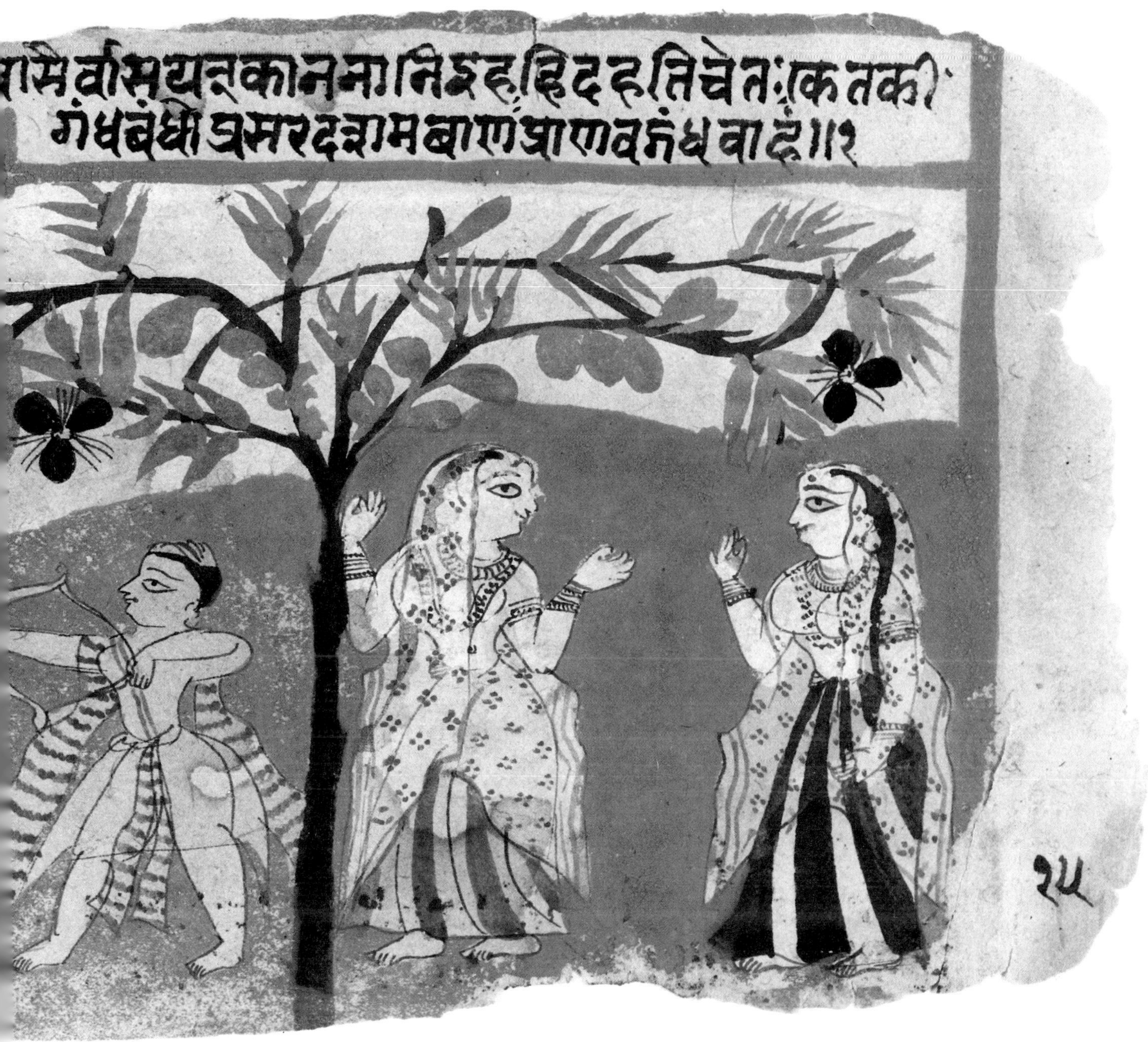

verse. He is in the next verse, however, as Love. The artist has equated Love with Kamadeva, the Indian Cupid. In the second composition, B, he is seen shooting an arrow at Krishna as two *gopi*s are conversing on the right.

While publishing another page, N. C. Mehta and M. Chandra (1962, pl. 3) suggested that this manuscript was copied and illustrated in Gujarat or Rajasthan in the last decade of the sixteenth century. The comparisons cited are unpublished, but there can be little doubt that this *Gitagovinda* is stylistically very close to a Jain manuscript of the *Samgrahanisutra* dated 1583 (Chandra and Shah 1975, pls. VIII–X). In fact, the figural forms in the two manuscripts are so similar that both may have been rendered by the same hand. A noteworthy feature in both manuscripts is the fact that the celestial beings are all dressed in Muslim attire. For instance, Kamadeva in B wears a tailored dress, as do the male celestial musicians and dancers in the 1583 manuscript. Other similarities between the two manuscripts abound. The 1583 *Samgrahanisutra* was painted at Matar, Gujarat, by an artist named Govinda, who also may have been responsible for illustrating this *Gitagovinda*.

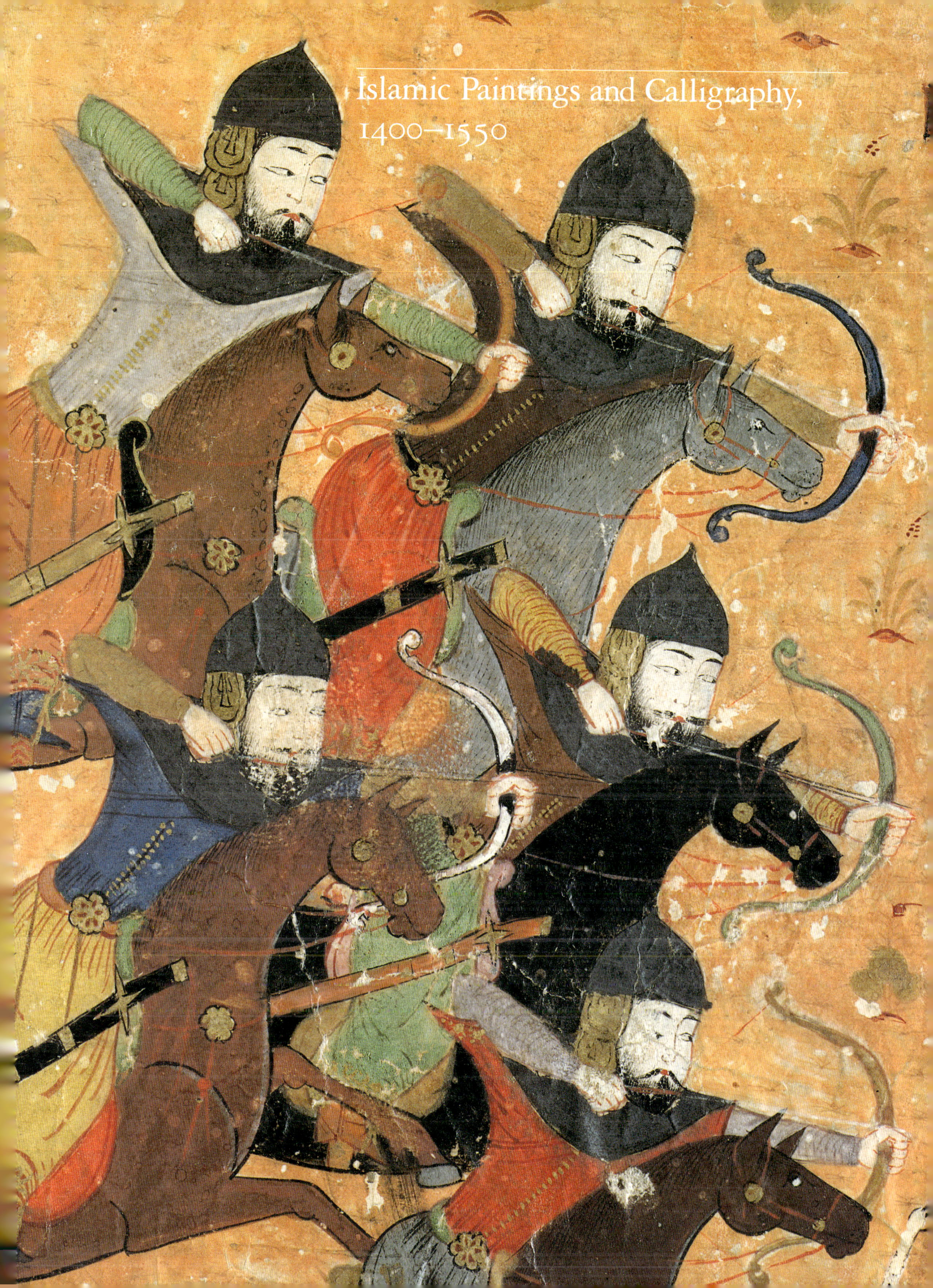

Islamic Paintings and Calligraphy, 1400–1550

(As for) the depiction of the form of each animal
which he draws upon the face of the paper,
the eye of the beholder considers it to be the real animal,
and every image which the pen of the painters of the
world draws upon the writing-board of the dust,
he writes it as beautifully as possible with a flowing
pen upon the face of water. . . . [1]

Introduction

The museum has a small group of Islamic paintings and calligraphy from the pre-Mughal, or Sultanate, period. These consist of isolated leaves from two Korans, the holy book of the Muslims, and several illuminated folios from two different secular books. One of these books is the great epic, the *Shahnama* (Book of kings), by the Persian poet Firdausi (c. 940–c. 1020) and the other a *Khamsa* (Quintet) by Amir Khusrau Dihlavi (1253–1325). All the manuscripts belong to the fifteenth or the early sixteenth century.

The earliest Muslim settlement on the subcontinent goes back to the eighth century, when Sind (Pakistan) was conquered by a group of Arabs. The kingdom they established remained, however, an isolated Muslim stronghold until the thirteenth century, when Islamic expansion across northern India began in earnest after the conquests of Shihab ad-Din Muhammad Ghori of Ghazni (Afghanistan) in 1192. Thereafter, several dynasties of Muslim rulers, known as sultans, ruled over different parts of the subcontinent for a little over three centuries until the Mughals came to power in northern India. Some of the sultans had larger kingdoms than others. It was during the Sultanate period that Delhi became the seat of central authority and the symbolic political center of much of northern India. The political influence of Delhi waxed and waned according to the might and authority of the sultan who sat on the throne. The Delhi Sultanate was dealt a devastating blow and the city sacked in 1398 during the invasion of Timur from Iran. By 1451 a semblance of normalcy returned to Delhi after the Lodi dynasty was founded. While the Lodis occupied the Delhi throne (until 1526), a number of powerful and influential Muslim kingdoms flourished elsewhere on the subcontinent. Prominent among these were the sultanates in Bengal, Malwa, Gujarat, and the Deccan.

The Muslims brought to India a new kind of interest in and reverence for the book. Owning a Koran was particularly important for most Muslims, and a cultured and educated Muslim was a bibliophile who took pride in his personal library. For a Muslim, copying a Koran is considered as worthy an act of piety as any other religious deed. The calligrapher therefore has always enjoyed an unusually exalted status in the Islamic world, as he is privileged to write the word of God. The Koran is written in the Arabic language and script, which is the common form of writing in the Islamic world, although the language spoken in a given area may be different. Thus, the two pages of the ornamental Koran in the collection [39] have the Arabic text with an interlinear Persian translation, presumably because its owner was more familiar with Persian than Arabic. Early Korans copied for Arab patrons are generally very simple. The tradition of adorning and illuminating Korans was due largely to Iranian influence. The arts of illumination and painting were less frowned upon in Iran than in the Arabic world.

There is disagreement among scholars about the provenance of what must have been a beautifully illuminated Koran, from which the two leaves in the collection came. While most scholars consider it to have been an Indian product, it has also been attributed to Anatolia as well as to Iran. It uses three different kinds of writing: the monumental *kufic,* the elegant *muhaqqaq,* and the cursive *naskh.* Though there is some doubt about the provenance of this Koran, there is none about that of a solitary leaf in the collection from a second Koran [40]. This Koran is written in a script called *behari,* which is considered to be an Indian variant of the *naskh.* As a rule *naskh* was not used for writing the sacred book in the Islamic world outside India, which makes *behari*'s adoption for this purpose in India unusual. Characterizing it as "a schoolroom script for provincials," J. P. Losty suggests that Indian scribes may have considered this script suitable for writing the Koran following Timur's invasion, which "destroyed the unity of the Delhi Sultanate and Delhi's metropolitan claims and contacts with the rest of the Islamic world."[2] While this may have been the case, it should be noted that the earliest surviving Koran in the *behari* script was copied in Gwalior, not far from Delhi, in 1399, only a year after Timur's invasion. Since few early Islamic books produced in India have survived, it would be imprudent to speculate on the origins of the script given the present state of our knowledge.

Timur's devastating invasion is not the only reason so little evidence of early Islamic painting has survived in India. Much figurative art in northern India may have been destroyed during the rule in Delhi of Feroz Shah Tughlaq (r. 1351–88), who issued a proclamation that all murals with animate subjects be obliterated from public buildings. In point of fact, the edict says nothing about illuminated manuscripts. Needless to say, Feroz Shah is unlikely to have destroyed illuminated Korans. So it is rather surprising that more Korans from the thirteenth and fourteenth century have not survived. Feroz Shah's predecessor, Muhammad b. Tughlaq (r. 1325–51), was a learned and cultured man, which means he was also an accomplished calligrapher. It is difficult to imagine that he did not have a workshop that prepared Korans as well as other Islamic books for him. Unfortunately, the Tughlaq library was looted during Timur's invasion. If the loot taken back to Iran by Timur included books produced in India, they appear not to have survived.

Citing Feroz Shah's ban on mural painting and an absence of literary allusions to illustrated manuscripts, K. Khandalavala has argued strongly that there was no tradition of either collecting or commissioning illustrated Islamic books in northern India before 1451, when the new dynasty of the Lodis was established in Delhi:

Had any such illustrated foreign or locally painted manuscripts whether of a courtly character or bourgeois character existed in the libraries of the Delhi Sultanate either belonging to the rulers themselves of the Mamluke {1192–1290} and Khalji {1290–1320} dynasties or any of the earlier Tughlaq rulers or any of their nobles or to the Muslim gentry or bibliophiles, Feroz Shah would without the slightest doubt have pointedly referred to them and ordered their wholesale destruction. This vital circumstance is often overlooked by Western writers.[3]

Clearly Khandalavala makes too much of a single edict, and it is naïve to conclude that the order must have been explicitly followed in every nook and cranny of the kingdom. Besides, the edict would have been enforceable only within the territories of the Delhi Sultanate. There were other sultanates and presumably cultured Muslims who owned books elsewhere on the subcontinent. More significantly, Khandalavala seems to have been unaware of earlier literary evidence, which has been thoroughly discussed by S. Digby. Apart from citing passages describing murals and royal picture galleries, Digby also quotes evidence of paintings on paper and cloth.[4] After discussing the passage by Ahmad Dabir quoted at the beginning of this section, Digby cites references to painting from the works of Amir Khusrau Dihlavi. In one of these, the *Dival Rani Khizr Khan,* occurs the following couplet: "From him, also, the picture of the Mughal has a pounce [Of the kind that] it does not come out even though the painter draws it."[5]

Pounces, made either of transparent vellum or paper, were used to make copies of outlines on either paper or cloth for transfer to another composition (see [44]). The use of a pounce implies a workshop situation and some demand for pictures. Moreover, other allusions by the poet to various kind of arts and crafts indicate that there very likely was a royal workshop in Delhi engaged in, among other things, producing illustrated books.

Amir Khusrau enjoyed the patronage of successive Delhi sultans beginning with Balban (r. 1266–87). One pre-Mughal illustrated leaf in the collection [41] is from a manuscript of the *Khamsa* composed by Amir Khusrau. Leaves from this copy of the *Khamsa* are now dispersed in many public collections, and all scholars agree that it was produced in India. In fact, there is no evidence that Amir Khusrau's works were illustrated outside the subcontinent. While most scholars cite fourteenth-century Egyptian and Iranian (Inju-style) illustrated manuscripts as the two possible sources for the style of pictures in this *Khamsa,* they consider it to have been copied and illustrated during the second half of the fifteenth century. This dating has been based primarily on R. Ettinghausen's suggested date of about 1450 for the calligraphy,[6] but this has been questioned by others. M. Beach has suggested a date of 1450 or earlier.[7] According to him, the closest stylistic parallel for these *Khamsa* illuminations can be seen in a manuscript painted in Shiraz, Iran, between 1330 and 1340. This of course does not mean that this *Khamsa* was painted at that date. A clue to its date is offered by a recently published *Shahnama* manuscript that is not unrelated in style to the *Khamsa* illustrations.[8] The pictures in this *Shahnama* (FIG. 13, p. 28) are more elaborate and reveal elements borrowed from other local modes, such as the Jain. Characterizing this *Shahnama* as a "Jainesque Sultanate" manuscript, B. N. Goswamy has dated it to about 1450. In that case, the *Khamsa* must be considered to be an earlier work since it shows very few Indian elements.

In addition to the uncertainty of its date, the manuscript's place of origin also remains obscure. Considering that Amir Khusrau was popular in Delhi, it could have been produced there. It may also have been copied and illustrated in the Bahmanid kingdom in the Deccan.

Whereas manuscripts such as this *Khamsa,* the newly discovered *Shahnama,* and a few others are indisputably of Indian origin, there are other illustrated books of the fifteenth and sixteenth centuries that are less obviously Indian. The collection has isolated folios from three such manuscripts, all of the *Shahnama,* whose attributions are difficult [42–44]. Manuscripts such as these that are strongly Persian in style but not always of the highest quality have been assigned to India, although they could have been produced in provincial centers in Iran or Afghanistan as well. The pioneering article about this so-called Sultanate group was published two decades ago, but since then some of its interpretations and attributions have been questioned.[9] There can be little doubt that calligraphers and artists from Iran and elsewhere in West Asia did come to India from time to time to seek their fortunes at some of the sultanate courts. Certainly the court of Muhammad b. Tughlaq must have attracted some of them, and Amir Khusrau could not have flourished in a literary vacuum. It is equally valid to assume that a certain number of finished books must have been imported for the Muslim bibliophiles on the subcontinent. There must have been individuals outside the courts who were interested in books. Despite the orthodox attitude of some of the Muslim sultans in Delhi and elsewhere, the Sultanate period was a highly productive one for literature in Arabic and Persian. A great many poets and writers of eminence, many of Iranian origin, flourished at the various courts, the most celebrated being Amir Khusrau. There must have been a strong demand among the Muslim literati for Persian books, both with and without illustrations.

In the individual catalogue entries for the museum's *Shahnama* leaves illustrated in a decidely Persian style, attempts have been made to point out a few of the details of landscape, architecture, or attire that may indicate an Indian origin for such manuscripts. By and large, however, such attributions must be regarded as highly tentative. Time and again, when a new artistic tradition arrived on Indian soil, it was modified sufficiently and rather rapidly so that its Indian flavor is unmistakable. If the books illustrated in a strongly Persian style were indeed prepared at Indian centers, they may have been prepared by Iranian artists who remained completely impervious to Indian influences. Or they may have been literally copied by Indian artists not trained in the foreign manner and with no mandate from their patrons to deviate from it.

A considerable number of illustrated Islamic manuscripts have survived from the second half of the fifteenth and early sixteenth centuries, some of which can be securely dated and whose Indian origins are in no doubt. Both their subject matter and style are Indian. One important center was Mandu, the capital of Malwa, where several manuscripts were illustrated in distinctive manners inspired by illuminated books from Shiraz and Herat. However, in such paintings the Indian elements are easily recognizable in figural forms, costumes, and architecture. One of the most outstanding illuminated manuscripts of the period showing a very successful assimilation of Persian and Indian elements is the Bombay *Laur Chanda* or *Chandayana* (FIG. 14, p. 29), a poetical romance written in the late fourteenth century in Avadhi, or eastern Hindi, current in eastern Uttar Pradesh and adjoining Bihar. The provenance of this beautiful manuscript is disputed, with most scholars favoring a northern Indian origin. It certainly shows stronger Indian features than, for instance, the slightly earlier manuscripts such as the *Nimatnama,* painted in Mandu.[10] While Persian elements are dominant in the Mandu books, the Bombay *Laur Chanda* manuscript as well as several others are recognizably Indian in their compositions, two-dimensionality, simplicity of landscape, figural forms, more intense coloring, penchant for greater ornamentation, and the highly decorative architectural designs and lively textile patterns.

Manuscripts illuminated in a strongly Persianized style have also survived from the Deccan, which had even closer links than the northern belt with West Asia, both the Arab and the Persian worlds. The first Muslim kingdom in the Deccan was founded in 1347 by an officer of the Delhi sultan, whose title, Bahman Shah, was the basis for the name of the Bahmanid dynasty. Toward the end of the fifteenth century five governors in the Bahmanid realm rebelled and established separate sultanates, only three of which—Ahmadnagar, Bijapur, and Golconda—survived. These flourished until Ahmadnagar was absorbed into the Mughal empire in 1636 and the other two by 1687. The early history of painting in these kingdoms is obscure as few works earlier than about 1550 can be attributed to the region. (Deccani paintings from 1550 to 1700 are included in a separate section of this volume.) As already noted, the *Khamsa* of about 1400–1450

[41] may have been prepared in the Deccan. The taste for exotic styles appears to have continued in the Deccani kingdoms well into the seventeenth century, even though recognizably Deccani styles had emerged earlier. It is not improbable therefore that the illustrated pages of the *Shahnama* of the fifteenth and sixteenth centuries belonged to books prepared for Muslim patrons in the Deccan, if they must be considered to be Indian rather than provincial Persian.

NOTES

1. Ahmad Dabir, as translated by S. Digby (1967, p. 54). Ahmad Dabir was a member of the chancellory of Sultan Giyas ad-Din Tughlaq (r. 1320–25).

2. Losty 1982, p. 38.

3. Khandalavala 1987, p. 85.

4. Digby 1967.

5. Ibid., p. 54.

6. Ettinghausen 1961, no. 1.

7. Beach 1981, pp. 42–46.

8. Goswamy 1988.

9. Fraad & Ettinghausen 1971; Ådahl 1981; and Brend 1986.

10. For examples of *Nimatnama* pictures, see Khandalavala & Chandra 1969, figs. 131–39, pls. 11–12. For more up-to-date discussions of painting during the Sultanate period, see Losty 1982; Khandalavala 1987; and Goswamy 1988.

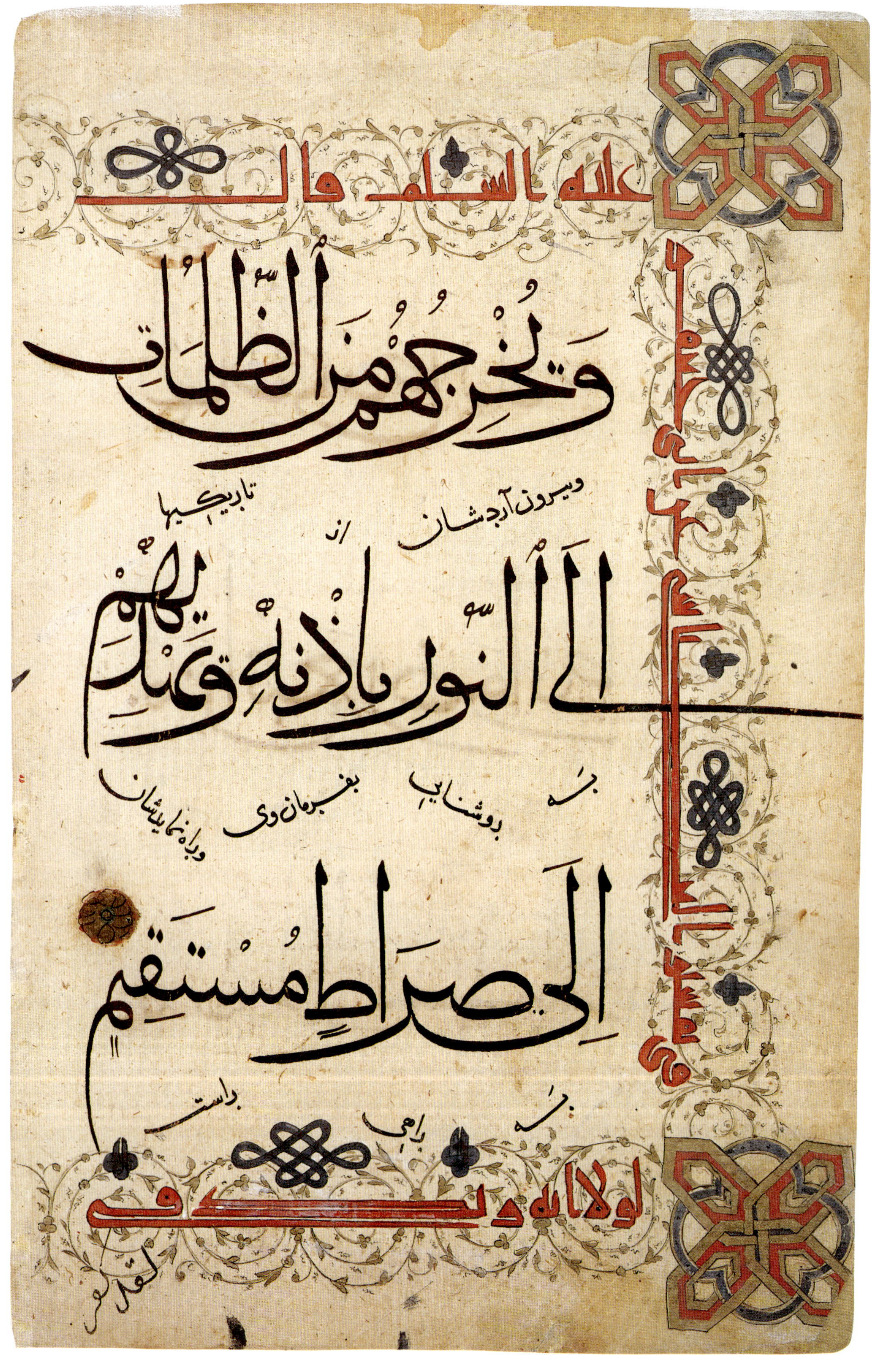

وَيُخْرِجُهُم مِنَ الظُّلُمَاتِ
وبيرون آرد شان از تاريكيها
إِلَى النُّورِ بِإِذْنِهِ وَيَهْدِيهِم
به روشنايي بفرمان وي وراه نمايدشان
إِلَى صِرَاطٍ مُسْتَقِيمٍ
به راهي راست

Catalogue

39 TWO FOLIOS FROM A KORAN

Provenance unknown; c. 1400
Ink, opaque watercolor, and gold on paper
Each, 11⅜ x 7¼ in (28.9 x 18.4 cm)
Christian Humann Asian Art Fund
M.86.186a,b

These two leaves are from a widely dispersed Koran whose colophon page is unknown, hence there is no certainty as to where, when, or for whom it was copied. Since it surfaced some years ago, the Koran has been attributed to fifteenth-century India. One publication has even suggested that it may have been copied in Delhi (Goswamy and Fisher 1987, p. 26). Recently, however, the Indian attribution has been questioned, and suggestions have been made that it was copied in Anatolia (James 1988, no. 119) or in Iran (Schimmel 1989, p. 309, fig. 13). In fact, A. Schimmel considers this to be a handiwork of the master Persian calligrapher Ahmed Suhravardi, one of the outstanding disciples of Yaqut (d. 1298), and suggests a late thirteenth- or early fourteenth-century date. Until more convincing evidence is forthcoming, for the present the Indian attribution will be adhered to, but the date could well be earlier, as suggested by Schimmel.

Although the exact place of origin is not known, the superb quality of the work almost certainly indicates that it was produced in a royal workshop. If it was done for one of the sultans in India, the calligrapher may have been an Iranian master. The calligraphy is elegant and refined, and the pages imaginatively designed.

All the elements that make Islamic art distinctive—calligraphy, the arabesque, and geometric configurations—are present on these pages. The principal text, comprising verses 15 and 16 of Sura V, is written in the large, bold script known as the *muhaqqaq*. The three lines of the Arabic text per page make a strong presence on the buff paper. The Persian translation is discreetly added below each line in smaller and more playful *naskh* letters. This contrast between the two kinds of lettering, one dignified and self-consciously somber and the other cursive and freely penned, adds to the visual appeal of the pages. The simple elegance of the lettering is emphasized by the elaborate designs surrounding the text on three sides. An interlaced flowering vine in gold forms a wide border. Superimposed on this rich arabesque are sayings from the *hadith* in the distinctive *kufic* script in red and blue on one side of each folio and in white on the other. Further embellishments are provided by a variety of blue knots randomly placed outside the *kufic* lettering. At the outside corners of each page is a pattern of interlocking geometric forms in red, blue, and gold.

CAT. 39 *(opposite)*
CAT. 39 *(overleaf)*

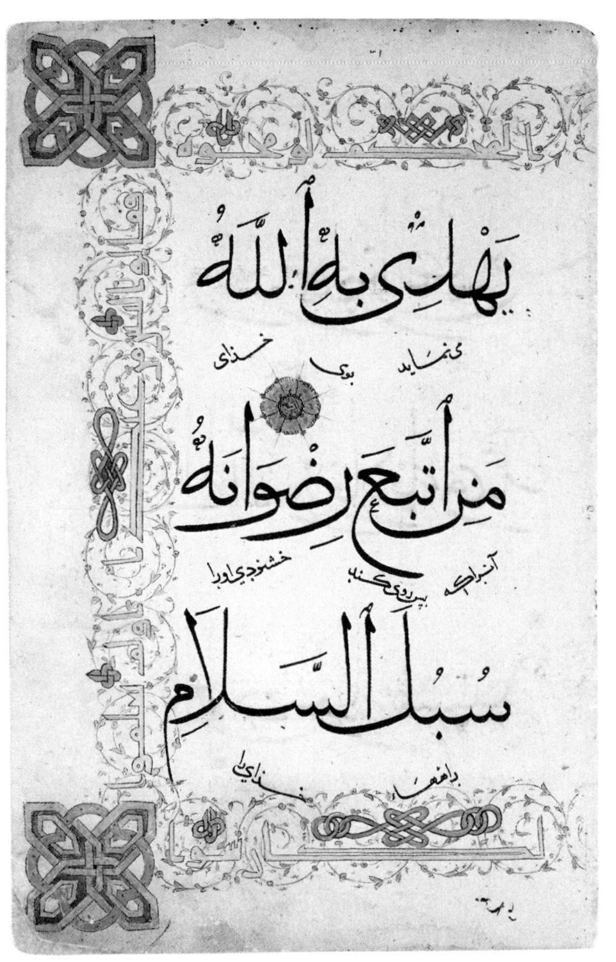
يهدي به الله
من اتبع رضوانه
سبل السلام

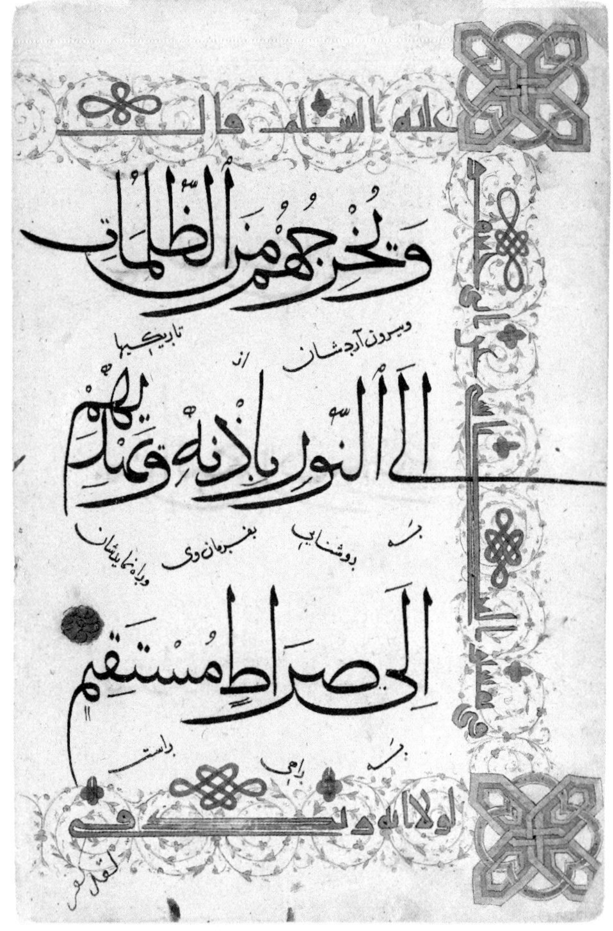
ويخرجهم من الظلمات
الى النور باذنه ويهديهم
الى صراط مستقيم

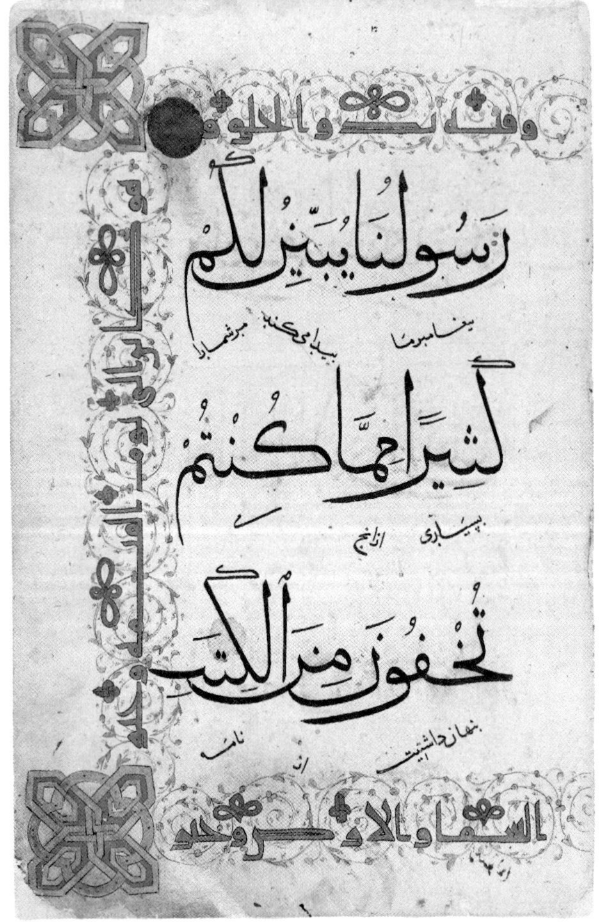
رسولنا يبين لكم
كثيرا مما كنتم
تخفون من الكتب

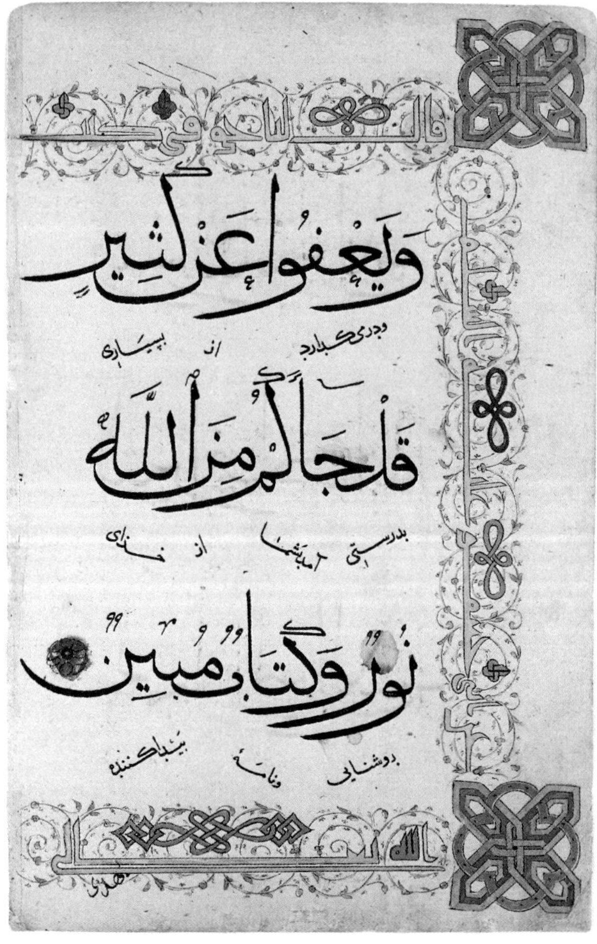
ويعفوا عن كثير
قد جاءكم من الله
نور وكتاب مبين

40 FOLIO FROM A KORAN

Northern India; 1400–1450
Ink, gold, and opaque watercolor on paper
Folio, 9⅛ x 6 in (23.2 x 15.2 cm)
Indian Art Special Purpose Fund
M.90.37

This folio is from a dispersed Koran, the whereabouts of the rest of the manuscript being unknown. The folio appears to be cropped, thereby making it impossible to determine whether it originally contained any marginal decoration. There are thirteen lines of text per page written in blue, black, and gold with a gold floral design serving as a punctuation mark. Although the pages are not as decorative and the writing not as bold as that on the folios from the other Koran [39], the use of lines in three alternating colors enhances the aesthetic appeal of the page. The writing is not exceptionally fine, but the overall page has a rhythmic pattern due to the flowing rhythms of the long, horizontal flourishes and the staccato, short verticals of the letters. The use of lapis lazuli would indicate that the Koran was copied for an affluent patron, even if the calligraphy is not of the highest quality.

This variation of the *naskh* script is known as the *behari* or *khatt-i behar* script. There is disagreement among scholars as to its origin. One view is that the term *behari* derives from the Arabic word for spring; alternatively, it may have been named after the Indian state of Bihar. However, why it should have been named after that region remains obscure since Bihar was not a major center of Islamic culture. As J. P. Losty has observed (1982, p. 38), it is difficult to understand why this rather provincial version of *naskh* that is "neither elegant nor monumental" should have been "elevated to the status of a Koranic script." The earliest datable use of this script is encountered in a Koran copied in 1399 in Gwalior (Losty 1982, pp. 55–56, no. 18), which is certainly nowhere near the state of Bihar.

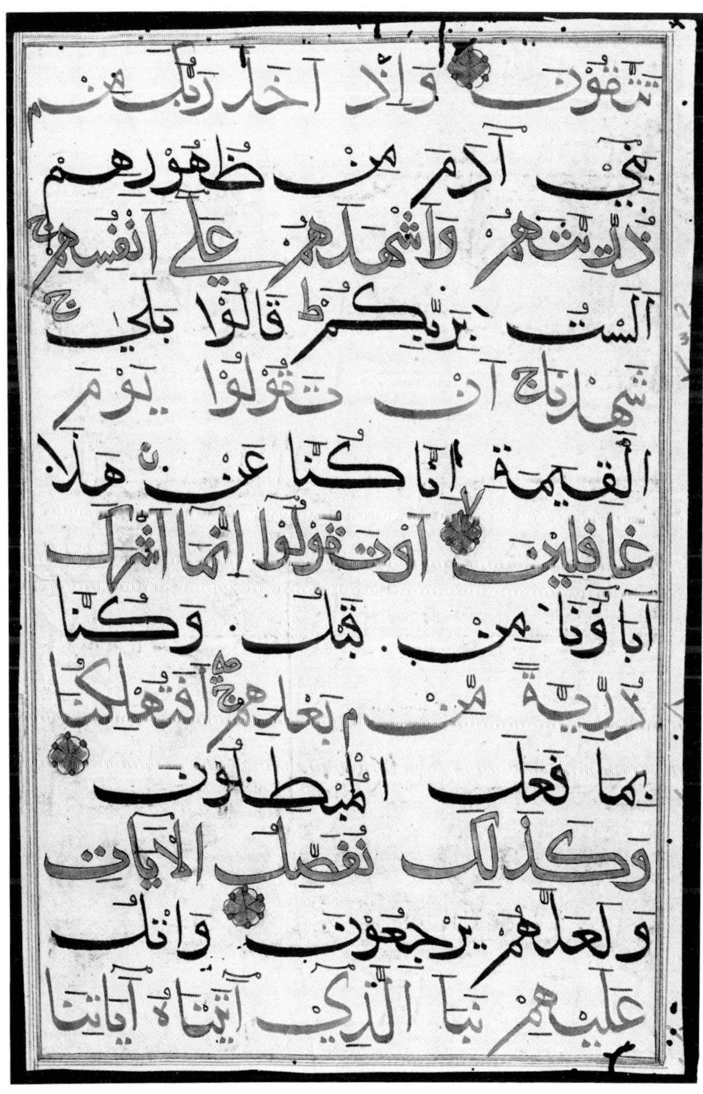

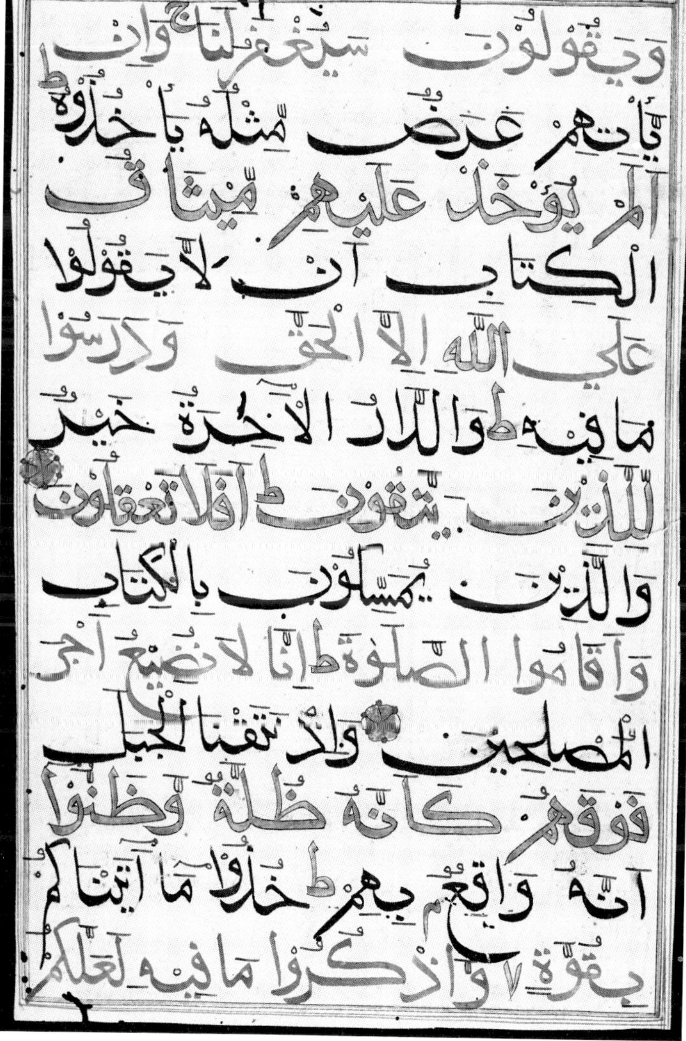

Northern India; c. 1400–1450
Ink and opaque watercolor on paper
Folio, 13½ x 10⅜ in (34.3 x 26.4 cm)
Illustration, 4½ x 8⅞ in (11.4 x 22.5 cm)
From the Nasli and Alice Heeramaneck Collection, Museum Associates Purchase
M.78.9.3
Literature: *Heeramaneck* 1966, p. 121, no. 145; Johnson 1972, p. 145, pl. LXXXIVc; Pal 1987, p. 113, fig. 69.

This leaf is from a dispersed but now well-known manuscript of the *Khamsa* (Quintet) by Amir Khusrau Dihlavi ("of Delhi"), who lived between 1253 and 1325. Amir Khusrau is the best known of all Indian poets who wrote in Persian, although his language does reflect influences from the Braj Bhasha, a dialect of Hindi current in Mathura. The text is written in black ink in the *nastaliq* script in four columns and is interrupted by the illustration. For other leaves of this manuscript and for a technical analysis of the pigments used in the paintings see Beach 1981 (pp. 43–45).

This folio is from the *Hasht Bihisht* (Eight paradises), one of the five stories of the *Khamsa.* The tale is recounted on Sunday in the Saffron Pavilion, the third paradise, by the Princess of Sistan. The wife of Hasan, a goldsmith, extracted from him the secret of how a golden elephant he made could be weighed. She then revealed the information to the wife of one of her husband's rivals. As a result Hasan was imprisoned in a tower for shortchanging the weight. Hasan instructed his wife to send him a silken cord tied to the foot of an ant. While Hasan escaped, his wife, who was holding onto the other end of the cord, was raised to the top of the tower. In the illustration the wife is stranded at the summit and is evidently being taunted by Hasan and others from the street below.

The composition is direct and simple. The richly attired figures display their emotions largely through their gestures, which are expressive enough for the viewer to appreciate the helplessness of the wife. Despite the overall simplicity, the postures and gestures of the figures as well as the disposition of their eyes contribute considerably to the liveliness of the composition.

There is considerable disagreement among scholars as to the date or the provenance of this manuscript. Some consider it to have been painted in the second half of the fifteenth century, while others prefer a date around 1450 or even earlier (Leach 1986, p. 16). Everyone, however, agrees that the illustrations are strongly influenced by fourteenth-century paintings of Mamluk Egypt or of the Inju school of Iran. Khandalavala and Chandra (1969, pp. 45, 46) characterize the manuscript as "a bourgeois manuscript of little artistic value" and consider it possibly an example of the art being "practised at Delhi during the last quarter of the fifteenth century." Leach (1986, p. 16) has suggested a possible Gujarati origin. It could have been made for a Bahmani ruler of the Deccan as well, considering the close ties between that region and Iran.

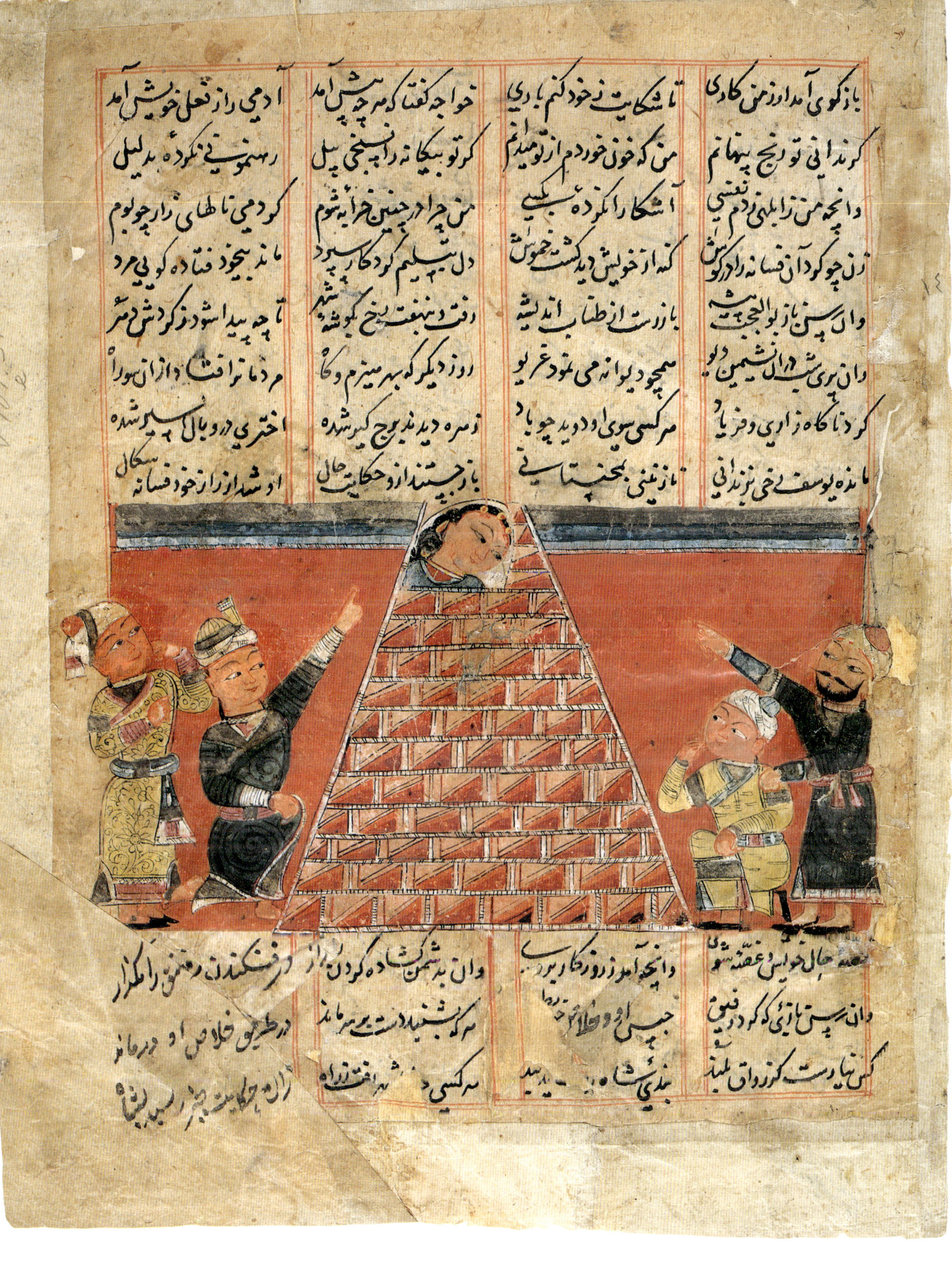

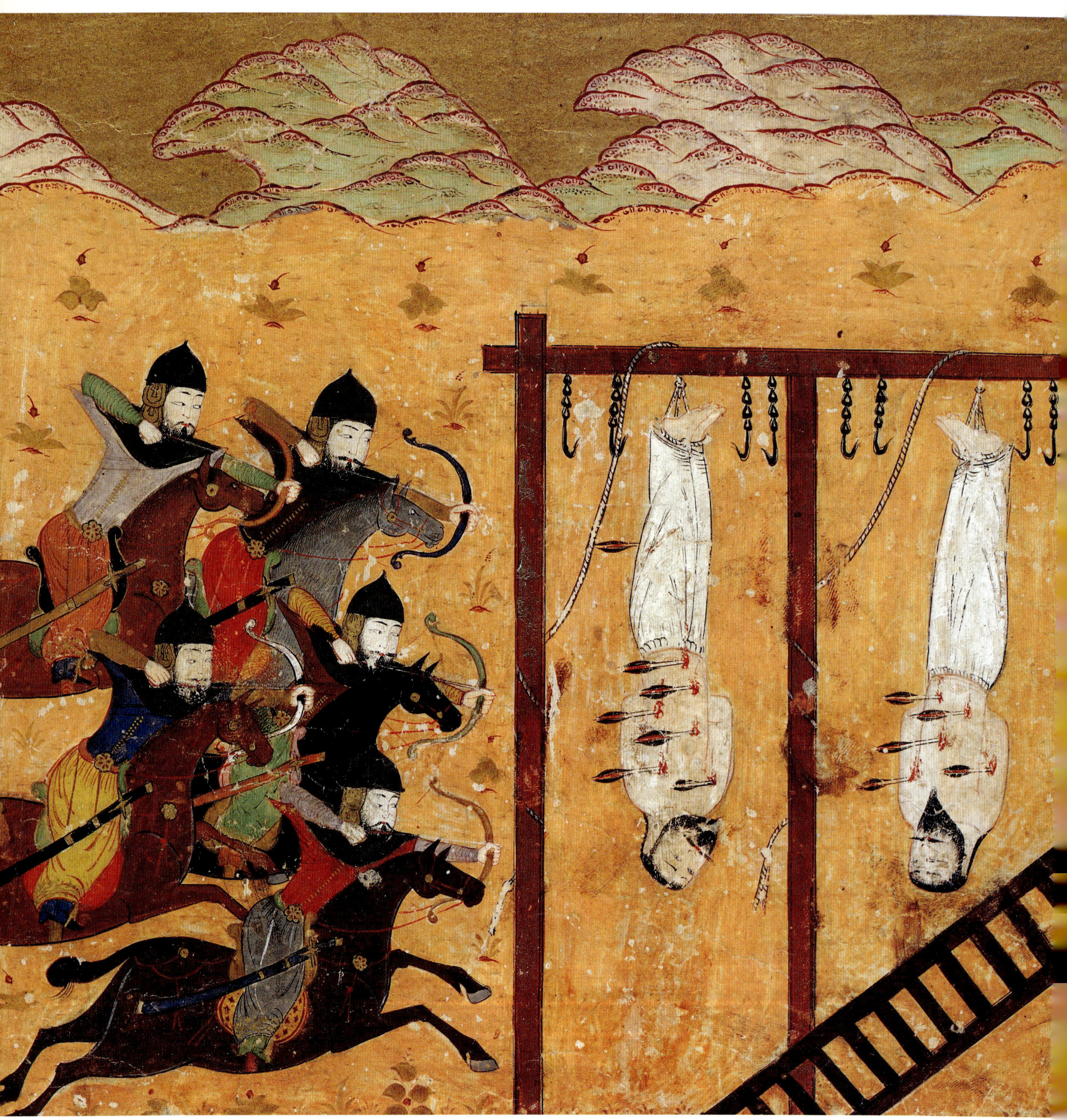

Provenance unknown; c. 1475
Opaque watercolor and gold on paper
Overall, 7 1/16 x 7 in (17.9 x 17.8 cm)
Folio, 10 1/16 x 9 13/16 in (25.6 x 24.9 cm)
Purchased with Harry and Yvonne Lenart Funds
M.85.189
Literature: Pal 1987, p. 114, fig. 71.

This illustration has been removed from a *Shahnama* manuscript and mounted as a picture. Several other examples have survived and are in various public and private collections (see Fraad and Ettinghausen 1971 , pp. 49, 51, where the pictures are listed as B10). Both their large size and square format make these illustrations rather unusual.

Because there is no accompanying text, it is not easy to identify the subject precisely. There are two alternatives. One is that the scene represents Iskander (Alexander) executing the two murderers of Dara (Darius Codomanus). In a painting of that subject from a 1482 Shirazi *Shahnama* in the Metropolitan Museum of Art, New York (acc. no. 40.38.1), the murderers are similarly shown hanging upside down. A second possibility is that the persons being executed are the two rebels who had risen successfully against Ardshir with the help of the Worm but were ultimately defeated and captured by the Sassanid monarch. However, a Timurid representation of this execution does not show the two prisoners hanging upside down on the gallows (see A. Welch 1972, p. 117). Thus, this picture very likely illustrates the first incident described above.

This rendering is more spirited than the two other pictures. From the fast gallop of the mounted archers, it appears as if they are involved in target practice rather than an execution. Also, there is a most unusual treatment of the distant hills of varying verdure against the gold sky. The background is painted in apricot color with sparsely distributed small plants in gold and a touch of red. Beyond the undulating horizon rise interestingly shaped mountain peaks like rearing hoods of serpents. The colors employed are white with a green tinge and purple along the crests. Similar forms with a penchant for purple, although not with the same flamboyance, appear in fifteenth-century Persian paintings (see Lentz and Lowry 1989, p. 132, no. 46, dated 1415–16; and A. Welch 1972, p. 109, dated 1482).

India (?); 1475–1500
Text in black and red ink
Folios, approx. 12 x $9\frac{1}{4}$ in (30.5 x 23.5 cm)
Gift of Major and Mrs. C. C. Moseley
57.17.7,.3,.10,.4

A *Fire Ordeal of Siyavush*
$5\frac{9}{16}$ x $4\frac{13}{16}$ in (14.1 x 12.2 cm)

B *Meeting of Two Generals*
$4\frac{3}{4}$ x $7\frac{1}{8}$ in (12.1 x 18.1 cm)

C *Bahram Gur and the Farmer's Family*
$5\frac{1}{8}$ x $4\frac{7}{8}$ in (13.0 x 12.4 cm)

D *King Khusrau and Barbad*
$5\frac{1}{16}$ x $6\frac{1}{16}$ in (12.9 x 15.4 cm)

The text is written in black script in six narrow columns; red ink is used for chapter headings and some marginal notations, mostly numerals. The illustrations are placed in a different position on each of the four pages. Such variations in the placement as well as the shape and size of the illustrations is a characteristic feature of Persian manuscripts. Not only do they enhance the interest of the illustrated pages as a whole, they also provide the artist with more challenging compositions. No less characteristic is the manner in which the composition sometimes is continued beyond the margin of the picture, in this instance with architectural extensions. In other examples both figures and landscape elements may overflow the margins.

A The fire ordeal of Siyavush is one of the more dramatic incidents of the *Shahnama*. The son of King Kay Kus, Siyavush was a handsome youth who aroused the carnal desires of his stepmother Sudabeh. Although he refused her, she accused him of violating her twice. The king ordered his son to prove his innocence by riding unharmed through a roaring fire. In this representation the virtuous prince charges through the fire on the right, watched by his father riding a horse, a group of courtiers behind the structure, and the anxious queen at upper left.

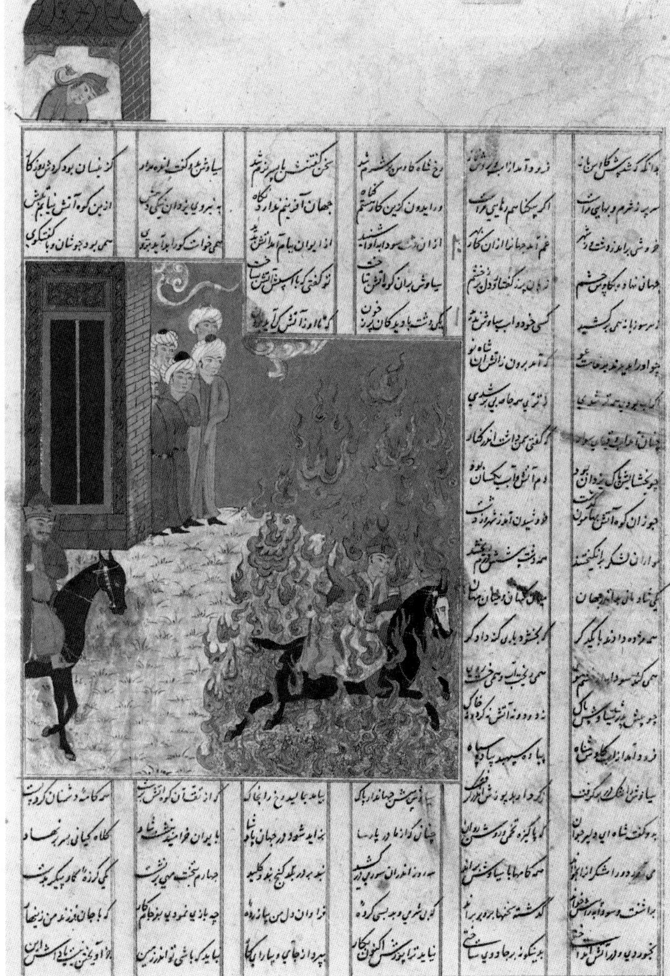

CAT. 43A

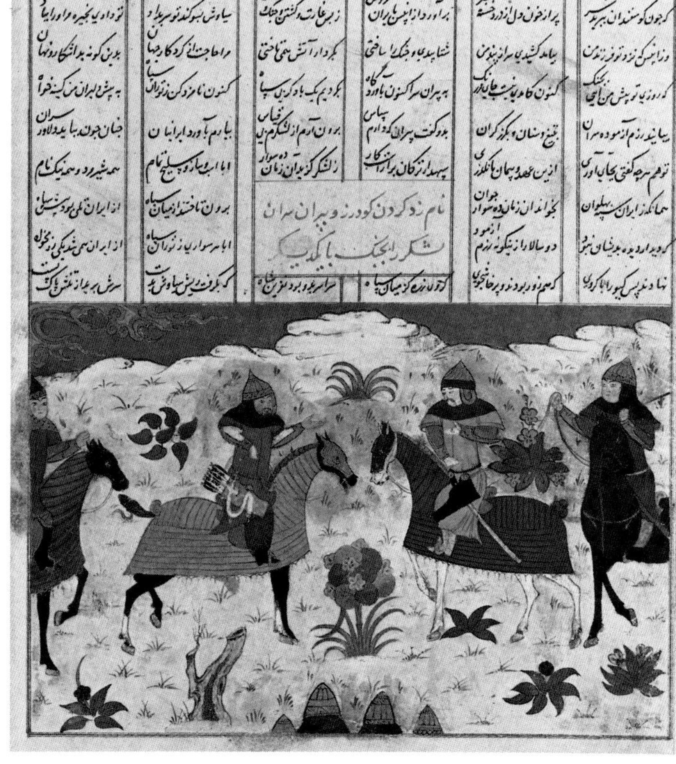

CAT. 43B

B The two generals meeting for a conference are Piran, the commander-in-chief of the Turanian army, and Goudarz, a general in the Iranian army.

C During a hunt Bahram Gur lost his dog. While searching for the animal, he came across a farm. The farmer invited him to meet his three daughters.

D This picture shows King Khusrau being entertained in a garden by the minstrel Barbad, who is hidden in the cypress tree. In the words of the text:

Now there was a cypress-tree all green with an abundance of foliage and with branches intertwined like the men at the battle of Pashan. Up into it with his lute at his breast went the minstrel, there remaining concealed while the Shah emerged from his portico on to the feasting-place, where the gardener had got ready a royal seat. . . . A page with a peri face approached and handed a cup to the Shah, who accepted wine from the Boy, the crystal of the cup disappearing before the red wines (Levy 1967, p. 387).

An ultramarine blue and a bright orange used primarily for garments are the prominent colors in all these pictures. The ground is green in C and D but buff in B. The sky is gold in D but blue in the others. The clouds in A and B are in gold with purple tinges. Noteworthy is the yellow in the garments of the daughter seated on the grass in C. It is certainly the intense Indian yellow called *peori,* which was made from cow's urine. The orange too has an unusually bright tonality for a Persian painting.

These four *Shahnama* illustrations generally reflect the style prevalent in the Herat region in the second half of the fifteenth century. They are closely related to a *Khamsa* of Nizami dated 1494/95 (Lentz and Lowry 1989, p. 277, no. 146) and the *Khavaranama* of 1477 (Welch and Welch 1982, pp. 60–61).

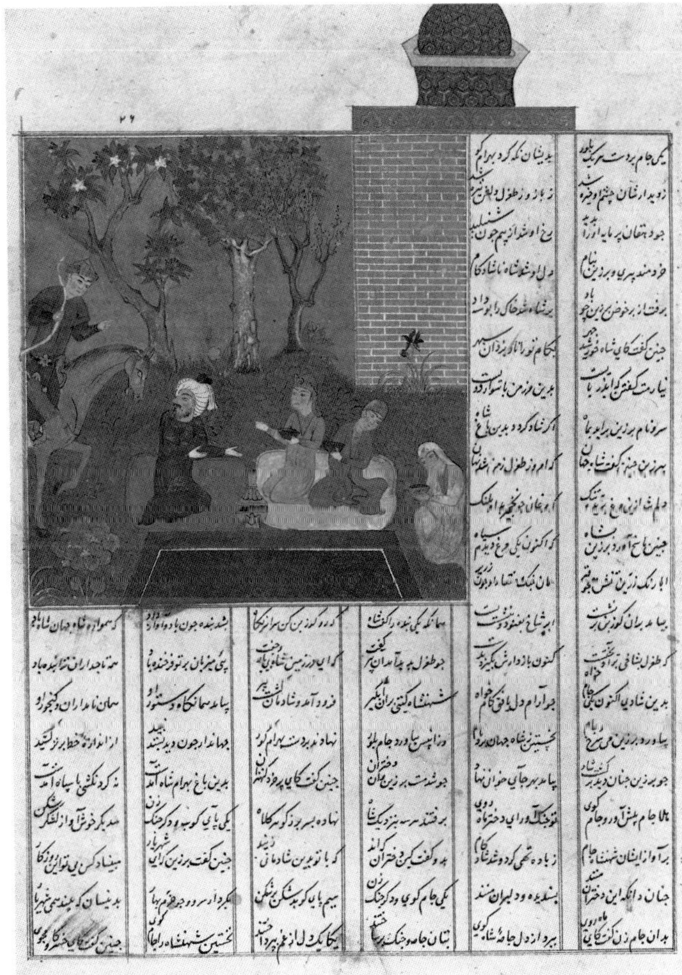

CAT. 43C

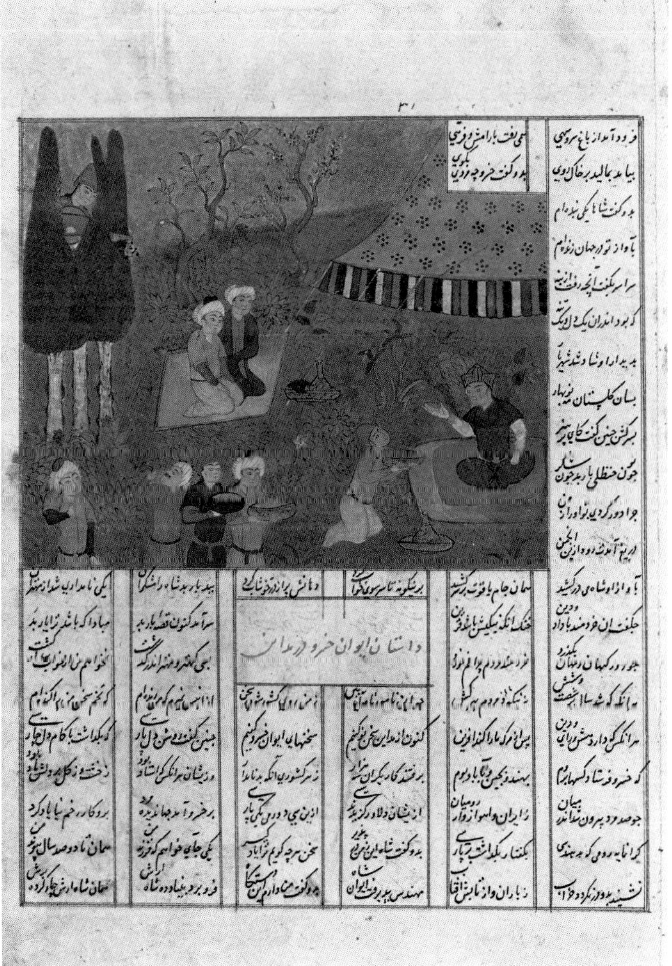

CAT. 43D

Northern India or Deccan; c. 1500
Opaque watercolor, gold, and ink on paper
Folio, 14 x 9¾ in (35.6 x 24.8 cm)
Illustration, 4¾ x 6⅛ in (12.1 x 15.6 cm)
Paul Rodman Mabury Collection
39.12.72
Literature: Pal 1987, pp. 114, 115, fig. 72.

The page with the illustration is glued to another page that, judging by the identical calligraphy of the texts, is probably from the same manuscript. The outer borders, however, are later than the pages; they are adorned with rather freely rendered, intertwined and meandering floral tendrils in gold. On both pages the text is written in black ink in the *nastaliq* script in four columns.

The illustration shows Rustam asleep on some rocks beside a stream. He wears a jacket of tiger skin and bright orange trousers. Another distinguishing trait of the hero, besides the animal skin, is the helmet consisting of a white feline head. His left hand grasps a golden lion-headed club, and a quiver of arrows rests on his right. To the right his spotted gray charger jumps on a lioness to save his master. Although the text describes a lion, the animal here is in fact a lioness. The symmetrical shape of the rising hill is disturbed by a twisting tree trunk slightly off center in middle ground. The tree is chocolate-colored, and the stream is gray with its borders in three shades of green. The hill is a light gray, and the daisylike flowers are the same color as Rustam's trousers. The sky is gold with a blue-gray, Chinese-style cloud form floating in the upper right corner.

Presumably the Indian provenance for this page is suggested primarily because of the pigments, especially the bright orange, whose tonalities are less subtle than those seen in contemporary Persian pictures. Moreover, the flowering plants display a stronger penchant for conceptualization, as do the multihued rock formations in the foreground, which are rather flattened, features that may reveal either a provincial Persian or an Indian provenance for this painting. The style of the picture is closely related to that in a *Shahnama* in the Museum of Fine Arts, Boston, that is considered to have been copied and illustrated in Sultanate India late in the fifteenth century (Fraad and Ettinghausen 1971, figs. 145–47).

Pounce holes are visible around the outlines of the horse and lioness, evidence that the forms were copied for transfer, a common practice in Islamic workshops. Indentations occur in the gold areas.

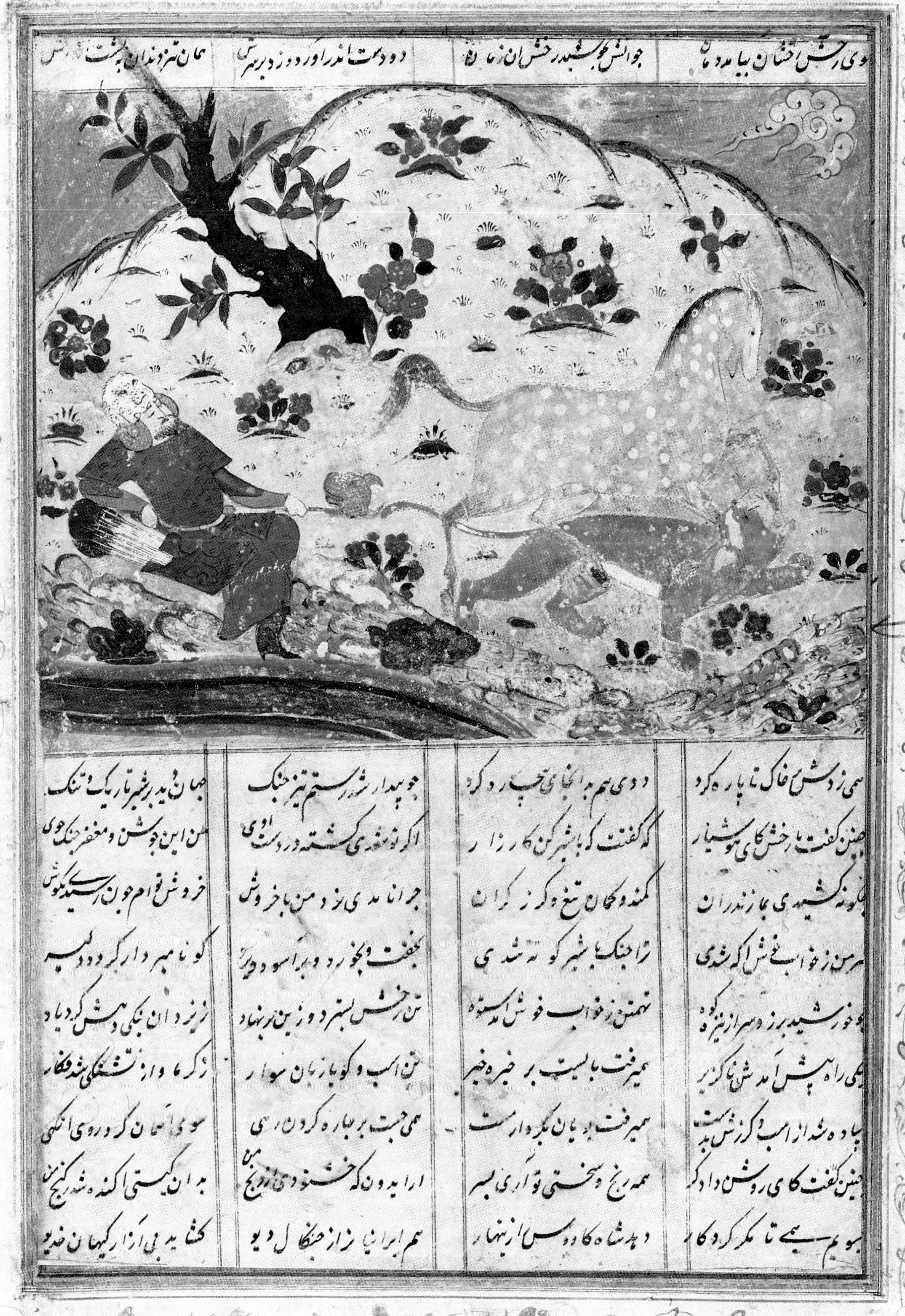

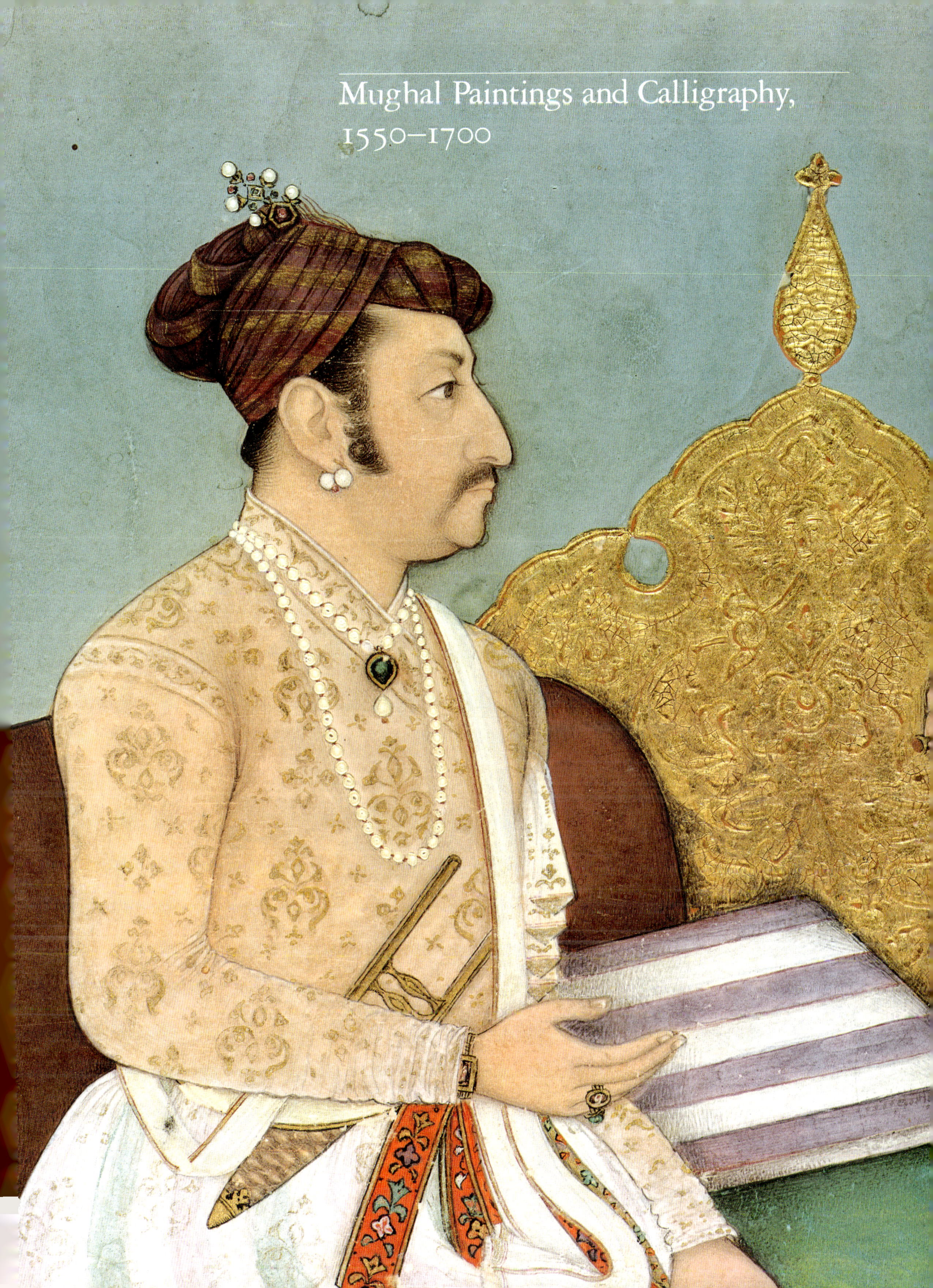
Mughal Paintings and Calligraphy,
1550–1700

Mughal art is no more "Muhammadan"
than Akbar was a "Muhammadan."
It is only as narrow sectarians, of the type
which Akbar and the saints alike condemn,
that we can make any attempt to segregate
the achievements of Mughal art
from the mainstream of Indian culture.
Those sixteenth and seventeenth century manuscripts
and albums are the Ajanta of our millennium;
and their delight is, like Ajanta's,
in the beauty of the visible world
at the noblest heightening of personality.[1]

Introduction

In 1526 a dispossessed chieftain from Farghana in Central Asia named Zahir ad-Din Muhammad Babur (1483–1530) occupied the throne of Delhi after defeating and killing Sultan Ibrahim Lodi. Although Babur ruled for only four years, his successors occupied the Delhi throne until 1858, when the British removed the last Mughal. The expression *Mughal* is derived from *Mongol* and became the appellation of the dynasty even though Babur was a Chaghatay Turk rather than a Mongol. He was descended on his father's side from Timur the Turk and on his mother's side from the Mongol Chingiz Khan. It was the Timurid heritage, heavily Persianized after Timur's conquest of Iran, that contributed significantly to the distinct culture that developed at the Mughal court. In its turn Mughal culture profoundly influenced both life-style and aesthetic taste across northern India until the British became the paramount power on the subcontinent in the nineteenth century. For Indian painting in particular Mughal culture and aesthetics proved to be of revolutionary significance. The Mughal paintings included in this catalogue were produced not only for the various Mughal emperors but also for others, whether associated with the court or not.

For most of his life Babur struggled to find a permanent home, and so it is unlikely that he had the time, the means, or the leisure to establish an art workshop. However, his military preoccupations did not distract him from collecting books or pursuing his interest in natural history and in his own language. He has left behind his memoirs, the *Baburnama,* which are regarded as a paradigm in this literary genre. Several references in it clearly demonstrate Babur's aesthetic sensibility as well as his interest in illustrated books and paintings. He was so fond of his books, some of which had been adorned by the greatest painters of Herat, that they traveled with him even while he was on the march.[2] His personal library was inherited by his son Nasr ad-Din Muhammad Humayun (1508–56), who was an even more ardent bibliophile. Humayun too carried a part of his library with him during military campaigns. At least two occasions are known when some of the precious books were looted or went astray. Fortunately they were recovered on both occasions. Two that have survived down to the present time are the Juki *Shahnama* and a *Zafarnama* that was transcribed by the famous Iranian calligrapher Sultan Ali and illustrated by Bihzad, the greatest Iranian painter.[3]

Humayun succeeded Babur in 1530 but ten years later lost his throne to Sher Shah Sur, or Sher Khan, an Afghan soldier of fortune. In the interim Humayun had conquered and lost Gujarat and Malwa in 1535–36, and from 1537 he was embroiled with Sher Shah in the attempt to save his kingdom. Nevertheless, he maintained his keen interest in books. As his sister Gulbadan Begum informs us in connection with a celebration that occurred soon after his accession, in one of the rooms in the palace at Agra, built by Babur, "an oratory had been arranged, and books placed, and gilded pen-cases, and splendid portfolios, and entertaining picture books [albums] written in beautiful character."[4] We have no way of determining whether at this stage Humayun was simply a collector of paintings and calligraphy or a patron of artists as well. If the memoirs of Jauhar, one of his court servants, are to be believed, then even in 1543, while he was in exile, he had a painter with him.[5] In that case there must have been others in royal employ during happier circumstances at Agra.

Upon losing his throne in 1540, Humayun wandered for some years in Sind and Rajasthan. Despite a nomadic existence in exile, he married, and his son Jalal ad-Din Akbar was born at Umarkot in 1542. He then managed to go across to Iran, where he was granted asylum by Shah Tahmasp. With the Iranian monarch's military aid Humayun conquered Kandahar and Kabul in 1545. The opportunity to regain his throne in India came ten years later, when civil war broke out upon Sher Shah's death. Humayun swiftly descended on the plains and captured Lahore, and shortly thereafter Delhi and Agra. His success was short-lived, however, for he died the following year as the result of a fall down the staircase of his library at Delhi.

Above and beyond helping him regain his kingdom, Humayun's exile in Iran proved to be of momentous importance for the development of Indian painting. He spent much of his time in Iran becoming familiar with his Timurid heritage, visiting holy places, seeing the various sights, and meeting leading literary and artistic personalities. He must also have been busy collecting books. It so happens that at about the same time Shah Tahmasp had lost interest in painting, which left his artists at loose ends. Humayun apparently was fairly confident about his own future, for he invited some of them to join his entourage. At least three seem to have done so. They were Mir Sayyid Ali, possibly his father Mir Musavvir, Abd as-Samad, and Dust Muhammad, also known as Mawlana (or Mulla) Dust. Unable to join Humayun while he was in Iran, they did so after he settled down in Kabul. There can be no doubt, therefore, about Humayun's genuine interest in painting. He is said to have taken lessons in painting from both Mir Sayyid Ali and Abd as-Samad.[6]

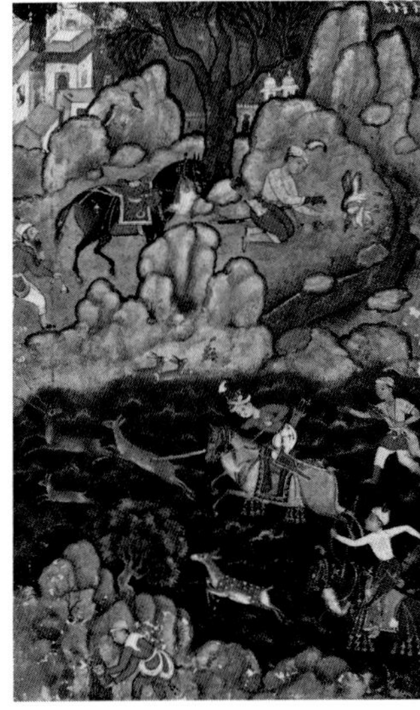

FIGURE 21
Prince Akbar Hunting a Nilgae,
Mughal, c. 1555, opaque watercolor on paper, 8¾ x 5⅜ in (22.6 x 13.8 cm), Syndics of the Fitzwilliam Museum, Cambridge.

Very little is known about the kind of work produced by these artists while they were in Kabul.[7] The museum's charming picture of a scholar by Mir Sayyid Ali [45] may well reflect Humayun's taste in painting. Several other pictures by Mir Sayyid Ali and Abd as-Samad and some possibly by Dust Muhammad were very likely rendered for Humayun, as they are strongly Persian in form and iconography and show little evidence of the innovations that one notices in the early Akbari pictures. More intriguing is a painting representing *Prince Akbar Hunting a Nilgae* from the Fitzwilliam Album (FIG. 21), dated by M. Beach to about 1555; the picture is said to record the occasion when Akbar hunted the animal at Salimgarh on 20 July 1555 on his way to Delhi.[8] Although it may have derived some of its iconographic features from earlier Persian representations of the royal hunt, the Indian flavor of this painting is unquestionable. If indeed it was rendered soon after the actual hunt, then one must conclude that the new style was already formulated during Humayun's brief reoccupation of the throne at Delhi. All the basic elements of the Mughal style, as evident in the *Hamzanama* [46], are present in the hunting picture. In any event, after his return to Delhi, Humayun did establish a studio with at least two Iranian masters, Mir Sayyid Ali and Abd as-Samad, producing pictures, although it is not known whether any manuscript was prepared. Some sort of experimentation with styles may already have begun under Humayun, but it was left to the genius of his son Akbar to inspire a new mode of artistic expression, which has come to be known as the Mughal style.

PAINTING UNDER AKBAR (r. 1556–1605)

Akbar, whose name means "the great," was only fourteen years old when he ascended the throne of what was a modest kingdom. At the time of his death in 1605 that inheritance had grown into the largest and most powerful empire the subcontinent had witnessed until then. This alone would have been achievement enough for most kings, let alone for a boy who had been born and raised in adversity and was unlettered. But Akbar was no ordinary man. He was at once a military genius and an astute administrator, a consummate politician and a brilliant statesman, a pragmatic ruler as well as a mystical philosopher, a keen sportsman and an avid patron of the arts and architecture. Above all he was a man of both imagination and vision, which contributed greatly to the creation of a new cultural ambience conducive to the nurturing of a new style of painting. Although a Muslim, he was conscious of the fact that most of his subjects were Hindus, of a completely different culture and with different values. He is probably the only Muslim ruler in the history of the subcontinent who genuinely attempted to establish a rapprochement between the two civilizations in all spheres of life. One of the means to achieve his goal was illuminated books.

Whether he could read or not, Akbar certainly inherited his father's interest in books and from the very start appears to have considered building a great imperial library just as important as expanding the kingdom. Judging by the fact that the preparation of manuscripts was undertaken early in the reign, the unexpected death of his father and his awesome regal responsibilities did not distract Akbar's attention from the studio. While in Kabul he had taken painting lessons from Abd as-Samad, and being an active child, he must have enjoyed the creative aspect of painting. Throughout his life he continued to display a keen interest in painting by examining weekly his artists' achievements, no matter how absorbed in other matters of state. He may well have found the experience both relaxing and therapeutic.

The most ambitious commission undertaken by the royal atelier was to prepare an illustrated copy of the *Hamzanama.* This was indeed a worthy project for a heroic ruler with an inventive mind. The task was entrusted to the leadership of Mir Sayyid Ali, but impatient with the slow progress, the emperor granted him permission to make the pilgrimage to Mecca and put Abd as-Samad in charge. Despite the fact that there were two different directors and a large number of artists trained in diverse traditions working on the project, the surviving pictures reflect a remarkably coherent style—as if a single person had envisioned the entire series. One suspects that a great deal of this coherence was due to Akbar's personal interest and his own vision. This is clear from the following passage from Mir Ala al-Daula Qazwini's book *Nafais al-Maasir* (Riches of glorious traditions) dealing with Akbar's reign:

It is now seven years that the Mir {Sayyid Ali} has been busy in the royal bureau of books . . . , as commanded by His Majesty . . . , in the decoration and painting of the large compositions . . . of the story of Amir Hamza . . . and strives to finish that wondrous book which is one of the astonishing novelties that His Majesty has conceived of. Verily it is a book the like of which no connoisseur has seen since the azure sheets of the heavens were decorated with brilliant stars, nor has the hand of destiny inscribed such a book on the tablet of the imagination since the discs of the celestial sphere gained beauty and glamour with the appearance of the moon and the sun. His Majesty has conceived of this wondrous book on the following lines.[9]

He then describes in some detail how Akbar had personally planned the format and disposition of the entire book. Clearly Akbar knew what he wanted and made sure his artists could transform his ideas into paintings. The passage also evidences a new kind of connoisseurship that the Mughals and their courtiers introduced during Akbar's reign. Other sources corroborate Akbar's deep involvement with painting, crediting specific technical innovations of the Mughal style to him. According to Abul Fazl,

*Drawing the likeness (*shabih*) of anything is called* taswir (painting, pictorializing). *Since it is an excellent source, both of study and entertainment, His Majesty, from the time he came to an awareness of things, has taken a deep interest in painting and sought its spread and development. Consequently this magical art has gained in beauty. . . .*

His Majesty has looked deeply into the matter of raw materials and set a high value on the quality of production. . . . As a result, colouring has gained a new beauty . . . , and finish a new clarity. . . .[10]

Thanks to Abul Fazl we also have a detailed account of the imperial workshop as it expanded and flourished under Akbar: "More than one hundred persons have reached the status of a master and gained fame; and they are numerous who are near to reaching that state or are half-way there."[11] He then names a number of the leading masters of the workshop, some of whom are represented in the collection: Mir Sayyid Ali [45], Basawan [57], Madhu [58B], probably Miskin [63], and possibly Abd as-Samad [55]. In addition there were calligraphers, illuminators, gilders, margin-makers, and bookbinders, all of whom had to work in unison and harmony to produce the great number of books that their demanding and discriminating patron wanted. Akbar was methodical in the way he examined and appreciated paintings. "Each week," his historian tells us, "the several *daroghas* (superintendents) and *bitikchis* (clerks) submit before the king the work done by each artist, and His Majesty gives a reward and increases the monthly salaries according to the excellence displayed."[12]

Akbar's primary artistic passion was to own beautifully adorned and illuminated books. Preparing lavish manuscripts therefore remained the principal task of his calligraphers and artists. His curiosity was insatiable: in addition to such traditional Persian literary works as the *Hamzanama* (Saga of Hamza; anon.), the *Shahnama* (Saga of kings; by Firdausi [c. 940–c. 1020]), the *Tutinama* (Tales of a parrot; by Ziya ad-Din Nakhshabi [d. 1350]), the *Khamsa* (Quintet) of Nizami (1141–1209), the *Gulistan* (Rose garden) of Sadi (1208–92), and others, Akbar and the Mughals who followed him were also interested in histories, of their ancestors as well as their own. And so books such as the *Chingiznama* (Saga of Chingiz Khan; by Rashid ad-Din [1247–1313]), the *Timurnama* (Saga of Timur; by Hatifi [d. 1521]), the *Zafarnama* (Saga of conquest; fifteenth century), the *Baburnama,* Babur's autobiography, and others of this genre were copied and illustrated. The *Baburnama,* which Akbar had translated from Turki into Persian, was especially admired, and several illustrated versions are known (e.g., [50]). As the one thousandth year of the Muslim calendar fell in his reign, Akbar commissioned a history of the first millennium of the Islamic era, the *Tarikh-i Alfi* (Millennial history), compiled between 1581/82 and 1593/94 [56]. In addition, Akbar had his aunt write an account of his father's life and had his own official history detailed by Abul Fazl in the *Akbarnama* [49]. Similarly, Jahangir's reign would be recorded in the *Jahangirnama,* and a superbly and lavishly illustrated copy of the *Padshahnama,* recounting the history of Shah Jahan's reign, is now in the Royal Library at Windsor Castle.

Nowhere is Akbar's keen interest in history more evident than in Abul Fazl's statement that Akbar ordered that an album be prepared with portraits of his courtiers and nobles so that those who were deceased would be remembered and the living might gain a sense of immortality. Akbar's sense of history, his own destiny, and the importance of the dynasty's achievements contributed a great deal to the kind of narrative accuracy and observed naturalism that distinguish Mughal painting from both the Persianate and the earlier Indian traditions. Akbar was the first Indian ruler to introduce realistic portraiture in Indian art. Although the genre was known in India from ancient times, most Indian portraits were highly idealized. Some degree of realism is reflected in the royal portraits on the coins of the Kushans, the Satavahanas, and the Guptas, but generally the sculpted and painted portraits that have survived depict the sitters not as they were but as they ought to have looked. They were kings and queens and had to be recognized as such. In Mughal portraits, even though some cosmetic touches are noticeable, by and large the face is not a mask, and we can easily distinguish one person from another. It should be noted, though, that frontal depictions are extremely rare, and the faces are usually presented in three-quarter view or in profile.

The production of a book involved a large number of people with specialized knowledge and talents, and presumably egos, and could not have been an easy affair. It must have been even more difficult when several artists had to work on a single illustration. For instance, apart from the overall planning of a book and its layout, which was often complex, especially when the text and illustration dovetail on a page, decisions had to be made before the writing began as to what was to be illustrated. Normally this supervisory work was undertaken by the head of the studio along with the calligrapher, but Abul Fazl informs us that Akbar himself determined the scenes to be painted. Mir Sayyid Ali was the first director of the workshop, but after he was relieved of his responsibilities, the mantle fell upon Abd as-Samad, who was probably a better administrator and a more sympathetic teacher. The former is evident from the fact that he was subsequently appointed the master of the mint and was posted to Multan in 1586 as the finance minister of the province. We do not know what happened to him thereafter or who assumed the leadership of the workshop. One possibility is Basawan, who was a versatile artist and highly regarded by Abul Fazl: "In designing (*tarrahi*), painting faces (*chihra kusha'i*), coloring (*rang-amezi*), portrait painting (*manind nigari*), and other aspects of this art, Basawan has come to be uniquely excellent."[13] Here again, however, there can be little doubt that Akbar's close supervision of the work of his artists had a lot to do with the smooth running of the atelier.

The marginal inscriptions on one of the pictures in the collection [58B], tell us that it was designed and painted by Tulsi and that the figures were drawn by Madhu. Although the division of labor is somewhat unusual, it does demonstrate how two or more artists worked together on a painting. Generally, a master was responsible for the design of the composition and a second artist, often junior, was entrusted with the task of coloring. While most novices were attached to a master during their apprenticeship, the opportunity to work with various eminent artists broadened the trainees' experience considerably. Often the son of an artist was initially trained by the father, as were Muhammad Sharif by his father, Abd as-Samad, Manohar by Basawan, and Abul Hasan by Aqa Riza. Thus, although they were employed by the imperial workshop, the traditional mode of the father teaching the son was continued. However, during their early years they were also assigned to more senior artists to work together on a picture. Artists who were born while their fathers were in the imperial service were especially favored as being "house-born" (*khanazada*).

The Akbari artists definitely represented in the collection are Mir Sayyid Ali, Basawan, Dharmdas [49], Sarvan [50A], Tulsi [58B], and Madhu [58B]. Several other works are attributed with reasonable certainty to Manohar [60], Kesu Khurd [61], and Miskin [63], and one painting may have been done jointly by Abd as-Samad and his son Muhammad Sharif [55]. Among them Basawan, Madhu, and Miskin were acknowledged masters, Basawan being the most versatile. An unusually gifted artist of the atelier was Dharmdas, who apparently had no arms and painted with his feet.[14]

The major task of the imperial atelier under Akbar was to produce books. Whether their subject matter was Indian or Persian, they were all written in Persian, and naturally the format continued to follow that of the bound codex. The two principal painters until about 1586 were Iranian, so it was only natural that the Persian aesthetic tradition would predominate. Unlike Humayun, however, Akbar had been born on Indian soil, and it was clear from his childhood that while proud of his Timurid heritage he was equally conscious of his Indian origin. Thus, as was the case with the buildings he raised and his life-style in general, his paintings too reflected a style that may have borrowed from the Persian tradition but at the same time had an Indian flavor. So even when Persian models were used—whether for compositions or for landscapes—the Mughal adaptations differed from the originals in significant ways. There can be no mistaking that the style of pictures of the *Hamzanama*, among the earliest Akbari paintings known [46], is noticeably different from that in which Mir Sayyid Ali was painting in 1555 [45]. The figural forms and attire as well as the flora and fauna are clearly Indian, natural forms are less flamboyant, and the gradations of color and tone differ strongly from those in Persian paintings.

Europe was another source that contributed significantly to the development of the Mughal pictorial tradition, especially after 1580. Thereafter there is a much keener interest in depicting forms with fuller volumes, representing a greater depth, and displaying a more conscious awareness of the effects of light and shadows. Even more important is the fact that European art made the Mughal artists realize the possibility of rendering their figures with greater psychological expressiveness than is the case with either the Iranian prototypes or the earlier Indian tradition.

This discovery of the European pictorial tradition was particularly timely, as it was in the 1580s that the imperial atelier became involved in producing the great historical works, the *Timurnama,* the *Chingiznama* [58], the *Tarikh-i Alfi,* the *Baburnama,* and the *Akbarnama.* As works of recent history or contemporary events, the last two required much greater topographical and narrative accuracy than was necessary for histories of the distant past, much less literary works. Babur was a keen naturalist with remarkably accurate powers of observation, and Akbar's own life was well documented. The illustrations for these works therefore, even if compositionally dependent on Persian models, are much more faithful to both nature and the material culture described in the books.

The penchant for using Indian motifs, natural forms, and plants as well as figurative types had also become necessary for the Hindu texts that Akbar wanted prepared in the 1580s. Akbar was a very eclectic man as well as being intellectually curious. Besides, he was the first Muslim ruler on the subcontinent to take a genuine interest in the culture, religion, and literature of the native population, especially of the Hindus, who formed the majority of his subjects. He had several of the better-known Hindu texts translated into Persian. From among them, the museum's collection includes leaves from a *Harivamsa* [48], Somadeva's *Kathasaritsagara* [51], a *Ramayana* [83], and a *Razmnama* (*Mahabharata*) [85]. While the *Harivamsa* and *Kathasaritsagara* leaves belonged to imperial copies of the books, the other two are probably from manuscripts done for such important courtiers as Abd ar-Rahim Khan Khanan. Akbar not only had copies made for himself but encouraged his grandees to own and read these Hindu texts in translation. Some orthodox Muslims may frown upon Akbar's expansive attitude, but the fact remains that for Akbar art served a variety of purposes, not the least of which was to apprehend the Creator. He sincerely believed that the Creator was responsible for the entire universe and not just one race or religious group. It is doubtful if any other patron has ever paid such a tribute to the artist as did Akbar when he said, as recorded by Abul Fazl, "It seems to me that a painter is better than most in gaining a knowledge of God. Each time he draws a living being he must draw each and every limb of it, but seeing that he cannot bring it to life must perforce give thought to the miracle wrought by the Creator and thus obtain a knowledge of Him."[15]

Over forty years ago the eminent Islamic art historian E. Schroeder used this passage to support his assertion that Mughal art was not simply "the fruit of a wholly secular mentality" but was inspired by Akbar's intense spirituality. "Such knowledge [as alluded to in the above passage, wrote Schroeder], and such knowledge alone, can explain the infinite variety of carefulness which we see in the best early Mughal art. The masterpieces of portraiture, the unequalled representations of the animal world, could never be made, as any painter knows, except in self-forgetting love."[16]

The Mughal style was sired by Humayun but nurtured by Akbar, whose catholic tastes and liberal attitude were largely responsible for its distinctive character. Three very different aesthetic traditions contributed to the formation of the style. One was the Indian tradition with its diverse aesthetic modes, as seen in various paintings included here ([36] and FIG. 10, p. 26). The second was the Persian tradition, which was reintroduced directly by Iranian masters and through first-rate illuminated books rather than through mediocre works from Sultanate India or from provincial Iranian centers. The third and perhaps the most influential tradition was the European, which was introduced largely through engravings, illustrated Bibles, paintings, and perhaps textiles. European hangings, possibly tapestries, were adorning the court as early as the time of Humayun, and European pictures and prints may have been introduced through the Portuguese as early as the 1560s.

It is neither easy nor profitable to separate the various artistic tendencies that were finally synthesized in the fully formed Mughal style that emerged in the 1580s. The Mughal pictures from between 1550 and 1570 that survive show tentative attempts at combining Persian formal and iconographic elements with native aesthetic norms and tastes. While the overall landscaping and compositional passages are derived from Persian pictures, the individual elements such as the flora and fauna are in keeping with local topography. The rock formations in Mughal painting never achieved the fantastically imaginary quality that one encounters in the great Persian paintings, and the trees are often local varieties, such as the mango or the plantain. The figures in Mughal painting are shown more often in profile than one encounters in Persian painting, and the figural forms as well as attire are Indian rather than Persian. Mughal artists were much more concerned with actual appearances and with conveying the plasticity as well as the sensuousness of the forms than were their Persian counterparts. The coloring in Mughal pictures also differs notably from Persian paintings in tonality and intensity as well as in application. The depicted space is still shallow, and even in the *Hamzanama* the use of perspective is ill understood and faulty.

By comparison, if we look at the *Harivamsa* pictures of the 1580s [48] or a work by Basawan [57], there can be little doubt that a dramatic change has taken place, particularly in the handling of space. The architecture is now presented three-dimensionally and individual figures and objects are more naturalistically modeled. Landscape backgrounds were often taken directly from European work [74] and European subjects and symbols were freely adopted [54]. Narrative themes are presented with verisimilitude, and the viewer is mentally drawn into a picture's pictorial space as if he or she is a direct witness of the action. The use of both foreshortening and shading to increase the representational accuracy of the picture was adopted from European works, which had reached the court by early 1580, when the Jesuits arrived. The fathers of the first Jesuit mission brought an illustrated Bible and presented a large painting of the Madonna to Akbar.[17] They saw with the emperor an atlas that he had received earlier from Goa. It is possible that he may have received European pictures from Portuguese Goa even before 1580.

One of the painters who appears to have taken a particular interest in European techniques was Basawan. More studies of European works by him have survived than by any other Akbari artist (e.g., [54]), and his enthusiasm must have been infectious, as is clear both from Basawan's influence in the studio, especially after Abd as-Samad's departure in 1587, and from the large number of studies of European works that were made by imperial artists. Indeed Abul Fazl's statement that the paintings of the Mughal masters are in no way inferior to those by European artists clearly demonstrates how European painting had replaced Persian painting as the measure of excellence.

PAINTING UNDER JAHANGIR (r. 1605–27)

Akbar died in 1605 and was succeeded on the throne by his eldest and only surviving son, Salim, who then assumed the title Nur ad-Din Muhammad Jahangir (*Jahangir* means "world seizer"). Like his two brothers, who died from overindulgence in liquor, drugs, and sensual pleasures, Jahangir was addicted to both wine and opium. Moreover, he could not hold either his drink or his drug and became very cruel when inebriated. These weaknesses naturally interfered with his ability to govern the realm, and most of his battles were fought for him by his son Prince Khurram, later emperor Shah Jahan, and his generals. In 1611 Jahangir married a widow called Mihr-u-nisa and conferred upon her the title of Nur Jahan ("light of the world"). She remained a strong influence in his life, and by assuming many of the imperial duties, she allowed him greater leisure to indulge in his passions, one of which was admiring paintings.

It would not be an exaggeration to state that Jahangir was the only Indian collector, connoisseur, and aesthete in India's past in the way we understand those words today. Like his father, his curiosity was insatiable, and his emissaries were always on the lookout for exotic animals and objects for him. Like his great-grandfather Babur, he loved nature and was interested in it both poetically and scientifically. Also like Babur, Jahangir wrote a memoir that is remarkably intimate and candid, although not as elegant and literary as Babur's. It is a good source, however, for illuminating Jahangir's aesthetic taste, which was responsible for guiding Mughal painting in a new direction.

Among the several allusions to painting in his memoirs, two passages are particularly revealing and relevant. Even though quoted often, they are well worth repeating, as they not only inform us about Jahangir's visual acuity but also why Mughal painting took a new turn under his patronage.

In one he claims to have become such an expert in distinguishing individual styles of painting that when a work was brought before him he could immediately recognize the hand without being given the artist's name, whether the artist were dead or alive. "And if there be a picture containing many portraits, and each face be the work of a different master, I can discover which face is the work of each of them," he claimed.[18]

Such claims not only reflect Jahangir's self-confidence in his extraordinary ability to judge a work of art but also introduce us to a new kind of connoisseurship. To Jahangir the individual skill and self-expression of the artist were both recognizable and important traits in a work of art. For this reason he was less fond of large books that were the result of cooperative effort. He commissioned fewer illustrated manuscripts and in those that he did he preferred that an artist should work alone on an illustration, which would inspire him to produce more inventive and expressive compositions. Jahangir clearly favored individual pictures to books and had such paintings assembled in sumptuous albums along with masterpieces of Persian calligraphy. The outer borders of these calligraphic pages were often illustrated by artists of his choice with genre subjects that allowed the artists great freedom of expression. Thus in this instance too the artists could express themselves in a more idiosyncratic and original manner than they could under Akbar.

Jahangir's second frequently quoted allusion to painting is in regard to the illness and death of Inayat Khan, one of his favorite courtiers and like him addicted to opium. Upon hearing that his friend was about to die, Jahangir had him brought to the court. The following passage from his memoirs records his reaction:

He appeared so low and weak that I was astonished. "He was skin drawn over bones." Or rather his bones, too, had dissolved. Though painters have striven much in drawing an emaciated face, yet I have never seen anything like this, nor even approaching to it. Good God, can a son of man come to such a shape and fashion? . . . As it was a very extraordinary case I directed painters to take his portrait. . . . Next day he travelled the road of non-existence.[19]

This kind of almost clinical interest in the world around him is evidenced by both his memoirs and surviving pictures. Jahangir took the same interest in the dying Inayat Khan, in his arch-rival Shah Abbas of Iran, in a turkey, and in the beautiful flowers he observed in his beloved Kashmir. When he dispatched an embassy to Shah Abbas, he sent along Bishandas (see [68]), one of his best portraitists, to take the ruler's portrait so that he could become better acquainted with his Iranian counterpart. When he was amazed to see a turkey or was thrilled with the spring flowers in Kashmir, he ordered one of his master artists, Mansur, to paint these marvels of nature. Observed realism, physical accuracy, and psychological insight were extremely important to Jahangir, and he was fortunate enough to have in his workshop a number of highly talented artists who could give him satisfaction.

A sensitive drawing in which the emperor is presented as he must have appeared to the artist [73] displays the kind of unvarnished truth that Jahangir preferred. Similarly, the rich assortment of marginalia with their vivid studies of men engaged in various activities [55] are excellent examples of the kind of psychological penetration that Jahangir expected to see in representations of human beings. The animal and flower studies done for him also reflect a lively accuracy and fidelity to nature unknown in Akbari painting.

Although we do not know how early in his life Jahangir's love for painting was manifested, there is no doubt that by 1588/89, when he was in his early twenties, the prince already had artists working for him and had developed a taste for Iranian pictures. In that year, or a little earlier, Aqa Riza had come to Agra from Iran and entered Akbar's employ. Moreover, one of Prince Salim's closest friends, perhaps from his childhood, was Muhammad Sharif, the son of the Iranian master Abd as-Samad. By 1600, when unable to wait any longer for the crown, Prince Salim rebelled and set up his own court at Allahabad, Aqa Riza became the most influential figure in the prince's studio. The studio functioned until 1604, when Salim returned to Agra to be near his dying father. In addition to Aqa Riza, his son Abul Hasan as well as another Iranian painter named Mirza Ghulam are known to have worked at Allahabad. The collection has at least two paintings that certainly were done for Salim during the Allahabad period [65A, 66], while a third [64] may also be added to the group.

Partly because of Aqa Riza's presence and partly because of Salim's own taste, there is a strong Iranian element discernable in the pictures painted at Allahabad. This is evident particularly in the greater delicacy and refinement of both the drawing and coloring as well as the introduction of typically Persianate themes such as the inebriated prince, with its metaphorical connotation [66]. Simultaneously, however, the strong influence exerted by European engravings available at the court is visible in a greater concern with the shading of the garments as well as the figural forms in the works of both the Jahangiri and the Akbari studios during the decade before Akbar's death. That the prince continued to admire European works is supported not only from the observations of foreign visitors and descriptions of murals decorating the palaces but also from the fact that even such a conservative Iranian painter as Aqa Riza began to copy European prints after joining Prince Salim's studio, as is evidenced by the Gulshan Album in Tehran.[20]

Nowhere is Jahangir's love of both the Persian and European manners more clearly manifest than in the decorations of the margins of the album pages. The very idea of the album containing fine examples of calligraphy and paintings was borrowed from Iran, and although we do know that Humayun possessed albums, we do not know what was in them. We do know, however, that Akbar had assembled albums containing portraits of his courtiers. What is different about the Jahangiri albums is the enormous diversity of their contents, which reflects his insatiable curiosity. This diversity is apparent not only in the pictures themselves but even more so in the margins. Here we witness the bold juxtaposition of styles and traditions in a novel manner. The background is often densely filled with rich arabesques or scrolling vines inhabited by fauna or with golden landscapes in a predominantly Iranian mode over which the master artists of Jahangir—such as Govardhan, Daulat, and others—have painted most lively, accurate, and intimately observed vignettes of men and women engaged in various activities. These are the true miniatures of Indian painting and are often more expressive and appealing emotionally than the larger pictures they surround. While the technical sophistication required for these representations was derived from European works, their thematic freshness and anecdotal directness must be attributed in a large measure to Jahangir's discriminating taste. Especially when these border representations depict ordinary people absorbed in everyday activities, the vignettes have been rendered appropriately with unglamourized spontaneity, which makes them particularly delightful [55].

Nothing could provide a greater contrast to the unaffected simplicity of these naturalistic gems on the album leaves' outer borders than the symbolic portrait of Jahangir in the collection [72]. This type of allegorical and highly artificial portrait began to appear after 1615, the year Sir Thomas Roe arrived at the court as ambassador of the British monarch James I (r. 1603–25). He brought with him examples of English allegorical portraits that apparently intrigued Jahangir, who ordered his artists to adopt the idea. From this time until his death twelve years later, Jahangir virtually ruled as a figurehead and much of the power was assumed by his astute queen Nur Jahan. Thus one can understand why such symbolic and flattering portraits, where he is portrayed not only as larger than life but as a divine figure, should have had particular appeal.

The collection contains one work bearing the names of two Jahangiri artists. This is a page from a *Shahnama* showing the collaboration of Bishandas and Inayat [68]. Not much is known about Inayat, who worked on the 1605 *Akbarnama* and painted a beautiful study of a mountain goat now in the Victoria and Albert Museum, London. In one of the *Akbarnama* pictures he is referred to as *khanazada,* "house-born," but his father's identity is not known. Bishandas, however, is a more familiar figure and was one of the leading painters of Jahangir's atelier; he was personally selected by the emperor to accompany his ambassador to Iran in 1613. In the words of Jahangir himself:

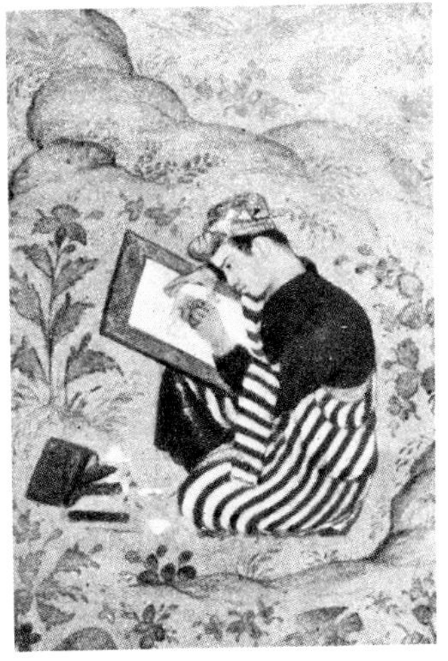

FIGURE 22
Portrait of Abul Hasan, from a border illumination in the Gulshan Album, by Daulat, Mughal, c. 1605–9, opaque watercolor on paper, Imperial Library, Tehran (after Godard 1936, fig. 11).

At the time when I sent Khan 'Alam to Persia, I had sent with him a painter of the name of Bishn Das, who was unequalled in his age for taking likenesses, to take the portraits of the Shah and the chief men of his State, and bring them. He had drawn the likenesses of most of them, and especially had taken that of my brother the Shah exceedingly well, so that when I showed it to any of his servants, they said it was exceedingly well drawn.[21]

It is interesting that despite expressing his confidence in Bishandas's talent, Jahangir had to have others verify how authentic the Shah's portrait was. This again shows how exacting Jahangir was on truthfulness in portraiture. He had never met the Shah and needed a penetrating psychological portrait to get to know him.

Among the other master painters of Jahangir who are represented in the collection are Abul Hasan [72, possibly 66], Manohar [60, possibly 73], and Govardhan [55B, 71]. Abul Hasan (FIG. 22), who was house-born, was undoubtedly the closest to the emperor and much admired. He was born after his father, Aqa Riza, joined Prince Salim's studio. Abul Hasan was honored with the title *nadir al-zaman,* "wonder of the age," and in his memoirs Jahangir praises him lavishly and says unequivocally that "at the present time he has no rival or equal."[22] His earliest surviving work is a drawing of Saint John copied from an engraving by Albrecht Dürer, the European artist most admired by the Mughals, now in the Ashmolean Museum, Oxford. Abul Hasan was only thirteen at the time. Not only does the drawing reveal how precocious he was, it also indicates how early he began studying European techniques, which he adapted with much greater assurance than his father. He was the first Mughal artist to understand the importance of shadows and was able to convincingly explore the interplay of light and shadows on the surfaces of objects in his pictures. From a portrait surviving in the Gulshan Album, we know that he was left-handed. He appears to have worked for a while for Shah Jahan early in his reign, but nothing is known of him thereafter.

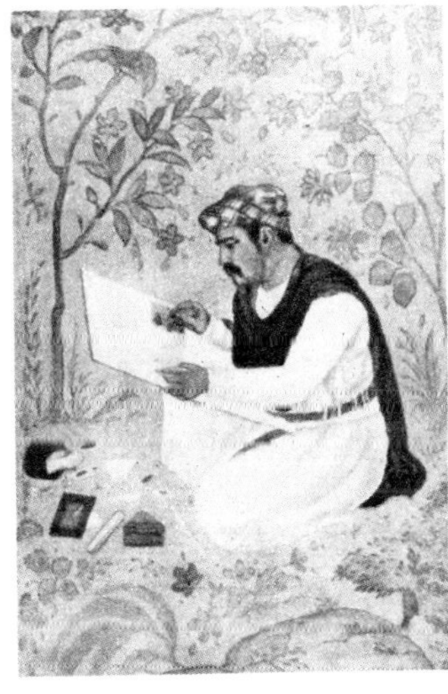

FIGURE 23
Portrait of Manohar, from a border illumination in the Gulshan Album, by Daulat, Mughal, c. 1605–9, opaque watercolor on paper, Imperial Library, Tehran (after Godard 1936, fig. 12).

Although not house-born, Manohar (FIG. 23) was also the son of a famous father, the Akbari master Basawan. He was probably born in the 1560s, and no work by him after Jahangir's reign has been recognized. He obviously received his early training from his father, following whom he became very interested in European works, which is evident from the charming study of two youths attributed to him in the collection [60], which may have been done for Prince Salim. The Gulshan Album includes a portrait of him, painted by Daulat early in Jahangir's reign. He must have then been in his forties and appears in robust health. Although not as sophisticated in his technique as Abul Hasan, Manohar was a versatile artist, as was his father, and was equally at home with manuscript illustrations, portraiture, and animal paintings. A. K. Das called him the most prolific of all Jahangiri artists, and the large number of his surviving works reveal his extraordinary range and quality sustained over four decades.[23]

Like Abul Hasan, Govardhan was a house-born artist, having been born while his father, Bhavani Das, was working for Akbar. He must have been born in the early eighties, as his earliest known pictures are in the 1604 *Akbarnama.* It is possible that he was recruited early for Prince Salim's studio, for like Abul Hasan, Govardhan was strongly influenced by European works. There is the further possibility that besides his father he was trained by Basawan, from whom he may have acquired his penchant for drawing holy men. Although Jahangir has nothing to say about him, Govardhan's studies of people are among the most sensitive and insightful in all Mughal art. As M. Beach has remarked, "no other Mughal artist of the period celebrates, with such sympathy and insight, the variety of humanity found in India."[24] He was equally at home in depicting princes [71], holy men [74], and people from all walks of life engaged in a variety of mundane activities [55B]. It should be noted, though, that very few signed works by this highly talented and somewhat eccentric artist have survived, and most of the paintings are attributions. However, his is one of the few highly individual styles that can be fairly easily recognized.

PAINTING UNDER SHAH JAHAN (r. 1628–58)

After eliminating his brothers, Prince Khurram succeeded his father in 1628, taking the title Shahab ad-Din Muhammad Shah Jahan (*Shah Jahan* means "world ruler"). He ruled for three decades, until one of his sons deposed him, and from 1658 until his death in 1666 Shah Jahan spent his years as a prisoner at the Agra Fort. His principal consolation during his confinement was the fact that from the palace he could admire his favorite building, the Taj Mahal. Partly because of the Taj and other highly visible architectural accomplishments, and partly because he did not leave any memoirs with copious comments about artists or the art of painting as his father did, Shah Jahan's interest in painting has been generally overlooked in histories of the Mughal art. A recent assessment of Shah Jahan as a patron of painting by J. Dye makes an important contribution in redressing this imbalance.[25] Like his grandfather Akbar, to whom he was very close, Shah Jahan's interest in the arts was wide ranging. Doubtless his principal passions were precious stones and architecture, but he was also interested in illustrated books and paintings. In fact, by the age of fourteen he had an album assembled for himself, and many paintings survive on which the names of the artists or his reaction to the work are recorded in his own hand.

Shah Jahan, however, was different in personality from both his father and grandfather. Although he was a more orthodox Muslim than both, he was not a bigot, as is clearly evident from his fondness for and approval of his liberal, philosopher son Dara Shikoh and his disapproval of the more austere but competent Aurangzeb. Like his grandfather, Shah Jahan was a brilliant military strategist and a man of action, but he lacked Akbar's open-mindedness and visionary qualities. He strongly disapproved of his father's indolent and lazy nature but was less spirited and down-to-earth than his grandfather. A formal man, he took the business of being an emperor very seriously.

Shah Jahan would, in fact, have been a perfect ruler for the age of television. He was a man who believed in his own destiny (after all, he had been born in the auspicious year of the millennium of the Islamic calendar and under the same conjunction of the planets as his great ancestor Timur), in his place in history, and in the power of image rather than substance. To him the universe was a paradise and he was at its center. And so his court, his architecture, and his paintings are all reflections of an idealized world rather than the real one. As Dye has pointed out, Shah Jahan continued some of the innovations of the Jahangir era, such as the polished refinement and technical virtuosity, a preference for individual paintings rather than manuscripts, and to a limited extent, the thematic categories, but otherwise Shah Jahani pictures reflect a dramatically different perception of the world. For instance, Shah Jahan was not as keen a naturalist as Jahangir and hence there are fewer animal and nature studies from the period. When we do encounter them, as in the margins of the albums [77–79], they are competently rendered but lack the spontaneity and freshness of Jahangiri works. Formal representations of courtly life from Shah Jahan's reign are more numerous than from the reigns of his two predecessors. Style rather than substance, outward appearance rather than inner character, decorative exuberance rather than restraint, technical virtuosity rather than spontaneous expressiveness are some of the salient features of Shah Jahani paintings.

There was apparently no change in the functioning of the imperial atelier under Shah Jahan. Early in his reign at least two manuscripts were commissioned, one of which, a *Gulistan* of Sadi, was sent to King Charles I as a gift. Several sumptuous albums that included a variety of pictures and portraits as well as superb examples of calligraphy (e.g., [77–79]) were prepared for the emperor. Unlike those in Jahangir's albums, the figures in the margins of the royal portraits in these albums seem to relate to the person depicted. Shah Jahan's eldest son, Dara Shikoh, was also a patron of painting and had assembled an album of brilliant pictures for his wife, which is now in the India Office Library, London. The crowning achievement of Shah Jahan's artists, however, is the magnificently illustrated history of his reign, the *Padshahnama,* now at Windsor Castle. Although lacking the drama and vigor of the *Akbarnama* manuscripts or the technical brilliance and subtlety of the *Jahangirnama,* it remains a landmark in Mughal painting for its ostentation and cool elegance.

Shah Jahan inherited a number of his father's artists, such as Abul Hasan, Manohar, and Govardhan. In addition to Govardhan, whose picture of four mullas [74] may well have been painted for Shah Jahan, other Shah Jahani artists to whom works in the collection may be attributed are Bichitr [75, 77B], Hashim [76], and Balchand [78B]. Except for Govardhan's characteristic study of the religious teachers, all these works are portraits from imperial albums. Govardhan's picture shows how well the Mughal artists had assimilated European elements by this time. As a matter of fact, the days of faddish interest in European pictures were over and no longer were European works regarded as novelties. Shah Jahan was less impressed than Akbar or Jahangir with the Europeans, their religion, or their art. The Shah Jahani artists were better able to integrate technical elements of European pictures in a less self-conscious manner. They also made subtle uses of European symbolic motifs and devices to express Shah Jahan's idea of divine kingship or the divine right to rule.

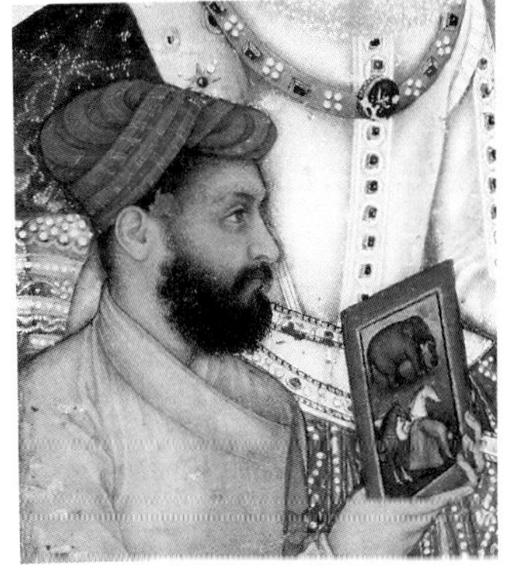

FIGURE 24
Self-portrait of Bichitr, detail of his *Jahangir Preferring a Sufi Shaykh to Kings,* Mughal, c. 1615–18, opaque watercolor and gold on paper, 10 x 7 1/8 in (25.3 x 18.1 cm), Freer Gallery of Art, Smithsonian Institution, Washington, D.C., 42.15.

Little or nothing is known about Bichitr except that from his name and his self-portrait in a painting in the Freer Gallery of Art, Washington, D.C. (FIG. 24), one can deduce he was a Hindu. He probably joined Jahangir's workshop, perhaps even in Allahabad, but his earliest work is of about 1615–20 and the latest of about 1645–50. After the departure of Abul Hasan, Bichitr must have been the leading painter of formal portraits for Shah Jahan. Although his portraits are said to be somewhat cold, there can be no doubt about his technical brilliance. Indeed, among the works of all Shah Jahani artists Bichitr's formal but sumptuous pictures, such as the meeting between Shah Shuja and Gaj Singh [75] and a portrait of the emperor himself that is possibly by the artist [77], best express Shah Jahan's aesthetic preferences. Although the former picture describes a historical occasion, the introduction of the two cherubs holding a canopy above clearly reflects the emperor's obsession with paradisiacal symbolism. Every detail of the picture reflects the opulence of the court, yet there is an almost palpable chill in the air. Similarly, in the portrait Shah Jahan's divine image is emphasized not only by the halo—which Jahangir had introduced into imperial portraiture, possibly from European sources—but also by the highly idealized and flawless form and the impassive, iconic expression. These characteristics are also found in a later picture in the collection, of about 1650 [79], when Shah Jahan was sixty-two years old. Except for the white beard his face shows no wrinkles and he seems hardly to have aged. Shah Jahan was very vain and was just as concerned about his appearance as he was about his portraits, all of which he probably personally inspected and approved. This portrait is very similar to another from the same album that is signed by Hashim.[26]

Whether or not the later Shah Jahan portrait in the collection is by Hashim, most scholars attribute the impressive representation of Mirza Rustam Safavi [76] to him. According to some Hashim may have been a Deccani artist who migrated to the Mughal court sometime during Jahangir's reign.[27] One reason for this suggestion is the survival of several portraits by him of Deccani personalities. However, the majority of his works, portraits of single figures, show very little direct Deccani influence. Whatever Deccani traits are discernible could very well have been adopted from Deccani pictures available at the Mughal court. In a fresh assessment of his work, J. Seyller very convincingly downplays the Deccani association and describes Hashim as an important artist who contributed significantly to perpetuating the established conventions of formal Mughal portraiture during the reigns of Jahangir and Shah Jahan without exhibiting undue concern about psychological nuances.[28]

PAINTING DURING THE AURANGZEB PERIOD (r. 1658–1707)

After deposing his father and waging a bloody fratricidal war in which he eliminated all his brothers, Aurangzeb occupied the throne in 1658 and took the title Muhyi ad-Din Muhammad Alamgir (*Alamgir* means "seizer of the universe"). He ruled for half a century, but the long reign was not encouraging for artistic production. A severe and orthodox man, Aurangzeb shunned luxuries and ostentation. Preoccupied as he was with economic and military problems, he had little interest in art and architecture. In a letter written in 1663, F. Bernier, who traveled in India between 1658 and 1663, painted a dismal picture of the state of the arts in Delhi in general, although he does state that "the artists . . . who arrive at any eminence in their art are those only who are in the service of the King or of some powerful *Omrah* (courtier), and who work exclusively for their patron."[29] The imperial atelier was thus still functioning, perhaps to produce Korans and official pictures. The history of Mughal painting under Aurangzeb is only vaguely known, and what can be said is that his indifference if not dislike for the art of painting had a beneficial effect on the development of the art in the Rajput courts.

Although a few pictures in the collection do belong to this period [80–82], there is no certainty that they were rendered at the imperial atelier or for the imperial collection. As a matter of fact, almost no scholarly work has been done on the production of painting in the imperial atelier during Aurangzeb's reign. It is generally believed that early in his reign Aurangzeb continued his predecessors' practice of patronizing painting, but slowly his attitude changed, and by the time he left for the Deccan in 1680 for a campaign, he had disbanded the studio for all practical purposes. The Deccan in fact remained Aurangzeb's principal obsession, and although he did succeed in annexing the region before his death, it proved to be a costly conquest. In the process the Mughal empire was ruined financially, and its subsequent decline was irreversible.

Some court artists, those that were retained, moved with the emperor to the Deccan, some probably remained behind in Agra and Delhi to do freelance work for whatever local patrons there were, and others moved to the provinces to work for both

Hindu and Muslim courts. It is also believed that those artists who went to the Deccan with the emperor naturally came in contact with Deccani artists and their works. As a result, the Mughal and Deccani traditions mutually influenced each other. One or two works in the collection [110A, 111B] may, in fact, reflect this exchange or assimilation of stylistic traits.

The portrait of Shah Alam, who succeeded Aurangzeb as Emperor Bahadur Shah I, was probably painted in Delhi or Agra shortly before Aurangzeb's departure for the Deccan [81]. The quality of the work points to its having been done by a court artist, perhaps for the prince himself. A second picture [80], dated 1674/75, which found its way into an album presented in the eighteenth century to Lord Clive, may well have been painted by an artist of the imperial studio, as it is an accomplished picture with the physical likeness of the sitter sensitively rendered. Less difficult to place is the portrait of Bibi Ferzana [82], which is stylistically close to several similar portraits attributed to the second half of the seventeenth century. Adequately painted, such female portraits are perfectly acceptable renderings of the subjects' appearance but lack both the psychological expressiveness of the Jahangiri portraits and the sumptuous but formal elegance of Shah Jahani representations. This type of idealized portrait of beautiful women, mostly courtesans, was introduced during the Shah Jahan period and continued to be popular. Except for portraits few other types of pictures of the period have survived, and the age of both richly illustrated manuscripts and lavishly assembled albums appears to have been over.

NONIMPERIAL MUGHAL PAINTINGS

Although the Mughal emperors were the principal patrons, there were others who commissioned or acquired illustrated books or individual pictures. The corpus of such works is not vast, and no systematic study about them has yet appeared. They are categorized in several different ways, such as provincial, popular, subimperial, or bazaar Mughal, but the differences between these are not always clear.

Around 1960 two basic styles of Mughal painting were recognized. In the words of P. Chandra:

Along with the refined and luxurious style of the Mughal court that was fostered in royal ateliers by imperial patrons there grew up a popular version of the same style patronised by the nobility, the commercial classes and others. For lack of better terminology they are referred to in this article as the Imperial and Popular Mughal styles respectively. The Popular Mughal style took on various aspects and forms, some close to the parent style, some apparently removed from it, but both of them heavily dependent on it.[30]

In 1973 E. Binney, 3rd, employed the category "subimperial style" in his catalogue of his own collection.[31] As Binney wrote, "'Popular Mughal' suggests a vulgar appeal to the masses which the sophistication of many of the examples belies. The 'Sub-Imperial Style,' a term coined by W. G. Archer, exactly describes the resultant pictures, varying from excellent painting to hackwork." (Binney does not, however, cite a source for Archer.)

To these two categories L. Y. Leach has added a third, "bazaar Mughal."[32] In her opinion subimperial pictures are less refined than but are related to those produced in the imperial ateliers and were generally done for the nobility. Popular Mughal pictures were rendered for "the next social level of patronage" and are "generally bright-colored, vital, and stiff." Technically, they are not as sophisticated as the imperial or subimperial pictures and reveal an aesthetic sensibility that is in keeping with the traditional mode of

Indian painting before the birth of the naturalistic Mughal style. Her next category, the bazaar Mughal style, represents inexpensive works rendered with a limited range of colors. These were apparently produced quickly in the bazaars of Agra or Delhi and "sold in great numbers from shops to townspeople for gifts, decorations, and so on." Although this may be a valid classification of nonimperial Mughal pictures, unfortunately Leach illustrates only one bazaar Mughal work, in the Cleveland Museum of Art, and nothing similar exists in the Los Angeles collection. It would be less confusing therefore to adhere to the two categories of subimperial and popular Mughal styles, to which most of the nonimperial Mughal pictures in the museum's collection belong.

Of the museum's subimperial pictures, the name of only one patron is known. He was Abd ar-Rahim Khan Khanan, from whose copy of the *Razmnama* two folios are in the collection [85]. Abd ar-Rahim, the Khan Khanan (commander in chief), was one of the most important courtiers during Akbar's reign, but he did not get along as well with Jahangir. He was very much a character in Akbar's mold, being a man of action as well as of culture. An avid bibliophile and a poet, he maintained a library well stocked with books, some of which were produced in his own workshop. However, he moved about a good deal, as he was given various appointments as governor of different provinces, and so must have been largely dependent on local talent. Although the names of several of his artists have survived, they were not the most eminent; the best in the realm naturally were attached to the imperial atelier. Nevertheless, many of the Khan Khanan's artists were loyal to him, for some of them worked on both his *Ramayana,* completed in 1598 (now in the Freer Gallery of Art, Washington, D.C.), and the *Razmnama* painted almost two decades later.[33] In fact, when he wanted his own illustrated copy of the *Ramayana,* he borrowed Akbar's copy to be used as a model by his artists. The style of his copy of the *Razmnama,* prepared between about 1615 to 1620, looks back to the Akbar-period *Ramayana* and reflects little awareness of contemporary Mughal painting that was being done for Jahangir. Clearly the Khan Khanan was not as passionately keen about paintings as were Akbar and Jahangir. This seems to have been generally true of most subimperial Mughal patrons. Most were more interested in books than in individual paintings as well as being unable to utilize the best artists.

There are two folios in the collection [83] from a *Ramayana* rendered in the subimperial style which is earlier than the Khan Khanan's *Ramayana.* It is not known who the owner of this manuscript was, but that he was a Hindu is evident from the fact that the text is in the original Sanskrit. The style of the illustrations makes it clear that the patron was close to the Mughal court and, although a Hindu, his taste was strongly influenced by the Mughal aesthetic. The artists who worked on this *Ramayana* were clearly familiar with imperial book production and may well have used a royal copy as a model, as was the case with the Khan Khanan's copy of the *Ramayana.* Like the earlier *Ramayana,* the *Story of Sukra and Rambha* [88] must have been done for a Hindu or Jain patron, but its style is not quite as sophisticated or naturalistic as that in which the two Hindu epics have been painted. This illuminated manuscript page is better characterized as popular rather than subimperial Mughal.

More difficult to place are three illustrations from two different *Shahnama* manuscripts [84, 86]. This Persian epic was popular with Muslim patrons of Iranian origin in India. The 1608 *Shahnama* picture [84] does echo elements of the imperial style but is more stridently colored. It uses an unusual shade of yellow that is not found in imperial manuscripts and is more akin to the brighter tonality encountered in popular Mughal pictures. Although the compositions of this picture and of paintings from other similar *Shahnamas* rely strongly on Persian models, the figural types, the costumes, the coloring, and the treatment of natural forms are distinctly Indian. The two illustrations in the collection from another *Shahnama* [86] are less elegant, and their landscape elements are quite coarse and archaic versions of Persian motifs. The coloring has neither the rich subtlety of imperial Mughal pictures nor the robust quality of the 1608 *Shahnama.* It is very likely that whereas the dated *Shahnama* was produced in Agra for one of the courtiers, the manuscript in the archaic style was done for a less affluent patron in a provincial center where the Mughal style was only vaguely familiar.

Apart from the illustrated page from the *Story of Sukra and Rambha,* all the examples of popular Mughal pictures in the collection illustrate poems describing musical modes. A musical mode is known as a *raga* and its derivatives as *ragini,* "wives of *raga,*" and *ragaputra,* "sons of *raga.*" The characteristics of each *raga* are described in verses in Sanskrit, Persian, and vernacular languages, which provided the artists with their verbal models. It is interesting that although music was appreciated by the Mughal royalty, no *Ragamala* (Garland of *raga*) series rendered in an imperial style has yet come to light. All known Mughal-style *Ragamala* series have been executed in what is now regarded as the popular Mughal style, and the genre seems to have become fashionable early in the seventeenth century, although the tradition of *Ragamala* pictures is much older. Many stylistic elements are shared with the imperial Mughal style, but by and large these popular Mughal pictures display sparser and simpler compositions, looser draughtsmanship, and less refined and subtle coloring. However, the popular Mughal idiom had a more direct bearing than the imperial Mughal style on the contemporaneous development of painting in the Rajput courts.

NOTES

1. Schroeder 1947, p. 85.

2. See Brand & Lowry 1985, pp. 87–105, for the collecting habits of the first three Mughals.

3. Ibid., pp. 88–92. The Juki *Shahnama* is in the Royal Asiatic Society, London, and the *Zafarnama* in the University Library, Johns Hopkins University, Baltimore (see Lentz & Lowry 1989, pp. 359, 338, for citations of studies of them).

4. Quoted in Beach 1987, p. 26.

5. Ibid.

6. Das 1978, p. 29.

7. For discussions of the development of early Mughal painting, see P. Chandra 1976; Brand & Lowry 1985; and Beach 1987.

8. Brand & Lowry 1985, pp. 27, 137; and Beach 1987, pp. 17–21.

9. Quoted in P. Chandra 1976, p. 180.

10. Quoted in ibid., pp. 182–83.

11. Quoted in ibid., p. 183.

12. Quoted in ibid., p. 182.

13. Quoted in ibid., pp. 183–84.

14. I am indebted to R. Skelton for this information.

15. Quoted in P. Chandra 1976, p. 184.

16. Schroeder 1947, p. 79.

17. E. R. Hambye, "The First Jesuit Mission to Emperor Akbar," in *Islam in India: Studies and Commentaries,* ed. C. W. Troll (New Delhi: Vikash Publishing House, 1982), pp. 3–13; see especially p. 11.

18. Rogers & Beveridge [1909–14] 1968, 2: 20–21.

19. Ibid., pp. 43–44.

20. Beach 1965.

21. Rogers & Beveridge [1909–14] 1968, 2: 116–17.

22. Ibid., p. 20.

23. Das 1978, pp. 188–92. For the latest assessment of Manohar, see McInerney 1991.

24. Beach 1978, p. 118.

25. Dye 1989.

26. Beach 1978, p. 127, no. 45.

27. See Seyller 1991, p. 118, n. 1, for relevant citations.

28. Seyller 1991.

29. Bernier [1891] 1972, p. 254.

30. P. Chandra 1960, p. 25.

31. Binney 1973, p. 57.

32. All quotations in this paragraph are from Leach 1986, pp. 106–7.

33. For the Freer *Ramayana* and a discussion of the Khan Khanan as a patron, see Beach 1981, pp. 128–55.

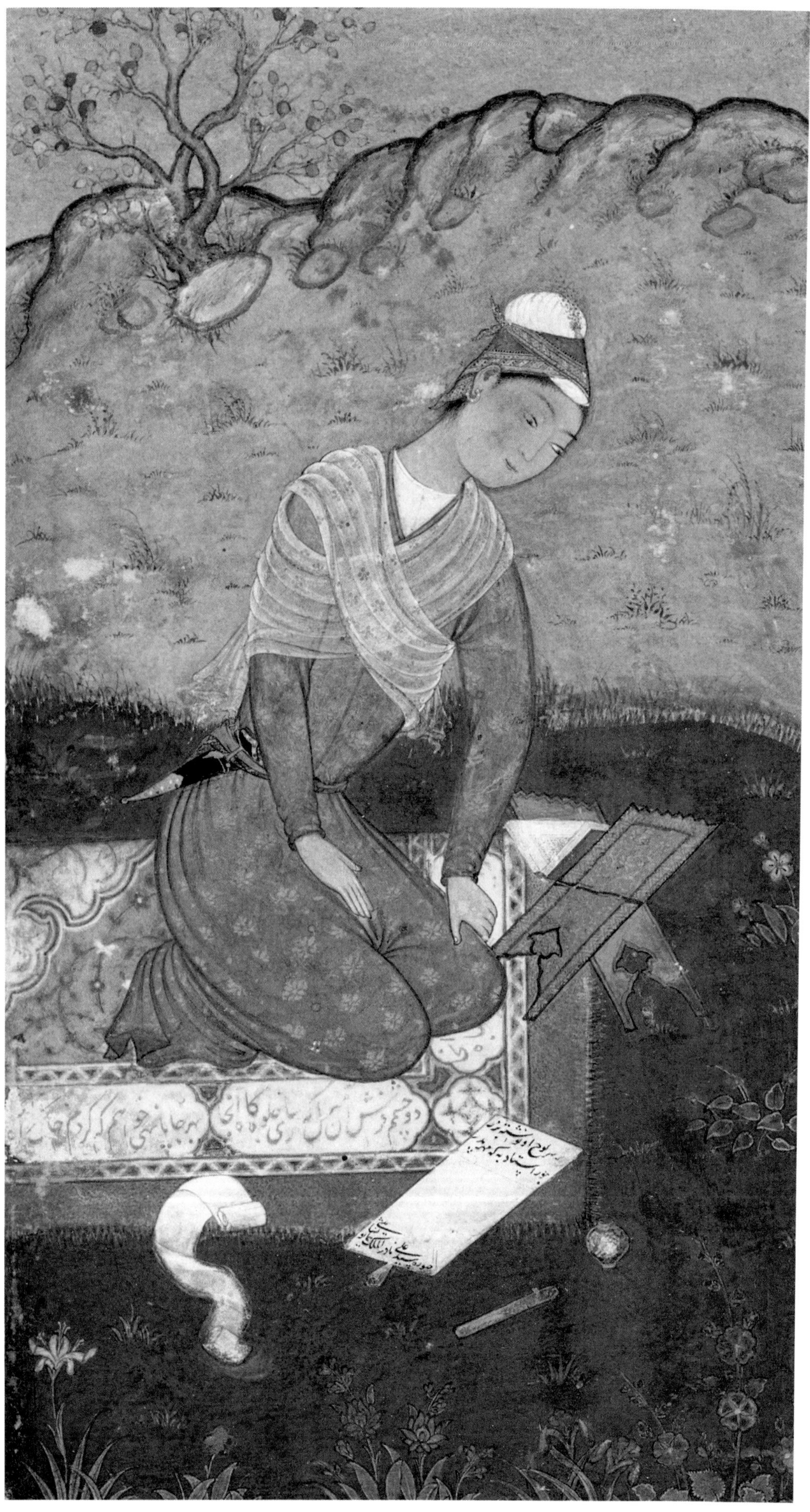

Catalogue

Imperial Mughal Paintings and Calligraphy

Unless otherwise noted, all pictures are painted in opaque watercolor and gold, all texts are written in ink, and all works are on paper. Because the imperial Mughal workshop and individual artists moved about, with rare exceptions only the regnal period of a work's creation is indicated.

45 PORTRAIT OF A YOUNG SCHOLAR

By Mir Sayyid Ali (active c. 1513–c. 1576)
Humayun period, 1549–56
Folio, 12 7/16 x 7 7/8 in (31.6 x 20.0 cm)
Illustration, 7 1/2 x 4 1/8 in (19.1 x 10.5 cm)
Bequest of Edwin Binney, 3rd
M.90.141.1
Literature: Grube 1968, pp. 39, 202, no. 90; Binney 1973, pp. 26, 30, no. 10; S. C. Welch 1973, pp. 88–89, no. 52; A. Welch 1975; P. Chandra 1976, pp. 20–21, pl. 64; Brand & Lowry 1985, pp. 24, 25, 137, no. 6; A. Welch 1990, pp. 91, 96, fig. 13.

According to W. M. Thackston, the inscription at the bottom of the writing tablet lying on the ground at the corner of the carpet reads: *sawwarahu Sayyid Ali Nadir al-Mulk-i Humayunshahi.* It informs us that the artist was Sayyid Ali, who worked for the emperor Humayun and enjoyed the honorific title *nadir al-mulk,* meaning "rarity of the realm." The couplet at the top of the tablet refers to the severity of a master being preferable to the affection of a father.

An Iranian artist, Mir Sayyid Ali was the son of Mir Musavvir of Badakhshan, a master artist who lived in Tabriz. Both father and son worked for the Safavid monarchs Shah Ismail and Shah Tahmasp. According to a Persian treatise on painters and calligraphers compiled by Qazi Ahmad in 1606, during his exile in Iran Humayun wanted to bring the father to India but settled for the son, "who in art was more clever than his father" (Minorsky 1959, p. 185). Mir Sayyid Ali joined the wandering ruler's temporary court at Kabul in Afghanistan in 1549. He accompanied Humayun to Delhi in 1555 and became the supervisor of the royal workshop. After Humayun's accidental death the following year, Mir Sayyid Ali continued to work in the same capacity for Akbar. He was in charge of the *Hamzanama* project [46] until about 1570, when he received the emperor's permission to go on Haj pilgrimage to Mecca. Nothing is known of him thereafter.

Unfortunately very little is known about the artist's personal life. He must have had his early training with his father, and generally he painted in the Safavid style that prevailed in Tabriz at the time. Like many other Iranian painters, he was also a poet and wrote under the pen name of Juda'i. However, his skill with paint was far superior to his facility with words. He has been accused of using others' ideas freely in his literary efforts.

CAT. 45 detail

Scholars disagree as to the date of this picture and where it was painted. Grube (1968, p. 202) is of the opinion that the form of the inscription clearly demonstrates that the picture was painted for Humayun, with which I concur. Even though it is not certain whether the inscription is a signature or an ascription, the characterization of the artist as "belonging to Humayun" would imply that it was painted for the scholarly Humayun, for whom the subject would have been particularly appropriate. As to the date Grube (p. 39) thinks it was painted before Humayun's death in 1556, E. Binney (1973, p. 26) considered the picture to have been painted in Kabul soon after the artist's arrival there. S. C. Welch (1973) suggested that it was done about 1555 (p. 88) and then stated specifically that it was "painted after the death of Humayun in 1556" (p. 89). P. Chandra (1976, pp. 20–21) is of the opinion that it was painted about 1556, as it has clear affinities to the *Hamzanama* "in the softly modelled rocks in the background and the fluffy texture of the scarf wound around the shoulders." Brand and Lowry (1985) state that it was painted "prior to Humayun's return to India" (p. 137) but also that it was executed between artist's arrival in Kabul and "Humayun's death" (p. 24).

In his discussion Chandra regards this as an important picture, "as the style of the work marks a new phase distinct from Persian painting, showing in the more vigorous movement of line, feeling for spatial depth, voluminousness, and boldness of execution, characteristics associated with the *Hamzanama.*" On one hand, there is no doubt that the picture does exhibit a flavor quite distinct from the kind of work Mir Sayyid Ali was doing in Tabriz about 1540 (cf. Beach 1987, p. 12, fig. 2). On the other hand, compared with a picture of a similar subject in the Fitzwilliam Album dated to 1555–60 by Beach (1987, p. 44, fig. 29), the portrait of the young scholar is distinctly more Persian. It is also interesting to compare this painting with a signed drawing by the master in the Musée Guimet, Paris (Okada 1989, p. 135, no. 27), where too the subject is a man reading. That drawing was done about twenty years later.

Compared with most other known paintings by Mir Sayyid Ali, this picture presents a few unusual features. While it shows the artist's particular penchant for shapes and features as well as design and ornaments, it certainly does not demonstrate his apparent flaw, which S. C. Welch noted, of seeing the world as still life. On the contrary, it stands out from other Safavid pictures of this genre for its whimsical touches. These are noticeable in the distinctive turban, which looks more Deccani than Safavid, the informal manner in which the young man wears his gossamer scarf, and the careless and unnaturalistic placement of the various scholarly apparatus in the foreground, all of which add to the composition's liveliness. Furthermore, the young man seems completely oblivious of his surroundings, so absorbed is he in his book. His keenness is expressed by his bent posture, which is as taut as a bow, while his rolling eyes betray his sense of wonder. Both the figural form and the facial expression are strongly reminiscent of figures in *The Meeting of the Clans,* an illustration that Mir Sayyid Ali painted for the Shah Tahmasp's *Khamsa* of Nizami between 1639(?) and 1643 (see A. Welch 1990, figs. 6, 7, 9).

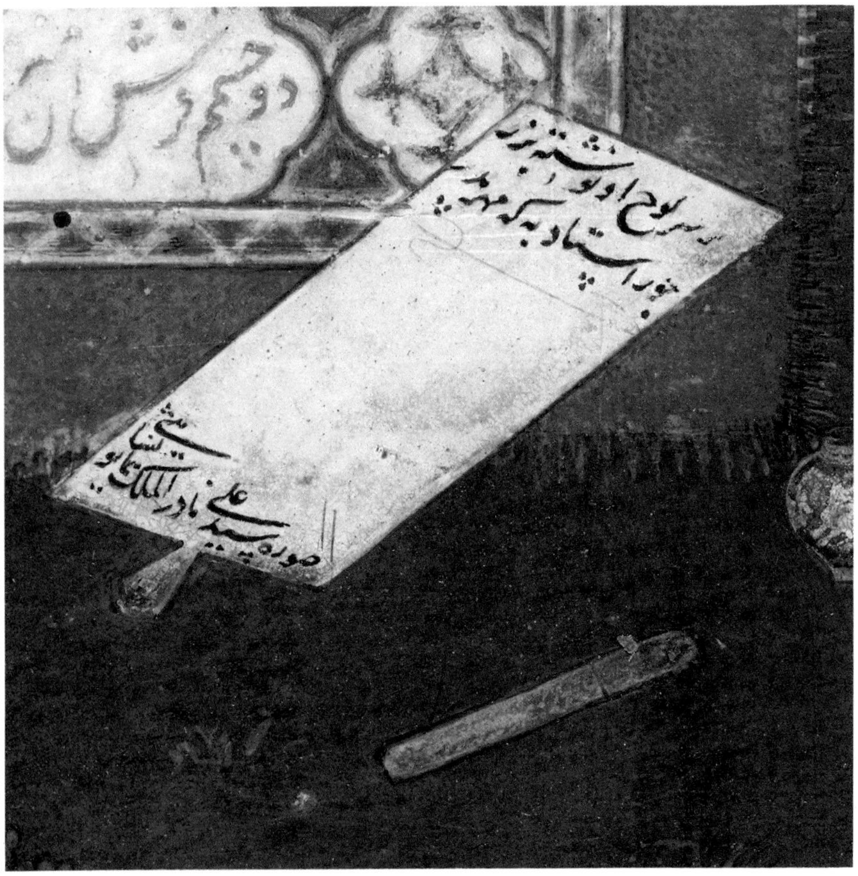

CAT. 45 detail

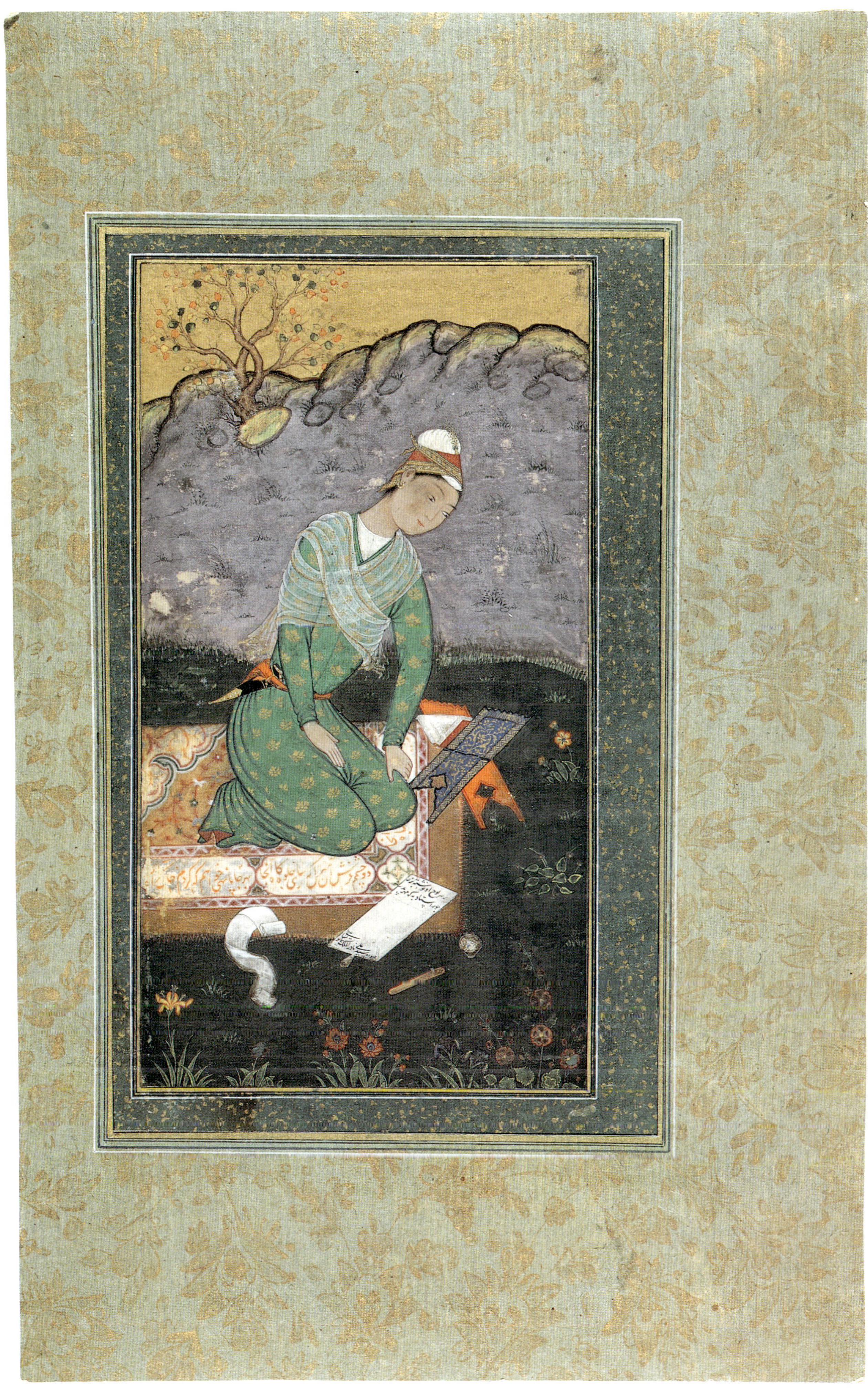

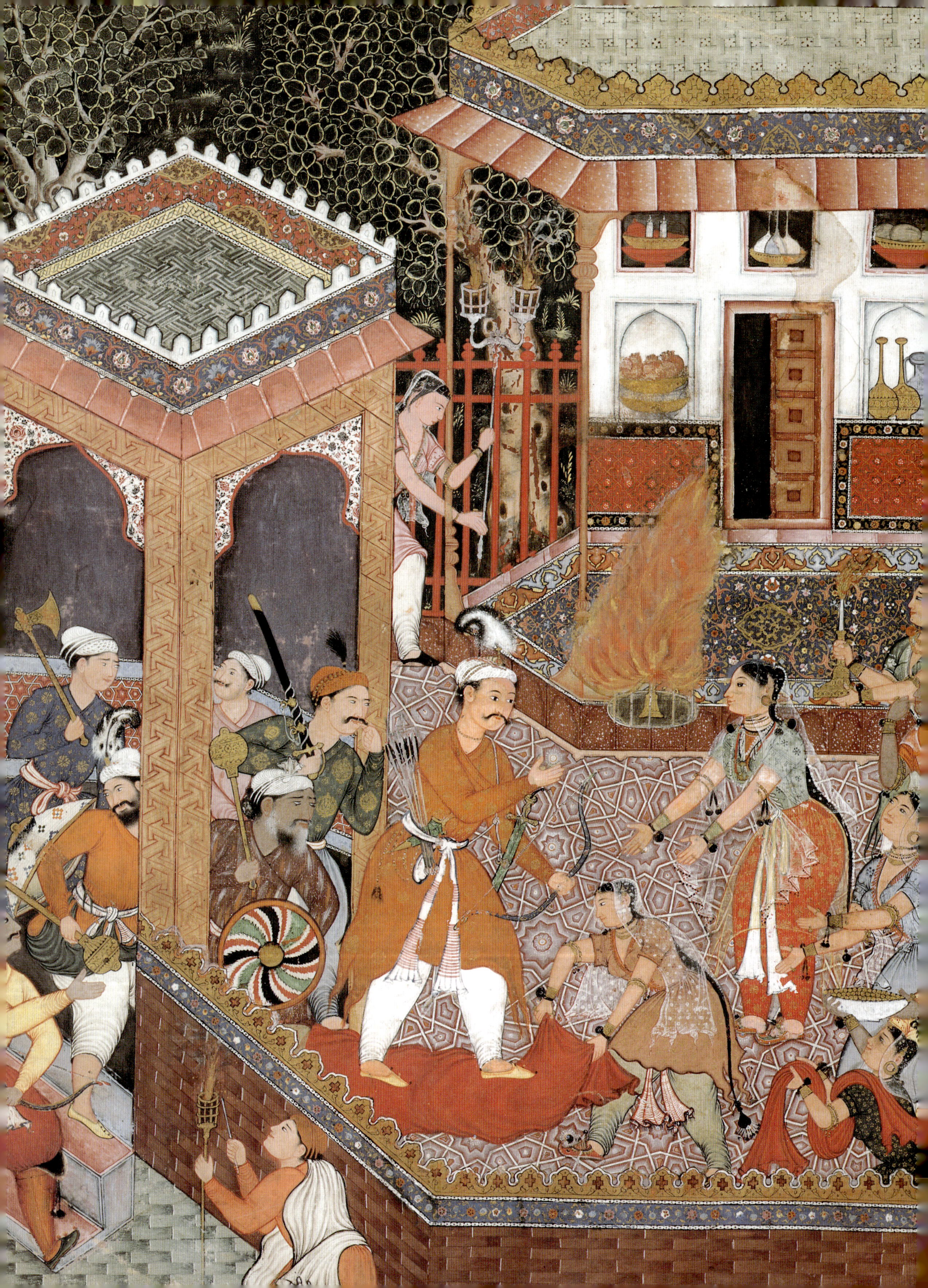

Akbar period, c. 1570
Illustration, opaque watercolor, gold, and ink, with mica, on cotton
Text, ink and gold on paper
Folio, 31 x 24⅞ in (78.7 x 63.2 cm)
Illustration and text, each, 26⅝ x 20¼ in (67.6 x 51.4 cm)
From the Nasli and Alice Heeramaneck Collection, Museum Associates Purchase
M.78.9.1
Literature: Pal 1982, pp. 8, 9, pl. 1; Pal 1987, pp. 116, 117, fig. 73.

Unlike most Mughal illustrated books, pictures in Akbar's *Hamzanama* (Saga of Hamza) were painted on cotton and the text was copied on paper and pasted on the back. Although examples of early Mughal paintings on cloth are not altogether unknown (S. C. Welch 1985, p. 143, no. 84), the *Hamzanama* is a unique production of the imperial Mughal workshop. The book was planned in fourteen (Abul Fazl mentions twelve) volumes, each consisting of one hundred folios. At present about one hundred fifty are known, none of which is in its original state. This particular folio is one of the best preserved and displays no sign of reworking. Each folio has a full-size painting on one side and the text, though not of the picture, on the reverse. The text relevant to this picture is in the Brooklyn Museum, as pointed out by Z. Faridany-Akhavan (personal communication). There is no edited text or translation of the *Hamzanama* into English, which makes it difficult to place the pictures in their proper narrative context.

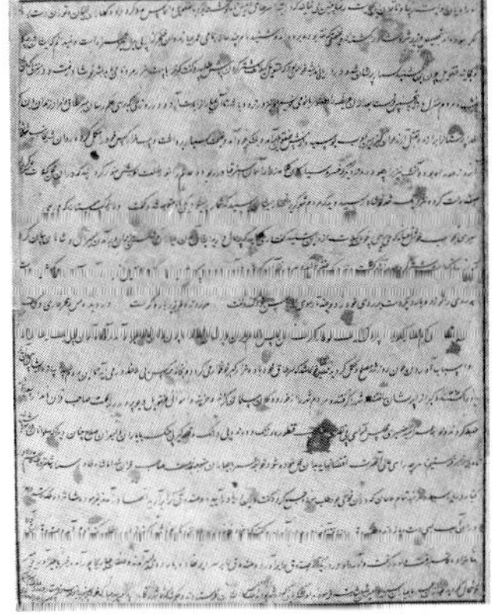
CAT. 46 text

The *Hamzanama* recounts the legendary adventures of Amir Hamza, a hero who is a conflation of an Iranian figure and an uncle of the Prophet Muhammad, in various Asian countries. These tales of adventure obviously had a great fascination for Akbar, which is why the *Hamzanama* was one of the earliest commissions. This particular illustration represents Sanubar Banu giving refuge to the champions of Iran and Turan who had killed the vizier of the city of Now-Shad and taken its treasure. The visitors are being enthusiastically welcomed by Sanubar Banu and other females of the mansion. One is spreading a red cloth for the heroes to walk on while another proffers a second piece. This must be the earliest known representation of this custom, which was probably adopted by the British and later spread to Europe. A third woman brings a bowl, while a fourth holds up a torch. A second torch is held by a servant at the back. A brazier burns dangerously near the blue carpet on the shallow platform leading into a pavilion.

CAT. 46

There is some disagreement among scholars as to the date this *Hamzanama* was prepared. Most agree that the series was begun in 1562 and completed in 1577. K. Khandalavala (1974, pp. 70–72), however, argues for a later start and completion: from 1566 until 1582. What does seem certain is that it took about fifteen years to complete the work. Mir Sayyid Ali supervised the project for the first seven years, until he left for Mecca, whereupon the task devolved upon Abd as-Samad.

Although there are conflicting opinions among the various contemporary sources regarding the statistics of the project, all are of the opinion that this was the single most ambitious undertaking of the imperial workshop. Most also credit Akbar for conceiving the idea. One source tells us that Mir Sayyid Ali "strives to finish that wondrous book which is one of the astonishing novelties that His Majesty has conceived of"; another source characterizes the emperor as "a designer of marvels" for ordering the illustrated copy of the *Hamzanama* (see P. Chandra 1976, pp. 180, 187). Akbar's role was probably more than seminal. Apart from selecting the episodes to be illustrated, he may even have contributed to the formation of the narrative style.

The large size of the paintings almost certainly indicates that they were held up in an assembly while the text was recited. This required a freer style with clearly recognizable figures rather than the richly detailed work that one encounters in smaller paper manuscripts. The *Hamzanama* paintings, despite their interesting spatial distortions and faulty perspective, express the energy and excitement of the action with dramatic intensity. Although the forms and motifs were borrowed from Persian paintings, they are given a distinctive Indian flavor. They are less delicate and precious and have an earthy quality that would be strange to an Iranian aesthete. The tonality of the vibrant and warm colors, particularly the yellow and orange, are recognizably Indian, as are the plants and the animals depicted, which are also treated with much greater naturalism than one finds in Persian paintings. Even more decidedly Indian are the figurative forms, which continue the robust sensuousness of earlier Indian paintings, although their naturalistic grouping and expressiveness are novel elements.

47 FOLIO FROM A *TUTINAMA* MANUSCRIPT

Akbar period, c. 1580
Folio, 10 x 6½ in (25.4 x 16.5 cm)
From the Nasli and Alice Heeramaneck Collection, Museum Associates Purchase
M.81.8.6
Literature: *Heeramaneck* 1966, p. 140, no. 193 (not illustrated).

A *Marriage of Ubayd (?)* (r)
7¼ x 4⅞ in (18.4 x 12.4 cm)

B *Merchant and His Partner Conversing* (v)
5⅞ x 4½ in (14.9 x 11.4 cm)

The *Tutinama* (Tales of a parrot) was composed by Ziya ad-Din Nakhshabi and completed in 1329/30. It is essentially a reworked version of an earlier Persian translation of a Sanskrit text known as the *Sukasaptati* (Seventy tales of a parrot). Nakhshabi's version consists of fifty-two tales. The stories are told by a parrot to amuse a lady and prevent her from seeking romance elsewhere while her husband is away. They are moralistic tales, although laced with humor as well as pathos.

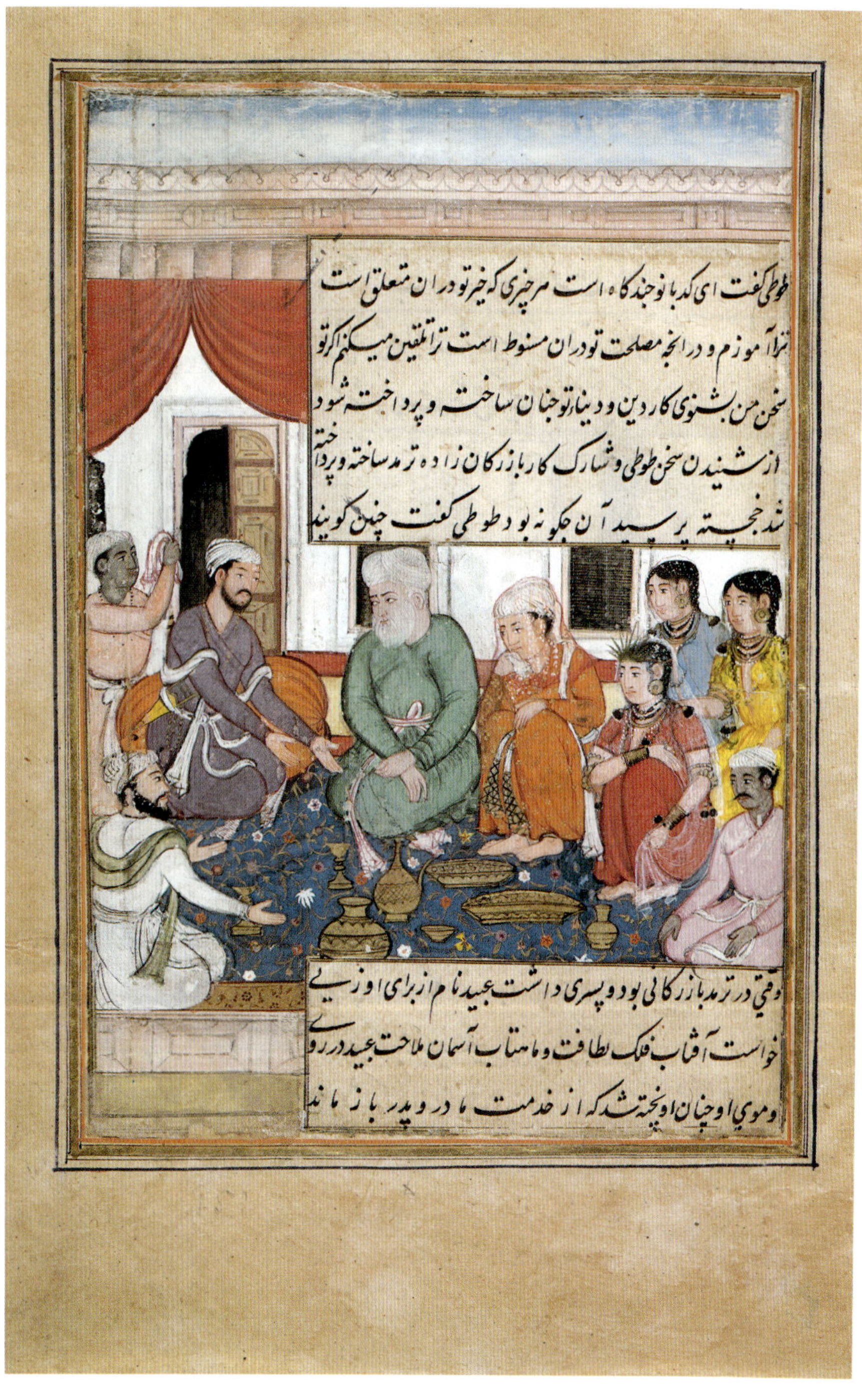

CAT. 47A

This folio is from a *Tutinama* manuscript, the bulk of which is now in the Chester Beatty Library, Dublin. Hence it is commonly referred to as the "Beatty *Tutinama*." It is generally considered to have been prepared in the imperial studio about 1580, perhaps for a literate lady of the imperial household.

Most scholars who have discussed this manuscript have commented on the simplicity of the illustrations, which certainly lack the complexity and sophistication of most manuscripts prepared for the emperor during the 1580s. Even compared with the *Kathasaritsagara* illustrations [51], these *Tutinama* pictures appear to be rather naïvely conceived in the use of landscape elements, coloring, and compositions. J. P. Losty (1982, p. 89, no. 60) finds close similarities between these illustrations and those in a *Darabnama* in the British Library. In both one encounters instances of rather immature work probably done by apprentices as well as work clearly by more practiced hands. While the names of the artists of the *Darabnama* are known, this *Tutinama's* attributions have been lost during subsequent rebinding.

The two pictures on this folio illustrate the early section of a tale narrated by the parrot on the forty-second night. It recounts the story of a merchant's son named Ubayd who loved his wife to excess and neglected his filial and professional duties. The merchant complained to his partner, who gave him a parrot and a myna bird. That night the birds narrated two different tales to Ubayd, as a result of which he realized his error and returned to his parents and his business (see Muhammad A. Simsar, *The Cleveland Museum of Art's Tuti-nama/Tales of a Parrot,* Cleveland 1978, pp. 258–65 for the story).

A It is difficult to identify exactly what is happening in the scene illustrated on the recto. The text gives no description of a wedding. All the figures are seated on a blue carpet, perhaps on a terrace. An old man with a white beard in the center of the picture listens to two men, both with black beards, who express themselves with rather forceful gestures of their arms. Beside the old man sit the groom and the bride with one male and two female companions. The couple is distinguished by the manner in which they sit—on their haunches rather than as the others—and the transparent veils over their heads. A number of golden dishes and pots containing refreshments are scattered on the carpet in the foreground. The artist has used a wide range of colors, especially for the attire of the figures, each of whom wears dress of a different hue.

B The composition on the verso is simpler, involving only three men. Within a pavilion the merchant and his friend are engaged in a lively conversation. Evidently the merchant is complaining to his partner about his son's infatuation with his wife. From the right a servant enters with a flask of wine. The tonality of the colors—particularly the blue, the orange, and the yellow—is identical in both illustrations.

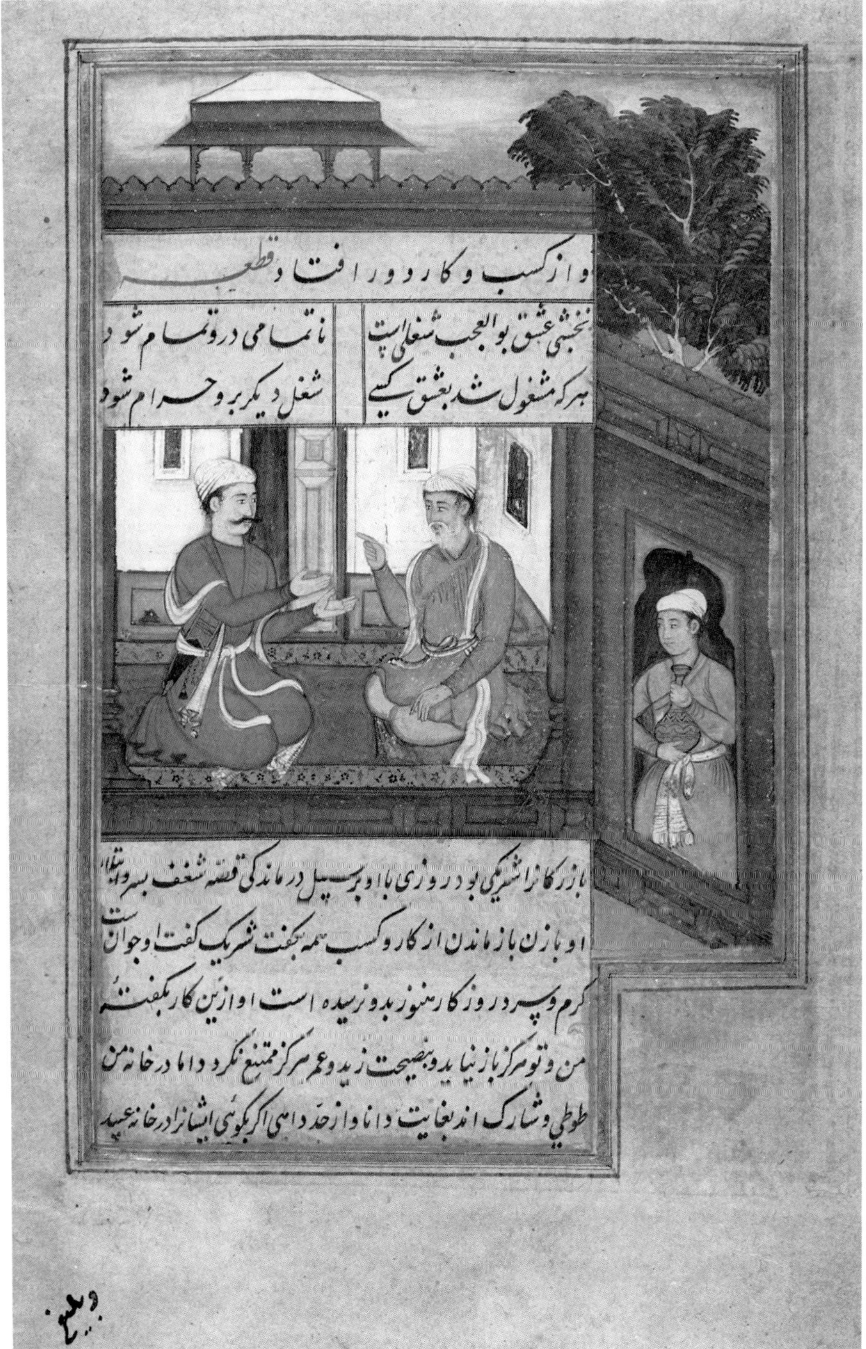

CAT. 47B

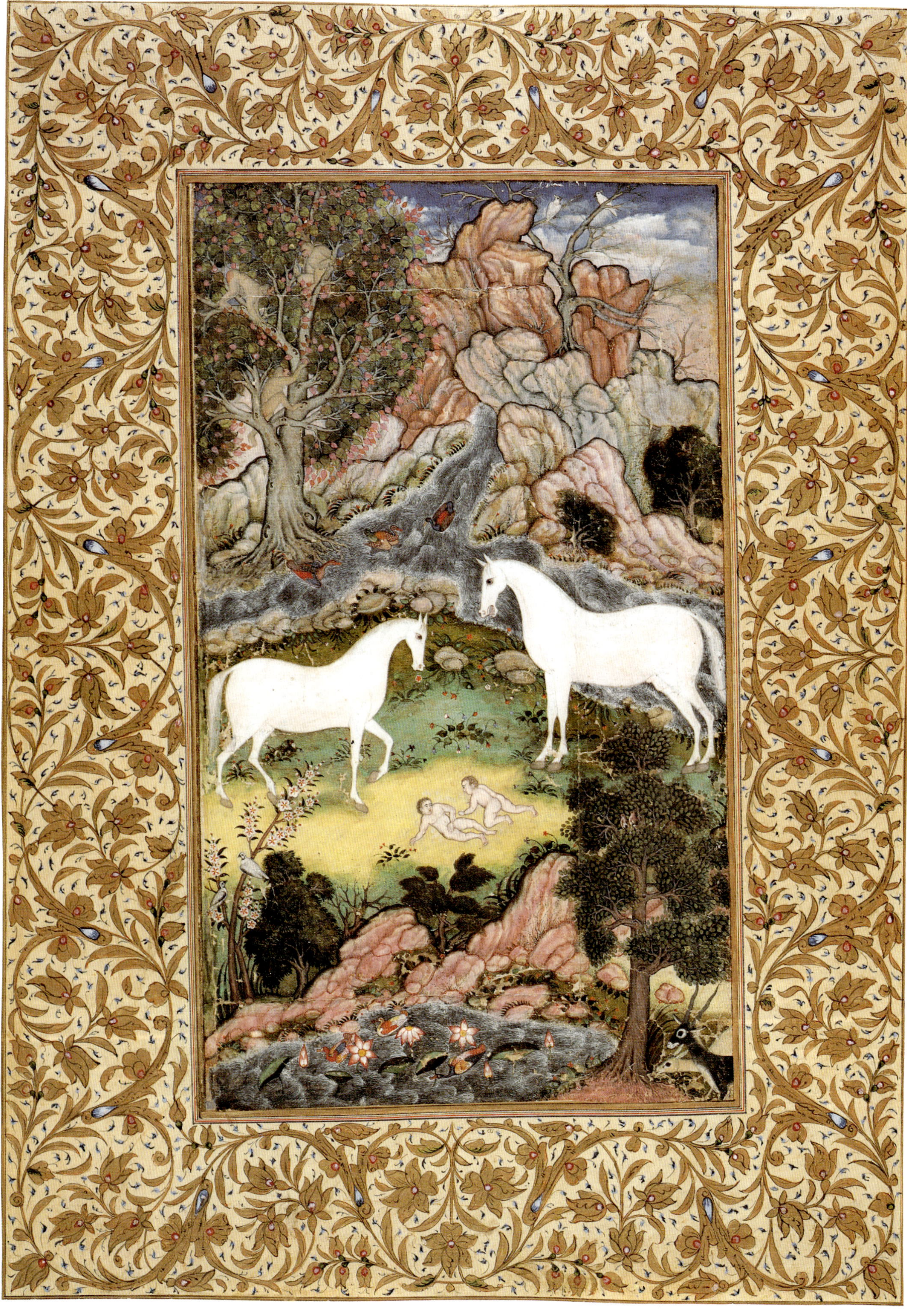

48 THREE FOLIOS FROM A *HARIVAMSA* MANUSCRIPT

Akbar period, c. 1585–90
Folios, approx. 16⅛ x 11¾ in (41.0 x 29.8 cm)
Illustrations, approx. 11¾ x 7 in (29.8 x 17.8 cm)
From the Nasli and Alice Heeramaneck Collection, Museum Associates Purchase
A, M.83.1.7; B, M.78.9.10; C, M.83.105.4
Literature: A, *Heeramaneck* 1966, pp. 144, 147, no. 199a; Heeramaneck 1984, p. 156, pl. 153; Pal 1986, cover, p. 15.
B, Ardeshar 1940, pp. 32–33, pl. 1; *Heeramaneck* 1966, p. 144, no. 199b (not illustrated); Johnson 1972, p. 145, pl. LXXXIIIa (detail); Hutchins 1980, pp. 49–51, 120; Pal 1982, pp. 12, 13, pl. III; Heeramaneck 1984, p. 156, pl. 152.
C, Pal 1982, pp. 14, 15, pl. IV; Heeramaneck 1984, p. 156, pl. 154.

A *Birth of the Celestial Twins*
B *Balarama Kills Dhenukasura*
Attributed to Basawan (active c. 1560–1600)
C *Pradyumna Kills Samvara*

These three folios, with illustrations on one side and text on the other, were removed from a *Harivamsa* manuscript and remounted in outer borders done about 1700. The borders are richly adorned with intertwined flowering tendrils in gold highlighted with touches of red, blue, and green.

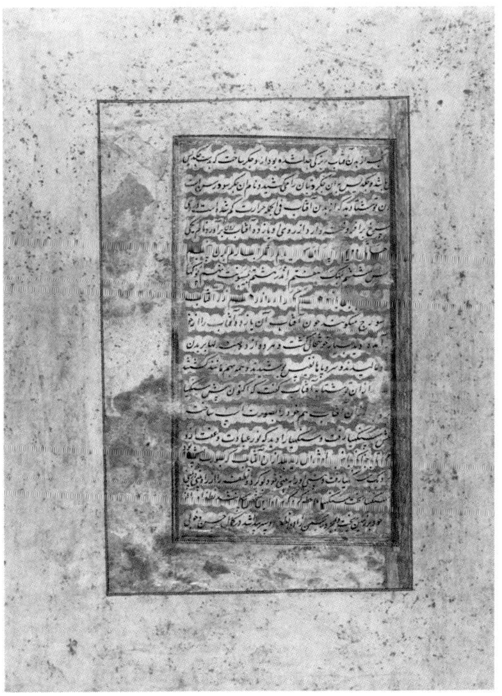

CAT. 48A text

The *Harivamsa* (Lineage of Hari [a synonym of Krishna]) is a sequel to the epic *Mahabharata* and was probably compiled in the early centuries of the Christian era. A Persian translation of this text was prepared for Akbar and was completed by February 1586, when Mulla Sheri, the translator, was killed.

Partly because of the date of the translator's death and partly because of archaisms in some of the paintings, it has been suggested that the illustrations were probably rendered as early as 1585 (Beach 1981, p. 71) rather than in 1590, the date preferred by R. Skelton (1970). Skelton, however, has argued at length to demonstrate how these *Harivamsa* illustrations are posterior to the Jaipur *Razmnama* and a different *Harivamsa*, which were illustrated by 1586. For the present therefore it seems appropriate to date the *Harivamsa* to which the museum's pictures belonged between 1585 and 1590. Unfortunately because of subsequent remounting the names of the artists are lost forever.

A This picture illustrates the birth of the celestial twins Asvinikumara described in chapter 9 of the text. The story goes that unable to bear the effulgence of the sun-god Vivasvat, his wife Samjna assumed the form of a mare and fled to the northern country known as Uttarakuru. Vivasvat found out where she was, changed himself into a horse, and mated with his reluctant spouse. The result was the birth of the twins who became known as Asvinikumara, "the mare's boys."

Although we do not know who the artists were, they expressed in a masterly manner the subtle nuances of the myth's symbolic meaning in the naturalistic Mughal style. In a landscape of rocks and streams in rich browns and greens and enlivened with cavorting monkeys and birds on trees, ducks and lotuses in the water, and a pair of antelopes in the lower right corner, the viewer's eye is inexorably led to the center of the composition, dominated by the two equine celestials. Appropriately, the horses are painted white, as they are symbols of luminosity, and the twins play against a radiantly yellow ground, as these celestial boys always make their appearance with the dawn. While the father remains slightly aloof, the mare appears to be more solicitous as she approaches the twins.

CAT. 48A

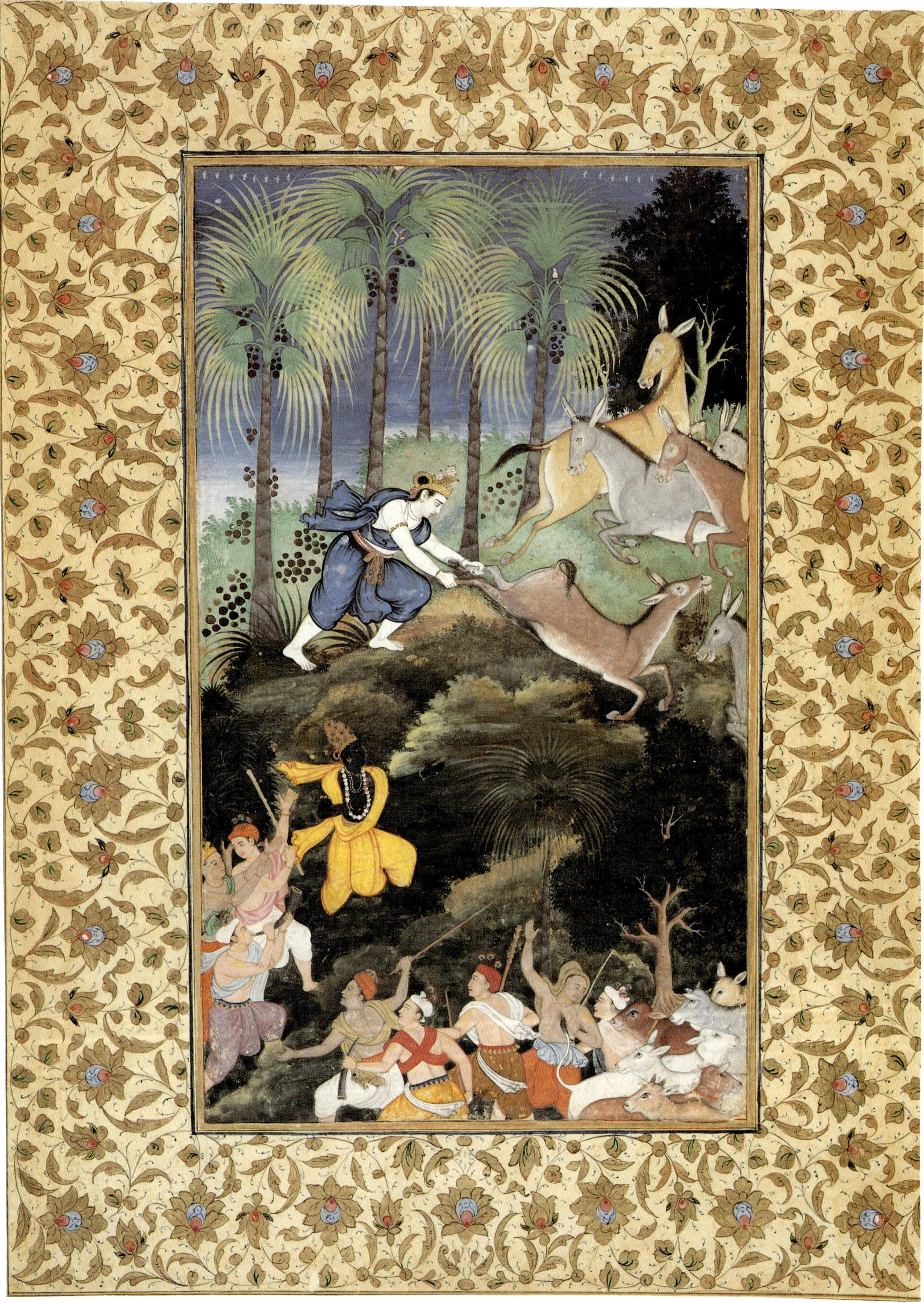

B The destruction of the ass-demon Dhenukasura is described in chapter 69 of the *Harivamsa.* Once Krishna and Balarama and their cowherd companions arrived at a palmyra palm forest that was deathly silent. The boys were unaware that the forest was occupied by the ass-demon Dhenuka and his cohorts. Unconcerned, the rambunctious boys began to bring down from the trees large and juicy nuts, which made a lot of noise as they fell to the ground. This upset Dhenuka, who rushed at Balarama. Balarama, however, picked Dhenuka up by his hind legs, and after swinging him a few times as if a hammer-thrower, hurled him at the top of the palmyra trees and so destroyed the demon.

One of the finest *Harivamsa* pictures, this is also one of the most dramatic. Both the composition and the strong contrast of light and dark heighten the drama of the occasion. The composition is, to use Skelton's expression, "organized along a swiftly moving diagonal" from the agitated figures in the lower left to the asses at the other end. Balarama's role in the incident has been given appropriate emphasis by distancing him from the others. The lower half of the picture, dominated by the bright orange garments of the blue-black Krishna, is painted in dark patches. All the excitement is confined to the figures in this section. The area occupied by Balarama and the asses is suffused with clear light, perhaps to emphasize the cosmic significance of the event. There is a strong possibility that Basawan (see [5 /]) had a hand in painting this picture.

C The myth of the feud between Pradyumna and Samvara is an important one and takes up four chapters (162–65) in the *Harivamsa.* Pradyumna was the son of Krishna and Rukmini and was in fact an avatar of Kamadeva, the god of desire. On the seventh day after his birth Samvara, a demon king, abducted the infant and took him to his wife, Mayavati. She, however, was the incarnation of Rati, the wife of Kamadeva, and at once recognized the beautiful child as her divine spouse. Later, after the child had grown up to be a handsome young man, Mayavati told him who he really was and how he had been abducted by Samvara. A battle ensued between the two, and Pradyumna killed Samvara and married Mayavati.

As is characteristic of Mughal pictures, the soldier demons are represented as fantastic creatures with animal or human heads, many-hued complexions, and spotted skins as if they all have the pox. Especially striking is the decapitated figure of the giant Samvàra, who is a bloody and fiery mess. The heroic Pradyumna watches the gory sight from a golden chariot to the right. Beyond some purple rocks and a green hillock is a palace, above which, against a blue sky enlivened with clouds painted in blue, white, purple, and green, are the four principal gods, Vishnu, Brahma, Siva, and Indra. They are showering garlands of victory from their floating thrones made of flowers. A few birds on the rocks and tree on the left seem totally disinterested in the gruesome events below.

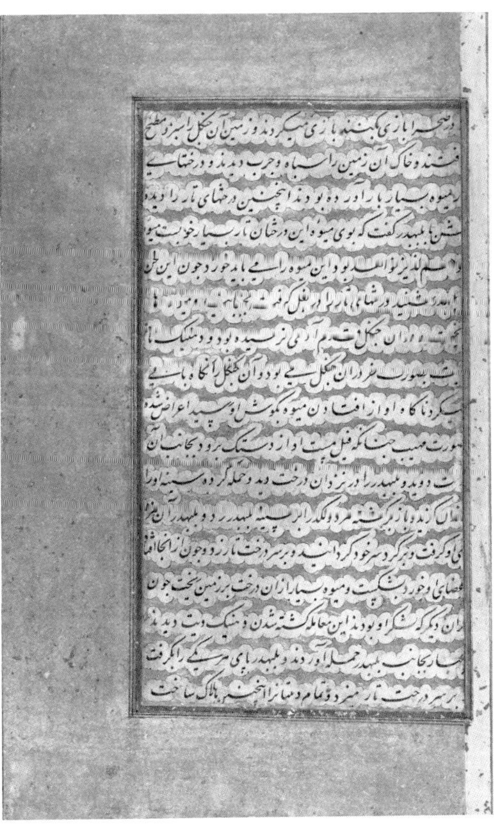

CAT. 48B *(opposite)*
CAT. 48B text *(right)*
CAT. 48C *(overleaf)*

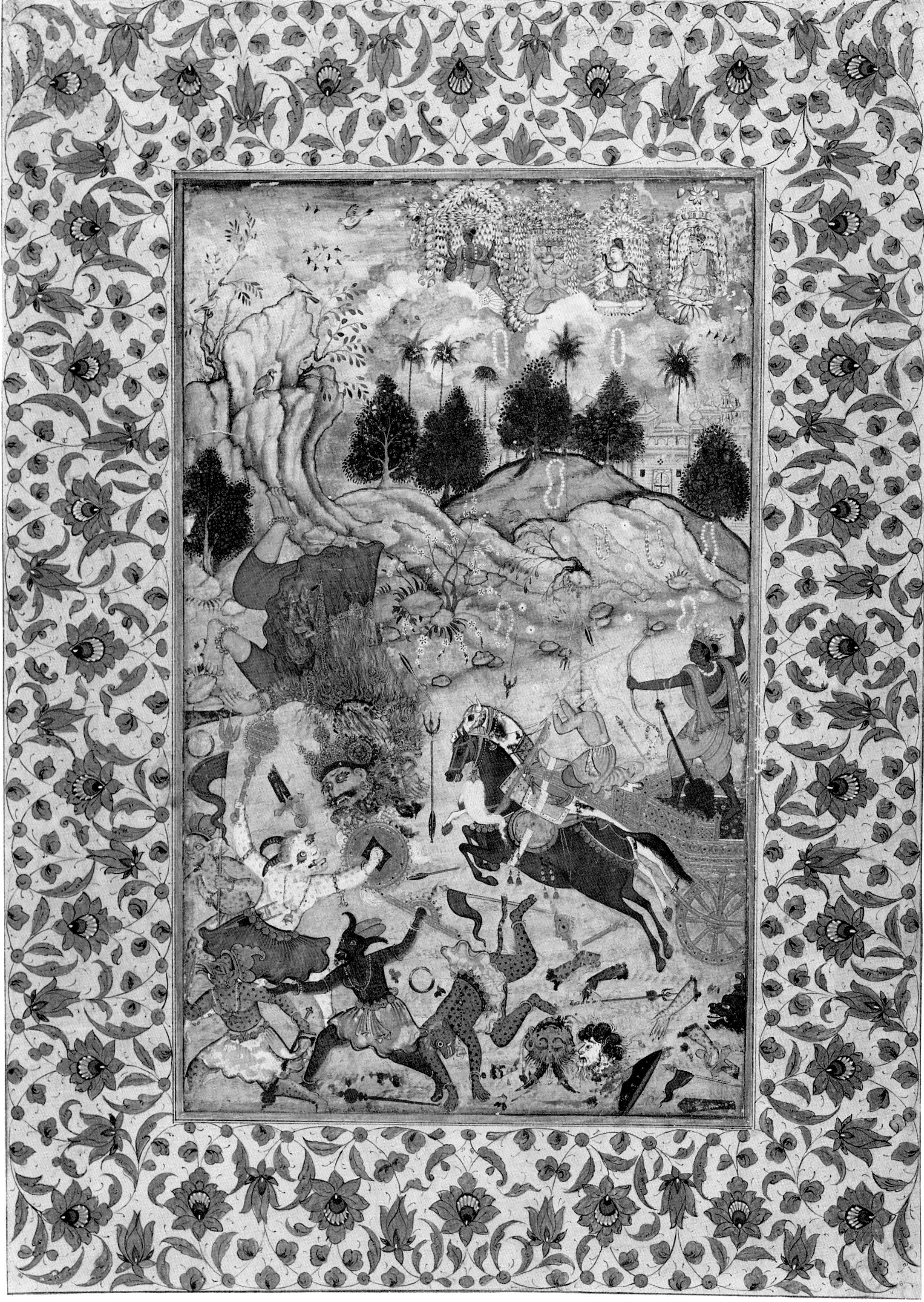

Inscribed to Dharmdas (active 1580–1610)
Akbar period, c. 1586–87
Inscription in red ink
Folio, 14½ x 9½ in (36.8 x 24.1 cm)
Illustration, 13 x 8¼ in (33.0 x 21.0 cm)
From the Nasli and Alice Heeramaneck Collection, Museum Associates Purchase M.78.9.6
Literature: *Heeramaneck* 1966, pp. 146, 148, no. 201; Pal 1982, pp. 10, 11, pl. II; Heeramaneck 1984, p. 159, pl. 179.

To sum up in a short space of time the breeze of salvation's morn breathed from fortune's ascension, and the brave warriors turned upon that mob and discomfited and scattered those hapless wretches by discharges of arrows. . . . The majesty of the royal wrath, and the onslaught of o'ermastering rage boiled over and an order was issued for plundering and burning Cambay. After that the pursuit of Sultān Bahādur was abandoned, and the army returned to Cāmpānīr.

So Abul Fazl wrote (H. Beveridge [1902] 1972, 1: 310) about the burning of the fort of Cambay, which has been illustrated here by Dharmdas for the first imperial copy of the *Akbarnama* (History of Akbar). This copy of the book is also known as the Victoria and Albert, or V&A, *Akbarnama*, as the majority of the illustrated folios are preserved in that museum in London. Because it recounts the story of Akbar's life, naturally it is one of the most lavishly illustrated of all the manuscripts prepared in the imperial atelier.

CAT. 49 detail

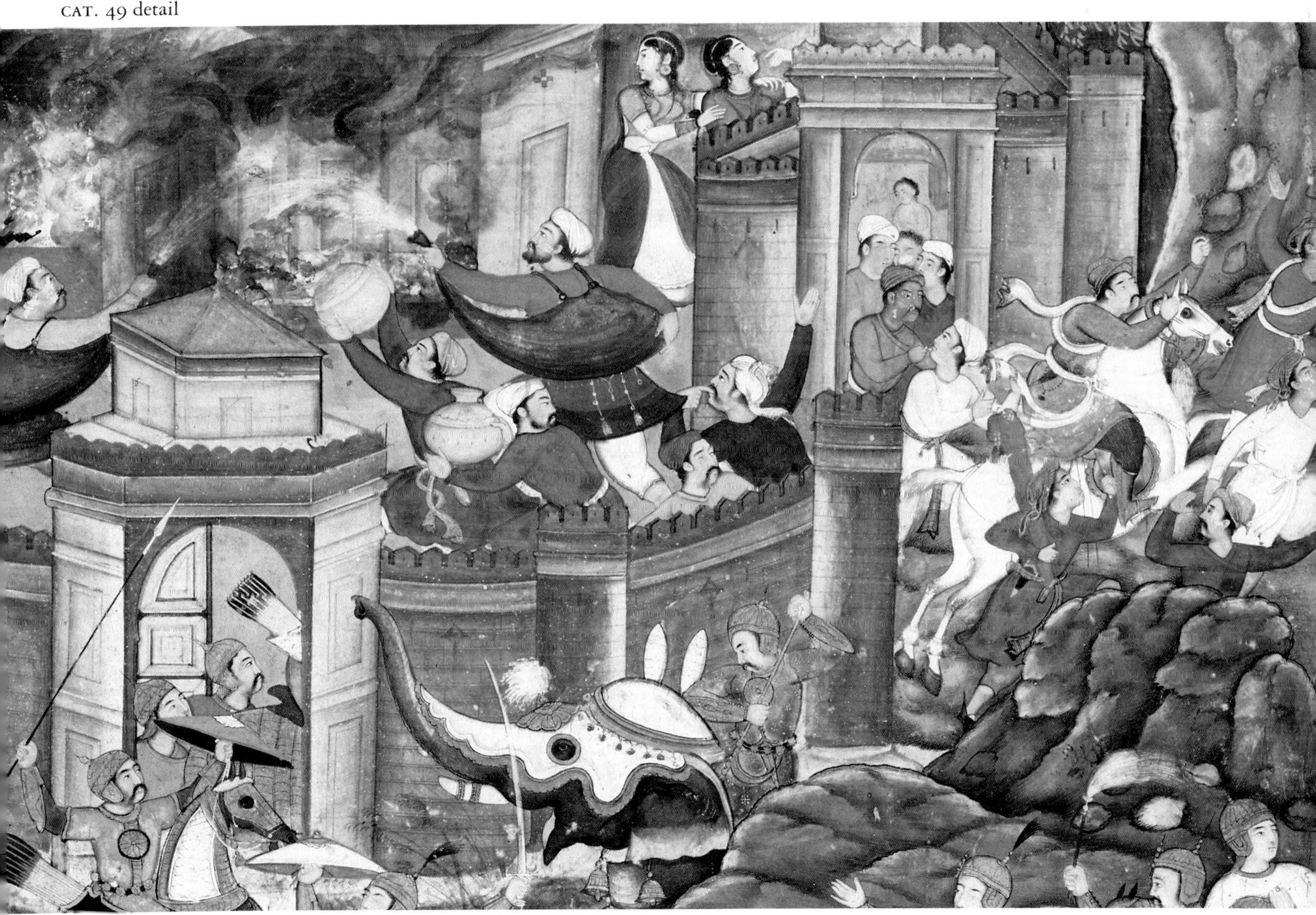

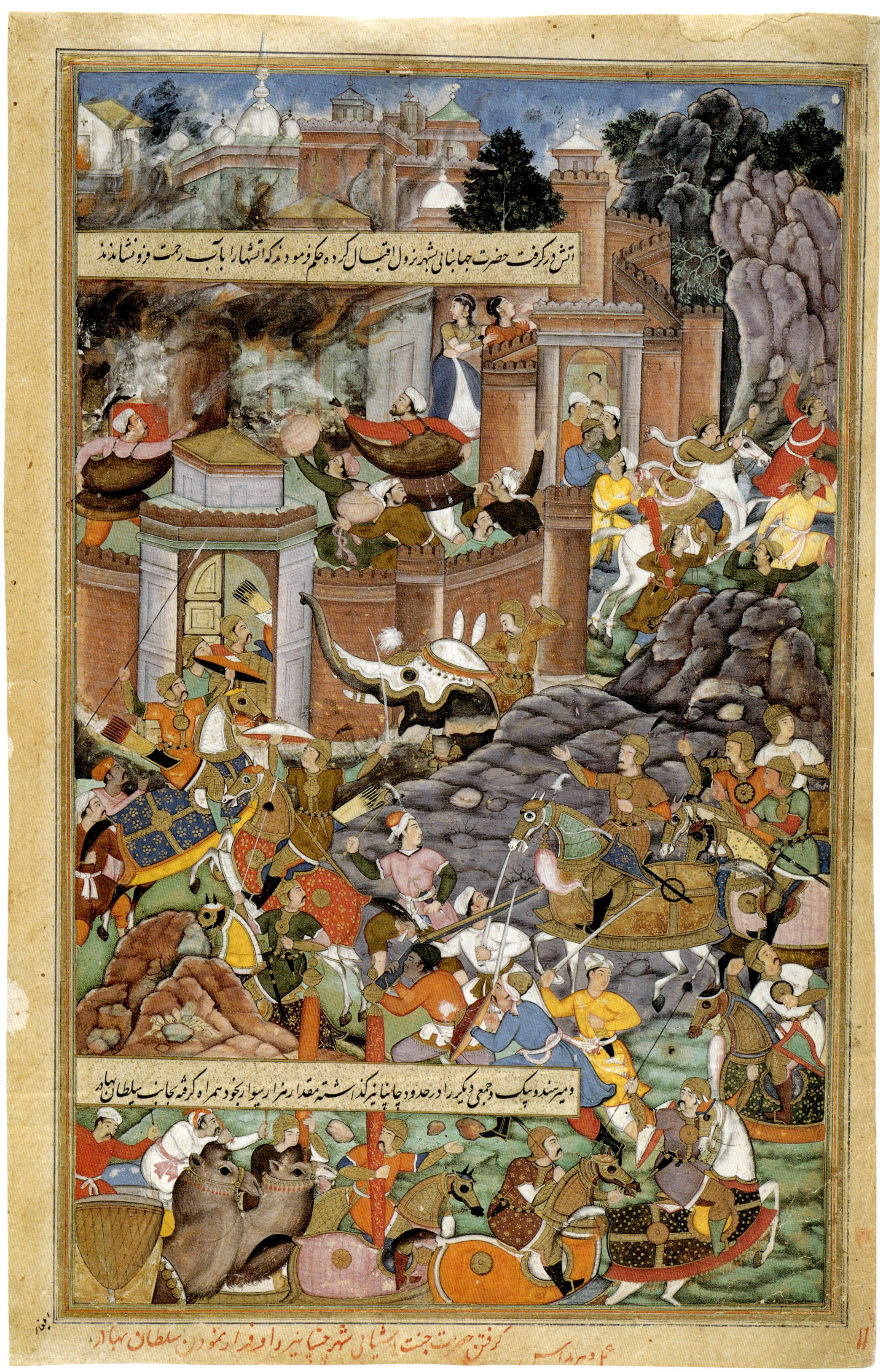
آتش درگرفت حضرت جهانبانی بشهر نزول اقبال کرده حکم فرمودند که آتشها را باآب رحمت فرونشاندند
و میر هندو بیگ و جمعی دیگر را در حدود چانپانیر گذاشته مقدار هزار سوار بخود همراه گرفته بجانب سلطان بهادر
گرفتن حضرت جنت آشیانی شهر چانپانیر را و فرار نمودن سلطان بهادر

According to an inscription in red ink along the bottom margin of the page, the artist responsible for this picture was Dharmdas. Although Dharmdas is not included among the seventeen masters of the imperial atelier listed by Abul Fazl, a review of all the inscribed works by him clearly demonstrates both his versatility and creative talent. What is even more fascinating is the fact (according to R. Skelton) that he had no hands and presumably painted with his feet. Not only was he responsible for painting portraits in many collaborative efforts for the principal Akbari manuscripts from about 1580 until 1604 (see Beach 1981, pp. 105–7 et passim), but often he worked on a painting with such masters as Basawan, Farrukh Beg, and Kesu the Elder. Even more significant is the fact that on several occasions he was given the responsibility for an entire illustration, as is the case with the example in the museum's collection. In addition, he painted three other illustrations among the known folios of this *Akbarnama* and rendered at least fourteen paintings for the 1604 copy. His later works, however, are less satisfactory than those done in the 1590s, when he was at the peak of his artistry.

As this picture demonstrates, Dharmdas was a master of design with a brilliant gift for organizing a complex composition that vividly expresses the drama of a situation. How skillfully he leads our eyes with the help of the diagonally moving figures to the fort on the upper left. The burning palace assumes great immediacy from the scurrying inhabitants rushing to quench the flames with water in hide bags and pots. The two women inside seem completely lost even as their brave master, Sultan Bahadur, deserts the palace on a horse. The impressive figure at the right lower center riding a richly caparisoned horse, heavily armored in a golden coat of mail and with his right arm stretched toward the fort, is clearly distinguished from the others and may represent Humayun himself. His face, shown in three-quarter view, is strongly individualized, which is what one would expect from Dharmdas, admired for his deftness in portraiture.

In 1969 Robert Skelton suggested that this copy of the *Akbarnama* was copied and illustrated about 1590. Most scholars since then have accepted Skelton's date except M. Beach (1981, p. 85), who first made the interesting suggestion that the style of the paintings indicates a date in the 1580s. He based his opinion on the close stylistic kinship between these *Akbarnama* pictures and those in *Tarikh-i Khandan-i Timuriyya* in the Khudabaksh Library in Patna, which was produced sometime between 1580 and 1585. In particular, Dharmdas's style in the two manuscripts is remarkably similar. L. Y. Leach (1986, p. 49) also follows Beach and states that the *Akbarnama* illustrations "follow the style of the major religious works produced in the late 1580s."

In a recent article John Seyller (1990) has very convincingly demonstrated that the illustrations in the V&A *Akbarnama* were, in fact, done for an earlier history and reused later to illustrate Abul Fazl's text. It seems Abul Fazl's text was considered the definitive history of the reign and was superimposed on the manuscript of an earlier history that carried these illustrations. After examining the codicological aspects of the V&A manuscript and closely comparing the style of the pictures with other illustrated manuscripts that can be firmly placed in the mid-1580s, Seyller concludes (p. 384) that "the 197 original paintings were probably executed in no more than two years within the period, most likely ca. 1586–87."

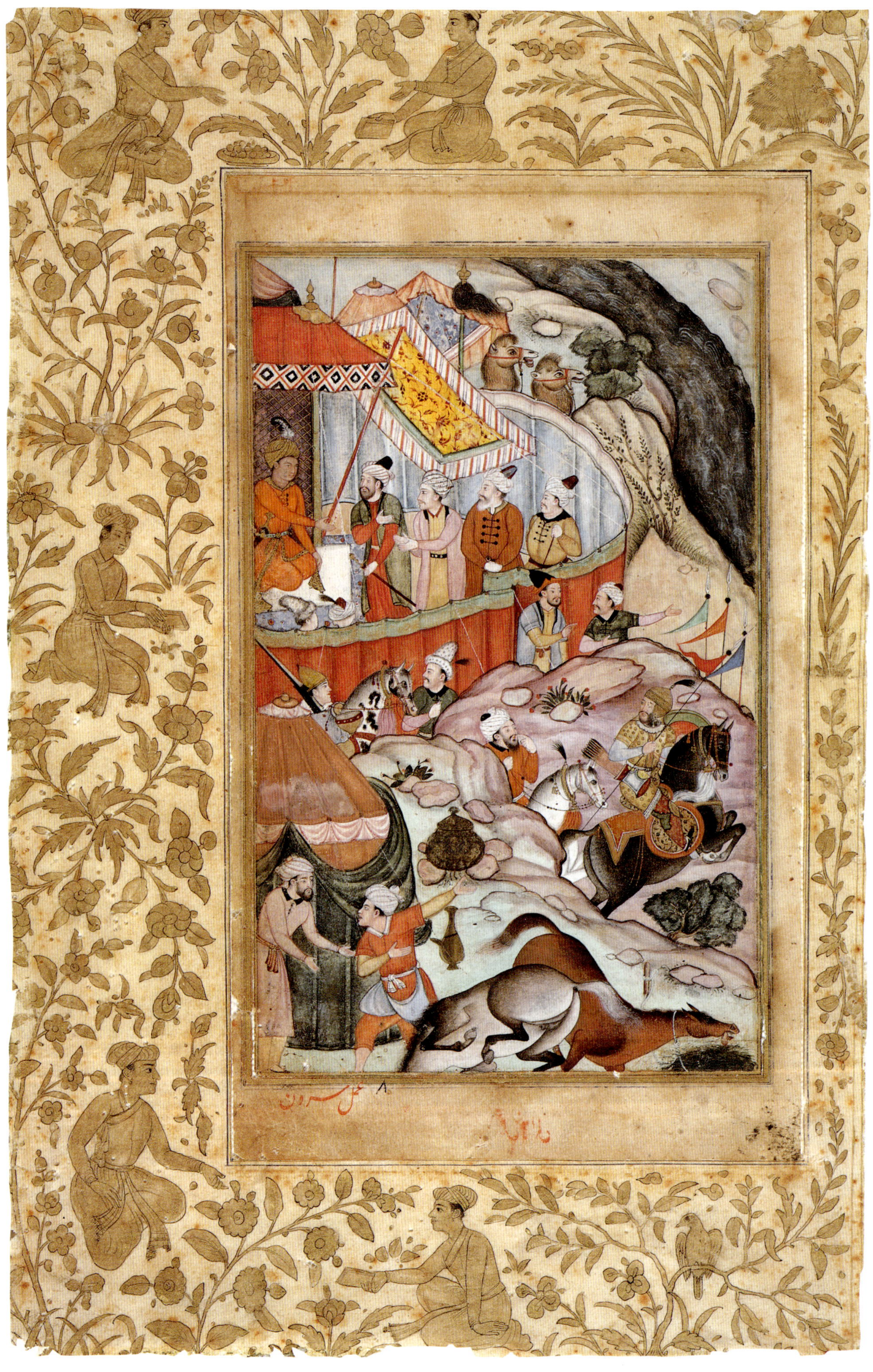

Akbar period, 1589–90

A *Disease at Qaba Disables the Horses in 1496*
By Sarvan (active 1580s)
Inscription in red ink
Folio, 13½ x 8¾ in (34.3 x 22.2 cm)
Illustration, 8¼ x 5⅛ (21.0 x 13.0 cm)
From the Nasli and Alice Heeramaneck Collection, Museum Associates Purchase
M.81.8.7
Literature: *Heeramaneck* 1966, p. 141, no. 195 (not illustrated); Heeramaneck 1984, p. 157, pl. 160.

B *Babur Marches from Kabul to Hindustan in 1507*
Folio, 10½ x 6⅝ in (26.7 x 16.8 cm)
Illustration, 8⅝ x 5⅞ in (21.9 x 14.9 cm)
Gift of the Walter Foundation
M.91.348.1
Literature: Pal 1971a, pp. 80, 83, fig. 12.

These two illustrated folios are from a manuscript of the *Baburnama* (Memoirs of Babur). Babur wrote in Turki, but as few of the Mughal court were familiar with the language, Akbar had several Persian translations made. One of these, supervised by Abd ar-Rahim Khan-Khanan, was completed and presented to Akbar in November 1589.

Four illustrated copies of the *Baburnama* were prepared successively for Akbar (see Smart 1973 and Smart 1978). The museum's two leaves are from the copy known as the "dispersed *Baburnama.*" Early in this century the manuscript was broken up and individual folios were set into borders from a *Farhang-i Jahangiri,* a Persian lexicon compiled for Jahangir (see [67]). Folio A has such an outer border but B does not. The border of A is richly adorned in gold with flowering tendrils and plants, including a pomegranate tree, a bird and a bee, and five seated male figures, four of whom hold books.

The dispersed *Baburnama* is the earliest of the four illustrated copies and is regarded as the copy that was presented to Akbar in 1589. Although the selection of the incidents to be illustrated was very likely made by Akbar when the scribes in the atelier began the planning, it is not known whether the illustrations were added as the work progressed. According to E. Smart, a specialist on these manuscripts, the illustrations could not have been done later than a year after the presentation date.

The manuscript is notable for the large number of double-page illustrations. Both the museum's pictures had facing compositions that cannot now be traced. A was a left half of such a double-page illustration and B was a right half. Whereas the majority of the illustrations were the results of collaborations between two or even three artists, some were rendered by a single painter, as is the case with A. An inscription in red ink at the bottom left just outside the picture's gold margin gives the artist's name as Sarvan. Nothing, however, is known about him except that he was an active member of the imperial atelier during the 1580s. No such marginal note is present on B.

A

The incident represented here occurred at a place called Qaba in Farghana. In the emperor's own words, Qaba has a stagnant, morass-like water, passable only by the bridge. As they were many, there was crowding on the bridge and numbers of horses and camels were pushed off to perish in the water. . . . Another thing was that such a Murrain broke out amongst their horses that, massed together, they began to die off in bands (A. S. Beveridge [1922] 1969, p. 31).

In the illustration Sarvan has not emphasized the dying animals, only two of which are shown in the foreground, but rather has given a picture of the lively campsite with its comings and goings. Note the improvised stove outside the kitchen tent, where one who seems to be the chef is pleading with a gesturing youth. The kneeling figure wearing orange dress within the larger tent in middle ground is very likely Sultan Ahmad Mirza, Babur's mother's half-brother, who had pitched his camp at Qaba. He is receiving a group of visitors. Although the bridge is not shown, the river is in the upper right corner. It is possible that other aspects of the incident, including the bridge and more dead horses, were included in the right half of the composition. Note how several of the figures express their concern for the epidemic with vigorous gestures, presumably pointing toward the bridge.

Sarvan was not a genius but a competent and observant artist evidently considered talented enough to handle an entire composition by himself.

CAT. 50A

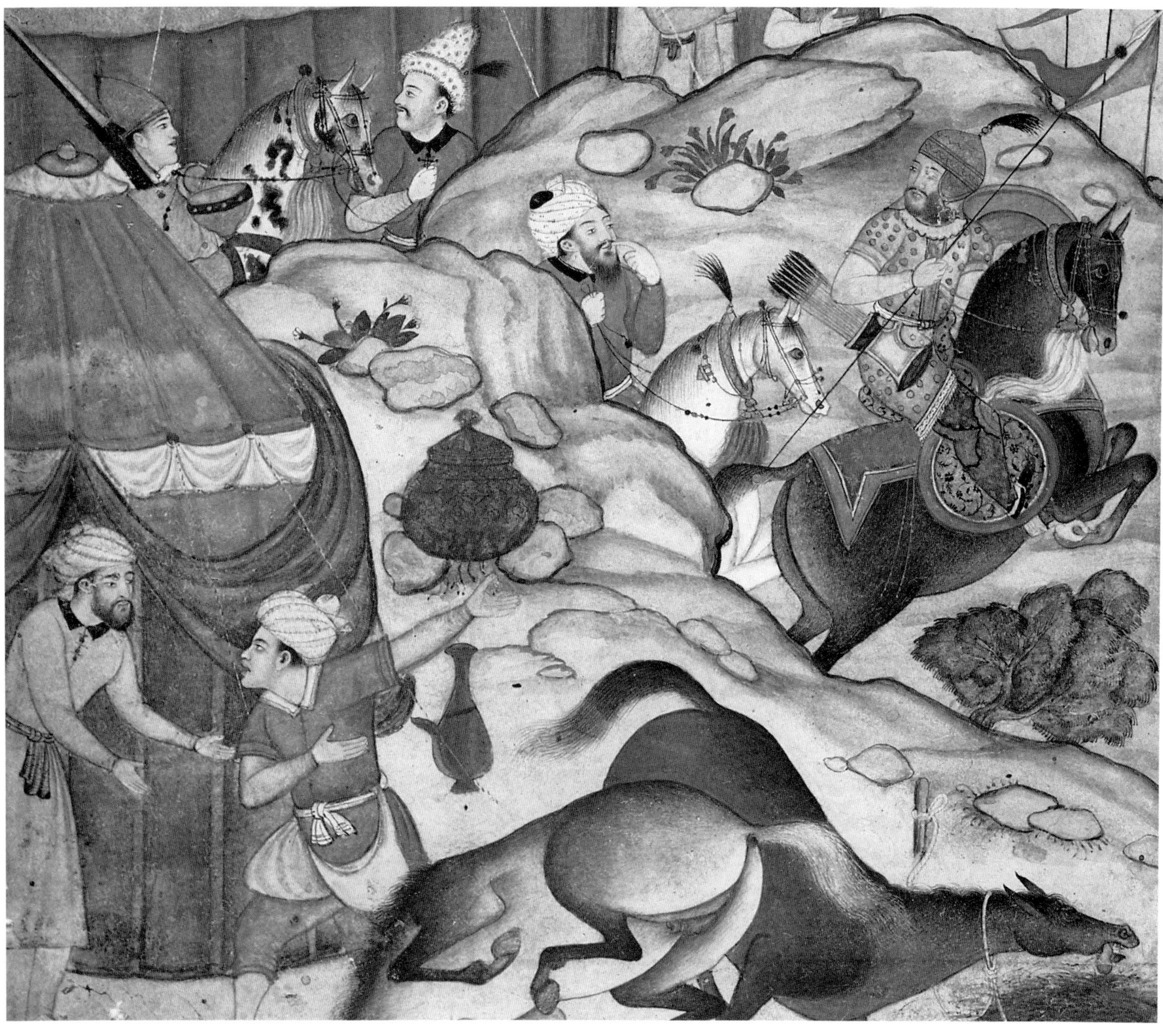

CAT. 50A detail *(above)*
CAT. 50B *(opposite)*

B The scene depicted here is Babur's second start for Hindustan (A. S. Beveridge [1922] 1969, p. 341). As Babur and his men marched out of Kabul, some Afghans, who were characterized by Babur as "thieves and abettors of thieves even in quiet times . . . blocked a pass . . . and advancing with the sound of tambour and flourish of sword began to show themselves off." Babur ordered his men to mount and set off at a gallop. The Afghans hesitated for a while and then took flight. "While I was on the mountain during the pursuit, [writes Babur,] I shot one in the hand as he was running back below me."

Clearly the artists or artist responsible for this illustration did not follow the text verbatim. That it is mountainous terrain is made explicit by characteristic rock formations. The two riders turning around to attack even as they flee are probably Afghans pursued by two of Babur's followers. The figure in the foreground is making the classic Parthian shot.

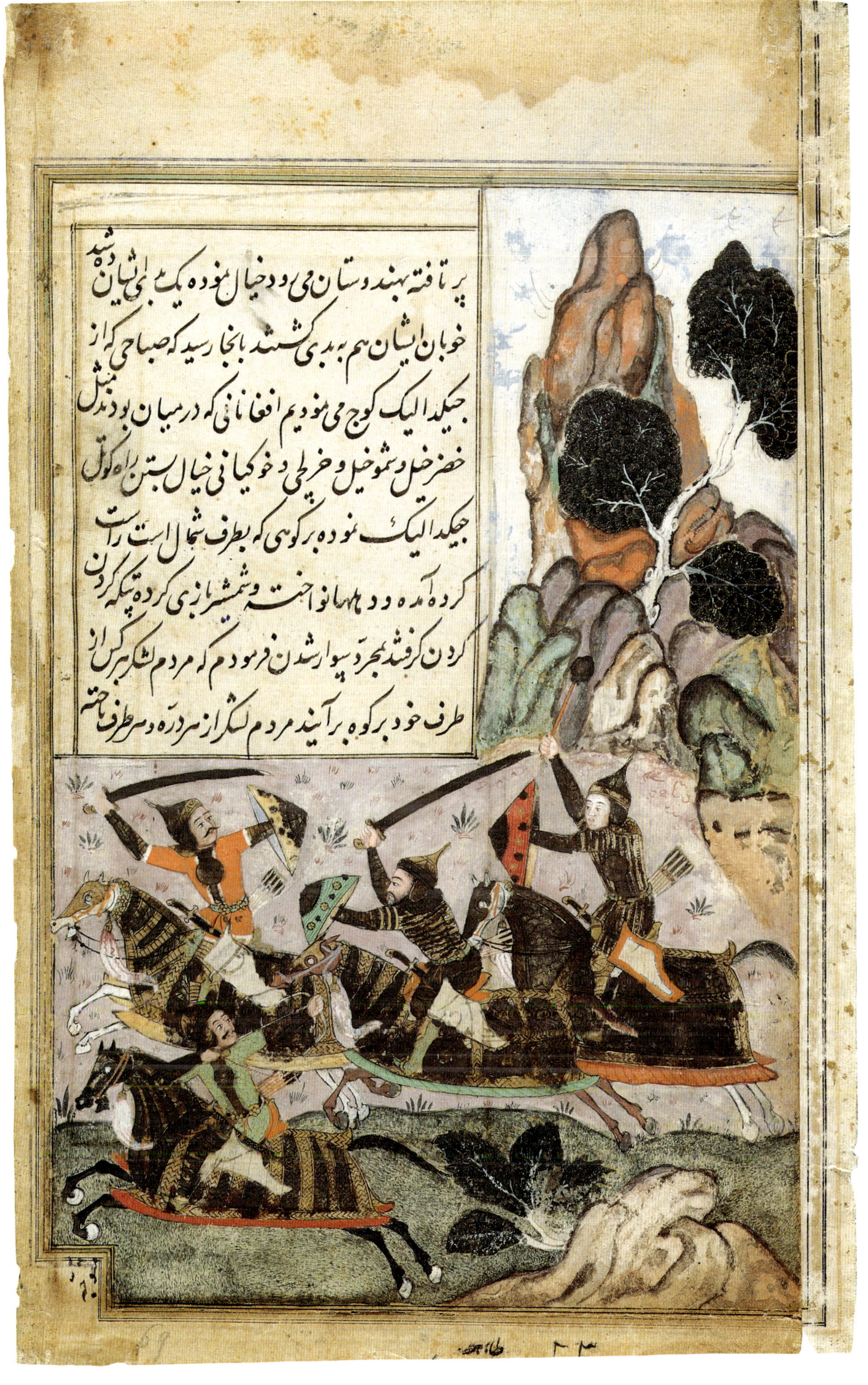
پر تافته بهندوستان می رود خیال نموده یک بدپی ایشان شده
خوبان ایشان هم بهدی گشتند بانجا رسید که صباحی که از
جگدالیک کوچ می نمودیم افغانانی که در میان بودند مثل
خضرخیل و شموخیل و خرلچی و خوگیانی خیال بستن راه کوتل
جگدالیک نموده بر کوهی که بطرف شمال است راست
کرده آمده دودها نواخته و شمشیربازی کرده تیکه کردن
گردن گرفتند بمجرد سوار شدن فرمودم که مردم لشکر بر کس از
طرف خود بر کوه برآیند مردم لشکر از سر دره و سر طرف تاخته

Akbar period, c. 1590
From the Nasli and Alice Heeramaneck Collection, Museum Associates Purchase
M.78.9.12,.13
Literature: Ardeshar 1940, p. 34, pl. 2 (A only); *Heeramaneck* 1966, pp. 142–43, no. 197 (A only illustrated); Sanford 1970; Johnson 1972, p. 145, pl. LXXXIVa (A only); Heeramaneck 1984, pp. 155–56, pls. 148, 149.

A *Tale of the Cunning Siddhikari*
6½ x 5¼ in (16.5 x 13.4 cm)
B *Tale of Somaprabha; text on verso*
5⅛ x 5⅜ in (13.0 x 13.7 cm)

These two illustrations, with cropped text pages on their reverses, once belonged to a manuscript of the *Kathasaritsagara,* which literally means "the ocean of streams of stories" but is generally translated as "the ocean of story." It is a vast compilation in the Sanskrit language by the Kashmiri poet Somadeva (eleventh century) of hundreds of stories of rogues and rakes, fools and wise men, gamblers and thieves, forest tribes and false ascetics, as well as faithful and adulterous men and women. Gathered from earlier sources and reembroidered, the stories were told by Somadeva to divert the mind of Suryamati, the queen of King Ananta of Kashmir (r. 1028–63). Very little is known about the translation made for Akbar, however. If the entire text were translated, it must have been a vast undertaking surpassed only by the *Mahabharata.* Only a dozen illustrated leaves of the translation seem to have survived, but even these have not been studied in depth yet. In addition to these two identifiable ones, a third cropped painting in the collection [52] may also have come from the same manuscript. Two other leaves from the manuscript are now in the San Diego Museum of Art (Binney 1973, p. 50, no. 26).

Because only a few illustrations have survived and none has any inscribed names, it is not possible to identify the artists who worked on this manuscript. Stylistically the pictures relate to illustrations in other manuscripts prepared in the imperial workshop around 1590. Similar pictures also occur in a copy of Anvari's *Divan* copied for Akbar in 1588 in Lahore. One particular illustration in that book, showing Anvari seated with a friend on a platform atop a tree (Schimmel and Welch 1983, pp. 77–80), is especially comparable to one of the two pictures in the collection (A).

A This picture depicts the story of the Siddhikari, who enters the service of a merchant in the guise of a maid in order to rob him. While fleeing with his treasures, she meets a *domba,* or a man of low caste, who intends to rob her. The cunning Siddhikari, however, pretends that she is running away from her husband and intends to commit suicide. She asks the *domba* how she should hang herself, and as the man obliges and shows her, she kicks the drum on which he is standing. While the man hangs from the tree, the merchant arrives with a servant. Seeing them, Siddhikari climbs up the tree but is followed by the servant. Siddhikari pretends to seduce him and bites off his tongue while kissing him. Screaming in pain the servant falls from the tree, and the merchant, thinking she is a witch, decides to call it a day.

As is clear, the picture faithfully follows the story except for a couple of minor details. The tree represented is the pipal (*Ficus religiosa*) rather than a *nyagrodha* (*Ficus indica*) described in the text. More serious is the omission of the drum that Siddhikari kicks. The painter may have forgotten it, or, as has been suggested, he may have taken the text literally in that Siddhikari is supposed to have smashed the drum to atoms (Sanford 1970, p. 43).

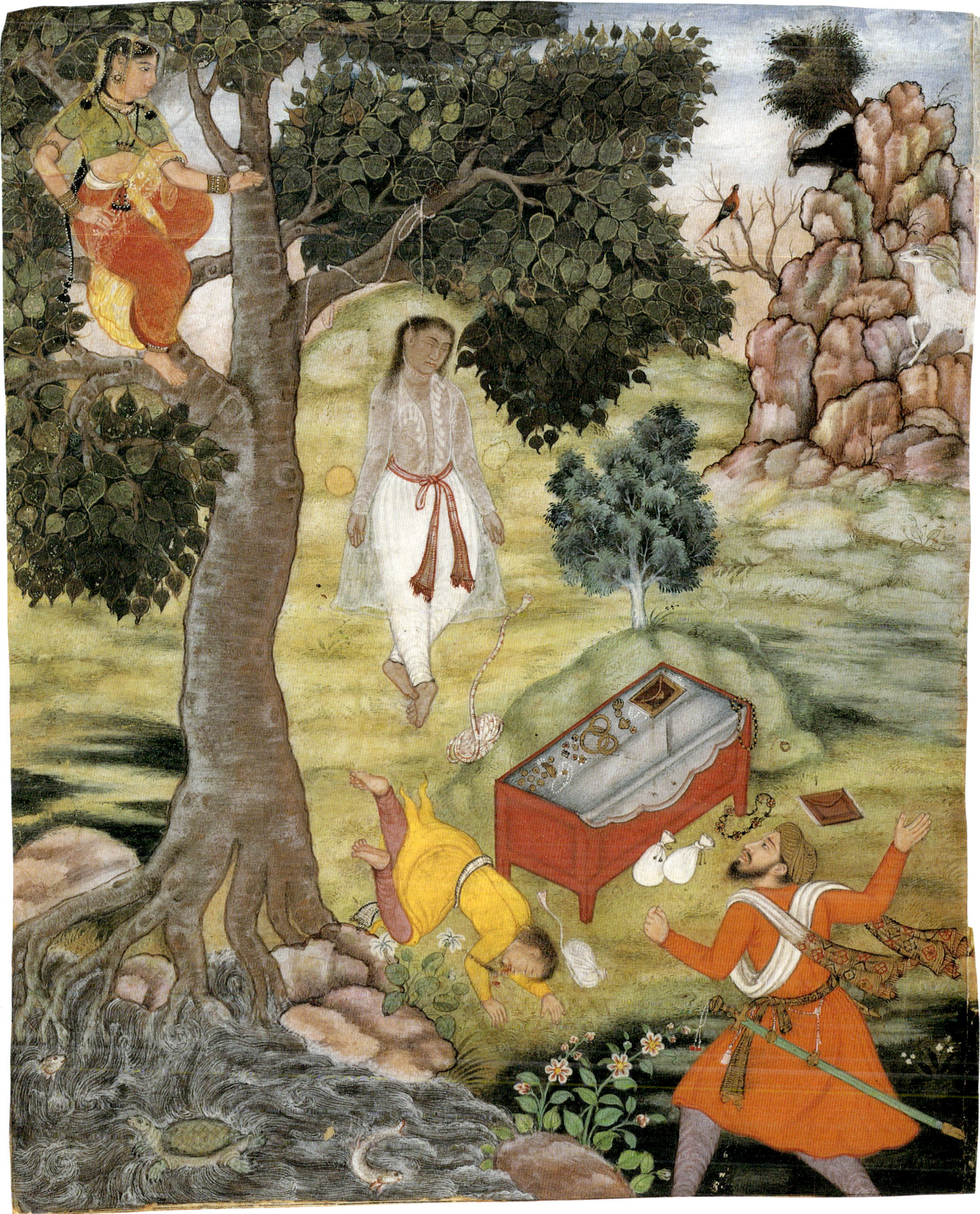

CAT. 51A

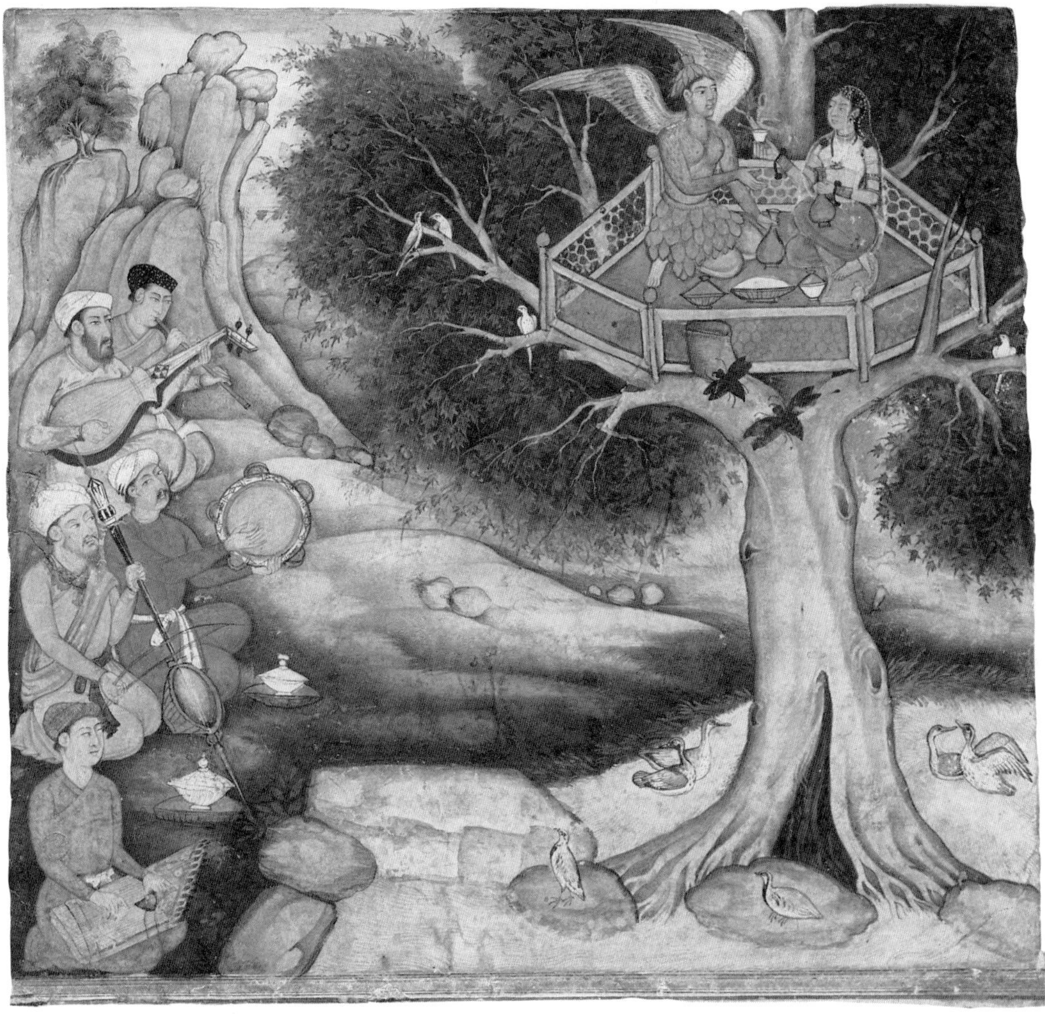

CAT. 51B *(left)*
CAT. 51B text *(right)*

B The story in this picture is that of a woman called Somaprabha. She is in reality a celestial nymph who is born in the human world because of a curse. After she grows up, she is given in marriage to the merchant Guhachandra on condition that they refrain from sleeping together. Each night, however, Somaprabha mysteriously leaves the house to return at dawn. This puzzles the husband, who recounts Somaprabha's behavior to one of the brahmans he feeds during the day. One of them gives him a charm, through which Guhachandra is able to gain the aid of Agni, the fire god. That night both Agni and Guhachandra change themselves into bees and follow Somaprabha. In the forest they come upon her listening to heavenly music with another beautiful nymph. Thereafter Agni advises Guhachandra to take a courtesan as a mistress, which he does. The jealous Somaprabha promptly accepts her conjugal duties.

In the picture Somaprabha and the celestial nymph, distinguished by her hairy body, wings, and a leafy skirt and hat, are seated on a platform on a tree rising by a pool. As the two black bees watch, Somaprabha offers a cup of wine to her companion. The music is provided by a group of five musicians, who are playing a flute; a *sarod;* a tambourine; another stringed instrument, perhaps a *sarangi,* played with a bow; and a *rabab.* The representations of the musical instruments are of interest historically. Here again the tree described in the text is the *nyagrodha,* but the artist has substituted a plane tree.

Akbar period, c. 1590
6 x 7½ in (15.2 x 19.1 cm)
From the Nasli and Alice Heeramaneck Collection, Museum Associates Purchase
M.78.9.7
Literature: *Heeramaneck* 1966, p. 152, no. 207 (not illustrated).

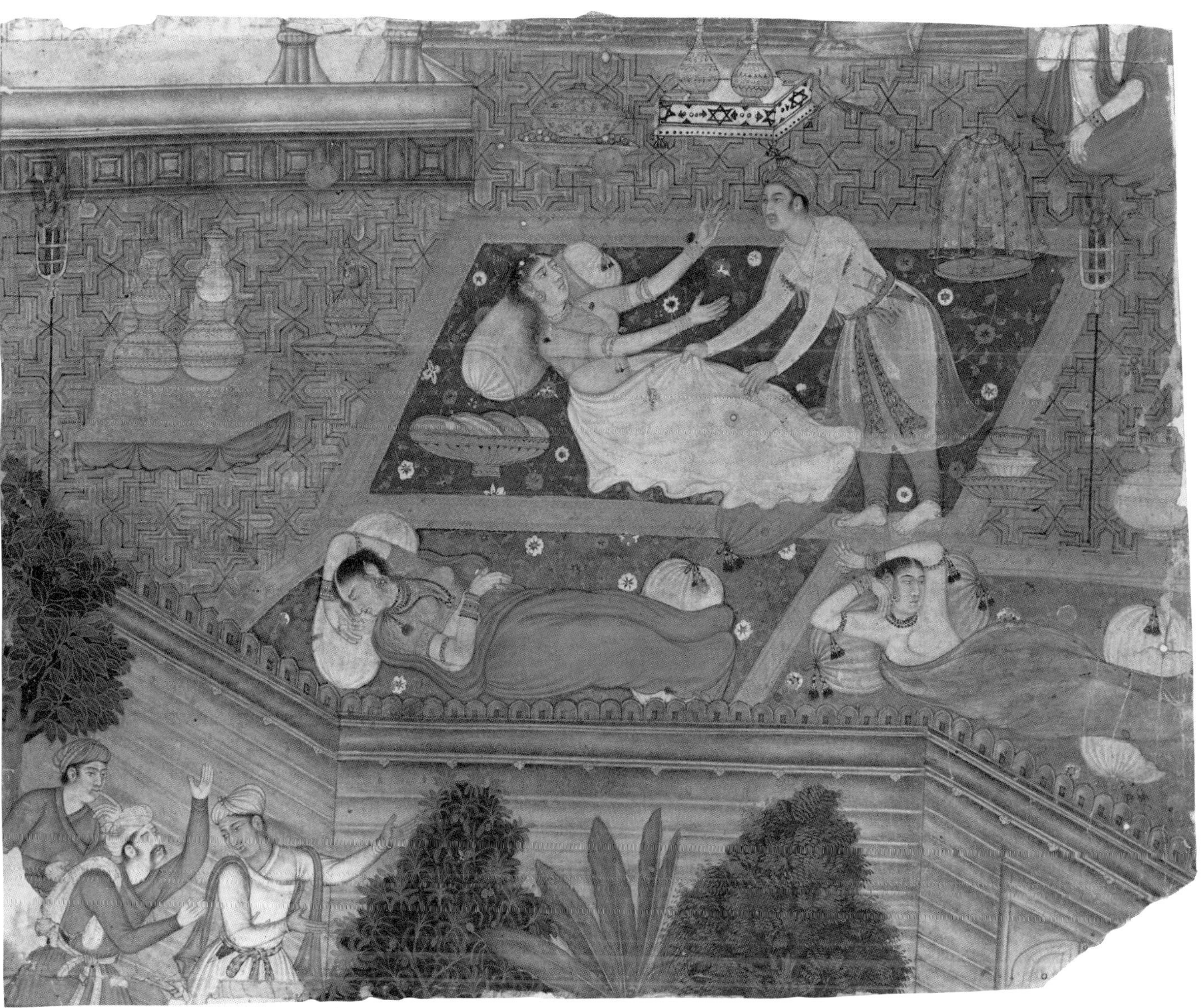

In 1966 (*Heeramaneck* 1966, p. 152) this picture was identified as a prince in a harem. The scene does take place within a walled enclosure, where a woman lying on a blue carpet on a tiled terrace eagerly welcomes her approaching lover, who has grabbed the white sheet covering her body. Two companions on two other carpets are fast asleep as if drugged, and a maidservant whose head is not visible is seated at the upper right corner. Burning torches indicate that it is a night scene—in fact a summer night since the lady is sleeping on an open terrace—but otherwise the picture is evenly illuminated. Whether or not the lover knows it, the behavior of the three men outside the wall in the picture's lower left corner clearly indicates that they are aware of his presence and are about to confront him. Thus, rather than simply illustrating the clandestine meeting of two young lovers, the scene may represent a morality tale, perhaps from the *Kathasaritsagara* (see [51]). Unfortunately there is no text visible on the back, as the picture has been pasted on a board.

The painting is interesting for the wide variety of objects strewn around the tiled floor of the terrace. Right next to the heroine's head is a golden bowl filled with watermelons. Diagonally across from it and also on the carpet is a tall tapering object with a translucent cloth cover. This is a screened nightlight that is draped with a cloth to lower the candle's intensity in the sleeping area. Farther away is another golden dish in which sits a blue-and-white Chinese bowl with cover surrounded by what look like red and yellow cherries. There are several other bowls and jugs of varied shapes. Some of the pots are for water and others probably for wine. Each of the three carpets—one of which is orangy red, one dusky rose, and one blue—has a wide golden border.

53 EUROPEANS EMBRACING

Akbar period, c. 1590
5 1/2 x 3 3/8 in (14.0 x 8.6 cm)
From the Nasli and Alice Heeramaneck Collection, Museum Associates Purchase
M.83.105.20

Watched by a bearded older European, two younger men embrace on a grassy knoll. Although the faces of the embracing pair do not betray much emotion, one gets the impression from the way the bright red shawl flies that this is an unexpected encounter. The sense of a joyous reunion is also expressed by the eager animal below held on a leash by the bearded man. Rather than a dog, the animal appears to be a mongoose, not an unusual pet in India with its reputation for snakes. All the men wear hats of different shapes and colorful costumes, stockings, and shoes. In the distance to the right is a group of buildings and on top of a rounded hill is a temple; beyond them are trees. Two other European travelers followed by a dog walk across the hills.

Undoubtedly this picture is based on a European model, which may have been a print. The subject matter, however, cannot be precisely identified. The figures are dressed in European costumes that display interesting modifications. For instance, the embracing figure with his back to the viewer is wearing a shirt that is too loose for European usage but still retains the lace cuffs fashionable in the Tudor age. Both embracing figures wear leather leggings known as buskins. The older man, however, wears baggy pants like pajamas, which are unlikely to have been worn by a figure in the European original. Normally, Europeans wore capes, which in this picture have been given the form of shawls. Thus, it seems as if the Mughal artist modified his model somewhat and gave the figures costumes that he may have observed on Portuguese visitors at court. The same urge to modification may have resulted in the transformation of a pet dog into the mongoose. The architecture has been Indianized, and it is interesting to note the artist's discomfort in representing the face of the figure facing the viewer. At least three other paintings showing similarly free adaptations of European engravings are known to exist (see Pinder-Wilson 1976, pp. 60, 61, no. 80). They all may be by the same Mughal artist.

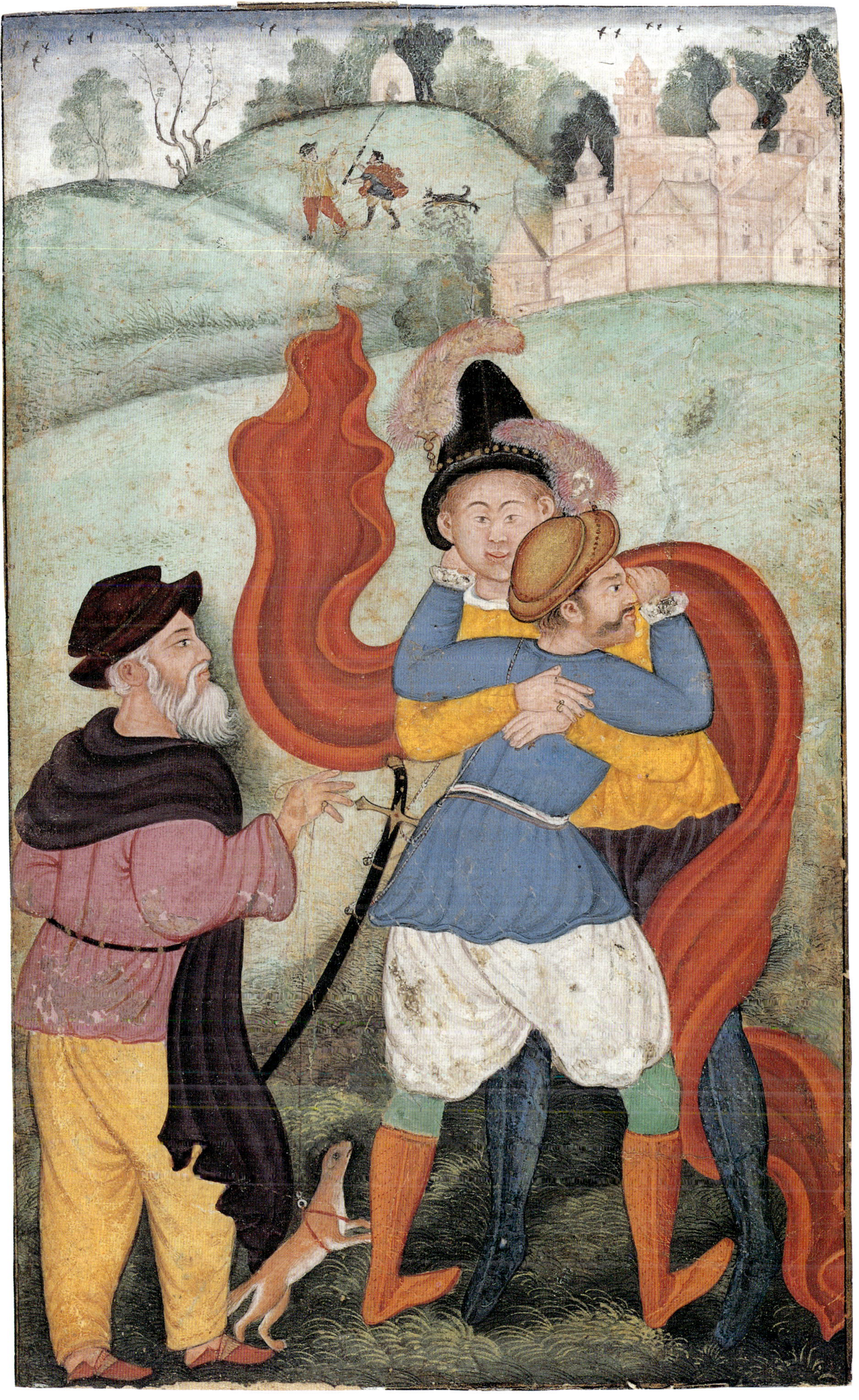

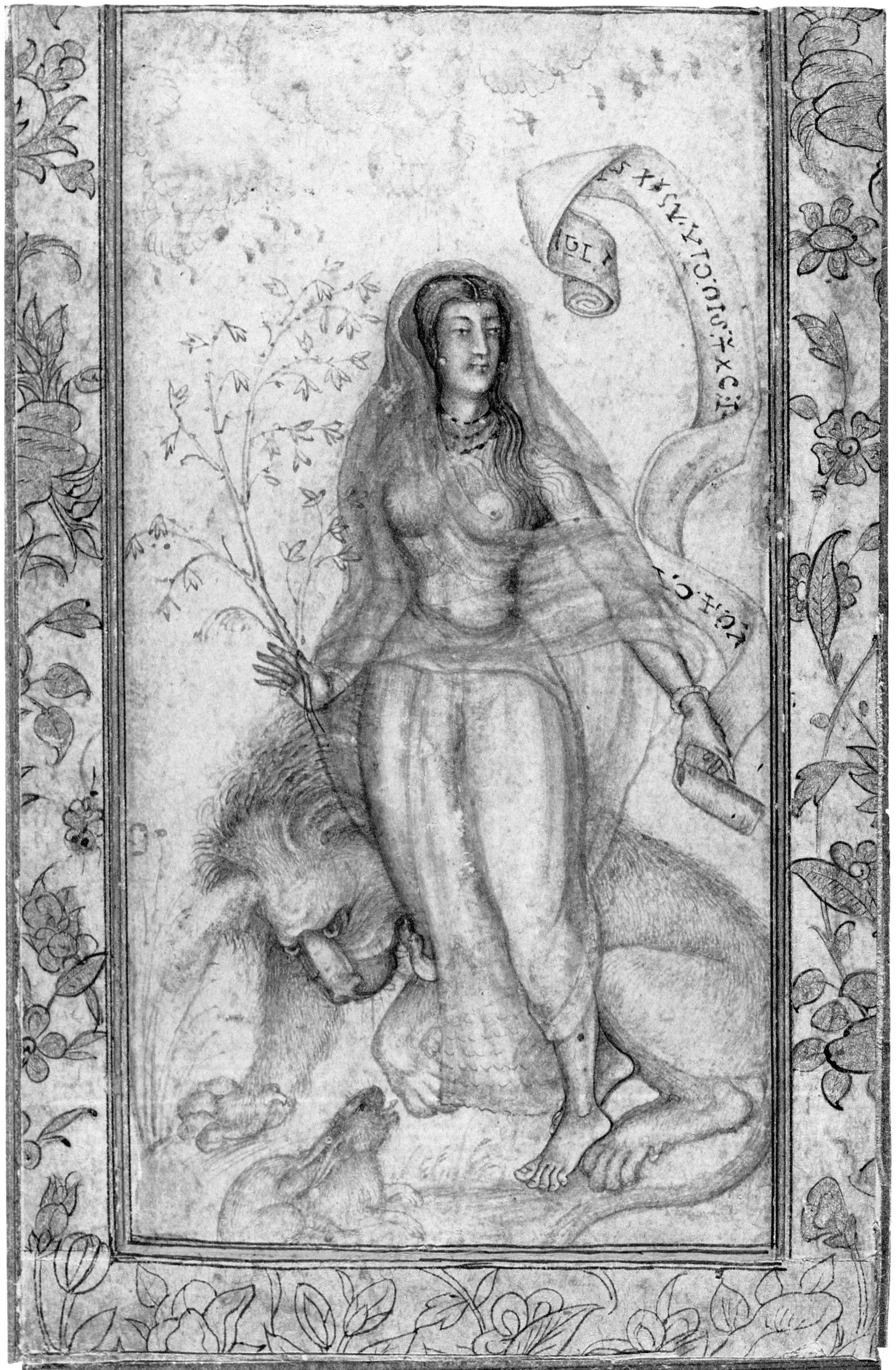

Attributed to Basawan (active c. 1560–1600)
Akbar period, c. 1590
Ink, color washes, and gold
Overall, $4^{3}/_{4}$ x $3^{1}/_{8}$ in (12.1 x 7.9 cm)
Illustration, $4^{1}/_{4}$ x $2^{1}/_{4}$ in (10.8 x 5.7 cm)
From the Nasli and Alice Heeramaneck Collection, Museum Associates Purchase
M.81.8.8
Literature: *Heeramaneck* 1966, pp. 151, 152, no. 205; Beach 1978, pp. 155, 157, no. 53; Pal & Dehejia 1986, p. 154, no. 154.

In his first publication of it (1966, p. 151) M. Beach wrote, "The sketch is likely to be an early work of the painter Manōhār, working under the strong influence of his father, Basāwan." In the second (Beach 1978, p. 157) he wrote, "A group of works roughly similar in style and subject is known; several are signed by Basāwan or Manōhar, although neither artist seems indisputably responsible for this example." This second opinion indicates how difficult it is to attribute even Mughal pictures, about which so much is known, to individual artists. Considering Beach's comments on Manohar's style, which relies on brilliant linear rhythms rather than on heavy shading to impart volume (see [60]), it seems highly unlikely that he had anything to do with this sketch. The sense of volume imparted by the figure's flowing draperies and the contrasting use of thin and thick shading as well as the drama created by the snarling rabbit and the open-mouthed lion are all characteristics of Basawan's technique. Indeed, this sketch is stylistically very close to at least three other signed drawings by Basawan in the Musée Guimet in Paris (see Okada 1989, pp. 188–93, nos. 54–56). In all four the modeling of the figures and the treatment of the clothing are very similar. Also noteworthy is the identical treatment of the clouds in this sketch and those in another study of an allegorical figure in the Musée Guimet (no. 54). There can thus be little doubt that all four sketches were probably made about the same time, about 1590.

Beach (1978, p. 157) is, however, correct in pointing out that the sketch was based on an engraving of Eve by the German artist Jakob Binck (1500–1569). It is known that many such European prints came to India through Antwerp, which Binck visited twice. In his engraving Eve strikes a similar posture in a landscape before a couchant lion, but she is naked and holds no attributes (F. W. H. Hollstein, *German Engravings, Etchings, and Woodcuts* [Amsterdam: Menno Herzberger, 1962], 4: 12). Basawan's figure is decorously clothed, although the modeling of the visible parts of the torso is similar to that of Binck's Eve. The Mughal artist has also added an oak branch in her right hand and an inscribed though unintelligible scroll in her left hand. The oak branch symbolizing *fortezza* (strength or fortitude) may have been borrowed from the allegory of Fortitude. The lion too is associated with Fortitude, who, however, is usually shown armored and carrying a spear. Generosity also leans against a lion, which symbolizes grandeur and courage, and is clothed in a similar fashion with part of her mantle of golden gauze flying near her left shoulder (Cesare Ripa, *Iconologia or Moral Emblems* [1709; rpt., New York: Garland, 1976], pp. 34–35). It should be noted further that Mercy holds a branch of cedar with her right hand, while an inscribed label is held by several allegorical figures (Ripa, *Iconologia,* figs. 232, 236, 266, 312, and 318). Clearly this particular figure is a concoction by Basawan, who had access to various European engravings of emblematic figures and preferred to make a whimsical study.

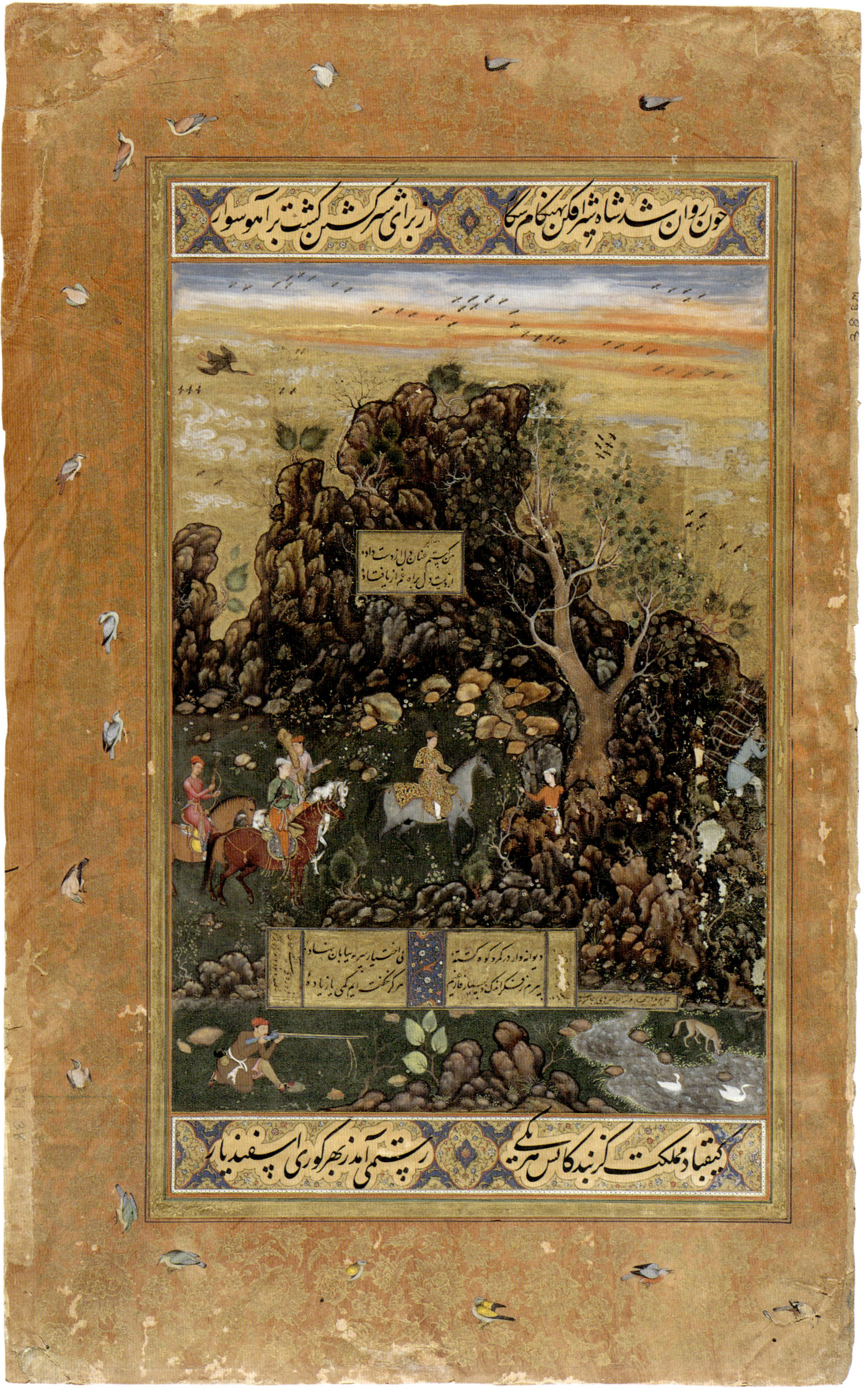

Folio and borders, Jahangir period, c. 1610
Folio, 16⅝ x 10½ in (42.2 x 26.7 cm)
From the Nasli and Alice Heeramaneck Collection, Museum Associates Purchase
M.78.9.11
Literature: *Heeramaneck* 1966, pp. 143–44, no. 198; Beach 1978, pp. 44–47, no. 5; Beach 1981, pp. 25, 26, 166, fig. 3; Heeramaneck 1984, p. 155, pls. 144, 145; Pal 1987, fig. 74 (B only); Soucek 1985, p. 164; Soucek 1987, pp. 171–72, fig. 4.

A *Hunters in a Forest* (r)
Signature of Sharif (active c. 1580–1615?)
Akbar period, inscribed date A.H. 999, A.D. 1590/91
10¼ x 7¼ in (26.0 x 18.4 cm)

B *Page of Calligraphy* (v)
Calligraphy, sixteenth century
10 x 6⅜ in (25.4 x 16.2 cm)
Border figures attributed to Govardhan (active c. 1600–1640)
Jahangir period, c. 1610

This folio with a painting from the Akbar period on one side and calligraphy on the other was part of an album prepared for Jahangir. The greater part of the album is in the Gulshan Library, Tehran, and is known as the Gulshan Album. The painting is mounted in a reddish-yellow outer border filled with golden floral arabesques inhabited by a variety of small, lively birds painted in color. The border around the panel of calligraphy on the verso is more elaborate. Several outstanding figure studies are deftly painted against a landscape in gold of knolls, rocks, plants, and birds.

A Although there are several inscriptions in the panels on the painting itself, they complicate rather than clarify the origin and attribution of the picture. The following translations are by S. Digby.

IN PAINTING FIELD

Upper panel
Allah is Great [added]
Who am I having loosed the rein of my heart from my hand?
From the hand [out of control?] *the heart having stumbled on the road of grief.*

Lower panels
Central horizontal panels
You have wandered madly in pass (?) and mountain
Helplessly you have set out towards the wilderness //
I am old (?) and have left off considering how little and how much
I have never said too little or too much

Extreme right horizontal panel
Work of the murid *standing in his place in the four ranks of devotion, Sharif.*

Right and left vertical panels
At the date of the {twenty-} ninth [partly obstructed with 36 (sic) written in numerals above] of the month //
Farwardi Ilah nine hundred ninety-nine // Hijri (?)
written by the slave Muhammad.

CALLIGRAPHIC PANELS

Above painting
When, at the season of hunting, the lion-overthrowing monarch set out
He rode on a deer to kill a lion.

Below painting
Kayqubad [an emperor] *of a kingdom*
each one of whose servants
Behaved as a Rustam [hero] *on account of*
the wild ass of Isfandiyar.

The figures referred to in the last two verses are characters in the *Shahnama.* Usually the wild ass is associated with Bahram rather than Isfandiyar. Farwardi Ilah is the Persian month used officially by Akbar and his immediate successors; Hijra year 999 corresponds to 1590/91.

A technical examination of the painting has revealed that it is made up of at least five different pieces. The question as to when exactly the various pieces were integrated is difficult to resolve. What can be stated certainly is that the final additions around the picture were completed about 1610, when it was selected to be included in Jahangir's album.

CAT. 55A

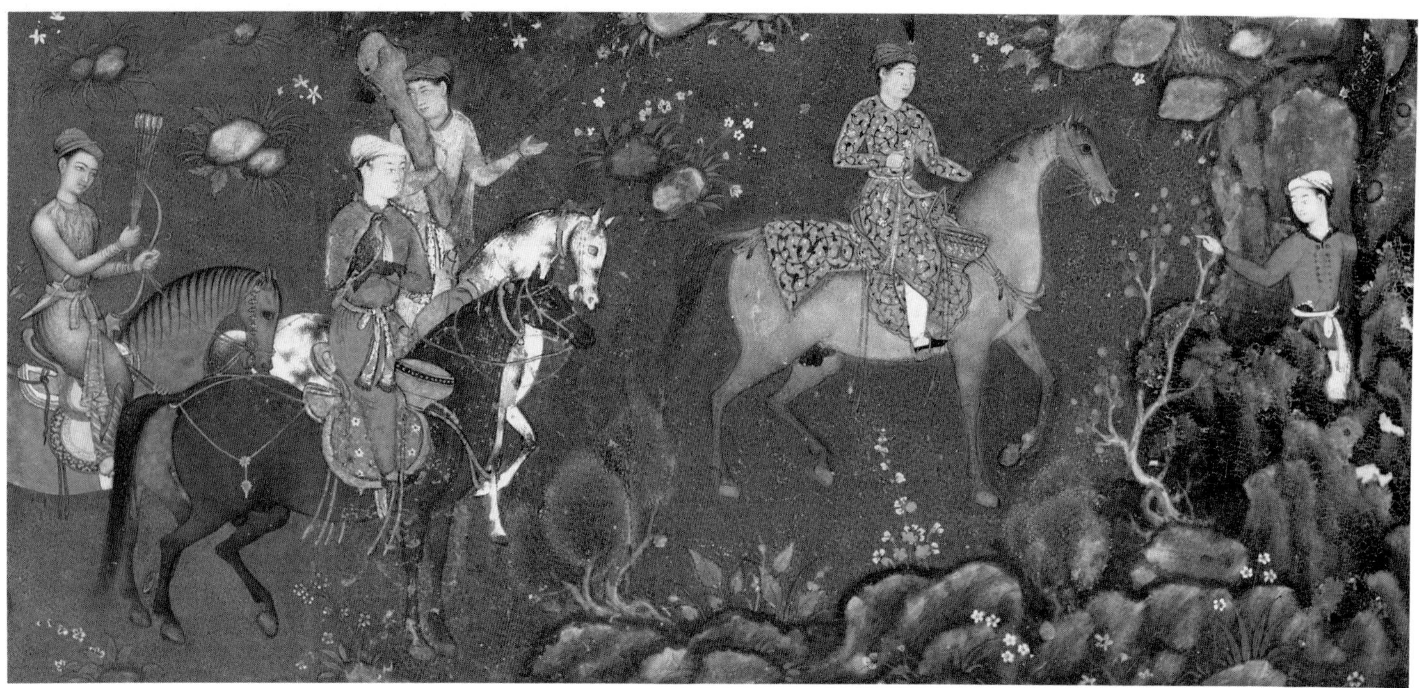

CAT. 55A detail *(above)*
CAT. 55B *(opposite)*

Sharif is identified as Muhammad Sharif, the son of Abd as-Samad and a personal friend of Jahangir. Similar inscriptions occur in two pictures in the Keir Collection (see Skelton 1976, pp. 240, 242). On the face of it therefore it seems that Muhammad Sharif was alone responsible for the painting. M. Beach (1978, p. 46) attributed the painting to both father and son but did not make it clear how the two cooperated. He found "the dark tonalities and the densely packed mountain forms, together with the heavy outlining" indicative of Abd as-Samad's authorship. He further stated that "from what little we know of Sharīf's work as a painter, however, it seems most unlikely that he is fully responsible for the painting seen here."

P. Soucek (1985, p. 164) regards the picture to be in a modified version of the father's style, as seen, for instance, in Abd as-Samad's signed painting in the Freer Gallery of Art, Washington, D.C. (see Beach 1981, p. 73, no. 16d). According to Soucek, "Despite the dramatic use of silhouette, particularly in placing the gold-clad prince against the dark landscape, greater emphasis is given to modeling with colors and less concern is shown for linear control." Two years later (1987, pp. 171–72) she wrote, "when compared to that of his father, Muhammad's work is freer in its use of modeling. His figures have a greater sense of corporeality than do those of his father, but they are rather expressionless."

Although it has been known for some time that the painting is a pastiche, the extent of the additions has not been settled yet. The core section including the central rider appears to have been an uneven piece to which various bits were added on all four sides. The gold panels with the inscriptions in the field, including the signature, also may not belong to the core. Furthermore, infrared photographs show some changes made in the position of the central rider's head. Until the technical examination is completed, it would be imprudent to arrive at any firm conclusion.

A possible scenario may have been as follows. Muhammad Sharif took a sketch of his father's and upon completing it added his signature and presented it to Jahangir in 1590/91. Almost twenty years later, when Jahangir decided to add it to the Gulshan Album, the picture was expanded further, either by Muhammad Sharif himself or someone else. The added portions definitely show different drawing and coloring from the core composition.

B This page of calligraphy is one of the most interesting of such pages for various reasons. The central panel with four text segments is a page from the *Divan* of Sultan Husayn (r. 1469–1506) composed in Chaghatay Turkish, the original language of the Mughals. This text is contained within blue borders with floral decoration, around which are pasted twenty-four small panels of miscellaneous examples of Persian *mathnavi,* or rhymed couplets. These couplets are separated by narrow floral dividers and eight panels containing lively, naturalistic representations of various kinds of birds. Additional borders with floral arabesques surround those calligraphic panels.

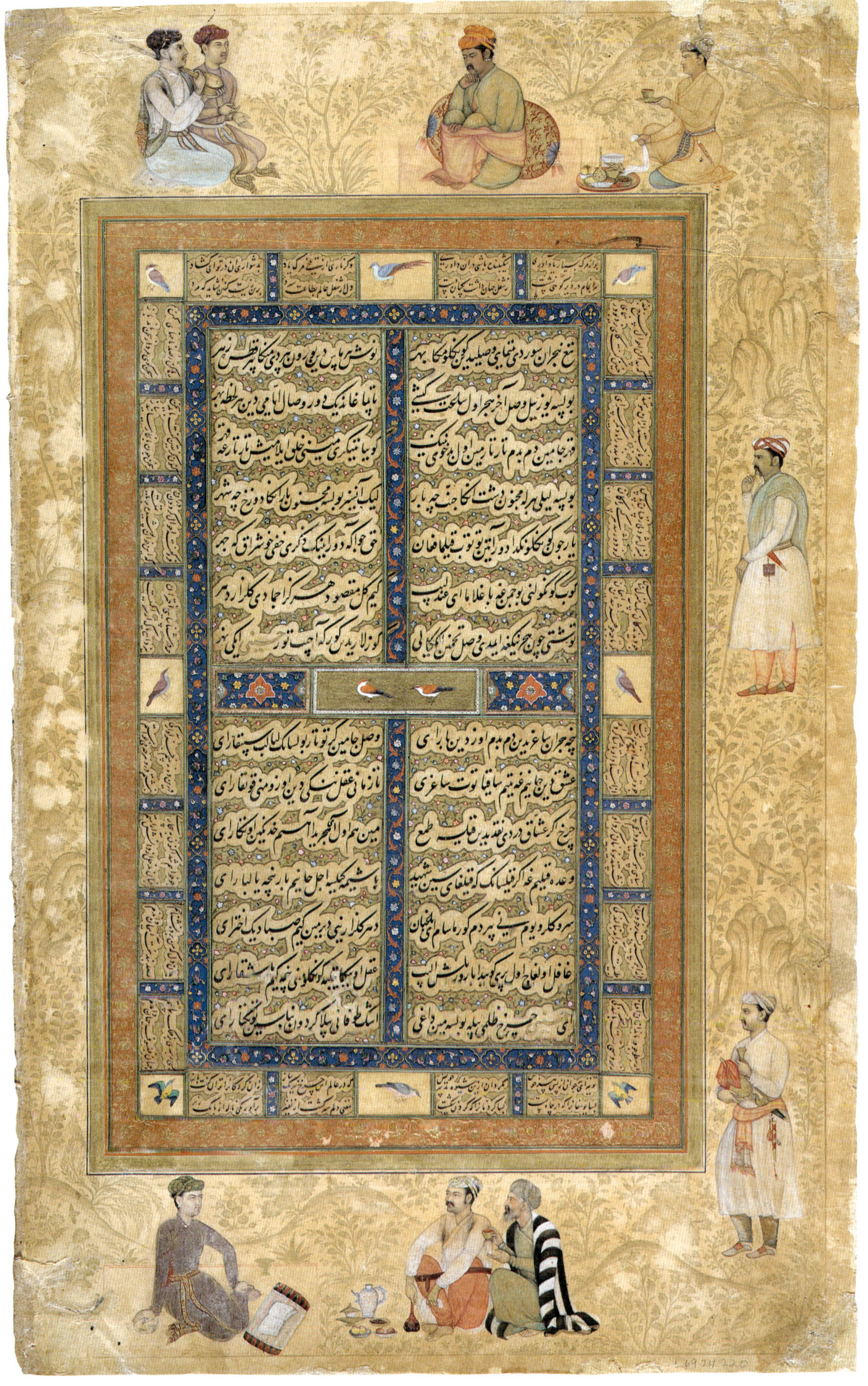

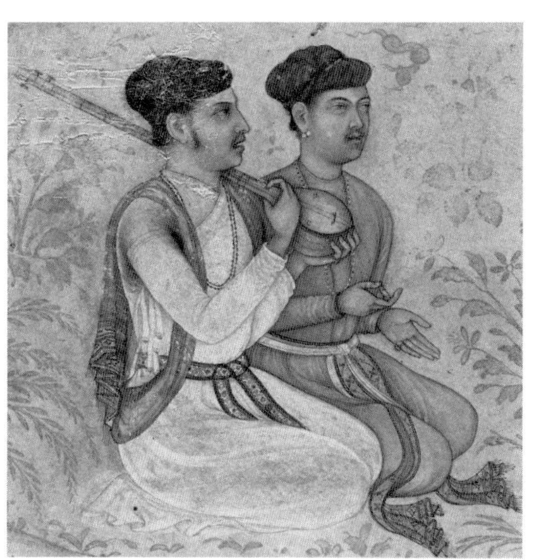

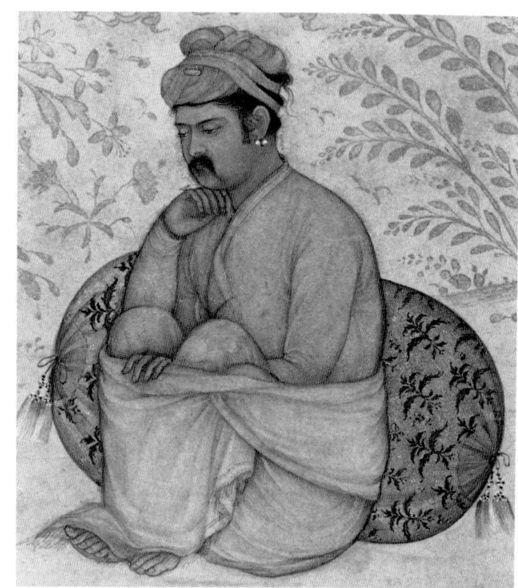

CAT. 55B details

Interesting as the design of the calligraphy is, even more striking is the outer border. Against a background delineated in delicate gold and representing landscapes with rolling hills, rock formations, and flowering shrubs and branches inhabited by birds are some of the most sensitive delineations of human figures found in Mughal art. Not only are these fully colored, they are so realistically portrayed that there can be little doubt that they were taken from life. It is generally agreed that these perceptive studies are by Govardhan, who was the acknowledged master of this genre (see [74]).

Along the top is a nobleman seated on a carpet against a bolster with his legs wrapped in a pink shawl. He is obviously in a pensive mood as he listens to two musicians perform. A servant behind him offers him a cup of wine. In the middle of the right-hand border a second man also in a thoughtful mood strikes a more formal posture. At the bottom a young man is reading a book while two others listen. The younger of the two is being offered a cup of wine by an older man, who sits slightly behind out of respect. Farther behind, a figure approaches with a jug held carefully by both hands. The spout of the jug, terminating in an animal's head, is covered with a piece of cloth.

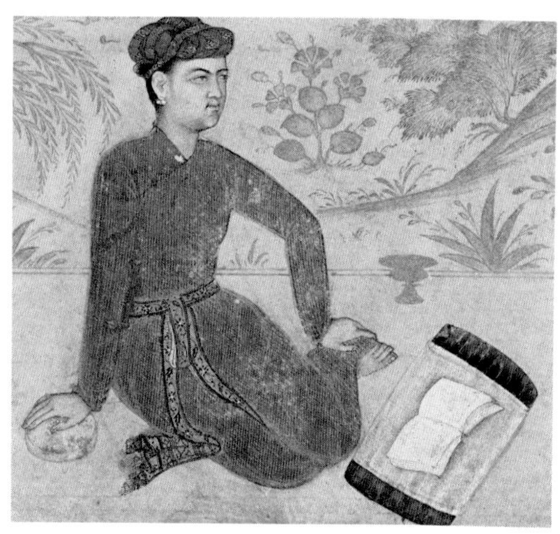

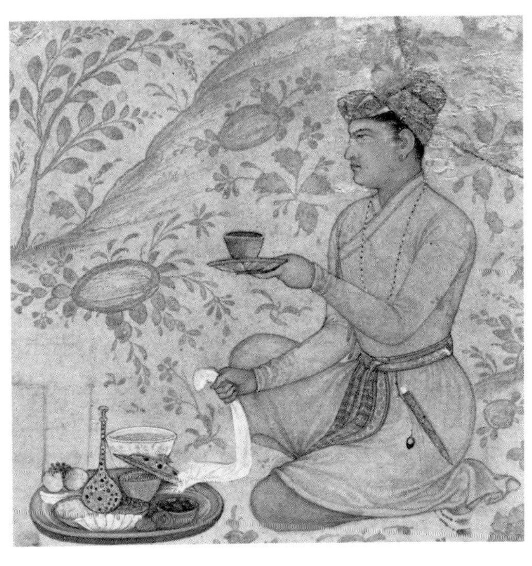
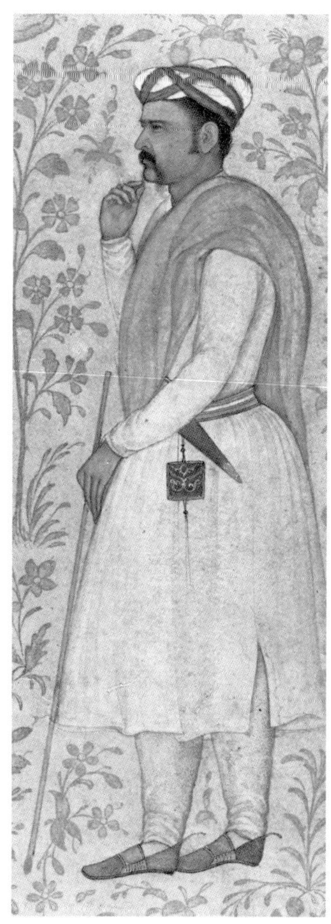
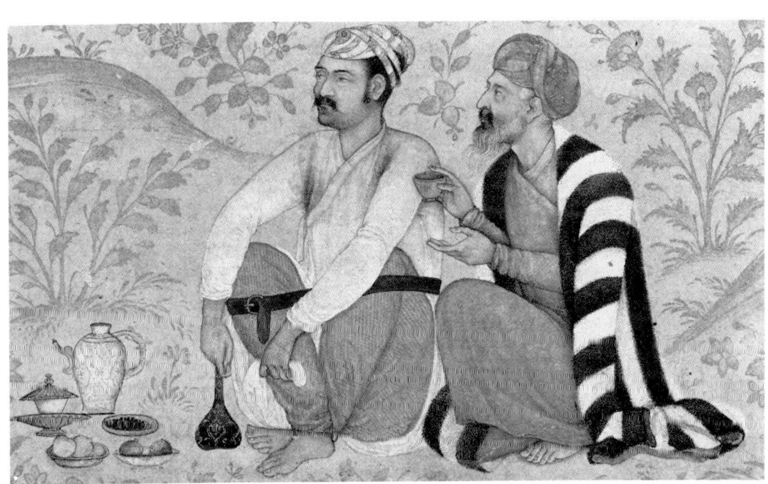
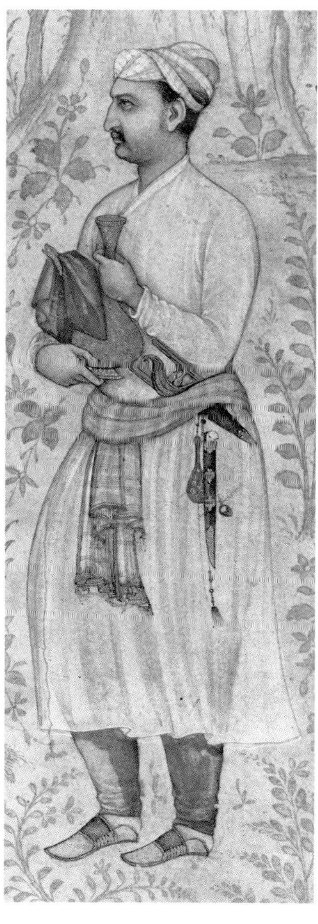

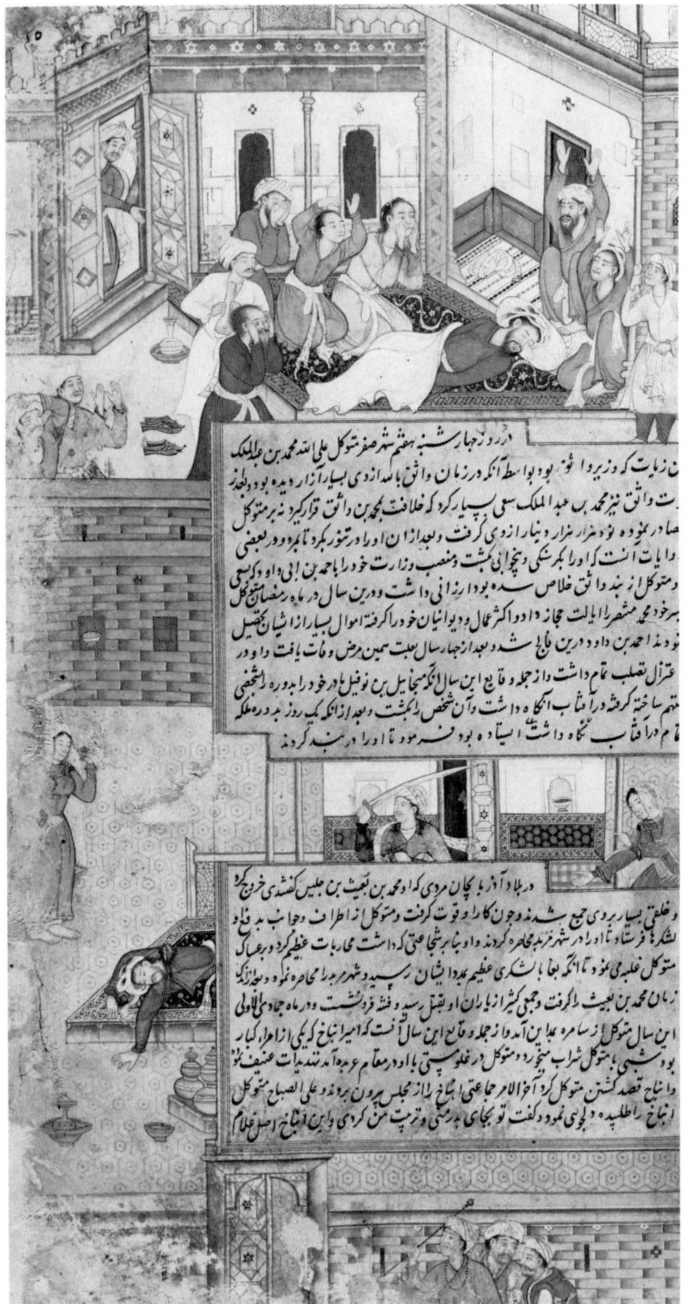

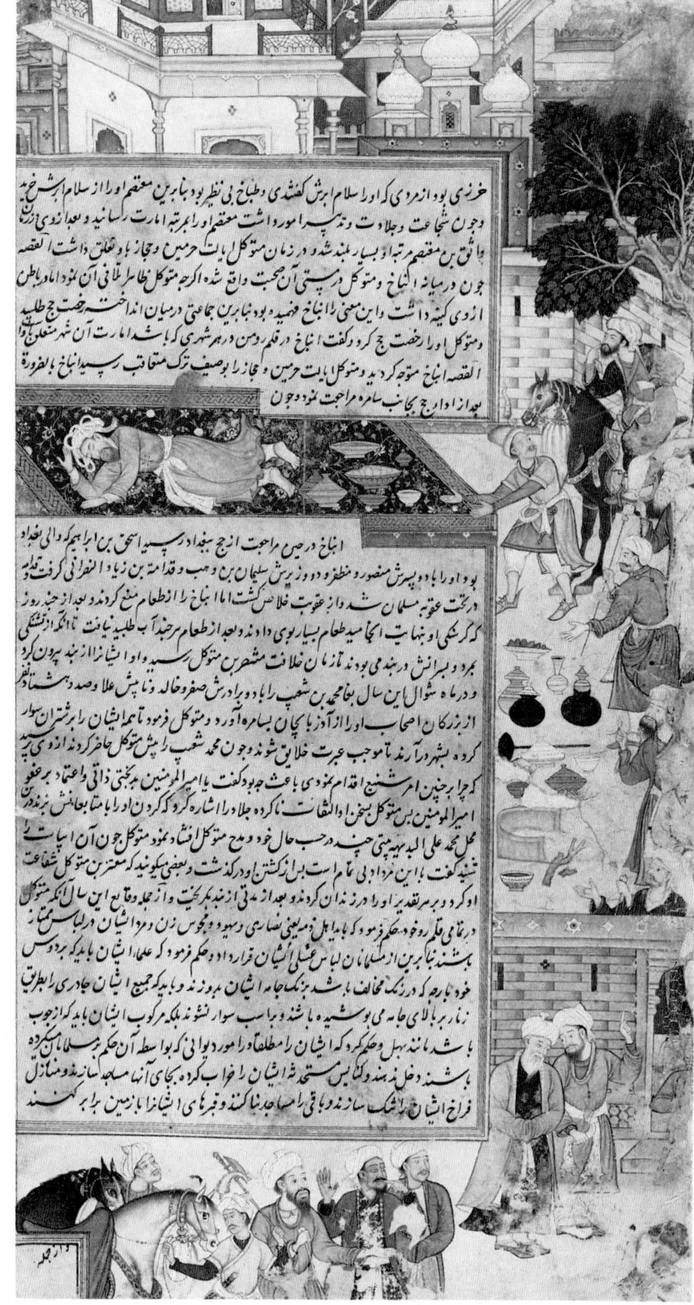

56 TWO FOLIOS FROM A *TARIKH-I ALFI* MANUSCRIPT

Akbar period, c. 1594
From the Nasli and Alice Heeramaneck Collection, Museum Associates Purchase
Literature: *Heeramaneck* 1966, pp. 141–42, no. 196 (A only illustrated); Johnson 1972, p. 141, 144, pl. LXXXa (detail of C); Heeramaneck 1984, p. 155, pls. 142, 143 (B and C only).

A *Deaths of al-Wathiq and Muhammad b. Baiis b. Jalis* (r)
B *Death of Anbakh* (v)
Overall, 16½ x 10 in (41.9 x 25.4 cm)
Illustrations, 16½ x 8¾ in (41.9 x 22.2 cm)
M.78.9.4
C *Attack of the People of Hams*
Overall, 16¾ x 9⅞ in (42.5 x 25.1 cm)
Illustration, 16¾ x 9¼ in (42.5 x 23.5 cm)
M.83.105.3

CAT. 56A detail *(above left)*
CAT. 56B detail *(above right)*
CAT. 56C *(opposite)*

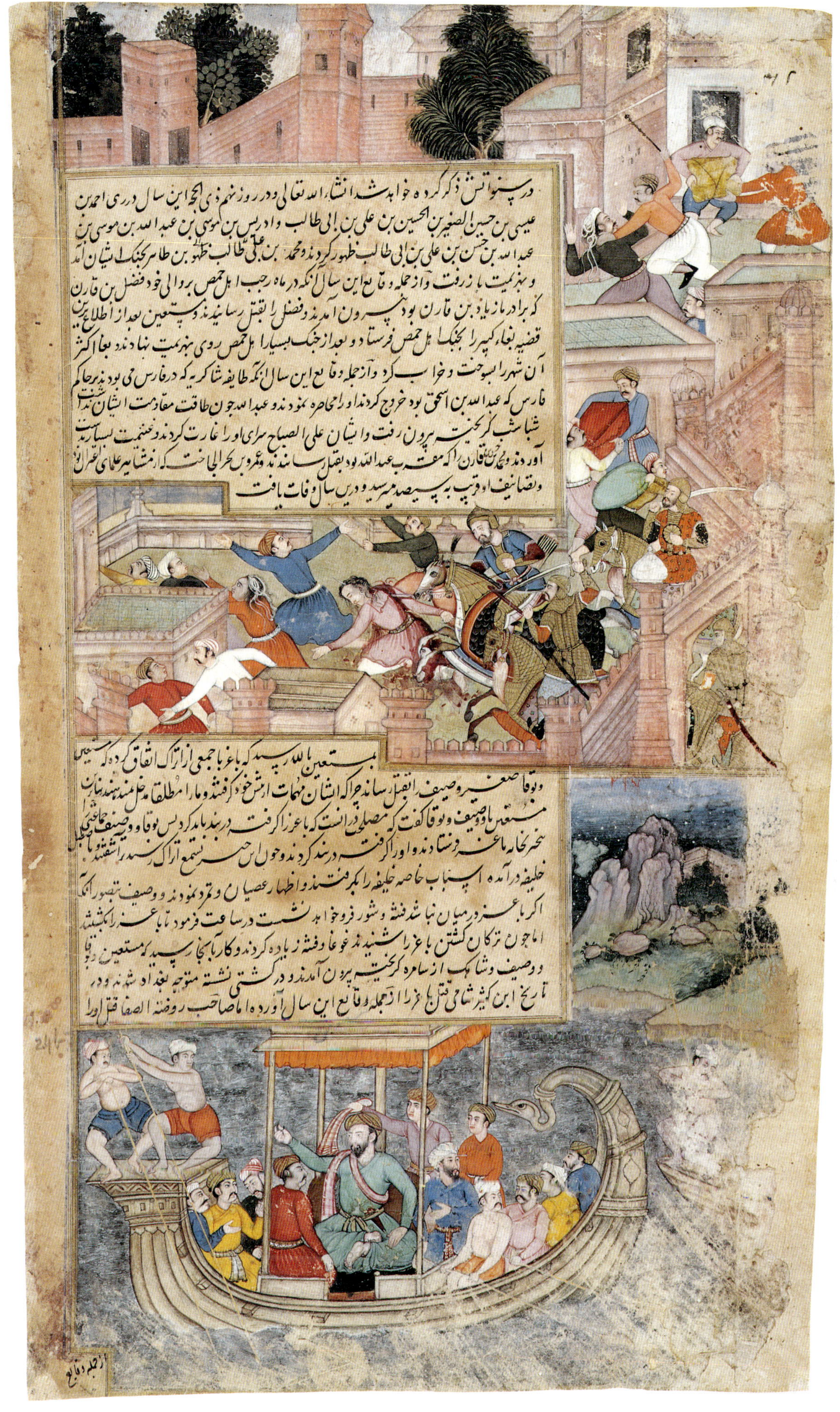
در سنه ثلث ذکر کرده خواهد شد انشاء الله تعالی و در روز نهم ذی الحجه این سال در ری احمد بن
عیسی بن حسین الصغیر بن الحسین بن علی بن ابی طالب و ادریس بن موسی بن عبد الله بن موسی بن
عبد الله بن حسن بن علی بن ابی طالب ظهور کردند و محمد بن علی بن ابی طالب ظهور [illegible] بن طاهر بجنگ ایشان آمد
و بهزیمت بازرفت و از جمله وقایع این سال آنکه در ماه رجب اهل حمص بر والی خود فضل بن قارن
که برادر مازیار بن قارن بود بیرون آمدند و فضل را بقتل رسانیدند و مستعین بعد از اطلاع برین
قضیه بغاء کبیر را بجنگ اهل حمص فرستاد و بعد از جنگ بسیار اهل حمص روی بهزیمت نهادند بغا اکثر
آن شهر را بسوخت و خراب کرد و از جمله وقایع این سال آنکه طایفه شاکریه که در فارس می بودند بر حاکم
فارس که عبد الله بن اسحق بود خروج کردند و او را محاصره نمودند و عبد الله چون طاقت مقاومت ایشان نداشت
شبا شب گریخته بیرون رفت و ایشان علی الصباح سرای او را غارت کردند و غنیمت بسیار بدست
آوردند و محمد بن حسن قارن را که مقرب عبد الله بود بقتل رسانیدند و عمرو بن بحر الجاحظ که از مشاهیر علمای اعتزال بود
و تصانیف او قریب به سیصد میرسید و درین سال وفات یافت

بمستعین بالله رسید که باغر با جمعی از اتراک اتفاق کرده که مستعین
و بوقا صغیر و وصیف را بقتل رسانند چرا که ایشان مهمات از پیش خود گرفته‌اند و ما را مطلقا دخل نمیدهند بنابران
مستعین با وصیف و بوقا گفت که مصلحت در آنست که باغر را گرفته در بند باید کرد پس بوقا و وصیف جماعتی را
بخرخانه باغر فرستادند و او را گرفته در بند کردند و چون این خبر بسمع اتراک رسید برآشفتند و باصطبل
خلیفه درآمده اسپان خاصه خلیفه را بگرفتند و اظهار عصیان و تمرد نمودند و وصیف تصور آنکه
اگر باغر در میان نباشد فتنه و شور فرو خواهد نشست در ساعت فرمود تا باغر را بکشتند
اما چون ترکان کشتن باغر را شنیدند غوغا و فتنه زیاده کردند و کار بآنجا رسید که مستعین و بوقا
و وصیف و شاهک از سامره گریخته بیرون آمدند و در کشتی نشسته متوجه بغداد شدند و در
تاریخ ابن کثیر شامی قتل باغر را از جمله وقایع این سال آورده اما صاحب روضة الصفا قتل او را

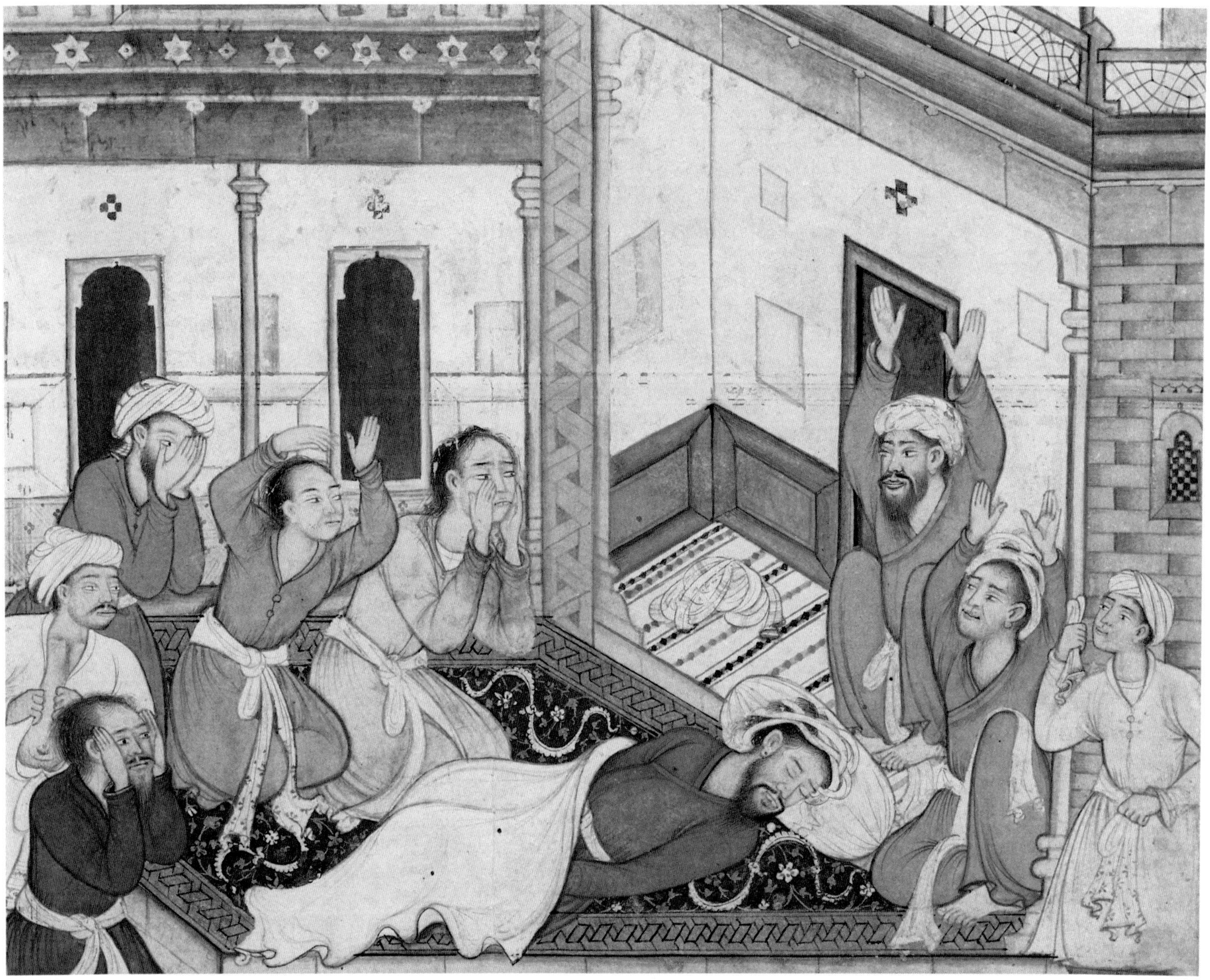

CAT. 56A detail

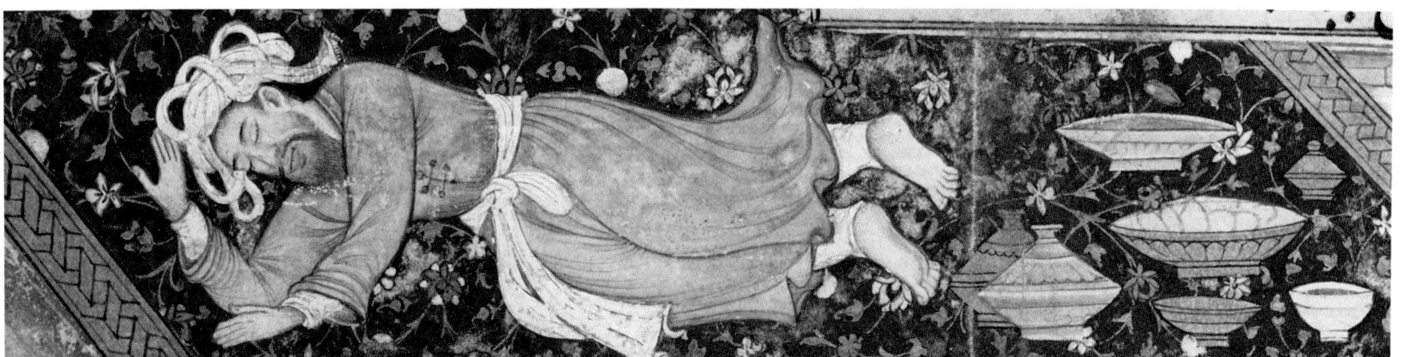

CAT. 56B detail

In several ways the *Tarikh-i Alfi* (Millennial history) is an unusual Mughal manuscript. The book was compiled expressly at Akbar's command, and its history is therefore well-documented (see Leach 1986, pp. 53–58; and Beach 1981, pp. 91–94). The compilation began in 1581/82 but was not completed until 1593/94. The person in charge of the task was Badauni, an eminent courtier and scholar. It is a history of the Muslim rulers during the first millennium of the Muslim era, which ended in 1591. Akbar wanted it to be a straight narrative devoid of any fantastic embellishment. As Badauni wrote,

The year 1,000 of the Hijrah era, which is in general use, being now of the point of completion, the Emperor ordered a history of all the kings of Islam to be written, which should in reality supersede all other histories, and directed that such a name should be given to the work as to denote the year of its completion. It was for this reason that the work was entitled Alfi. *He . . . employed seven persons to undertake the compilation . . . .* (as quoted in Beach 1981, p. 91).

As a matter of fact, more than seven persons were involved in the compendium, and most of the work appears to have been done in Lahore. As L. Y. Leach has observed (1986, p. 56), this undertaking had particular significance for Akbar and was part of his overall program of infusing Islam with his brand of liberalism. It was also intended to demonstrate that he was the *Imam Mahdi,* or the prophesied reformer who, it was believed, would appear at the end of the first millennium to forestall the apocalypse. Indeed, the work was considered so heretical that one of the compilers was murdered, and the assassin hinted that even Abul Fazl and Akbar himself might suffer the same fate.

There is some disagreement among scholars as to when exactly this manuscript was prepared. Suggested dates range from 1585 to 1595. However, since Badauni's revisions were completed by 1594 (the year he died) and assuming that the dispersed copy to which these leaves belong is the one presented to Akbar, then 1594 would appear to be *terminus ante quem* for the illustrations. Stylistically the pictures are considered to be earlier than the 1596 *Chingiznama* [58] but later than the Victoria and Albert *Akbarnama,* which is dated to c. 1586–87 (see [49]).

As in several other Akbari manuscripts, the text and the pictures are organized differently on different pages. On all three illustrated pages in the collection the text is written in two irregularly shaped blocks separated by painted passages. (The reverse of C is text only.) Sometimes different scenes are clearly separated, as in A and C, but in B a single incident occupies the entire composition. As was customary in the preparation of such illustrated manuscripts, more than one artist collaborated on each page, but unfortunately the names were lost in later cropping at the bottom. However, so similar are the compositions and the three dead figures on the three identical beds that there seems little doubt the two sides of one folio (A/B) were painted by the same artists.

A Both scenes depicted on this page are concerned with death. In the upper composition al-Wathiq of the Abbasid dynasty (r. 842–47) has died in his sleep on a carpeted bed. He is surrounded by a number of men, who display their emotions in a variety of expressive ways. The death of al-Wathiq cleared the road for al-Mutawakkil to succeed (r. 847–61). In the lower composition al-Mutawakkil brandishes a sword, having just killed Muhammad b. Baiis b. Jalis. Two women look on, one of whom stands impassively on the left while the other expresses some concern by extending her arms. At the bottom of the page three men with anxious faces huddle together outside the wall.

B On this page also a man's death is the focus of the story. The incident occurred during the reign of Caliph Mutasim (r. 833–42). A man named Anbakh had arranged a great feast but unfortunately died of dehydration before the event could take place. In the picture Anbakh is shown dead on the carpet in a narrow panel sandwiched between the two blocks of text. In the courtyard several people are busy preparing for the feast while others look curiously at the dead host. The rider is very likely the leader of the group, perhaps representing the guests, who anxiously await news from inside the palace.

C The upper composition depicts the people of Hams in Syria attacking the palace of governor Fazal, the son of Qarn. The Caliph Mustain (r. 862–66) sent an army against the people of Hams. Apparently the army was dispatched by sea. The large figure in the center of the boat may represent the caliph himself and the others his generals. While the scene above does convey the violence involved in the attack, that below seems to represent a joyride by a convivial group rather than the movement of an attacking army.

The fourth page, the reverse of C, consists only of text.

By Basawan (active c. 1560–1600)
Akbar period, c. 1595
Overall, 11¼ x 6 1/16 in (28.6 x 15.4 cm)
Illustration, 10⅜ x 5¾ in (26.4 x 14.6 cm)
From the Nasli and Alice Heeramaneck Collection, Museum Associates Purchase
M.79.9.12
Literature: Heeramaneck 1984, p. 162, pl. 201 (reproduced in reverse); Pal 1987, pp. 116, 118, fig. 77.

This leaf with an illustration on one page and text on the other is from a manuscript of the *Gulistan* (Rose garden) of Sadi, one of the great Persian poets, whose life may have spanned all of the thirteenth century except the last decade. Some consider the *Gulistan* to be the most famous work in Persian literature. It is a collection of moralistic tales on a wide variety of subjects, including human nature; conduct in life, sex, and religion; royal manners; and morals of dervishes, among others. It has no counterpart in Europe. In India the great Sanskrit poet Bartrihari (fifth century), whose poems reveal the same kind of insight into human nature and express moral aphorisms with both wit and elegance, may be regarded as Sadi's counterpart.

Ten other illustrated folios of this copy of the *Gulistan* are known; eight of them are in the Cincinnati Art Museum (Smart and Walker 1985, pp. 17–23, no. 3). E. S. Smart and D. S. Walker's discussion of them has rejected the earlier belief that these stray leaves once belonged to a manuscript of the *Gulistan* copied in Bukhara in 1567/68 and preserved in the British Library, London. Although M. Beach (1981, p. 227) dated the Cincinnati and Los Angeles folios to about 1600, Smart and Walker prefer a date around 1595. What does seem certain is that the manuscript was prepared in the 1590s rather than in the following decade.

The museum's painting illustrates a crucial moment from a story about misplaced trust by an indulgent vizier (chapter 1, tale 4; see Rehatsek 1966, pp. 68–71). A band of robbers was captured and brought to court. Among them was a small boy, the son of one of the robbers, who attracted the attention of the kindly vizier. He pleaded with the monarch to spare the boy's life on the promise that he would raise and educate the boy to be an honest man. The cynical ruler reluctantly agreed after cautioning his vizier. The vizier spared no effort in bringing up the boy properly, but two years later the boy connived with a band of local robbers, helped to kill the vizier, and absconded with his benefactor's wealth. The moral of the story, in the words of the king, is, "How can a man fabricate a good sword of bad iron?"

A marginal inscription ascribes the picture to Basawan, one of the most accomplished artists at the imperial court. Both the masterly composition and the psychological acuity in the rendering of the characters undoubtedly confirm the ascription. The focus of the composition is the vizier, who stands on the elegant carpet and pleads with his monarch. Beside him stands the sweet, innocent-seeming boy with his arms crossed against his chest, a picture of repentant humility. The older robbers are grouped in the front, and on either side the courtiers participate actively in the deliberations. Rather interesting are the type of people who constitute the court. Among others are a man holding a book, a falconer, a bowman, and two musicians. Characteristic of Basawan's compositions, the scene is infused with high drama, and the viewer inexorably becomes a participant who shares in the excitement of the event. The picture is a superb example of the elegant and highly refined style that characterizes the manuscripts prepared in the imperial atelier in the 1590s. (For Basawan, see S. C. Welch 1961, Okada 1986, and Okada 1991a).

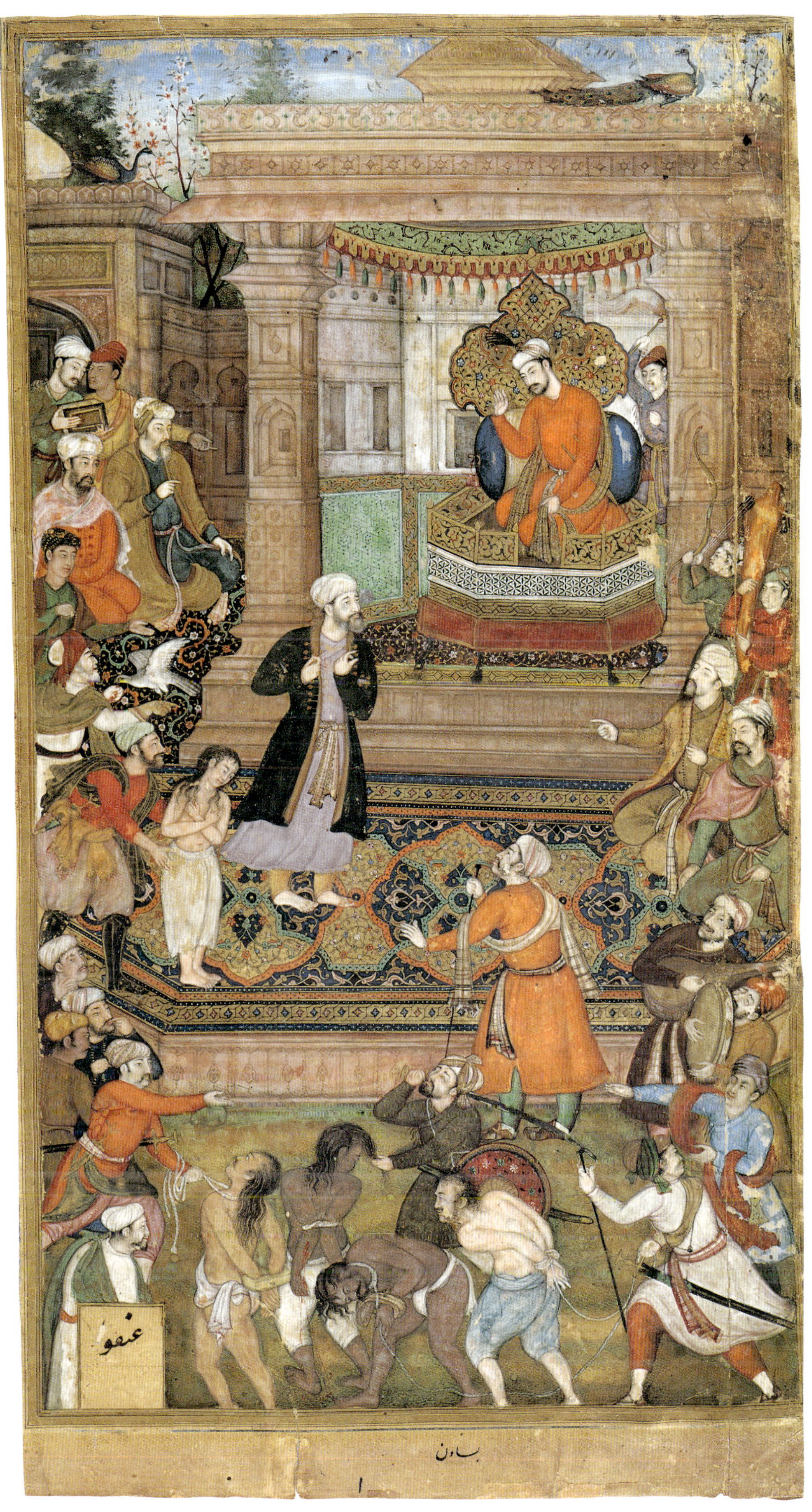
عفو
بساون
١

Akbar period, manuscript dated 1596
Text in black and red ink
From the Nasli and Alice Heeramaneck Collection, Museum Associates Purchase
M.78.9.9,.8
Literature: *Heeramaneck* 1966, p. 150, no. 202 (A only illustrated); Johnson 1972, p. 145, pls. LXXXIa, LXXXIIIb,c (A only); Heeramaneck 1984, p. 158, pls. 162, 163; Brand & Lowry 1985, pp. 16, 136, no. 2 (A only).

A *Alanquva and Her Three Sons*
13⅜ x 8¼ in (34.0 x 21.0 cm)

B *Toda Mongke and His Mongol Horde*
Designed and painted by Tulsi (active 1575–96); portraits by Madhu (active 1575–1604?)
Folio, 15 x 10 in (38.1 x 25.4 cm)
Illustration, 12⅜ x 8 in (31.4 x 20.3 cm)

These two leaves are from an illustrated manuscript of the *Chingiznama* (Saga of Chingiz Khan), which is a section of the well-known world history the *Jami at-Tavarikh* by the great historian Rashid ad-Din (1247–1313). In point of fact the section deals with the history of the Mongol dynasty rather than with Chingiz Khan alone. As the Mughals were descended from Chingiz Khan, it was natural that Akbar would be particularly interested in possessing a copy of this portion of the history. The bulk of the manuscript, which includes the colophon page with the date of completion as 1596, is in the Gulistan Library, Tehran. The two pages of the museum's folios not illustrated here have only text.

A The incident depicted in this illustration had a special significance for Akbar in particular and the Mughals in general. Alanquva was a mythical ancestor of the Mongols and was accorded an almost divine status. Apart from emphasizing her purity, Abul Fazl compared her with the Virgin Mary. Like that of the Virgin, Alanquva's conception was regarded as miraculous since a divine light is said to have impregnated her. Unlike Mary, however, Alanquva gave birth to triplets. The descendants of all three boys were known as *nairun,* or light-produced. The light that Akbar inherited came down from the youngest of the triplets through Chingiz Khan and Timur.

In the picture the artists have given us a well-observed scene within a large enclosure. In front of the tents Alanquva is seated on a carpeted platform with her three sons, around whom are spread bowls and dishes of food. Several ladies mill about watching the encounter and talking among themselves. All the men, some with offerings and others with horses, are kept outside the enclosure. Several carafes, bowls, and goblets rest on a table below the tree, beyond which are a pair of peafowls. It is interesting that one of the triplets is much larger than the others, and he may represent the youngest son, the most important from the Mughal point of view. Unfortunately the marginal notes have been cropped, and so the artists' names have been lost. In many ways, however—in the composition, the placement of the two blocks of text, and the design of the carpet and the figural forms—the picture closely resembles an illustration designed by Basawan (Brand and Lowry 1985, p. 75, no. 35).

B The text on this page was kept to a minimum, causing little distraction from the illustration. The scene shows Toda Mongke (r. 1280–87), who succeeded Mongke Timur (r. 1267–80) on the Mongol throne, riding with his followers in a hilly landscape outside a town. He is probably on his way to his accession ceremony. One of the curious details of this and other pictures from this manuscript is the unusual feathered headdress worn by some of the Mongols. It is unclear whether this was the figment of the imagination of someone in the imperial workshop or was adopted from some unknown Central Asian source. The same headdress is given to the Mongol princes in an illustration designed by Basawan (Brand and Lowry 1985, p. 75, no. 35). Otherwise the representation of the figures, the architectural details, and the landscape all reflect contemporary influences rather than those of the period depicted.

CAT. 58A

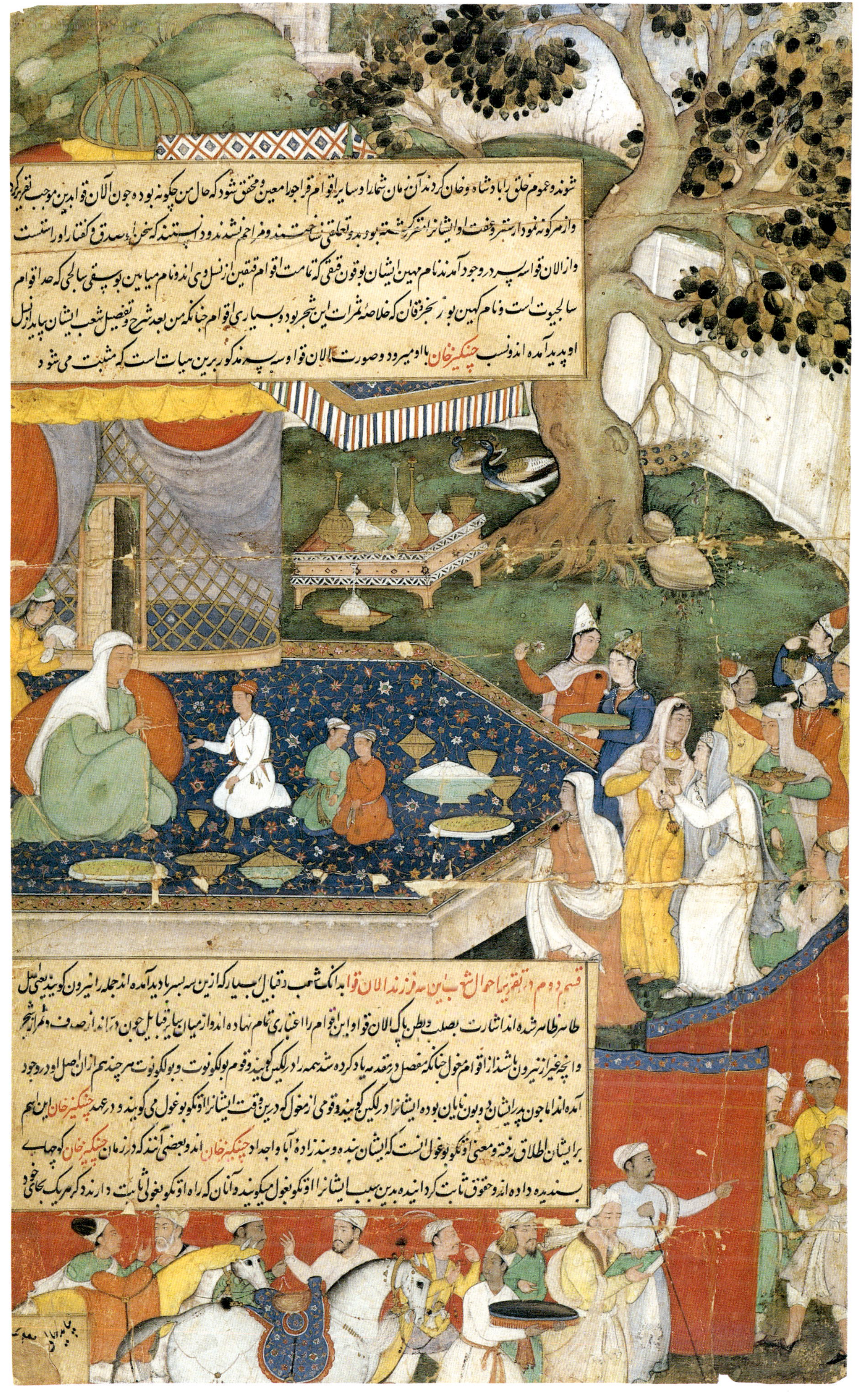

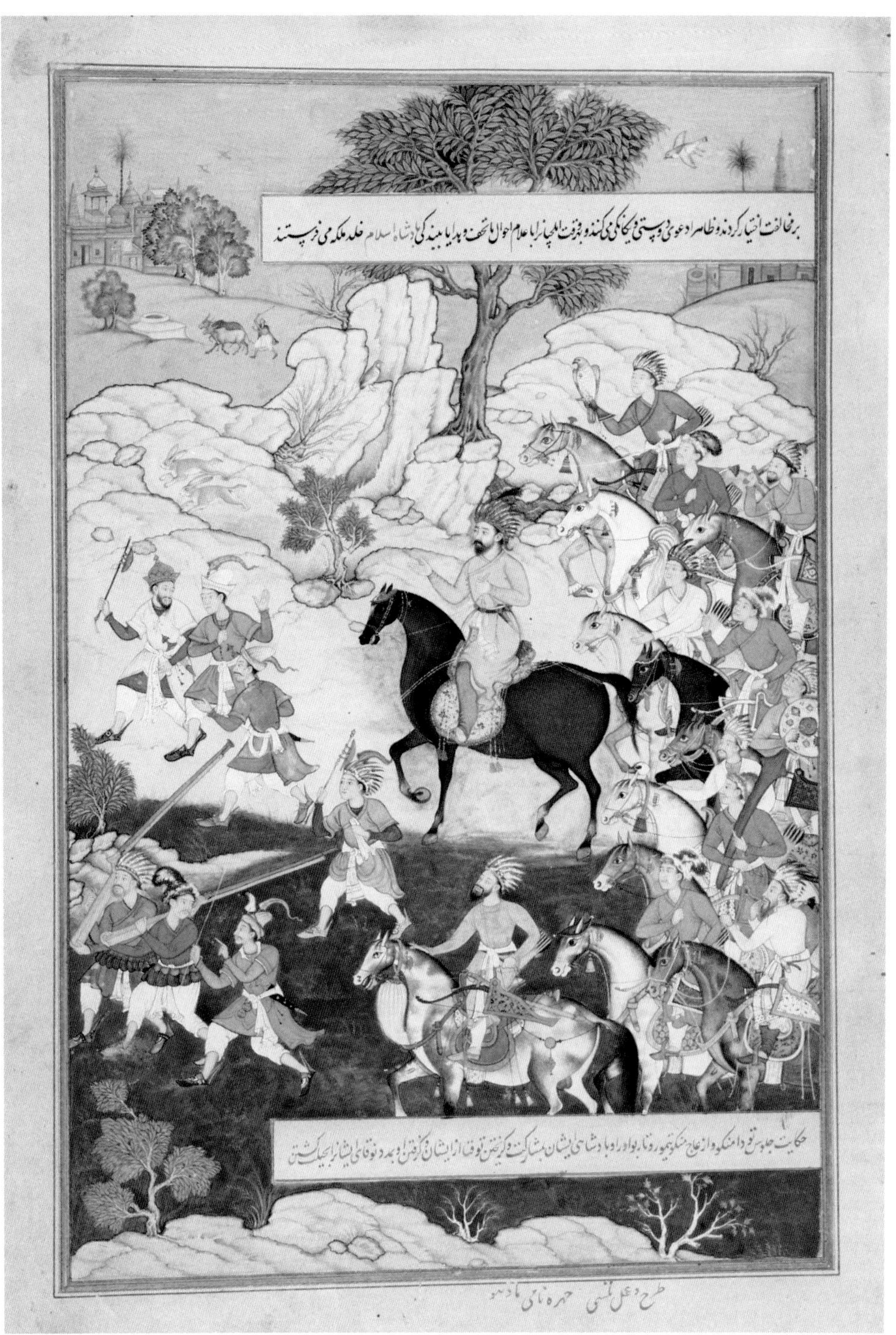

CAT. 58B

Marginal notes inform us that this illustration was designed and painted by Tulsi and that Madhu was responsible for the portraits. Both were well-known artists and in addition to the *Chingiznama* worked on several other Akbari manuscripts. Little, however, is known about them except that Madhu was listed by Abul Fazl as one of the leading painters of the imperial workshop. There is another leaf from this manuscript that also was designed by Tulsi now in the San Diego Museum of Art (see Binney 1973, p. 42, no. 17). On it too the text is limited to two lines in almost identical positions. In both, the principal figure is placed in the center, otherwise the two compositions are quite different. Tulsi, however, did not color the San Diego page. That Madhu was a gifted portraitist is evident from Toda Mongke's face, which has been rendered with greater care than those of the soldiers and courtiers forming his retinue. A second Madhu is known to have worked for Abd ar-Rahim Khan Khanan. The person responsible for this painting is known as Madhu Kalan, or Madhu the Elder.

Akbar period, 1590–1600
Overall, 9 x 6¾ in (22.9 x 17.1 cm)
Illustration, 4⅞ x 3 in (12.4 x 7.6 cm)
Gift of Christopher Perkins and Wanda and Don Stein through the 1989 Collectors Committee
M.89.60
Literature: Leoshko 1990.

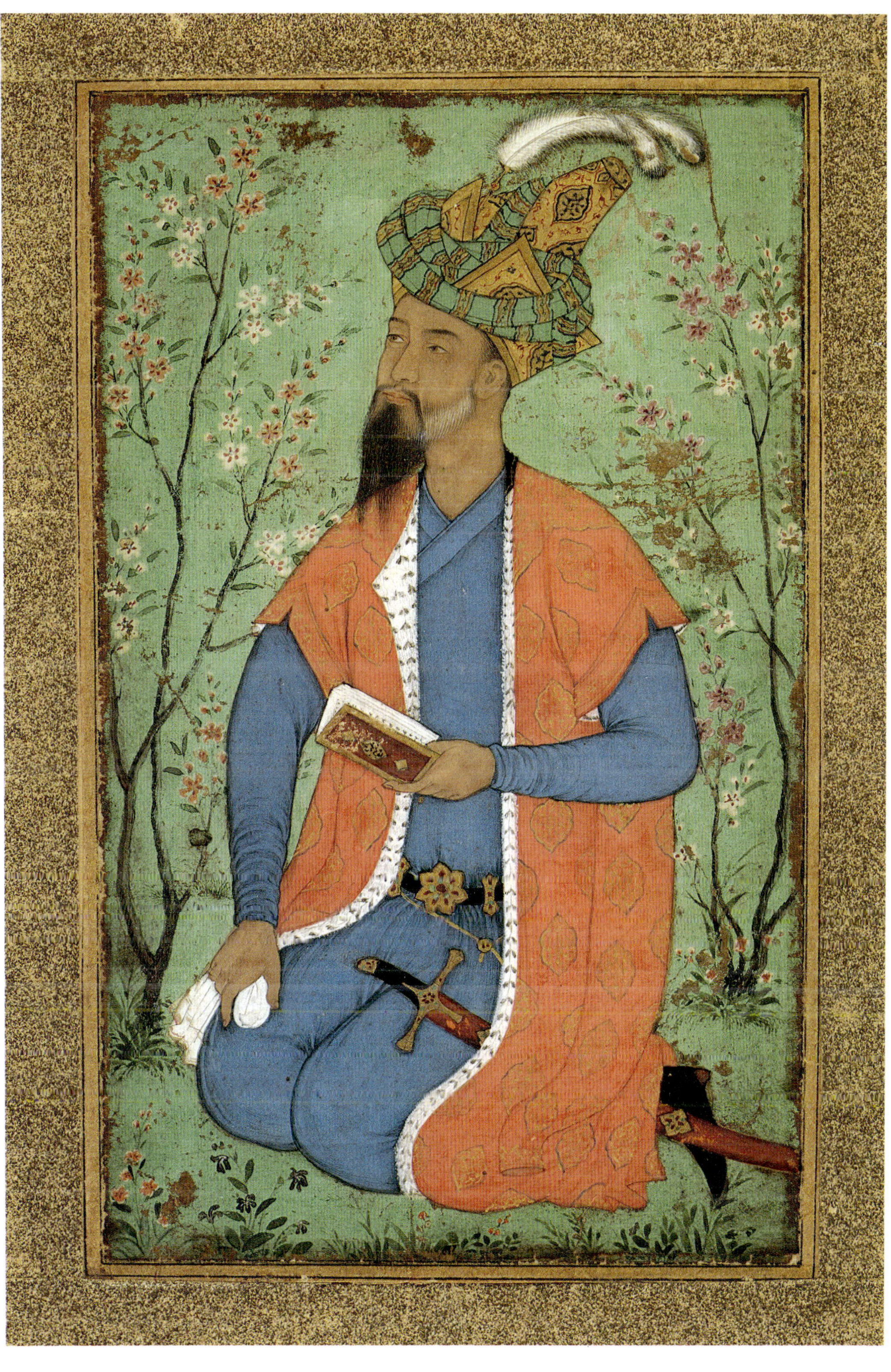

CAT. 59 detail

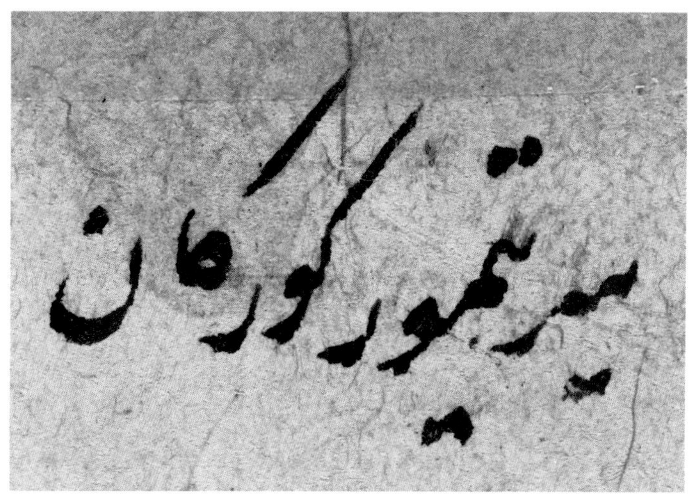

CAT. 59 reverse, detail

A Persian inscription on the back of the painting has been read by T. W. Lentz as *mir Timur qurqan,* which would identify the figure as the monarch Timur, an ancestor of the Mughals. It is very likely, however, that the inscription was added much later and the person represented is not Timur at all but an early Mughal prince. This particular type of turban decorated with feathers and known as a Chaghatay cap was favored during the reign of Humayun, and usually he and his brothers and courtiers are depicted wearing such turbans (cf. S. C. Welch 1985, pp. 143–45, nos. 84, 85). Even in a later portrait showing Timur with Babur and Humayun (Goswamy and Fischer 1987, p. 91, no. 40), only Humayun and a brother or a courtier are given the distinctive Chaghatay cap, while the other two have quite different turbans. Moreover, in most Mughal representations Timur's physiognomy varies considerably, clearly indicating that there was no realistic model available to the Mughal artists. The face of this figure, however, is so distinctly individualized that the artist must have been personally familiar with the model or had at his disposal a naturalistically drawn representation of him.

Indeed, the sensitively rendered face of the figure, with its well-groomed black-and-white beard and expressive dreamy eyes, is not unlike that of Humayun himself. But more likely the portrait represents one of his brothers, perhaps Mirza Hindal. The face resembles that of one of the brothers portrayed in a splendid picture attributed to the Iranian master Dust Muhammad (S. C. Welch 1985, p. 145, no. 85).

Depictions of a prince with a sword and a book, signifying the Timurid virtues of courage and wisdom, or of a scholar in a garden, which is indicated by delicately painted flowering trees that do not overwhelm the figure, was a popular genre in sixteenth-century Persian painting. The mode was adopted by Mughal artists, but characteristically their representations are less idealized delineations of the sitters. Some Mughal examples of the genre that have relevance to this picture are reproduced in S. C. Welch 1985, no. 107, and Okada 1989, nos. 26, 33, and 44. The last is a sketch of a man writing in a garden painted by Lal in the last decade of the sixteenth century. It reveals much stronger influence of European technique than does this lyrical portrait, which still retains a Persian flavor in its linear treatment and romantic mood. Indeed, in the delineation of the background and the flowering plants the picture is comparable to that in a work in the Musée Guimet, Paris, signed by an artist named Husayn, who was a talented painter of the Akbari atelier during the last two decades of the sixteenth century (Okada 1989, p. 206, no. 64). Especially noteworthy is the similar treatment of the foliage in the two pictures. The two differ somewhat in coloring, however. In the Musée Guimet picture Husayn used warm, intense reds and a bright yellow background, whereas the museum's portrait is painted in cooler colors, the background being the typical green of Akbari portraits.

Attributed to Manohar (active c. 1580–1620)
Akbar period, c. 1600
3⅞ x 4⅛ in (9.8 x 10.5 cm)
From the Nasli and Alice Heeramaneck Collection, Museum Associates Purchase
M.81.8.4
Literature: *Heeramaneck* 1966, p. 151, no. 204 (not illustrated); Meister 1968, pp. 112–13, fig. 14; Glynn 1974, pp. 70, 71–72; Beach 1978, pp. 131, 134, no. 46; Heeramaneck 1984, p. 160, pl. 191.

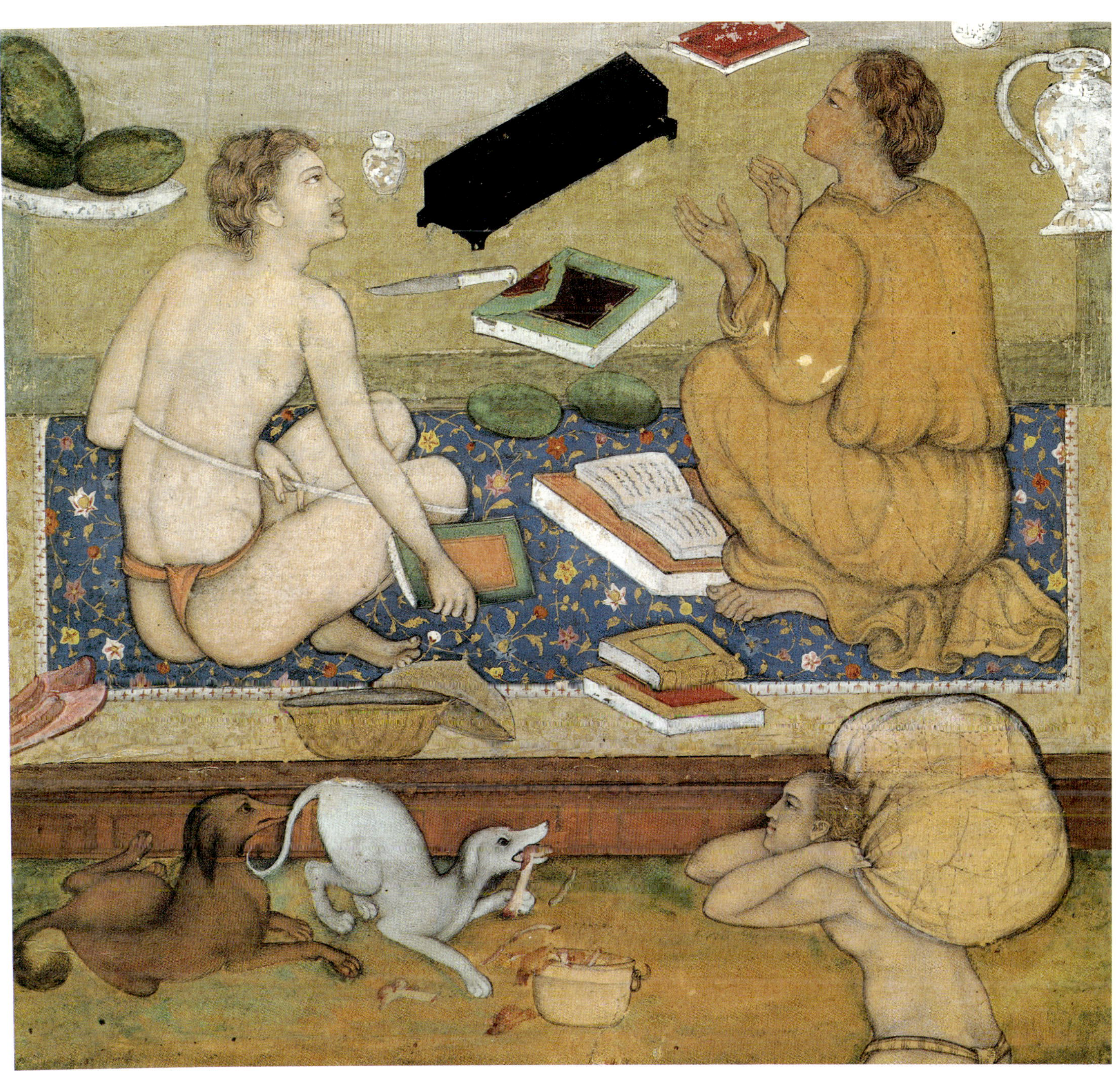

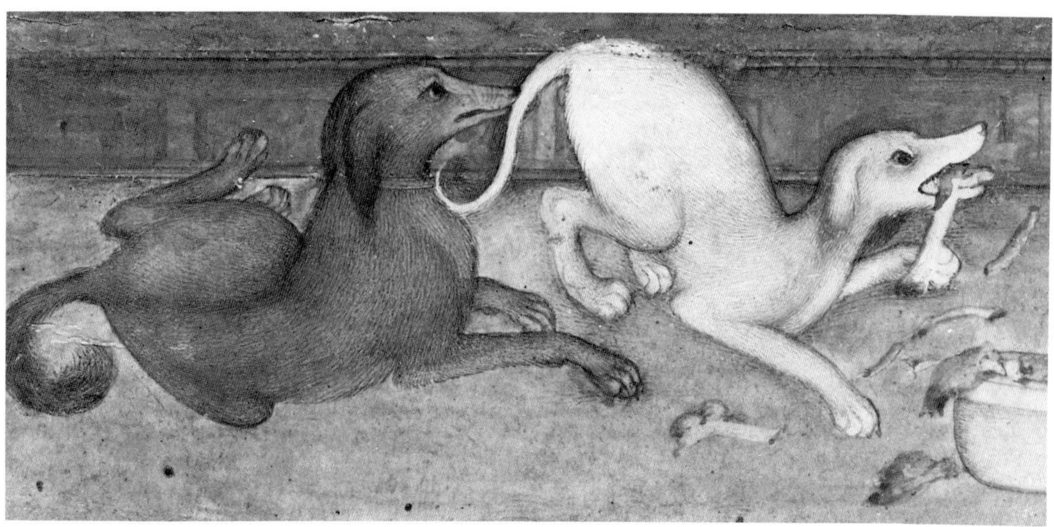

CAT. 60 detail

Although fragmentary, this small picture is a fine example of the kind of pastiche that the Mughal artists loved to produce as a virtuoso exercise drawing from various European sources. All three human figures have doubtless been adopted from European works, but the seminaked blond youth on the left has been transformed into a Hindu ascetic. The presence of the dogs, one of which chews upon a bone while scattering others, and of the man bearing a load seems somewhat incongruous next to two young scholars apparently engaged in a serious religious discussion. Less anomalous are some of the other items strewn around the composition, which include fruit, a basket, porcelains, and books. The clothed man has an open book placed on a board before him and the other holds one in his right hand. It is curious that a pair of slippers should be placed on the platform rather than on the ground.

In its present cropped condition it is difficult to identify the scene precisely or suggest a context. It may have been done as a technical exercise in which the artist was demonstrating his skill in adopting European ideas and may have been presented as a New Year's Day present to either Akbar or Jahangir, which was a common practice. The latter seems the more likely recipient. Although adapted from European models, the two young scholars probably represent a Hindu and a Muslim, the nearly naked person being the former. They are obviously engaged in a discussion, although the inclusion of scattered bones seems somewhat strange in the presence of a Hindu ascetic. Even if a Hindu ascetic did sit down for a discussion with a Muslim scholar, it is unlikely that the two would have shared a meal. In any event, considering that neither really is an Indian, the picture may have nothing to do with reality. Indeed, by showing one figure almost naked and the other fully dressed, it would seem the artist was demonstrating his ability to model both naked and clothed bodies. That this might have been a technical exercise is also suggested by the way he has handled the inanimate objects, almost as still-life compositions.

Several Mughal artists, including Miskin, Basawan, and his son Manohar, were fascinated with European works. In her article published in 1974, C. Glynn pointed out several details in this study that occur in pictures by Miskin. However, she did not attribute the painting directly to that artist, although the implication is there. Since then the painting has been firmly attributed to Manohar by G. D. Lowry (in Beach 1978, pp. 133, 134), but it was not included in the study of this artist by T. McInerney (1991). Comparing the techniques of the father and the son, Lowry considered this work to emphasize "linear interplay of the various forms on the surface of the painting," a characteristic of Manohar, rather than to express the sense of volume through heavy shading that is Basawan's trademark. Moreover, this picture lacks the sense of drama that is so predominant in Basawan's work (cf. [57]). Manohar's compositions are less emotionally charged and possess a quieter mood. Although his admiration for European works was no less intense than his father's, he appears to have been less seduced by their painterly technique. Nevertheless, as Meister (1968, pp. 112–13) remarked about this picture, "Each student is delicately drawn, the soft robe, the wavy hair, their rapt expressions done with subtle understanding. Translucent flesh, the worn, faded patchwork of the bundle carried in the foreground, the warm blood on bones torn at by the dogs are all painted in by a most exceptional hand."

Folio, 11⅝ x 7½ in (29.5 x 19.1 cm)
From the Nasli and Alice Heeramaneck Collection, Museum Associates Purchase
M.83.105.5
Literature: Trabold 1975, pp. 35–36, no. 48 (A only); Beach 1976–77, p. 46, fig. 14 (A only); Larson et al. 1980, p. 119, no. 24.

A *Felicitation of the Virgin and Child* (r)
Attributed to Kesu Khurd (active c. 1580–c. 1600)
Akbar period, c. 1600
Ink and color washes
7⅜ x 4¾ in (18.7 x 12.1 cm)

B *Page of Calligraphy* (v)
By Mahmud b. Ishaq al-Shihabi al-Haravi
Iran; c. 1565
6⅛ x 3¼ in (15.6 x 8.3 cm)

The gold-speckled borders of the two works are probably of the eighteenth century. It is not possible to determine whether the drawing and calligraphy were mounted together in an earlier imperial album or were placed back to back when the eighteenth-century album was assembled. As is usually the case with such albums, there is no relation between the picture and the calligraphy. The latter in fact is an example of calligraphy from Iran that predates the lightly colored drawing by a number of years. Such tinted drawings are known in Persian as *nim qalam,* and they were popular with both Iranian and Mughal patrons.

A While the exact identification of the subject matter is unclear, the composition shows some sort of felicitation or adoration of the Virgin and Child. The Virgin sits slightly off center on a low chair and supports the child on her left thigh. The lollipoplike object in her right hand cannot be identified but is very likely a rattle for the child. They are surrounded by a large number of women engaged in various activities, some simply gesturing, some holding books or boxes, others engaged in conversation, and one holding a censer in front of the divine couple. Several men are included in the lower section of the picture. A group is led on the right by rather a large man walking jauntily and holding a cylindrical object in his right hand and his hat in the other. The direction of his gaze is unclear, but there is no doubt that the dog is looking at him with interest. In the foreground a youth wearing a Scythian hat points both his arms toward the group entering from the right as he converses with a woman holding two flasks. More vessels sit on a table, and a spittoon and a candlestick stand on the floor. A second woman holding a cup and pointing toward the scene above is partially visible behind the woman with the flasks.

M. Beach (1976–77, p. 46) has attributed this painting to Kesu Khurd, or Kesu the Younger. Presumably the epithet was meant to distinguish him from another Kesu, a leading member of Akbar's atelier who was referred to as Kesu Kalan, or the Elder. Like his older namesake, Kesu Khurd also had a distinctive personal style but was less gifted. Most of his surviving work is from several of the Akbari manuscripts dating from the 1580s or later. Few single paintings or drawings by Kesu Khurd have survived. This drawing, tinted sparingly with pink and brown, is quite close to another similarly crowded interior composition with the Virgin and Child bearing his signature and now in the Chester Beatty Library, Dublin, as has been discussed by Beach. It is difficult to agree, however, that Kesu Khurd was unable to draw eyes or that his treatment of cloth is stiff and "unclothlike." If anything he has drawn a remarkable variety of eyes in this drawing registering different moods and expressions, even though generally his faces do appear to be somewhat impassive. Nor does one note any particular lack of ability in the use of shading to impart volume to his figures as well as their attire. Indeed, the bustle of the attendants and the flow and swirl of drapery enhance the vitality of the figures and make the scene remarkably animated.

What is clear is that Kesu Khurd did not copy a single European source but created a pastiche of his own. The enthroned Virgin and Child have been placed in an unrecognizable court setting, and the Virgin is distinguished from the others only by her halo. She does not have her traditional blue or red robes. As Rebecca Gowen has written (in Larson et al. 1980, p. 119), the Virgin and Child appear as "an island of tranquility amidst the bustling activity" around them and yet are presented more as "a part of the community of 'everyday life' than was ever conceived in the West."

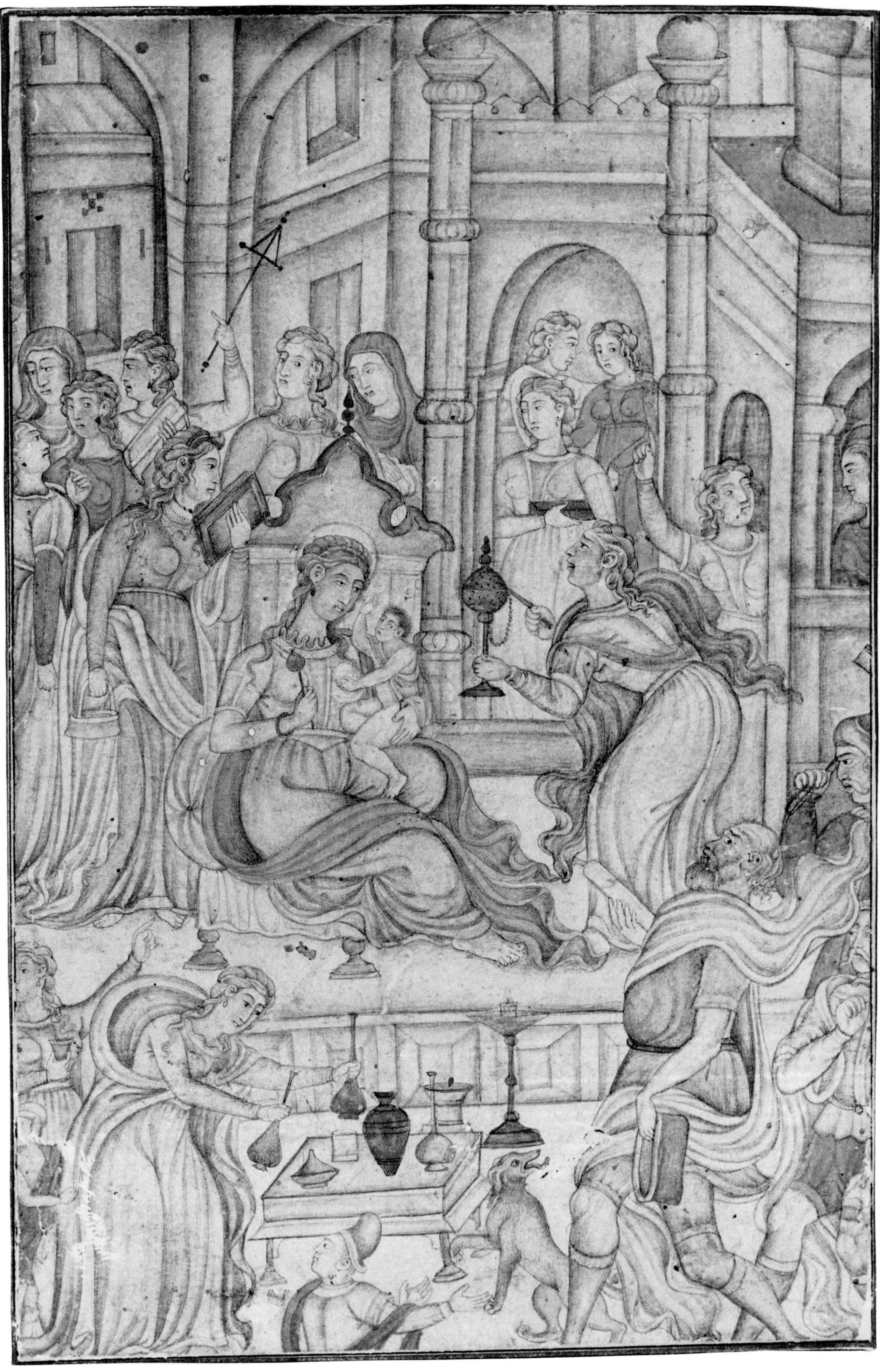

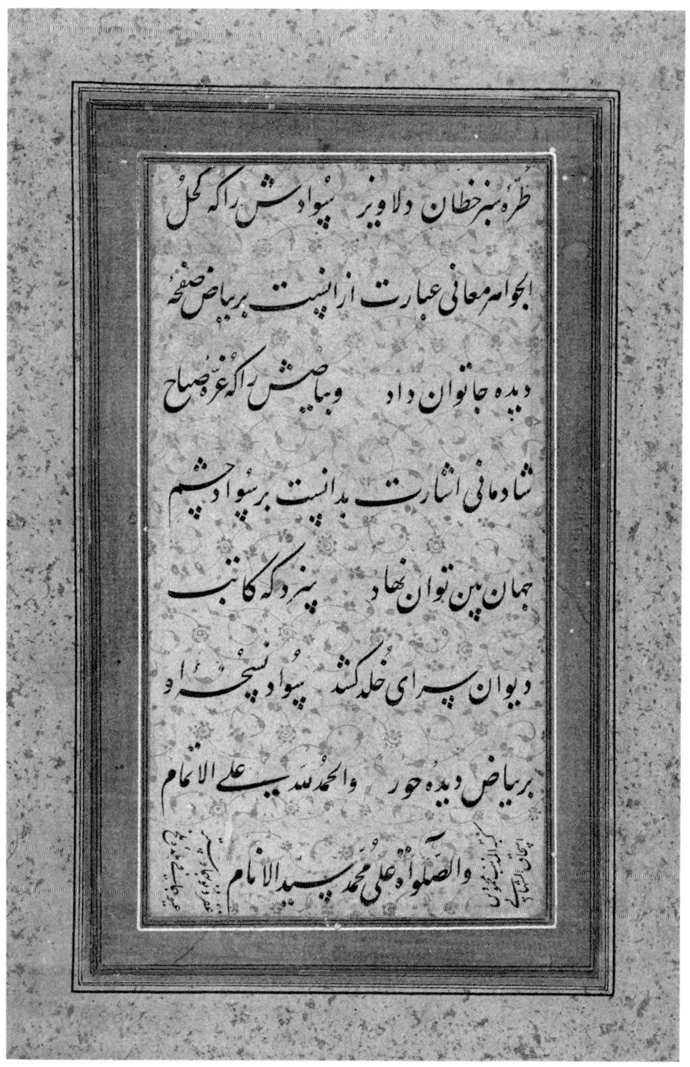

CAT. 61A *(opposite)*
CAT. 61B *(right)*

B The calligraphy on this page consists of a verse describing the good qualities of a calligrapher, such as Mir Ali of Herat (see [77A, 78A]), who was the calligrapher's teacher. Mahmud b. Ishaq al-Shihabi al-Haravi was a native of a small village near Herat, now in Afghanistan. His father, Ishaq, was the mayor of Herat. When Ubayd-khan Uzbek captured Herat in 1528–29, he took away Ishaq and his children to Bukhara. The well-known calligrapher Mir Ali was in the same company and accepted Mahmud as a pupil. So talented was the pupil that later Mir Ali himself said, "I have acquired a pupil better than myself" (Minorsky 1959, pp. 131–32). After some years Mahmud moved from Bukhara to Balkh, where he appears to have led a leisurely life. When Qazi Ahmad wrote his treatise on painters and calligraphers in 1606, Mahmud's calligraphy had already become scarce. He was also an accomplished musician.

The verse is very likely a composition by the calligrapher himself. It is written in black ink on a buff page enlivened with a lightly drawn *rinceau* in gold. The writing, however, is straightforward *nastaliq* with no fancy embellishments. Considering the rarity of specimens of Mahmud's calligraphy, it is possible that this page was a gift to either Akbar or Jahangir by a visitor from Central Asia or Iran.

Akbar period, c. 1600
Border, probably nineteenth century
Folio, 13 x 8 1/16 in (33.0 x 20.5 cm)
Illustration, 6 1/8 x 3 7/8 in (15.6 x 9.8 cm)
From the Nasli and Alice Heeramaneck Collection, Museum Associates Purchase
M.80.6.7
Literature: *Heeramaneck* 1966, p. 152, no. 206 (not illustrated); Heeramaneck 1984, p. 160, pl. 186 (reproduced in reverse).

The identities of both the figure and the instrument he is playing are uncertain. Seated beneath a tree on a tiger skin, the man, with a curly beard and fur-trimmed hat, seems to be a European. At least he has been adapted from a European source, as is clear from his pink garment and blue cape. The landscape also echoes Flemish compositions even though individual elements such as the form of the gnarled tree, the impressionistic rendering of the leaves, the birds in the sky, and the cluster of buildings representing a settlement have been Indianized.

The tiger skin is usually used by ascetics, particularly of the Hindu faith. Rarely, however, do ascetics function as musicians, and certainly the attire is inappropriate for a Hindu or even a Muslim ascetic. But a European is unlikely to go barefooted, and no shoes are visible anywhere. No less intriguing is the musical instrument he is playing. It seems to be a composite of at least three different instruments, a harp or lyre—which has a golden peacock decorating the termination of the body—combined with a resonating gourd of a vina and a bagpipe, which the musician is blowing.

This picture seems to be the kind of whimsical pastiche that the Mughal artists loved to create, selecting from various European sources available to them. However, the perceptively realistic rendering of the face could indicate a live model. Such pictures could easily have been made for Jahangir's amusement while he was still a prince.

The picture is surrounded by two narrow borders decorated with intertwined flowering vines of two different forms in gold. The outer border is adorned with boldly rendered flowering plants of three different species. This border is of a much later period, probably the nineteeth century.

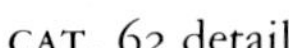

CAT. 62 detail

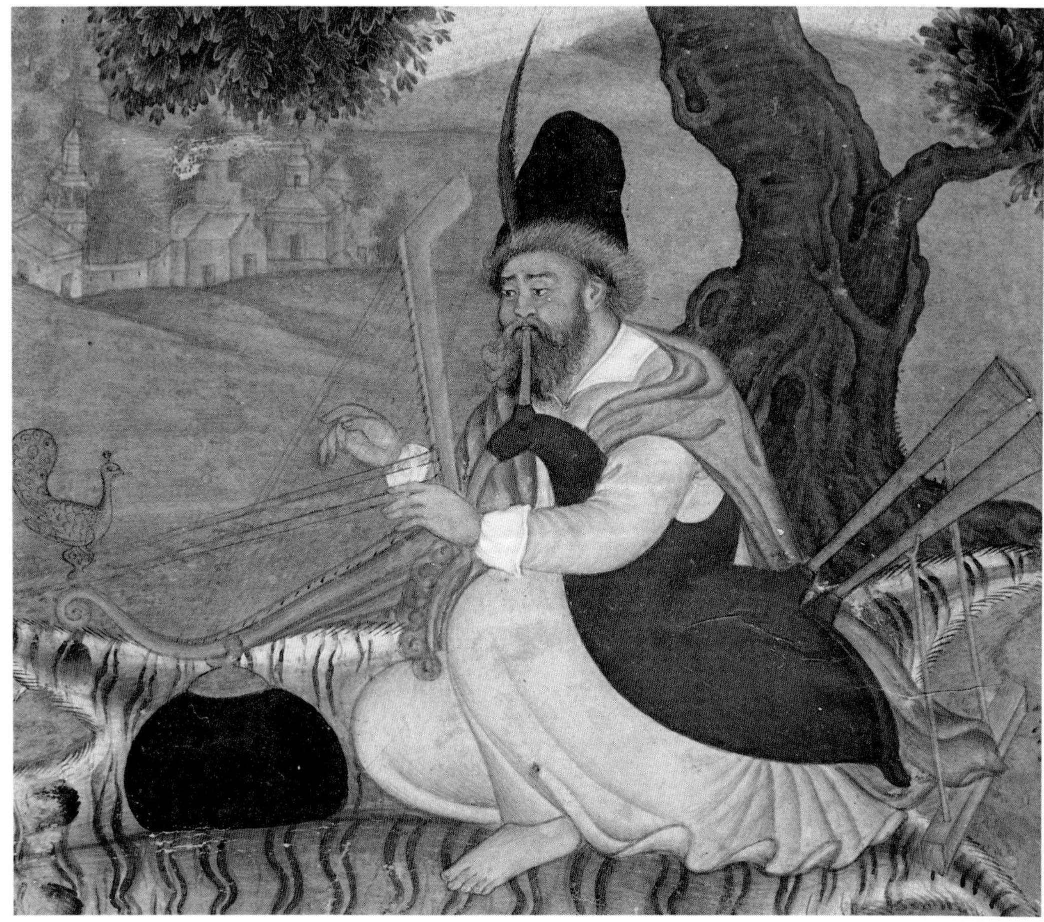

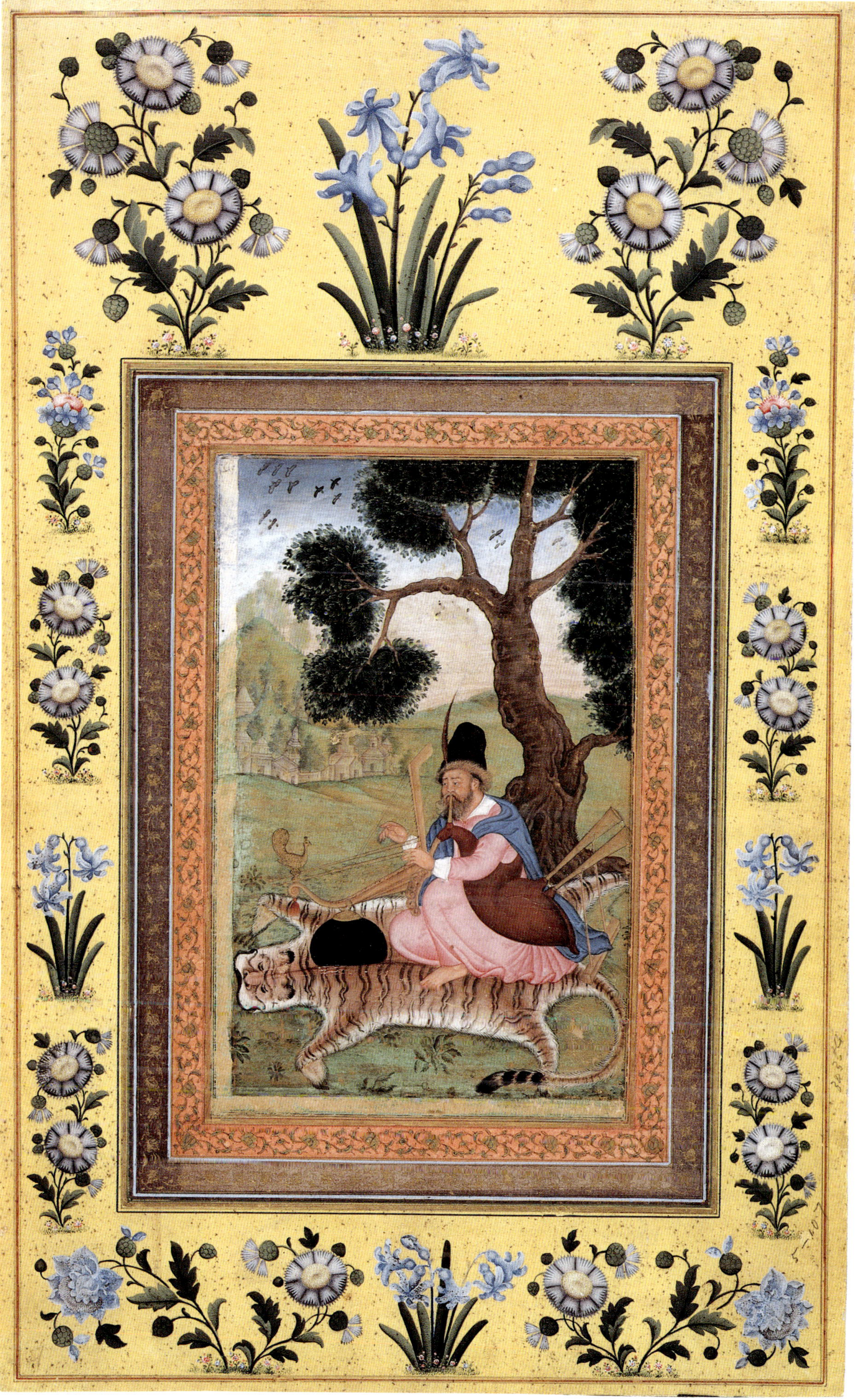

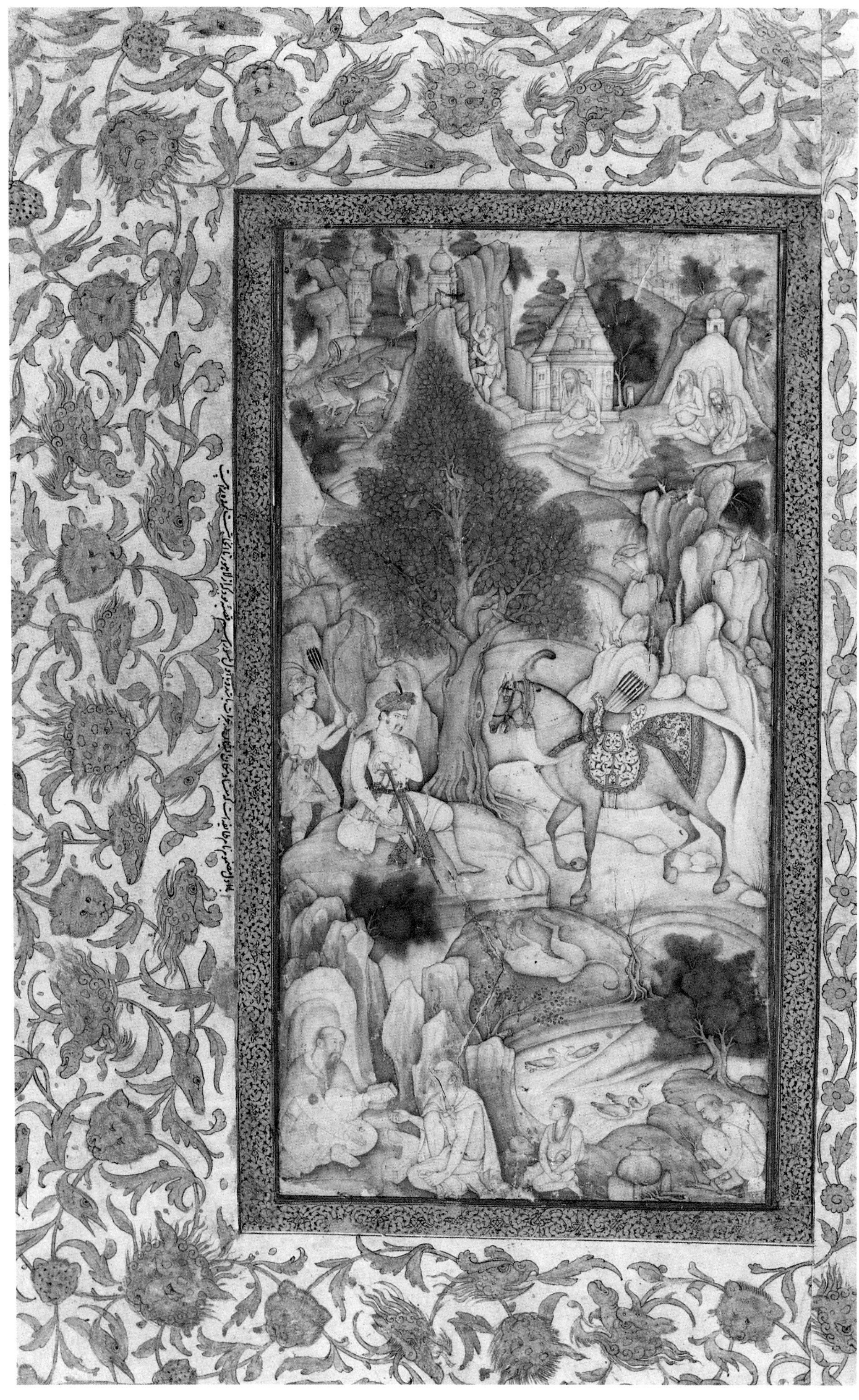

Drawing, Akbar period, c. 1600–1605
Attributed to Miskin (active c. 1580–c. 1610)
Ink, opaque watercolor, and gold
Border, Jahangir period, c. 1608
Folio, 13½ x 8⅜ in (34.3 x 21.3 cm)
Illustration, 9¼ x 4⅝ in (23.5 x 11.7 cm)
From the Nasli and Alice Heeramaneck Collection, Museum Associates Purchase
M.84.32.7
Literature: *Heeramaneck* 1966, p. 146, no. 200; Glynn 1974; Heeramaneck 1984, p. 159, pl. 173.

This lightly colored drawing *(nim qalam)* is mounted within a border that once adorned a *Farhang-i Jahangiri,* a dictionary prepared for Jahangir (see [67]). The Persian inscription on the left relates to the dictionary and not to the drawing.

The picture was the subject of an article (Glynn 1974) in which a convincing case was made that the well-known imperial artist Miskin may have been responsible for it. Compositionally as well as in the style of draughtmanship the drawing is indeed closely related to several works either signed by the artist or firmly attributed to him. M. Beach (1978, p. 42) also attributes this picture to Miskin, considering it to be one of his late works, contemporary with the 1604 *Akbarnama* illustrations.

Miskin was the son of Mahesh, one of the leading masters of Akbar's studio. His brother Asi was also a painter. Although they were Hindus, belonging to the *kahar,* or palanquin-bearer, subcaste, both brothers were given Arabic epithets as names, probably after Mahesh joined the imperial studio. Miskin too came to be regarded as a master painter, and his name is included in Abul Fazl's list of leading court artists. Miskin may well have worked on the *Hamzanama,* but his participation in the 1582–86 *Ramayana* is certain. In recognition of his talents he was assigned joint projects with both Dashwanth and Basawan, the two greatest Akbari masters. Thus, in addition to his father, he had the opportunity to learn from two other masters and perhaps also Abd as-Samad. (See Vaughn 1991 for an extensive discussion of Miskin's development.)

While there is no disagreement as to the authorship of this picture, the subject matter is not entirely clear. That the seated man is a prince is in no doubt, but is he Salim, later emperor Jahangir? And if it is he resting during a hunt, where is his retinue? Even more intriguing is the representation of the dog on a rock in front of the royal hunter, who seems, in fact, to be helplessly watching the animal as it goes into convulsions before death, if it is not already dead. In the foreground, separated from the prince by a stream and some rocky outcrops, two elderly scholars, almost certainly based on a European source, are engaged in a conversation while a young man listens. They could hardly have been drawn from life if this were a historical occasion. In the lower right corner a man is busy cooking. At the top four Hindu ascetics are seated in front of a temple, while a fifth climbs up some steps leading to a smaller shrine. Except for the green foliage, some coloring of garments, and the light gray horse's saddle, much of the picture is tinted in various shades of tan and browns.

Once more we are confronted with a picture that seems to offer a composition that is a pastiche of different themes. The seated hunter could have been modeled after Prince Salim, if the picture were done for him. Both the synthetic character of the composition and the intriguing symbolism of the subject matter could well have appealed to him. Certainly the contemplative nature of the occasion with a prince watching a dead dog while ascetics and scholars discourse above and below conveys a philosophical mood. There is an earlier hunting *nim qalam* picture in the Cleveland Museum whose theme is characterized by L. Y. Leach (1986, p. 42) as "a sophisticated, philosophical one." She goes on to comment that "related compositions suggest that at one time there existed a series of pictures devoted to various types of hunting in rocky landscapes." It is not unlikely that an album of hunting pictures, both historical and symbolic, was prepared for Jahangir, and it may well have included the tinted drawing as well as the more action-filled painting in the collection [65].

Akbar period, 1600–1605
Overall, 5⅞ x 3¾ in (14.9 x 9.5 cm)
Illustration, 5⅝ x 3⅜ in (14.3 x 8.6 cm)
From the Nasli and Alice Heeramaneck Collection, Museum Associates Purchase
M.83.1.4
Literature: S. C. Welch 1963, pp. 31, 165, pl. 19; Khandalavala 1962, pp. 11–12, fig. E; *Heeramaneck* 1966, p. 151, no. 203; Trabold 1975, p. 35, no. 46; Skelton et al. 1982, p. 35, no. 34; Heeramaneck 1984, p. 159, pl. 181 (reproduced in reverse).

Wearing red pajamas with a matching turban and a long durbar coat of dazzling figural silk, a youthful figure stands with his falcon against a green background. The band of sky above is rendered in gray, perhaps indicating clouds, and is enlivened with tiny impressionistic birds. Both the figure and the falcon are so realistically rendered that they must have been sketched from life.

We do not know who the falconer is, but it is unlikely that anyone but a member of the imperial family would have worn such spectacular dress. Khandalavala (1962, pp. 11–12) suggested that the portrait may be a later copy and that the falconer has been "passed off as young Emperor Akbar." Others have verbally suggested, without questioning the picture, that the figure may represent Prince Salim in his youth. It should also be pointed out that one cannot rule out his brother Prince Daniyal. The two looked remarkably alike. Both the size and quality of the picture recall similar and informal royal portraits such as that possibly of Mirza Hindal in the collection [59] or that of Babur reading a book in the British Museum, London (Pinder-Wilson 1976, p. 66, no. 102, pl. not numbered). In the latter Babur wears a short jacket made with a somewhat similar silk brocaded with plants and animals.

These coats were probably made of imported Iranian silk. The *Akbarnama* (H. Beveridge [1902] 1972, 1: 439) mentions how such figural silks from Yezd and Kashan were presented to Humayun by Shah Tahmasp (for a surviving example see Skelton et al. 1982, pp. 94–95, no. 252; see also [75] for the use of one in a canopy). Similarly designed material is also depicted in a tent by Mishkin in an illustration for a *Khamsa* of the 1590s (see Losty 1982, pl. XXIV [left]). The design of the fabric in the museum's portrait is particularly elaborate and consists of a landscape of hills with plants inhabited by a wide variety of animals and birds. In one portion a lioness has pounced on a stag, elsewhere a mountain lion is chasing what looks like a goat. While the inclusion of a bird of paradise (*simurgh*) on the left shoulder indicates the fabric's Iranian origin, in the hands of the Indian artist the landscape as well as the fauna have become Indianized.

The precise and lively rendering of the animals on the coat as well as the highly naturalistic drawing of the jessed falcon clearly indicates a master such as Abul Hasan or Mansur. Both were working for Jahangir at Allahabad at this time, although Abul Hasan was in his teens. His portraits are noteworthy for the sumptuousness of textiles and for his rendering of the designs and textures of the material with remarkable finesse. Mansur was extraordinarily skillful in not only representing the precise outer appearance of animals and birds but also expressing their nature. Certainly in this portrayal the hawkishness of the falcon is made clear by the bird's restlessness.

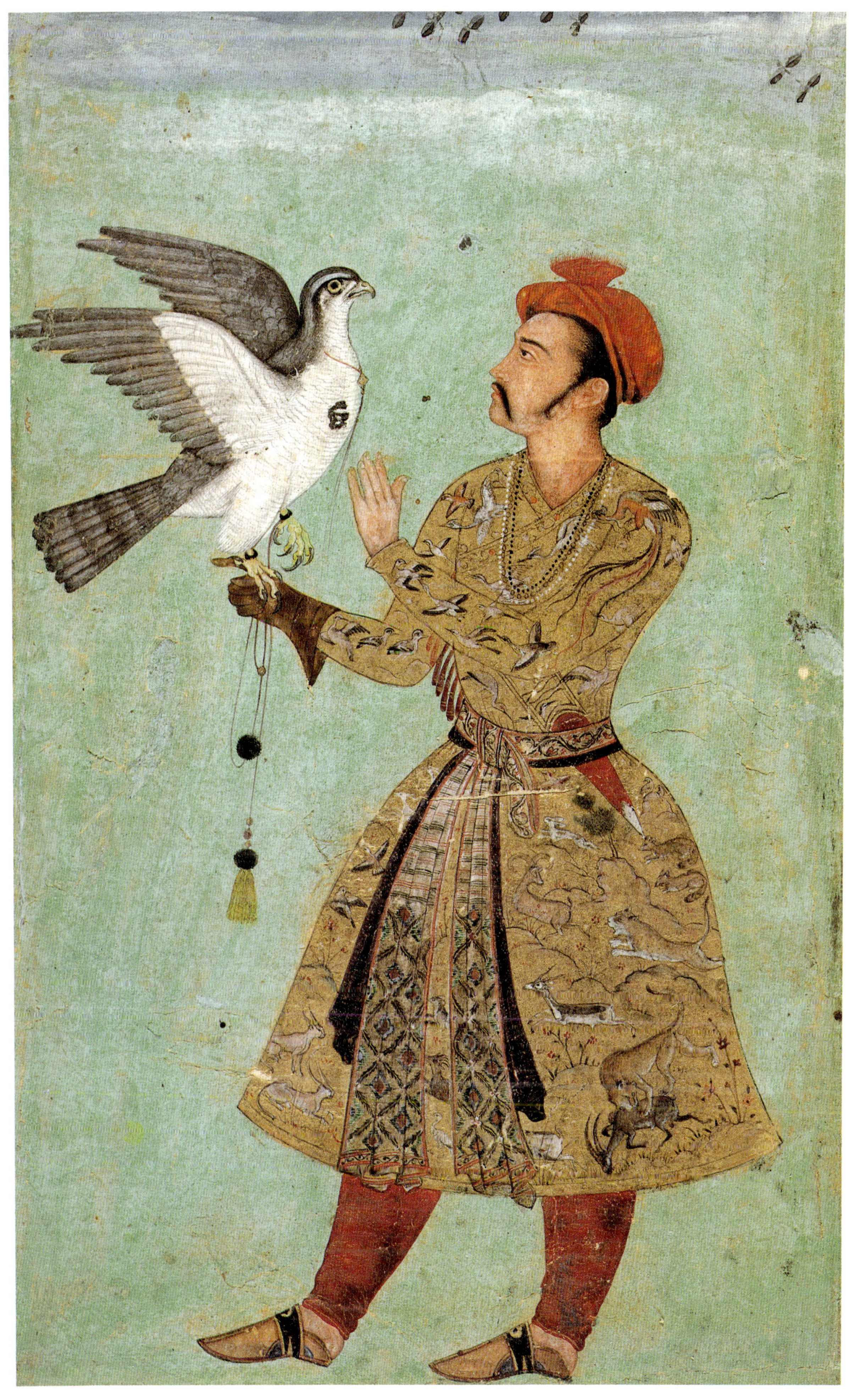

Overall, 14¾ x 10½ in (37.5 x 26.7 cm)
Purchased with funds provided by
The Ahmanson Foundation
M.83.137
Literature: [S. Canby], "Recent Acquisitions: Indian Art," *Los Angeles County Museum of Art Member's Calendar* 21, no. 10 (October 1983): cover, inside front cover; Pal 1987, p. 118, fig. 78.

A *Prince Salim at a Hunt* (r)
Akbar period, Allahabad, Salim's studio, 1600–1604
7¾ x 4⅝ in (19.7 x 11.7 cm)

B *Page of Calligraphy* (v)
By Muhammad Nasir al-Munshi
India or Persia
8½ x 4⅜ in (21.6 x 11.1 cm)

Both the picture and the calligraphic panel on the reverse have been removed from their original borders and remounted on a plain board. Two other hunting pictures, probably from the same album and now in the collections of the San Diego Museum of Art (Binney 1973, p. 72, no. 45) and the Cleveland Museum of Art (Leach 1986, pp. 73–76, no. 19, pl. V), also are no longer in their original borders. Unlike the museum's example, however, those pictures do not have any calligraphy attached to the back.

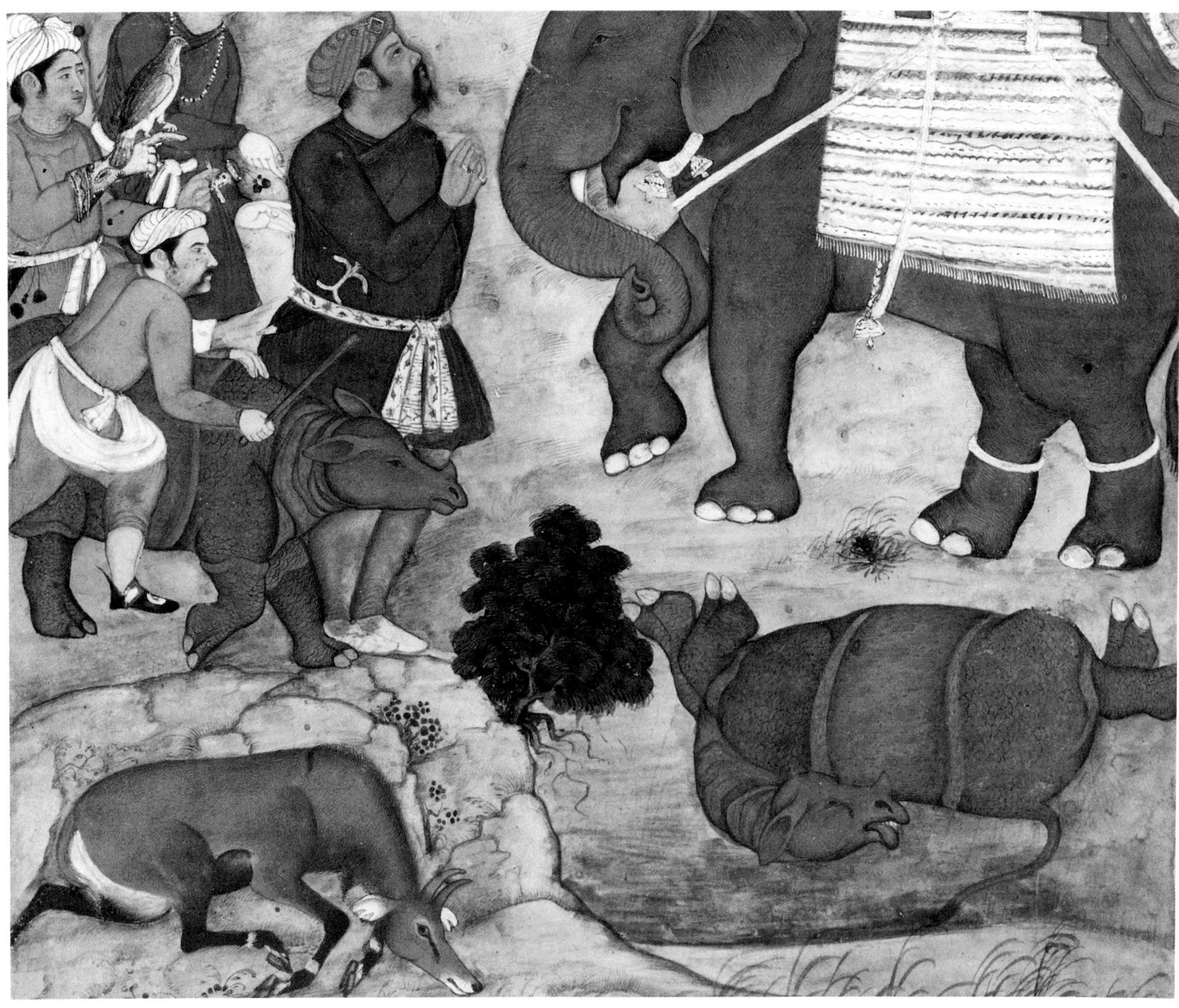

CAT. 65A detail

A It appears that a number of pictures were done for Jahangir showing him hunting at various periods of his life, both as a prince and as the emperor, and they may all have been kept together in an album (see [63]). Jahangir was as fond of hunting as he was of having his experiences in the fields and forests recorded in paintings. He was skillful with various weapons and hunted with guns, bows and arrows, swords, and spears, as well as trained cheetahs and falcons. Because of Jahangir's love both for hunting and for naturalistic representations, these pictures were often rendered by artists who were particularly adept in depicting animals. However, the Cleveland picture is signed by Govardhan, who is known for his perceptive studies of humans rather than animals. While the museum's picture bears no signature, S. Canby (see Literature above) attributed it to Manohar because of "the brilliant treatment of the surface and the sensitivity to the animals and their motions." S. C. Welch, in a personal communication to Canby, opined that the painting may have been done by Bichitr about 1603.

What is certain, however, is that this picture was done in Prince Salim's Allahabad studio, very likely by the same artist who painted the San Diego painting. This is clear from the similar compositions of both pictures with their open simplicity, the placement of the figures against the background, the almost identical groupings of figures in exactly the same position to the upper right, as well as the similarity of Salim's position in the pictures (even though in the San Diego painting he stands on the ground). No less telling are such details as the identical postures of the dead antelope in the bottom left of this picture and of one of the antelopes in the San Diego picture, the identical leaping deer in exactly the same position in the upper left of both, and the astonishingly similar vignette showing the cheetah bringing down an antelope. The last is the exact mirror image in the San Diego picture. Salim's portrait—the details of the face, the forward tilt of the body, the gesture of the hands, and the identical turban—leaves no doubt that the same artist was responsible for both pictures. What is also clear is that he was equally at home in drawing humans as well as animals.

That these hunting pictures were done for the rebellious Prince Salim at Allahabad is clear from a comparison with manuscripts illustrated in his studio in that city. For instance, in the use of soft colors, the naturalistic, open space, a somewhat awkward understanding of perspective, and in the well-modeled forms defined by freely rendered outlines, the museum's picture bears close stylistic relationship to at least three illustrations, one of which represents a hunting scene, in a manuscript of the *Divan* of Hasan Dihlavi painted for Jahangir at Allahabad in 1602/3 (Beach 1978, pp. 34, 37, 38).

In the museum's picture the hunt is over and Salim is being presented with what may be a young orphaned rhinoceros, its mother lying dead in the foreground. The prince is seated in the howdah on the elephant with his gun resting against his shoulder. In representing Salim the artist did not seem to have considered the space required for accommodating the lower part of his body. In addition to the dead rhinoceros there is a dead antelope in the lower left corner. Much more lively activity is depicted in the background. One cheetah has brought down an antelope, while another is giving chase to a deer. These attacks keep the two attendants of the cheetahs busy. Noteworthy are the expressive faces and lively interaction among the prince's hunting companions in both groups.

B On the reverse is a quatrain of Persian poetry written by the scribe Muhammad Nasir al-Munshi, about whom nothing is known. The text is contained in four separate, irregularly shaped cartouches floating against a golden background adorned with delicate vines supporting green leaves and pink and blue flowers. The following translation is by Z. Faridany-Akhavan:

O Beloved
O your magnanimity is like a roof from the corner
of which nine firmaments hang like candles.
On the battle-field your sword overthrows an elephant
like a pawn.

The use of chess as a metaphor is interesting. In the original Indian game the elephant was used in place of the bishop.

CAT. 65A,B details *(overleaf)*

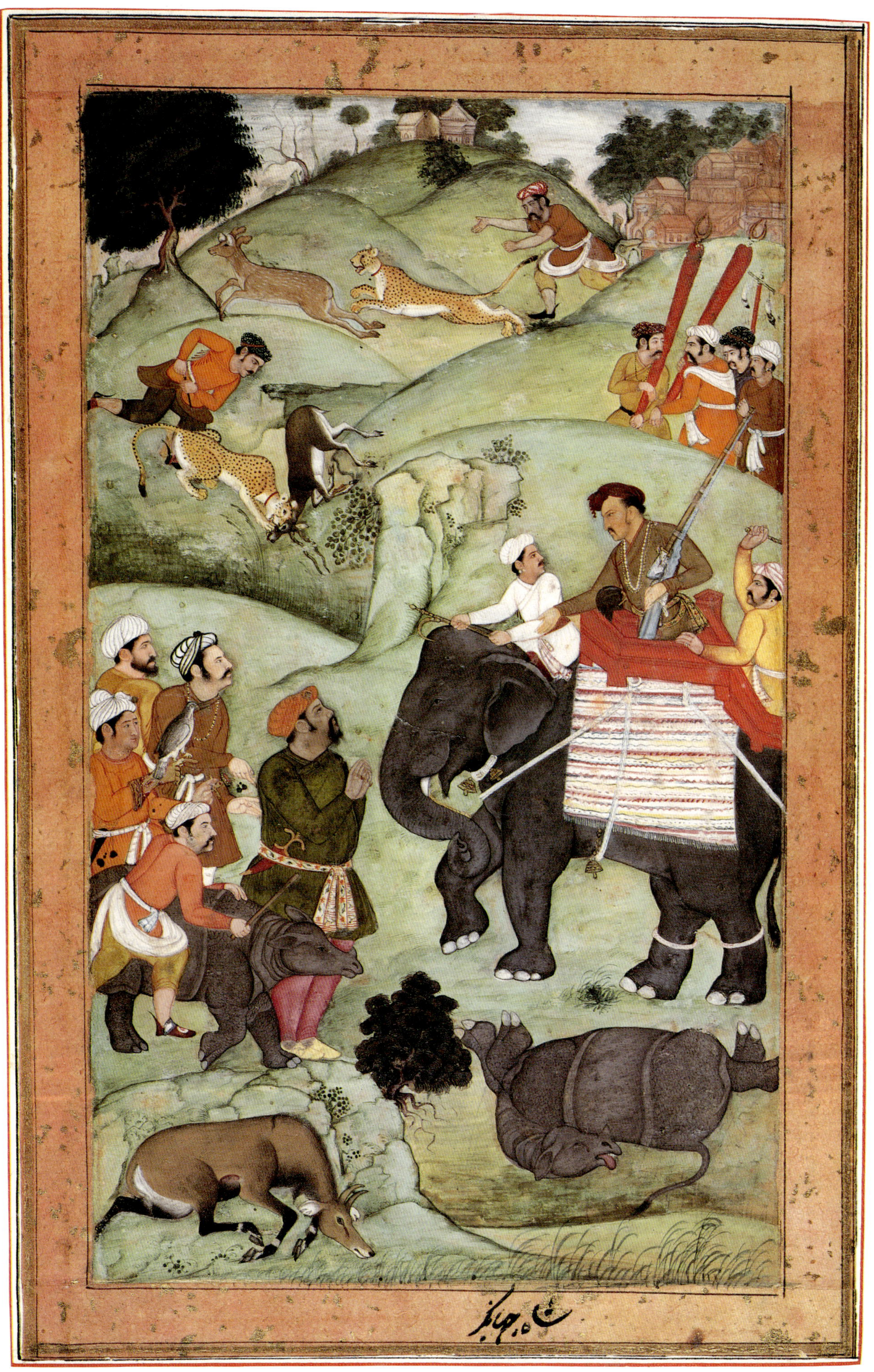
شاه جهانگیر

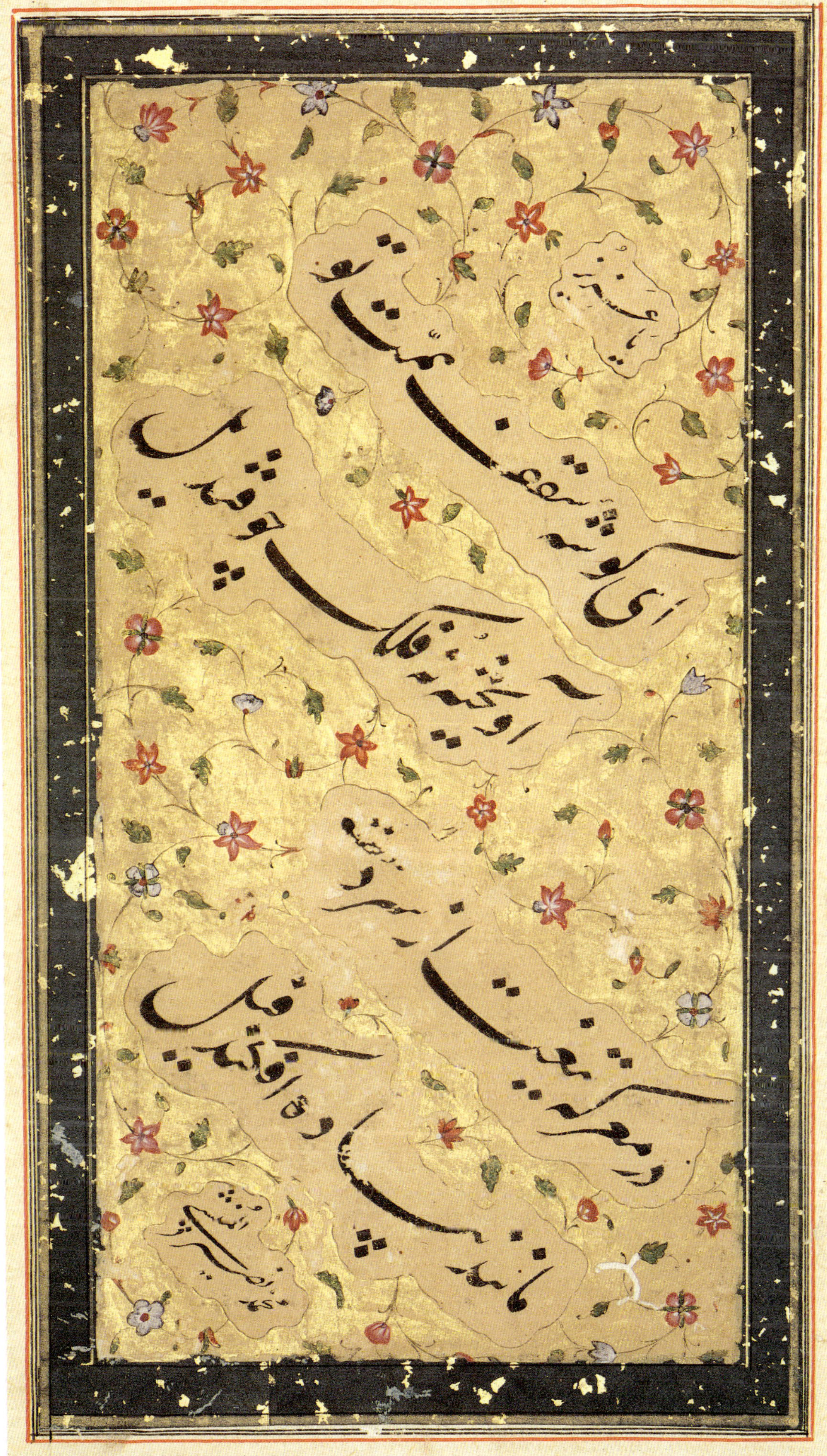

Possibly by Aqa Riza (active in India c. 1588/89–at least 1604) or Abul Hasan (b. 1588/89, active 1600–c. 1635)
Akbar period, Allahabad, Salim's studio, 1600–1604
Folio, 9 3/16 x 5 7/8 in (23.3 x 14.9 cm)
Illustration, 3 7/8 x 2 1/8 in (9.8 x 5.4 cm)
From the Nasli and Alice Heeramaneck Collection, Museum Associates Purchase
M.81.8.12
Literature: Strzygowski 1933, fig. 208, pl. 76; *Heeramaneck* 1966, p. 152, no. 210 (not illustrated); Beach 1978, pp. 116–18, no. 39.

The inscription in the two panels is of a verse, perhaps by the Persian poet Hafiz, which has been translated by R. Skelton as follows:

I have seen my beloved's reflection in the cup,
O, ignorant man, you do not understand why
I am constantly intoxicated.

Two other small inscriptions are in the field of the painting. The one above reads *Shah Salim* and the one below *amal-i-ghulam*. The small picture is surrounded by a pink border decorated with gold flowering vines and is mounted on a beige sheet adorned with golden geometrical patterns enclosing floral motifs.

The picture shows an elegantly dressed youth seated on a high, golden stool against an undulating ground subtly delineated in two shades of green. He wears slippers, blue pajamas, a yellow *jama* (long-sleeved tunic) with a red lining, a pink coat with a fur collar, and a white turban. He looks down at the ground with a pensive expression and holds a cup in his right hand and a blue ceramic flask in the other. Therefore the verse and the picture convey the same message, the anguish of a jilted lover who finds consolation in wine.

The inscription *Shah Salim* makes it quite clear that the picture was painted for Jahangir when he was still a prince. The use of the title *Shah* indicates that it was done after he had rebelled against his father and set up his own court at Allahabad. This is also evident from both the subject matter and the style of the picture with its strong Iranian resonances, which characterize the works produced at the Allahabad studio, where the Iranian master Aqa Riza was the preeminent figure. The subject is quite typical in Persianate painting, where such studies of solitary youths reading, reflecting, drinking, or strumming a mandolin are said to be earthly reflections of divine beauty or are considered metaphors for the soul drunk with divine love. It may have also had a particular significance for Jahangir, whose love for wine was well known. This is the kind of picture that an artist would present to his patron as a birthday or New Year's gift.

While there seems no doubt about the picture's patron, there is some disagreement among scholars regarding the artist involved. The inscription *amal-i-ghulam* can be interpreted in two ways. It can either mean "work of Ghulam" (a proper name) or "work of the slave." It is not uncommon for artists and others in the employ of an Islamic ruler to express humility by describing themselves as slaves of their masters. Besides, both Aqa Riza and Abul Hasan are known to have signed some of their works in a similar fashion, as discussed by M. Beach (1978, pp. 116–17).

The only scholar who has written at length about this painting is Beach. Others have given their opinions verbally. Interpreting the word *ghulam* as a proper name, Beach (1978, pp. 117–18) has attributed the painting to Mirza Ghulam, an artist who seems to have flourished for a very short time during the first decade of the seventeenth century. Beach compared this picture with several others, both inscribed and attributed to Mirza Ghulam, and found all these works to reflect a consistent style. Those who have given verbal opinions include A. K. Das, an authority on Jahangiri paintings, who concurred with Beach. R. Skelton, however, has suggested that the painting could be by Aqa Riza or by Abul Hasan, an opinion shared by B. N. Goswamy.

The largest number of works inscribed to Mirza Ghulam occur in the *Anvar-i Suhayli* in the British Library, London (Wilkinson n.d., pls. IX, XXVII, XXXVI, and possibly VIII), but the stylistic correspondences between these and the museum's portrait are not as clear as Beach suggests. They differ noticeably in the treatment of the background, the coloring, and the modeling of the figures. The museum's figure does, however, show a remarkable likeness to a youth reading a book in a picture now in the British Library that has been attributed to Aqa Riza (Pinder-Wilson 1976, pp. 65, 66, no. 101). A second example in which the same model was used is considered to have been done either by

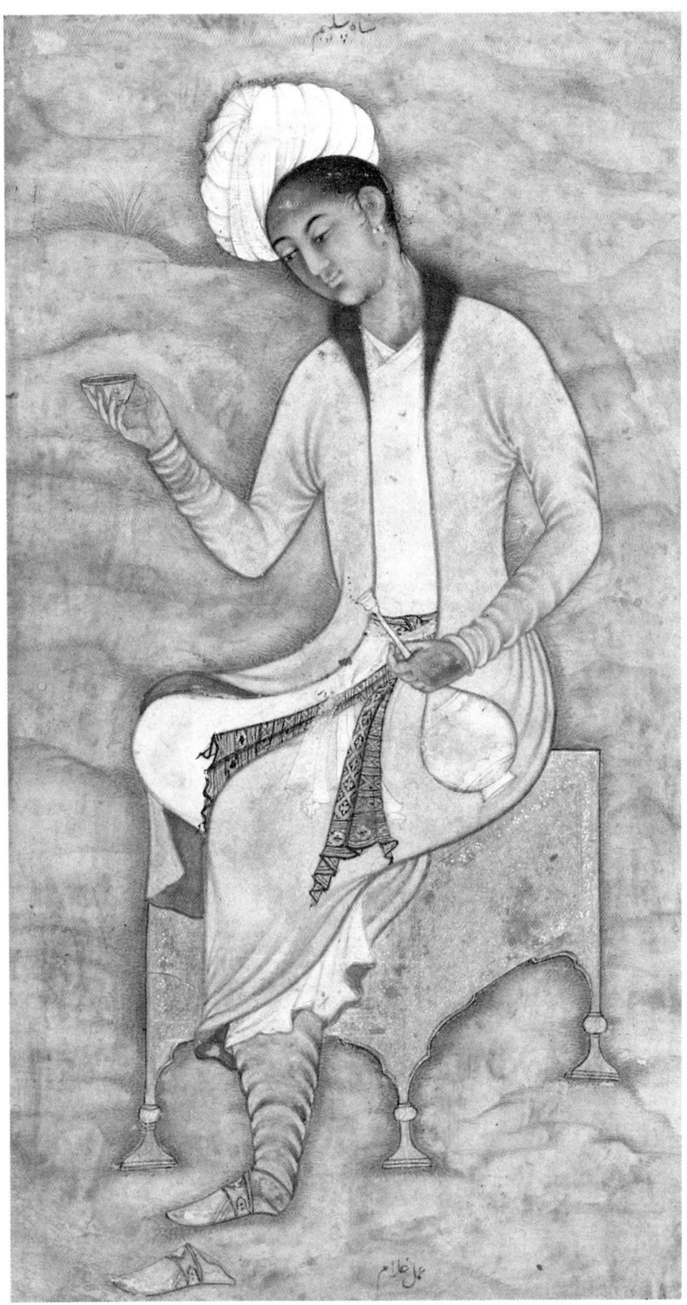

CAT. 66 detail

Farrukh Beg or Aqa Riza (Sotheby's *Important Islamic Manuscripts and Miniatures*, 7 April 1975, lot 111.) A third picture of this genre has been attributed to Muhammad Ali (Falk and Archer 1981, fig. 36). The faces in all three pictures are almost identical, except that here it is more heavily shaded, a technique preferred by Aqa Riza's son, Abul Hasan. Indeed, the other pictures are much more Persian both in technique and aesthetic sensibility, whereas here the artist conveys a better sense of spatial depth, as well as of modeling and expression, all of which point to Abul Hasan. Abul Hasan frequently used the epithet *ghulam* to describe his relationship to Jahangir. Interestingly, in 1966 (p. 152) Beach had written, "The work is of the type associated with Āqā Rizā Jahangiri, and comes from an album of which additional pages are in the Chester Beatty Library, Dublin, and an American private collection."

CAT. 66 *(overleaf)*

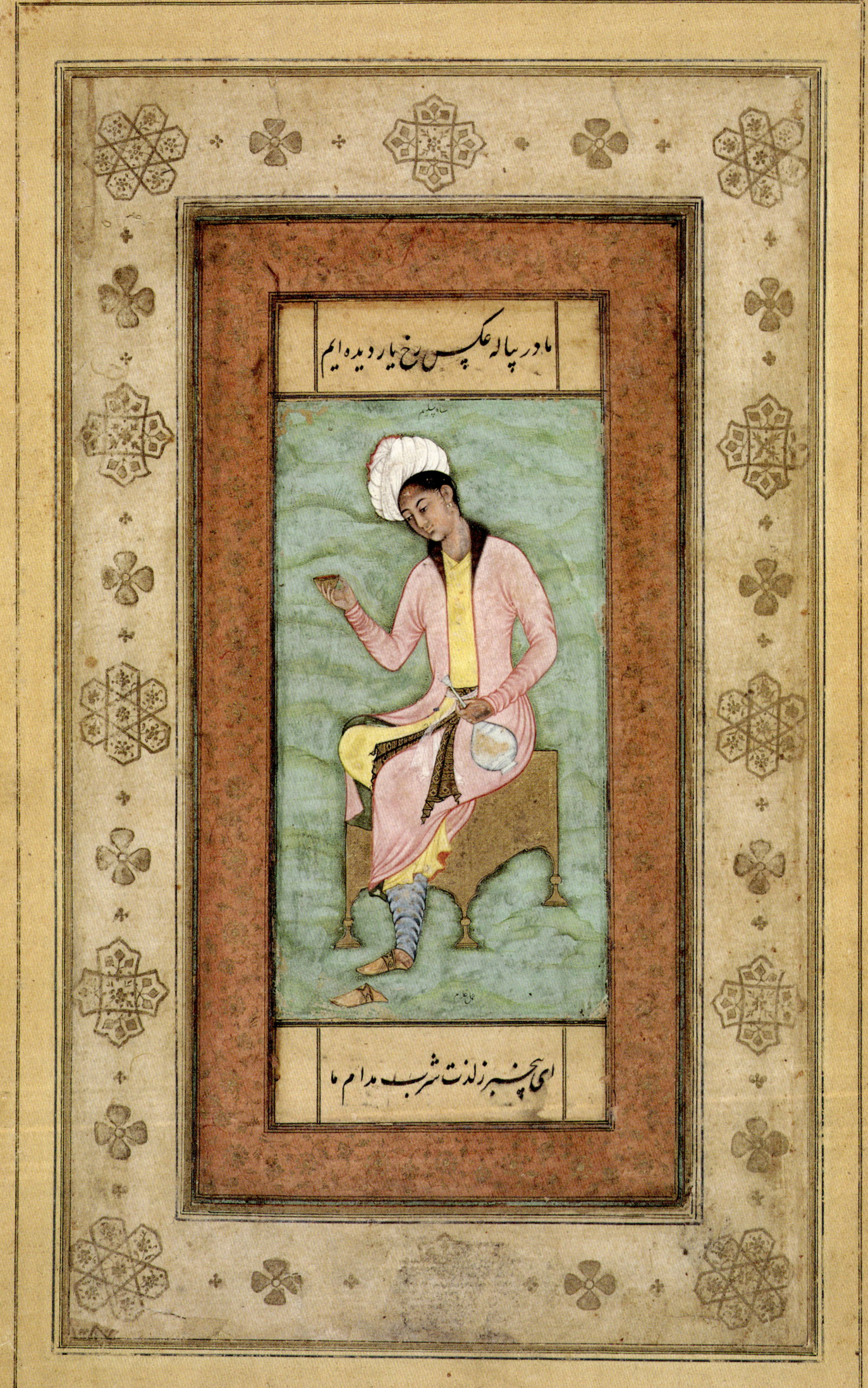
ما در پیاله عکس رخ یار دیده ایم
ای بیخبر ز لذت شرب مدام ما

Jahangir period, c. 1608
Gold and black and red ink
Each, approx. 13½ x 8¾ in (34.3 x 22.2 cm)
The Nasli M. Heeramaneck Collection, gift of Joan Palevsky
M.73.5.535–.537

These borders are from a copy of a Persian dictionary entitled the *Farhang-i Jahangiri* that was compiled for the emperor by Mir Jamal ad-Din Husayn Inju and presented in 1608. In the 1930s these folios came into the possession of the dealer L. Demotte, who removed the text and used the borders to mount Mughal pictures (e.g., [50A, 63]).

Mir Jamal ad-Din belonged to the Sayyids of Shiraz, who were a renowned family and associated with the Safavid rulers. Mir Jamal ad-Din came to the Deccan, whose kings had frequently intermarried with the Injus. Later on he entered Akbar's service and became a favorite of Prince Salim. He had a distinguished career under Jahangir, who made him governor of Bihar and in his eleventh regnal year (1616) honored him with the title Azududdaula (pillar of the state). He was pensioned off in 1621 because of his advanced age. He died in Agra, but the date of his death is not known.

Although the dictionary was compiled by the Mir, it was probably copied and illuminated in the imperial workshop, as it was meant for the emperor. Both the drawing and the gilding are of very high quality. The designs of the borders are in gold and are of astonishing variety, as can be seen from a comparison of these three examples as well as the two others in the collection. Two of these borders are adorned with meandering and intertwined tendrils with leaves, flowers, and blooms in the form of animal heads (A, B). In the third (C) is a landscape with hillocks, flowering plants, and birds. Along the bottom are two *saras* cranes, one of whom reaches for food while the other looks up, perhaps distracted by the cackle of the flying geese, who appear to have been attacked by a falcon.

By Bishandas (active c. 1590–1640) and Inayd Inayat (active c. 1590–c. 1615?)
Jahangir period, c. 1610
Text with red ink
Folio, 13⅝ x 9 in (34.6 x 22.9 cm)
Illustration, 5⅞ x 4¼ in (14.9 x 10.8 cm)
From the Nasli and Alice Heeramaneck Collection, Museum Associates Purchase
M.78.9.5
Literature: Strzygowski 1933, fig. 225, pl. 84; *Art of India and Southeast Asia,* exh. cat., Krannert Art Museum, University of Illinois, Champaign, n.d., p. 71, no. 91; *Heeramaneck* 1966, p. 152, no. 208 (not illustrated); Johnson 1972, pp. 141, 144, pls. LXXXIa, LXXXIIb (details); Leach 1986, p. 80, fig. 21(A); Heeramaneck 1984, p. 157, pl. 158.

This illustrated folio from a manuscript of the *Shahnama,* very likely prepared for Jahangir about 1610, is framed by an elegant inner border decorated with a floral motif. The illustration is placed between panels of text in four columns above and below. In addition, portions of text have been accommodated in two angular projections intruding from the inner border into the outer one, which is adorned with a golden landscape inhabited by golden birds and animals both real and fabulous. In design and execution this elaborate border is very similar to those adorning Jahangir's dictionary of 1608 (see [67]). Inscriptions at the bottom of this border provide the names of Bishandas and Inayd Inayat, who worked together on the illustration.

Both artists were important members of Jahangir's atelier, although Bishandas was the more famous. He is one of only four artists whose names are included in Jahangir's memoirs. He was selected by Jahangir to accompany Khan Alam, his ambassador to the court of Shah Abbas of Iran. Jahangir wrote, "At the time when I sent Khan 'Alam to Persia, I had sent with him a painter of the name of Bishn Das, who was unequalled in his age for taking likenesses. . . ." (Rogers and Beveridge [1909–14]1968, 2: 117). This embassy was sent in 1613 and returned seven years later. Very little else, however, is known of the life of this master portraitist, whose Indian name must have been Vishnudas. He was a nephew of Nanha, a leading Akbari artist, and had a long career stretching for over half a century. Bishandas probably was trained by his uncle, and the two are known to have collaborated on an illustration now in the Victoria and Albert Museum, London, from the *Baburnama* of about 1590. Thereafter he seems to have joined Prince Salim's Allahabad studio (see Das 1971; and Beach 1978, pp. 107–11), where he would have worked with both Aqa Riza and Abul Hasan under the personal supervision of the prince. By 1613 Bishandas had obviously become so adept at painting portraits that he was sent off to Iran. He is the only Indian artist of the period known to have visited a foreign land.

Bishandas's career after his return from Iran in 1620 seems to have been considerably less spectacular. While Beach does suggest that he continued working on such royal works as the *Jahangirnama* of about 1625 and the Windsor *Padshahnama* of the 1630s, he may have left the imperial atelier in the 1640s.

Nothing is known about Inayd Inayat except that he also worked on the 1604 *Akbarnama.* He collaborated with Nanha, Bishandas's uncle, on a painting now in the British Library, London, and assumed individual responsibility for two illustrations now in the Chester Beatty Library, Dublin (Beach 1981, p. 228). A splendid study of a mountain goat now in the Victoria and Albert Museum, London, may have been painted by Inayat for Jahangir (Das 1978, p. 142, pl. 59). It would show him to be an accomplished animal painter. In the museum's *Shahnama* illustration he may have been responsible for the design as well as the overall execution, while Bishandas concentrated on the figures.

The style of the painting clearly reflects Jahangir's Persianized taste, as discussed by L. Y. Leach (1986, p. 80) in connection with a folio from the same section of the *Shahnama* in the Cleveland Museum of Art. (For two more illustrations from the same manuscript, see *Persian and Mughal Art* 1976, pp. 174–76, 203, no. 88).

The incident represented is Faridun striking Zahhak with his animal-headed mace. Zahhak was an Arab sovereign who became king of Iran when Jamshid's fortunes declined. However, Zahhak had come under the influence of Iblis, the devil, and became an oppressive ruler. In order to rid the world of him, a hero named Faridun was born. Learning of his birth, Zahhak killed the father but failed to find Faridun. When Faridun grew up, he obtained a specially made mace and went to seek revenge against Zahhak, who was away from his capital at the

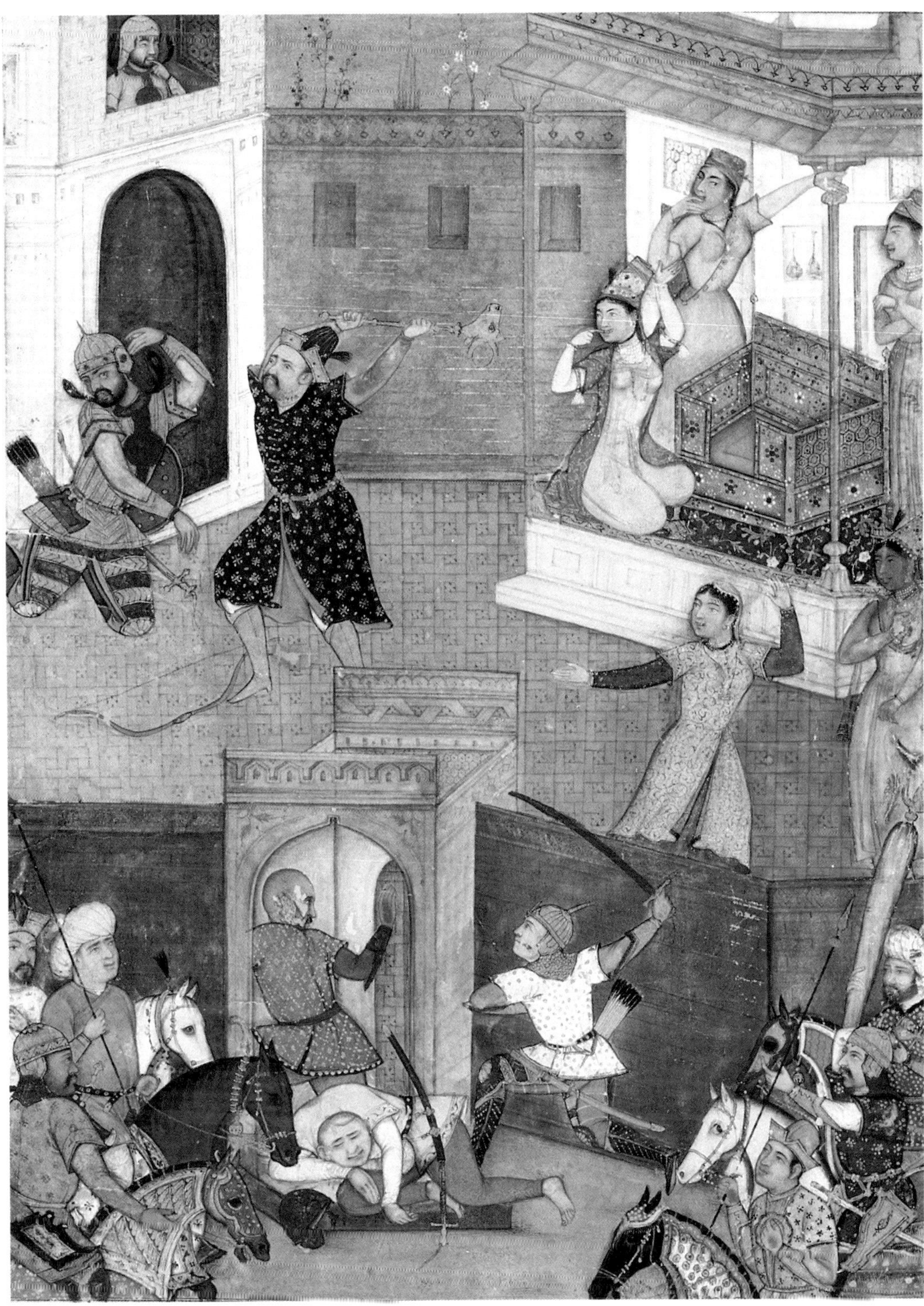

CAT. 68 detail

time. When the king heard that Faridun had not only occupied his palace but was also enjoying his two wives, the enraged Zahhak returned and surprised Faridun. In the illustration, while Zahhak's men engage Faridun's followers at the gate, Faridun is striking Zahhak, who is fully armored and on his knees. He is also distinguished by two black serpents emerging from his shoulders, which had led to his reputation as the dragon king; these two reptiles became attached to his shoulders when he allowed the devil to kiss him. On the right surrounding the throne are women from Zahhak's harem, including his two wives.

CAT. 68 *(overleaf)*

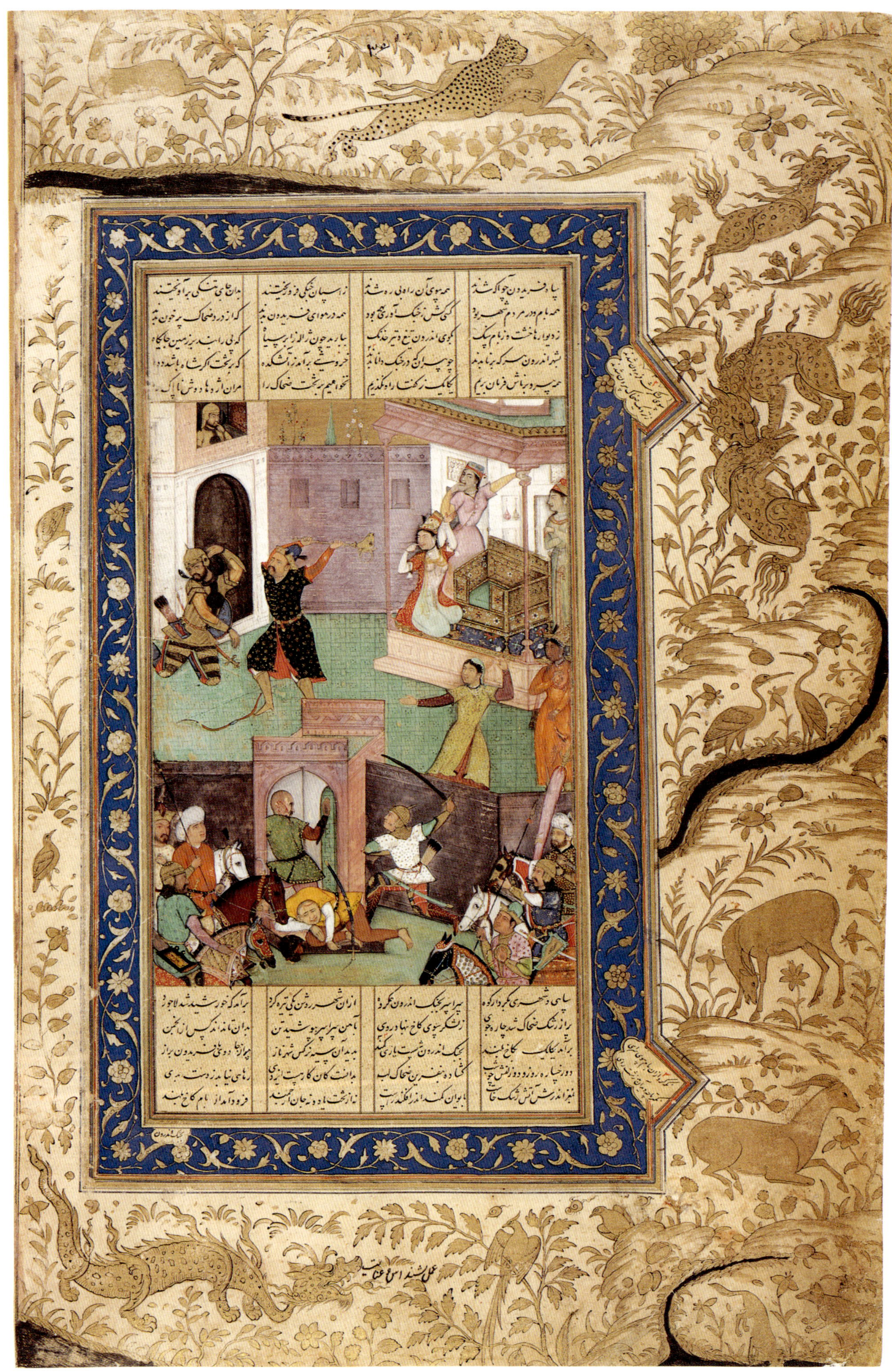

69 HOLY MAN

Jahangir period, c. 1610
Overall, $6\frac{7}{8} \times 3\frac{3}{8}$ in (17.5 x 8.6 cm)
Illustration, $2\frac{1}{4} \times 1\frac{3}{4}$ in (5.7 x 4.4 cm)
Gift of Myrna Smoot and Peter Smoot
M.84.228.2

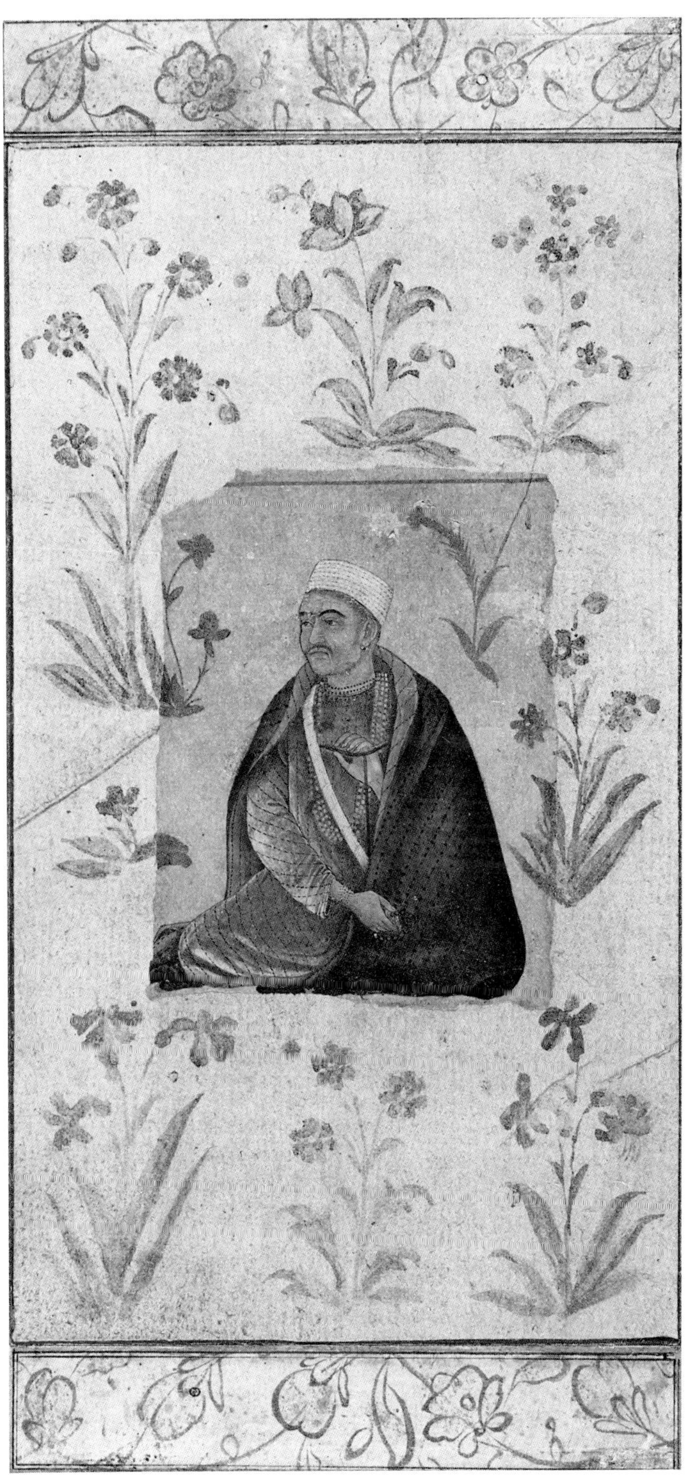

The figure of a seated man holding a crutch in his left hand is painted on a fragmentary piece of thin, transparent paper that has been pasted on a section of a mount adorned with golden floral motifs. Gold flowers on the mount and some apparently already on the tissue of the drawing were joined after the drawing was laid down. The portrait is certainly of the Jahangir period, but the mount is perhaps later. The panels above and below with sketchily rendered flowers are of a later date.

Judging by his necklaces of beads, his crutch, and his attire, there seems little doubt that the man represents a holy personage. He is of a pink complexion and wears a gray *jama* and a thick, brown shawl or blanket lined in red. The face and the hands are superbly modeled, indicating that this is a sensitive study from life. Several artists of Jahangir's studio excelled in rendering animated, perceptive portraits for the borders of albums. They included such masters as Govardhan and Daulat. The latter could have been responsible for this charming study, although depicting holy men appears to have been a specialty of Govardhan (see [74]).

Jahangir period, c. 1610
Ink with touches of color and with gold and opaque watercolor illumination
Folio, 9 3/8 x 6 3/8 in (23.8 x 16.2 cm)
Illustration, 4 3/4 x 3 in (12.1 x 7.6 cm)
Paul Rodman Mabury Collection
39.12.76
Literature: Canby 1983, no. 4, fig. 3.

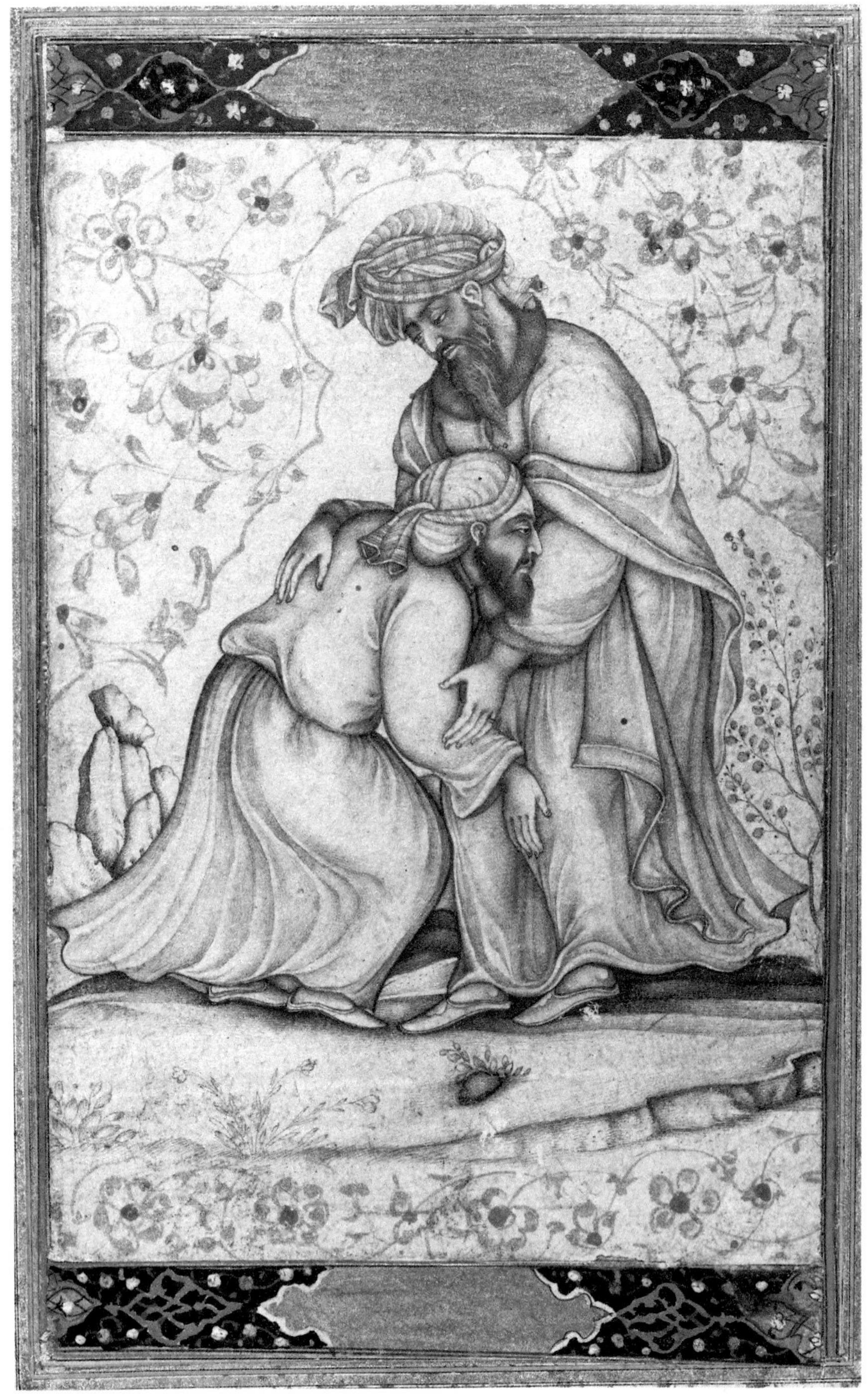

CAT. 70 detail

That this is a copy of a European print is in no doubt. The two figures may well represent Mordecai and King Ahasuerus of Persia, two principal characters in the Book of Esther. Mordecai was a cousin of Esther, who was the queen of Ahasuerus. Haman, the king's vizier, insisted that Mordecai bow down before him, as did the king's servants, which, however, he refused to do. The enraged Haman decided to kill not only Mordecai but all the other Jews in Persia. Mordecai persuaded Esther to intercede with her husband, who had just ordered Mordecai rewarded for an earlier act of allegiance and who asked Esther what she wished done. Haman was executed and the Jews allowed to destroy their enemies. The Jewish festival of Purim, also called the Day of Mordecai, celebrates this deliverance. In the drawing Mordecai bows before the king, who helps him to rise.

Biblical themes were very much liked by Jahangir, and this drawing was probably meant for him. Although the name of the artist is not known, the quality of the drawing and the modeling clearly indicate his excellent craftsmanship and mastery of European technique. He made heavy use of shading to make the faces expressive and to indicate the volume of the garments. This heavy shading is reminiscent of a drawing of an inebriated musician attributed to Basawan (Beach 1981, p. 198, no. 25). The artist responsible for the museum's drawing could well have been a pupil of the Akbari master. The golden floral arabesques around the two figures, however, are probably by a later hand.

71 DALLIANCE ON A TERRACE

Attributed to Govardhan
(active c. 1600–c. 1640)
Jahangir period, c. 1615 or later
Folio, 13 1/8 x 8 1/8 in (33.3 x 20.6 cm)
Illustration, 7 3/8 x 4 9/16 in (18.7 x 11.6 cm)
From the Nasli and Alice Heeramaneck
Collection, Museum Associates Purchase
M.83.1.6
Literature: Stchoukine 1935, pp. 167–76, pl. 56; S. C. Welch 1963, pp. 12, 73, pl. 32; Khandalavala 1962, p. 9, fig. A; *Heeramaneck* 1966, p. 154, no. 212; Carroll 1972, pp. 19, 168–69; Beach 1978, p. 125; Heeramaneck 1984, p. 163, pl. 205.

CAT. 71 detail

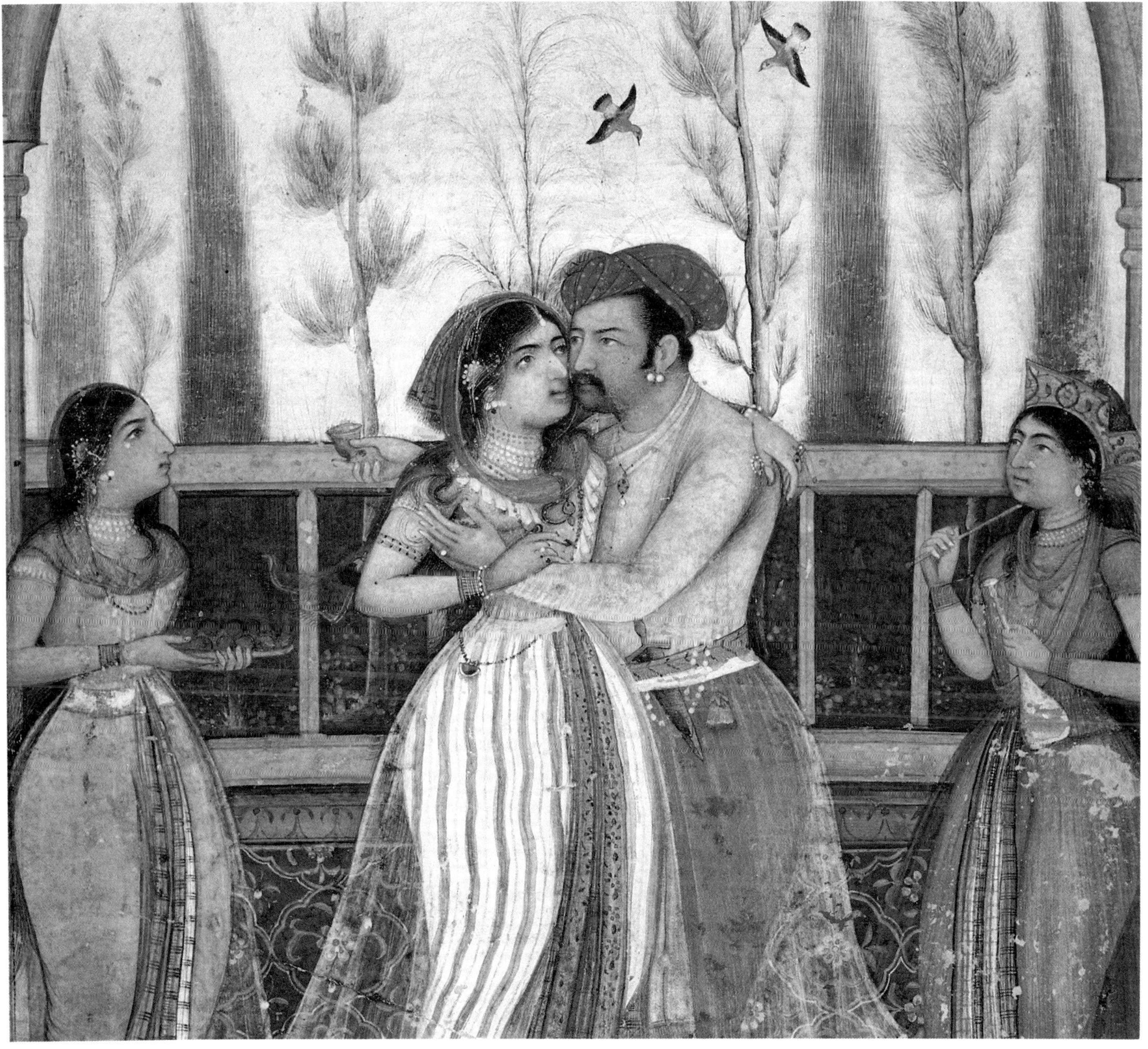

When it was first published, this picture was attributed to Govardhan by I. Stchoukine, an attribution subsequently accepted by S. C. Welch and most other scholars; K. Khandalavala has questioned the attribution and furthermore regards this as a late seventeenth-century painting (see Literature above). Scholars such as R. Skelton, B. N. Goswamy, and A. Okada who have looked at the picture have not questioned the attribution or the date. The outer border of the picture is beautifully adorned with very naturalistic flower studies that can hardly be later than the early Shah Jahan period. The folio may, in fact, have formed part of an album assembled for that emperor. The two seals on the upper corners of the painting have been read by Goswamy and Skelton as *Abdullah* (left) and *Hasan Ali* (right), who were probably later owners. In any event, a late seventeenth-century date is unlikely, and despite the erotic flavor of the subject, there is no reason why it could not have been painted in the first quarter of the seventeenth century. Although Khandalavala asserts that such pictures were not done until the end of the century, the Minto Album, for instance, includes a representation of a prince drinking with a lady on a terrace inscribed to Govardhan and probably painted toward the end of Jahangir's reign. In fact, it is attached to a similar border with delicate floral studies (see Goetz 1964, pl. facing p. 227). The faces in the museum's picture, however, are not quite as heavily modeled as they are in the one in the Minto Album.

It was also Stchoukine who first suggested that the two lovers in this picture may represent Jahangir and Nur Jahan. Agreeing with him, S. C. Welch (1963, p. 73) wrote: "Passionate and intimate in mood, this miniature brings Jahangir so far down from his throne that one wonders as to its meaning. Does it portray love as a ritual act of Kings? Or is it an intensely personal document intended only for the eyes of the emperor and his beloved?" Khandalavala does not deny that the male looks like Jahangir but does not accept that the female represents Nur Jahan. The only contemporary representation of the empress is in the Freer Gallery of Art, Washington, D.C. (Beach 1981, p. 205, no. 32). The two depictions do differ considerably. It should be noted that the man in the museum's picture wears earrings. Jahangir had his ears pierced in his ninth regnal year (1614/15), hence the figure is likely to represent him. (However, others too had their ears pierced, following the emperor.) Jahangir does look rather young in this picture, and one wonders if it might not have been painted later in his life as an idealized, imaginary piece.

Whatever the exact identification of the lovers, the picture remains one of the earliest Mughal representations of this genre, which gained greater currency in the reign of Shah Jahan. Although intimate, it is not entirely an informal rendering. The strictly symmetrical composition with the embracing lovers in the center flanked by two attendants is reminiscent of a Hindu image. The iconic character is also echoed by the stately trees behind framed by the arch above. Thus even though the picture is meant to represent a private moment, the composition as well as the rather impassive faces of the two figures relate this to the more stately and symbolic portraits of the emperor. Another picture that shows this kind of mixture of intimacy and imperial majesty is in the Chester Beatty Library, Dublin, and depicts Jahangir playing Holi with palace ladies (Arnold and Wilkinson 1936, 3: pl. 56).

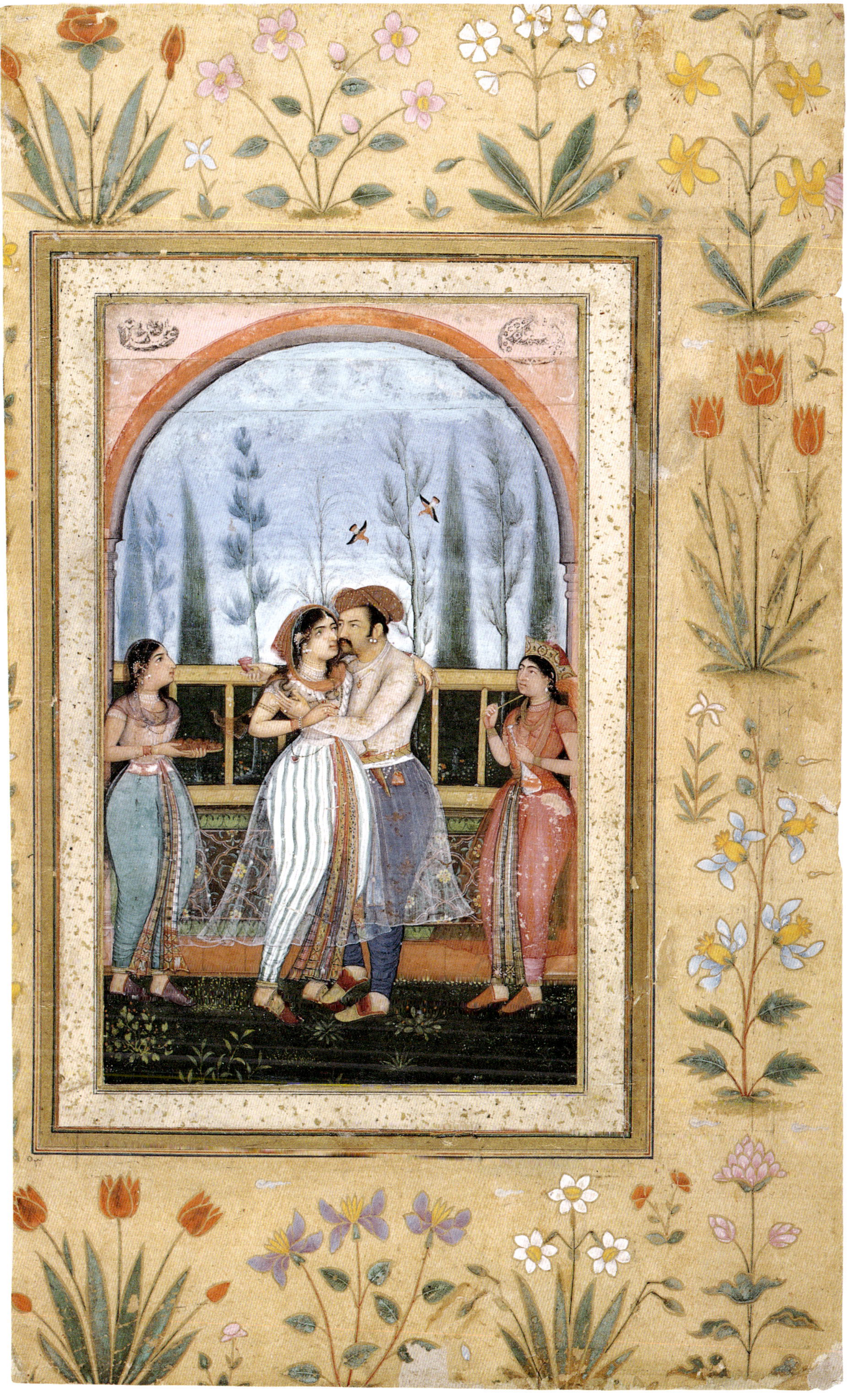

Attributed to Abul Hasan (b. 1588/89, active 1600–c. 1635)
Jahangir period, c. 1620
Folio, $14\frac{1}{2}$ x $9\frac{11}{16}$ in (36.8 x 24.6 cm)
Illustration, $9\frac{3}{8}$ x 6 in (23.8 x 15.2 cm)
From the Nasli and Alice Heeramaneck Collection, Museum Associates Purchase
M.75.4.28
Literature: Kahlenberg 1972, p. 154, pl. XCII; Beach 1978, p. 92; Skelton et al. 1982, p. 40, pl. 48; Heeramaneck 1984, p. 163, pl. 204; Desai 1985, pp. 26–27, pl. 24; Skelton 1988, p. 185, fig. 5.

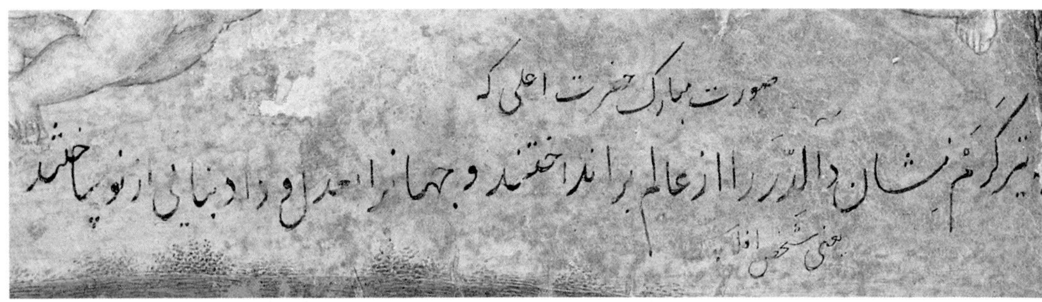

CAT. 72 details *(above and opposite)*

The inscription in the upper right of the portrait, as translated by Z. A. Desai, is as follows:

The auspicious portrait of his exalted majesty, who by the arrow of generosity eradicated the trace of Daliddar—the very personification of poverty—from the world and laid the foundation of a new world with his justice and munificence.

"His exalted majesty" is Jahangir, who stands on a lion that sits amicably with a lamb on a globe. The globe is supported by a man stretched out on a giant fish. He wears a yellow *dhoti* and shawl and extends his left arm toward a book. Jahangir, his head surrounded by an enormous nimbus representing heavenly light or the solar disc, shoots an arrow at a dark, naked, and emaciated man with white hair and beard. Another arrow has struck the old man's left eye, and a cherub offers three more shafts to the emperor. A second cherub emerges from the clouds at the upper left corner holding a chain with alternating bells and pink flywhisks, which is attached to a post on a platform. On the other side two more cherubs fly down with a crown.

Part of the rich symbolism of this painting is explained in the inscription. The target clearly symbolizes poverty. Justice is represented by the coexistence of the lion and the lamb, the chain descending from the heavens, and the figure on the fish. While the tradition of the fish supporting the earth is encountered in Islamic cosmology, the figure lying on the fish, as pointed out by Skelton (1988, p. 185), is certainly Manu, the Hindu lawgiver. This is obviously a concession to the Hindus, who formed the vast majority of Jahangir's subjects. The celestial chain is reminiscent of the "chain of justice" that hung from a palace window in the Agra Fort; it could be pulled by any aggrieved subject who felt he had been denied justice in a regular court. However, here it must have an additional reference, as the chain clearly connects the earth and the heaven and may symbolize Jahangir's direct line of communication with God.

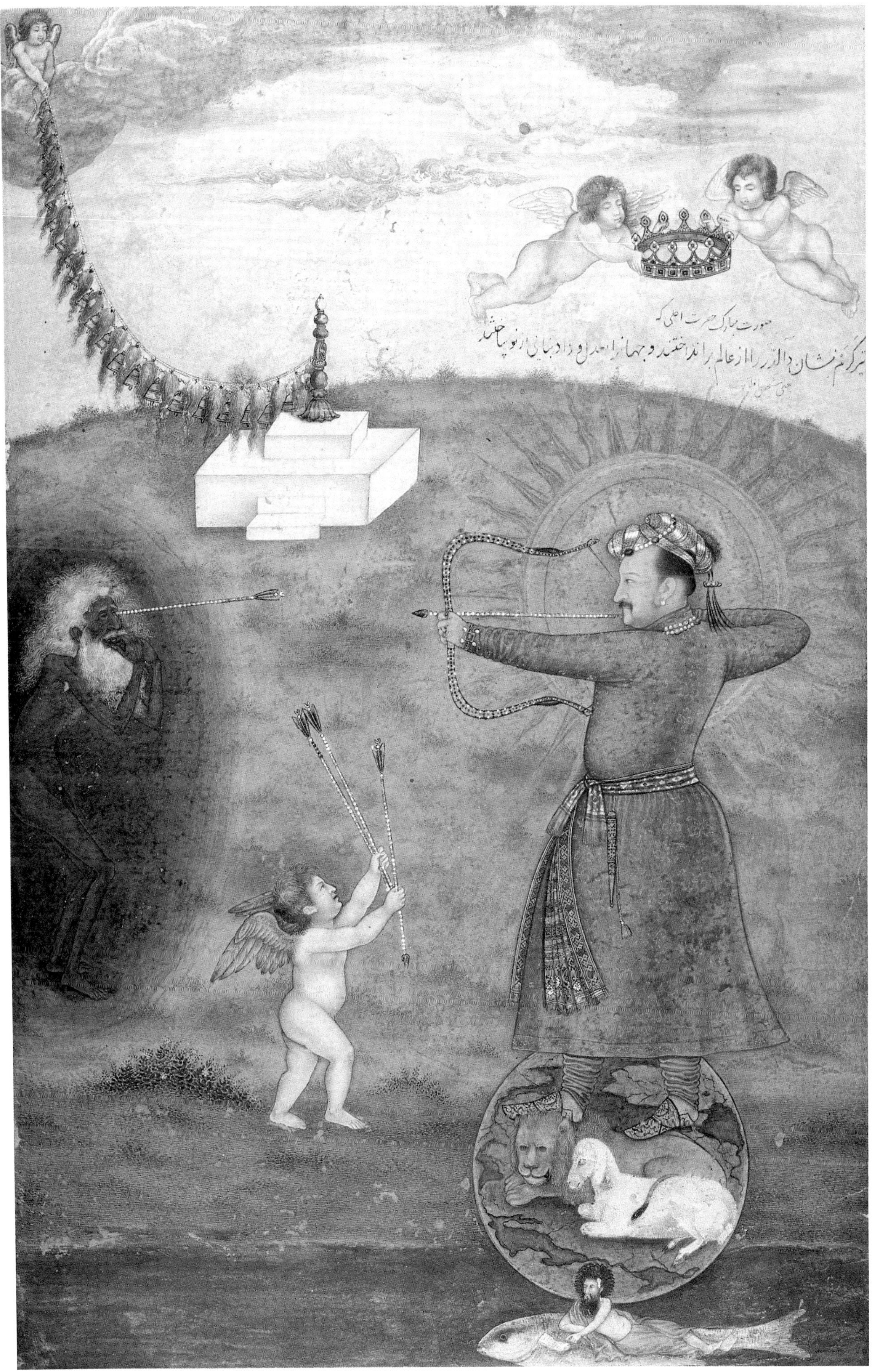

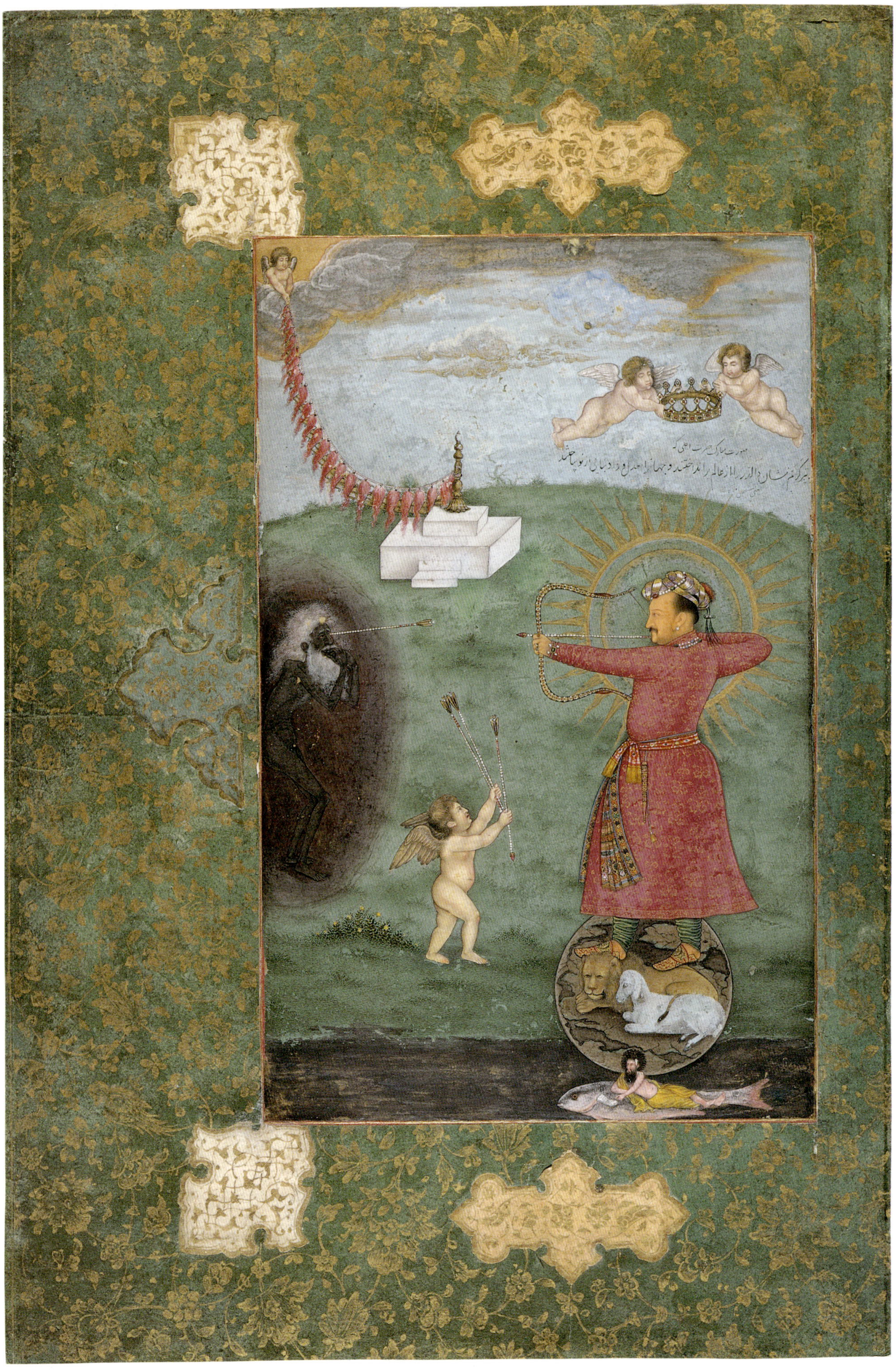

In fact, the entire iconography of this painting was devised to emphasize not only Jahangir as a just king but also his divine right to rule. This is clear from the fact that a crown is being brought down from the heavens by cherubs, an idea probably borrowed from a Christian painting of the Coronation of the Virgin. The chain of justice too emphasizes Jahangir's direct connection with God and probably implies that the justice he dispenses is no different from divine justice. Even in his effort to abolish poverty from his realm, the ruler is helped not by his economic advisers but by a cherub. Could Jahangir be also presented as the personification of Eros or Kamadeva, the Hindu god of love?

Most scholars agree that the painting was rendered by Abul Hasan, one of the emperor's favorite artists, whom he honored with the epithet "wonder of the age" (*nadir al-zaman*). He was the son of Aqa Riza, the Iranian master from Mashhad, who had entered Prince Salim's service in Allahabad. Abul Hasan must have shown signs of his talent very early in life: one of his earliest surviving works is a drawing of Saint John, copied from an engraving by Albrecht Dürer, now in the Ashmolean Museum in Oxford; Abul Hasan was only thirteen at the time. Not only did he catch Jahangir's eye, but in his memoirs the emperor claims to have played a role in the young boy's artistic development, saying, "My connection is based on my having reared him, till his art arrived at his rank" (quoted in Beach 1978, p. 86). Abul Hasan's surviving oeuvre reveals wide-ranging interests, but he was particularly good at rendering symbolic images such as the present example. Two similarly elaborate allegorical portraits of Jahangir are in the Freer Gallery of Art, Washington, D.C., and one is in the Chester Beatty Library, Dublin (see Skelton 1988 for a comparative discussion of all three).

While most scholars agree that Abul Hasan painted this picture, why and when he did so are not settled matters. In 1982 (p. 40) Skelton wrote, "The picture belongs to the end of Jahangir's reign and may reflect his mood in 1624 when he ordered that the blind, maimed or sick should be driven from his sight when he left the palace." While this is not to be ruled out, the picture really expresses a positive sentiment and the artist is emphasizing the emperor's achievements. As the inscription says, he refashioned the world by banishing poverty. Moreover, the face of the monarch shows no signs of age, dissipation, or illness, but rather is extremely close to that seen in the Chester Beatty portrait, which has been convincingly dated by Skelton to the year 1617, when the emperor was forty-eight. V. N. Desai (1985, pp. 26–27) accepted Skelton's date of about 1625 and suggested that the museum's picture may have been painted at a time when Jahangir was increasingly preoccupied with "unrest in the north" and with Prince Khurram's rebellion in 1622. In any event, considering the closeness of the face in the Chester Beatty painting of 1617 to that in this picture, one can hardly separate them from each other by a wide margin. While the Freer and the Chester Beatty portraits are associated with specific events in Jahangir's life, the museum's picture provides a generalized vision intended to emphasize Jahangir's divinity. Abul Hasan may have rendered it on the occasion of the Hindu festival of Diwali as an appropriate gift for his patron. Diwali is the festival of light that triumphs over darkness, when the goddess Lakshmi, or good fortune, drives away poverty. The light symbolism calls to mind Jahangir's appellation Nur ad-Din, "light of the faith," an aspect reinforced by the halo. As Skelton (1982, p. 40) commented, the use of the Hindi word *daliddar* (*daridra* in Sanskrit) to denote poverty in the inscription may be significant. The intent here may have been to represent Jahangir as the very embodiment of good fortune.

Possibly by Manohar (active 1582–c. 1625) or Abul Hasan (b. 1588/89, active 1600–c. 1635)
Jahangir period, 1620–25
Ink with touches of color
4 1/8 x 2 1/8 in (10.5 x 5.4 cm)
From the Nasli and Alice Heeramaneck Collection, Museum Associates Purchase
M.83.1.5
Literature: *Heeramaneck* 1966, pp. 155, 156, no. 214; Trabold 1975, p. 35, no. 47 (not illustrated); Beach 1978, pp. 158, 160, no. 58; Heeramaneck 1984, p. 158, pls. 165, 166; Markel 1987, p. 124, fig. 85.

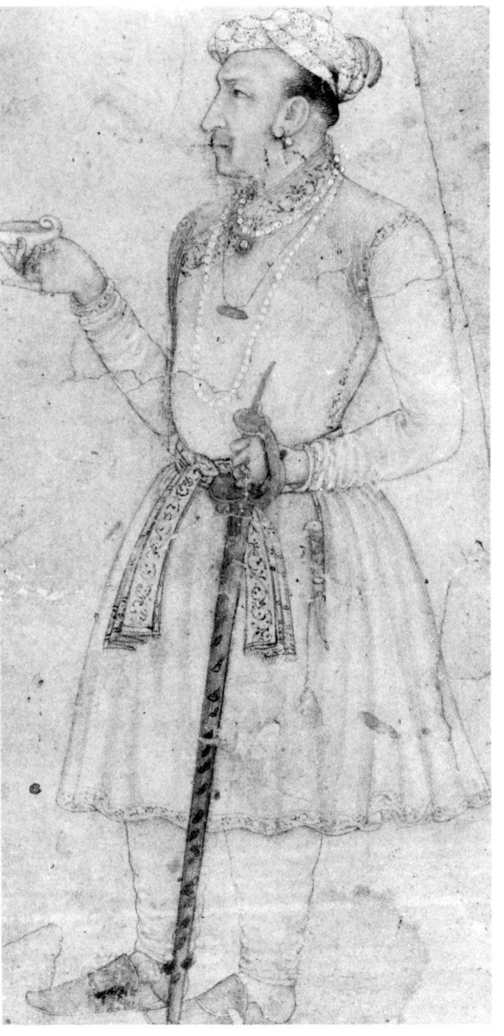

This lightly colored sketch of the emperor, like two others known (T. Lentz in *A Handbook of the Museum of Art* [Providence: Rhode Island School of Design, 1985], p. 154, fig. 67), was very likely taken from life as a preparatory drawing for a more formal portrait. All three sketches are basically similar in their compositions and the emperor's posture. Although he stands formally, holding the sword with his left hand, and is similarly attired and adorned with quiet elegance, the faces in the three are quite distinct and are the result of careful observation. Unlike the more ceremonial portrait in the collection [72], here the emperor is presented as a mere mortal stripped of all cosmetics, so to speak. Not only is the face more expressive, every detail has been rendered meticulously. With his right hand he holds a jade wine cup of a type familiar in Mughal art.

In 1966 (p. 155) M. Beach dated the sketch to about 1620 but in 1978 (p. 158) moved the date earlier by five years. He finds the Jahangir of this sensitive drawing to be "markedly younger" than his portrait in the durbar painting of about 1620 in the Museum of Fine Arts, Boston. A careful comparison of the two pictures, however, indicates that precisely the opposite is true. In the durbar scene Jahangir has a fleshy face, obviously idealized, and black moustache and hair. In this portrait, the face is quite drawn, as one finds when a person has been ill for some time, the lines at the end of the eye are clearly visible, the moustache is almost completely gray, and the hair is thinner and a mixture of gray and black. These considerations lead me to suggest a date closer to 1625 rather than 1615.

Among the artists who could have made this sketch, two probabilities are Abul Hasan and Manohar. Both were particularly favored by the emperor for painting formal portraits and must have been permitted to sketch his likeness from life. As a matter of fact, while the formal representations of state occasions flattered the emperor, such intimately observed pictures could have been done for his private viewing. As is evident from his memoirs, Jahangir was a remarkably candid man who did not care to hide behind a mask. Especially noteworthy is the delicate and elegant rendering of the right hand, something not always found in such portraits. Both Manohar and Abul Hasan were good at drawing hands naturalistically.

74 FOUR MULLAS IN A DISCUSSION

Attributed to Govardhan (active c. 1600–c. 1640)
Shah Jahan period, c. 1630
Folio, 13⅛ x 8³⁄₁₆ in (33.3 x 20.8 cm)
Illustration, 8³⁄₁₆ x 5¼ in (20.8 x 13.3 cm)
From the Nasli and Alice Heeramaneck Collection, Museum Associates Purchase
M.85.2.3
Literature: P. Brown 1924, pl. LXVII; S. C. Welch 1963, pp. 102–3, 170, no. 46; *Heeramaneck* 1966, pp. 155, 156, no. 215; Beach 1978, pp. 122, 123, no. 43; Heeramaneck 1984, p. 164, pl. 211; Pal et al. 1989, pp. 116, 118, fig. 117.

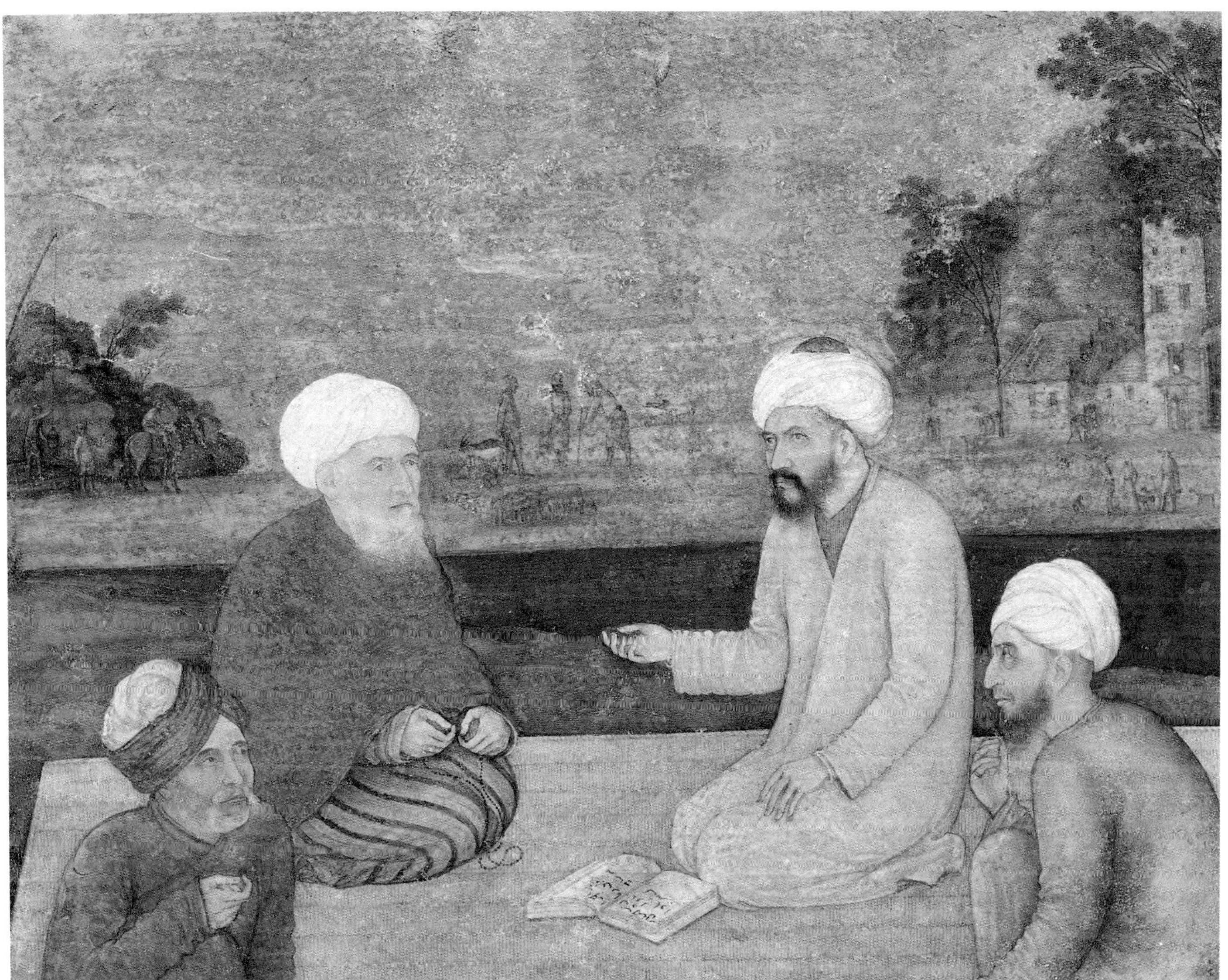

CAT. 74 detail

The picture depicts four mullas (theologians and experts in Islamic religious laws) engaged in a discussion while seated on a platform covered by a mat in a meadow. Immediately behind them is a stream, beyond which is a partly Indianized Dutch or Flemish landscape with tiny figures. On the left are a horse and rider and two men at a well before a clump of trees. In the middle a goatherd stands conversing with two men as his goats graze around them. On the right are European buildings before a clump of trees and villagers milling about. The foreground is adorned with a variety of flowering plants. The four mullas are all dressed in different colored garments—purple, green, chocolate brown, orange, and very light yellow. Otherwise, the predominant colors are various shades of green for the ground, black for the water, and blues and grays for the sky. The painting was enlarged at all four margins, probably to fit the required size of an album. The present outer border is not original, however, but is from another Shah Jahani album. The remounting was done in this century by the French dealer Demotte. The first line of the left-hand page of the open book on the mat gives the name of Shah Jahan, according to B. N. Goswamy.

The painting was first attributed to Govardhan by S. C. Welch (1963, p. 170), though he did not give any specific reasons. Subsequently this attribution was confirmed by M. Beach (1978, p. 42) because of the stylistic similarity of the figures in this painting with those in a signed work by Govardhan. In a recent essay (1989, p. 116–17), J. Dye has reconfirmed the attribution in the context of a brief discussion of the artist's paintings for Shah Jahan. In addition to the very perceptive characterization of his figures, Govardhan was also very skillful in integrating European landscape elements in his pictures. An almost identical group of figures and goats can be seen behind the principal figures in a picture in the Cleveland Museum of Art that also has been attributed to Govardhan (Leach 1986, fig. 28*i*, pl. VIII).

According to Dye (1989, p. 116) Govardhan was "perhaps Shah Jahan's greatest painter," and in Beach's opinion (1978, p. 118), "No other Mughal artist of the period celebrates, with such sympathy and insight, the variety of humanity found in India." Govardhan was the son of Bhavani Das, a minor artist who worked in Akbar's studio. He not only excelled his father but became a brilliant portraitist with a particular penchant for drawing realistic portraits that are concerned as much with the subjects' outer appearance as with their character and personality. Although Abul Hasan was no less brilliant technically, Govardhan's portraits are noteworthy both for their spontaneity and expressiveness, especially in revealing the inner feelings of his subjects. At the same time, however, in such group pictures as this one often notices that each figure seems to be an individual study displaying little emotional interaction with the others. Govardhan's development into a sensitive and insightful portraitist of human character must have been due as much to Jahangir's aesthetic sensibility as to his own gift for catching the fleeting expression. His genius lies in his uncanny ability to combine realistic representations of figures and idyllic and exotic landscapes with compelling visual aplomb.

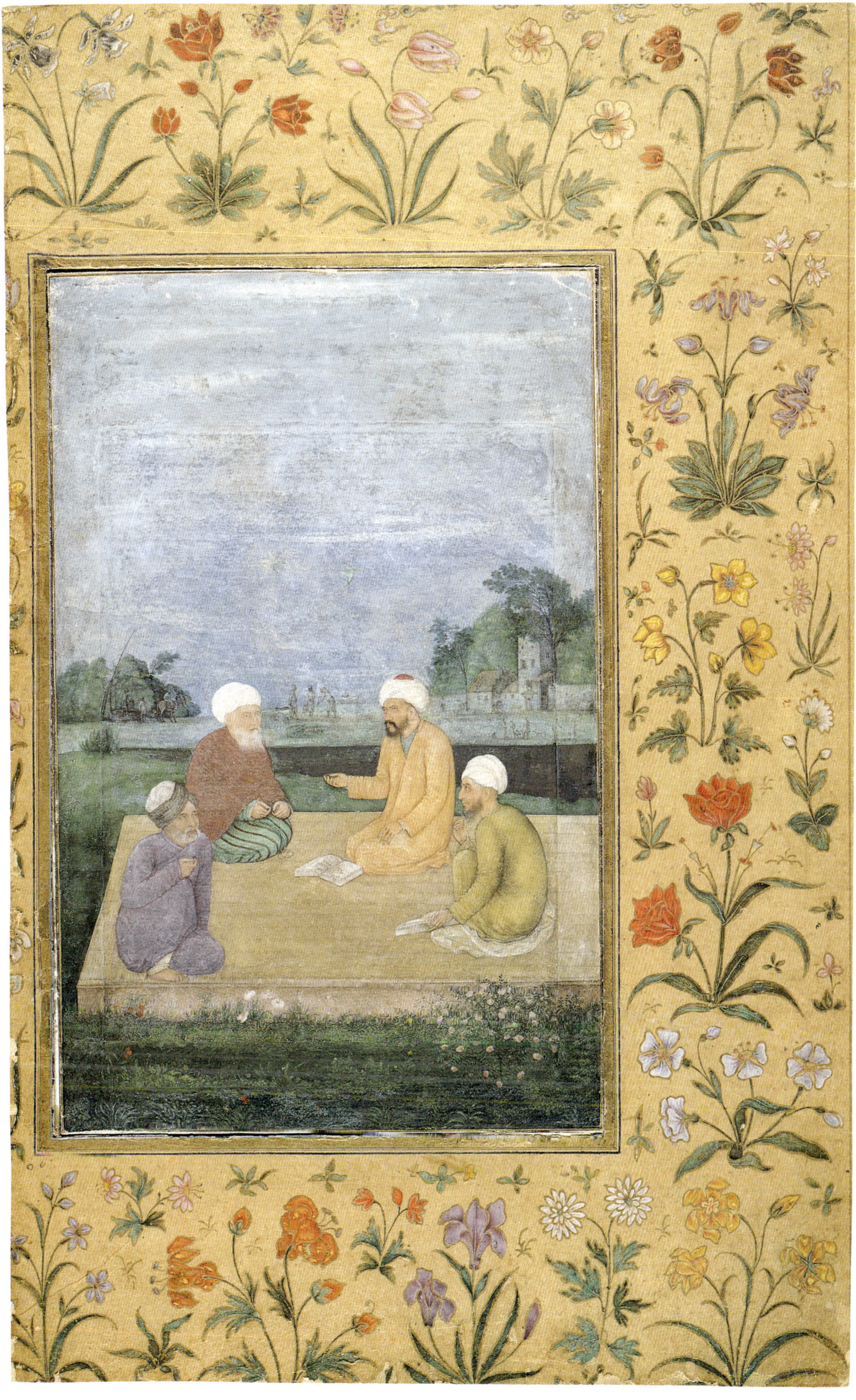

Attributed to Bichitr (active c. 1610–c. 1650)
Shah Jahan period, c. 1638
Opaque watercolor, gold, gesso, and ink
Folio, $17\frac{3}{4}$ x $13\frac{1}{2}$ in (45.1 x 34.3 cm)
Illustration, $9\frac{7}{8}$ x $7\frac{1}{4}$ in (25.1 x 18.4 cm)
From the Nasli and Alice Heeramaneck Collection, Museum Associates Purchase
M.80.6.6
Literature: S. C. Welch 1963, pp. 102, 169, no. 44; *Heeramaneck* 1966, pp. 155, 157, no. 216; *A Decade of Collecting,* exh. cat., Los Angeles County Museum of Art, 1975, pp. 29, 150, no. 15; Beach 1978, pp. 96–97, 102, 103, 105, no. 34; Heeramaneck 1984, p. 165, pl. 220; Pal et al. 1989, p. 112, fig. 26.

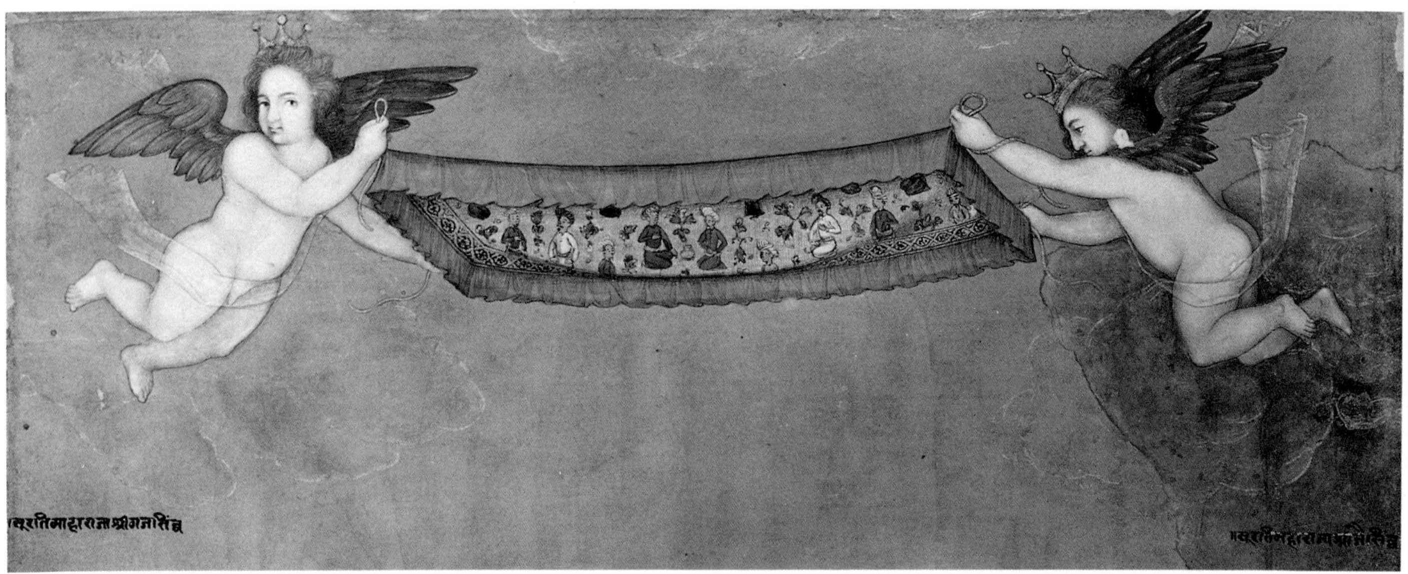

CAT. 75 details *(above and opposite)*

The Devanagari inscriptions above the two figures identify them as Maharaja Gaj Singh (left) and Maharaja Jai Singh (right). While the identification of the figure on the left in these later inscriptions is correct, that on the right is wrong. From many other known portraits he can be identified as Shah Shuja (1616–60), Shah Jahan's second son. Gaj Singh was the ruler of Marwar, the capital of which was Jodhpur, and a cousin of the Mughal prince. Very likely the painting later entered the Marwar royal collection, where a librarian was able to identify his former ruler but could not recognize the other.

That this is a formal state portrait is evident. Both men are seated as equals against bolsters on an elaborately adorned and gilded thronelike seat placed on a carpet. A container with prepared betel leaves lies open between them. The fact that Shah Shuja offers one to Gaj Singh while holding a second for himself in his left hand clearly shows that he is the host. The expressions on both faces are somewhat cold and stern as the two stare into each other's eyes, as if they are uncertain of the other's intentions. Interestingly, the canopy above is held by two putti, as one would expect in a symbolic portrait of the emperor. Why these two princes should be exalted in such a fashion is not clear.

S. C. Welch (1963, pp. 102, 169) suggested that the portrait was painted about 1633 "in commemoration of their service together in the Deccan." M. Beach (1978, p. 102), however, has more convincingly demonstrated that the

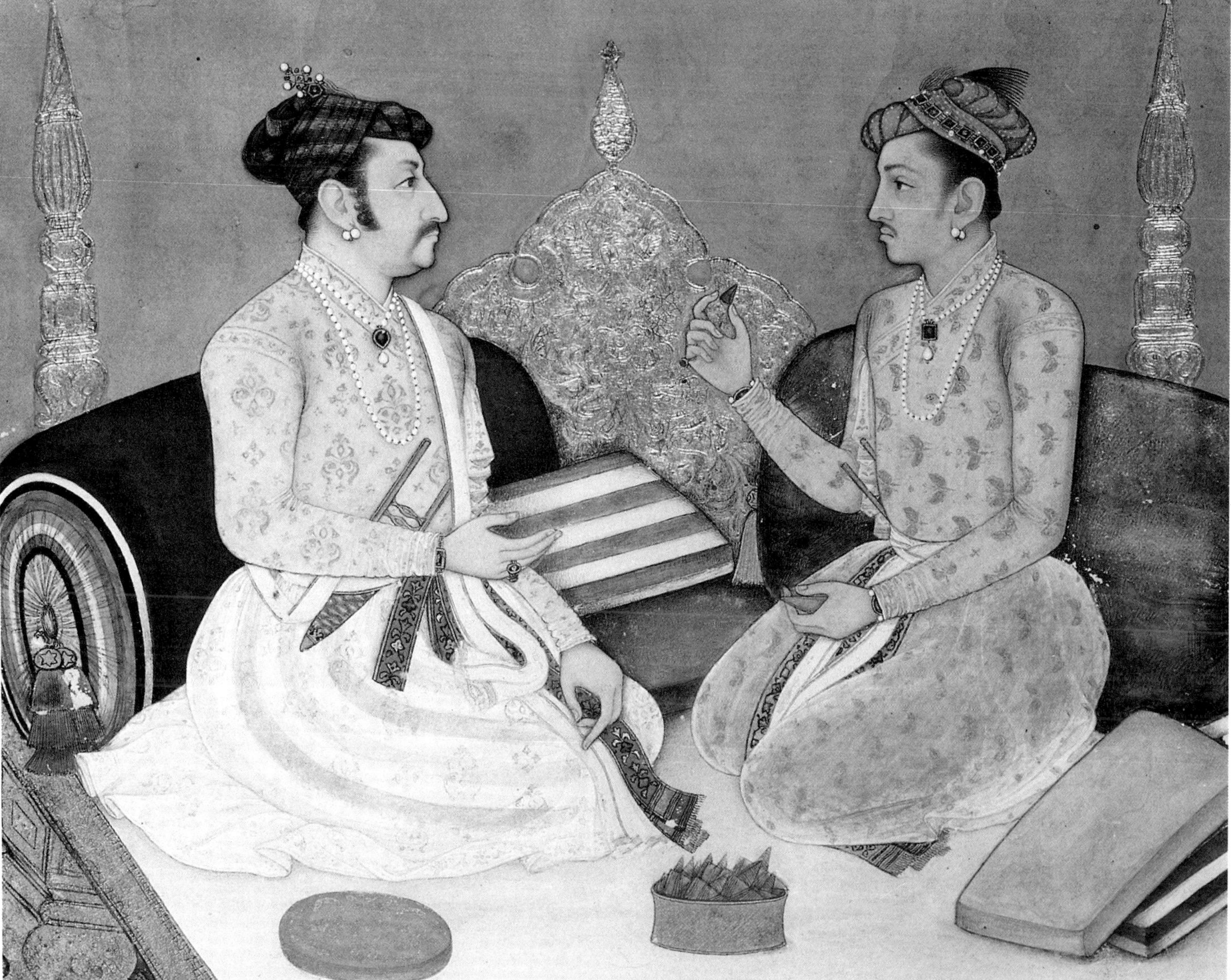

occasion must have been their meeting in 1638 shortly before Gaj Singh's death in May of that year. The Rajput ruler had been recalled to Agra to accompany Shah Shuja on the Qandahar campaign. Moreover, in 1633 Shah Shuja was only seventeen, but in this picture he looks older. The prospect of the difficult campaign ahead may explain the serious expressions on their faces, characterized by Welch as displaying a shared emotion—anxiety.

Welch was the first to attribute the painting to Bichitr. Beach has confirmed this by comparing it closely with other known works of Bichitr. From a self-portrait (FIG. 24, p. 185) we do know what Bichitr looked like, but almost no information is available about his background. His earliest known work listed by Beach (1978, p. 105) is a painting done for Jahangir between 1613 and 1620. According to Welch (1978, p. 82), "Bichitr was a brilliant young follower of Abu'l Hasan." Both artists were admirers of European works, from which they acquired a great deal of their technical skills. There is no doubt that both were capable of painting a wide variety of subjects effortlessly. Note how accurately and elegantly Bichitr has executed every detail in this painting, whether of the gold relief work of the seat, the opulent carpet and canopy made with figural Iranian material, or the impassive faces of the two princes. Indeed, this is one of the most perfect examples of the Shah Jahani taste in pictures.

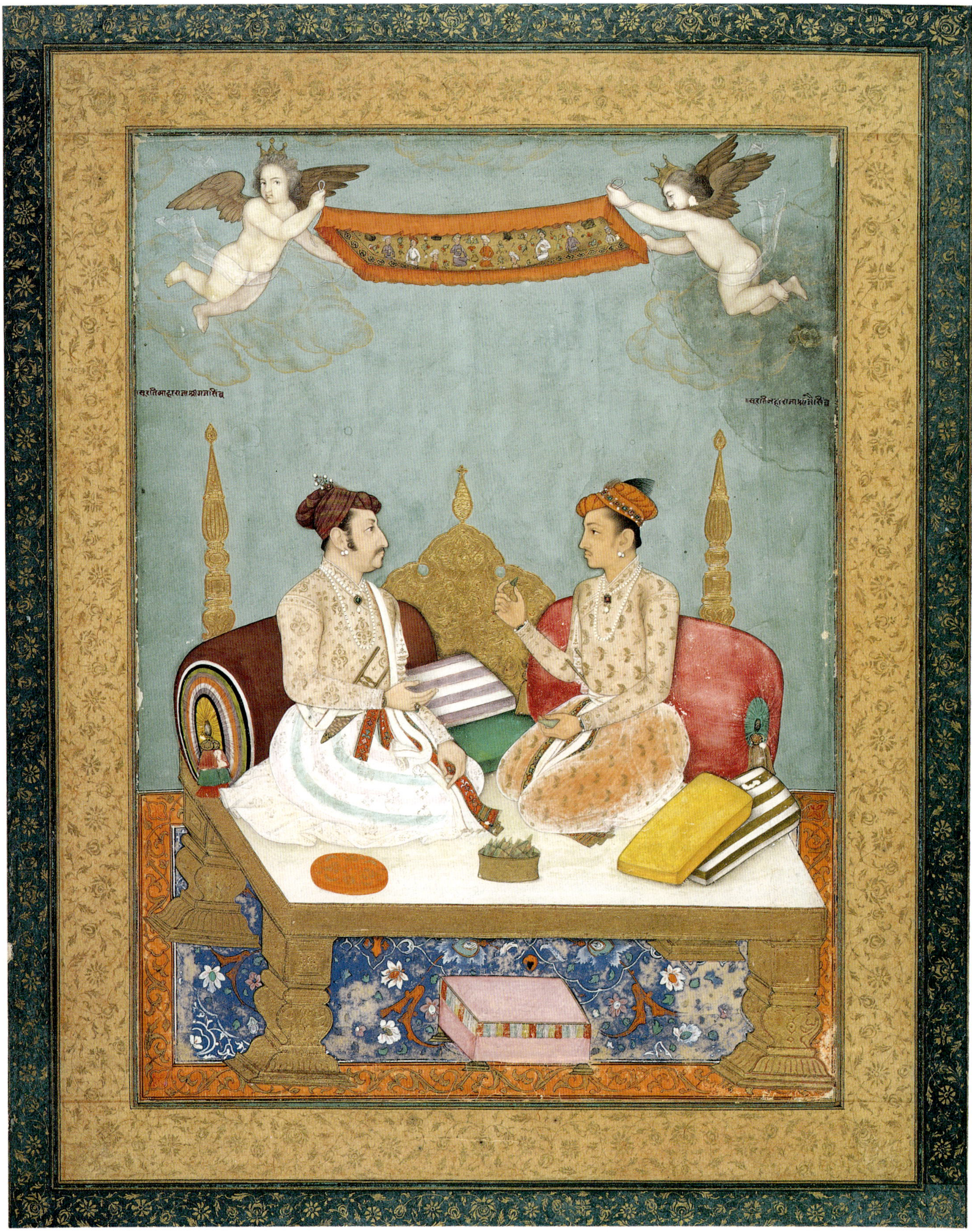

CAT. 75 detail

Attributed to Hashim (active c. 1615–55)
Shah Jahan period, c. 1635–40
6 9/16 x 3 3/4 in (16.7 x 9.5 cm)
From the Nasli and Alice Heeramaneck Collection, Museum Associates Purchase
M.78.9.14

Literature: S. C. Welch 1963, p. 169, no. 45; *Heeramaneck* 1966, pp. 157, 158, no. 217; Heeramaneck 1984, p. 161, pl. 194; Pal et al. 1989, p. 97, no. 92; Seyller 1991, pp. 105, 116, 117, fig. 14.

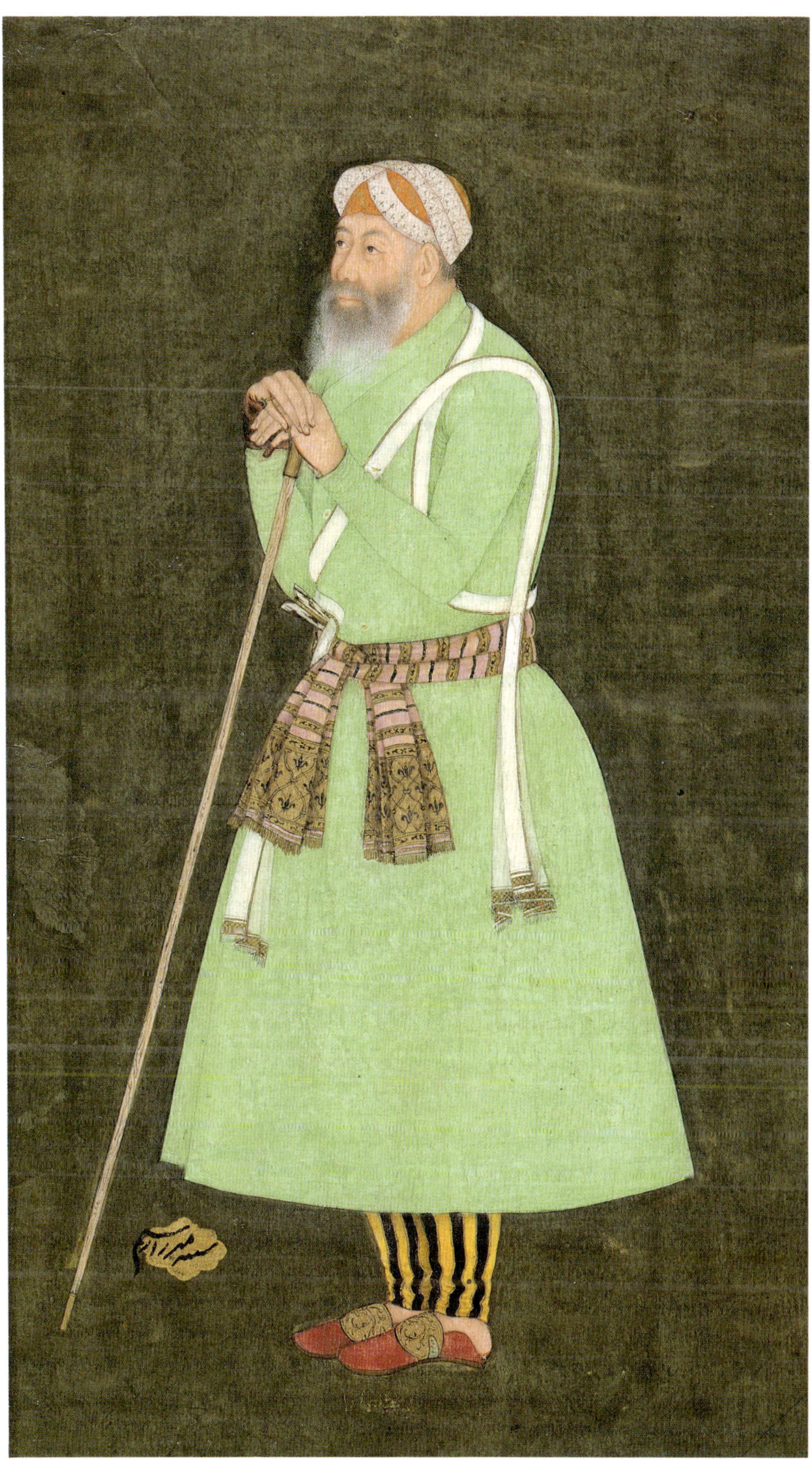

The inscription in the cartouche reads "portrait of Mirza Rustam." Mirza Rustam was related to the Safavid royal family and was the brother of Mirza Muzaffar Husayn of Qandahar, whose daughter was Shah Jahan's first wife. Because of trouble with his brother at home, Rustam went to India in 1592, during Akbar's reign, and was soon appointed the governor of Lahore. He faithfully served three generations of Mughal emperors in various capacities until he was retired by Shah Jahan. He was also related to the imperial family through matrimonial alliances. One daughter was married to Prince Parviz, the second son of Jahangir, and another to Dara Shikoh, the eldest son of Shah Jahan (see [79]). A highly cultured man, Mirza Rustam was a poet and used the pen name Fida'i. He died in 1641 at age 72, and this portrait may have been painted shortly before his death.

Perhaps intended for an imperial album, this formal portrait continues the Akbari tradition of representing the figure against a monochrome background. However, instead of the ubiquitous Akbari green, the hue here is a dark olive-gray. His face portrayed in three-quarter view, Mirza Rustam stands with his hands resting on a long and slender walking stick. The three-quarter profile for individual representation is not very common in this period, and Hashim seems in this instance to have mastered the technique. The posture of standing and holding a stick follows a common convention, especially for portraits of older men. Mirza Rustam wears a green *jama,* a brocaded sash, pajamas with orange and black stripes, and red shoes with gold embroidered medallions. A neatly folded shawl of light, white material with a gold border crisscrosses his torso elegantly. The red-and-white turban is arranged in an unusual manner.

Abul Fazl characterized Mirza Rustam as "a man of the world" who "understood the spirit of the age" (Blochmann [1927] 1939, 1: 329). Hashim has presented him as a tall and elegant man with a slightly weary expression on his face. His eyes seem to be gazing into the future with almost a dreamy look. Characteristic of Hashim's works is the particularly sensitive rendering of the hands. As J. Seyller (1991, p. 116) suggested in a recent study of him, Hashim was like other Mughal artists, who emphasized the idiosyncratic features of the faces "and supplied complementary portrait elements—the figure's stance, physique, dress and weapons, and hands—from their own formal repertoires." Noteworthy is the fact that unlike royal portraits, in this instance the figure is not overwhelmed with sumptuous attire; here it is only modestly elegant. Also typical of Hashim are the strong contours of the figure that define the form articulately against the dark background. It is worthwhile noting that Mirza Rustam is represented at least twice in the Windsor *Padshahnama* (Smart 1991, figs. 2, 10). Both portraits are by Balchand, but their closeness to Hashim's portrait in the museum's collection makes it likely that the latter was the model for the *Padshahnama* renderings.

77 FOLIO FROM THE LATE SHAH JAHAN ALBUM

Folio and borders, Shah Jahan period, c. 1650
Folio, 14½ x 10 in (36.8 x 25.4 cm)
From the Nasli and Alice Heeramaneck Collection, Museum Associates Purchase
M.78.9.15
Literature: Trubner 1950, p. 61, no. 102 (B only); *Heeramaneck* 1966, pp. 157, 158–59, no. 218a (A only illustrated); *Aesthetics of Calligraphy,* exh. cat., Fine Arts Department, University of Southern California, 1977, pl. 43; Beach 1978, pp. 72, opp. 72, 74, 75, no. 23; Heeramaneck 1984, pp. 164, 165, pls. 212, 218; Pal et al. 1989, pp. 51, 141, figs. 37, 144 (B only).

A *Page of Calligraphy* (r)
Probably by Mir Ali (d. c. 1544)
Iran; 1500–1544
7¾ x 4 in (19.7 x 10.2 cm)

B *Portrait of Shah Jahan* (v)
Attributed to Bichitr (active c. 1610–50)
Shah Jahan period, 1630–50
8 x 4⅞ in (20.3 x 12.4 cm)

This and two other folios in the collection [78, 79] once belonged to an album that was assembled for Shah Jahan, perhaps about 1650, which is why it is generally referred to as the Late Shah Jahan Album. As is characteristic of this album, the calligraphy is set in a border ornamented with motifs from nature, while the portrait is in a border with figural representations, mostly of standing courtiers and attendants, or of fauna. In many instances the human figures seem to have some kind of association with the central portrait. Here, for instance, some attend upon the emperor even though they are placed on the border. Although most such marginal figures as well as many of the larger portraits were painted when the album was assembled, some of the representations, such as this one of Shah Jahan, were done somewhat earlier, perhaps in the early 1630s.

A Within the triangle at the lower left of the central panel, the scribe describes himself as *al-fakhr, al-muzahib,* meaning "a poor sinner." The poem in this panel, as translated by Z. Faridany-Akhavan, is as follows:

A flood came and destroyed life,
and the measure of life began to be filled.
O Khwaja, be prudent for the carrier of time
has deceivingly drawn your face from the house of life
[is taking your life away from you].
Speak, O learned man,
for tomorrow there will be no pen for the mute.

The couplet on the left margin reads: "When a lion who has a strong neck falls like a fox, a dog is better than he." The couplet on the right margin reads: "Dispute with others and then accept their opinions, don't accept the remnants of the dispute of others." The calligraphy is very likely by Mir Ali of Herat, who often signed his works with epithets expressive of humility rather than his name (see [78A]). For similar folios with calligraphy by Mir Ali from the same album, see Pal et al. 1989, figures 105 and 109.

The calligraphic cartouches are set off against a rich gold background filled with tiny flowering vines painted in colors. The entire central panel is surrounded by a narrow peach margin adorned with flowering vines in gold, bordered by a narrower gold margin. The outer border is beautifully decorated with interconnecting vines supporting delicately painted flowers, buds, and leaves that are inhabited by naturalistically painted birds and symmetrically placed deer. Unlike those on some Jahangiri borders (e.g., [67]), the design here is more open and restful and is reminiscent of an exquisite piece of embroidery.

B In this formal portrait Shah Jahan stands facing to the left and holds a jeweled turban ornament with his right hand. The emperor wears a plain, white, diaphanous *jama,* which shows off the other jewelry and gem-encrusted weapons as well as the brocaded sash to advantage. Indeed the intent of the portrait was to show the emperor as a great connoisseur of gems and jewelry, which he was. This is emphasized by the inclusion of two jewelers or attendants along the bottom of the outer border, who are laying out various items for the emperor's inspection. The bearded face and turbaned head of the emperor is set off against a green halo fringed with golden rays. The ground is rendered realistically with flowering plants, and the background is painted blue-green with a multihued sky. This kind of elaborate, vivid sky is common in Shah Jahani pictures (cf. [79]), and was exploited with even greater exuberance in later Mughal paintings, from which the technique was adopted for Rajput pictures. The formal elegance and rather cold brilliance reflected by the emperor as well as the courtiers in attendance are quite characteristic of such court pictures of the period. Of the three courtiers standing on the right, the bearded man in the middle holding a spear may represent Nasir Muhammad, as suggested by Wayne Begley in conversation. The upper portion of the border has been rendered as a sky filled with uniformly golden curlicue clouds, but the flying birds were depicted naturalistically. The same admixture of naturalism and fantasy, symmetry and opulence, is evident in the representation of the animals and floral arabesques in the margins.

The picture probably shows Shah Jahan at about age forty. Although it bears neither an inscription nor a signature, it may have been painted by Bichitr (cf. Stchoukine 1929, pl. XXXIX; S. C. Welch 1963, no. 43; and [75]). All these pictures share the highly controlled technique, the formal elegance, and the brilliant finish that are hallmarks of the artist's works.

CAT. 77A,B *(overleaf)*

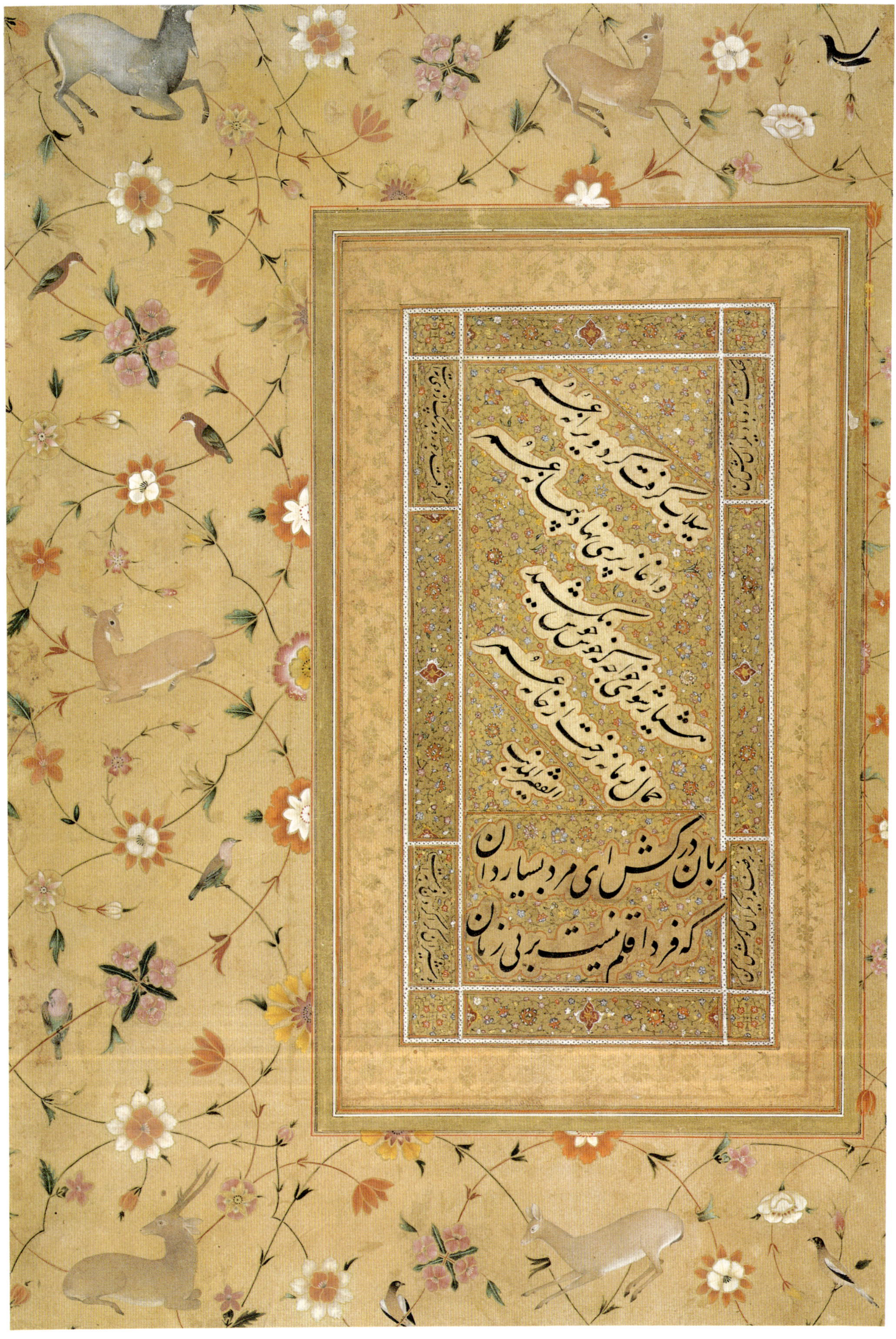
زبان درکش ای مرد بسیار دان
که فردا قلم نیست بر بی زبان

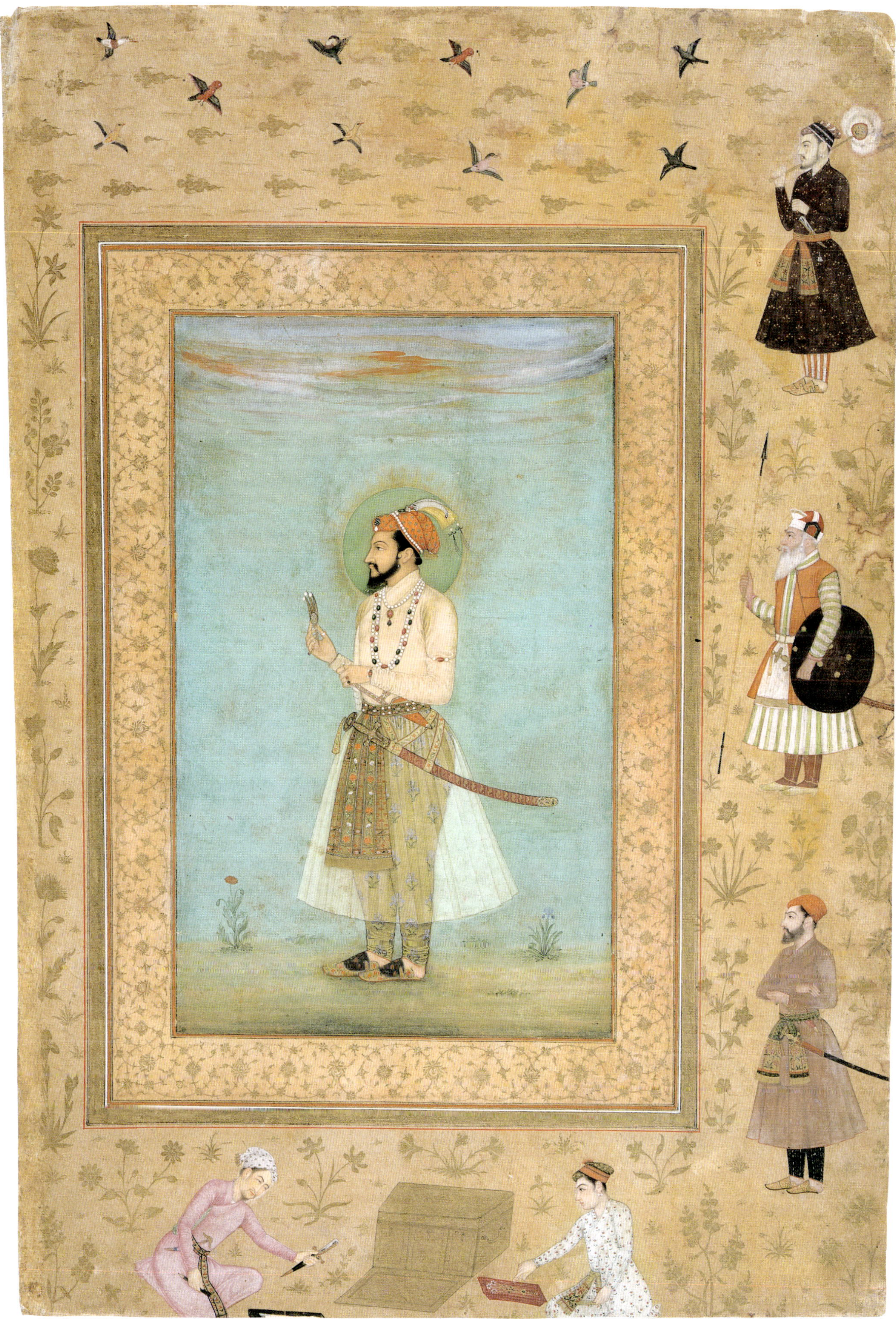

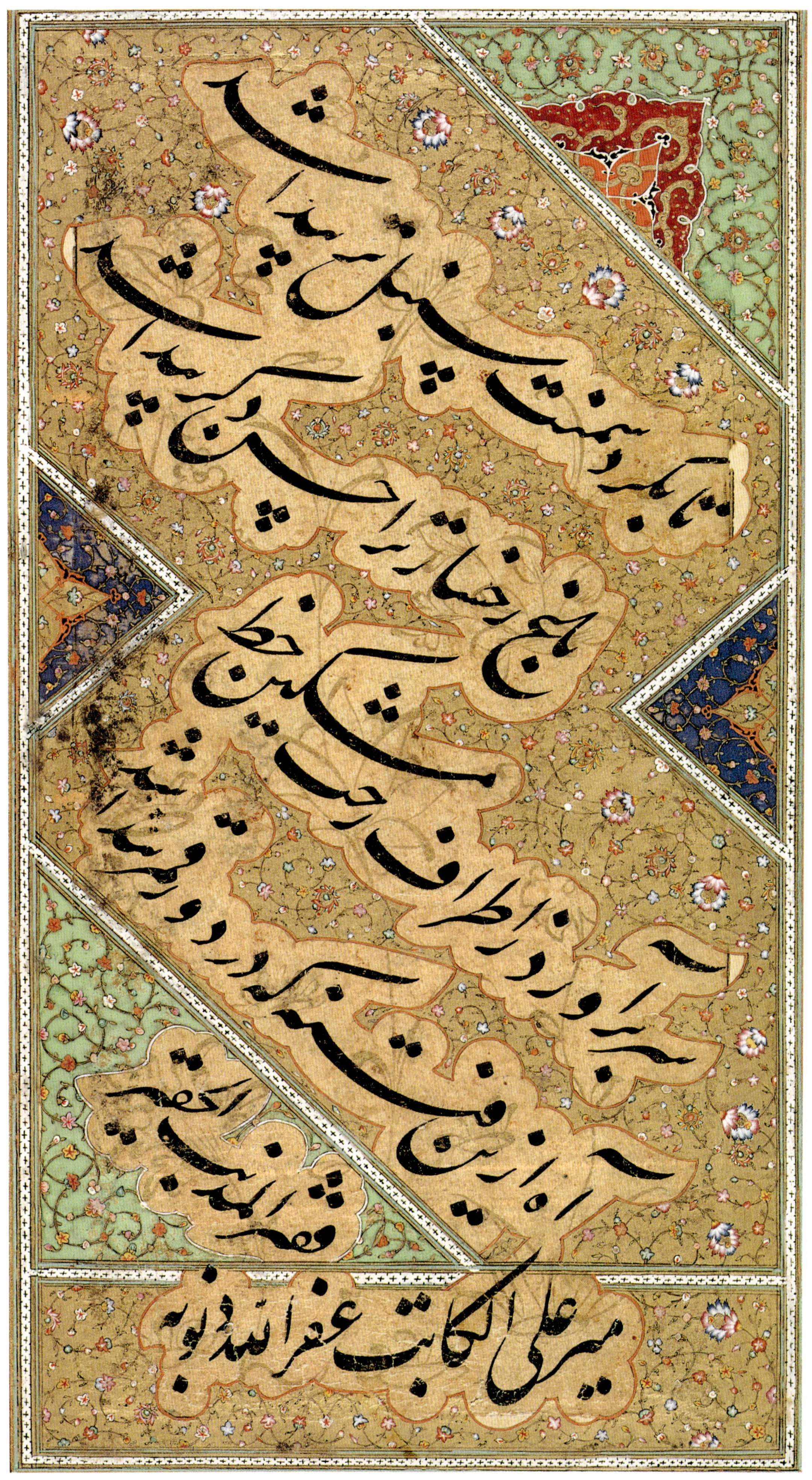
میر علی الکاتب غفر الله ذنوبه

Folio and borders, Shah Jahan period, c. 1650
Folio, 15 1/8 x 10 7/8 in (38.4 x 27.6 cm)
From the Nasli and Alice Heeramaneck Collection, Museum Associates Purchase
M.83.1.3
Literature: *Heeramaneck* 1966, p. 157, no. 218b (not illustrated); R. Skelton, "A Decorative Motif in Mughal Art," in Pal 1972, pl. LXXXVIIb (A only); Heeramaneck 1984, p. 165, pl. 213 (B only); Pal & Dehejia 1986, p. 169, no. 176 (detail of border of A).

A *Page of Calligraphy* (r)
By Mir Ali (d. c. 1544)
Iran; 1500–1544
7 1/2 x 4 1/8 in (19.1 x 10.5 cm)

B *Portrait of Chattarsal of Bundi (?)* (v)
Possibly by Balchand
Shah Jahan period, 1640–50
8 1/2 x 4 7/8 in (21.6 x 12.4 cm)

A The cartouches with calligraphy are placed in a field enlivened with intertwined vines with polychromed flowers. The design of the panel is further variegated with interestingly placed triangular sections with varied designs in gold and colors. A more lightly delineated floral scroll pattern, also in gold, decorates the narrow borders immediately surrounding the calligraphy. The outer border is adorned with a variety of flowering plants that have been naturalistically delineated and are among the finest examples of Shah Jahani flower studies.

The calligraphy is by Mir Ali of Herat (al-Haravi), who was much admired by the Mughals. Many specimens of his work are included in this later album of Shah Jahan (see A. Welch 1979, pp. 191–92 and no. 83, for the calligrapher; and Welch and Welch 1982, pp. 220–22, no. 73, for another example from this album). Mir Ali flourished in Herat and Bukhara and died in about 1544. His writing style was not only considered to be perfect, but he is credited with having introduced innovations in the *nastaliq* script. The poem and inscription have been translated by Z. Faridany-Akhavan as follows:

While a ringlet encircled your enemy,
Another virtue appeared on the garden of your countenance
A black line is visible around your face
Woe from this calamity which appeared around the moon.
The poor insignificant sinner
Mir 'Ali the scribe, dust beneath the lord.

B The formal central portrait showing a portly man with a dark complexion is very likely Chattarsal, who was the ruler of Bundi, a Rajput state, from 1631 until 1658. He was, in fact, put on the throne by Shah Jahan and served the emperor loyally and literally with his life. Until his death he remained the governor of Agra but also participated in many military campaigns. During the war of the brothers vying for the crown in 1658, he fought for the emperor and Dara Shikoh and was killed in battle. As J. Tod ([1832] 1957, 2: 389) wrote, "Rao Chutter-sal had been personally engaged in fifty-two combats, and left a name renowned for courage and incorruptible fidelity." Like his Mughal master, he was interested in architecture and made additions to his palace and built temples in his kingdom.

Not only is Chattarsal appropriately dressed as a Rajput with the *jama* tied on the left rather than the right, as would be the case for a Muslim, but most of the figures in the margin appear to be Rajputs as well. The artist emphasized Chattarsal's military career by providing him with a conspicuous shield and a large sword. His companions in the margins cannot be identified, but all except two bear swords. Shields are provided for the two figures seated above. Of the two figures at the bottom, the bearded fellow on the left has a bow and arrows, while the man with the striped shirt has only a dagger. In his left hand he holds a string of beads. The standing figure beside him is shown in three-quarter profile.

Although the name of the artist is not inscribed, it is possible that the central portrait as well as the marginal figures were rendered by Balchand. Balchand was a brother of Payag, and both had long careers spanning most of the first half of the seventeenth century (Smart 1991). Balchand's earliest known work goes back to the 1590s, and he remained active into the 1650s. He seems to have enjoyed Shah Jahan's confidence, and besides being a leading artist of the imperial atelier, he may also have held other administrative positions (Beach 1978, pp. 95–101). Like Bichitr, Balchand was technically brilliant but "a more fastidious recorder of human physiognomy and psyche" (Smart 1991, p. 148), as is evidenced by the variety and sensitive renderings of the portraits in this album leaf.

CAT. 78A detail *(opposite)*
CAT. 78A,B *(overleaf)*

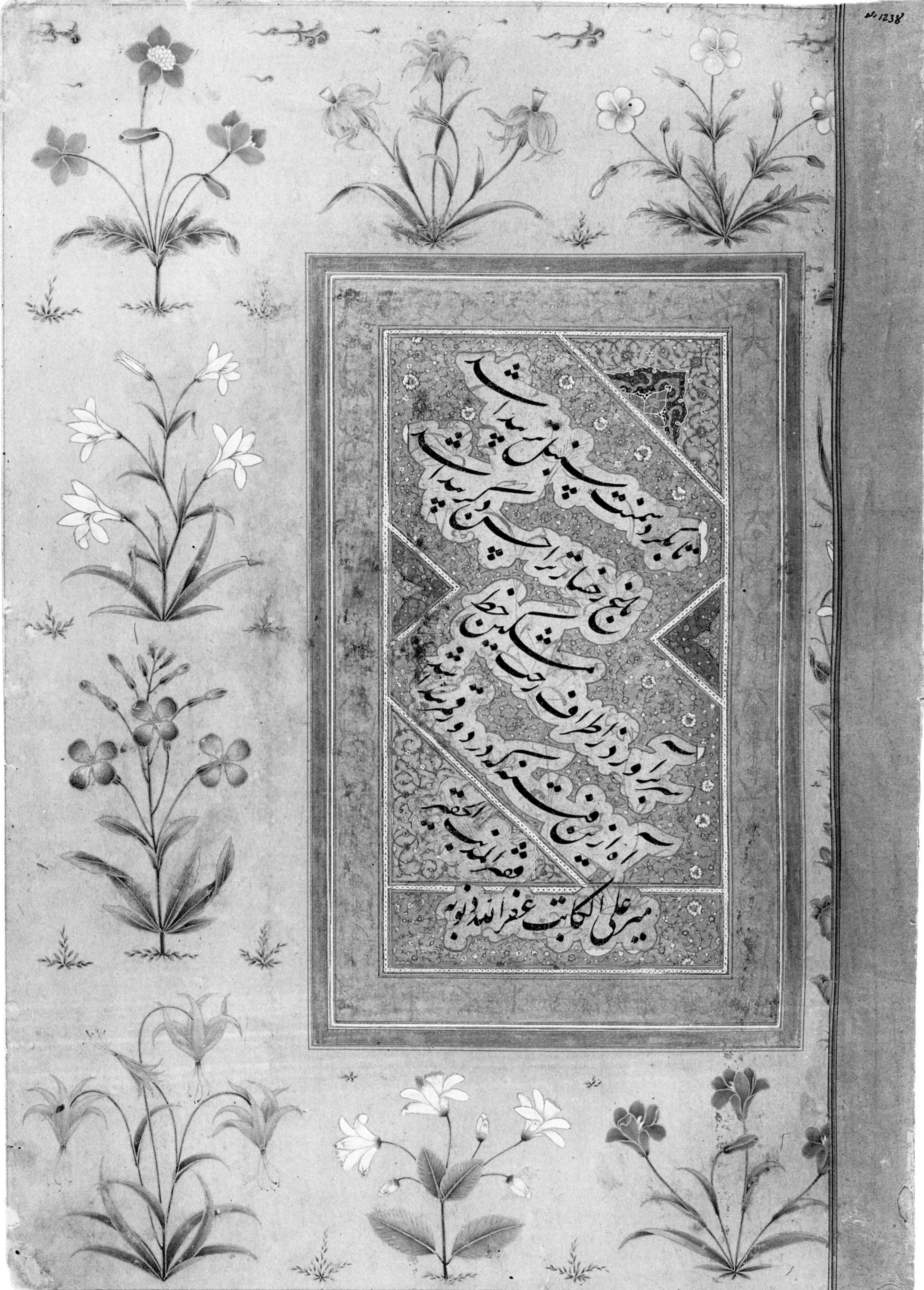
میر علی الکاتب غفر الله ذنوبه

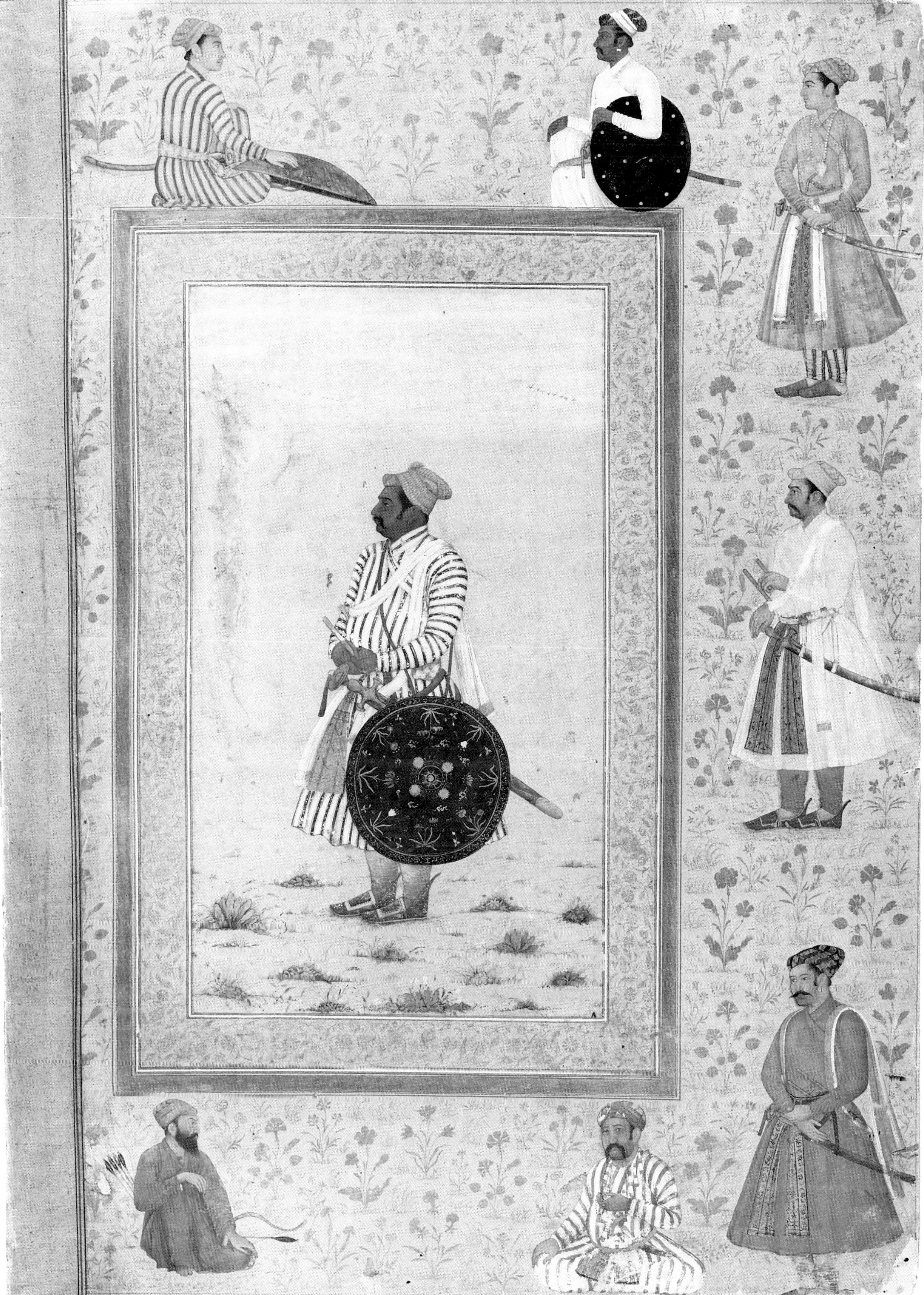

Folio and borders, Shah Jahan period, c. 1650
Overall, 14⅝ x 10 in (37.1 x 25.4 cm)
Illustration, 10⅛ x 7⅞ in (25.7 x 20.0 cm)
From the Nasli and Alice Heeramaneck Collection, Museum Associates Purchase
M.83.105.21
Literature: Strzygowski 1933, fig. 109, pl. 70; Trubner 1950, p. 62, no. 104; Johnson 1972, p. 144, pl. LXXXIIa; Trabold 1975, pp. 36–37, no. 50; Pal 1982, pp. 16, 17, pl. V; Heeramaneck 1984, p. 165, pl. 217 (reproduced in reverse); Pal & Dehejia 1986, p. 167, no. 172 (detail of border); Pal 1987, p. 118, fig. 75; Pal et al. 1989, p. 32, fig. 24; Bhatia 1990, pl. 1.

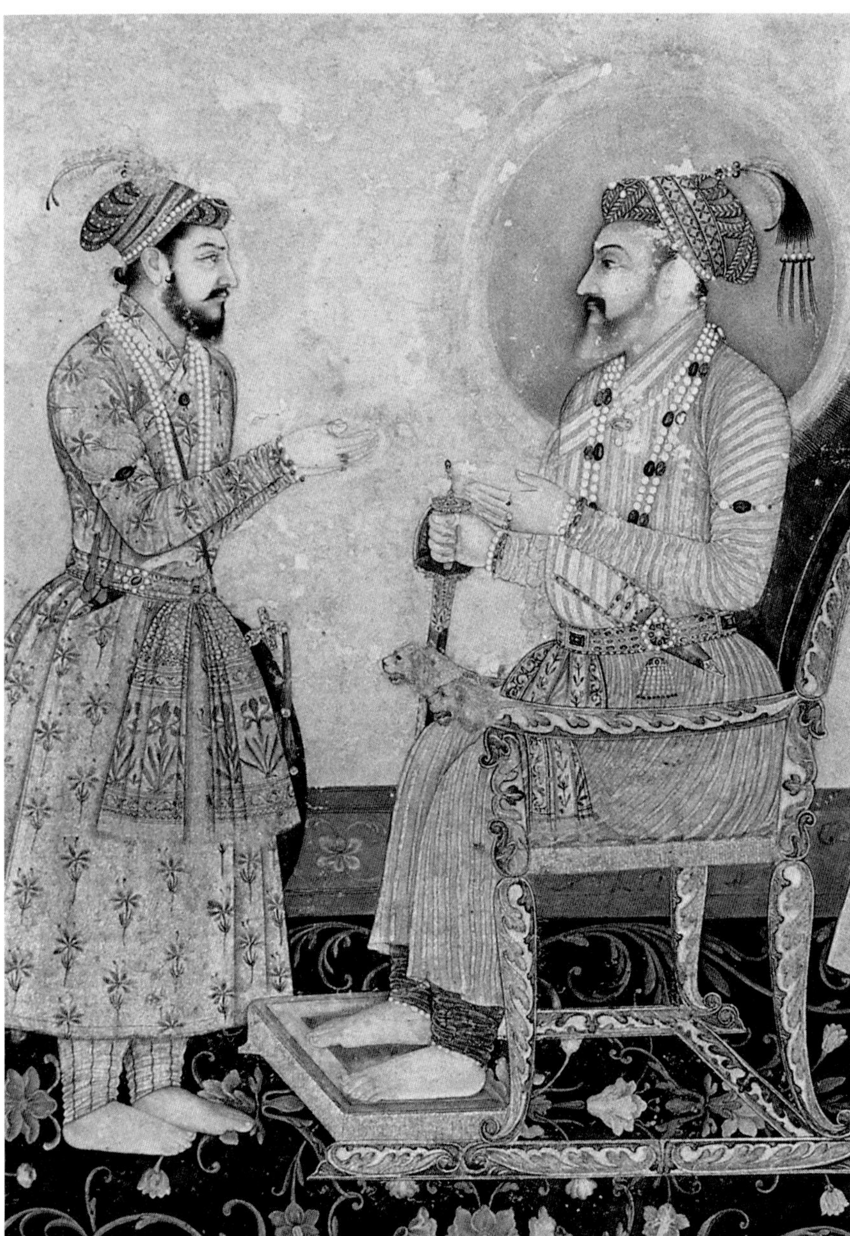

CAT. 79 detail

This formal portrait is mounted in borders beautifully adorned with a variety of flowering plants and birds rendered with exquisite naturalism. In addition, stylized, decorative clouds share the upper border with the flying geese, a *saras* crane, and a long-tailed bird.

Shah Jahan is seated on an ornate chair with lion arm terminals and inlaid with ivory. The chair rests on a European carpet with floral designs. A small covered container, perhaps a spittoon, rests on a tray along the border of the carpet in the foreground. Shah Jahan's head is set off against an effulgent green nimbus. Immediately behind the chair a courtier holds a yak-tail flywhisk. In front stands Dara Shikoh, Shah Jahan's eldest and favorite son, with his hands held in supplication. Behind the prince stands another courtier in the same attitude. Shah Jahan has a partly white and partly black beard but a black moustache. Except for the beard, his smooth and wrinkle-free face betrays no sign of age. Unlike Jahangir (see [73]), Shah Jahan was extremely self-conscious about his age and seems not to have allowed himself to be portrayed as he really looked.

It is not known if this picture records a particular occasion or is simply a generalized representation of a formal meeting between the father and the son. In the album this picture faced a similar formal depiction of Jahangir receiving his prime minister and brother-in-law Asaf Khan (Pal et al. 1989, p. 32, figs. 23, 24). Both paintings were probably painted by the same artist. The artist, however, remains unknown, although both Bichitr and Hashim are possibilities (cf. Beach 1978, pp. 127, 129, no. 45, by Hashim; and Seyller 1991, figs. 9, 11, by Hashim).

This is the only portrait of Dara Shikoh (1615–59) in the collection. He was mystically inclined and probably more interested in philosophy and poetry than in politics. Although he was the legitimate heir, he lost both his throne and his life to one of his siblings, Aurangzeb, during the fratricidal war of succession.

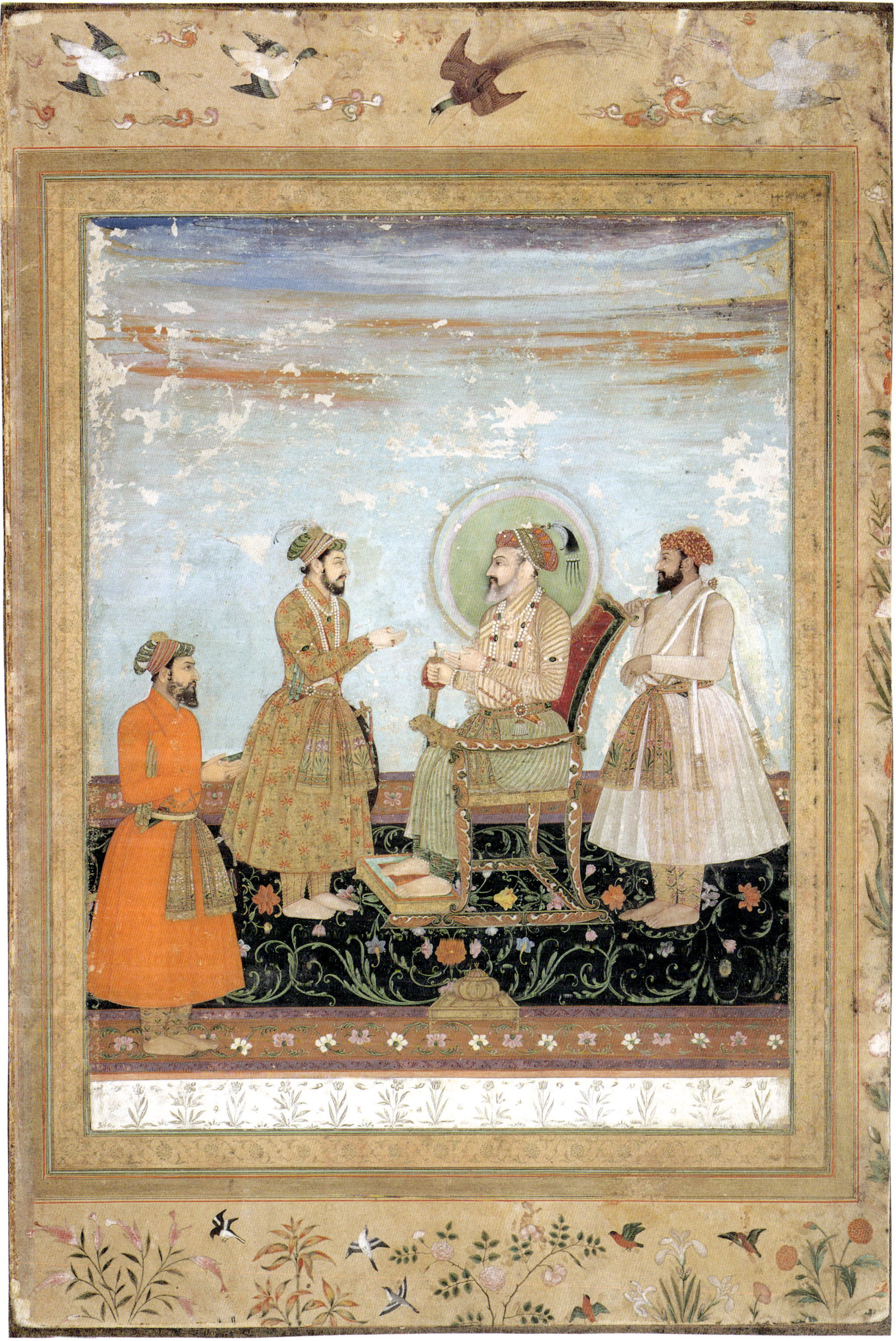

Painting, Aurangzeb period, dated A.H. 1085, A.D. 1674/75
Folio, 14 3/8 x 9 9/16 in (36.5 x 24.3 cm)
Illustration, 6 1/4 x 3 5/8 in (15.9 x 9.2 cm)
Purchased with funds provided by Dorothy and Richard Sherwood
M.72.88.9
Literature: Canby 1983, no. 5, fig. 4.

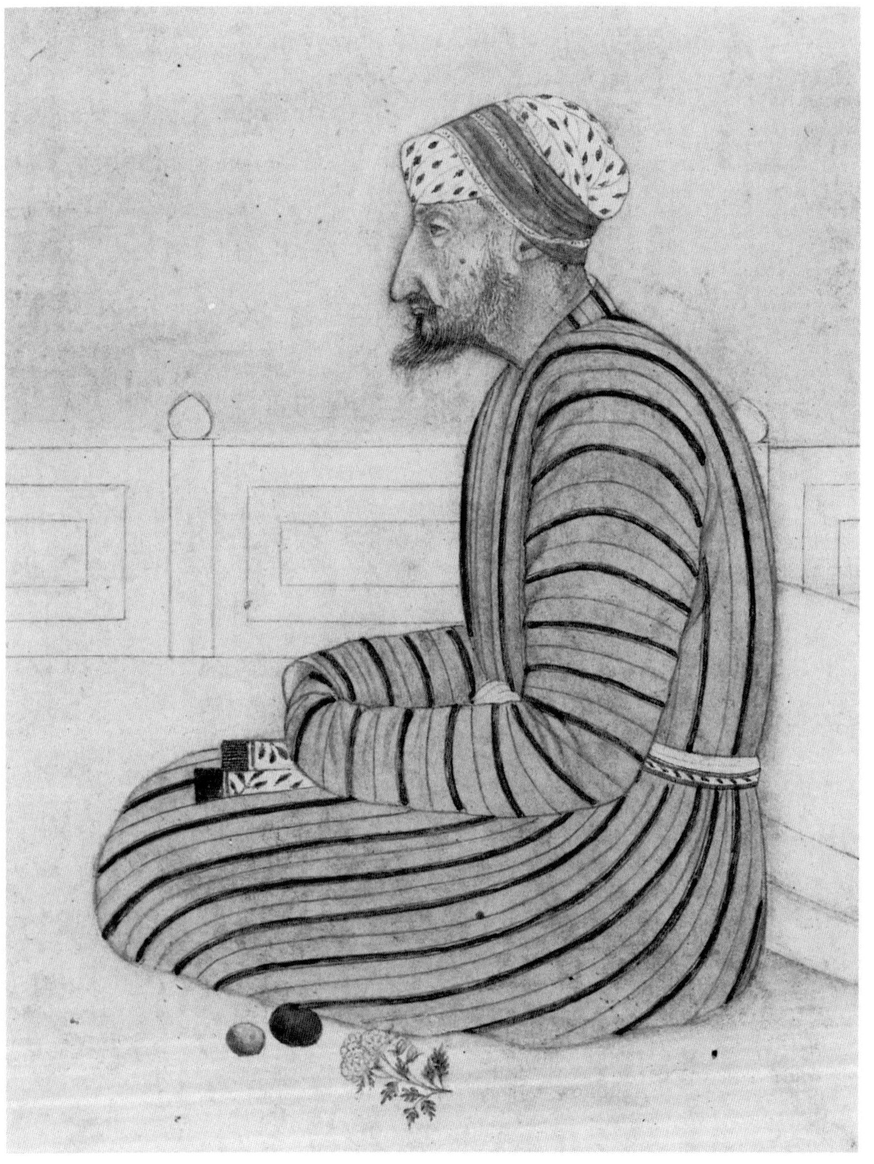

CAT. 80 detail

This album leaf is from the Small Clive Album, the bulk of which is preserved in the Victoria and Albert Museum, London. The album was assembled and given by Shuja-ud-daulla, the ruler of Oudh, to Lord Clive during his final visit to India (1765–67). Clive had restored the kingdom to Shuja-ud-daulla, who had been defeated by the British at Buxar in 1764. Although the album was assembled between 1765 and 1767, it included paintings that were done much earlier.

The seal at the back of this picture reads, according to Robert Skelton, *Ashraf Khan* and *Padshah Alamgir,* the latter of which was Aurangzeb's title. The date given is A.H. 1085, which corresponds to A.D. 1674/75. Thus, the painting was clearly executed during Aurangzeb's reign (1658–1707), but whether it was meant for an imperial album is not certain; by this date Aurangzeb was losing interest in painting. The subject of the portrait may well be a religious person, a mystic or a Sufi.

The narrow borders immediately surrounding the portrait are adorned with golden floral tendrils, while the outer border is decorated with two floral motifs whose outlines were certainly drawn with pounced designs dating from the Shah Jahan period. The portrait itself was delicately drawn by a very competent artist. It is an expressive face whose features are articulately delineated. Sitting with a flower and some fruit beside him, the bearded, elderly man is clearly in a contemplative mood. The swelling gray clouds in the sky seem somewhat menacing, but otherwise the mood is tranquil.

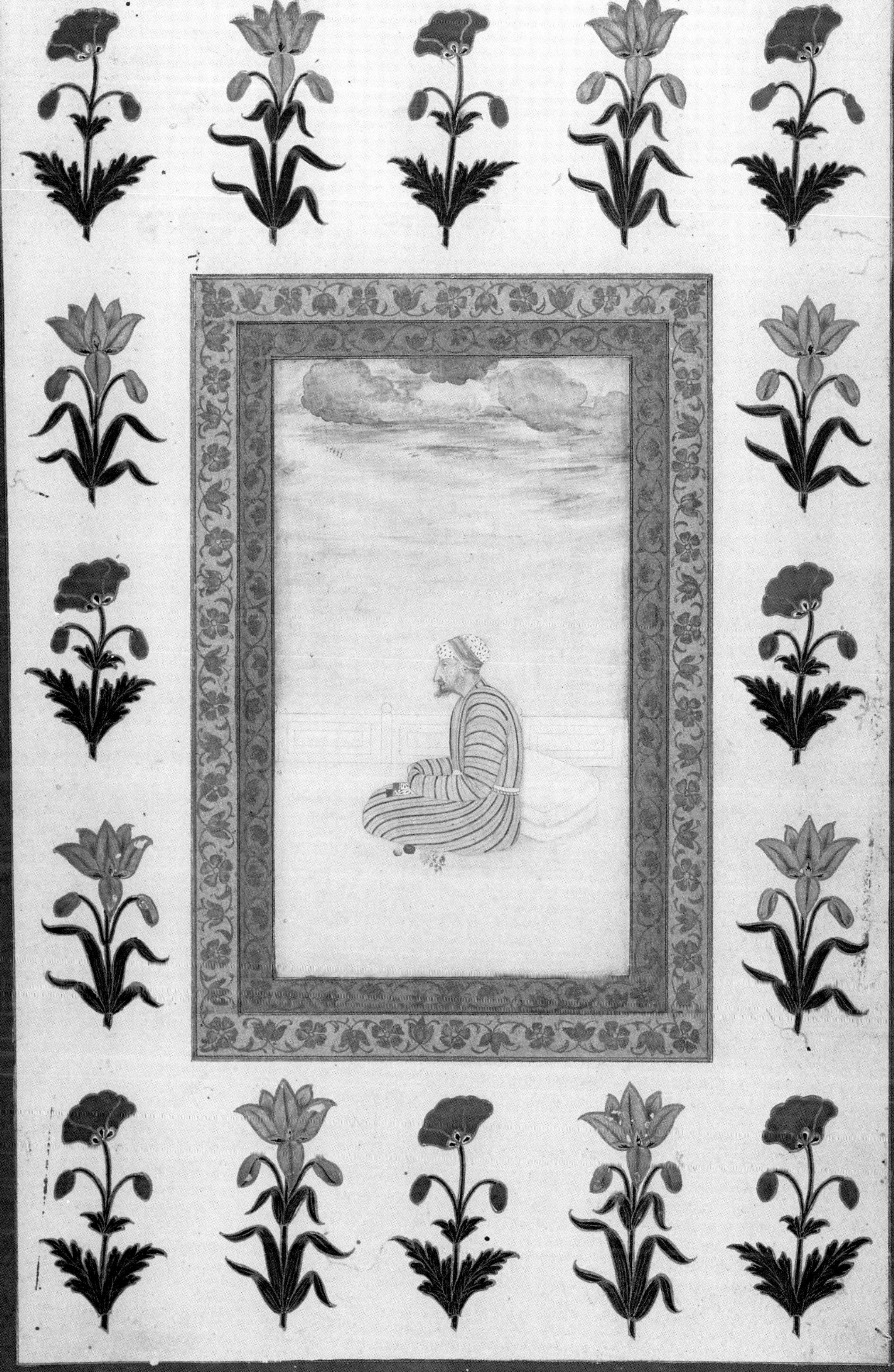

Aurangzeb period, c. 1675
Ink, opaque watercolor, and gold
7 1/16 x 4 15/16 in (17.9 x 12.5 cm)
Gift of Paul F. Walter
M.74.123.5
Literature: Pal 1971a, p. 95, no. 84; Pal & Glynn 1976, p. 11, no. 2.

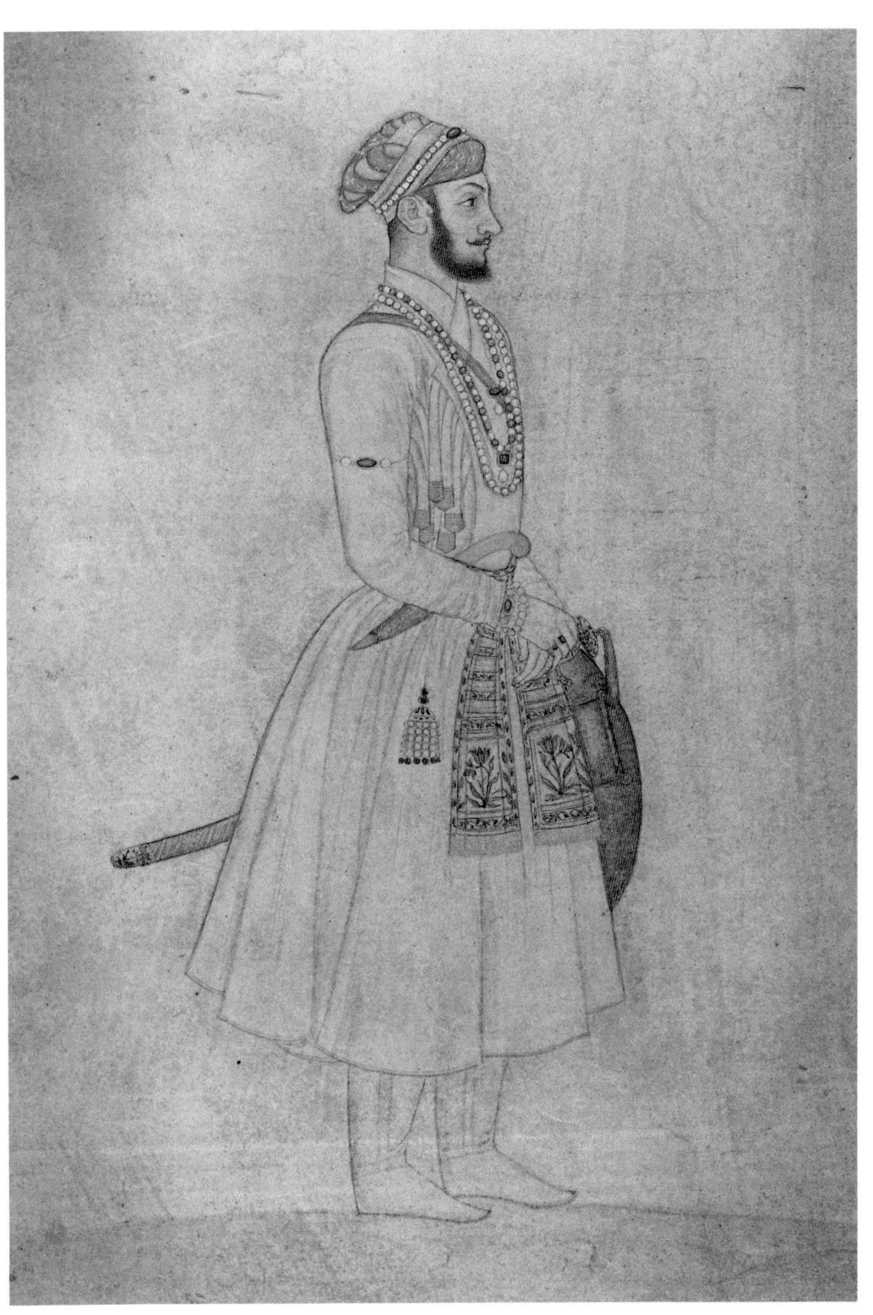

The words *Shah alam* are written on the back in both Devanagari and Arabic. Because of the style of the drawing, which is close to that of Shah Jahan–period portraits, as well as a comparison of his facial features with other known representations, the figure can be identified as Muhammad Muazzam (1643–1712), the second son of Emperor Aurangzeb, who succeeded his father in 1707 as Shah Alam Bahadur. Also known as Bahadur Shah I, he had a reign of only five years.

This well-drawn and lightly colored portrait was probably painted about 1675, when the prince was thirty-two years old. It was very likely rendered by an artist of the imperial atelier. He was a proficient draughtsman and had a keen eye for details, as is clear from the face, the turban, and the sash. The same artist who was responsible for a contemporary portrait of Aurangzeb as if he were a young man, now in a private collection (Falk et al. 1978, p. 87, fig. 29), may have done this portrait of Shah Alam.

Aurangzeb period, c. 1675
Folio, 15 3/8 x 9 5/8 in (39.1 x 24.4 cm)
Illustration, 9 5/16 x 5 1/2 in (23.6 x 14.0 cm)
Purchased with funds provided by Dorothy and Richard Sherwood
M.72.88.4

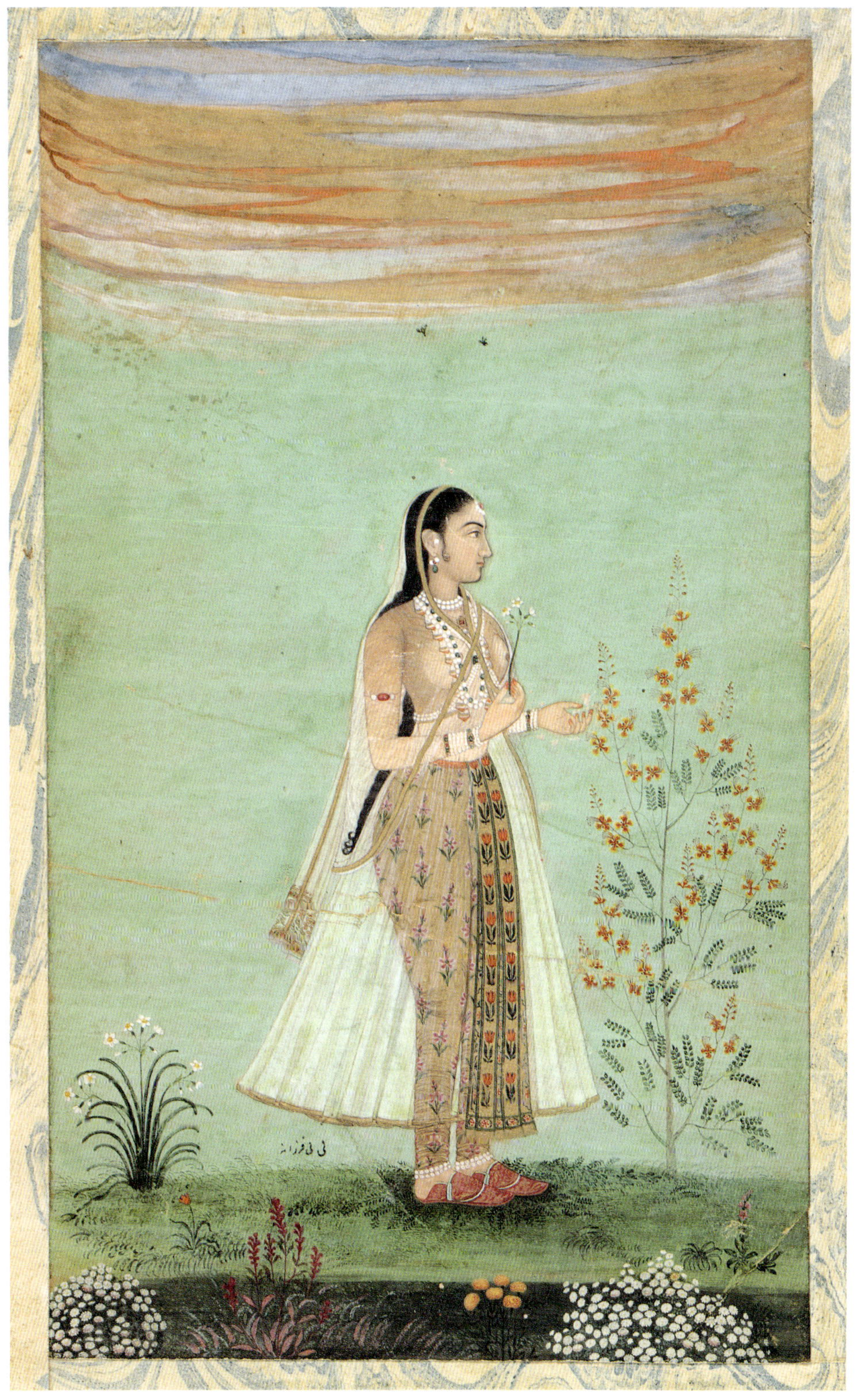

CAT. 82 detail

The inscription below the flowing dress of the lady identifies her as *Bibi Ferzana*. While generally the word *bibi* means "a lady," it can also be applied to a wife or a mistress. Here very likely it means that Ferzana was a courtesan. Her name implies that she was Muslim. The portrait has been remounted with strips of marbled paper serving as inner borders.

Wearing a very transparent dress through which one can see her torso and arms as well as her flowered silk pants, she stands looking to the right. She wears red shoes, a sash of brocade with orange tulips, a transparent shawl (*odhni*), and a fair amount of jewelry. Her left hand reaches out to a tree with small red flowers, while in her right hand she holds a flower of the kind that is behind her. Various other forms of flowering plants adorn the foreground, which is painted in dark green. She stands on a lighter green ground, and a third shade of green represents the background. The sky is colorfully rendered with streaks of red, orange, purple, gold, and blue.

Portraits of individual women were rare during the reign of Akbar and Jahangir. They became more fashionable under Shah Jahan, whose life and court were dominated by women. The portraits do not differ fundamentally from those of men but are even more idealized, since the subjects were not usually accessible. This is why portraits of royal ladies are extremely scarce, and as J. Dye (1989, p. 97) has stated, "likenesses of female subjects were almost totally confined to the pleasurable realm of fantasy." Although this charming representation of Bibi Ferzana is dated here to about 1675, it is basically no different from another portrait of a lady in the Virginia Museum of Fine Arts, Richmond, attributed by Dye (1989, p. 100, fig. 95) to about 1640.

Other Mughal Paintings and Calligraphy

Unless otherwise noted, all pictures are painted in opaque watercolor and gold, all texts are written in ink, and all works are on paper. Because the imperial Mughal workshop and individual artists moved about, with rare exceptions only the regnal period of a work's creation is indicated. Nonimperial works are in the following order: subimperial, popular Mughal, and calligraphy.

83 TWO FOLIOS FROM A *RAMAYANA* MANUSCRIPT

Subimperial Mughal, Akbar period, c. 1595
Text in black and red ink
Folios, approx. 11⅛ x 7⅜ in (28.3 x 18.7 cm)
Illustrations and text, each, approx. 9⅜ x 7½ in (23.8 x 19.1 cm)
From the Nasli and Alice Heeramaneck Collection, Museum Associates Purchase
M.82.6.6,.5
Literature: *Heeramaneck* 1966, p. 153, no. 211 (B only illustrated); Beach 1981, pp. 130, 134, fig. 18 (A only); Heeramaneck 1984, p. 161, pl. 197 (B only, reproduced in reverse).

A *Hermitage in a Forest*
B *Rama Chastises Bali*

These two folios are from the Book of Kishkindha of a *Ramayana* manuscript. On the reverse of each folio is the Sanskrit text in the Devanagari script, which demonstrates that the manuscript was almost certainly prepared for a Hindu patron. A Muslim was more likely to own a Persian translation of the text. The patron was very likely a courtier at the imperial court, as the style of the pictures is close to that noted in manuscripts illustrated by artists belonging to the imperial atelier (see P. Chandra 1957–59 for a discussion of other folios from this manuscript). The partially preserved impression of a rubber stamp on the reverse of A indicates that it was once in the possession of a Rajput palace library. Unfortunately the name of the state has been deliberately obliterated. Both folios are damaged at the bottom. As is clear from the preliminary drawing of outlines in red at the bottom of B, at some time in the past an attempt to restore the picture was begun.

Very likely these two leaves belong to the same manuscript from which twenty-four folios are in the Prince of Wales Museum, Bombay (P. Chandra 1957–59). Those folios are damaged in a similar fashion and have the text written in Devanagari on the reverse. Moreover, some of those illustrations show similar traces of attempts at repair. In his article on them P. Chandra characterized the paintings as popular Mughal and dated them to about 1590. In a subsequent publication (P. Chandra 1960, p. 38), however, in the text he dated the series to the late Akbar period, which would make it 1600–1605, but the caption gave the date as about 1610. E. Binney (1973, p. 48, no. 24) assigned one folio from the same manuscript to 1590–95 and characterized it as an imperial manuscript, which is unlikely considering the language and script on the reverse. However, Binney published a second folio, probably from the same series, that he dated to about 1605–10 (1973, p. 60, no. 34). M. Beach (1981, p. 130, fig. 18) places the series in about 1595, a date with which R. Skelton has concurred verbally.

Indeed, a date around 1610 seems much too late when compared with other popular Mughal pictures of the period discussed by Chandra himself or with others in the museum's collection. Although lacking the finish and rich coloring characteristic of the imperial manuscripts of the nineties [56, 57], the complex compositions, the treatment of architecture and of the natural forms, as well as the expression of mood and atmosphere are strongly reminiscent of such manuscripts as the *Harivamsa* [48] or the *Kathasaritsagara* [51].

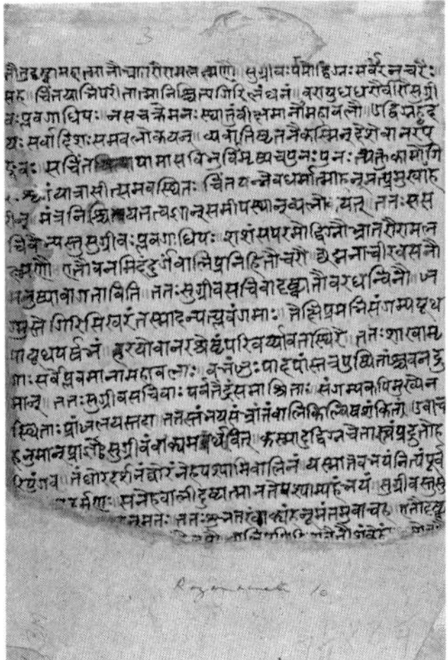

CAT. 83A text

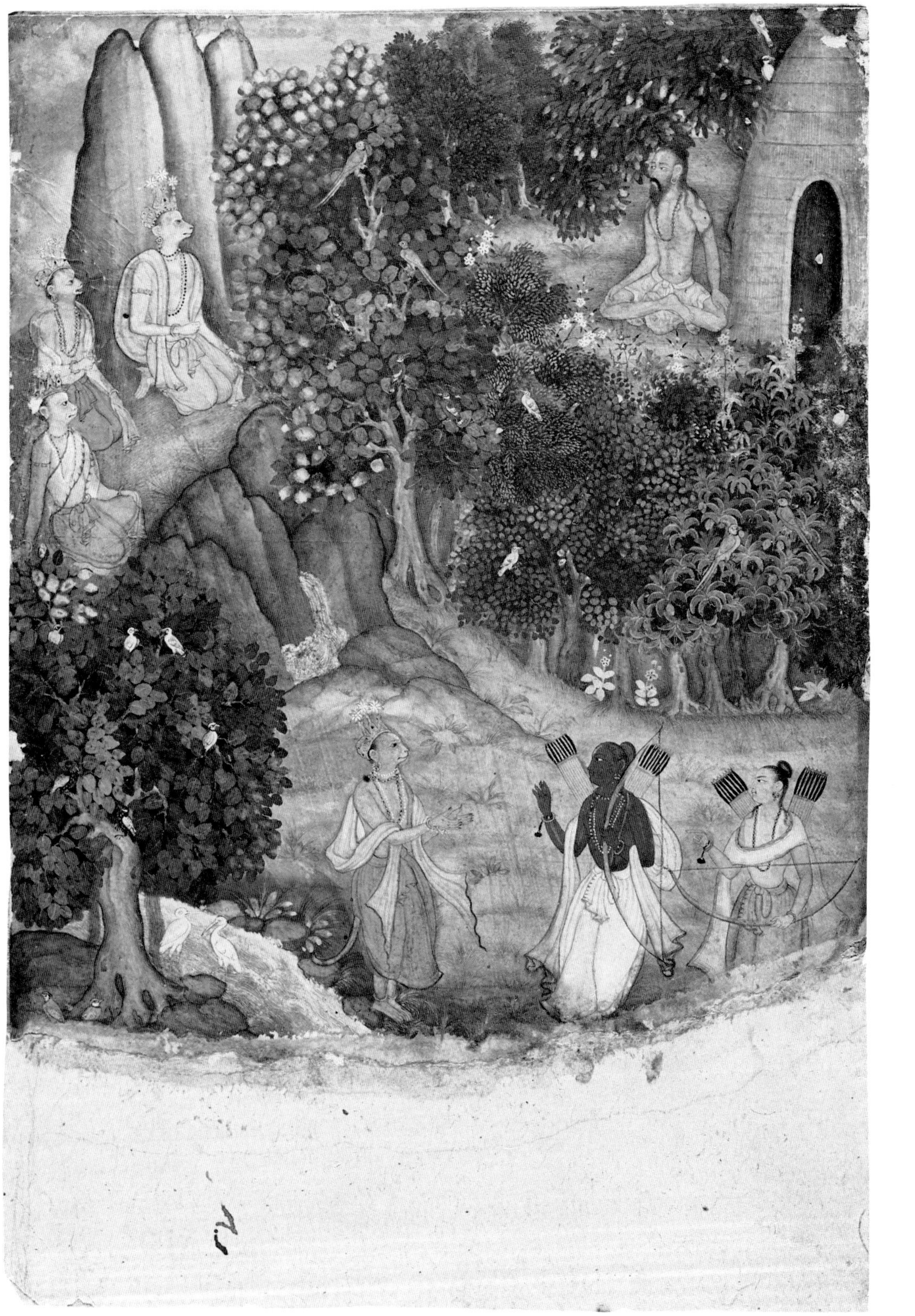

CAT. 83A *(right)*
CAT. 83B *(opposite)*

A The exact identification of this illustration is uncertain, as the text for it would have been on the previous page. Along the bottom of the composition a monkey prince is greeting the brothers Rama and Lakshmana. Three more monkeys wearing tiaras sit on a rock at the upper left and converse with an ascetic seated beside a hut and across from them (although the placement of the tree in the middle would appear to obstruct their line of vision). There is no doubt that the incident depicted is from the early section of the Book of Kishkindha. Whether the simian who meets the two heroes is Hanuman or Sugriva is not clear; nor is the identification of the scene above. Chapter 13 of the Book of Kishkindha describes the hermitage of Saptajanas as being occupied by several ascetics, but here only one is shown.

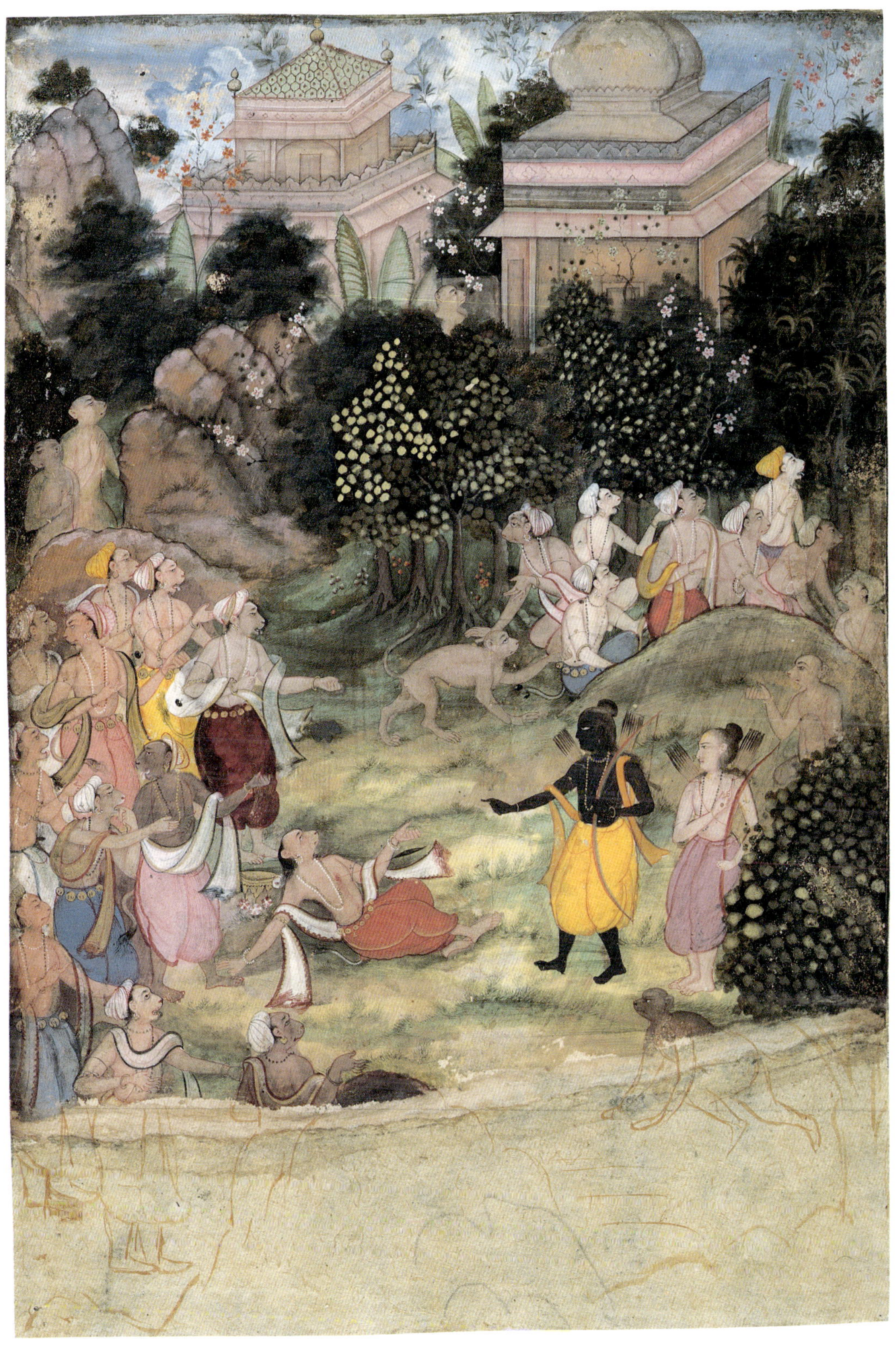

B This is clearly the scene (chapter 18) in which, after he has fallen from Rama's arrow, Bali reproaches Rama for striking him from behind. Curiously, in the illustration the arrow pierces Bali's chest from the front. In any event, Rama chastises Bali by reminding him that he has received just punishment for seducing his brother Sugriva's wife. That Rama is reproving Bali is clear from the gesture of his right hand.

84 FOLIO FROM A *SHAHNAMA* MANUSCRIPT: RUSTAM SLAYS THE WHITE DIV

Subimperial Mughal, Jahangir period, manuscript dated 1608
Folio, $9^{1}/_{4}$ x $5^{3}/_{4}$ in (23.5 x 14.6 cm)
Illustration, $6^{3}/_{4}$ x $4^{3}/_{4}$ in (17.1 x 12.1 cm)
Gift of the Michael J. Connell Foundation
M.71.49.3

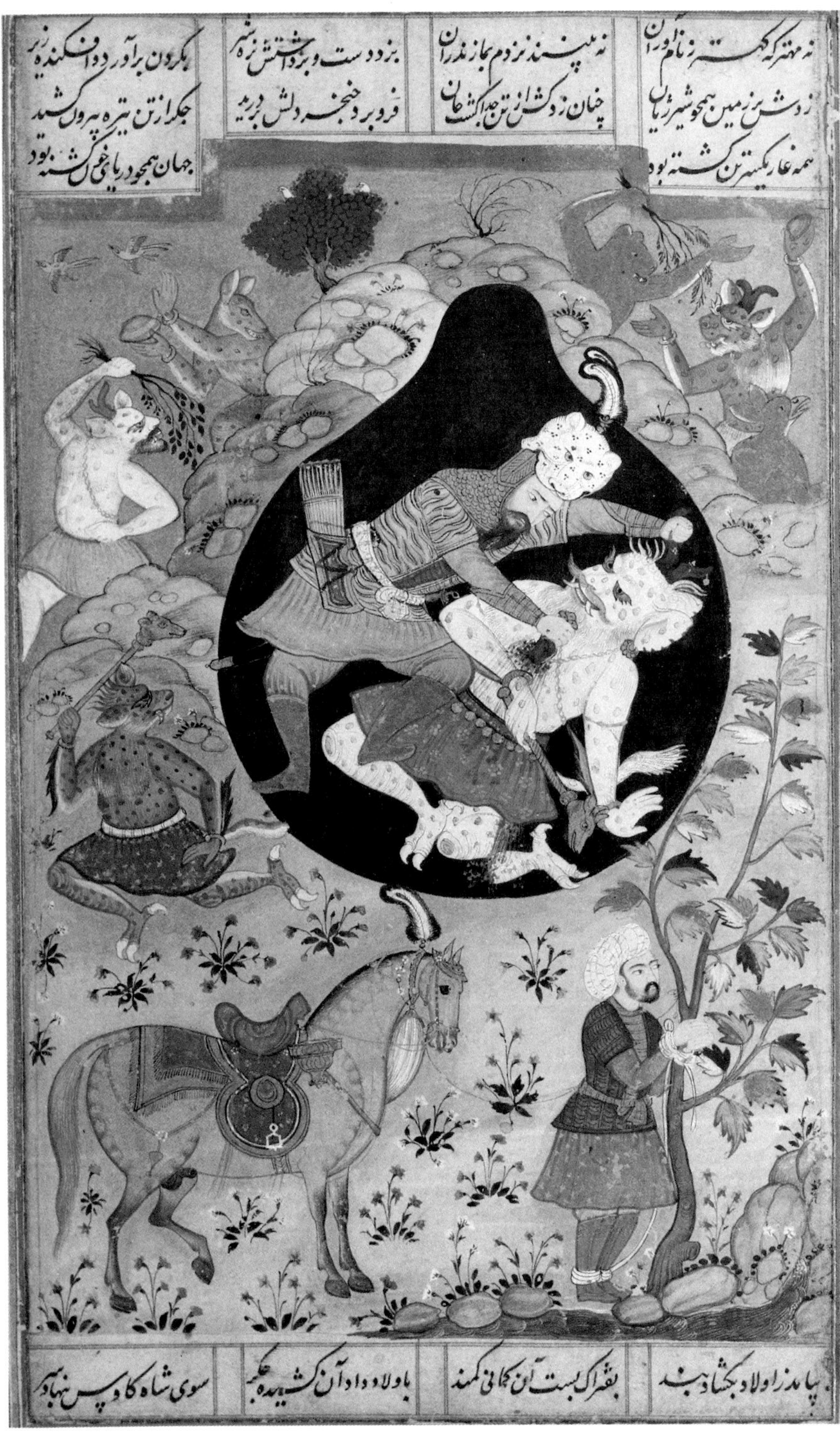

This folio is from a *Shahnama* manuscript that is said to have been copied in 1608. The whereabouts of the bulk of the manuscript are not known, but a second illustrated folio is now in the San Diego Museum of Art (Binney 1973, p. 58, no. 32). Another illustrated folio in the San Diego museum (Binney 1973, pp. 62–63, no. 37), although dated by E. Binney to about 1620, very likely belonged to the same manuscript. Both folios were correctly characterized as subimperial by Binney; the manuscript must have been commissioned by a Mughal courtier for his personal use. The colors, especially the yellow, have a different tonality than those encountered in imperial manuscripts. They seem more strident and less subtle in their application. The iconographic program as well as the composition of the picture generally follows the Persian convention, but in addition to the coloring, individual figures and motifs—such as the flowers on the ground, the stream of water, and the horse with its trappings—are recognizably Indian.

The scene represented here is Rustam's destruction of the demon, the White Div. This episode is one of seven heroic labors Rustam performed on his way to Mazandaran on behalf of King Kay Kaus, who had been taken prisoner by the White Div. In the picture the King is tied by his hands and feet to a tree. Behind him stands Rustam's favorite horse, Raksh. The cave is represented as a pear-shaped black area. Distinguishable by his helmet of a leopard head and jacket of tiger skin, Rustam thrusts his dagger into the chest of the monstrous White Div. The demon's companions surround the cave and attack Rustam in vain.

On the verso is text only.

85 TWO FOLIOS FROM A *RAZMNAMA* MANUSCRIPT

Subimperial Mughal, Jahangir period, 1610–20
From the Nasli and Alice Heeramaneck Collection, Museum Associates Purchase
A, M.75.4.27; B, M.74.5.15
Literature: *Heeramaneck* 1966, pp. 154–55, no. 213 (A only illustrated).

A *Disguised Vishnu and a Brahman*
Folio, 14⅞ x 8¾ in (37.8 x 22.2 cm)
Illustration, 14⅜ x 8⅛ in (36.5 x 20.6 cm)

B *Prince Chandrahasa and a Goddess*
Overall, 8⅞ x 9 in (22.5 x 22.9 cm)
Illustration, 7⅞ x 8¼ in (20.0 x 21.0 cm)

CAT. 85A detail

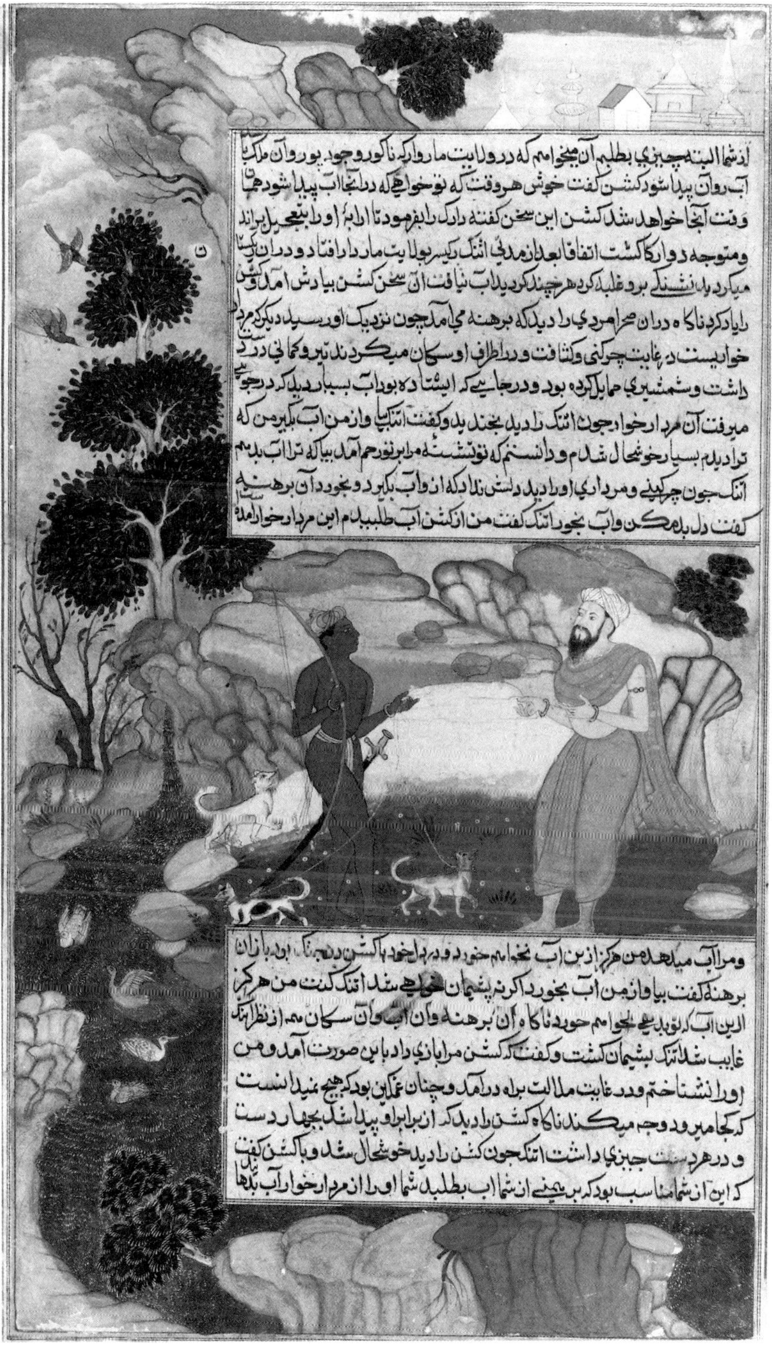

The *Razmnama* is the Persian title of the *Mahabharata,* the celebrated Hindu epic. The massive work was translated into Persian at Akbar's request, and several illustrated copies were produced for the emperor. The copy from which these folios came was prepared for Abd ar-Rahim, the Khan Khanan ("commander in chief"), one of the leading Mughal courtiers, who served both Akbar and Jahangir. As well as being an able administrator, he was a man of letters and bibliophile who had his own workshop for producing books. Like Akbar, Abd ar-Rahim was a liberal Muslim interested in Hindu literature as well. His illustrated copy of the *Ramayana,* the other Hindu epic, is now in the Freer Gallery of Art, Washington, D.C. (see Beach 1981, pp. 128–55). The copying and illustrating of that manuscript took more than a decade. Unfortunately the colophon page of the *Razmnama,* as well as much of the text, is lost. However, a few pages bear the dates 1616 or 1617, and considering that this epic is much larger than the *Ramayana,* it may have taken even longer to prepare, or may not have been completed.

The colophon of the Freer *Ramayana* clearly states that Abd ar-Rahim borrowed Akbar's copy of the *Ramayana* to be used as a model by his own artists. And in fact, many compositions of the Khan Khanan's *Ramayana* are based on the imperial copy, but the style of the paintings differs considerably. His *Razmnama,* however, seems not to have been dependent on the imperial copies. It has been suggested that the manuscript may have been prepared while the Khan Khanan was in the Deccan and hence had no access to the imperial library (Leach 1986, p. 106). In fact, he was in a number of places during the years it took to prepare this manuscript. Nevertheless, there seems little doubt that the artists of Abd ar-Rahim's *Razmnama* did use his *Ramayana* manuscript as a model, because of the similar Akbari manuscript mode of the distribution of text panels and illustrations in both. What is curious is how uninfluenced the *Razmnama* illustrations are by the prevailing Jahangir period taste, which seems to have had no effect on the Khan Khanan.

Aesthetically the pictures in this copy of the *Razmnama* are less polished and sophisticated than the illuminated manuscripts done for both Akbar and Jahangir. This difference is attributable to the Khan Khanan's needs rather than his purse. It seems that he was more interested in the text than in the illustrations. He was less discriminating than both Akbar and Jahangir in selecting his artists and probably less demanding a patron as well.

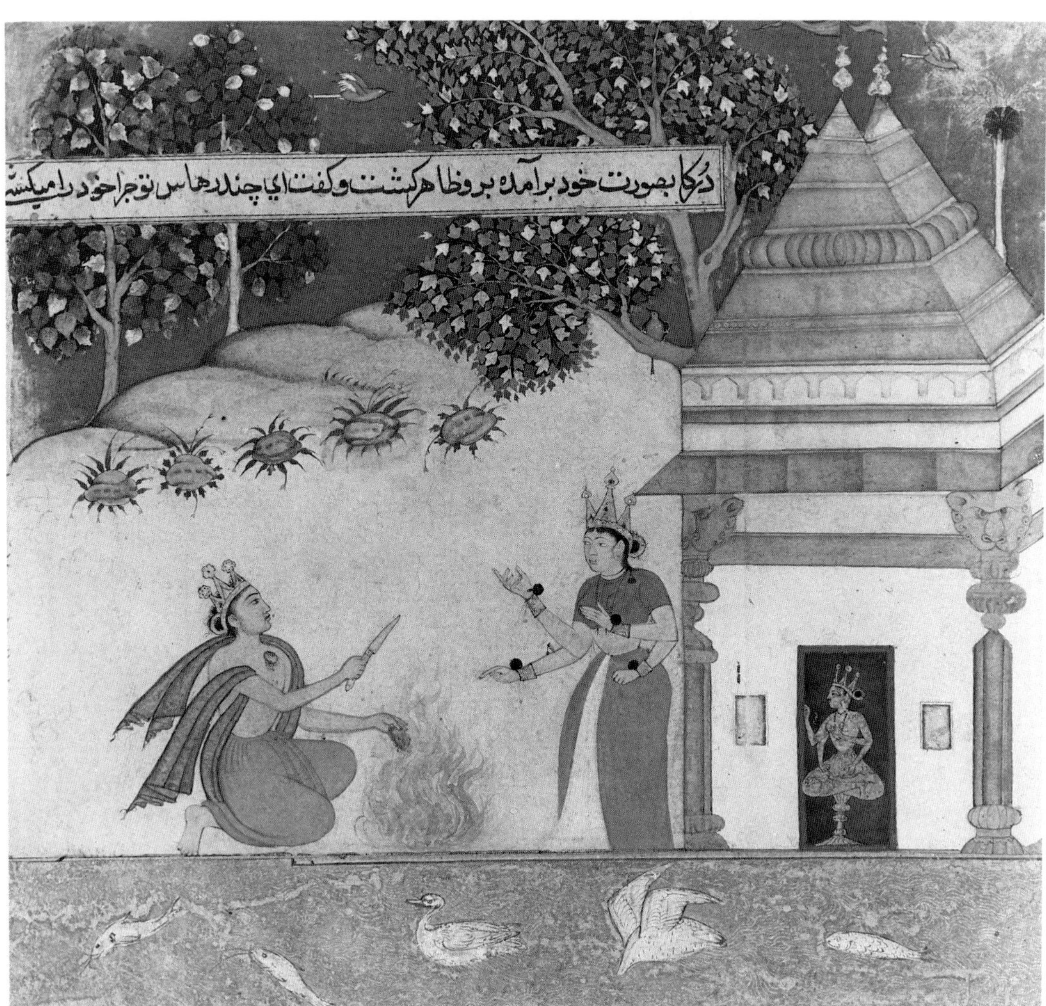

CAT. 85B detail

A This leaf has text on one side and a picture with two text panels on the other. The illustration is quite elaborate and shows two figures conversing on the bank of a stream. The story encapsulated in this picture is quite long. Once, while returning to Dwarka from Hastinapur, Krishna met the ascetic Uttanka, who prevailed upon Krishna to show him his universal form and praised the god. Krishna granted Uttanka a boon that would allow him to have water simply by thinking of Krishna. Later Uttanka became thirsty while wandering in the desert and thought of Krishna. A naked and dirty outcast (*chaṇḍāla*) carrying a sword and a bow and arrows appeared with a pack of dogs. Copious streams of water issued from his urinary organ, which he offered Uttanka. Uttanka, however, refused and the outcast disappeared. Krishna then appeared and told Uttanka that the outcast was the god Indra in disguise and had offered elixir to Uttanka. In the picture the stream of water does not appear from the outcast's urinary organ but from the earth. Moreover, instead of a desert the artist has depicted a rich landscape with vegetation and rocks of various shapes. One can also glimpse a city in the distance in the upper right corner. Birds fly across a cloudy sky and ducks swim in the stream. The dogs form a lively group, with one of them curious about the ducks.

B This page has been cropped and separated from the text that would have been on the other side. Only one line of text is incorporated in the illustration. The story is that of Chandrahasa, who has cut a piece of flesh from his chest and offers it as an oblation into the fire. A four-armed goddess whose image is shown within the shrine appears in person to dissuade the young man. In the foreground is a stream or a water tank with a pair of ducks and fishes rendered naturalistically. In contrast, the landscape is treated in rather a flat manner with little depth and with the five artificial rocks placed decoratively on the yellow ground.

Subimperial Mughal, Jahangir period, 1620–25

A *Meeting of Warriors*
Folio, 11⅝ x 7¼ in (29.5 x 18.4 cm)
Illustration, 8⅜ x 6 in (21.3 x 15.2 cm)
Gift of Gursharan and Elvira Sidhu
M.90.160.1

B *Gorgin Leads Bizhan Astray*
Folio, 10⅝ x 7¼ in (27.0 x 18.4 cm)
Illustration, 6⅞ x 4¾ in (17.5 x 12.1 cm)
Gift of Doris and Ed Wiener
M.75.52

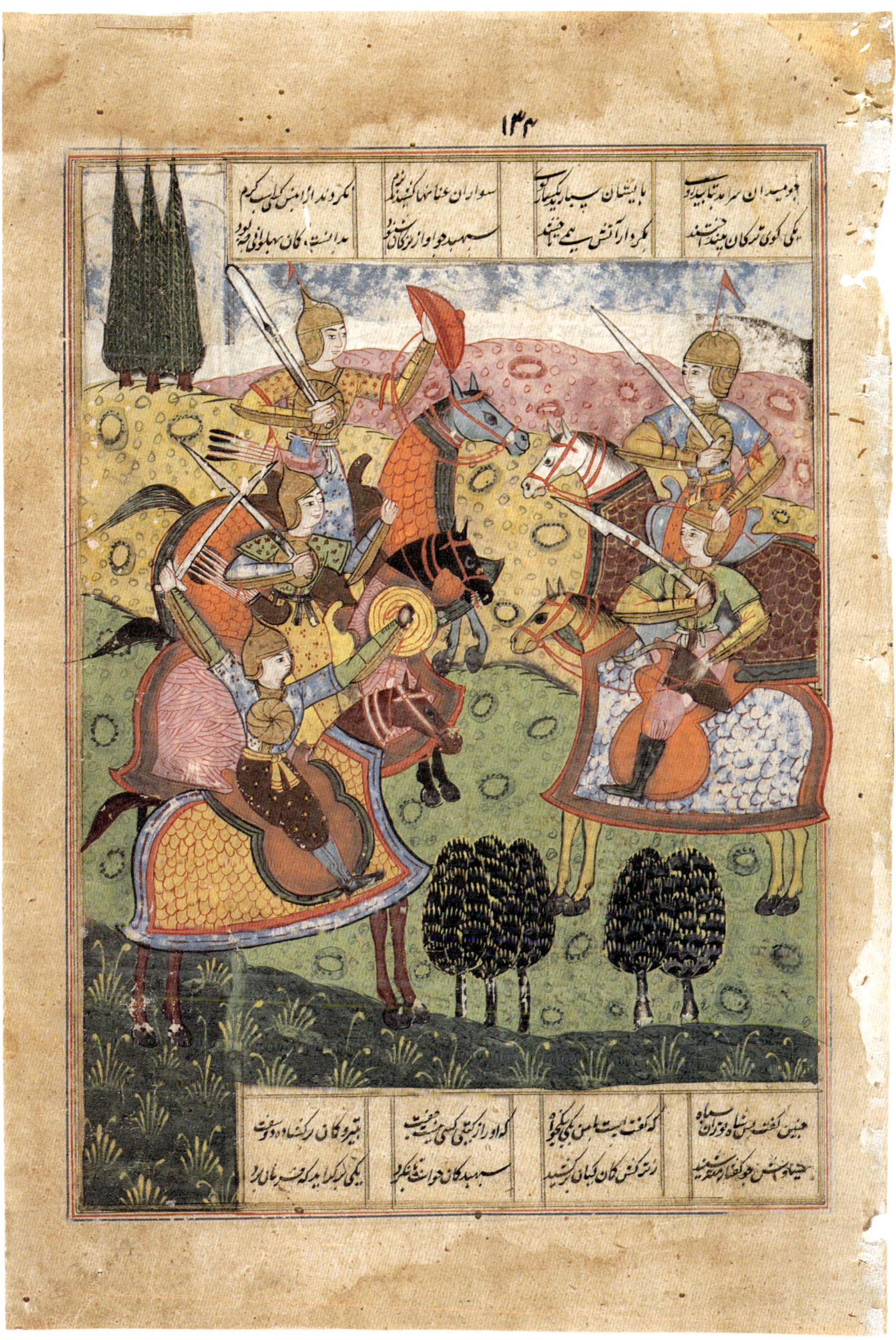

CAT. 86A

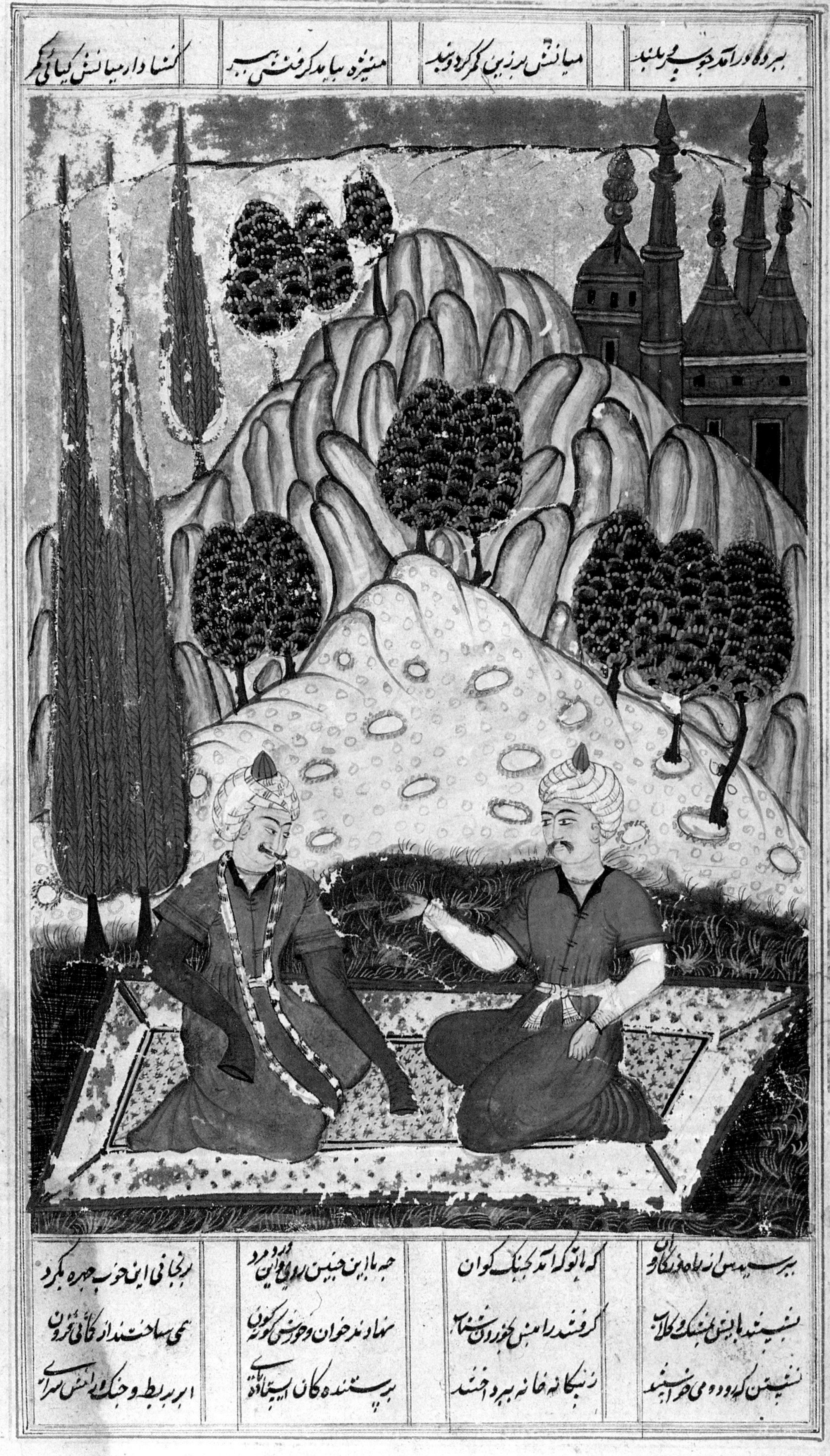

These two folios are from a dispersed manuscript of Firdausi's *Shahnama*. Each leaf comprises a page of text and a page with text and an illustration. One other illustrated folio from the same manuscript has been published (Pal 1971a, pp. 80–81, no. 36; and S. C. Welch 1973, pp. 86–87, no. 51), but the whereabouts of the rest of the leaves are not known.

A The few lines of text on the page do not help in readily identifying the scene represented. However, the chapter heading in red on the reverse does indicate that the scene is from the story of Siyavush, which constitutes the seventh book of the *Shahnama*. The two confronting armies may be those of the Iranian Siyavush and Afrasiyab, the Turanian.

The meeting takes place in a mountainous landscape with four receding layers of hills in four different colors. Two shades of green are followed by yellow and mauve. A white band separates the mauve hill from the indigo sky. Everything in the picture is depicted in a rather stiff and naïve manner, whether the trees, the legs of the horses, or the posturing of the warriors. The horses are, in fact, remarkably wooden looking. The large saddle blankets are rendered in a wide variety of colors and designs, which considerably compensates for the rigidity of the figures and the trees.

B This episode is from the tenth book of Firdausi's epic. The Armenians had petitioned the Iranian king Khusrau to rid them of wild boars that were ravaging their lands. The king offered a rich reward, and the warrior Bizhan accepted the challenge. With his companion Gorgin he went in search of the boars. After they arrived, however, Gorgin refused to help Bizhan since the latter usually received all the credit for and rewards from their joint ventures. Having exterminated the boars alone, Bizhan joined Gorgin, who then proceeded to lead his companion astray by telling him about a paradisiacal spot a day's journey away where they could capture comely maidens for the king.

In the illustration the artist has treated the subject with brevity. Gorgin and Bizhan are seated on a carpet in a meadow. Behind them rise two rather symmetrical tiers of hills. The lower hills are in white with blue boulders of different sizes and typically Indian trees, mostly on the ridges. An area of gold separates the purple hills and the band of blue sky. Although the composition was probably based on a Persian model, it lacks the imaginative asymmetry or exuberant coloring of the original. The entire mountainscape is rendered as a decorative backdrop and lacks the idyllic character of similar passages in Persian paintings.

When a few isolated leaves of this dispersed manuscript first appeared on the market about two decades ago, it was thought to belong to the Sultanate period (see Pal 1971a, pp. 80–81, no. 36; and S. C. Welch 1973, pp. 86–87, no. 51). In fact, S. C. Welch was of the opinion that the manuscript may have been copied and illustrated in Lahore in the mid-sixteenth century. Apparently these *Shahnama* pictures have some stylistic similarity with a group of "Persianized" paintings occurring in a *Darabnama* manuscript, now in the British Library, London, done for Akbar in the 1580s and with others in a recently published *Shahnama* manuscript of 1590 (Sotheby's, London, *Islamic and Indian Art—Oriental Manuscripts and Miniatures*, 29–30 April 1992, lot 354). Both R. Skelton and S. Digby have verbally questioned a Sultanate attribution and consider the manuscript to have been assembled in a provincial center sometime in the first quarter of the seventeenth century. This date seems to be consistent with the Indian elements in the illustrations and the patternization of natural forms. The trees and the grass, for instance, are more akin to those seen in Malwa pictures than in Sultanate-period paintings. The flattened, decorative treatment and the coloring show a degree of Indianization that one does not find in those Sultanate pictures in a strongly Persian style. The architectural forms in B and in the third published illustration are reminiscent of those in Deccani rather than Mughal pictures. The manuscript could have been done for a patron in central India or the northern Deccan.

CAT. 86B detail

By Muhammad Taqi
Mughal style
Ink and color
Folio, 14½ x 10½ in (36.8 x 26.7 cm)
Illustration, 9 x 6⅛ in (22.9 x 15.6 cm)
From the Nasli and Alice Heeramaneck Collection, Museum Associates Purchase
M.83.1.8
Literature: Ettinghausen 1956, fig. 16; S. C. Welch 1963, pp. 24, 163, no. 6; Khandalavala 1962, pp. 11–12, fig. c; *Heeramaneck* 1966, pp. 140–41, no. 194.

Of the four art historians who have published this lightly colored drawing (see Literature above), only Khandalavala has questioned its authenticity. On the lower left corner of the picture is inscribed the name of an artist called Muhammad Taqi, whom S. C. Welch (1963, p. 163) tentatively identified with Ali Quli, a leading artist of Akbar's atelier. However, he did not cite any reason for his suggestion. Khandalavala claims to have purchased "an exact copy [of this drawing] . . . perhaps slightly finer, bearing the signature Muhammad Aqa" and to have seen at least two more copies with signatures. While these other copies have not been published, it must be stated that other scholars who have seen the drawing have not doubted it except R. Skelton.

No other work by an Indian Muhammad Taqi is known, nor has his signature appeared in any other work in India. However, Muhammad Taqi was the name of one of the sons of Shaykh Abbasi, an Iranian artist who flourished between 1650 and 1683, first under the patronage of the Iranian monarch Shah Abbas II (r. 1642–66). Shaykh Abbasi is said to have traveled to India and may have been employed at Golconda in the Deccan. Muhammad Taqi may have accompanied his father. While in India he may have seen an Akbari picture of Dara and the herdsman and copied it as an exercise, in which case the museum's picture may be this later seventeenth-century copy of an earlier original. However, the signature here differs considerably from that in an authentic painting by Muhammad Taqi (Sotheby's, London, *Catalogue of Important Oriental Manuscripts and Miniatures,* 7 April 1975, lot 46). An alternative is that this is a still later copy of an Akbari original and the artist's name was added by the copyist. It was not uncommon in the eighteenth and nineteenth centuries to copy earlier pictures and to add names of famous masters. However, no Indian artist of any eminence by the name of Muhammad Taqi is known.

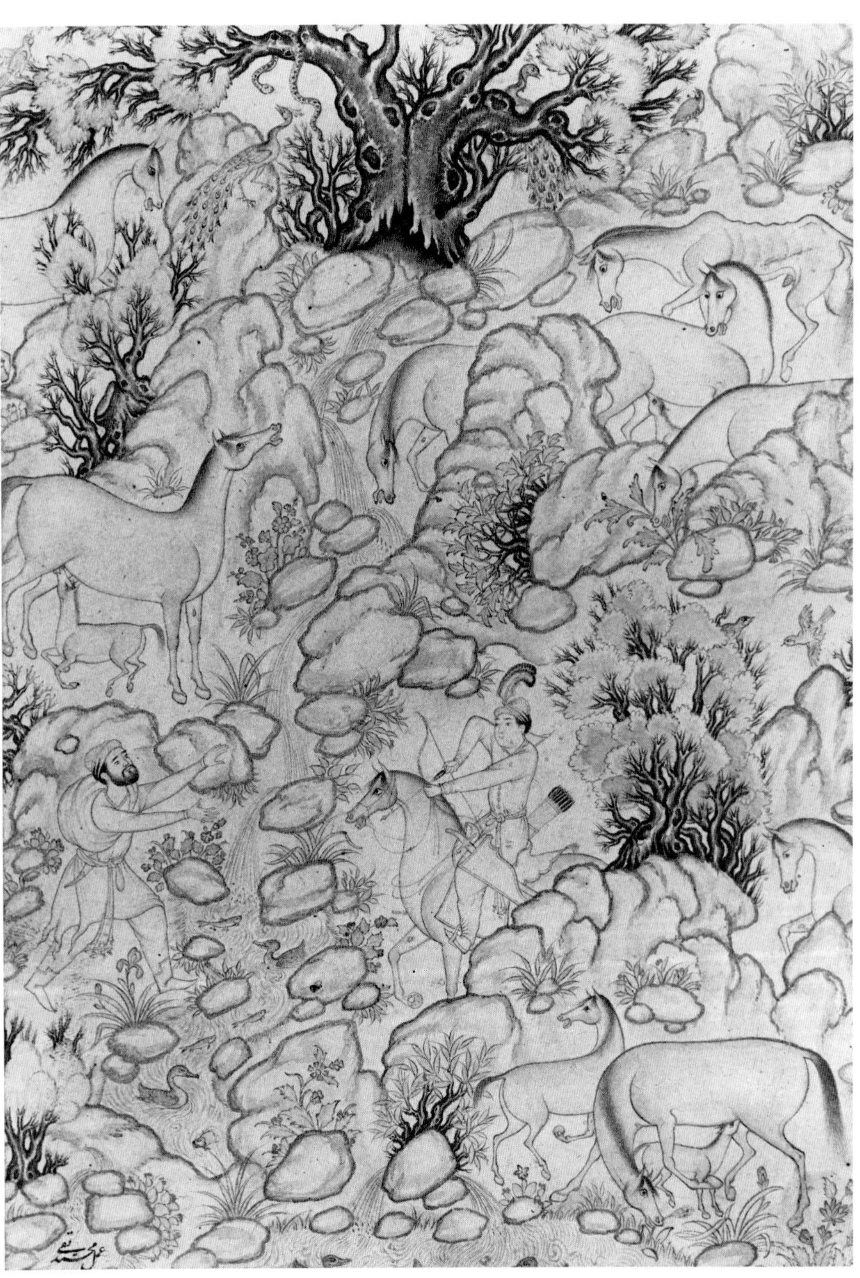

CAT. 87 detail

Popular Mughal, 1600–1625
Text in gold
Folio, 11⅛ x 5¼ in (28.3 x 13.3 cm)
Illustration and text, each, 8½ x 3⅞ in
(21.6 x 9.8 cm)
Purchased with funds provided by
Christian Humann
M.86.61.2

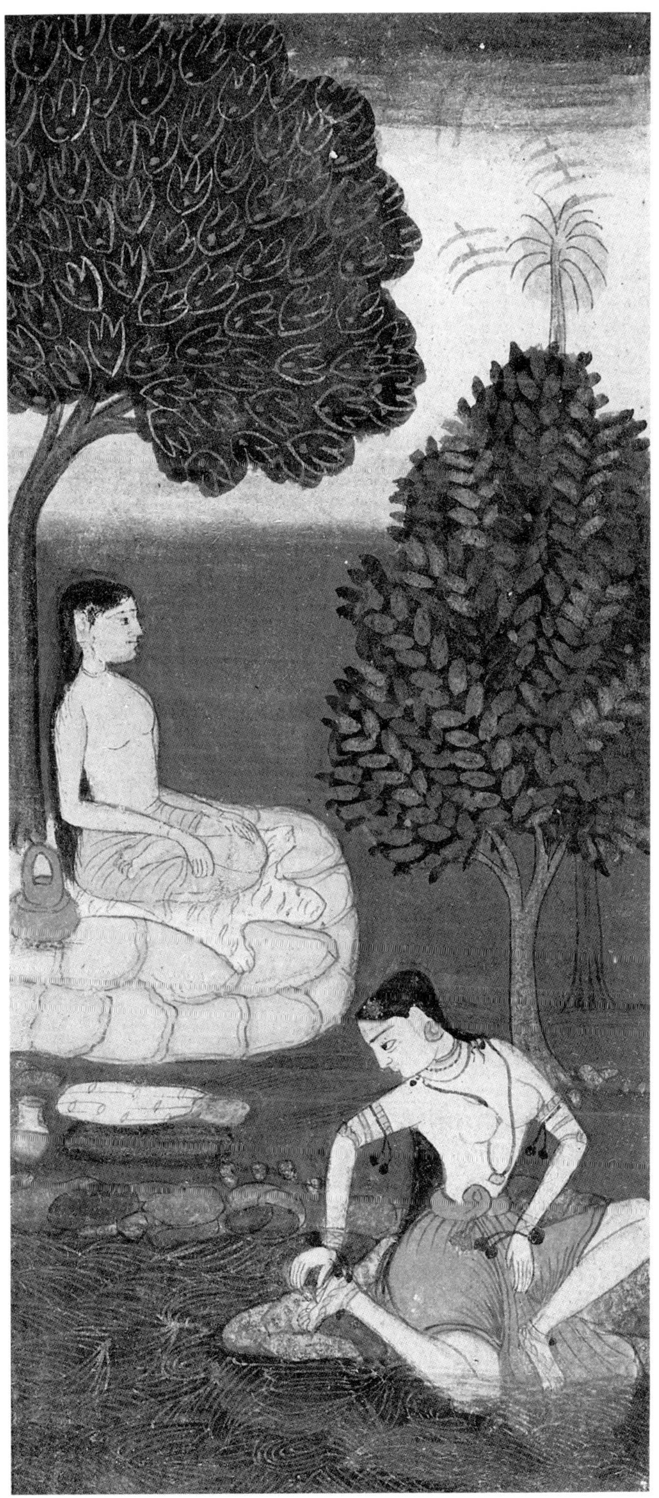

CAT. 88 detail

This leaf is from a manuscript entitled *Story of Sukra and Rambha (Sukra Rambha Samvada)*. The text is written on one side, which lacks a page number, and the illustration occurs on the other side. Both the text and the picture are contained within margins of black, gold, green, and red lines. The text is written in Devanagari script and consists of two verses and commentaries, both in Sanskrit. The verses are written in larger, bolder letters and are numbered 17 and 18. The first verse is spoken by Sukra and the second constitutes Rambha's response. The commentaries are numbered 11 and 12. Both Rambha and Sukra are well-known figures in Hindu mythology. Rambha is a celestial dancer, while Sukra is the priest of the *asuras*, or titans.

In the illustration a young ascetic is seated in meditation on a tiger skin atop a platform of boulders below a tree. It is not easy to determine the figure's sex. The face and the long hair indicate a female but the chest is flat. The second figure, about whose femininity there is no ambiguity, sits on the edge of water and seems to be attending to the sole of her right foot. She seems to be picking a thorn from her foot, which is a very ancient motif in Indian art. The ground is painted in olive green, and the sky above is yellow, white, and blue-gray.

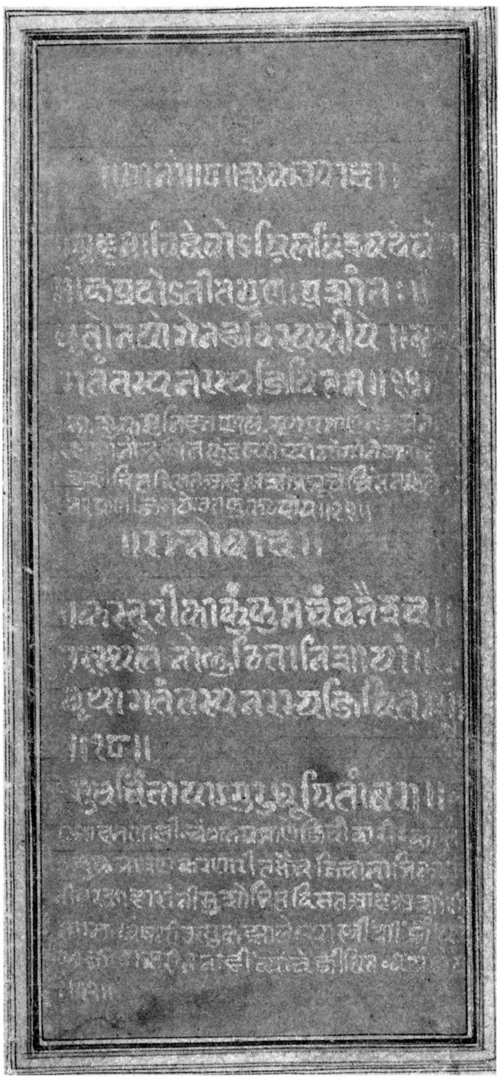

CAT. 88 text detail

The text is written in gold letters against a red ground, as one encounters in Jain manuscripts. Moreover, although both text and picture are vertically oriented, the shape and size of the folio are comparable to those of Jain manuscript leaves. The format of the manuscript, the fact that it was not bound, and the colors of the text page would indicate a western Indian origin or at least the scribe's acquaintance with Jain illuminated manuscripts. The illustration, however, does not reveal any relationship to the kind of painting that was being done in Gujarat during the first quarter of the seventeenth century, which is when this manuscript was probably prepared. A number of artists trained in the Mughal manner were employed in a wide area including Rajasthan, Madhya Pradesh, and Uttar Pradesh during this period.

The book from which this leaf came could have been made for a Hindu or a Jain patron. More likely he was Hindu who was either attached to the Mughal court or had acquired a taste for the Mughal style. The picture's style is closely comparable to a popular Mughal *Ragamala* painting in the Khajanchi Collection, Bikaner (P. Chandra 1960, fig. 18, pl. x). Recently some Pahari pictures of this theme, probably based on the manuscript to which the museum's folio belongs, have been published in a portfolio (K. Khandalavala, *A Heavenly Romance: Sukra Rambha Samvada* [New Delhi: Lalit Kalā Akademi, 1991]).

89 TWO FOLIOS FROM A *RAGAMALA* SERIES

Popular Mughal, Akbar–Jahangir period, series dated 1605/6

A *Gaudi Ragini*
Folio, 8½ x 6¼ in (21.6 x 15.9 cm)
Illustration, 6¼ x 4½ in (15.9 x 11.4 cm)
From the Nasli and Alice Heeramaneck Collection, Museum Associates Purchase
M.74.5.14
Literature: *Heeramaneck* 1966, p. 152, no. 209 (not illustrated).

B *Meghamallara Raga*
Folio, 8⅝ x 6⅜ in (21.9 x 16.2 cm)
Illustration, 6⅜ x 5 in (16.2 x 12.7 cm)
Gift of Paul F. Walter
M.86.345.1
Literature: Pal 1978, pp. 56–57, no. 5.

A The Sanskrit couplet above the picture describes the ragini as a lady whose beauty is enhanced by her splendid attire, who is adorned with a girdle of sweet-sounding bells, whose hands hold two sprays of the divine tree, and who always gives pleasure. Then follows the numeral eight and the title *Gaudi Ragini*. The second, smaller inscription on the right margin in a different hand states *guchinananga,* whose meaning is not clear; below is the numeral *8*. In the picture the female personification of Gaudi stands in the center of the composition and looks to her left. A peacock with its wings spread as if about to take off stands on the right. The bird is not mentioned in the text above. The landscape is enlivened with a stream or pool in the foreground in which are a duck and lotuses. Two cranes and several smaller birds fly across the sky.

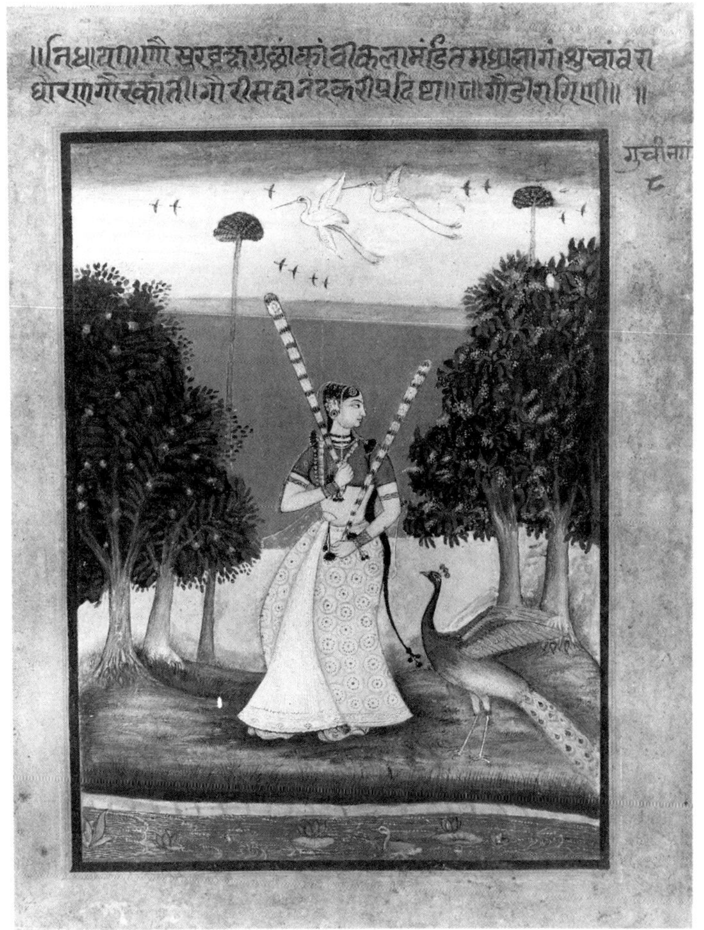

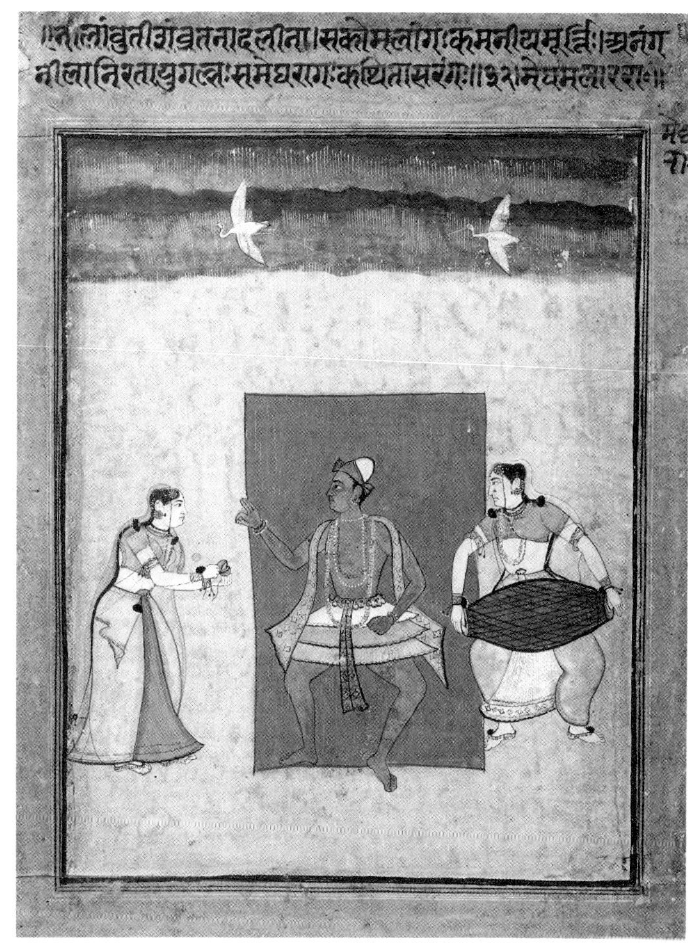

CAT. 89A *(left)*
CAT. 89B *(right)*
CAT. 89A detail *(overleaf)*

The placement of the trees provides considerable depth of field, which is a distinctive characteristic of Mughal painting. The middle band, however, is painted red, following the native tradition.

B The verse above describes Meghamallara Raga as the god of love, who is of a splendid blue complexion, of tender body and lovely form, proud as well as playful, and fond of the roar of the rain cloud. The author of the verse is Saranga, also known as Sarangadeva, who lived in the thirteenth century and composed a text on music called *Sangita Ratnakara*. In the representation Meghamallara is shown as a young male of light blue complexion dancing in the rain that comes down from the sky, which is painted in dark and light blue and across which fly two cranes. The figure of the raga is set off against a red rectangle. The background is a flat gray. The same light blue is used for Meghamallara's complexion and the sky. He wears a three-tiered short skirt of mauve, yellow, and white and a yellow shawl over his shoulders.

Four other pictures from this series are in the Museum für Indische Kunst, Berlin (Waldschmidt and Waldschmidt 1975, pp. 427–31, figs. 63, 109, 133, pl. 1). One of them is dated 1605/6. Although these pictures are characterized as popular Mughal, they in fact show a mixture of both Mughal technical sophistication with the simplicity preferred by Hindu patrons. For instance, whereas the representation of Gaudi Ragini (A) has been rendered in the more naturalistic Mughal style, in the figures are presented in a single plane against a flat background with no attempt to create any sense of pictorial space. The mode of distinguishing the central figure by a red rectangular panel is a characteristic of a contemporary *Bhagavatapurana* series generally attributed to the Rajasthani state of Bikaner (Pal 1978, p. 55, no. 4a), which is why this picture was given a Bikaneri attribution when published earlier, and a possible Bikaneri provenance should not be ruled out altogether. The Sanskrit text clearly indicates that the *Ragamala* series was produced for a Hindu patron, who probably was attached to the Mughal court.

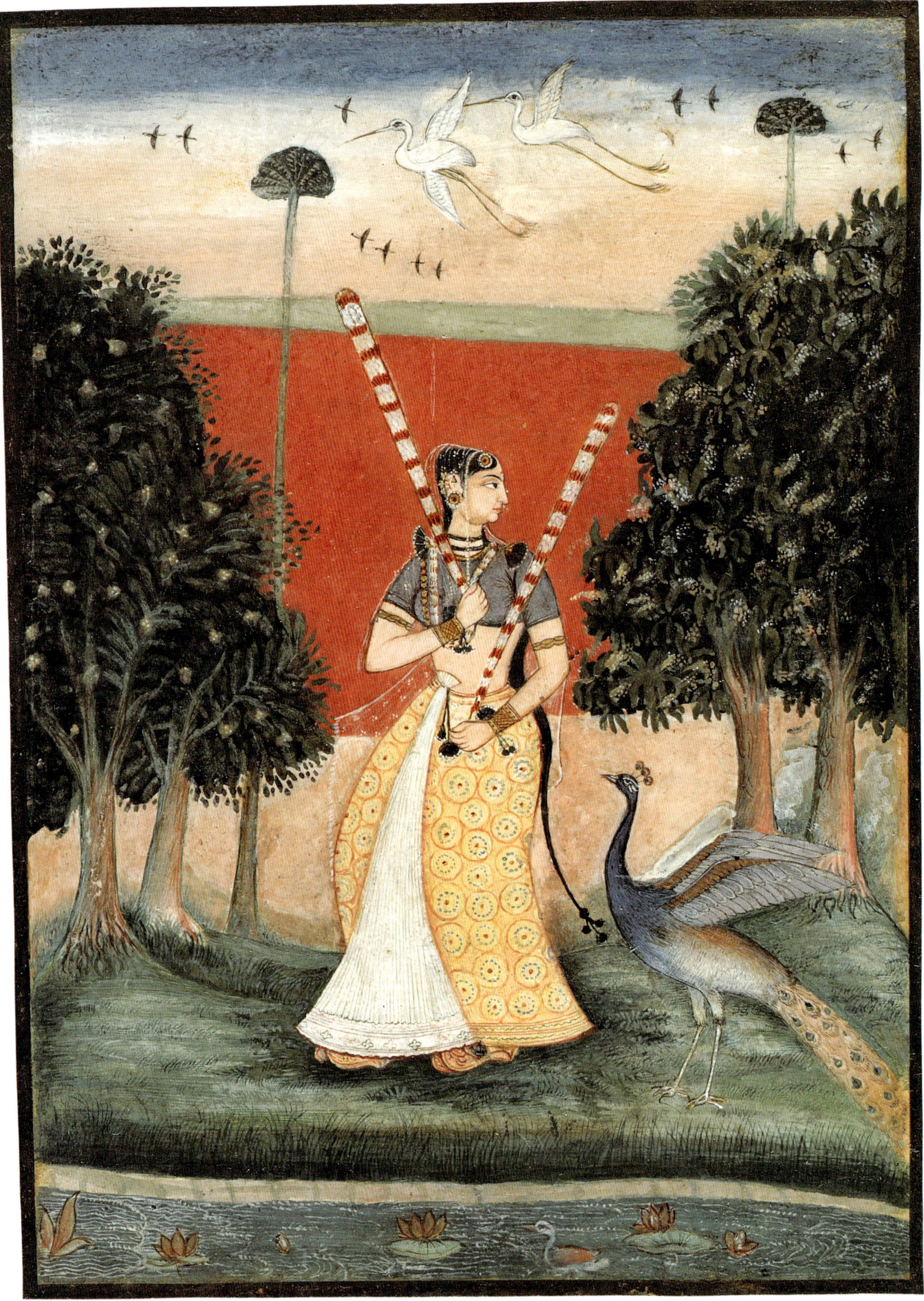

90 FOLIO FROM A *RAGAMALA* SERIES: SRI RAGA

Popular Mughal, Jahangir period, c. 1625
Text in black and red ink
Folio, 9½ x 7½ in (24.1 x 19.1 cm)
Illustration, 8⅝ x 7¼ in (21.9 x 18.4 cm)
Gift of John Ford
M.70.59

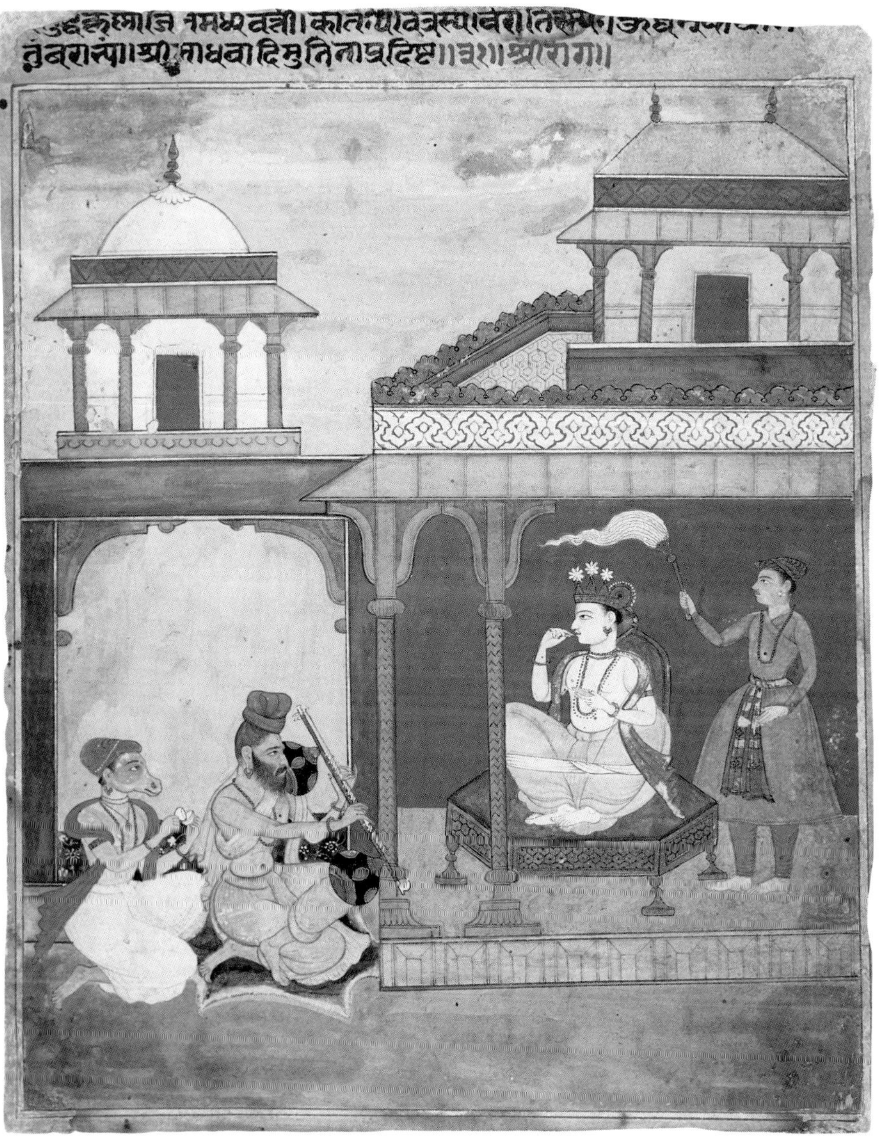

The Sanskrit verse written above the picture in black and red ink identifies the musical mode as Sri Raga and describes him as a man of matchless beauty and as lovely as the autumn moon who, seated on an elegant throne, listens to the stories sung by Narada and Tumburu. The verse is ascribed to Madhava and other sages.

Appropriately, a white-complexioned lord wearing a tiara is seated, with his legs held in position by a sash, on a throne within a pavilion. He is putting something, which he may have picked up from the shallow dish in his left hand, into his mouth, while a servant stands behind him and fans him with a flywhisk. In front the sage Narada sits on an animal skin and plays his vina. Narada is a celestial musician who also acts as a divine messenger. Behind him is the horse-headed Tumburu with a pair of cymbals. Tumburu is a semi-divine being called a *gandharva* and is given the head of a donkey or a horse. The iconography as well as the text above are fairly standard for this raga and are encountered in several Rajasthani and popular Mughal *Ragamala* series (see Ebeling 1973, pp. 118–24, 239, no. 180, for a picture with similar text and iconography).

This painting and three others from the same series in a private collection (Pal 1971b, p. 33, no. 31) are closely related stylistically to other *Ragamala* series of the early seventeenth century that are regarded as provincial or popular Mughal (Stooke and Khandalavala 1953; Khandalavala et al. 1960, figs. 26, 28; and Falk and Archer 1981, no. 64). As a matter of fact, the representation here is somewhat more flattened with local areas of color clearly demarcated. The sky is not quite as lively as one finds in most popular Mughal pictures, but the faces of Narada and the servant are rendered with finesse characteristic of the Mughal style. It is possible that the series was painted by a Mughal-trained artist for a Rajput patron in Rajasthan rather than in Delhi or Agra or other centers of Mughal painting.

Popular Mughal, Shah Jahan or Aurangzeb period, 1650–75
Ink with color
Overall, 8⅞ x 6¼ in (22.5 x 15.9 cm)
Illustration, 8½ x 6¼ in (21.6 x 15.9 cm)
Gift of Paul F. Walter
M.76.149.1
Literature: Pal & Glynn 1976, pp. 10, 11, no. 1.

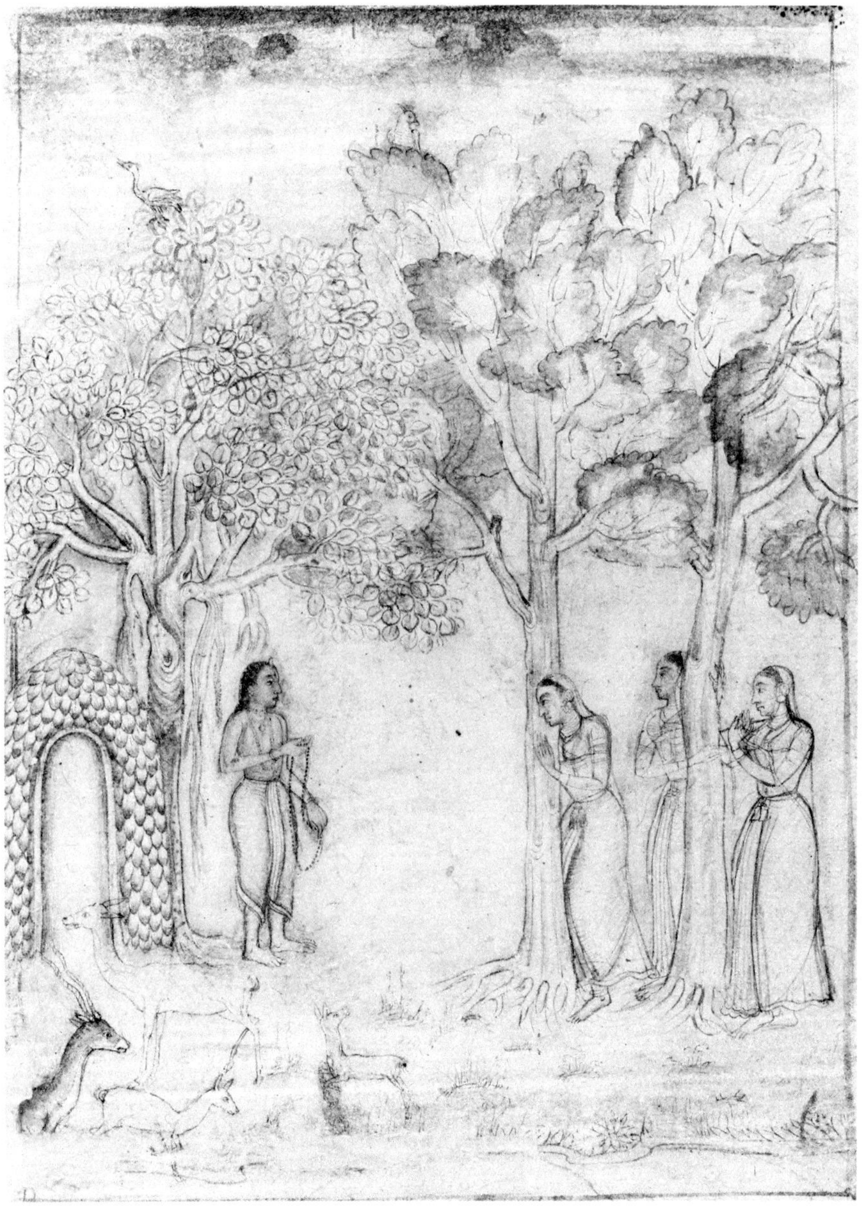

The scene represents a hermitage in the woods where a young Hindu ascetic stands before a leafy hut below a banyan tree. He holds a large rosary with both hands. A group of deer are in front of the hut, and a stream is indicated in the foreground. Three women on the right are approaching hesitantly or watching him discreetly.

A close examination of the youthful ascetic reveals that a horn projects from his forehead. Clearly therefore he represents the ascetic Rishyasringa, one of the most fascinating characters in Indian mythology. He was born with a horn because his father had once seen the nymph Urvashi and spilled his seed in the water. A doe drank the potent water and gave birth to Rishyasringa. Brought up in his isolated hermitage by his father, the young Rishyasringa led a very sheltered life and never encountered a woman. Once there was a prolonged drought in the neighboring kingdom, and the ruler was told that only Rishyasringa could bring rains. So the king sent a beautiful courtesan and her companions to bring the innocent youth to his land. The women abducted Rishyasringa and took him to the king. The drought finally ended, and Rishyasringa married the king's daughter, Santa. In this picture the artist illustrated the moment when the women approach stealthily to kidnap the young ascetic.

Whether this was intended to be a part of a series of pictures depicting this story, which is included in both the *Ramayana* and the *Mahabharata,* is not known. The Khan Khanan's *Ramayana* in the Freer Gallery of Art, Washington, D.C., contains an illustration of the tale (Beach 1981, p. 136, no. 15b) that is similar. Because of the unfinished state of the museum's illustration, one can appreciate the unknown artist's accomplished draughtmanship. Not only does the drawing reveal great verve, but judicious use of shading has made the forms both naturalistic and lively. Although not as dramatic as some of the genre scenes with ascetics that began to appear during the reign of Shah Jahan, this charming sketch is refreshingly original for its subject matter and is rendered in an expressive manner.

Northern India (?); sixteenth century
Ink on brown paper
3½ x 6⅞ in (8.9 x 17.5 cm)
Gift of Mr. and Mrs. Robert D. Mathey
M.84.224.4

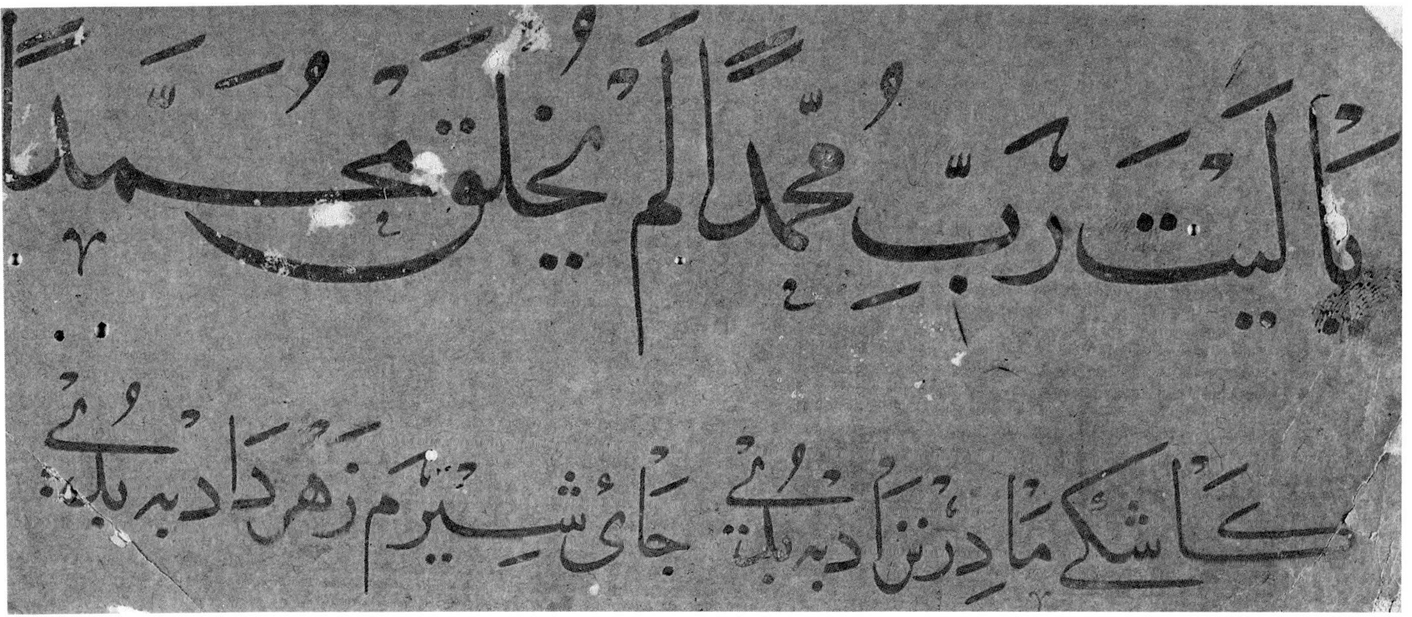

The text written in large letters in the upper line is in the Arabic language, while that in smaller letters in the lower line is in Persian. S. Digby has translated the text as follows:

Upper line
Would that Muhammad's God had not created Muhammad!

Lower line
Would that {my} mother had not given birth: it would have been better would that she had given me poison instead of milk! It would have been better.

According to Digby there are errors of grammar in both the Arabic and the Persian. The poet responsible for the text is not known, but his cynical mood is transparent in his composition.

The script is the *thuluth,* which was used frequently on Indian Islamic buildings for monumental calligraphy because of its dignified appearance and well-proportioned and uniformly thick letters. Although the calligraphy in this example is not of high quality, especially when compared with the best examples of Persian calligraphy, it is a rare specimen of sixteenth-century *thuluth* script from Mughal India.

Calligraphy by Shamsa Kashmiri
Rajasthan, Ajmer; dated A.H. 1024, A.D. 1615
Black and red ink and gold
Folios, 8 x 5 1/8 in (20.3 x 13.0 cm)
Texts, 4 1/4 x 2 3/8 in (10.8 x 6.0 cm)
Covers, 8 1/4 x 5 5/16 in (21.0 x 13.5 cm)
Indian Art Special Purpose Fund
M.87.21

A *Opening Pages*
B *Colophon Page with Seals*

This volume has eight folios with fourteen pages of text inset in central bordered panels. The first page has irregular calligraphy and three round seal stamps. No illustrations. There are five lines of text in black and red ink per page, except for page two, which has a heading in red and three lines of text in black and three lines in red ink. The text is written on buff paper; around it are narrow bands of gold, ink, and white pigment. There are four instances of marginal notes or addenda. The text insets are mounted onto coarser tan paper, which has been lengthened, widened, and repaired in places. Numerous worm holes are evident. The covers of cardboard covered in red fabric and black leather with gold embellishment are from the nineteenth century. The inside of the back cover has an Arabic inscription in gold leaf.

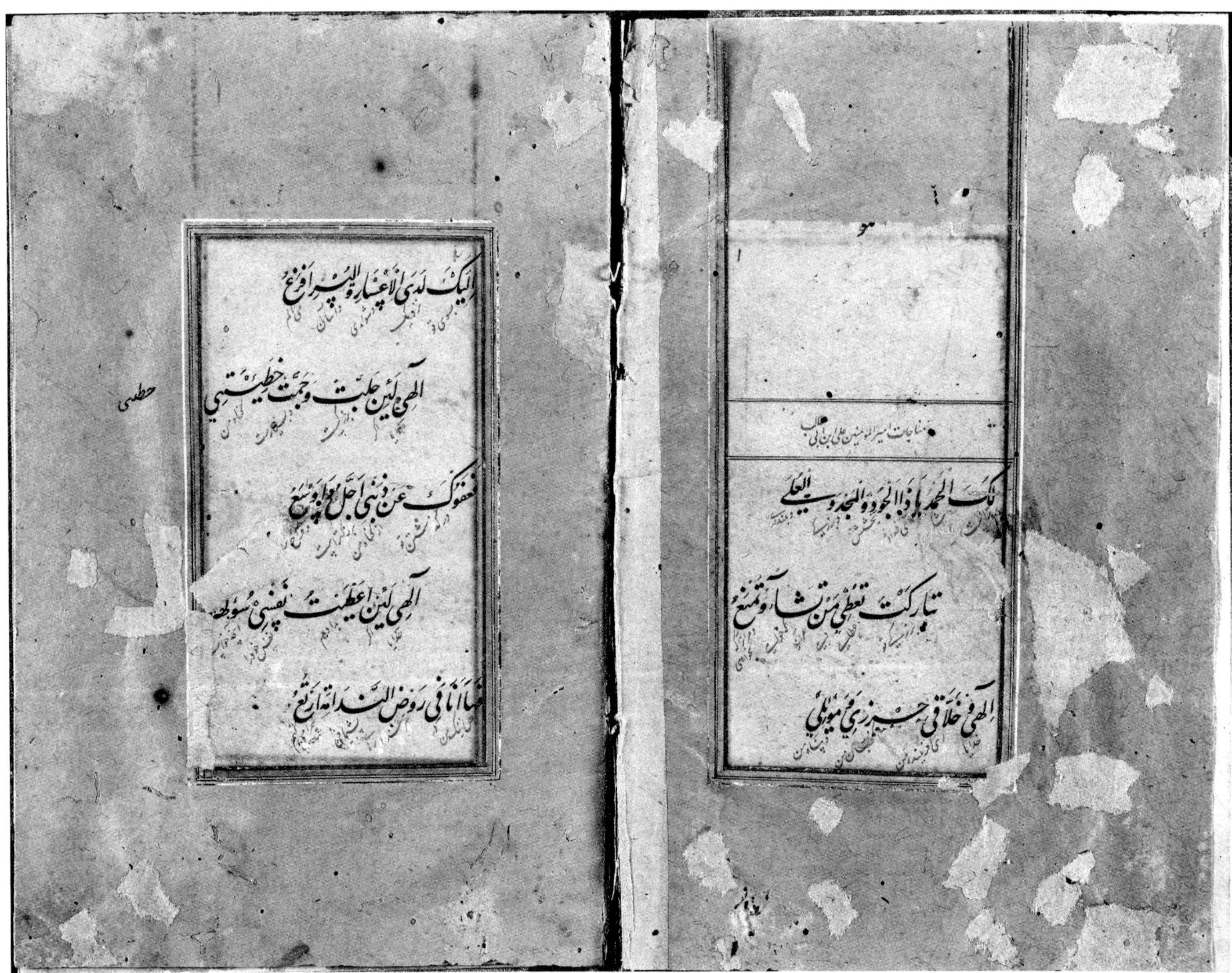

CAT. 93A

The script used is the *nastaliq*. The text is of the *munajat* (silent and fervent prayer) to Ali, with the Arabic in black ink and Persian translations in red below it. The colophon informs us that the book was copied on the eleventh of Jumada II in the Hijra year 1024 (A.D. 8 July 1615) at the tomb of Khwaja Mu'in al-Haqq wa'd-Din (Muin ad-Din Chishti) by "the needy, the little, the sinner Shamsa Kashmiri." Nothing is known of Shamsa except that he was from Kashmir and presumably had settled in Ajmer at the shrine of the Chishti saint or was a visitor there.

Among the various notes contained on the first page, the owner's name is given as Muhammad Yusuf, who declares himself to be a disciple or follower of Nur ad-Din Jahangir Shah. On 16 September 1632 the book was presented by the owner, presumably to Shah Jahan's library, as there are notations that say Shah Jahan saw the book three times, on 17 April 1635, 24 May 1637, and, finally, during August-September 1639. There is a seal giving the following information: "Nizam al-Mulk, the devoted slave of Muhyi ad-Din [A.H.] 1133" (A.D. 1720/21). This Nizam al-Mulk may well be the founder of the Asafiya dynasty of Hyderabad (1671–1748). He was the Mughal viceroy in the Deccan in 1720/21 and may have received the book as a present from Emperor Muhammad Shah (r. 1719–48). *Muhyi ad-Din* ("reviver of the faith") was part of the reign name of Aurangzeb (r. 1658–1707) as well as being the name of Ibn Arabi, the great Sufi mystic (1165–1240), and one wonders if Nizam al-Mulk might not have been a follower of his.

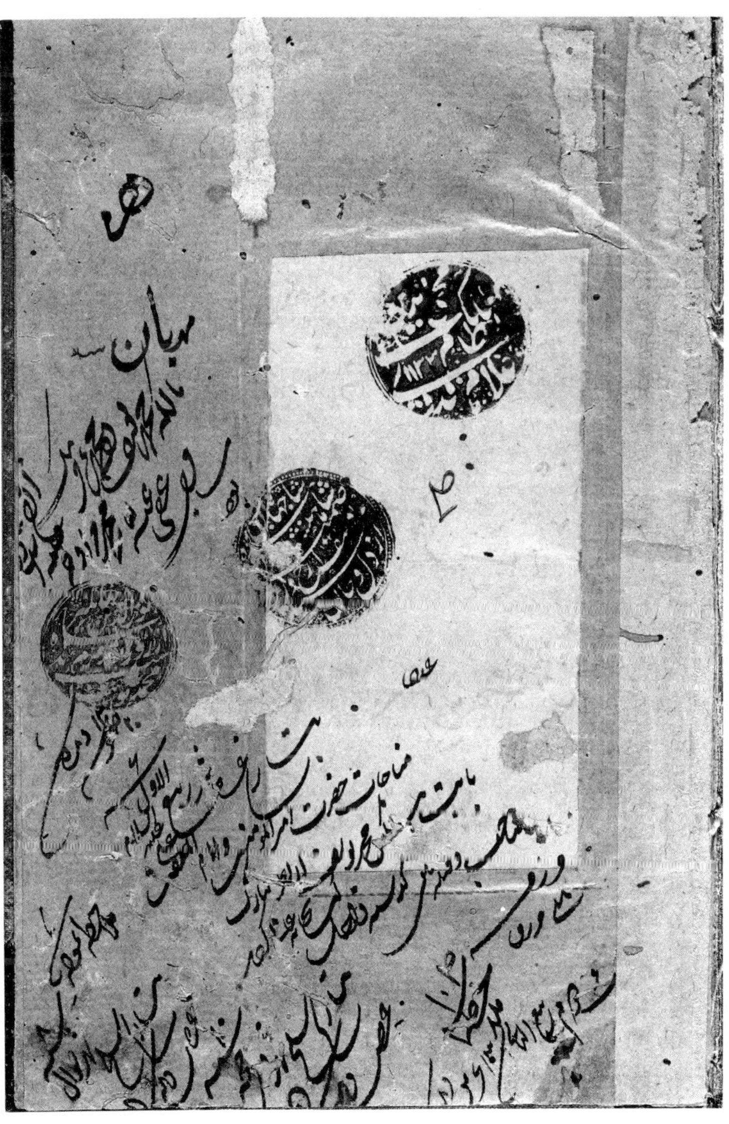

CAT. 93B

94 TESTIMONIAL LETTER

Aurangzeb period, dated A.H. 1095, A.D. 1684
With border, 18¼ x 7⅞ in (46.4 x 20.0 cm)
Text, 10¾ x 4⅜ in (27.3 x 11.1 cm)
Indian Art Special Purpose Fund
M.85.37.1

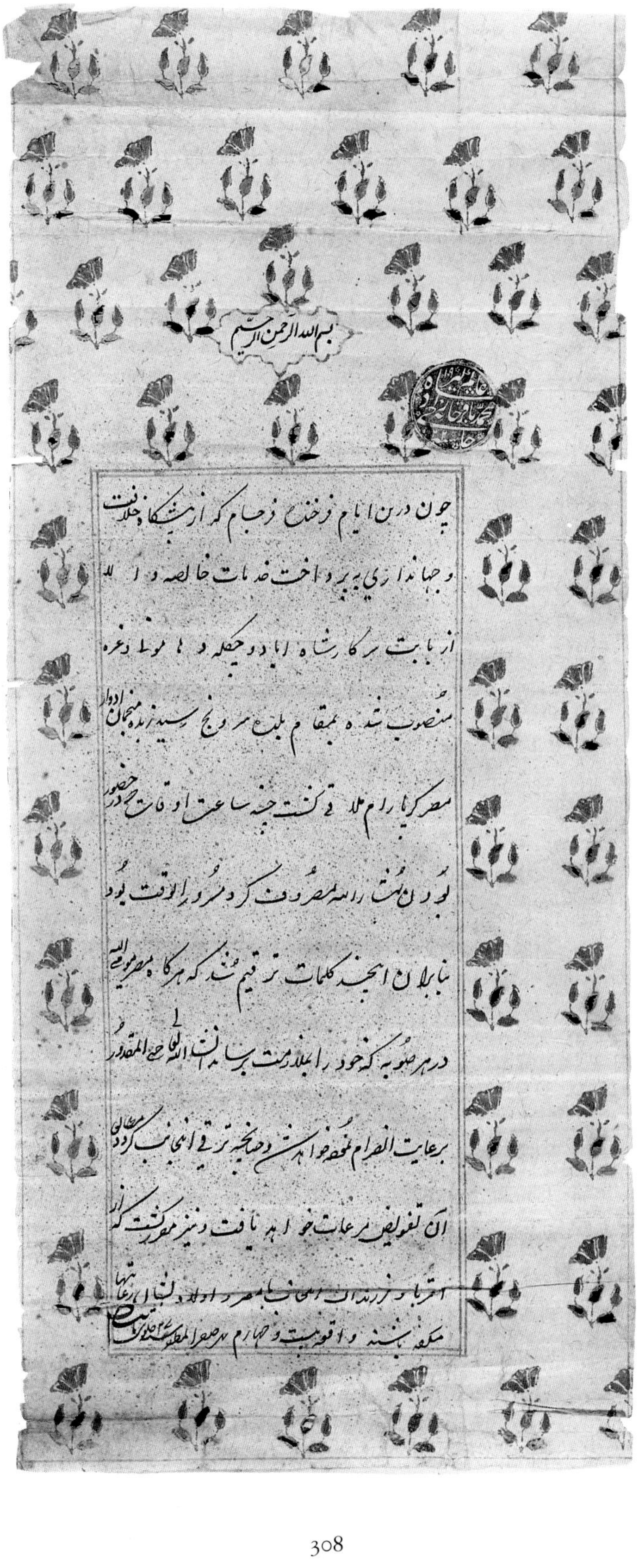

As read and translated by Z. A. Desai, the seal and the text of the letter are as follows:

SEAL

Haji Muhammad Baqir, house-born servant of Shah Alamgir {regnal} year 22, {A.H.} 109{0} {A.D. 1679/80}

TEXT

When in these days of happy ending, proceeding from the forecourt of caliphate and sovereignty on {way to take charge of} the duties of the royal Khalisa *lands relating to the* Sarkar *of Shahabad and* chakla *Dhamoni {in Madhya Pradesh}, I reached Sironj {Madhya Pradesh}, the cream of astronomers of ages Misra Kirpa Ram met me. The few hours of time that passed in the company of the aforesaid, I thoroughly enjoyed them. Consequently, these few words have been written so that any time the said Misra comes to {meet me} in any province, God willing as far as possible, he will be shown consideration, and, when I get promotion, he will also receive {further} consideration accordingly. And it is also resolved that from my kinsmen and offspring also, {everyone} will show favors to Misra and his offspring. This took place on the twenty-fourth of the month of victorious Safar, {regnal} year 27.*

The regnal year 27 cited in the text is A.H. 1095, and 24 Safar 1095 corresponds to A.D. 12 February 1684.

This testimonial letter was written on behalf of an esteemed Hindu astrologer of Sironj in Madhya Pradesh by the Mughal administrator Haji Muhammad Baqir, who also claims to have been house-born, that is, his father too served the Mughal court, where the letter-writer was born. He may have written the letter himself but more likely dictated it to a scribe and endorsed it with his seal. The script is the *nastaliq*. It is interesting to note how even an ordinary letter has been mounted and decorated with a floral border as if it were an album leaf (compare the border with that of [80]).

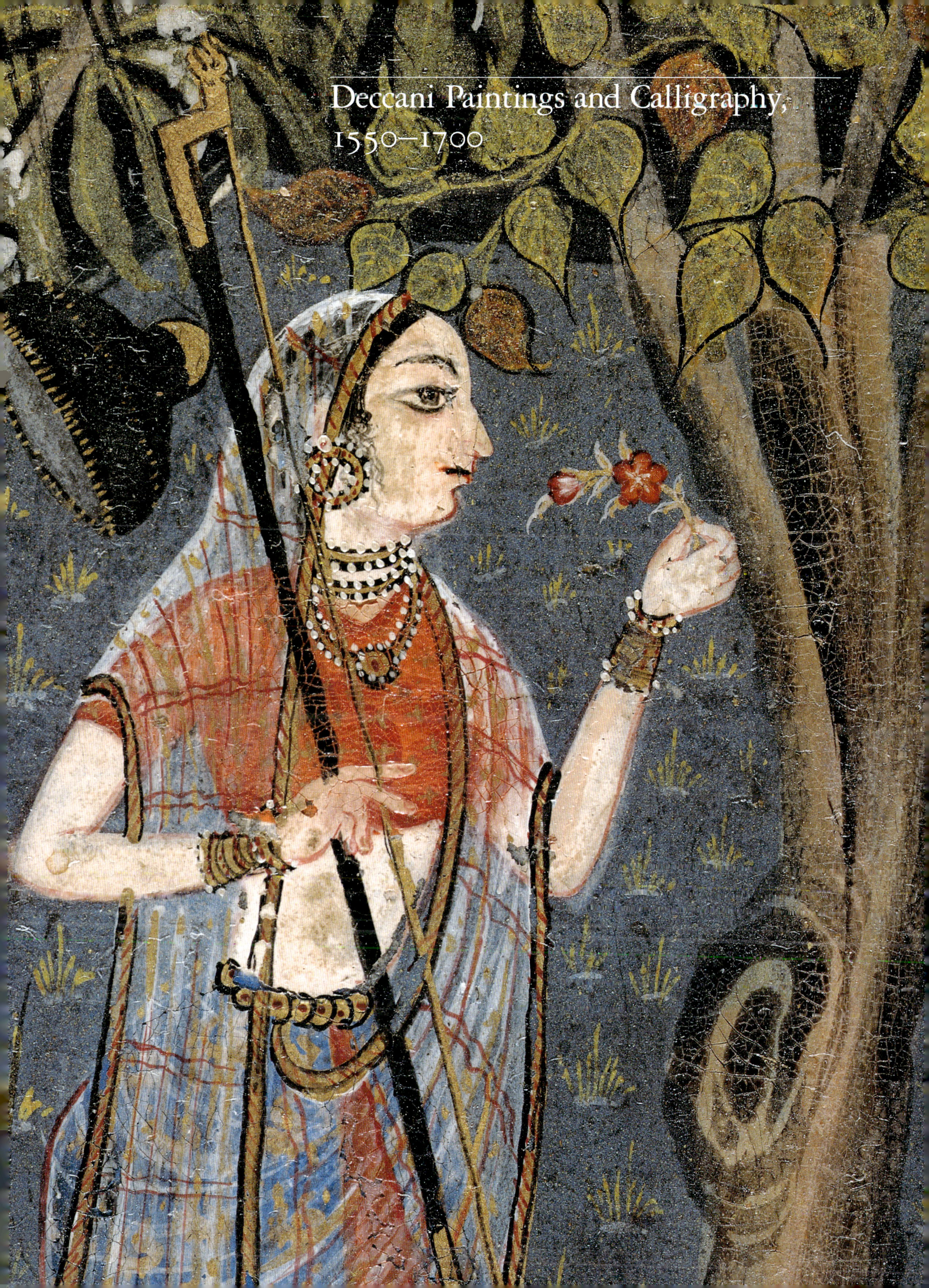

Deccani Paintings and Calligraphy, 1550–1700

Although the background of both {the Mughal
and Deccani} schools was Safavid Persian,
each created a new world of art:
dynamic, tangible, realistic, a world teeming
with action in conquered space, in the Mughal studio;
a kingdom of sated nostalgia, abandoned to
scents and dreams, lingering in flowers,
glowing in colors, calm and deep, in the Deccan.
In this world of enchantment, modeled bodies,
voluminous garments, and inserts of
European distant views occupy or float in a
picture space of deep tenderness.[1]

Introduction

The first Muslim kingdom in the Deccan was founded by an officer of the Delhi sultan in 1347. From his title Bahman Shah, the dynasty came to be known as the Bahmanid dynasty. Toward the end of the fifteenth century five governors in the Bahmanid realm rebelled and established five separate sultanates, only three of which survived. These were Ahmadnagar, Bijapur, and Golconda, which flourished until Ahmadnagar was absorbed into the Mughal empire in 1600 and the other two in 1686 and 1687, respectively.

The founder of Ahmadnagar, Ahmad Nizam Shah Bahari I (r. 1490–1510), was one such rebellious Bahmanid governor and the son of a Hindu slave who had converted to Islam. Yusuf Adil Shah of Bijapur belonged to the Ottoman dynasty of Istanbul and was a political refugee. Quli Qutb Shah, the founder of Golconda, was a Black Sheep (*Qara Qoyunlu*) Turkman prince who had fled to India for political reasons. It is therefore not surprising that the courts of Bijapur and Golconda should have been partial to the cultures of Turkey and western Iran. They also attracted large communities of Turks, Iranians, Arabs, and Africans for both commerce and cultural enrichment, and hence these foreign elements have remained a strong presence in Deccani courts and societies.

The early history of painting in these kingdoms, founded at different times, is obscure, as few works earlier than about 1550 can be attributed to the region. However, considering the interests and tastes of many of the rulers, it is difficult to believe that they were indifferent to painting. For instance, writing about the second Adil Shahi Sultan of Bijapur, Ismail (r. 1509–34), the historian Ferishta commented: "He was an adept in the arts of painting, varnishing, making arrows and embroidering saddle-cloths. In music and poetry he excelled most of his age. He was fond of the company of learned men and poets, numbers of whom he munificently supported at his court. . . . He was fonder of the Turkish and Persian manners, music and language, than the Decanny: he seldom made use of the latter tongue."[2]

If this description of Ismail's cultural accomplishments and inclinations is no exaggeration, then one can assume that a royal workshop must already have been established in Bijapur by the founder of the kingdom. How else could his successor have learned to paint, presumably when he was a child? No less interesting is Ferishta's claim that Ismail preferred the Iranian and Turkish manners to the Indian. Most surviving illuminated books of the third quarter of the sixteenth century, from both Bijapur and Golconda, such as al-Qazwini's work in the collection [95], either directly imitate imported styles or are strongly influenced by them. It is interesting to note that while a Deccani artist was illustrating the al-Qazwini manuscript in 1570, others from the region were busy contributing to the *Hamzanama* at the Mughal court at Agra. The taste for exotic styles appears to have continued in the Deccani kingdoms well into the seventeenth century, even though recognizably Deccani styles had emerged earlier.

The majority of the examples of Deccani pictures and calligraphy of the Mughal period in the collection are from either Bijapur or Golconda. Only one painting [112] has been attributed to the third Deccani sultanate, Ahmadnagar, although scholarly opinion on it is not unanimous. With two, or possibly three, exceptions all the Deccani paintings belong to the seventeenth century. The exceptions are two illustrated folios from an Islamic book probably produced about 1570 [95], a slightly later *Gauri Ragini* [112], and a *Female Ascetic* [96A].

The book, an *Ajaib al-Makhluqat* (Wonders of creation and oddities of existence) of al-Qazwini, was copied and illustrated in Bijapur. At the time it was made, the Akbari studio in the north was creating the Mughal style of painting. Unlike the *Hamzanama,* the 1570 Bijapuri book is not painted in an innovative style but, like the Sultanate-period *Khamsa* [41], harks back to West Asian paintings of an earlier period. The style of the *Ajaib* illustrations has little to do with Bijapuri painting of the period, as seen in several illustrated manuscripts rendered for Ali Adil Shah I (r. 1557–79), who did establish an atelier to produce books. Instead it shows close similarities with the late-fourteenth-century West Asian manuscripts of the same text, particularly with the Sarre manuscript. In fact, the two manuscripts have the same conflations of subject matter, and there can be little doubt that the Bijapuri artist had at his disposal either the Sarre manuscript or another like it to use as a model. Whether the artist was an Iranian or an Indian is less easy to discern. The more crudely rendered illustrations from another *Ajaib* manuscript [113] done a century later than the Bijapuri one reflect the Deccani artists' continued dependence on earlier foreign models.

That Iranian art should have served as a paradigm for Deccani patrons is not surprising. As in the northern courts, so also in those in the Deccan—Iran was the role model for social behavior as well as cultural matters. The Deccan still remains the most important center of Arab learning on the subcontinent.

There are other works in the collection besides the al-Qazwini manuscript that either show direct Iranian influence or reflect their patrons' highly Persianized taste. While a *Shahnama* illustration [97A] does reveal Indian characteristics despite its strong Persian flavor, there is disagreement among scholars about the origins of two other pictures. If the *Youth Dressed in Green* [98] was rendered in Bijapur, an artist trained in Safavid Iran must have been responsible for painting it. Similarly, although some scholars attribute the charming picture of a delicate dancing lady [105] to either Turkey or the Mughal north, it was probably painted in Golconda, where at least one artist working early in the seventeenth century appears to have been fond of copying conventional Safavid subjects.[3] In fact, one finds that during the sixteenth and the first half of the seventeenth century both strongly Persianized and distinctively local styles existed concurrently in all three Deccani kingdoms.

Of the three, information about Ahmadnagar is the most meager. Not only was the school short-lived, little of its output has survived. Only one picture in the collection is attributed to Ahmadnagar [112], although M. Zebrowski prefers a northern Deccani provenance for it. Representing a musical mode, this vivacious picture does exhibit stylistic features seen in Ahmadnagar painting, in particular in a manuscript prepared for the court early in the reign of Murtaza Nizam Shah I (r. 1565–88).

Whether produced in Ahmadnagar or in the northern Deccan, it represents the Deccani pictorial tradition at its best. With its vibrant coloring and unusual treatment of natural forms, *Gauri Ragini* epitomizes a romantic world where the lyrical mood is more important than realistic representation. This is expressed as much by the humans portrayed as by the forms of nature, which are often fanciful creations. The effusively whimsical rendering of nature clearly apparent in the candylike outcrops along the lower section of the *Gauri Ragini* was to remain a distinguishing characteristic of Deccani painting even after contact with the more naturalistic Mughal tradition during the last quarter of the seventeenth century. Deccani artists never quite surrendered their penchant for visionary landscapes with phantasmal, exuberant, or even turbulent rock and cloud formations; for the bold distortion of shapes and forms to create configurations of fantasy rather than reality; for flat but lively compositions; for highly stylized but luxurious foliage; and for luminous, sensuous colors. Some of these elements reflect a continuous admiration for West Asian pictorial traditions among Deccani patrons. As Zebrowski summed up, "the delicate rhythms of Persia, the lush sensuality of Southern India, the restraint of European and Ottoman Turkish portraiture all contributed" to the uniqueness of the Deccani aesthetic.[4] Despite the fact that the three kingdoms were politically independent, there was good deal of cultural exchange among them. Although the styles developed at the courts are recognizably different, they have in common the basic traits of Deccani painting enumerated above. It is not unlikely that artists moved about freely among the three states in search of patronage.

Several of the Deccani paintings in the collection once belonged to albums that perhaps were assembled in the eighteenth century. As was the case in the Mughal tradition, usually an album leaf consists of a portrait on one side and a page of calligraphy on the other. Some of the portraits are of rulers, although not necessarily taken from life, while others are of nobles or religious leaders. The earliest album leaf has not strictly a portrait but a fine representation of a yogini [96A], a subject that was especially popular in Bijapur. Most portraits in the collection, whether from Bijapur or Golconda, are fairly straightforward depictions with both Deccani and Mughal features. Two of the Bijapuri portraits depict Muhammad Adil Shah [99A, 100B], and a third portrays Ibrahim Adil Shah II [101]. While the former two may have been done during the ruler's lifetime, the latter is certainly a posthumous portrait, probably based on an earlier model. Although not as sumptuous and elaborate as the well-known sixteenth-century portraits of Ibrahim Adil Shah, it is more characteristically Deccani than the other two. For instance, the ruler is depicted with a swagger that is typically Deccani, as also are the three-quarter view of the face, the absence of the nimbus found in contemporaneous Mughal royal portraits, a greater idealization of the features, and the interest in details of attire, which is of a local design.

By contrast, the influence of Mughal portraiture is evident in both portraits of Muhammad Adil Shah. In the group picture [99A] the strict profile representation, the formal and somewhat stiff posture, as well as the halo, are adaptations of Mughal conventions. However, the inclusion of a boy (in others it may be a woman) holding a spittoon, or more commonly a cloth fan, is characteristically Deccani and is seen in the Golconda portraits of rulers [103E,F,G] as well as other regal figures [107, 114]. The representations of the rulers in the Golconda manuscript [103] are clearly imaginary, and they differ from the others in the collection in their attempts at flattering portrayals. Most of the other late-seventeenth-century Golconda portraits [106, 110A, 111B] are strongly Mughal in their simple composition, the coloring of the background, and a strong emphasis on capturing the likenesses of the subjects. The increase in Mughal influence at this time is not surprising given the fact that in the mid-1680s Aurangzeb finally gained control of the Deccan. Mughal influence is also evident in the depiction of Rai Jabha Chand [108], but the rest of the picture shows typically Deccani characteristics.

Like other cultured Muslim patrons, those in the Deccan were highly appreciative of examples of calligraphy. Although none of the examples in the collection is by a well-known Iranian master, as one finds in imperial Mughal albums, at least two appear to have been done by calligraphers of some renown [100A, 110B], as is indicated by their titles. It is difficult, however, to determine whether they were Indians or foreigners. One of the examples of calligraphy [109] is by Abul Baqa al-Musavi, who was a court calligrapher of the Mughal Emperor Aurangzeb, but nothing else is known about him. He may have been in the Deccan at the time he copied this piece, or it may have been done farther north and collected by an admirer in the Deccan. With one exception all the examples of calligraphy are in the *nastaliq* script, which obviously was the most popular in the Deccani courts as it was with the Mughals. The exception is a page of the more cursive and whimsical *shikasta* script done by Nadir al-Zaman [100A]. It is a rare and handsome example of the aesthetic use of this script. It should be noted that little work has been done on Deccani calligraphy.

This brief introduction of the museum's holdings of Deccani paintings and calligraphy may be brought to a close with a few words about marbled paper, which appears to have had particular attraction for local patrons. Examples of marbled paper in the collection reveal three different uses. In one instance marbled paper has been used as a mount for a drawing and a calligraphic page [96]. The rich design of the marbled paper acts as a foil for the simplicity of both the drawing and the calligraphy. In a second example also marbled paper has been employed in a mount for a lightly colored drawing, but this time it forms a discreet inner border around the figure [105]. Indeed, this album page is a fine example of how effectively picture, calligraphic panels, marbling, as well as figurative and geometric decorative motifs have been harmoniously combined to create a coherent, collagelike composition. In the third example the calligrapher has very attractively floated his *nastaliq* letters on a piece of marbled paper, which enhances the animated quality of the writing [111A].

Where and when the art of marbling was invented is not known. China remains a possibility. By the early 1500s, however, marbling was known both in Iran and Turkey, whence the technique must have reached India, as it did Europe. The Persian and Turkish words for marbling are *abri* and *ebru,* respectively, both meaning "cloud art," from which the Indian term *abar* is derived. Both Mughal and Deccani artists adopted the technique, although it appears to have been more popular in the south. In fact, the Deccani artists also employed the process to create paintings with marbled images. As there are only eighteen such pictures known, it has been suggested that they may have been done by a single artist or workshop.[5] It was certainly more common to use marbled paper as background for calligraphy and borders for pictures.

NOTES

1. Kramrisch 1986, p. xvii.

2. Quoted in Zebrowski 1983, p. 60.

3. Ibid., p. 174.

4. Ibid., p. 10.

5. See C. Weimann, "Techniques of Marbling in Early Indian Paintings," *Fine Print* (October 1983): 134–37, 164–66.

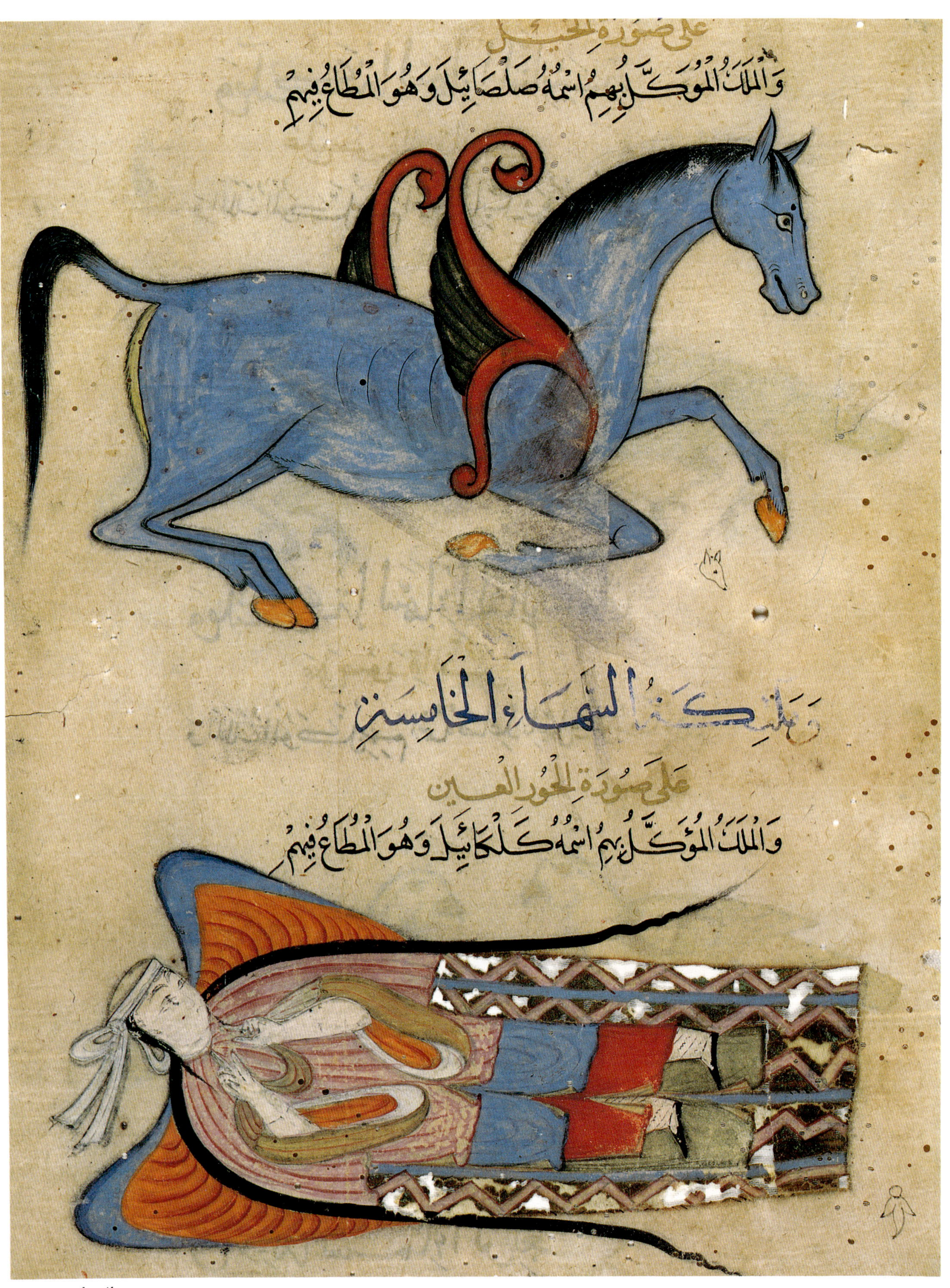

CAT. 95B detail

Catalogue

Bijapur

Unless otherwise noted, all pictures are painted in opaque watercolor and gold and all texts written in ink on paper.

95 TWO FOLIOS FROM A MANUSCRIPT OF AL-QAZWINI'S *AJAIB AL-MAKHLUQAT*

Karnataka, Bijapur; c. 1570
Text in ink, gold, and opaque watercolor

A *Pairs of Eagles and Falcons*
B *Winged Horse and Angel*
Text in black and red ink
Folio, 11 x 8½ in (27.9 x 21.6 cm)
Text and illustration, 9¹¹⁄₁₆ x 7⁵⁄₁₆ in (24.6 x 18.7 cm)
The Nasli M. Heeramaneck Collection, gift of Joan Palevsky
M.73.5.585
Literature: Pal 1974, p. 102, no. 187 (A only illustrated); Badiee 1978; Pal 1987, pp. 119, 120, fig. 79 (A only illustrated); Blair & Bloom 1991, p. 83, no. 16c (B only).
C *Winged Feline and Cow*
D *Two Winged Angels*
Folio, 11 x 8⅞ in (27.9 x 22.5 cm)
Text and illustration, 9⅞ x 7⅝ in (25.1 x 19.0 cm)
Gift of Dr. and Mrs. Pratapaditya Pal
M.88.213.8

Although the measurements of the two leaves vary slightly, very likely they are from the same manuscript of al-Qazwini's *Ajaib al-Makhluqat wa-Gharaib al-Mawjudat* (Wonders of creation and oddities of existence). Two folios from an *Ajaib* in the San Diego Museum of Art may belong to the same manuscript (Binney 1973, p. 152, no. 126).

A two-volume work on cosmology and geography, the *Ajaib* was written by Zakariya b. Muhammad b. Mahmud Abu Yahya (1203–83). He came to be known as al-Qazwini because the family had settled in Qazwin in Iran. The book was written in Arabic and subsequently translated into both Persian and Turkish (Atil 1975, p. 115); the museum's folios are from a copy in Arabic. An encyclopedic work, the book is divided into two parts, which discuss celestial and terrestrial phenomena, respectively. The first part includes a substantial discussion of the heavenly bodies, such as the planets and the stars, and the inhabitants of the heavens, such as angels. The second volume describes earthly phenomena, such as the elements, minerals, flora, fauna, and the human species. It also includes much geographical information about the earth.

Both folios in the collection represent different types of angels in the various heavens. As Qazwini wrote, "God the Almighty has created them in various forms and differing shapes to put his creation in order and to populate his heaven" (quoted in Badiee 1978, p. 51). The text describes seven different heavens inhabited by various types of angelic creatures.

CAT. 95A,B *(opposite top)*
CAT. 95C,D *(opposite bottom)*

In her article (1978) Badiee discussed at length the source of these illustrations' style and their provenance. Stylistically the illustrations are very similar to those in another manuscript of the same book most likely copied and illustrated in Bijapur in 1571/72 and now in the India Office Library, London. That manuscript was prepared for b. Kamal ad-Din Husayn, who may have been a courtier both in Golconda and after about 1565 in Bijapur. An inscription in Mecca describes him as a collector of books. It is unlikely that he would have wanted a second copy, but he could have had a second presentation copy prepared.

Indeed, this copy of the *Wonders of Creation and Oddities of Existence* may have been owned by Ali I, the ruler of Bijapur (r. 1557–79), for whom Kamal ad-Din worked. According to Rafi ad-Din Shirazi's history of Bijapur until 1612, Ali I "had a great inclination toward the study of books and he had procured many books connected with every kind of knowledge, so that a coloured library had become full. Nearly sixty men, calligraphers, gilders of books, book binders, and illuminators were busy doing their work the whole day in the library" (quoted in Zebrowski 1983, p. 61). It is not improbable therefore that Kamal ad-Din's copy may have been commissioned after he saw another with his patron. Considering the fact that Ali I "procured many books connected with every kind of knowledge," a copy of al-Qazwini's work would have been a desideratum. Significantly, another dated Deccani manuscript of the period is of the *Nujum al-Ulum,* which is concerned with magic, animals, weapons, and astronomy, but it is rendered in a local style (Zebrowski 1983, p. 63, figs. 43, 44).

Shirazi's statement about Ali's interest in books also explains why the illustrations in the museum's folios exhibit no local influences but hark back to fourteenth-century illustrated manuscripts of the text, as discussed by Badiee (1978). Obviously the royal library did possess an earlier copy of the work that had been written and illuminated in West Asia, such as the Sarre Qazwini now divided between two American collections (see Badiee). The court artists of Ali I simply used it as a model when a copy was needed. This was not only the practice during the Sultanate period but also among Mughal artists, who often modeled the compositions of their illustrations on West Asian prototypes.

Without examining all the illustrations it is difficult to conclude whether the artist responsible for the illustrations was an Indian or an Iranian. In the museum's four illustrations only the cow looks somewhat Indian. Otherwise, in neither the coloring nor in the drawing, or for that matter in the figural forms, does one encounter any specifically Indian trait. If the artist was an Indian, he copied his Iranian models faithfully. The coloring reflects the lustrous brilliance of the Iranian palette rather than the sensuous warmth of Indian pigments.

On both leaves the portrayals are highly conceptual but lively. The winged horse (B), representing the angels of the fourth heaven, is a spirited portrayal with a body of vibrant royal blue, orange hoofs, black mane and tail, and red-and-gray wings. The supine angel, representing the angels of the fifth heaven, has a very Iranian face with lightly indicated features. He has orange-and-blue wings and wears multicolored garments of mauve, blue, red, white, orange, and brown. On the reverse of the first leaf (A) are conceptually rendered pairs of eagles and falcons representing the second and third heavens. On C the first two heavens are symbolized by a winged feline and a cow, neither of which is very naturalistically drawn but which are more convincing than the birds. The feline is almost colorless except for a few patches of gray. The cow by contrast has a bright red body with gray hooves and blue horns. Noteworthy is the fact that the wings of the feline are not at all integrated with the body but rather serve as a backdrop. Likewise, the red wings of the green angel on page D are not grafted to the body, but those on the shoulders of the blue angel are. The green angel has black spots on his body. He seems to be falling over his companion, who has a light blue body with wings in a different shade of blue. Both angels have black hair.

The text on the leaves has been translated by Z. A. Desai as follows:

And the angels of the second sphere are in the likeness of the eagle [uqab], *and the name of the guardian angel for them is Mikhail, and they are accountable to him.*

And the angels of the third sphere are in the likeness of the eagle [nasr], *and the name of the guardian-angel for them is Saidhail, and they are accountable to him.*

And the angels of the fourth sphere are in the likeness of the horse, and the name of the guardian-angel for them is Salsail, and they are accountable to him.

And the angels of the fifth sphere are in the likeness of the peri (hur), *and the name of the guardian-angel for them is Kalkail, and they are accountable to him.*

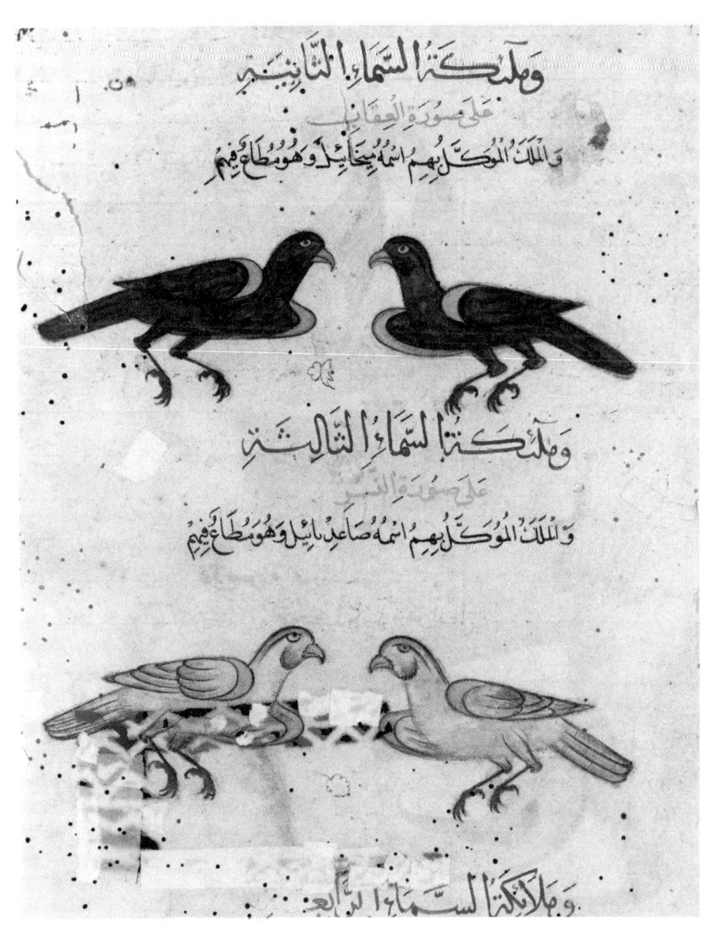

وملائكة السماء الثانية
على صورة العقبان
والملك الموكل بهم اسمه ميخائيل وهو مطاع فيهم
وملائكة السماء الثالثة
على صورة النسور

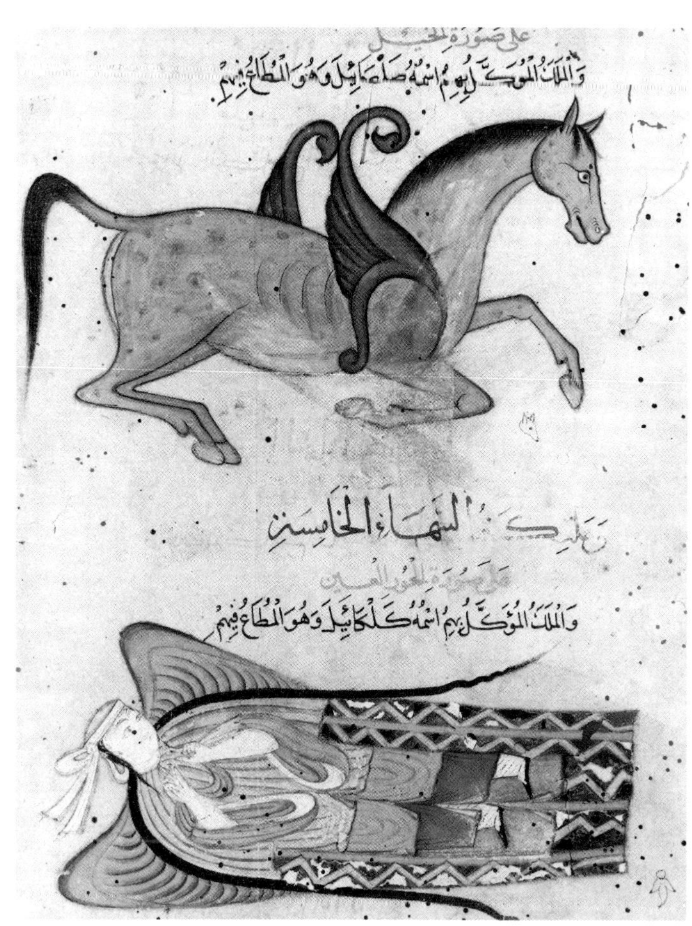

على صورة الخيل
وملائكة السماء الخامسة
على صورة الحور العين
والملك الموكل بهم اسمه كلكائيل وهو المطاع فيهم

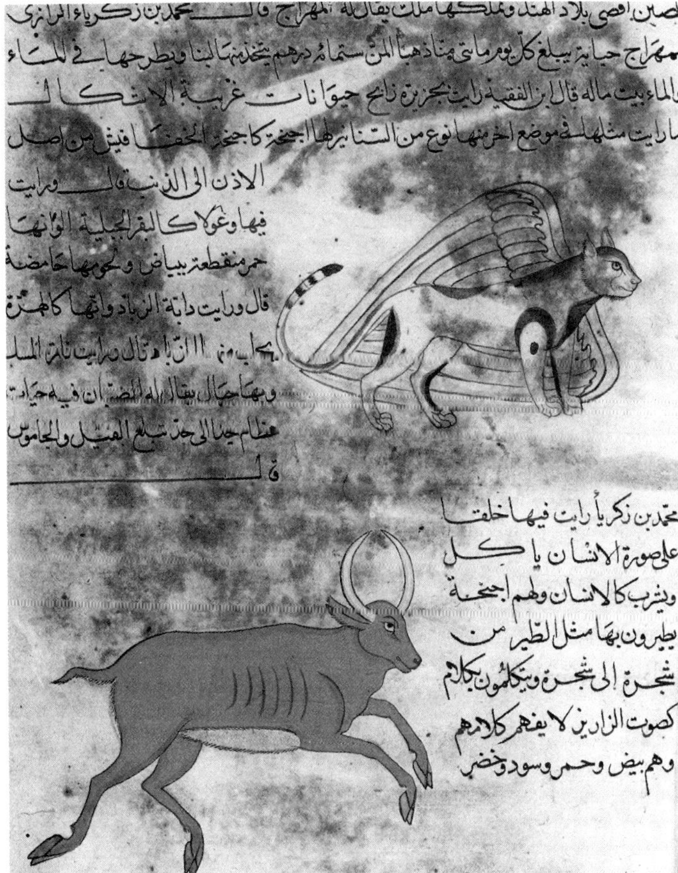

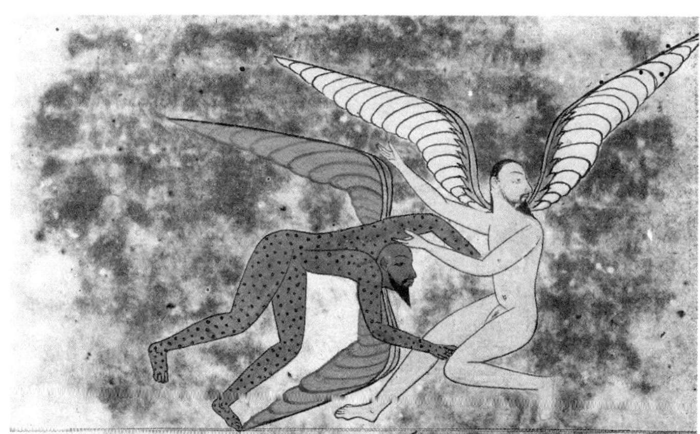

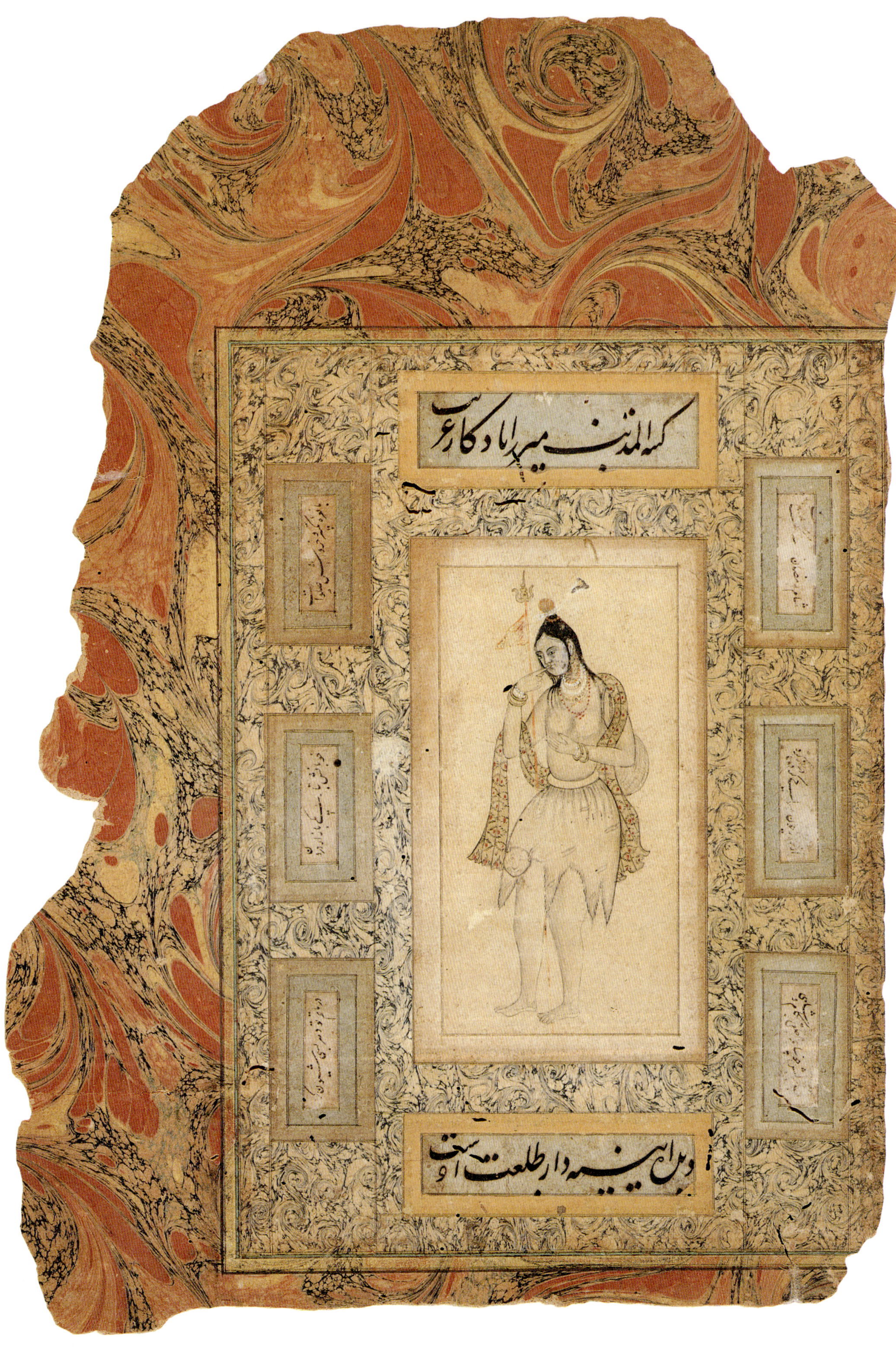

Folio, 14½ x 10⅛ in (36.8 x 25.7 cm), irregular
Bequest of Edwin Binney, 3rd
M.90.141.3

A *Female Ascetic*
Karnataka, Bijapur; 1600 or slightly earlier
5¼ x 2¾ in (13.3 x 7.0 cm)

B *Page of Calligraphy*
Iran or India; seventeenth century
7 x 3½ in (17.8 x 8.9 cm)

Both the picture and the page of calligraphy are surrounded by sumptuous borders of marbled paper. Despite its damaged condition this album leaf remains a remarkably rich document of the variety of marbling used in the Deccan. The outside border of A is adorned with bold patterns of swirling, energetic forms of crimson surrounding a more delicate and densely packed pebble pattern in light blue, and that of B is decorated with the more familiar curled combed pattern of variegated hues, with crimson patches dominating. A narrow margin painted in gold separates the outer borders from inner ones. Here again the design of the marbling is different on the two sides, being quieter and less obtrusive on the page of calligraphy (B). On both sides small rectangular panels of calligraphy have been pasted around the central image or page. Those above and below the picture are in bold *nastaliq* lettering, as is the calligraphy on the page on the other side.

A The picture shows a slightly slouching female standing against an unpainted background. She wears a blouse made of fine, transparent material, an elegant scarf (*dupatta*), and some jewelry. She also wears a skirt of animal skin and a string of *rudraksha* beads (literally, "Rudra's [Siva's] eyes"), which are also used as rosary beads; these together with her hairstyle indicate that she is a yogini or a mendicant. The trident she holds with her right hand and the *rudraksha* string further indicate that she may be a Saiva yogini. The exact meaning of the gesture of her right hand is uncertain.

Representations of female ascetics, often in single portraits, are fairly common in seventeenth- and eighteenth-century Deccani paintings, especially from Bijapur (see Nigam n.d.). Some, such as this, are straightforward depictions of Saiva yoginis, but others, dressed in Muslim attire, are more enigmatic. Citing literary evidence, particularly a *mathnavi* called *Sahrul Bayan* written by Mir Hasan Dihlavi of the late eighteenth century, M. L. Nigam has shown that it was customary for "ladies of princely families, who otherwise lived in *purdah*," to go out of their homes "in the guise of *yoginis* of certain Saivite sects." Nigam then goes on to suggest that these pictures of "yoginis" wearing Muslim attire were included in large numbers in albums prepared for Muslim courts in order to emphasize the ideal of spiritual love rather than to serve as actual portraits. The yoginis of the Deccani pictures therefore may symbolize the wandering human soul in search of divine reality.

Despite the somewhat awkward rendering of the left hand, the yogini here is presented as an attractive lady rather tall for an Indian woman. The picture essentially is a drawing except for the coloring of the scarf, the black hair, and the jewelry. However, the outline, the attire, and the bag attached to her back have been generously shaded to impart a sense of volume.

The calligraphic panels around the picture are pasted-on cutouts and bear no relation to the yogini. The following discussion about the calligraphic panels on both sides of the folio summarize information provided by Z. A. Desai.

The large panel with bold calligraphy above the picture informs us that it was written by Mir Yadqar Gharib. The word *gharib* literally means "a stranger" and may have been the calligrapher's poetical conceit. The Persian hemistich at the bottom written by Mir Yadgar Gharib reads: "The eye is the mirror-holder of his/her countenance."

The six panels on the sides of the picture contain six Persian hemistiches, or three verses. However, they do not form a single poetical unit as they are composed in different meters. They are very likely parts of different *ghazals,* judging from their subject matter. The calligraphy of these marginal panels and those on the reverse are in the same hand.

CAT. 96A

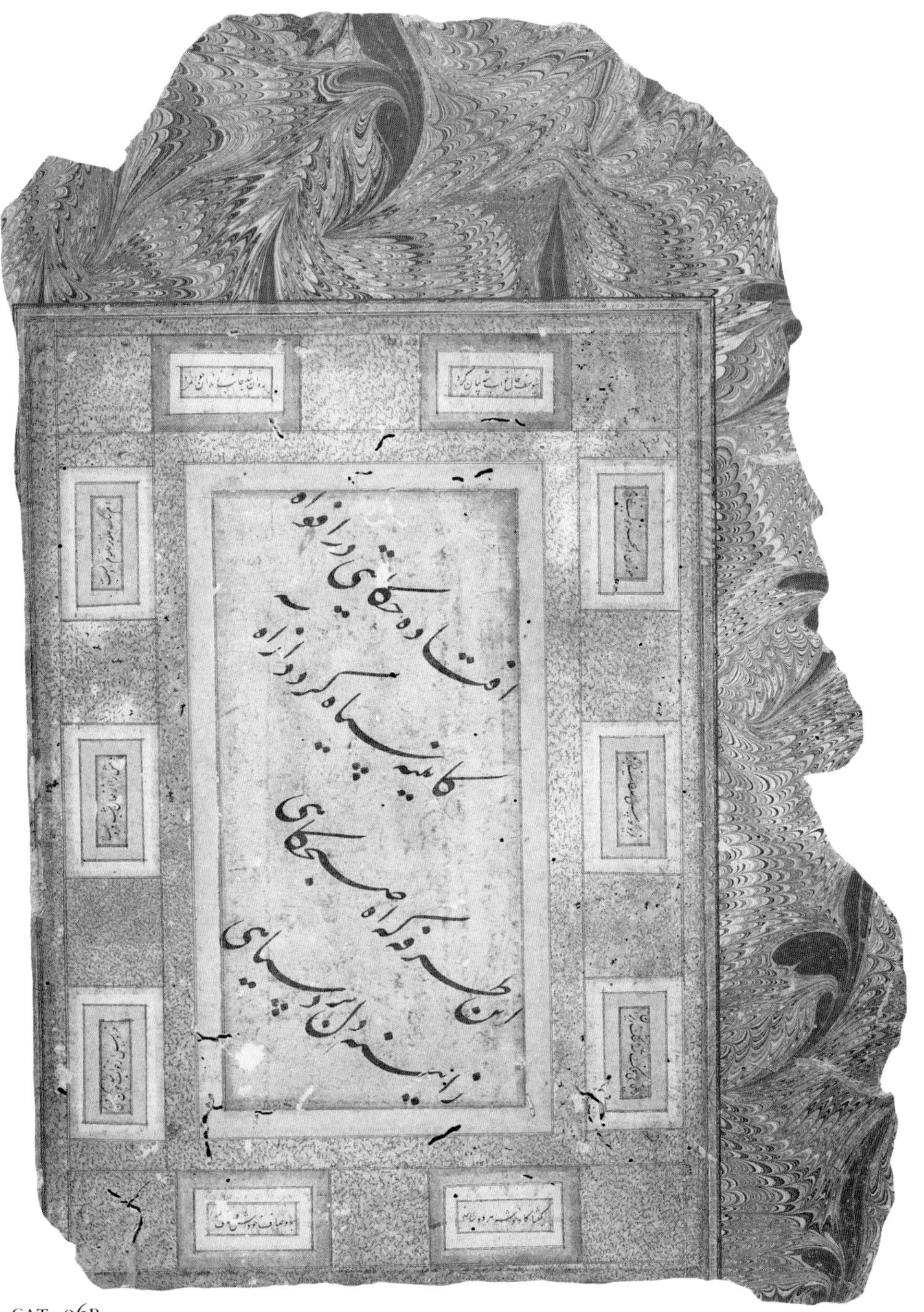

CAT. 96B

B The four hemistiches in the central panel constitute two verses from a *mathnavi.* Desai's translation is: "There is a tale on the lips (of people) that a mirror gets darkened, by the sigh (of oppressed or distressed persons or lovers). But it is curious that (here) the sigh of the time of dawn removes blackness from the mirror of the heart."

The ten marginal panels containing five verses are in the same meter and may or may not belong to the same *mathnavi.* At least five of them, constituting two-and-a-half verses, are from the *Yusuf u Zulaykha* of Mawlana Abdul Rahman Jami, a well-known Persian poet (1414–92). The verses refer to queen Zulaykha, the dream of the king of Egypt, and the king's emissary going to consult with Yusuf (Joseph) for the interpretation of the dream. Of the remaining two-and-a-half verses, one refers to the tail of a dog tied to the door-ring, another to a rooster raising its neck to give a call.

Karnataka, Bijapur; c. 1610
Black and red ink, opaque watercolor, and gold on brown paper
Folio, 8 x 4¾ in (20.3 x 12.1 cm)
Text and illustration, 5¼ x 2¾ in (13.3 x 7.0 cm)
Purchased with funds provided by Dorothy and Richard Sherwood and the Indian Art Special Purpose Fund
M.81.12a,b

A *Bizhan Visiting Manizha*
B *Page of Calligraphy*

These two folios are from a dispersed *Shahnama* manuscript, most of the others being in private collections, the Metropolitan Museum of Art, New York, and the Rietberg Museum, Zurich (see McInerney 1982, p. 49, no. 18, for two other illustrated pages reproduced in color). The two folios published here are not consecutive. The text is arranged in four columns and written in *nastaliq* in small letters in black ink on buff paper dusted with gold. The chapter headings are in red ink on gold panels. The surrounding margin is dyed brown. Only one of the four pages is illustrated, and the lettering on that page is contained in cloud bands.

The illustration depicts the meeting of Bizhan and Manizha, the daughter of Afrasiyab, in her tent as described in chapter 5 of book 10. As the text informs us, "They washed his feet in musk and rose water, then hastened to prepare a meal. Soon they set down a tray covered with viands of every kind to which they pressed him ever and anon. Afterwards they seated themselves for music and wine, having cleared the pavilion of all others" (Levy 1967, p. 157).

CAT. 97A detail

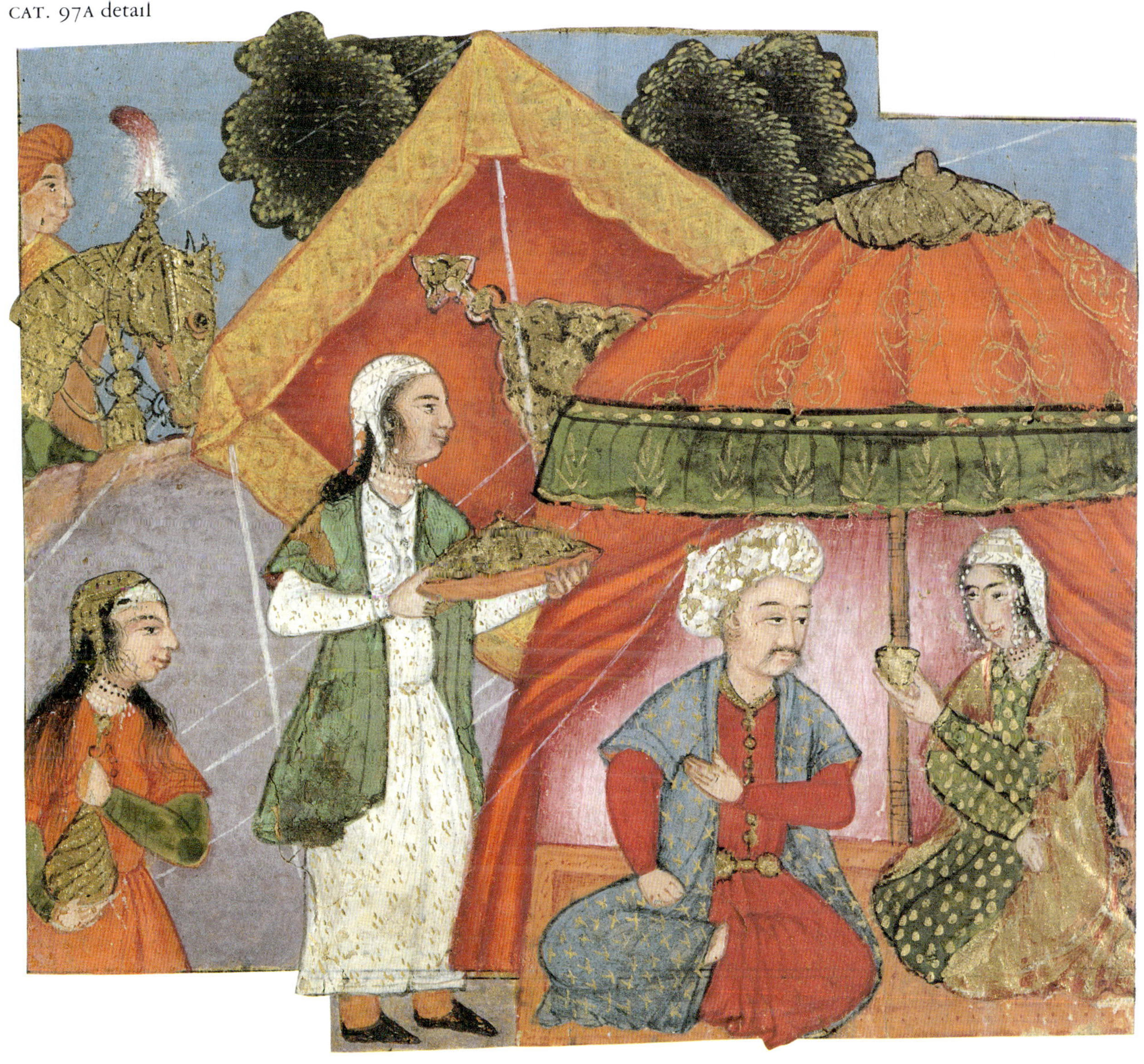

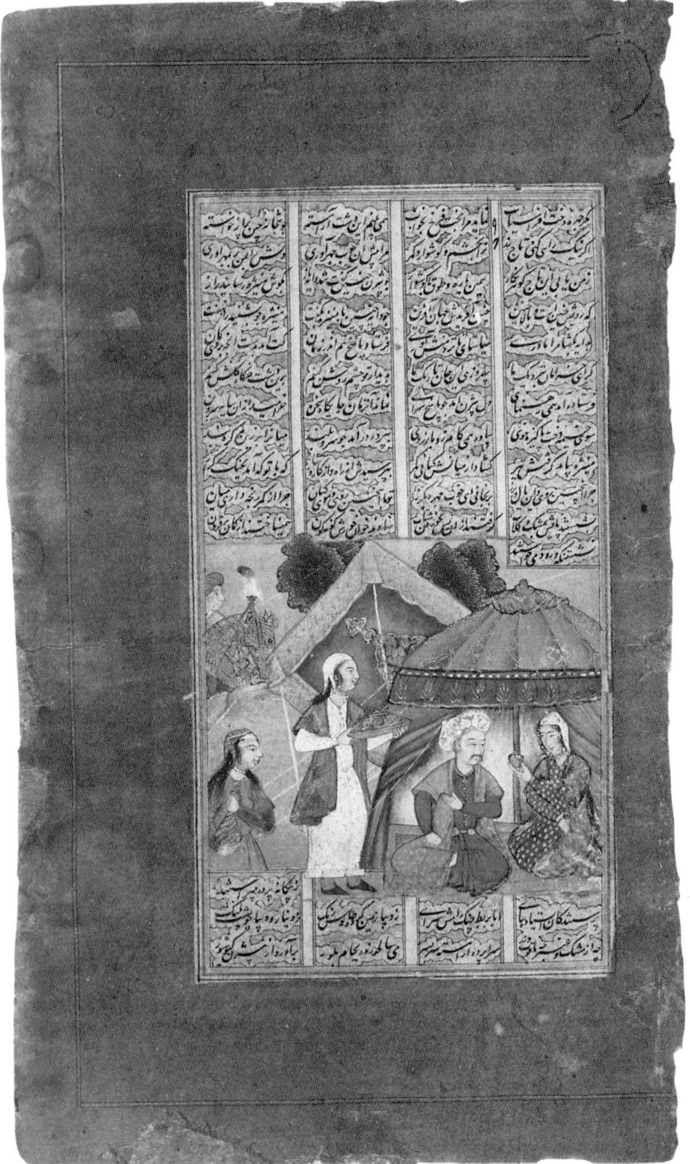

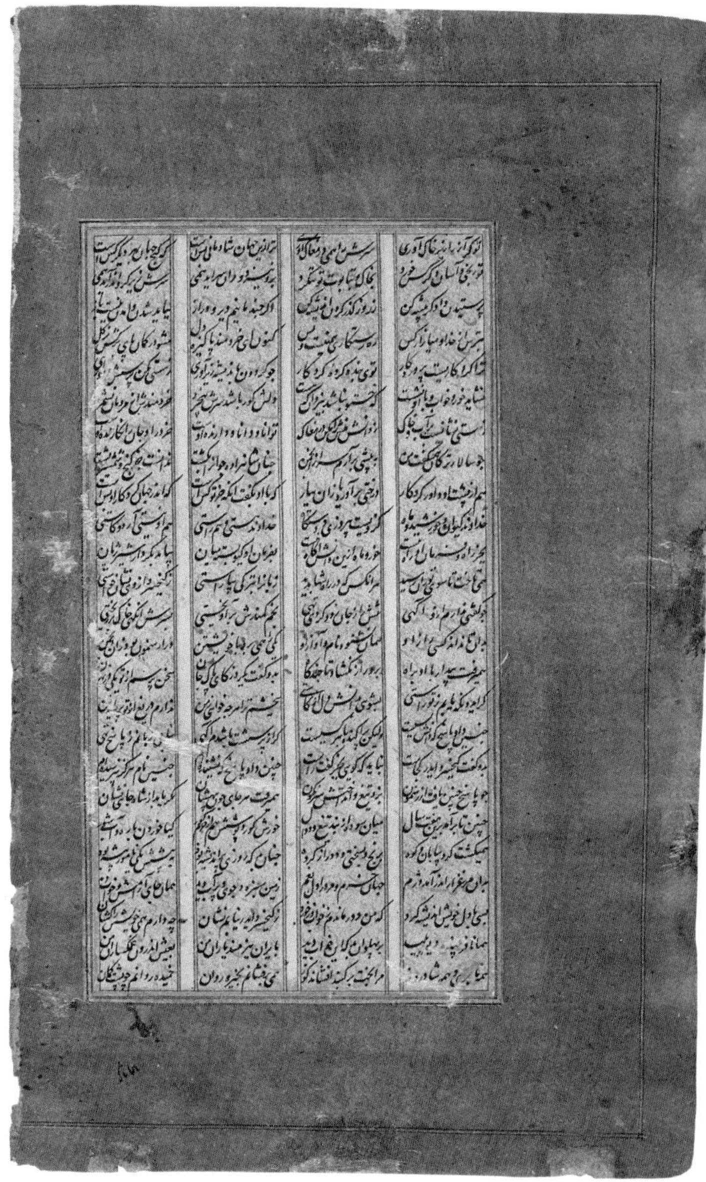

CAT. 97A *(left)*
CAT. 97B *(right)*

The composition is simple, with Bizhan seated on a carpet in a tent rather than a pavilion and turning his head toward Manizha, who proffers him a cup of wine. Two attendants approach the tent from the other side, one holding a tray with a gold cover and the other a gold flask of wine. In the middle ground is a hill mostly in mauve with pink boulders along the top and a gold-and-red rectangular canopy rendered in awkward perspective. Beyond, against a blue sky, are a partially seen horse and man and some trees. All the figures are dressed in the Persian mode.

The pocket size of the book indicates that it was intended to be easily handled and perhaps more frequently read than larger tomes. The lavish use of gold and the high quality of the illustrations point to an affluent if not a royal patron. Though the unknown artist may have borrowed compositional features and individual motifs from contemporary Iranian paintings, the figurative forms and the tonality of the colors are Indian. T. McInerney (1982, pp. 49–50) is probably right in suggesting that the book was created for the Bijapuri court. Comparable in size and to some extent in the style of the illustrations is the *Pemnem* (Toils of love) manuscript now in the British Library, London, probably produced for Ibrahim Adil Shah II early in the seventeenth century. Although somewhat later, this *Shahnama* could have come out of the same workshop but was illustrated in a more consistent and homogenous style than the *Pemnem,* where at least three different hands can be recognized (Losty 1982, p. 73, no. 52). Although not as flamboyant in the distortion of natural motifs and sumptuous coloring as the best Bijapuri paintings of this period, these *Shahnama* illustrations do possess a lyrical mood that is typically Deccani.

Karnataka, Bijapur (?); 1600–1650
Folio, 13½ x 8½ in (34.3 x 21.6 cm)
Illustration, 6⅞ x 3$^{1}/_{16}$ in (17.5 x 7.8 cm)
The Nasli M. Heeramaneck Collection, gift of Joan Palevsky
M.73.5.453
Literature: Pal 1974, p. 147, no. 265.

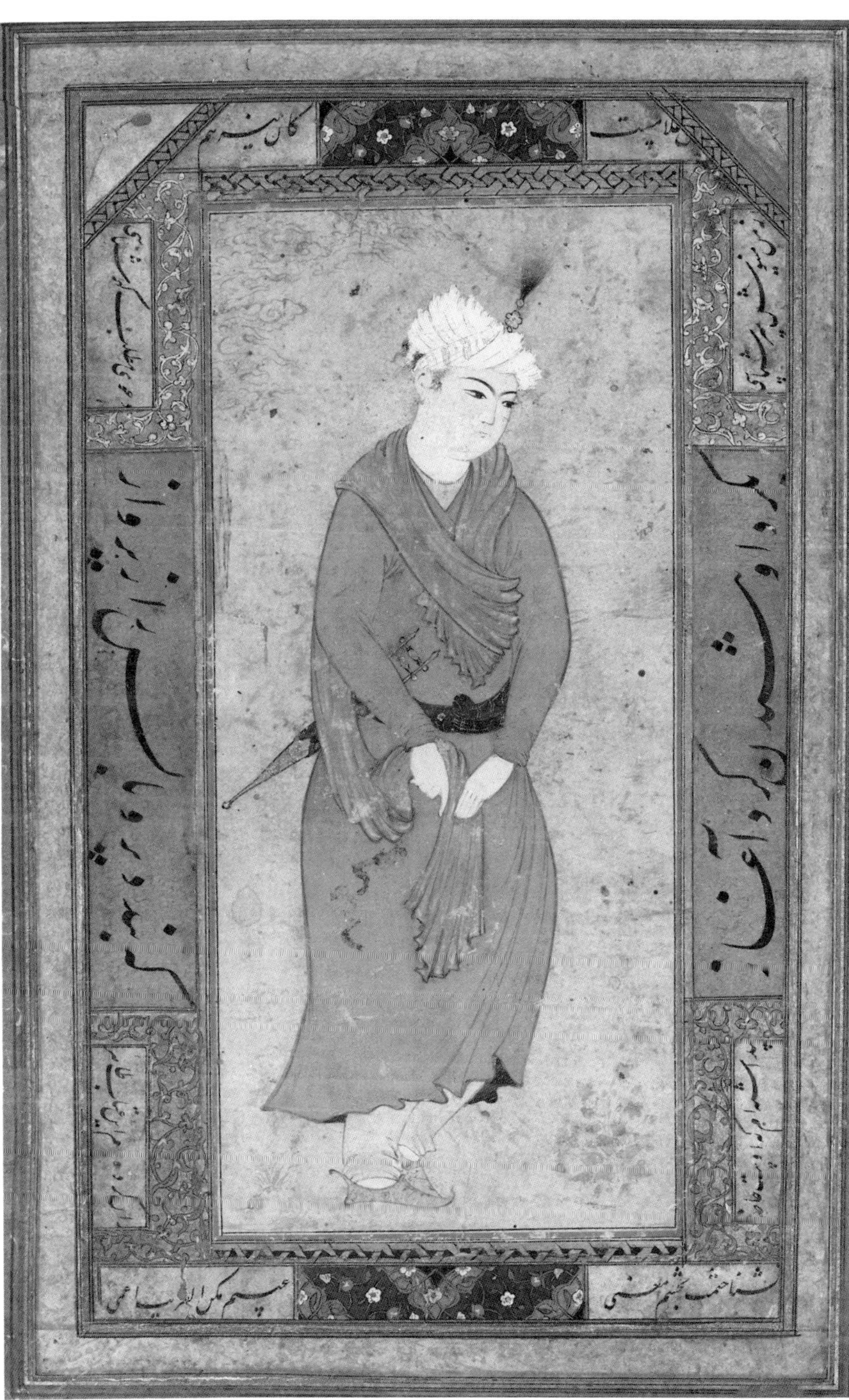

CAT. 98 detail

Mounted as an album leaf with panels of calligraphy, arabesques, and ornamental designs in blue and gold, the picture depicts a youth standing somewhat ill at ease, with his hands awkwardly handling the pleated end of his scarf or shawl. He wears white pajamas, a green *jama,* a gray shawl, a black sash, and a white turban with a plume. A dagger of the type known as *katar* is secured to his waist by the sash. Except for gold clouds above and golden grass and foliage below, the background is left plain.

When the picture was first published, E. Binney wrote (1974, p. 147, no. 265), "The *katar* at his waist, his Bijapuri-like turban, and the folds of the youth's scarf reinforce a Deccani provenance." This attribution has not been accepted by all visiting scholars who have examined the painting; it has been attributed both to Iran and Turkey. However, the presence of the *katar,* an Indian weapon, as well as the manner in which the scarf is draped around the shoulders are elements one would expect from an artist in India who was perhaps copying a Persianate model. It should be noted that the hands and the hem of the *jama* have been rendered rather crudely, and one is not sure exactly how the scarf is wrapped around the shoulders.

The *nastaliq* calligraphy in the surrounding panels is well executed. The verses have been translated by Z. Faridany-Akhavan as follows:

Large letters
{It} began to weave around him/her
So as to tie his/her wings and
feathers and prevent him/her from flying.

Bottom
I did not recognize you with my spirit's eye,
Do not blame me, O blind stranger

Bottom right
I had thought that he/she was present

Bottom left
That is why I have come out with this protest

Top right
Understand the extent of my gratefulness

Top left
Do not wish for a quarrel if
you recognize the essence {the jewels}

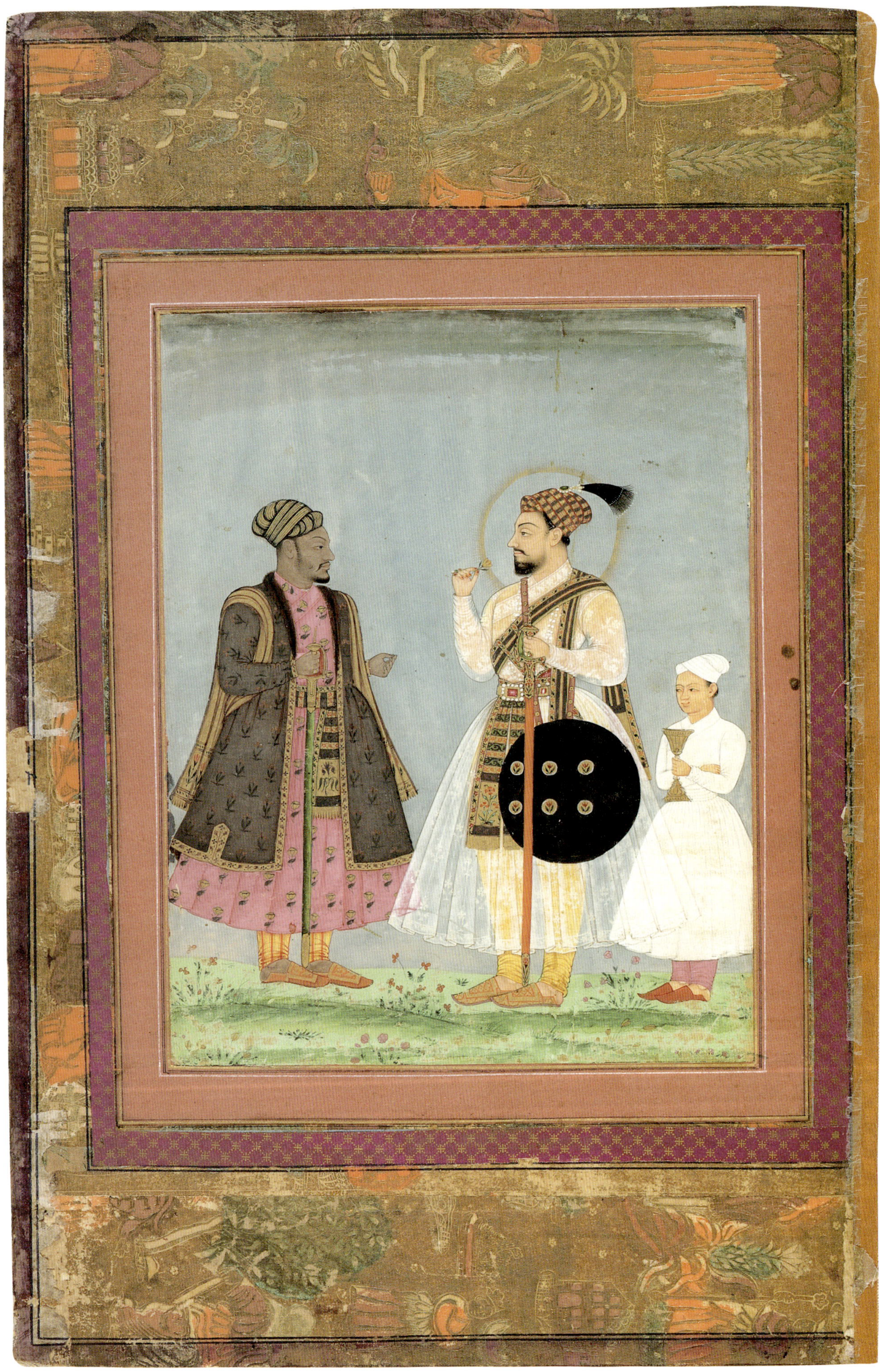

Folio, 17 3/8 x 11 3/8 in (44.1 x 28.9 cm)
From the Nasli and Alice Heeramaneck Collection, Museum Associates Purchase
M.76.2.35
Literature: Heeramaneck 1984, p. 167, pl. 234 (A only).

A *Muhammad Adil Shah and Ikhlas Khan*
Karnataka, Bijapur; 1650–75
9 5/8 x 7 5/8 in (24.4 x 19.4 cm)
Border, embossed with gold, with hand-coloring

B *Page of Calligraphy*
Iran or India; seventeenth century
5 7/8 x 2 7/8 in (14.9 x 7.3 cm)
Border, embossed with gold

A This formal portrait is surrounded with two inner borders in different shades of purple and mounted as the recto of an eighteenth-century album leaf. The richer purple inner border is decorated with a gold design. The outer border appears to be made of Chinese (?) paper block-printed with figural and landscape motifs. (The folio in [110] is from the same album.)

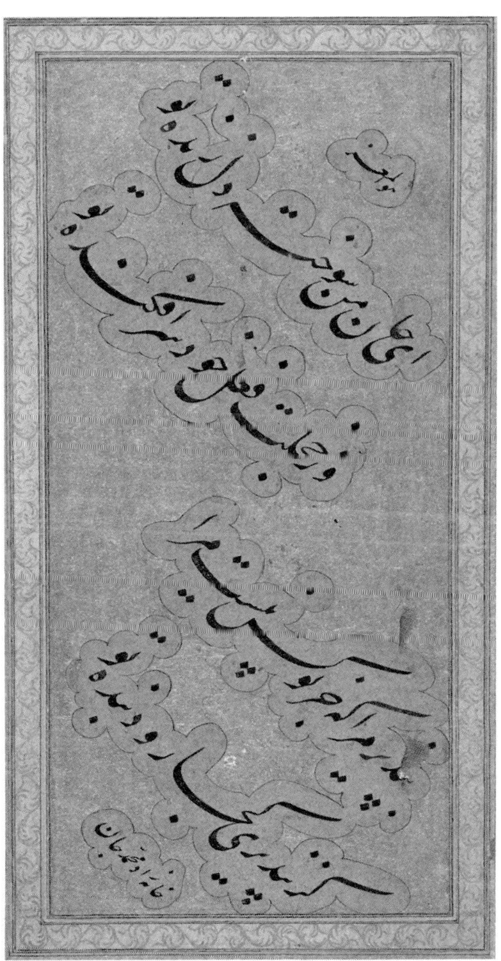

CAT. 99A *(opposite)*
CAT. 99B detail *(right)*

The figures in the painting stand on green, uneven ground with flowering plants. The background is gray with darker streaks at the top indicating the sky. Sultan Muhammad Adil Shah (r. 1627–56) is distinguished by a golden halo and holds a flower in his right hand. He wears a superfine white muslin *jama* over yellow pajamas. His sash and scarf are of gold brocade, strands of pearls adorn his chest, and a feathered plume is on his turban. He holds a sword with his left hand, and a black shield hangs from a strap that goes over his right shoulder. He also has a *katar* tucked in his cummerbund. The dark figure facing him is attired less ostentatiously but no less elegantly and holds only a sword. He wears a mauve *jama* with gold flowers over bright yellow pajamas with red stripes. In addition, an elegant jacket with gold borders and fur-trimmed collar announces his importance. A golden shawl circles his shoulders. The page behind the ruler is dressed mostly in white and holds a golden spittoon.

The dark figure can be identified as Muhammad Adil Shah's African Prime Minister Ikhlas Khan from a comparison with at least three other known portraits (Zebrowski 1983, figs. 96, 97, 100). This formal state picture of the meeting of the sultan and his prime minister may well have been done before the former's death in 1656. The halo for the ruler is clearly a legacy of Mughal imperial portraits, and in fact, in one of the three comparative pictures cited (fig. 100), the sultan is provided with a similar halo. That picture is signed by Haidar Ali and Ibrahim Khan, one of whom could have been responsible for this stately portrait.

B This page of *nastaliq* calligraphy is surrounded by a narrow margin in peach with a gold arabesque, a wide border in plain gray, and a third inner border of the same rich purple paper with a gold diamond-shaped design as on the other side. The outer border has a purple margin around the edges and is adorned with large, bold floral patterns block-printed in gold. The calligraphy is written neatly on light gray cloud bands on a gold ground. This translation of the poem is by Z. Faridany-Akhavan:

O my life burns for your wisdom and from its deed hangs its head in shame before you,

For if you do not accept me, where shall this follower of yours go?
The child of the slave Muhammad Yar.

Folio, 16 3/16 x 10 5/8 in (41.1 x 27.0 cm)
Purchased with funds provided by the Smart Family Foundation through the generosity of Mr. and Mrs. Edgar G. Richards
M.87.61

- A *Page of Calligraphy* (r)
  By Nadir al-Zaman Mahdi(?)
  Deccan; dated A.H. 1130, A.D. 1717/18
  5 3/8 x 2 7/8 in (13.7 x 7.3 cm)
- B *Muhammad Adil Shah* (v)
  Attributed here to Muhammad Khan
  Karnataka, Bijapur; 1650 or later
  5 7/8 x 3 13/16 in (14.9 x 9.7 cm)

A This page of unconnected couplets and quatrains in Persian calligraphed in the *shikasta* script is surrounded by an inner border adorned with flowering vines in gold. Deriving from the *taliq* ("hanging") and the *nastaliq*, the *shikasta*, which means "broken form," is a more playful script that depends on exaggerated density and the idiosyncratic arrangement of the lines to create its aesthetic effect. An inscription at the bottom of the leaf reads *kar-i-nadir-al-zaman Mahdi*(?), "the work of the wonder of the age, Mahdi(?)." Whether the calligrapher was an Iranian or an Indian is not known, nor is it

CAT. 100A

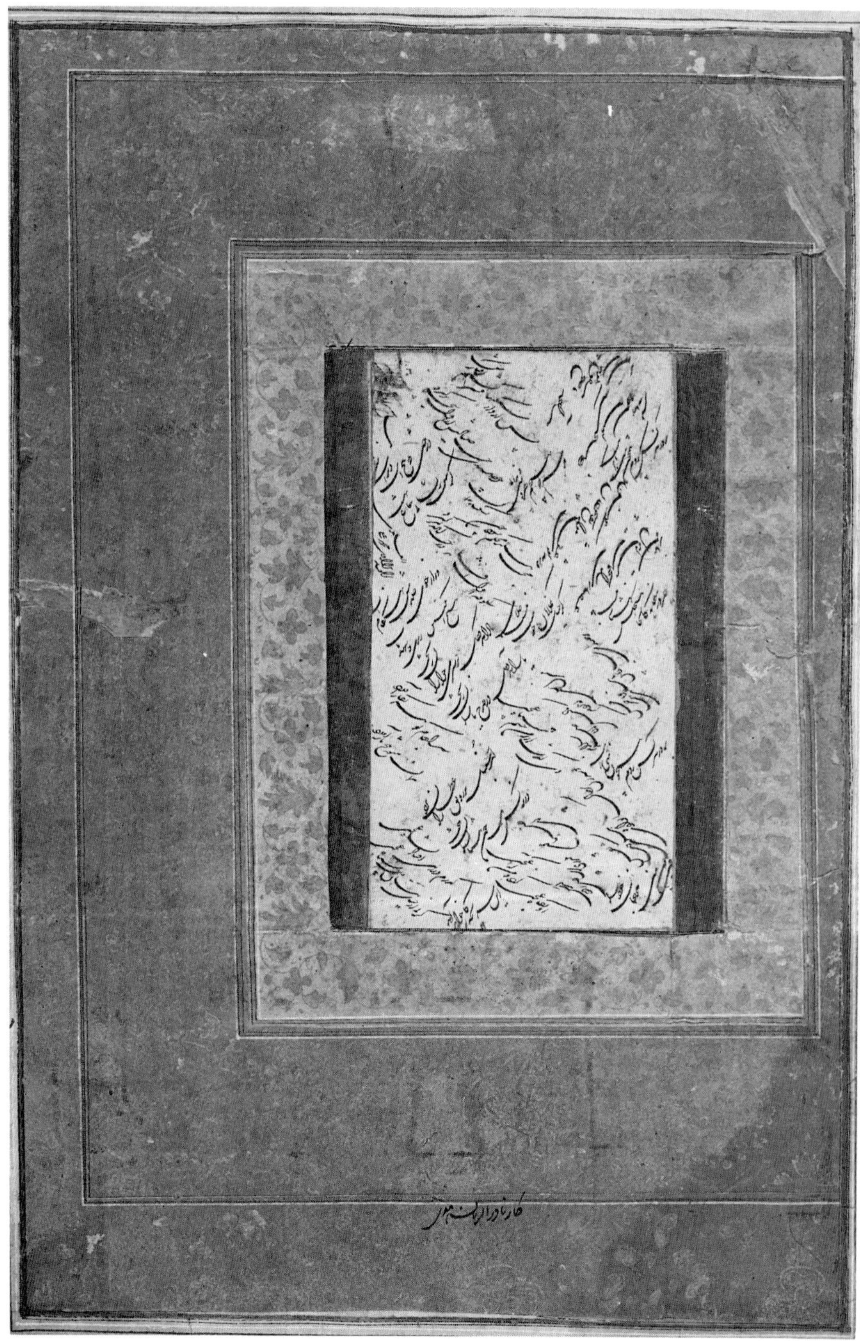

certain whether the page was written in India or in Iran. The expression *kar,* signifying "work," is found in other Deccani paintings (see Zebrowski 1983, p. 113). A signature at the top left corner of the page seems to have been deliberately mutilated. However, there is a date that can be read as A.H. 1130, which corresponds to A.D. 1717/18.

B Just below the inner borders is a brief inscription in a Deccani or Gujarati variety of the Devanagari script that states *padshamirasha. Mira Shah* was a title of Muhammad Adil Shah of Bijapur, who had a long and prosperous reign of almost three decades (1627–56). He was put on the throne when he was only fifteen, after his elder brother, the rightful heir, was blinded by the ambitious machination of two nobles. Muhammad Adil Shah resisted the advances of Shah Jahan's forces for a number of years, but in 1636 he was forced to sign a treaty of submission with the Mughal emperor. In exchange for a large tribute to the imperial treasury, Bijapur gained some territories from the dismembered Ahmadnagar, which brought in additional revenues. Indeed, under Muhammad Adil Shah Bijapur attained its greatest geographical extent and political power. He was also a generous patron of the arts and an ambitious builder like his imperial overlord.

CAT. 100B

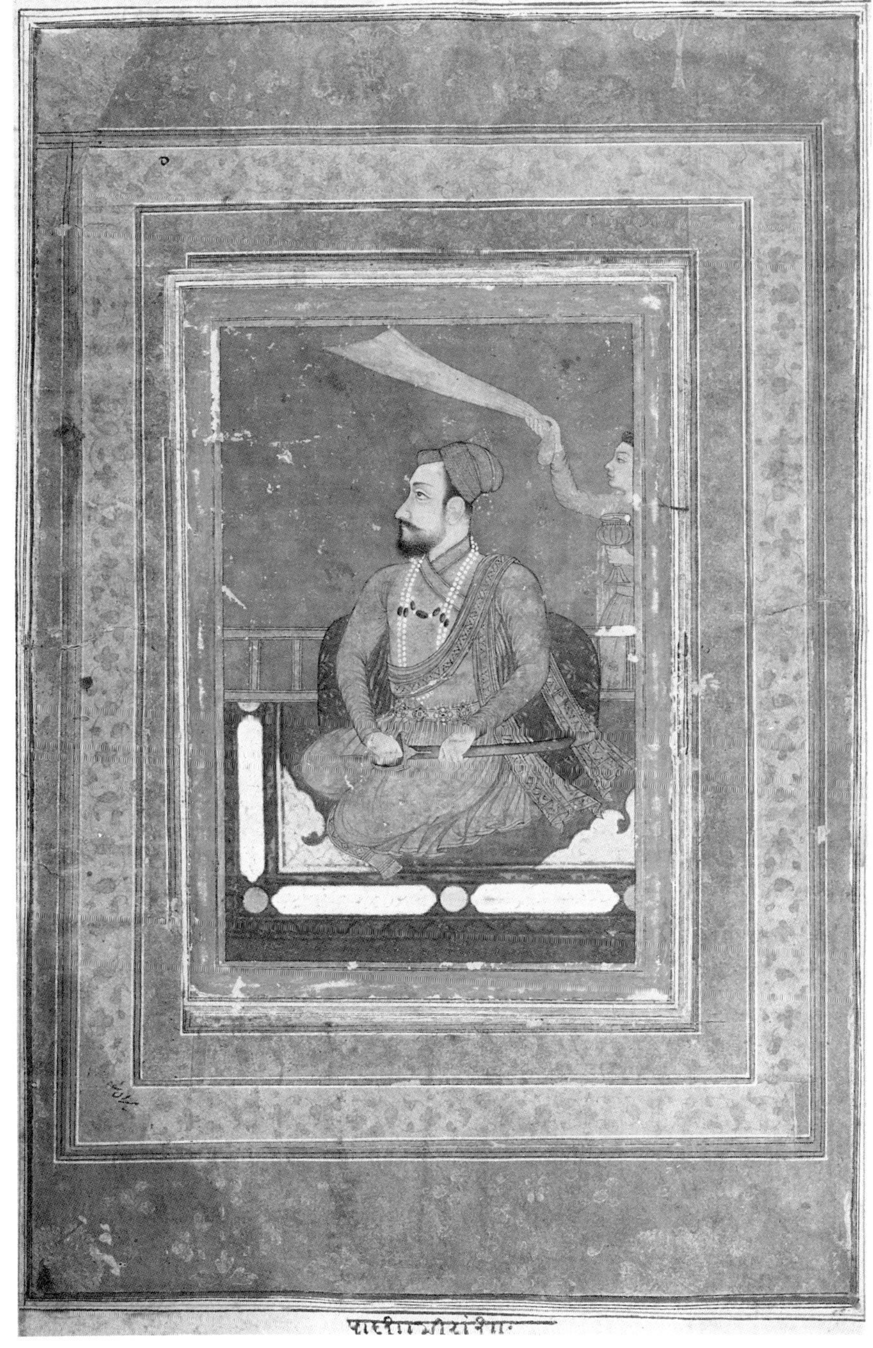

The portrait shows the ruler seated informally with his legs folded underneath him, against a bolster. His hands resolutely hold a sword as if he were about to draw it from the scabbard. Behind him is a servant holding what appears to be a gold spittoon in his left hand as he fans his monarch with a piece of cloth serving as a flywhisk or *morchal,* also an insignia of royalty. Unfortunately the inscriptions on the white cartouches on the carpet are much too faded to be legible.

Stylistically the representation is very close to a durbar scene painted by Muhammad Khan in 1651 now in the City Palace Museum, Jaipur (Zebrowski 1983, fig. 95). There too the shah sits in the same manner, supported by a bolster, with his left hand placed on his sword. A servant holding a spittoon and a fan stands behind the ruler in a similar position. In another portrait of the ruler by the same artist, also in the same collection, a rectangular panel at the bottom right carries the artist's signature (Zebrowski 1983, fig. 94).

The face of the sitter, with almond shaped eyes and well-groomed beard, has been sensitively rendered. There is a resolute expression on his face, as if the artist wanted the viewer to see the ruler as a heroic figure. This is also evident from his broad shoulders and the way he grasps the sword. The details have been carefully rendered, and the artist's fondness for luxurious effects is apparent from the fact that every article of royal apparel is painted in gold. The carpets and the bolster are in a rich purple. A similar carpet occurs in another portrait of the ruler attributed to Muhammad Khan (Zebrowski 1983, fig. 99), and in it too cartouches with inscriptions are placed beneath the throne in the foreground of the picture. The servant is dressed in gray and waves a pale yellow cloth. If Muhammad Khan did not paint this portrait then certainly the artist used his work as a model.

There seems little doubt that the album from which this folio came was assembled sometime after 1717/18, perhaps in the northern Deccan. It also included of a large number of Mughal paintings (see Pal 1983, pls. M22, M23, M25, M32, M33–35).

101 IBRAHIM ADIL SHAH II

Karnataka, Bijapur; c. 1675
8⅛ x 4⅝ in (20.6 x 11.7 cm)
From the Nasli and Alice Heeramaneck Collection, Museum Associates Purchase
M.83.105.2
Literature: Heeramaneck 1984, p. 167, pl. 235; Pal 1987, p. 120, fig. 80.

Ibrahim Adil Shah II (r. 1579–1627) came to the throne when he was only nine, and by the time he died at the age of forty-eight, he had ruled for almost four decades. The first decade was characterized by constant intrigues among the various regents, but once he assumed authority at the age of twenty, Bijapur entered a prosperous phase that was particularly conducive to its cultural enrichment. Although not as practical or militarily aggressive as his Mughal contemporary, Akbar, like him Ibrahim was a remarkably eclectic, tolerant, and liberal man. He was an ardent connoisseur of music and would often fall into a trance while listening to a great performance. Unlike Akbar, he was literate, and he was a poet with a mystical streak. His *Kitab-i-Nauros* (Book of nine *rasas*) is an anthology of songs written in Deccani Urdu. A great patron of the arts and literature, his poet laureate was Zuhuri, who arrived in the Deccan in 1580/81 from the Iranian court of Shah Akbar and who after serving at the Ahmadnagar court moved on to Bijapur soon after 1595. Although

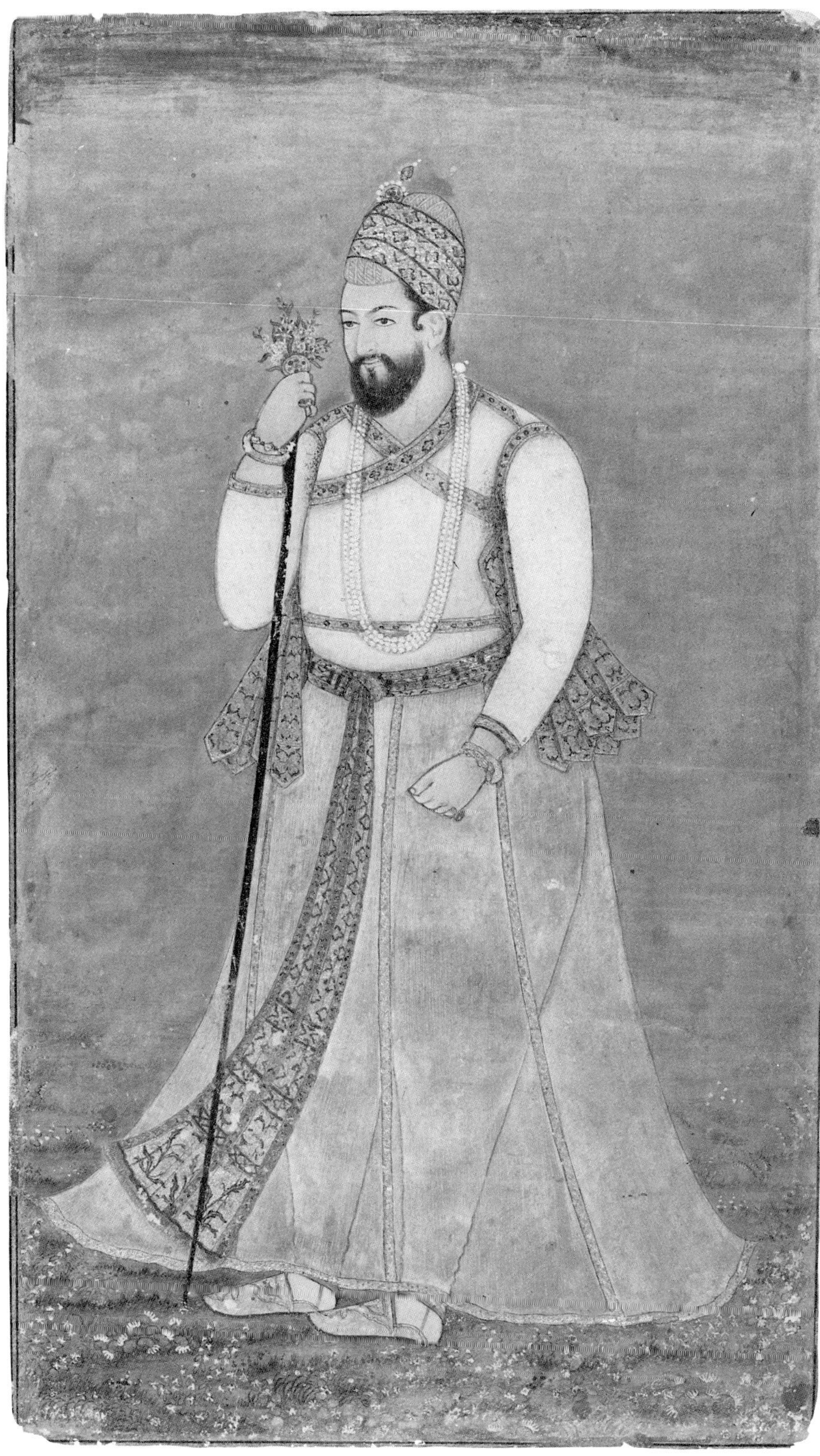

music was Ibrahim's first love, according to Zuhuri (quoted in Zebrowski 1983, p. 69): "In the art of painting he excels the painter. . . . While placing the looking glass before him he paints his own picture. . . . He is also an expert calligraphist." No wonder many consider him the greatest patron of the arts among the Muslim rulers of the Deccan.

This formal portrait in the typically Bijapuri manner shows a three-quarter view of Ibrahim standing. With his right hand he holds a long, black staff and a bouquet of flowers, and the left is held closed against his thigh. The transparent *jama* flares around him stylishly and the brilliant brocade sash swings elegantly to the left, adding a sense of movement. The brocaded pleats under each arm hang like pendants from a chandelier. The conical turban characteristic of Bijapur is wrapped in matching gold brocade. The ground below is carpeted with white flowers, grass, and tiny stones. The background is a light blue, which sets off his white *jama* and pink trousers. The sky is indicated by a darker shade of blue.

Although a fine portrait, it was not painted during his lifetime but perhaps about 1675, when Sikander Shah was on the throne of Bijapur. Interestingly, the necklace of *rudraksha* beads seen in most portraits of Ibrahim is replaced here by three strands of pearls. The presence of Mughal influence as well as a greater idealization of the face, without his prominently curved nose, also point to a date in the second half of the seventeenth century. The proportions of the figure, the shape of the legs, and the swing of the sash are reminiscent of the well-known early-seventeenth-century portrait attributed to the Bodleian painter and now in the British Museum, London (Zebrowski 1983, pl. VIII). There too the nose has been straightened out and the features cosmetized. A comparable later portrait perhaps done in Golconda but based on a more elaborate Bijapuri original is in a British private collection (Zebrowski 1983, fig. 67). The museum's portrait, however, may have been rendered by either Kamal Muhammad or Chand Muhammad, who collaborated on a splendid formal picture of the sultans of the Adil Shahi Dynasty at about the same time (Zebrowski 1983, pl. XVII). Although the hands here are not as well done and the eyes are more idealized, there are strong stylistic similarities between the museum's portrait and the representation of Ibrahim Adil Shah in the group picture.

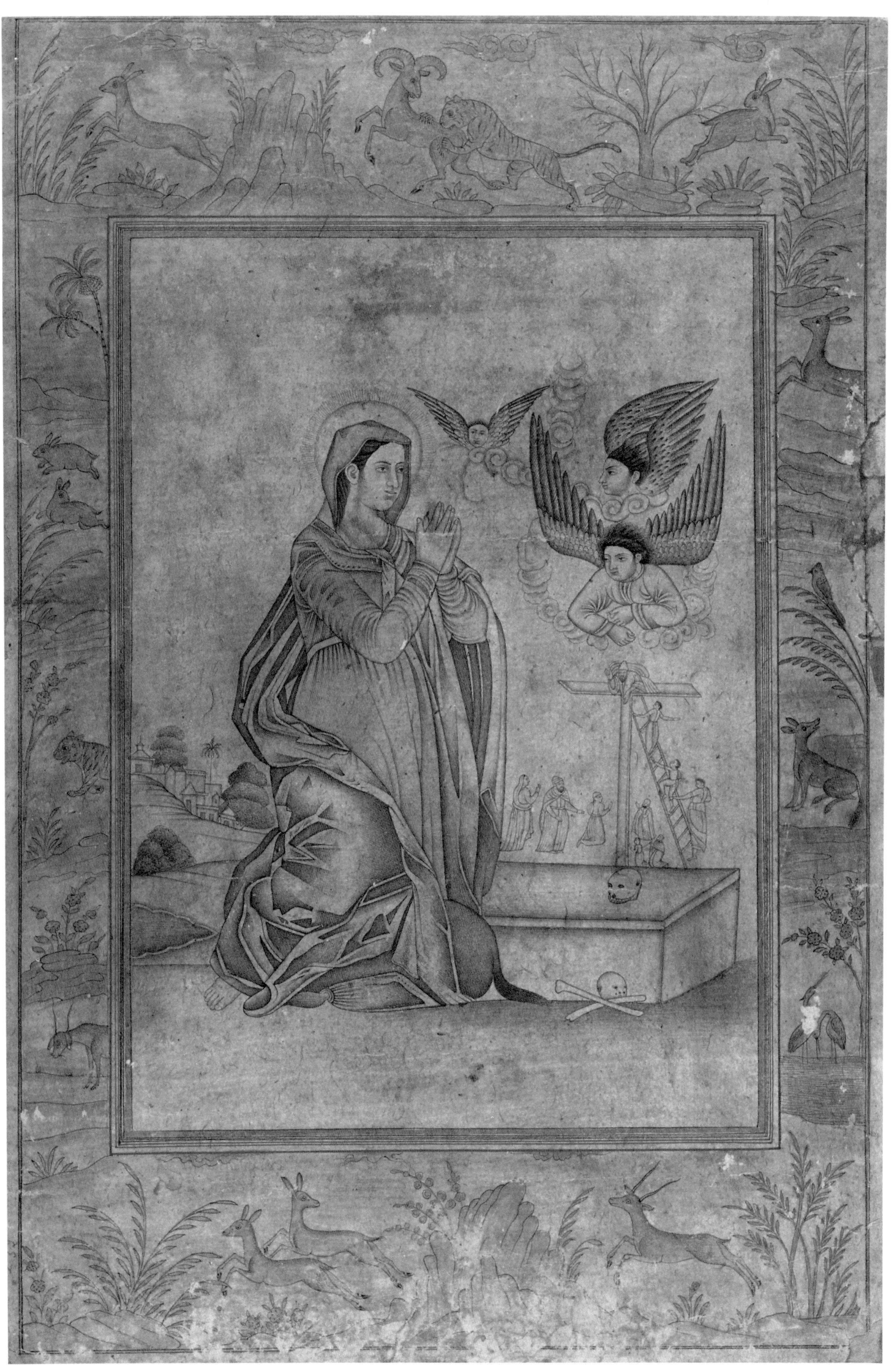

Deccan, Bijapur (?); c. 1675
Ink with color washes on paper
Folio, 11 7/8 x 7 3/4 in (30.2 x 19.7 cm)
Illustration, 7 5/8 x 5 3/8 in (19.4 x 13.7 cm)
Purchased with funds provided by Julian C. Wright Bequest, Christian Humann Fund, Felix and Helen Juda Foundation, Paul F. Walter, Valley M. Knudsen Estate, the de Anda-Fast family, and Dr. Ronald M. Lawrence
M.82.289

Fewer pictures with European subjects have survived from the Deccan than from the Mughal court, and they are less varied. Moreover, very little has been written on the subject (see Falk and Archer 1981, pp. 238–39, nos. 442–45, 448, for the largest group). No Deccani patron appears to have been as curious about European art as were Akbar and Jahangir.

This particular tinted drawing is an intriguing rendering of a Christian subject for several reasons. In the characteristically Deccani manner the principal figure is shown as a colossus in comparison with the other figures, including the animal whose hindquarters can be seen emerging from the front of her gown. Indeed, the position of the animal, which probably represents an ass, is most peculiar and is encountered in this strange fashion neither with the Virgin Mary nor with Mary Magdalene, the two persons with whom the figure has been identified. She appears to be genuflecting, and the animal seems to be hiding in the folds of her robes. Her dress is in a shade of light pink but the blue veil over her head along with the halo would tend to identify her with the Virgin rather than the Magdalene, who is associated with *memento mori* but whose distinctive attribute—the jar of ointment—is not present here. However, it should be noted that blue apparel, signifying constancy, is also associated with the Magdalene. There is no association between the ass and the Magdalene but there is with the Virgin. An ass, along with an ox, was present at the Nativity, and she did ride an ass during the Flight into Egypt. Why, however, the animal should be included in the scene depicted in this picture is unclear.

As a matter of fact, it is very likely that the scene is a pastiche of more than one European print, as were made by Mughal artists (see [61]). If the Virgin is kneeling at Golgotha, as is indicated by the skulls and the crossbones, then the shape of the single cross and the goings on around it are very strange indeed. The cross seems to be a post supporting a flat plank from which rises the bust of a cap-wearing Muslim mulla with his right hand raised. He is obviously not Christ nor God the Father. A dhoti-clad man followed by a child and another person climb up a ladder placed against the unusual cross. Around the post four Muslims kneel in prayer, while a man clearly dressed in Bijapuri costume and a woman stand reverentially. Whatever is occurring here has little if any relation to the events surrounding the Crucifixion of Christ. Certainly the characters have been altered. The larger-than-life Virgin seems to be greeting the three angels appearing in the clouds. Behind the Virgin are rolling hills with trees and buildings.

Apart from the iconographic hotchpotch, the manner of rendering the Virgin's shawl seems disingenuous at best. Clearly the lower section that wraps her right leg is so artificially arranged that it must reflect some kind of misunderstanding of the artist's source. It would almost seem that he had unsuccessfully attempted to combine two different modes in representing the garment. This may also explain the strange inclusion of the animal below the folds. In addition to the figure dressed in the Bijapuri manner, the wings of the angels are very similar to those seen in a picture attributed to the Deccan of about 1700 (Zebrowski 1983, fig. 195). One may compare the treatment of the garments in this picture with a Madonna on the crescent moon in the India Office Library, London, dated to the mid-seventeenth century (Falk and Archer 1981, no. 443).

No less interesting than the picture are the margins, which have been filled with animals in a landscape, following the Persian convention. There are prancing deer, a goat, rabbits, tigers, storks, and a *bulbul* bird. In one instance a tiger is pouncing on a mountain goat with impressive horns. Gold has been generously applied to the water, the vegetation, the boulders, the rocky escarpments, and the clouds. The rest of the ground is painted with light washes of green and blue. (For a similarly painted outer border with animals and birds in gold used as a mount for a later picture, see Binney 1973, fig. 169.)

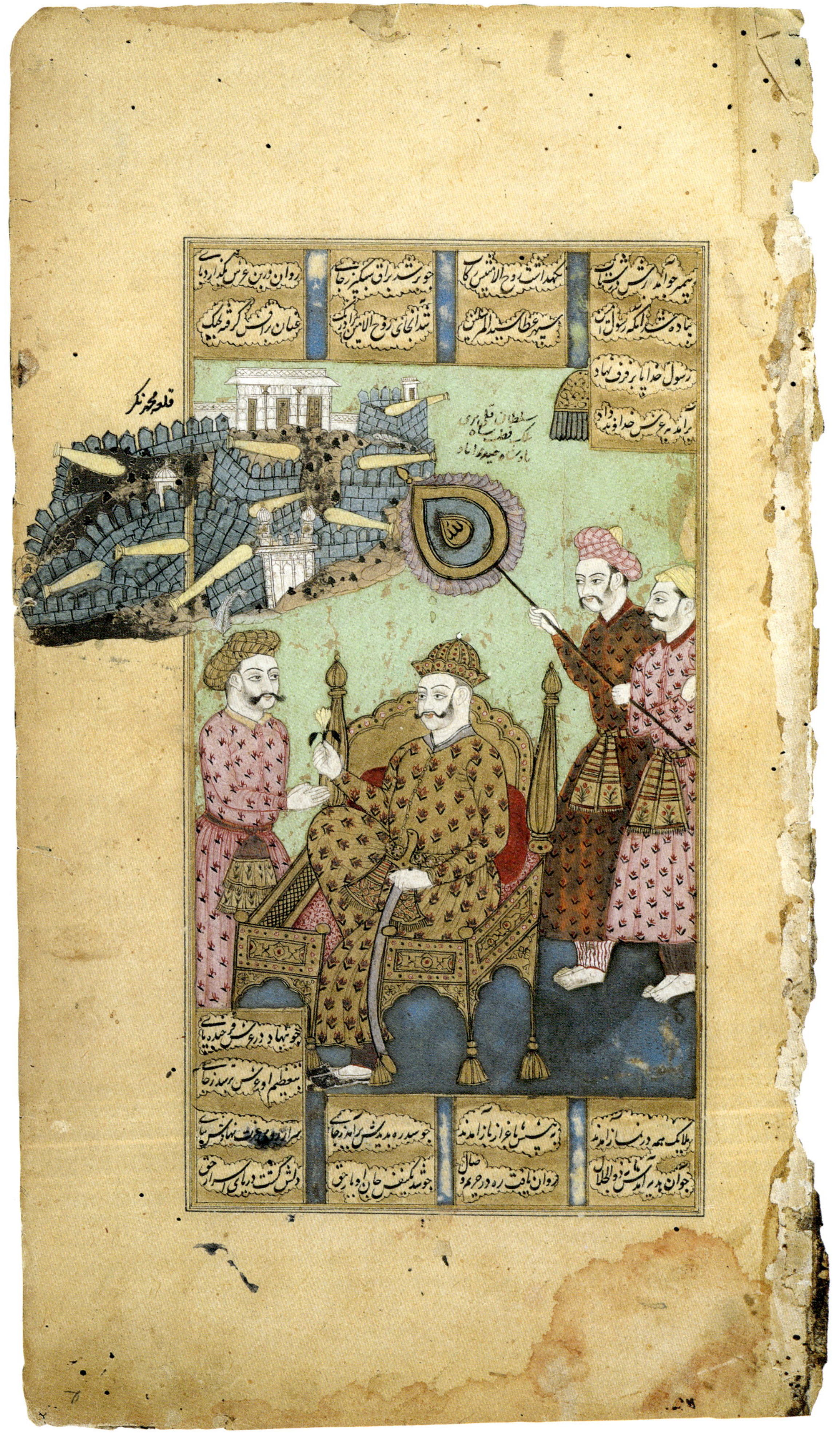

قلعه محمدنگر

Golconda and Hyderabad

103 ILLUSTRATED MANUSCRIPT OF THE *HISTORY OF THE QUTB SHAHI SULTANS OF GOLCONDA*

Andhra Pradesh, Hyderabad; manuscript dated A.H. 1019, A.D. 1610/11
Folios, 12½ x 7⅛ in (31.8 x 18.1 cm)
Text panels, approx. 8⅞ x 4½ in (22.5 x 11.4 cm)
Anonymous gift
M.89.159.4

A *Title Page*
B *Page with Seals and Notes*
C *Illuminated Frontispiece*
D *Sultan Quli Qutb Shah (?)*
6⅜ x 6¹⁄₁₆ in (16.2 x 15.4 cm)
E *Sultan Abdullah Qutb Shah*
6½ x 4½ in (16.5 x 11.4 cm)
F *Sultan Ibrahim Qutb Shah*
5¹¹⁄₁₆ x 4½ in (14.4 x 11.4 cm)
G *Sultan Muhammad Qutb Shah (?)*
6⅛ x 5 in (15.6 x 12.7 cm)
H *Sultan Muhammad Quli Qutb Shah*
7 x 5⅛ in (17.8 x 13.0 cm)
I *Page with Colophon*
J *Page with Seals and Inscriptions*

Complete manuscript with 450 pages, five of which have illustrations. Illuminated double frontispiece with decorative borders. Text written in black ink on buff paper with inset captions in red ink; text on the two illuminated pages and those with illustrations contained within white clouds in a gold field. The majority of text pages have twenty lines of text in four vertical columns surrounded by narrow borders in ink and gold; other pages have varying numbers of lines of text, often written inside square or rectangular compartments. Several hands discernible. Numerous marginal notes. Both end-pages have several seal-stamps in red, black, and blue ink. Cover of cardboard covered in brown and red leather with embossed floral decoration on the outside.

The loosely bound folios are very brittle, frequently stained, and several are worm-eaten. The tooled leather binding, very likely of the nineteenth century, is much damaged. A large number of owner's seals indicate that the manuscript changed hands several times and was considered a proud possession. The illustrations of five of the seven rulers of the dynasty are probably not contemporary with the manuscript. All translations given below are by Z. Faridany-Akhavan.

CAT. 103D

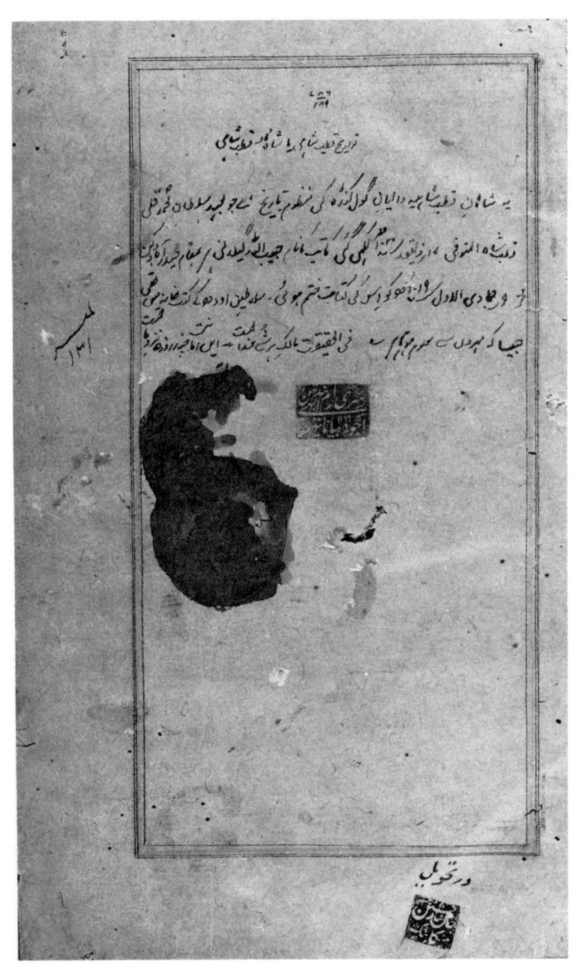

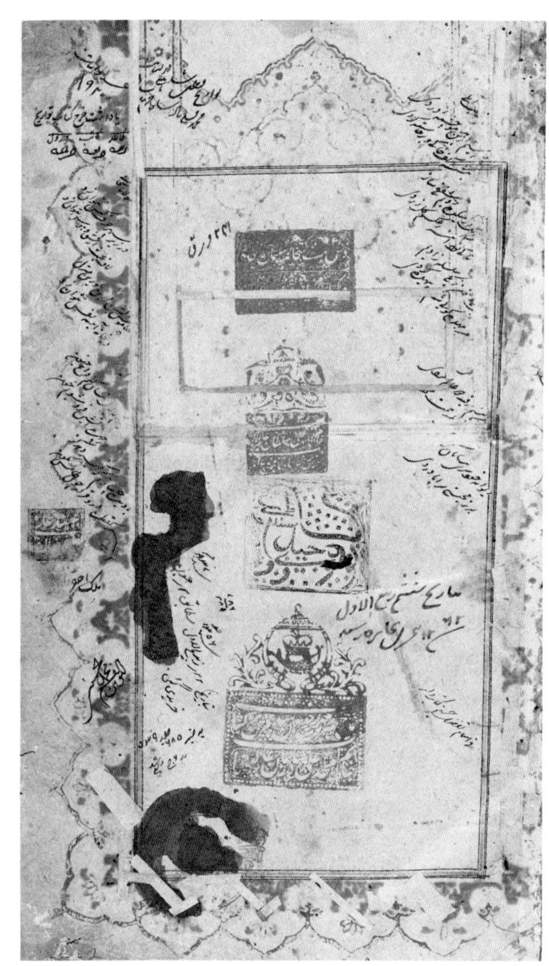

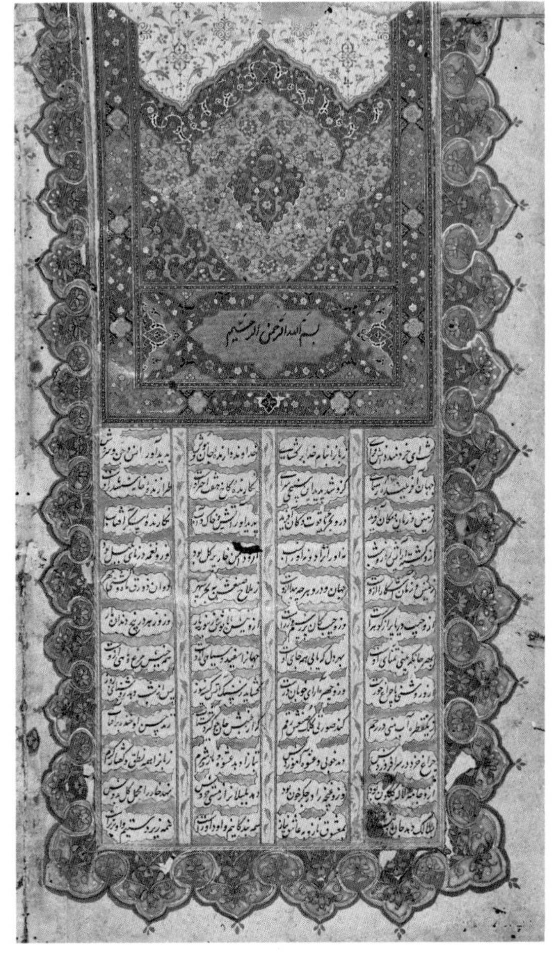

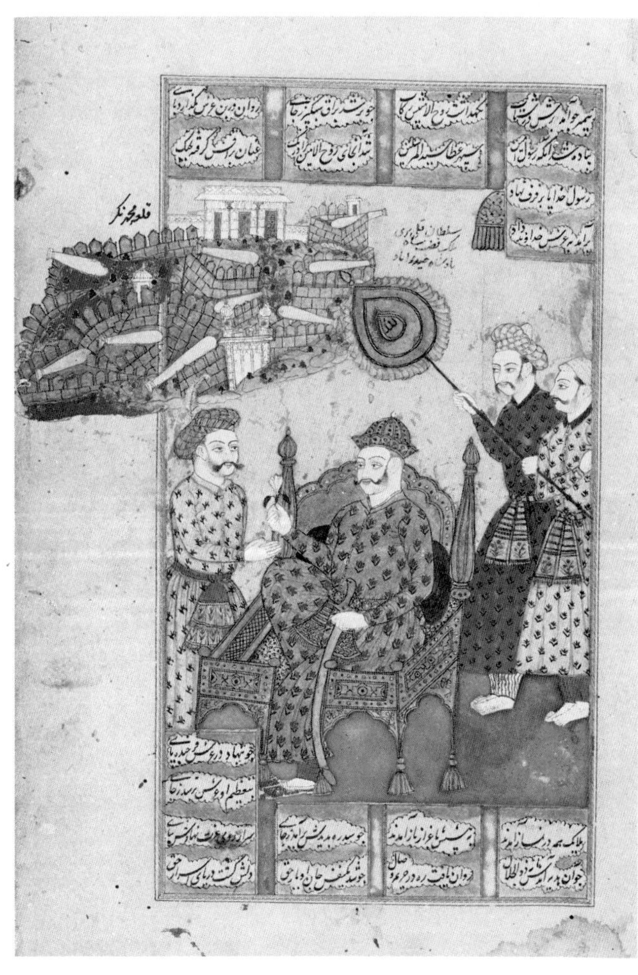

A

The Qutb Shahi Histories, Padshah . . . Qutb Shahi . . . The Shahs of Qutb Shahieh . . . history . . . Sultan Muhammad Quli Qutb Shah . . . , named the scribe Habibullah Gilani to the rank of Haydar-abad . . . On the first of Jamadi . . . the rulers of Oudh . . . in truth the ruler is God (?) But these few days . . .

SEAL
A.H. 1199 [A.D. 1784/85]

LOWER SEAL
received by . . . Hussein A.H. 1123 [A.D. 1711/12]

B
Center panel, top left
The Qutub Shahi history in the library of Muhammad Quli, the padshah of {Haydar-abad?}.

On this page there are a number of seals and librarian's notes as well as poems and aphorisms.

C This brilliantly illuminated page with its elaborate chapter heading (*unwan*) is quite characteristic of Islamic books. The intricately designed illuminated panel at the top is rendered in bright turquoise and gold and adorned with flowering vines and arabesques in light colors and white. The border on three sides is decorated with cusped arches in green and blue and contains flowering vines. This marginal decoration also occurs on the facing page. It appears to have been added to both pages at a later date. The text is contained within white clouds in a gold field.

D The title above the standard reads "Sultan Quli . . . Malik Qutb Shah Padshah of Haydar-abad." The inscription outside the frame at the upper left identifies the fort as Mihr Nagar Fort. *Mihr Nagar* literally means "city of the sun." Apparently this was once the name of the Golconda fort, which is what this characteristically Deccani depiction of an architectural mass must represent. It gives sort of a distant bird's eye view of the fort, its walls painted gray, the rocks and ground in brown and purple, and the buildings in white. The figure below seated on a golden throne and holding a flower must be Sultan Quli Qutb Shah (r. 1512–43), the founder of the dynasty and of the fort. Unlike other Deccani rulers, who wear turbans, he is given a crown as one sees monarchs in fifteenth-century Persian paintings wearing. Quli Qutb Shah was a Black Sheep (*Qara Qoyunlu*) Turkman prince who had emigrated from Iran to Bidar when it was the capital of the Bahamanids. The artist probably had no portrait of the founder at his disposal and modeled it on a generalized representation of a king in Timurid paintings. His manner of sitting on the throne too is reminiscent of fifteenth-century Persian paintings. The throne, the sultan's garment, and his crown are all in gold. The floor below is painted indigo, and the background is the same green as one sees in the portrait of Ghazi ad-Din Bahadur Khan in the collection [110A].

E The inscription above the doorway reads: *Sultan Abdullah Qutb Shah.* Abdullah Qutb Shah (r. 1626–72) was the penultimate ruler in the dynasty and was a child when this book was completed. There are several known portraits of him, but this representation is much more idealized and hence less easily recognizable than the others. However, in all these portraits he is distinguished by the feathered plume that rises prominently from his distinctive turban (Zebrowski 1983, figs. 149–51). Elegantly dressed in gold attire, he stands somewhat stiffly with his left hand on his sword and the gloved right supporting a falcon. A maid offers him a tray with flowers, and two more females, one of whom also holds a spittoon, stand behind him waving cloth *morchals.* Bottles of blue and red glass adorn the niches in the whitewashed door frame behind him. Beyond the open door is a tree and a blue sky.

F The inscription on the roof identifies the figure as *Ibrahim Qutb Shah.* Dressed in yellow, he is seated on his haunches on a polygonal golden throne and holds a flower with his right hand. In front of him a woman stands in supplication or adoration, and behind stands a second woman fanning him with a cloth. The door frame behind him contains no doors and is painted as a green patch. Trees and blue sky may be seen beyond the white wall and the porch.

No contemporary portrait of Sultan Ibrahim Qutb Shah (r. 1550–80) is known, even though he is considered to be the first Golconda monarch to patronize painting. It is not possible therefore to determine how close this portrait is to a true likeness. The face does show a distinctive shape, and possibly some earlier representation was available to the artist.

G The inscription above the ruler simply says *Qutb Shah.* As this is the designation of the dynasty, it is of not much help in identifying the sitter. However, since the following portrait (H) is identified as Sultan Muhammad Quli Qutb Shah, by process of elimination this painting could represent his successor Muhammad Qutb Shah (r. 1612–26), Abul Hasan Qutb Shah (r. 1672–87), or even the second member of the dynasty, Jamshid Quli Qutb Shah (r. 1543–50). There is no known portrait of Sultan Jamshid, and he is probably the least likely of the three. Despite the schematic nature of the representation, this portrait is more similar to those of Muhammad Qutb Shah than to those of Abul Hasan Qutb Shah. The manner in which

CAT. 103A,B *(opposite top)*
CAT. 103C,D *(opposite bottom)*

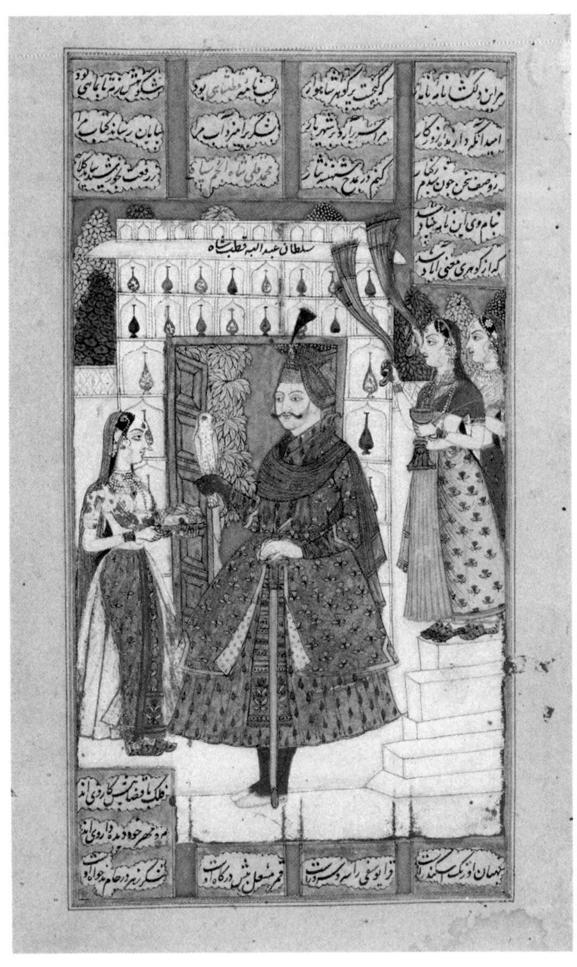
سلطان عبدالله قطبشاه

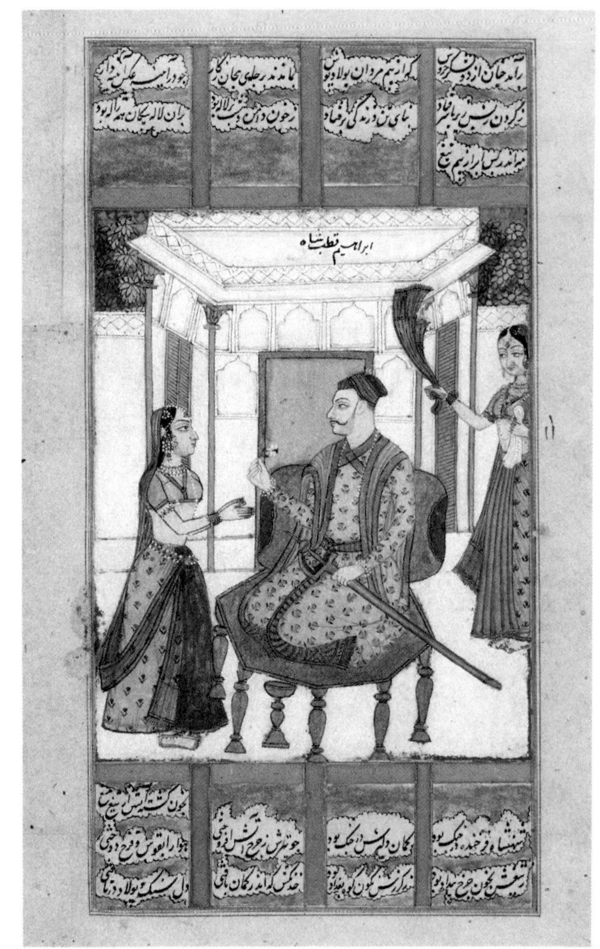
ابراهیم قطبشاه

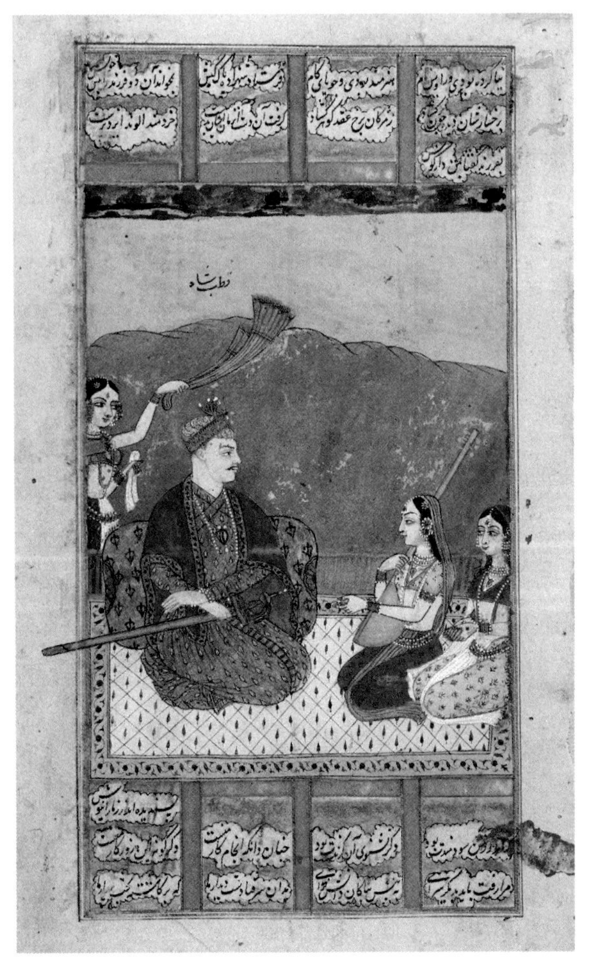
قطبشاه

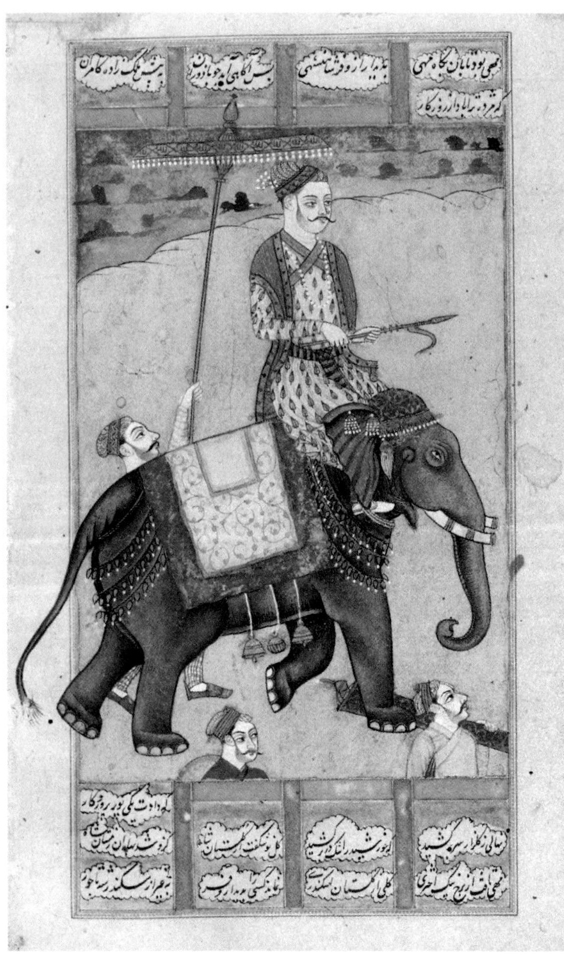

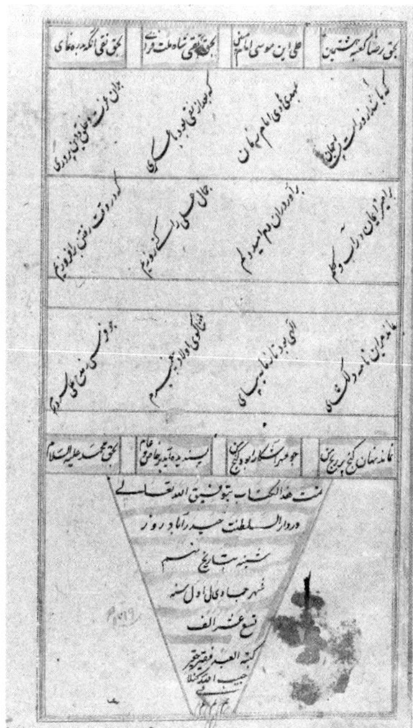

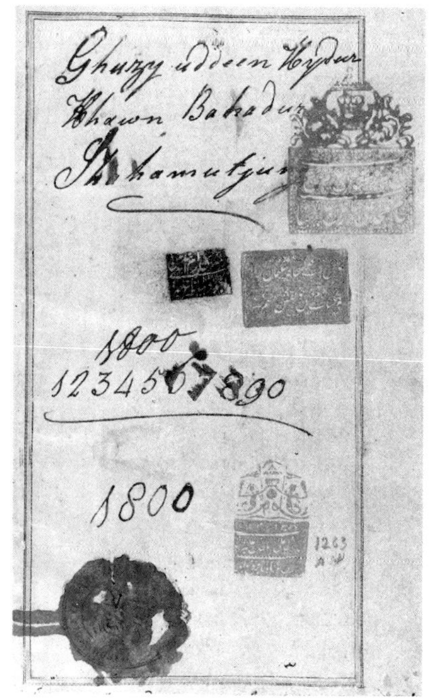

CAT. 103E,F *(opposite top)*
CAT. 103G,H *(opposite bottom)*
CAT. 103I,J *(above)*

the turban is tied, the form of the moustache, and the shape of the nose closely resemble these features in known portraits of the monarch (Zebrowski 1983, figs. 142, 143).

If this is indeed a portrait of Muhammad Qutb Shah, then we are given a clue to a hitherto unknown dimension of his personality. The fact that he should be portrayed listening to music could indicate his renown as a music lover. The musician's companion seems to be doing nothing, and a third woman keeps the prince cool. The background immediately behind them is rendered as the side of a blue hill, above which is a band of green surmounted by a narrow, dark sky with slightly menacing clouds.

H An inscription on top of the page of the fifth picture identifies the monarch as *Sultan Muhammad Quli Qutb Shah* (r. 1580–1612), for whom this history was prepared. Holding an elephant goad, he rides an elephant before a green hill and gray sky with patchy blue clouds. He wears a purple garment and is dressed less sumptuously than other sultans. Three men walk alongside, one holding the royal parasol above the monarch's head. He sports whiskers and a prominent moustache. The text on the page mentions "Muhammad Quli Shah with an army as [numerous] as the stars." Unfortunately no contemporary or later portrait of the ruler has yet come to light, which makes it difficult to determine how faithfully this representation might preserve his features.

The colophon of the manuscript states in words the date A.H. 1019, which corresponds to A.D. 1610/11. Thus, the book was copied for Muhammad Quli Qutb Shah by, according to the colophon, Habibullah Gilani, who was probably the author as well. It appears, however, that for some reason the book was not illustrated at the time it was copied. This is clear not only from the inclusion of portraits of the later rulers Muhammad and Abdullah Qutb Shah but also from the style of the illustrations, which is more consistent with that prevailing in Hyderabad toward the end of the seventeenth century rather than the beginning. The inclusion of Abdullah Qutb Shah and not of his successor Abul Hasan (r. 1672–87), the last ruler of the dynasty, might lead one to conclude that the illustrations were added during the former's reign. However, the fact that even Abdullah looks so different from his known portraits indicates that the artist was not too familiar with his subject. The ubiquitous use of Mughal green for the background would tend to confirm a date after the Mughal occupation in 1687. The illustrations are adequate; both the weak coloring and the unenterprising compositions lack the finesse that one sees in first-rate Golconda or Hyderabadi paintings even during the last quarter of the seventeenth century (cf. [110A, 111B]). The colors are applied in a flat manner, and the extravagant picturesqueness of the landscape that is the hallmark of Deccani painting is absent from these pictures. While the illustrations could have been executed by a mediocre artist during the reign of Abdullah Qutb Shah, more likely they were added about 1700 by an artist who was used to working in the Mughal rather than the Deccani manner.

Andhra Pradesh, Golconda; c. 1630
Folios, 10⅛ x 6¹⁄₁₆ in (25.7 x 15.4 cm)
Illuminations, approx. 6½ x 3⅝ in (16.5 x 9.2 cm)
Gift of Dr. and Mrs. Pratapaditya Pal
M.83.255.2
Literature: Pal 1987, pp. 120, 121, fig. 81.

Detached from the book they once adorned, these two sumptuously illuminated pages once served as a frontispiece. The central panel on each leaf is a colorful composition of various shapes filled with arabesques with several types of flowers. Gold and blue are the predominant colors, but there is some use of green in the top panel and red has been employed, especially for the flowers in the surrounding margins. The outer borders are particularly attractive, with brilliantly feathered birds perched on equally colorful flowering plants. The outlines of these birds and flowers have been drawn in gold, and the

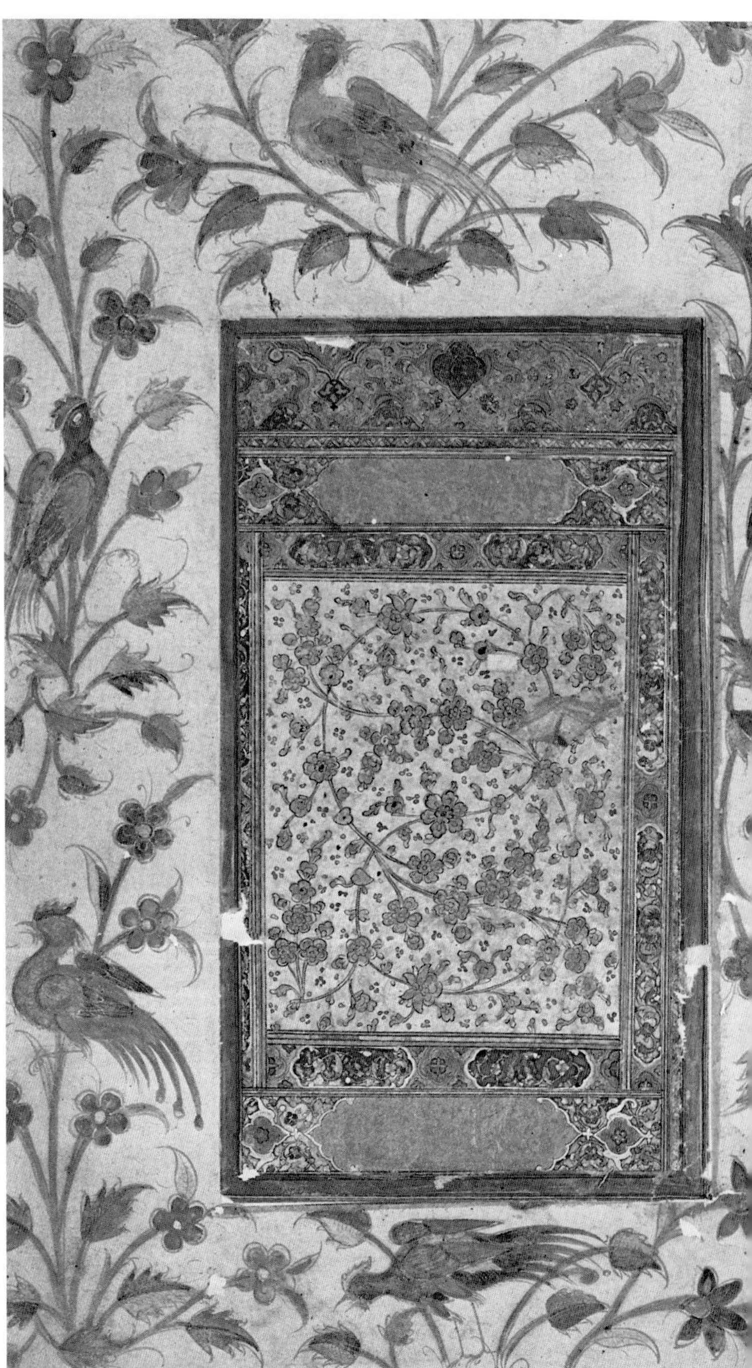

colors—red, orange, green, purple, and blue—have a particularly rich and vibrant tonality. Indeed, the delightfully decorative forms of the borders have the quality of fantasy as well as a rhythmic vitality that is characteristic of Deccani paintings, whereas the more restrained central panels are reminiscent of Persian manuscripts.

The closest parallels to these two leaves can be seen in a similarly illuminated but unillustrated manuscript of the *Fawaid-i-Qutb Shahi* in the National Museum, Delhi (see Bukhari 1967). That manuscript is incomplete, and some leaves from it are in the San Diego Museum of Art (Binney 1973, p. 149, no. 125). While the measurements of the folios in that manuscript (22 x 13.8 cm) differ from those of the museum's leaves, the decorative design of the margins—with birds, animals, and flowers—is very similar in both. A collection of useful codes for rulers, elegant prose, and Persian verses, the *Fawaid* was compiled by Mawlana Uwair Munshi at the order of Sultan Abdullah Qutb Shah (r. 1626–72) of Golconda and completed in 1631. There can be little doubt that the same illuminators responsible for the lavish marginalia of the *Fawaid* manuscript also executed the outer borders of these two leaves, if they did indeed belong to a different book, which also must have been produced for the sultan.

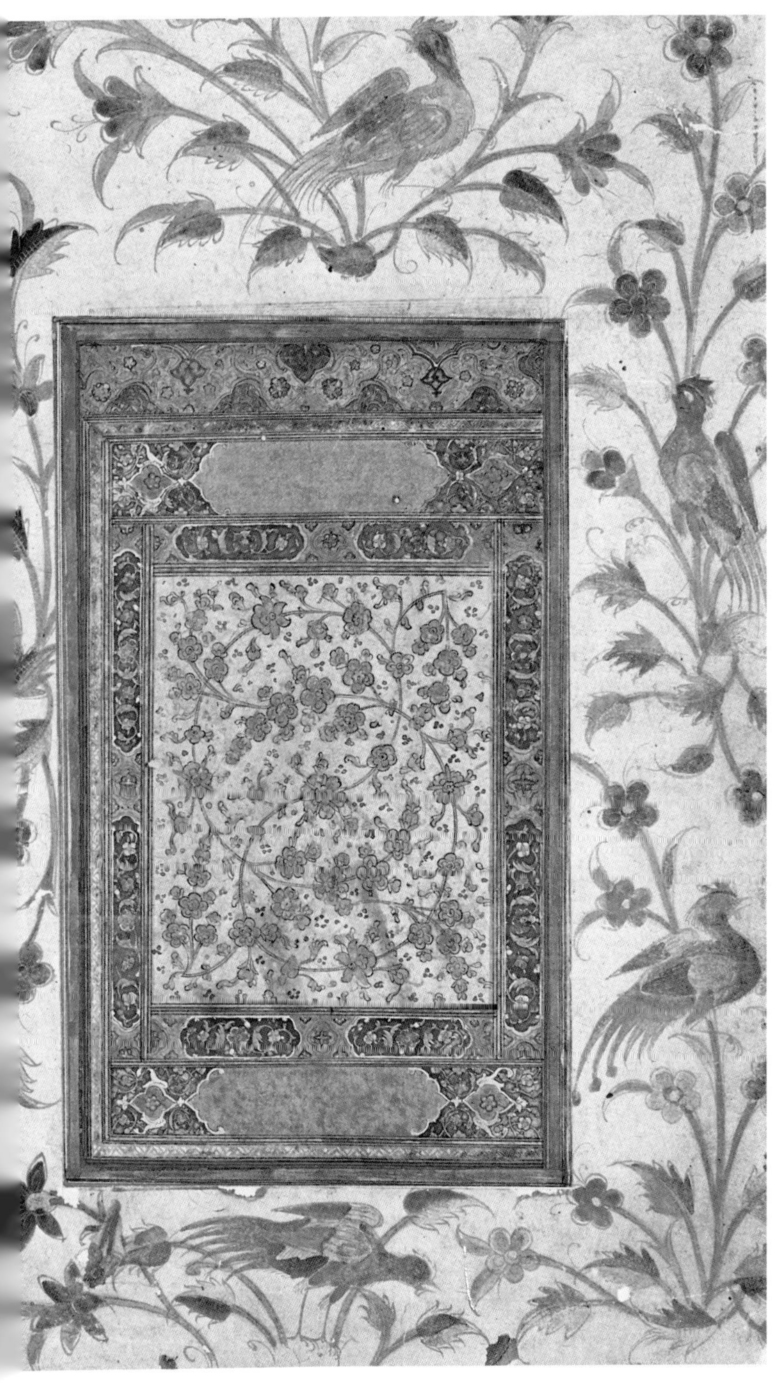

Deccan, Golconda(?); c. 1650
Ink with color washes and gold on paper
Folio, $9\frac{3}{4}$ x $5\frac{9}{16}$ in (24.8 x 14.1 cm)
Illustration, $5\frac{1}{4}$ x $2\frac{5}{8}$ in (13.3 x 6.7 cm)
The Nasli M. Heeramaneck Collection,
gift of Joan Palevsky
M.73.5.466
Literature: Pal 1974, p. 148, no. 266.

This lightly colored drawing is in an elaborate mount with two prominent calligraphic panels at the top and the bottom. Immediately surrounding the image is a border of marbled paper, around which is another border with a golden flowering vine on a peach background. In the calligraphic panels the text is accommodated within clouds, and the rest of the space is painted in gold with light arabesques. At each end is a small square containing a pair of golden beasts against a blue background. In each instance the beasts, most of which seem to be mythical creatures, are attacking each other. Two are serpents or dragons, two appear to be avian creatures, and one is clearly a deer. The verse has been translated by Z. Faridany-Akhavan as follows:

{O Lord, whoever} found {Thee} knows thee,
{O Lord,} finding Thee is our wish but comprehending Thee . . .

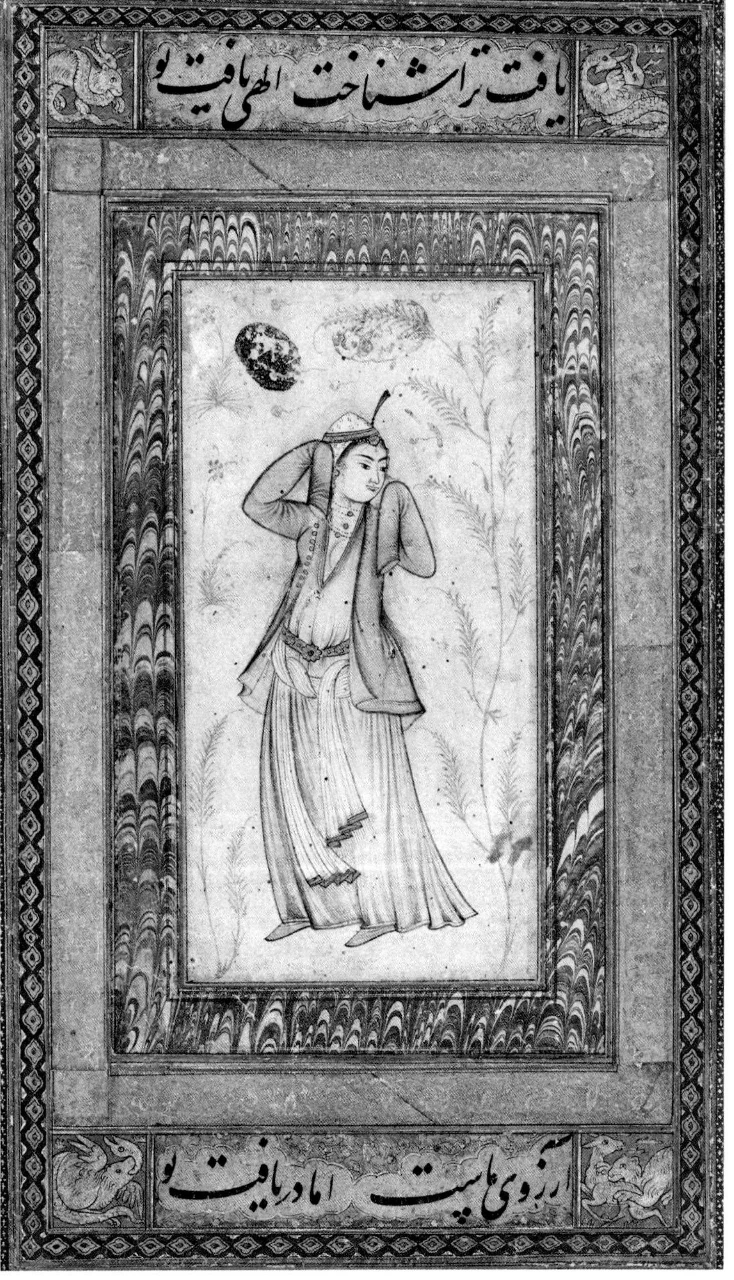

The picture depicts a young woman dressed in Persian costume with her arms raised and her sleeves dangling. Although her shape and proportions are those of a Persian lady, the way her breasts are shown may reflect an Indian fashion. The garments have been quite heavily shaded. Beside her rise two golden plants, and tufts of vegetation have been added on the left. It is possible that the lady represents a Sufi in search of God, in which case the poem would be relevant to the picture. Usually dancing Sufis are portrayed with their arms withdrawn in their sleeves.

There is some difference of opinion among scholars as to where this picture was rendered. E. Binney (1974, p. 148, no. 266) suggested a Deccani provenance, but others who have examined it have disagreed, verbally attributing it either to northern India, Iran, or even Turkey. In a written communication Z. Faridany-Akhavan stated she feels that the tinted drawing is Deccani rather than Mughal or Turkish. It should be noted that the shape of the face and the features as well as the turban with a single plume are very close to those of a young prince attributed to a Golconda artist by Zebrowski (1983, pp. 173–74, fig. 139). Active during the first few decades of the seventeenth century, this artist appears to have been infatuated with foreign sources, from which he borrowed compositions but added local flavor in coloring and rhythmic patterns. The lady in the museum's painting is also quite close to another in a composition with lovers adapted by the unnamed Golconda artist from a Safavid model (Zebrowski 1983, fig. 140). Although the museum's picture lacks the sensuous exuberance of nature or the brilliant coloring of the more elaborate compositions, it could have been done by the same artist as a less ambitious exercise in copying a Persianate model.

106 MULLA RAOZA

Andhra Pradesh, Golconda; c. 1675
Opaque watercolor, gold, silver, and ink on paper
Overall, 9 x 5 in (22.9 x 12.7 cm)
Illustration, $8\frac{11}{16}$ x $4\frac{3}{4}$ in (22.1 x 12.1 cm)
Gift of Paul F. Walter
M.75.113.2

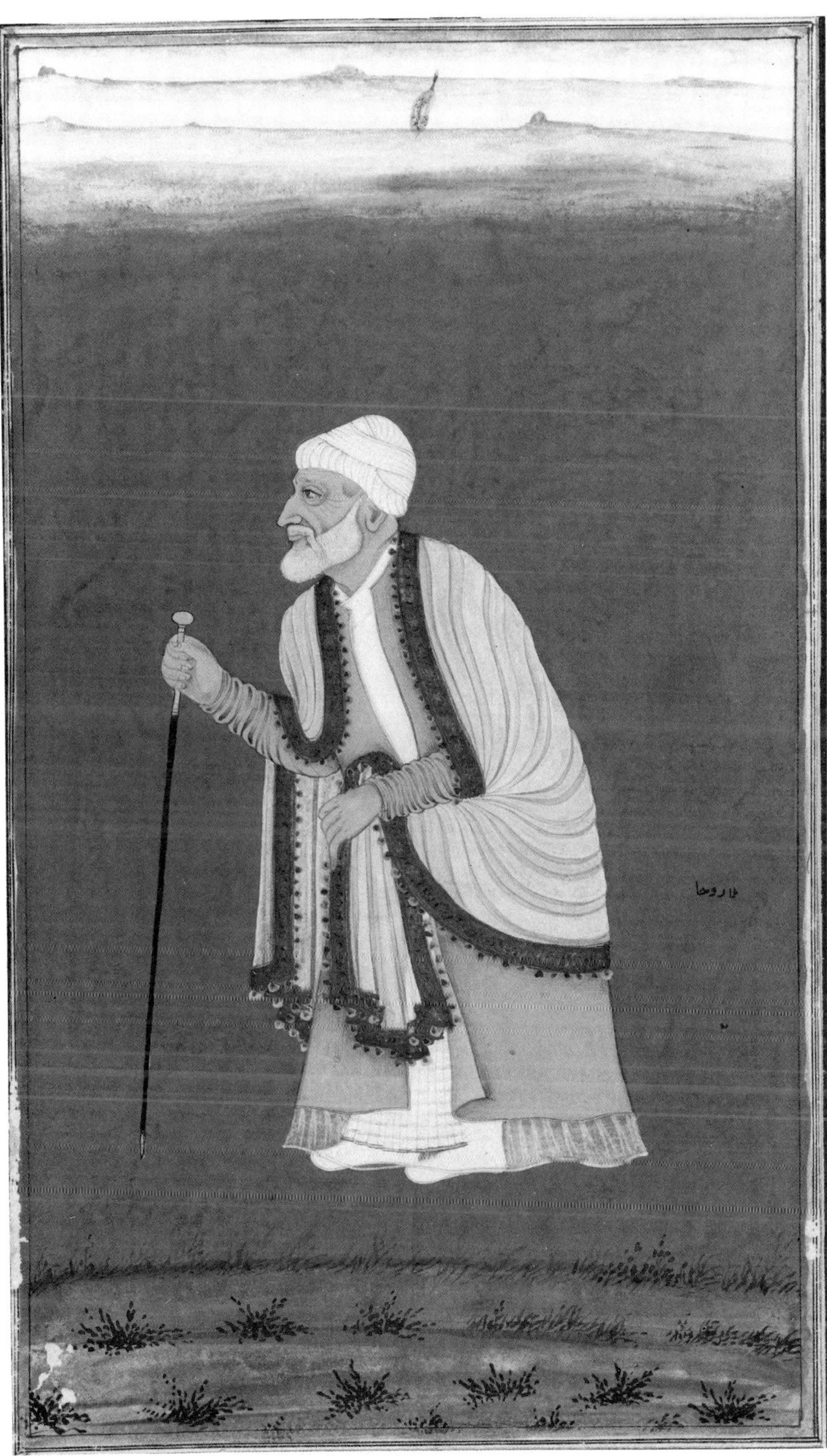

A small inscription to the right of the figure identifies him as *Mulla Raoza.* Written in English in what appears to be nineteenth-century script on the back of the painting is *Molla Roeha of Mal Rucha.* If Mal Rucha is the name of a place, it cannot be identified at present. There is apparently a portrait of the same person in the Royal Library, Copenhagen (Codex Orient Rotuhe III), where he is identified as Molla Somi'a of Golconda. Either there is a misidentification on one of the two portraits or the mulla in fact had two names, which is not improbable. Nothing, however, is known about him.

Although a light green patch of ground with dark green sprays of vegetation is rendered at the bottom of the picture, the aged mulla is shown standing higher up against the chocolate-colored middle ground. He stands hunched over, supporting himself with a staff. He is dressed in several layers of clothing, the most prominent being a long coat in green over a white *jama.* Over this is draped a fine Deccani shawl with a sumptuous gold border with flowers (cf. Zebrowski 1983, fig. 142; and Binney 1973, no. 139a).

It is possible that the portrait illustrated by Zebrowski (fig. 142)—that of Sultan Muhammad Qutb Shah of Golconda—is by the same artist who painted this sensitively rendered but slightly mechanical portrait of the aged mulla. While the sultan's visage is more idealized, here the artist has given us a realistic rendering of the face with its wrinkles, lines, shadows, and the distinctive and noble nose. In the other portrait as well the figure is strongly contrasted against a dark background and the sky indicated sparingly, even more so. Both paintings show a similar delight in the rendering of the attire, although appropriately the ruler is more luxuriantly robed. Two portraits now in the San Diego Museum of Art, one representing Shaykh Muhammad Khatun and the other Sultan Muhammad Qutb Shah of Golconda (Binney 1973, pp. 162–63, no. 139a, recto and verso), are certainly by the same artist. In fact, this portrait is very likely from the same album as the San Diego pictures.

Andhra Pradesh, Golconda; 1675–1700
8¼ x 4⅛ in (21.0 x 10.5 cm)
Gift of Doris and Ed Wiener
M.75.114.3

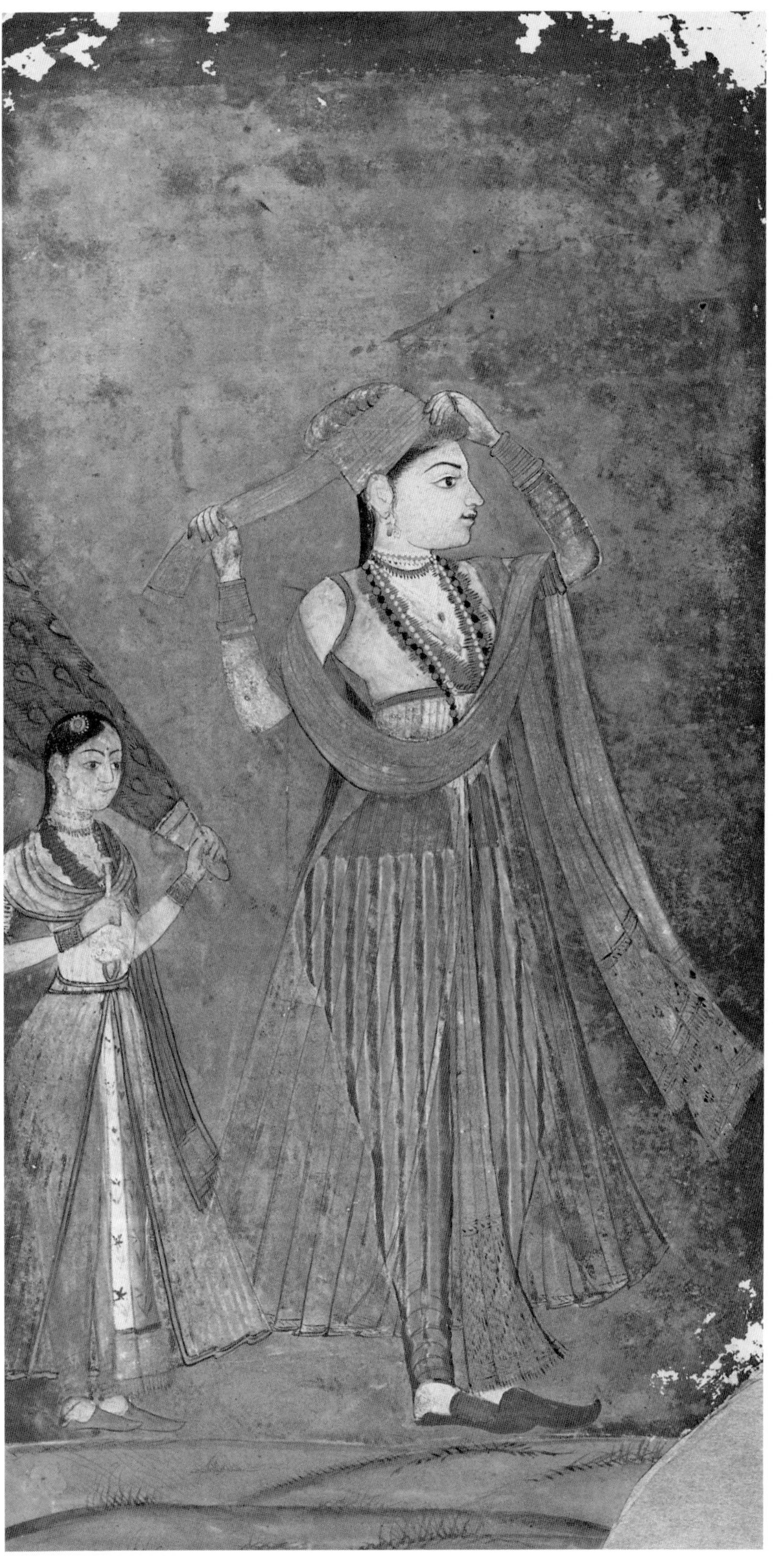

An elegantly dressed lady is busy wrapping her turban while a servant girl stands stiffly behind holding a carafe with her right hand and a green peacock-feather *morchal* with the left. The inclusion of a *morchal*-bearer would indicate that the lady is a princess of the realm. Whether this is a portrait taken from life or simply an idealized representation is more difficult to ascertain. Certainly the individualized face would make one think it a portrait. Rather curious is the fact that she is wrapping her turban outside, indicated by the ground, rather than inside a building. Is the viewer to assume from the expression on her face and the direction of her gaze, however, that a mirror exists beyond the margin of the picture?

Both women are clothed in a similar fashion, but the apparel of the mistress is obviously much more luxuriant. Her red-and-green-striped pajamas are prominent beneath the diaphanous dress. Her shoes match the red of the pajamas. The turban and the scarf are of the same gold fabric. That the maid is of local origin is indicated by her face and the ornament in her hair. This item of jewelry is seen in several late-seventeenth-century pictures attributed to Golconda (Zebrowski 1983, figs. 176, 177). Curiously, both figures stand slightly above the green ground against a blue-gray middle section. Along the top is a band of dark gray, some of the pigment of which has peeled off.

Such genre studies of women engaged in various mundane activities are more common in Mughal than in Deccani art. However, in the Deccan they appear to have been in some demand in Golconda during the last quarter of the seventeenth century (Zebrowski 1983, figs. 165, 166, 168, 177, 179). It may be recalled that after 1687 the kingdom was overrun by the Mughals. Stylistically the examples in Zebrowski's book are quite different from the museum's picture, which exhibits some of the formal characteristics seen in works of an artist called Rahim Deccani. Although it may not have been painted by him, the picture does belong to the artistic milieu of Golconda of the last quarter of the seventeenth century.

108 RAI JABHA CHAND AT A JAIN SHRINE

Andhra Pradesh, Golconda; 1675–1700
8⅝ x 12¼ in (21.9 x 31.1 cm)
Gift of Mr. and Mrs. Michael Douglas
M.81.271.5
Literature: Zebrowski 1983, p. 218, fig. 189; Pal 1987, pp. 120, 121, fig. 82.

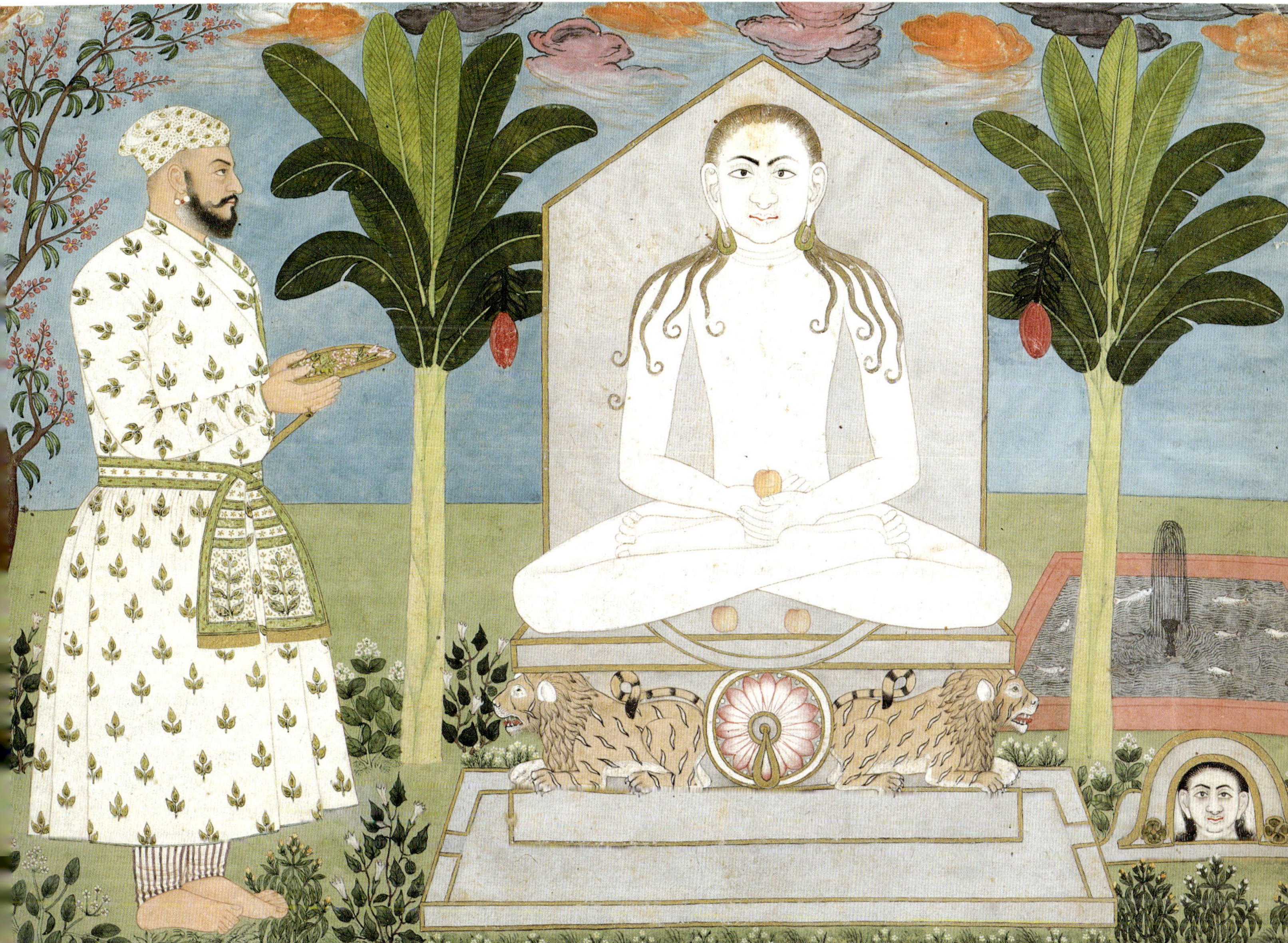

CAT. 108

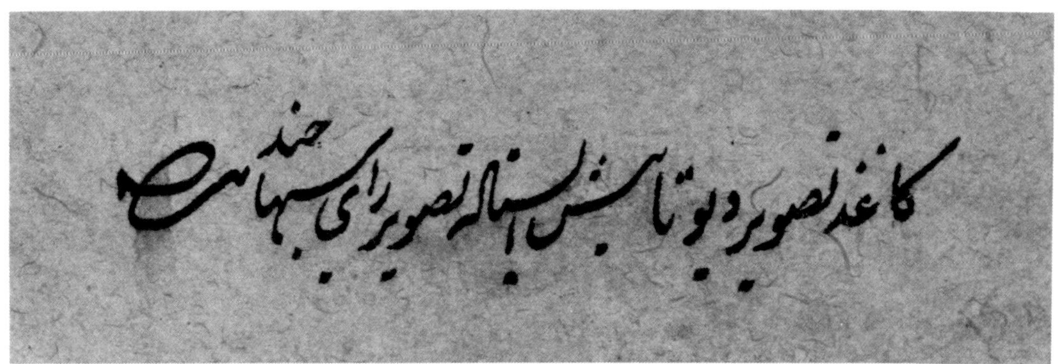

CAT. 108 reverse detail

This is a rare and unusual Deccani painting because of its subject. According to S. Digby the Arabic inscription on the back may be translated as, "Standing in front of the picture [or image] of the deity (*devata*) is Rai Jabha Chand." M. Zebrowski (1983, p. 218) read the name tentatively as "Rai Sahai (or Bihari?) Chand." The deity in this instance is Rishabhanatha, one of the twenty-four enlightened teachers known as Jinas and venerated by the Jains. Apart from his name, we know nothing about the worshipper. He may have been a nobleman attached to the Golconda court or a Jain merchant.

The picture shows Rai Jabha standing rather formally to one side with a dish full of flowers as an offering to the marble statue of Rishabhanatha. Except for his two earrings, the Jina is naked; his hair is colored golden. He is seated in the posture of meditation on a throne that is edged with gold and supported by a pair of animals that are a combination of a tiger and a lion. Between the animals is a lotus medallion. An unusual feature is the placement of three apples as an offering to the Jina: one of the fruits is placed in the palm of his right hand. Noteworthy also is the awkward manner in which the Jina's left hand is rendered. Traditionally, it should be placed below the other. The statue is flanked by two banana trees, and on the right is a pool with a fountain and fish. In front of the pool is a rather unusual stone niche, framed in gold, containing only a human head with flowing hair. An attractive flowering tree rises behind the devotee, and the foreground is decorated with a formal arrangement of a variety of flowering shrubs in two rows. The blue sky above is adorned with cloud formations in orange, purple, and mauve.

In his discussion of this painting Zebrowski correctly points out that the style here is considerably influenced by the Mughal tradition, especially in the naturalistic representation of the noble devotee and his attire. Zebrowski has also suggested its close stylistic kinship to another picture (Zebrowski 1983, fig. 190) bearing the signature of an artist called Ali Reza, who may have worked in Bikaner before migrating to the Deccan during Aurangzeb's reign, when interest in painting diminished at the Mughal court. Whether or not he was trained in the Mughal school, there is no doubt that Ali Reza's style is much more restrained than that preferred in Golconda just before its capitulation to Aurangzeb. His preference for strictly symmetrical composition and a sense of order may well reflect a Jain patron's taste. (For another version of the same subject, see *In the Image of Man* 1982, p. 179, no. 291).

109 PAGE OF CALLIGRAPHY

By Abul Baqa al-Musavi (c. 1625–1700)
Andhra Pradesh, Hyderabad; 1675–1700
Folio, 9 x 6 in (22.9 x 15.2 cm)
Text, 7 3/8 x 4 1/4 in (18.7 x 10.8 cm)
Purchased with funds provided by Lizabeth Scott
M.91.1.1

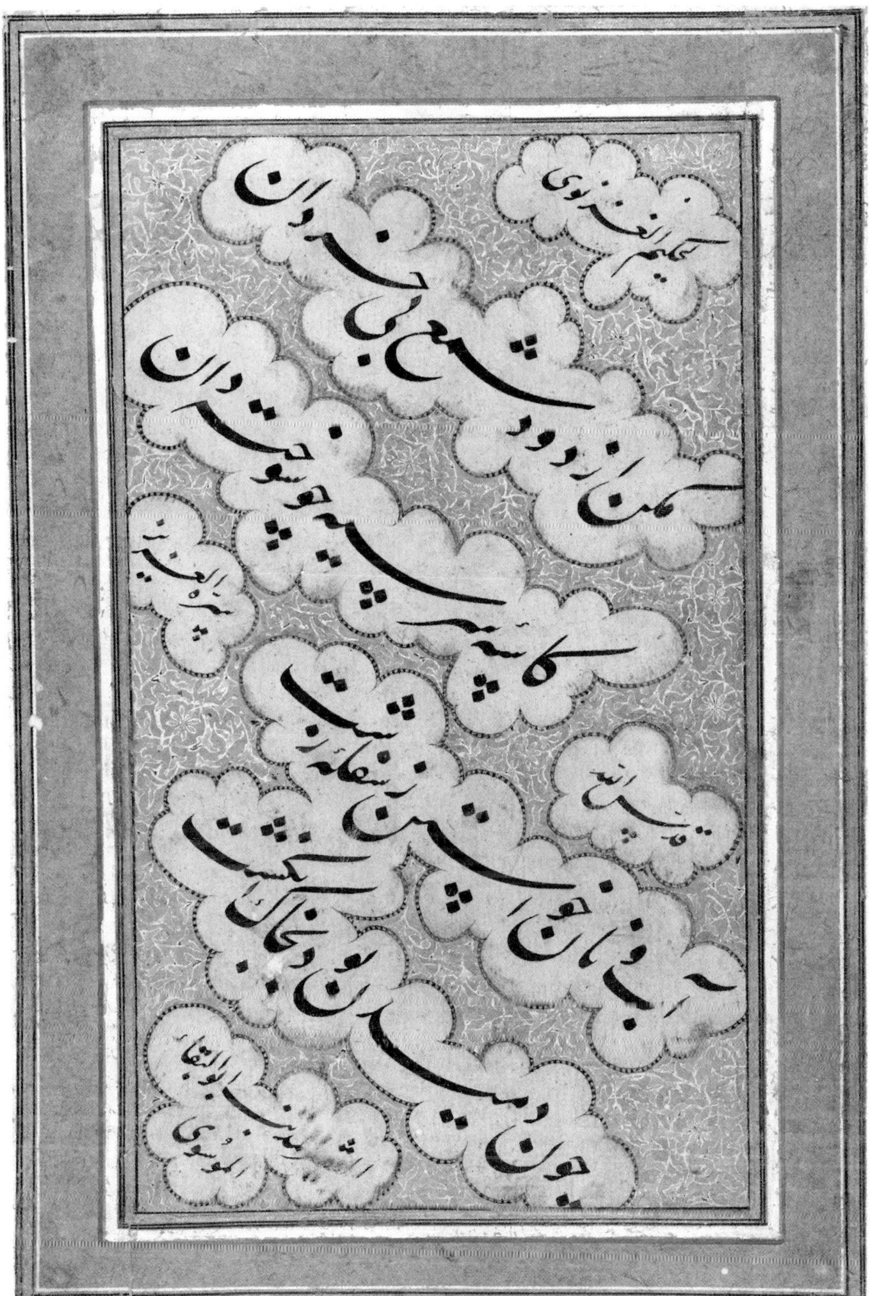

Bold *nastaliq* letters written in black ink are accommodated within beige cloud bands floating diagonally across a gold ground adorned with a delicately rendered white flowering vine enlivened with blue specks. The name of the calligrapher is included in the cloud band in the lower left corner. Abul Baqa al-Musavi was a court calligrapher of the Mughal Emperor Aurangzeb, and he may have been in the Deccan during the siege of Bijapur and Golconda.

The text has been translated as follows by S. Digby:

To Hakim Ghaznavi {i.e., verses of Hakim of Ghazni}

VERSES
Make not black from the smoke of the unwise
The cup of {your} skull like an ash-tray {container}.

SMALL CARTOUCHES
May Allah the Almighty sanctify his secret
{i.e., the poet Hakim Ghaznavi}

VERSE
Asking for water and bread from the ugly (and) base
Would be like breathing on {?} one's finger in the dust.
The sinful faqir Abul-Baqa al-Musavi.

Andhra Pradesh, Golconda or Hyderabad
Folio, 17 3/8 x 11 1/4 in (44.2 x 28.6 cm)
From the Nasli and Alice Heeramaneck Collection, Museum Associates Purchase
M.81.8.9
Literature: *Heeramaneck* 1966, p. 160, no. 219 (A only illustrated).

A *Portrait of General Ghazi ad-Din Bahadur Khan Firuz Jang* (r)
c. 1690
9 7/8 x 6 1/4 in (25.1 x 15.9 cm)
Border, embossed with gold, with hand-coloring

B *Page of Calligraphy* (v)
By Haidar Beg, Roshan Qalam
Seventeenth century
4 3/8 x 2 in (11.1 x 5.1 cm)
Border, embossed with gold

CAT. 110A

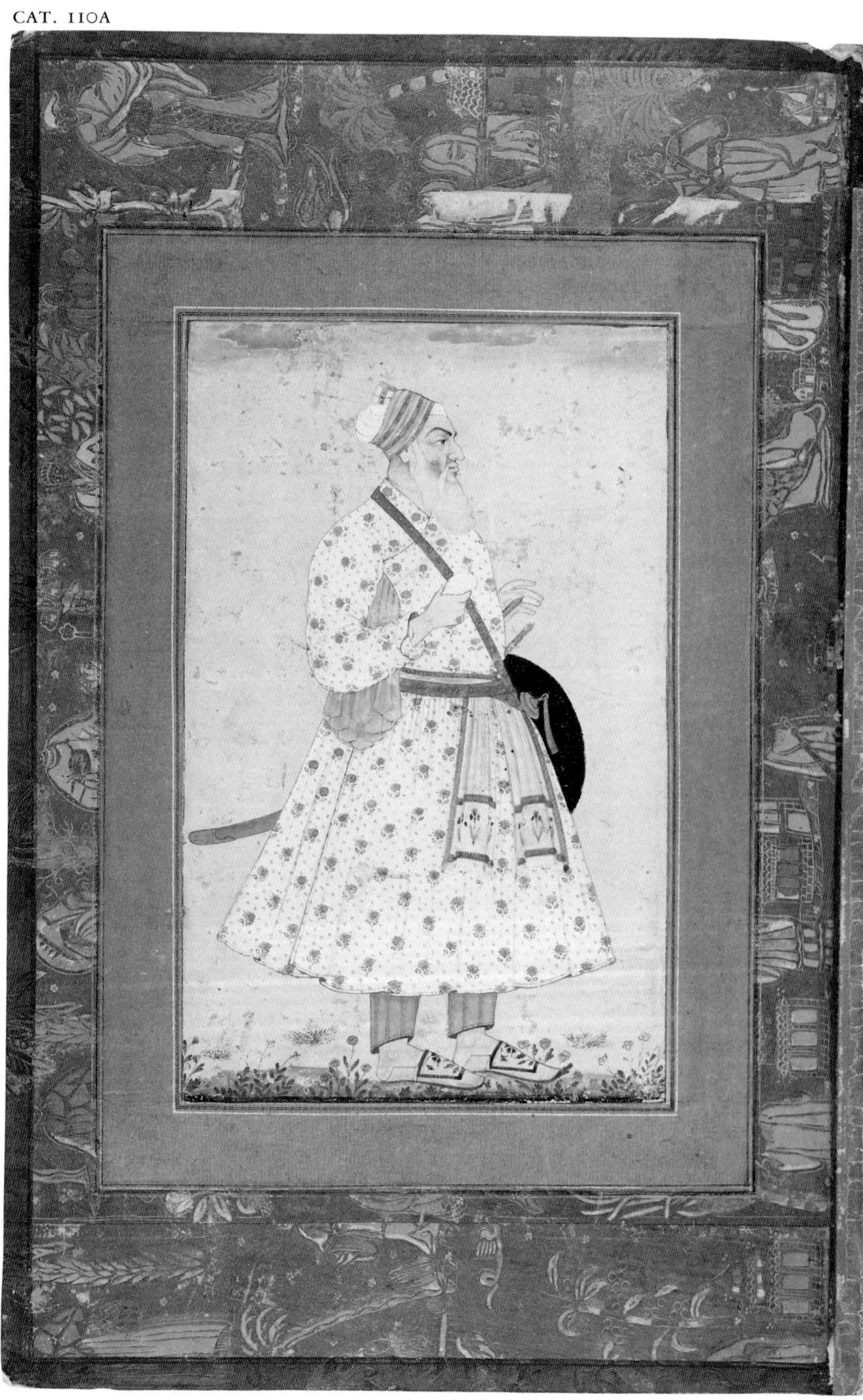

This folio is from the same album as another in the collection [99], as it has the same use of printed, embossed paper for the outer borders. Two folios now in the San Diego Museum of Art (Binney 1973, pp. 160–61, no. 136) may have belonged to the same album. The album seems to have contained formal portraits of both local and Mughal notables and may have been assembled in eighteenth-century Hyderabad. The calligraphic panel, B, includes a mention of the regnal year 1, which may refer to the first year of the rule of the first nizam of Hyderabad, 1724. The album could have been assembled for him, as this particular portrait is of his father.

CAT. 110B

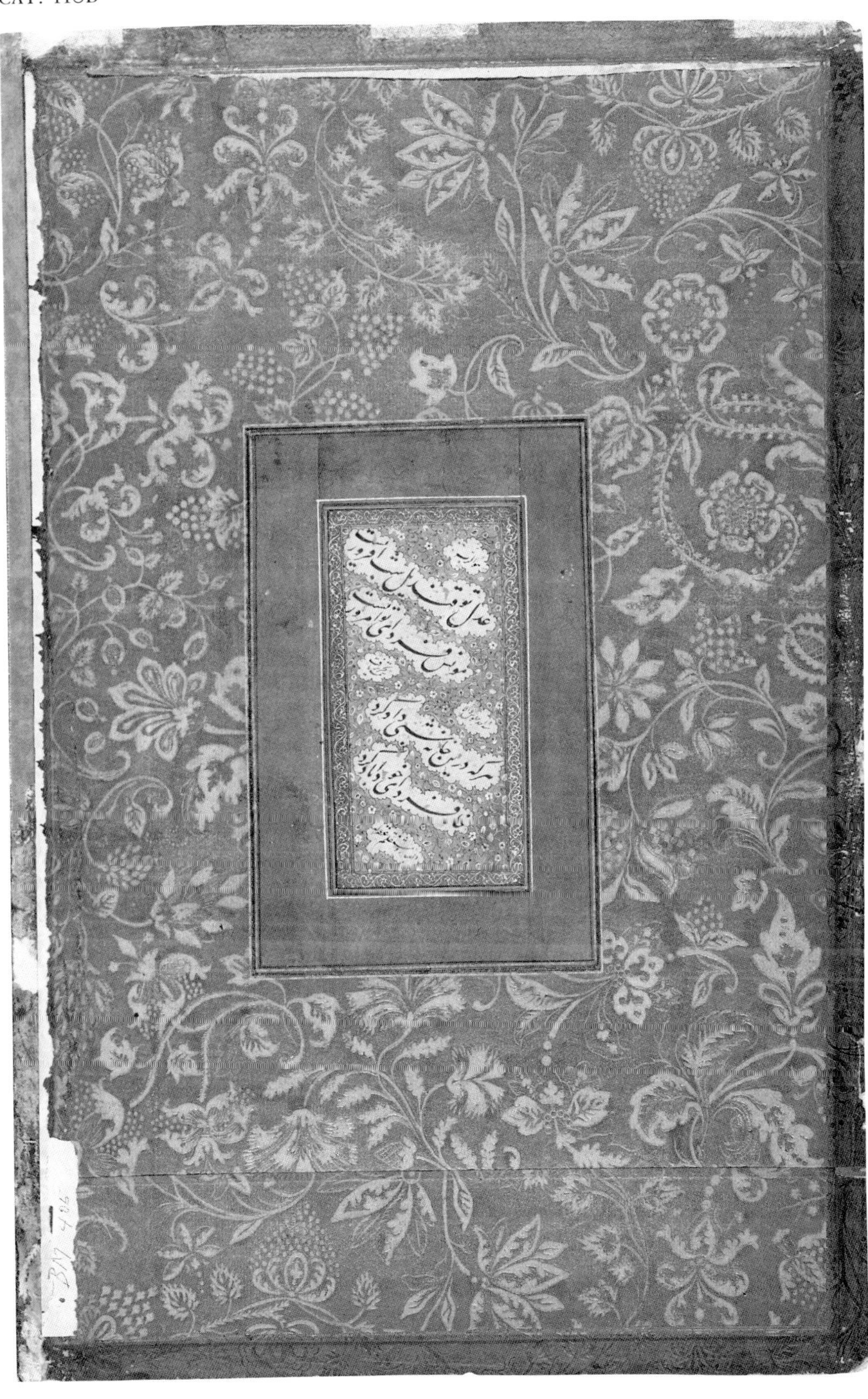

A The subject of the portrait was identified by M. Beach (1966, p. 160) as the Mughal general Ghazi ad-Din Bahadur Khan Firuz Jang from comparison with an inscribed portrait in the Rijksmuseum, Amsterdam. Known originally as Mir Shihab ad-Din, Ghazi ad-Din arrived at Aurangzeb's court from Iran in 1669 and remained in the emperor's service until his death. He was a skillful general who fought many of Aurangzeb's battles. In 1685 he was sent by the emperor to relieve Prince Azam when the latter was overtaken by a famine during a siege of the Bijapur fort. By then he had been honored twice, with the titles Ghazi ad-Din Bahadur Khan and Firuz Jang. Two years later he participated in the siege of Golconda and captured Hyderabad. For a time he was appointed administrator of Berar. In 1724 one of his sons founded the Asaf Jahi dynasty of Hyderabad, and he may have owned this portrait.

This is a standard example of the kind of Mughal-influenced portraiture that became popular in Golconda after its capitulation to Aurangzeb. Against a typically Mughal dull green background the aged general, with a pink complexion and a white beard, is portrayed as a figure of large proportions. A yellower green is used for the ground and the sky above. Flowers of different hues of purple adorn the foliage on the ground, his shoes, his *jama,* as well as his yellow sash. He holds a piece of cloth in his right hand. The general's distinguished face with a prominent nose has been rendered with considerable care and with naturalistic details. The portrait could well be by the same hand responsible for another Deccani portrait now in the National Museum, New Delhi (Zebrowski 1983, fig. 186).

B The calligraphy on the reverse gives the title of the calligrapher as Roshan Qalam, who is undoubtedly the same calligrapher whose full name occurs on a calligraphic panel probably from the same album in the San Diego Museum (Binney 1973, no. 136). There the name is given as Haidar Beg Roshan Qalam. *Roshan Qalam* is obviously his title; E. Binney translates it as "golden pen." However, the word *roshan* is better translated as "bright." He was obviously a much-admired calligrapher and was probably attached to the court at Hyderabad.

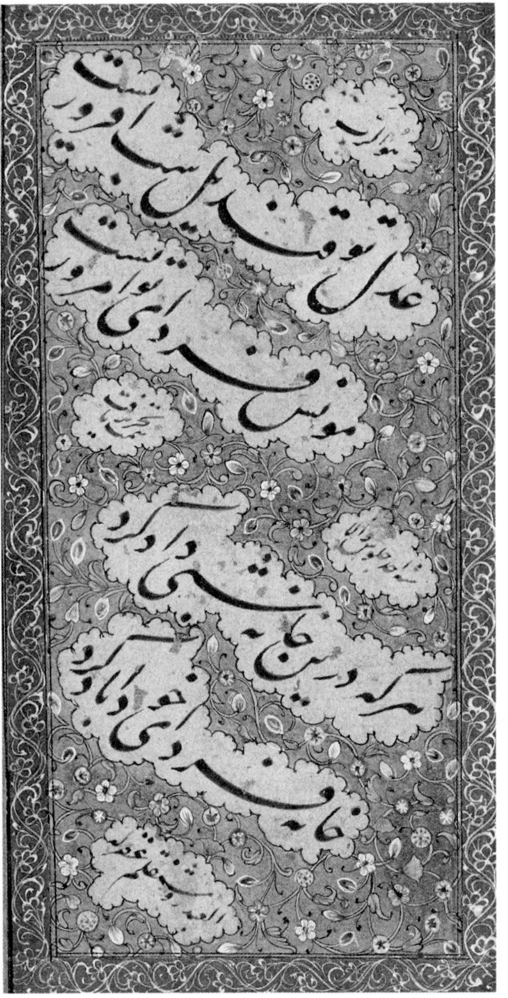

CAT. 110B detail

The panel is quite small and is mounted in a border with floral patterns in gold. The text itself is written in fine *nastaliq* of two sizes in cloud bands placed diagonally on a gold background. The rest of the field is covered in delicately rendered flowering vines. A second flowering vine in white adorns the narrow blue margin immediately around the panel. The following translation of the text is by S. Digby:

He is the Lord.

VERSE
Your justice is a lamp to light the night
Your today is the comforter of tomorrow.

SMALL PANELS
{This} attained inscription {in} the first year of one exalted reign.

VERSE
He who one night administered justice in this house
Made fair the abode of his tomorrow.
The slave Roshan Qalam
—May {God} pardon him.

111 FOLIO FROM AN ALBUM

Andhra Pradesh, Golconda; c. 1690
Folio, 12 3/4 x 8 1/4 in (32.4 x 21.0 cm)
Purchased with funds provided by Lizabeth Scott
M.87.20.1

A *Page of Calligraphy* (r)
By Nur ad-Din Muhammad al-Lahiji
Ink on marbled paper
6 1/2 x 3 in (16.5 x 7.6 cm)

B *Portrait of Sharza Khan* (v)
4 3/8 x 3 5/16 in (11.1 x 8.4 cm), oval

A Five lines of text are written diagonally across marbled paper in bold, black *nastaliq* letters. The marbling consists of swirling forms in light blue and white and is a beautiful foil for the calligraphy. In fact, the marbling creates the illusion of water on which the black letters float like boats. The first narrow border around the panel is blue with a gold twisted form that almost looks like a snake hood. The second border is painted yellow. The outer border is dyed bright pink and is adorned with gold leaves.

Nothing is known of the calligrapher Nur ad-Din Muhammad al-Lahiji. The calligraphic panel may, in fact, be from either Bijapur or Golconda. This translation of the verse is by S. Digby:

May your body have no need of the proud airs of physicians
May your delicate existence remain unharmed by injury
Seek healing from the sugar-scattering speech of Hafiz
May you have no need of treatment with rose water and sugar candy.
Written by Nur ad-Din Muhammad al-Lahiji

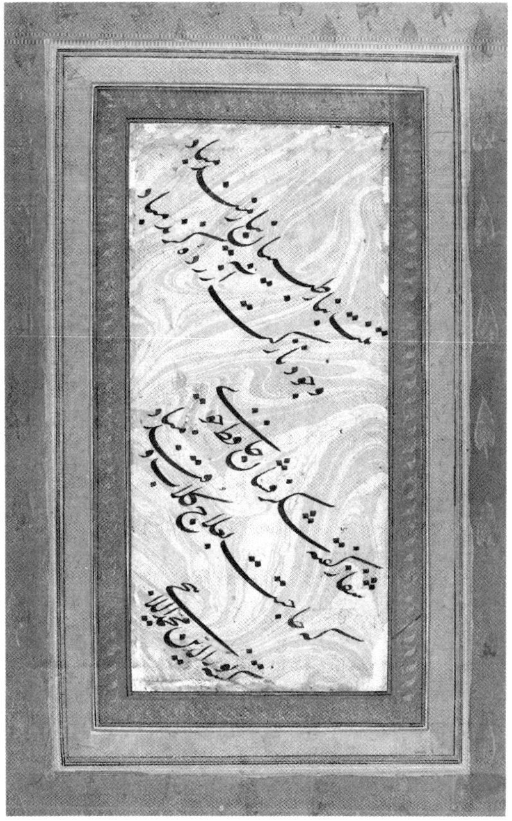

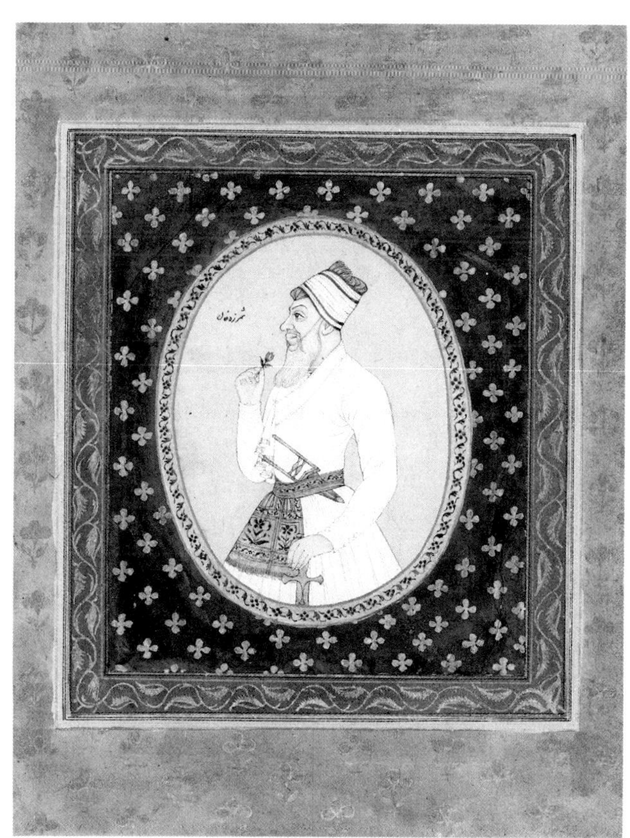

CAT. 111A detail *(left)*
CAT. 111B detail *(right)*

According to Digby these are the first and last couplets of a *ghazal* of the celebrated Persian poet Hafiz (1327–90) (*Diwan-i Hafiz,* M. Qazwini and Q. Ghani, eds. [Tehran, 1942], pp. 72–73, no. 106).

B The inscription near the face identifies the figure as *Sharza Khan.* Sharza Khan was a Pathan from the northwest of the subcontinent and was the general of the Bijapuri army during Aurangzeb's campaign. He is mentioned by the Venetian traveler N. Manucci as someone who tried to avoid a war with the Mughal emperor but without success (Manucci 1981, 2: 131). His courage earned him the title of Rustam Khan from Aurangzeb. He was captured in 1689/90 by the Marhattas and incarcerated until 1704/5. He was then appointed deputy governor of Berar and named full governor in 1707/8. This portrait was very likely made sometime around 1690. It is interesting that Manucci himself owned a portrait of the general. The museum's portrait is related stylistically to several others, all within oval frames, which appear to have been done after the Mughals occupied Golconda (Zebrowski 1983, fig. 160; and Weber 1982, nos. 44–47). The oval frame may have been adopted directly from European miniatures or from Mughal paintings. As Zebrowski observed (1983, p. 194), "It was the custom at Golconda for painters of modest talent to produce albums of Deccani and Mughal notables for sale in the bazaar to European and other foreign travellers."

Very little in this portrait is specifically Deccani. There is less shading than is usual in such Deccani portraits, but nevertheless it could easily be mistaken for the sort of conventional Mughal portraits produced during Aurangzeb's time. Wearing a white *jama,* the pink-complexioned Sharza Khan stands against a dull green background. His sash is in gold with red-and-green floral motifs, and the brightest patch of color in the picture is the yellow turban. A close stylistic parallel with the painting is the portrait of Mulla Raoza in the collection [106]. Very likely the two were rendered by the same artist and may once have belonged to the same album.

In imitation of a framed miniature, the oval frame, adorned with a border of flowering vine, is surrounded by a deep violet ground with gold flowers, which in turn is within a border of gold vine with split palmette on blue ground. The outer border of the folio is the same pink as that on the other side, but here has gold flowers rather than leaves.

यंतीश्रवणेवतंसमानाकुरकोकिलनादहृष्टा॥ शामामधुस्वादनघूर्णनेत्रागो
धुका किलकोहलेन॥३॥ तरुणारुणसंकाशवसना विचित्रकंचुका॥ सहकारव
स्यांतः क्रीडंतीस्वसखीयुता॥४॥

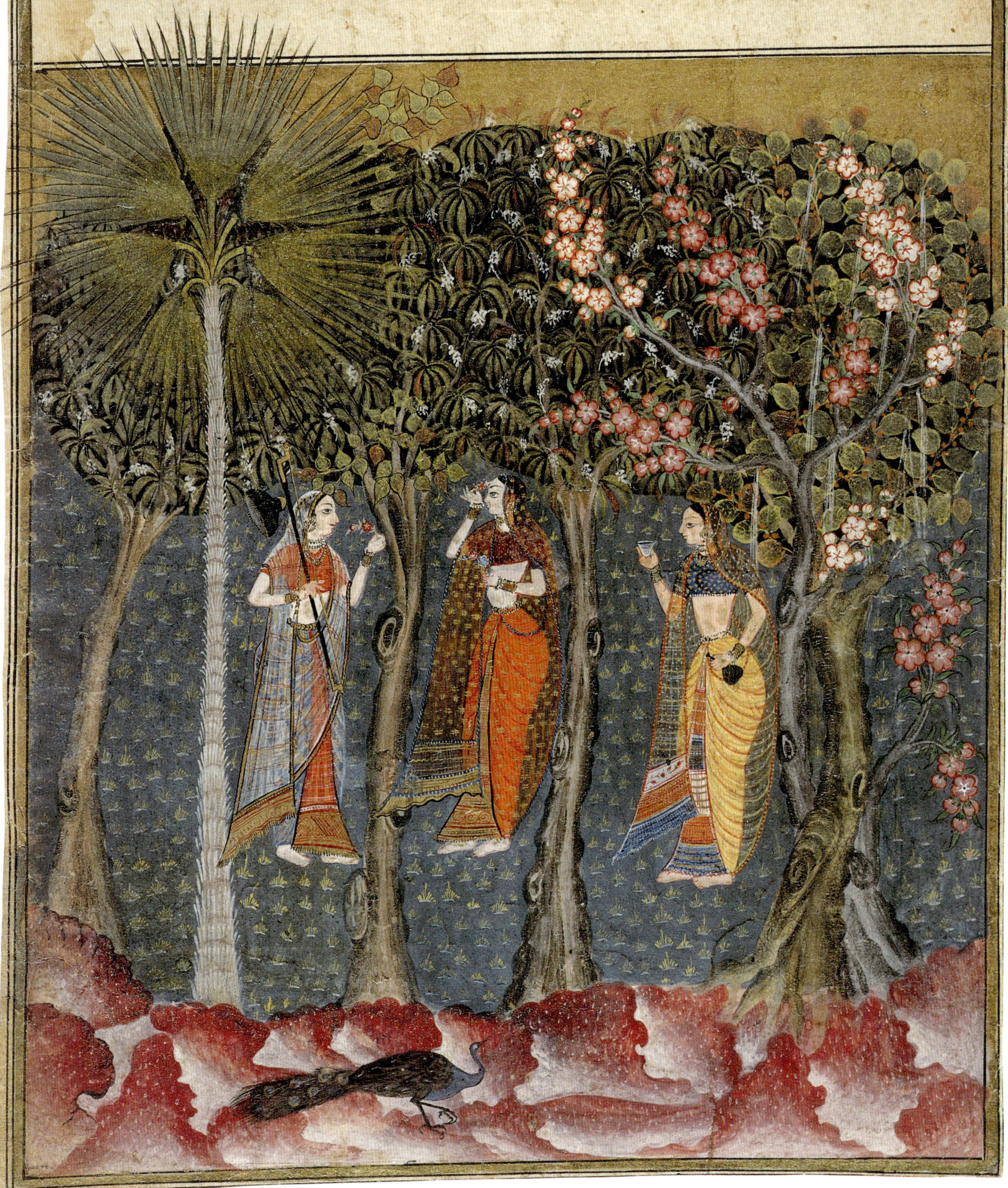

Other Deccani Centers

112 THE MUSICAL MODE GAURI RAGINI

Deccan, Ahmadnagar (?); 1575–1600
Folio, 9¾ x 7½ in (24.8 x 19.1 cm)
Illustration, 8 x 7 in (20.3 x 17.8 cm)
Bequest of Edwin Binney, 3rd
M.90.141.2
Literature: Binney 1973, pp. 141, 150, no. 118; S. C. Welch 1973, pp. 126–27, no. 75; Ebeling 1973, p. 157, fig. 14; A. Welch 1975, fig. 1; Binney 1979, pp. 802–4, fig. 19; Zebrowski 1983, p. 40, fig. 25, pl. IV.

One of the most important Deccani paintings in the collection, this is also the most enigmatic. Although it has been frequently published and discussed, there is no consensus as to where precisely it was painted. There is no disagreement, however, that the painting was executed in the Deccan sometime in the late sixteenth century. Only S. C. Welch (1973, p. 127) has suggested a more precise date, the decade of 1580–90.

The painting represents a female musical mode known as a *ragini,* who is described in the text on the band above. Written in the Devanagari script, the verse is in Sanskrit, but its exact source is not known. Although part of the text is damaged and no name is recognizable, very likely the mode depicted is Gauri or Gaudi. *Gauda* was a designation of a part of Bengal (West Bengal and Bangladesh) and also of the capital in the Maldah district of West Bengal. The musical mode probably originated in that region. The text describes the *ragini* as a beautiful young girl dressed in gorgeous costume the color of the rising sun. Her eyes are swimming from drinking liquor, and she frolics with her companions in the mango grove while the cuckoo sings a mournful tune. The artist has followed the description fairly closely. Gauri stands in the middle separated from the others by two tree trunks. Holding a flower to her forehead and wearing a bright red sari, she faces the companion who holds a musical instrument. The other stands behind her and offers her a cup of wine. Tufts of golden grass decorate the gray ground, giving it the appearance of a carpet. The foreground is a band of mulberry-colored rocky forms that are definitely a Deccani trait. Across this puffed sugarcandy-like landscape struts a solitary peacock, but no cuckoo is to be seen anywhere. Except for the two intertwined trunks at the right, the other trees are placed at regular intervals, almost like columns, framing the three ladies. The mango and the palm, adding a southern touch, are clearly recognizable, but the flowers are decorative.

One cannot even be certain whether this picture is a singular work or belongs to a *Ragamala* series. Only about a score of similar paintings, all depicting musical modes, are known, but they do not belong to one series (see Ebeling 1973, pp. 155–58). Most have Sanskrit inscriptions in Devanagari, but some also have short texts in Arabic script. The general assumption at present is that they are single pictures and were done mostly for Hindu patrons. Their stylistic similarities do indicate that they all may have been done in the same region, if not the same workshop. M. Zebrowski (1983, pp. 45–46) believes that rather than Ahmadnagar or Bijapur the paintings were rendered somewhere in the northern Deccan between Malwa and Aurangabad. He recognizes features that one encounters in the illustrated *Nimatnama* done in the Mandu court. S. C. Welch (1973, p. 127) opined that "stylistically the [museum's] picture emerges from the earlier illustrations to the *Tarif-i-Husayn Shahi,* a manuscript celebrating the reign of Husayn Shah I (1553–1565) of Ahmadnagar, a state in Northern Deccan." According to him this would account for some of the Rajput elements "in the costumes, gestures, and formulae for the foliage, which recall the Chaurapanchasika style."

That the picture is Deccani is in no doubt, and its stylistic kinship to the *Tarif-i Husayn Shahi* (cf. Zebrowski 1983, pp. 17–18, figs. 1, 2, pl. 1) is clear. As a matter of fact, it is difficult to agree with Zebrowski (1983, p. 45) that all these *Ragamala* paintings display a naïve charm and "possess an exquisitely fresh, rural mood, full of the sounds and smells of the countryside, quite unlike the courtly atmosphere of other great Deccani paintings." Certainly the female figures in the museum's picture, with their ivory-white complexions and tall, graceful proportions, cannot be compared with country women. Moreover, the paintings display an elegant and sophisticated aesthetic sensibility on the part of the patron and a complete mastery of technique as well as boldness of vision on the part of the artist. Only a master painter with enormous self-confidence could have been aware of so many different modes and yet could have painted in so brilliantly original a manner. While the picture could have been rendered somewhere in the northern Deccan, an Ahmadnagar provenance cannot be ruled out altogether. It could have been painted for a prince of the realm by an artist trained in the same workshop that produced the royal history of Husayn Shah. According to K. Khandalavala (1985, pp. 41–42), both the Ahmadnagar and Bijapur courts could have patronized these early *Ragamala* pictures of the Deccan. He further thinks that "they may be the work of a guild or guilds of Vijaynagar artists who had settled in Ahmadnagar and Bijapur after the fall of Vijaynagar in A.D. 1654 and had absorbed various influences into their Deccani styles and Deccani rulers such as Ibrahim Adil Shah II of Bijapur and Burham II of Ahmadnagar may have acquired their works for their libraries complete with Sanskrit inscriptions got written by a scribe."

Finally, it might be worth quoting what E. Binney—who owned the painting before it came into the museum's collection—thought of this beautiful picture in comparison with the other *Ragamala* paintings: "It is exceptional in several ways. First, it is as lovely as any of the others! More important, it is the only *original* example in a 'Western,' as opposed to Indian, collection. Finally, it is probably my finest Deccani miniature" (Binney 1979, p. 804). There is no doubt that it is the finest Deccani painting in the museum's collection as well.

113 FOLIO FROM A MANUSCRIPT OF AL-QAZWINI'S *AJAIB AL-MAKHLUQAT*

Deccan; c. 1675
Inscriptions in red ink
8½ x 5¾ in (21.6 x 14.6 cm), irregular
Gift of Mr. and Mrs. Michael Douglas
M.85.283.1

A *Constellations: Large Dog and Small Dog* (r)
B *Constellations: Ship and Hydra* (v)

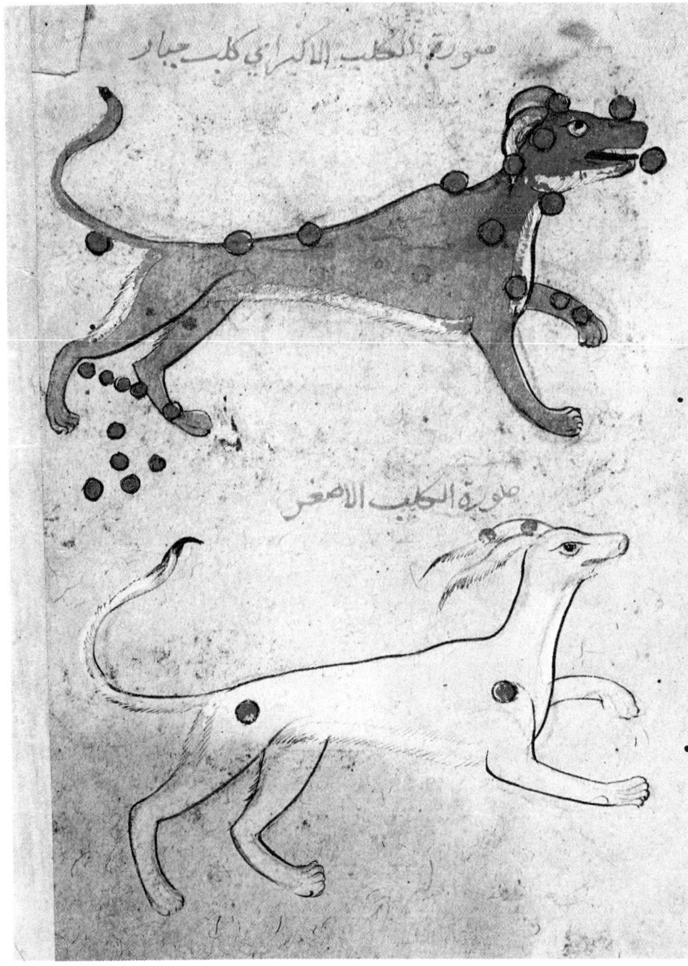

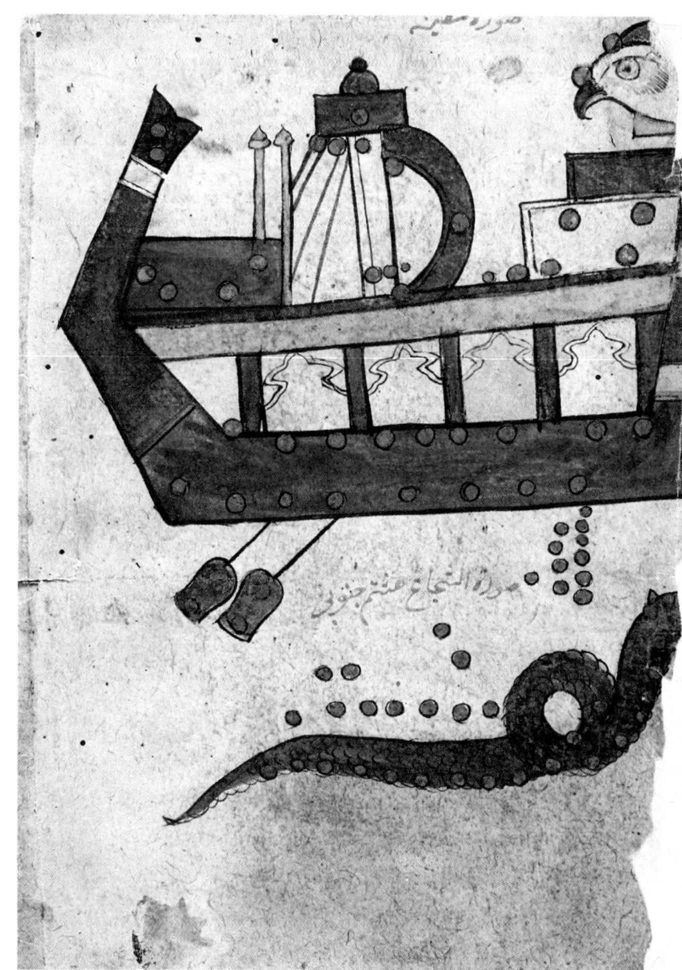

CAT. 113A *(left)*
CAT. 113B *(right)*

Unlike the folios from the earlier Bijapuri manuscript of this book [95], this folio contains no text. On both sides only short inscriptions in red ink serve as labels for the pictures, which represent the various constellations. Two images are accommodated on each side, but it is clear that on the side with the ship and the Hydra (B) the image was spread over two facing pages. According to W. M. Thackston, the short Arabic inscriptions give the following information:

A *al-kalb al-akbar,* Canis Major, the large dog
al-kalb al-asghar, Canis Minor, the small dog

B *safina,* Argo, the ship
al-timsah, Hydra

It should be noted that the folio entered the collection as having belonged to a manuscript of al-Qazwini's work. But in point of fact it could be from some other astronomical book, such as the *Treatise on the Fixed Stars* by Abd ar-Rahman as-Sufis of Shiraz (d. 986).

The folio entered the collection as belonging to a manuscript copied in 1675. However, no evidence of the colophon is known. Even though that date would make this a century later than the much better illustrated Qazwini manuscript folios in the collection, the representations here seem even more archaic. Once again the artist may have been simply copying an earlier illustrated model from West Asia.

The colored images are on beige paper and are rather modest efforts at representation. For instance, the fawn-colored Canis Minor on A looks more like a composite of a canine, a deer, and a goat than a dog. Canis Major is colored gray and is a more convincing canine but has horns. The tail end of the Hydra is found on B, but the ship is elaborately designed and colored with gray, yellow, orange, magenta, and pink. A well-executed head of a parrot has survived on top of the ship.

Gray pellets are added to each representation to indicate the configuration of the stars in the constellation.

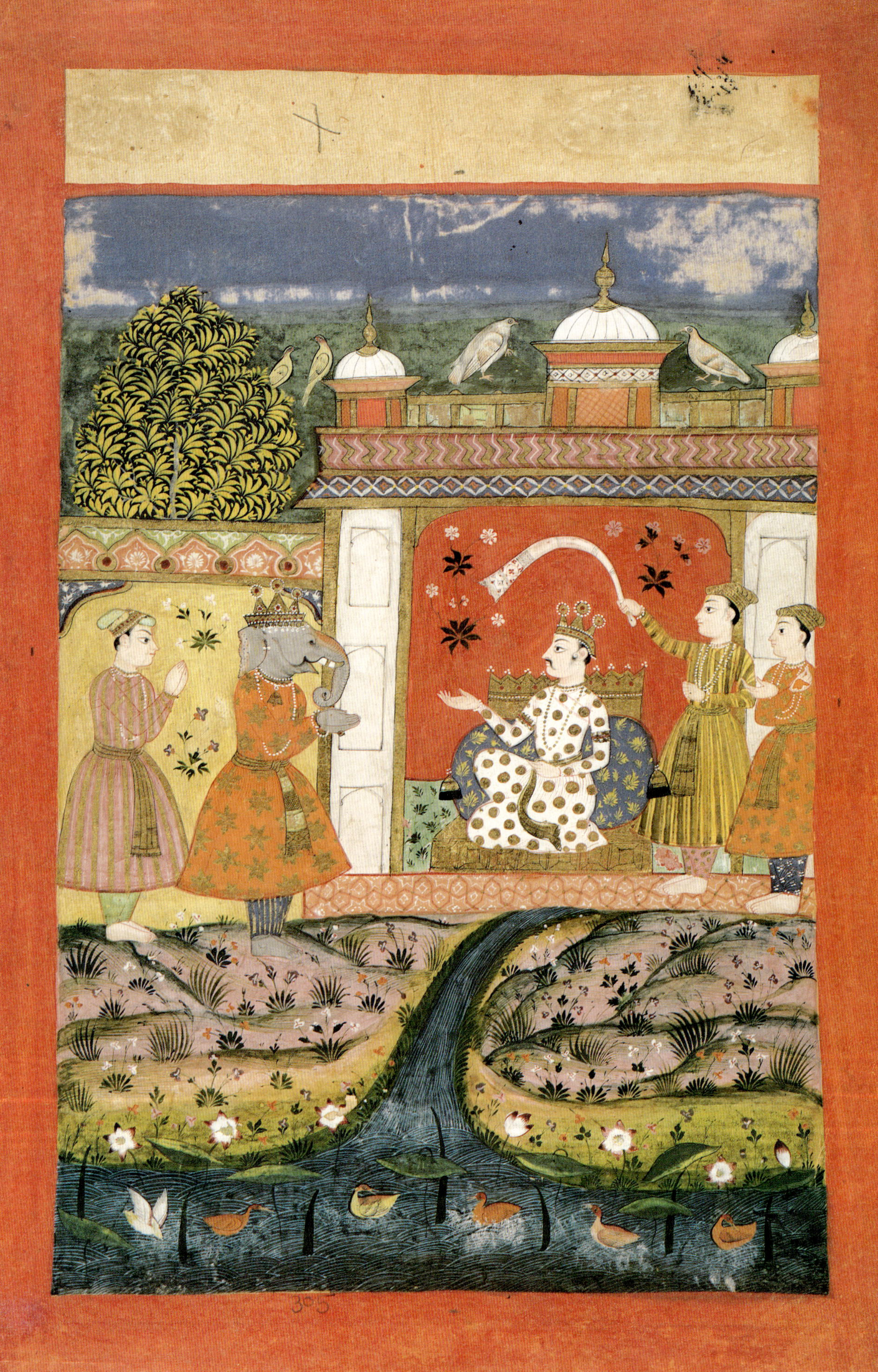

114 ILLUSTRATION OF THE MUSICAL MODE SANKARABHARANA RAGAPUTRA

Maharashtra, Aurangabad; c. 1675
Folio, $13\frac{1}{2}$ x $9\frac{3}{16}$ in (34.3 x 23.3 cm)
Illustration, $10\frac{1}{2}$ x $7\frac{5}{8}$ in (26.7 x 19.4 cm)
Gift of Mr. and Mrs. Harry Kahn
M.74.105.1
Literature: Pal 1987, pp. 120, 122, fig. 83.

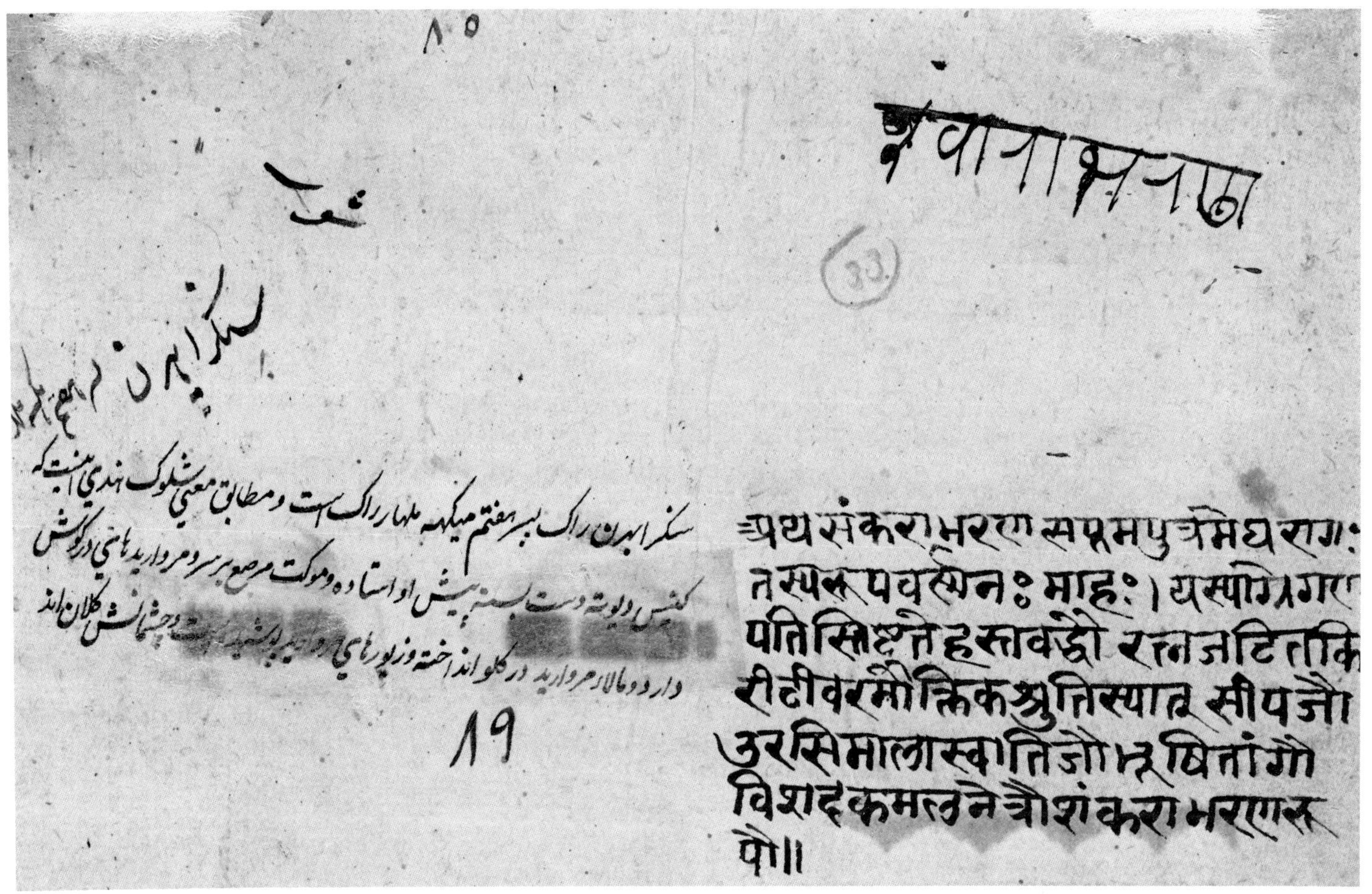

CAT. 114 reverse detail

On the back are a long inscription and a short one in both the Arabic and Devanagari scripts. The long inscription in Devanagari is of a Sanskrit text, and the other is a translation of it into Persian. Also, the title *Sankarabharana* is written rather carelessly in both scripts, probably in a later hand. The Persian numbers *85* and *89* are above and below. The number *33* has been added in pencil. The longer text characterizes Sankarabharana as the seventh son of Megharaga. The brief description says that before Sankarabharana stands Ganapati (Ganesa), adorned with a gem-encrusted crown, his body ornamented with garlands, with lotus eyes and hands joined together.

The composition shows a king seated on a throne within a pavilion and receiving homage from Ganesa and his human companion. One of the attendants to the seated king holds a cloth fan, which appears like a canopy above his master's head. Ganesa's form matches the textual description. The scene takes place in a garden with uneven ground rendered in pinks, mauves, and greens with flowers and vegetation beside a pool that is fed by a stream emerging from the bottom of the pavilion. The pool is adorned with lotuses and inhabited by waterbirds. Pigeons and falcons sit on the roof and the tree.

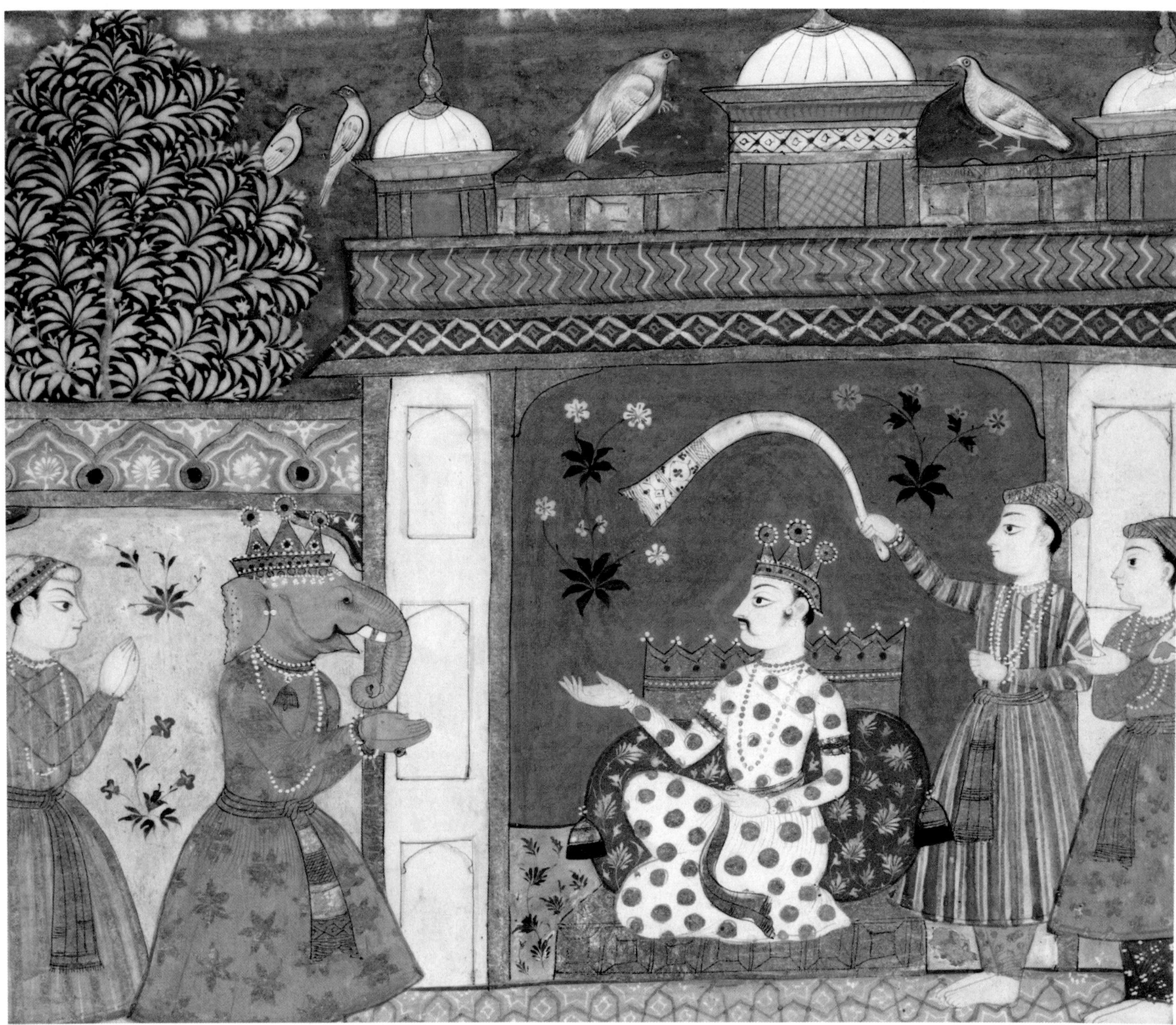

CAT. 114 detail

The iconography of this version of Sankarabharana does not correspond with other known depictions. Sankarabharana is usually described as a *ragini* and only in one instance as the son of Megha (see Ebeling 1973, pp. 146, 193, 247, 284). Even in the latter instance the iconography is quite different. Moreover, this is the first known *Ragamala* painting to incorporate the image of Ganesa in its iconography.

There can be little doubt that the style of this *Ragamala* picture is related to the mixed mode of painting that was developed primarily for Rajput patrons in the train of the Mughals in the northern Deccan in the last quarter of the seventeenth century. There appear to have been two centers—at Aurangabad and Daulatabad—where the artists, borrowing freely from the Mughal, Rajput, and Deccani traditions, created a style that is less lyrical and fantastic than the Deccani mode and not quite as naturalistic as the Mughal manner (see Doshi 1972). It should also be noted that even at Golconda during the reign of Abul Hasan (1672–87) there was considerable expansion of Hindu influence. This *Ragamala* painting, along with others (Smart and Walker 1985, nos. 23, 24), shows strong Rajput influences in the figural forms, particularly in the wide eyes, and in the flat areas of strident colors within rectangular shapes that clearly relate it to the pictures done at Aurangabad about 1650. Very likely the artist was following a Hindu textual tradition but the patron was a Muslim, for whom the Persian text was added.

Deccan; 1675–1700
Folio, 14 11/16 x 11 1/4 in (37.3 x 28.6 cm), irregular
Purchased with funds provided by Paul F. Walter
M.90.86.2

A *Scene with Bovines and Demons*
12 1/4 x 8 5/8 in (31.1 x 21.9 cm)

B *Page of Calligraphy*
Black and red ink on paper
9 7/8 x 5 1/8 in (25.1 x 13.0 cm)

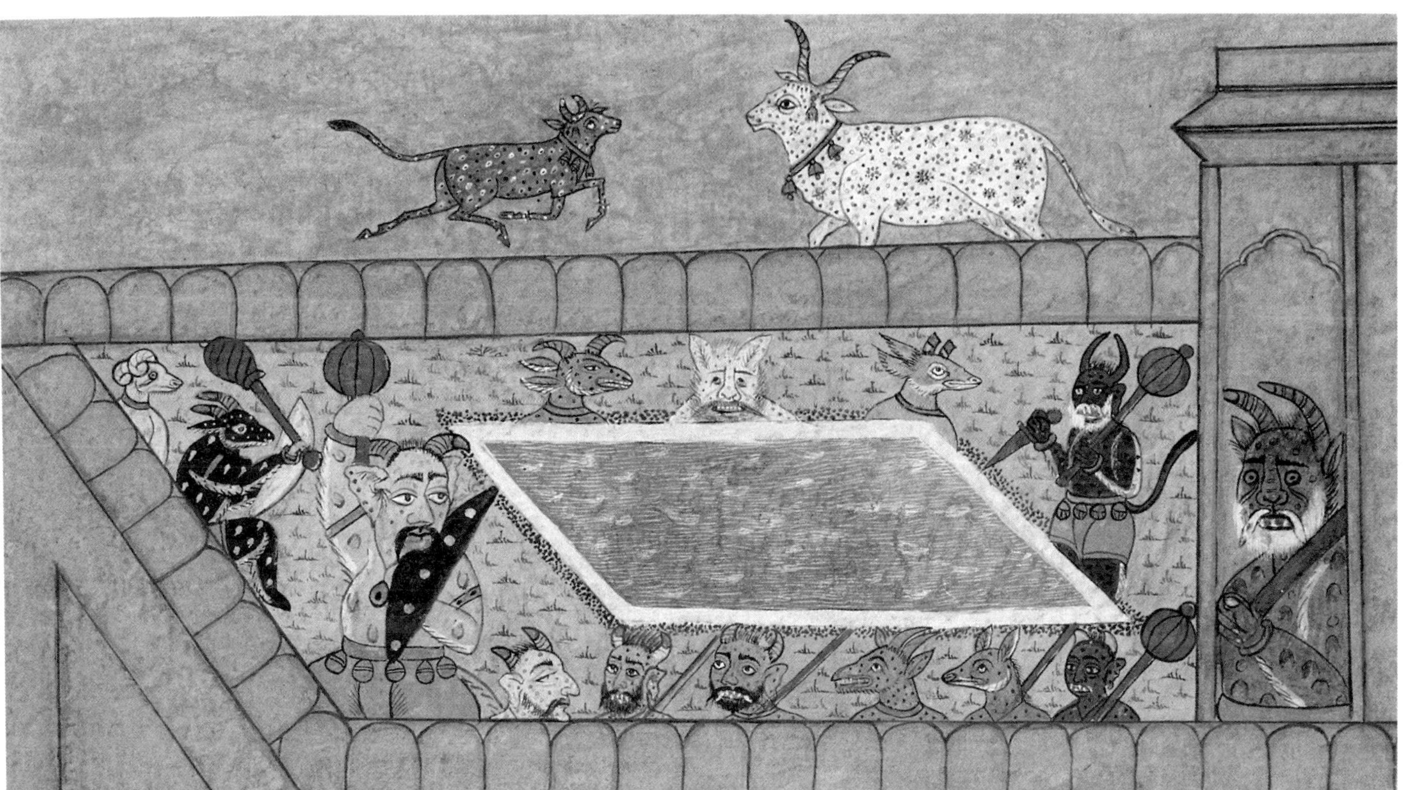

CAT. 115A detail

This folio is from an illustrated manuscript of a Persian translation of the *Bhagavatapurana.* It is distinguished by its large size, which allowed the artists to paint rather impressive compositions. On this folio the text is accommodated on the recto and the illustration on the verso. Although the text has been read and fully translated by Z. Faridany-Akhavan (see below), the scene has not been precisely identified. The painting is surrounded by two borders, the inner with blue flowers and the outer with dull red circles containing bright red flowers. The lower section of the composition shows a highly imaginative mountain formed from mauve rocks rising like a beaker or a basin with a wide rim. Both this formation and the light green ground from which it rises are speckled with small tufts of grass. Behind the rocky escarpment is what appears to be a fort whose enormous walls are painted in light brown. Within is a tank of water on a lawn on which are animal-headed demons, some of whom appear to be in a belligerent mood. Beyond the further wall of the fort are two spotted bovines, presumably cows, against a bright orange background. The larger one is white, and its body is decorated with multi-colored flowers and polka dots. The smaller one is similarly adorned but is brown in color. The sky is represented with a white and a blue band.

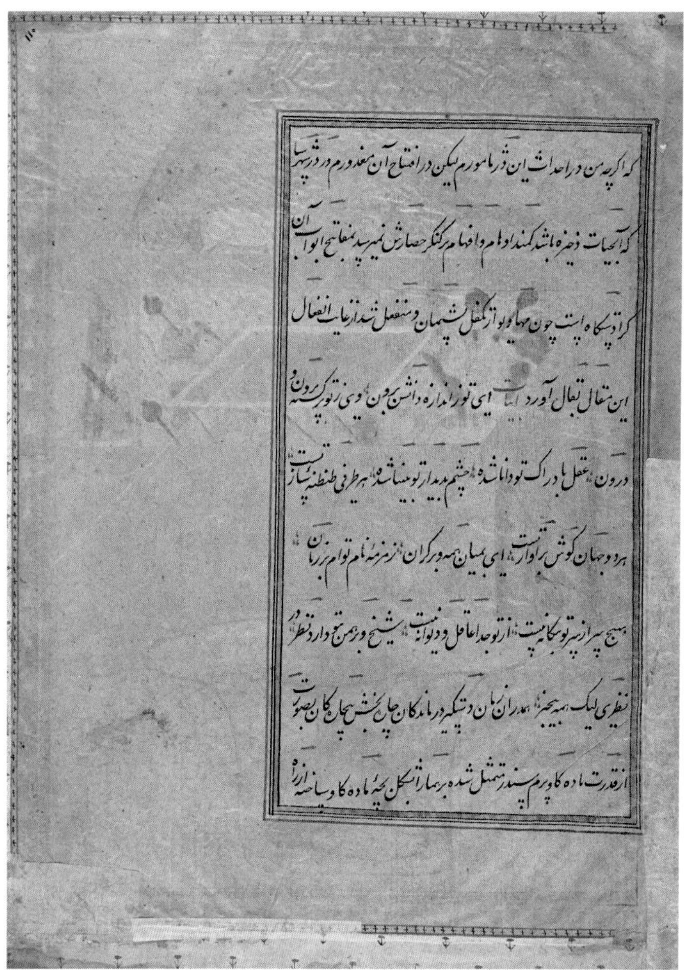

CAT. 115B *(above)*
CAT. 115A *(opposite)*

B The text on the other side as translated by Z. Faridany-Akhavan is as follows:

Even though I am involved in the invention of this fortress on a hill, I am excused from its commencement in the city fortress of Sahrsa {Shahr Sa} where life-giving water is stored and where the snare of suspicions and opinions cannot reach the battlements of its fortress. Keys have been manufactured for its gates.

When Mahiya Div {Mahadeva} became remorseful and ashamed of . . . from the force of his shame he spoke these words:

O one whose knowledge is beyond limit,
You who are rich within and without,
The mind has become intelligent through you.
From the sight of you the eye is all-seeing,
From all around voices speak of you,
Amongst all gatherings is the murmuring of your name.
Both worlds listen for your voice,
No one is a stranger on account of you,
No one is separate and negligent of you,
Shaykh and brahmin alike look to you
You resemble everyone yet awares

From the strength of the she-cow my wings resemble amber.
Always made like the calf of the she-cow {?}.

The National Museum in New Delhi has a folio from a Deccani *Bhagavatapurana* (Gupta 1985, p. 105, no. 139) that very likely is from the same manuscript as the museum's folio. On the published page the illustration surrounds the text. Although that folio is dated to about 1700 in the catalogue, it may in fact be somewhat earlier. The Persian text makes it clear that this Hindu book was translated for a Muslim patron. The most propitious time for this appears to have been during the reign of Sultan Abul Hasan of Golconda (1672–87), who was particularly supportive of Hindus. In addition to appointing Hindus to high administrative offices, he was also a patron of Telegu literature. His guru was the famous saint Shah Raju, whose son Akbar Shah Husayni was a mystical poet and, like Shah Jahan's son Dara Shikoh, was seriously interested in Hindu philosophy (see [79]). Akbar Shah was thoroughly versed in Sanskrit and translated Hindu books (Zebrowski 1983, p. 189). Whether or not this is his translation, the manuscript may have belonged to him.

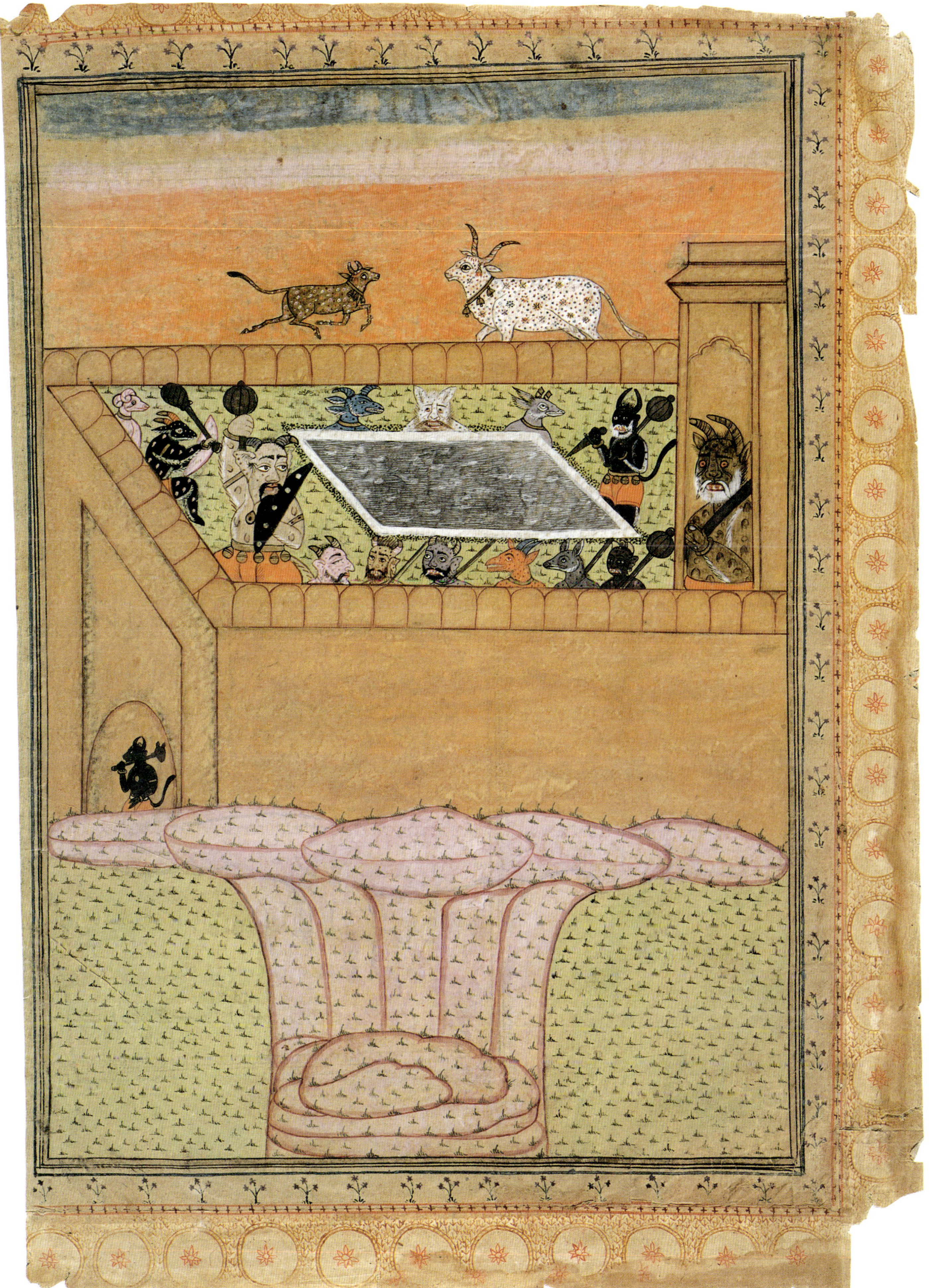

Appendix

Colophons of Buddhist and Jain Manuscripts

Read and translated by Dr. Gouriswar Bhattacharya

Buddhist Manuscripts

1

PRAJNAPARAMITA MANUSCRIPT

Inscription
deyadharmmo='yaṃ pravara-mahayana-yāyinyāḥ paramopāsikāyāḥ kāyastha-śrīkumāra-patnī-tejokāyā yad=atra puṇyaṃ tad-bhavatv=ācāry-opādhyāya-mātāpitṛ-[pūrvaṅgamaṃ kṛtvā sakala-satva-rāśer= anuttara-jñā]nā-vāptaya iti || mahārājādhirāja-parameśvara-paramabhaṭṭāraka-paramasaugata-śrīman-mahīpāla-deva-rājye pravardhamāna-vijaya-rājye samvatsare saptaviṃśa . . .

Translation
This is the pious gift of Tejoka, who is a devout follower of the excellent Mahāyāna and the wife of the scribe Śrīkumāra.

Whatever merit there is in this gift, let it accrue to their teacher, to their parents, to all their ancestors, as well as to all sentient beings. In the twenty-seventh year of the great king of kings, the great Lord, the great worshipful one, the great follower of the Buddha, Mahīpāla.

Newari Inscription
tra dvam bhāṣā lekhaya patra sa[ankhya?] 194 samvat 355 śrāvaṇa śuddhi 5 vijaya dine rājye rājā prameśvara śrī abhayama[lla]-deva svavityanaḥ 2udayavarmana.

Translation/Commentary
Because it is incomplete and not correctly written, the Newari inscription is difficult to translate. It mentions that the manuscript containing 194 pages was written in the Newari Samvat 355 [A.D. 1235], when King Abhayamalla was the king, as well as mentioning the name Udayavarman, whose function is not clear.
P.P.

3

DHARANISAMGRAHA MANUSCRIPT

Inscription
deyadharmo='yaṃ pravara-mahāyāna-yāyinaḥ paramopāsaka-nepālī-rāmajīvasya | yad=atra [etc.] | paramabhaṭṭāraka-mahārājādhirāja-parameśvara-paramasaugata-śrīman-nayapāla-deva-vijayarājye 14 phālguna-dine 13 || śrī-nāland-āvasthita-lekhaka-svamesvarasya likhitam-iti ||

Translation
This is the pious gift of Rāmajīva, who is from Nepal and who is a devout follower of the excellent Mahāyāna. Whatever merit there is in this gift [etc., same invocation as in the previous colophon].

On the thirteenth day of Phālguna [February–March] of the year fourteen of the victorious reign of Śrī Nayapāladeva, who is the great worshipful one, the great king of kings, and a great follower of the Buddha, [this manuscript was dedicated or consecrated]. The scribe Svamesvara of Nalanda copied it.

5

PRAJNAPARAMITA MANUSCRIPT

Inscription
deyadharmo='yaṃ pravara-mahāyāna-yāyinaḥ malaya-deśa-vinirgata-śākyabhikṣu-sthavira-pūrṇacandrasya asya śiṣya-sthavira-trailokyacandrasya | yad=atra [etc.] mahārājādhirāja-śrimad-rāmapāladeva-rājyasamvat ||18|| śrīmad-āpanaka-mahāvihār-āvasthita-vāmatanaka-jayakumāreṇa likhita iti |

Translation
This is the pious gift of the elder monk Trailokyacandra, who is steadfast in the Mahāyāna, and who is the disciple of the elder monk Pūrṇacandra, who has come from the Malaya country. Whatever merit there is in this gift [etc., same invocation as in the previous colophons]. In the eighteenth regnal year of the great king of kings Śrī Rāmapāladeva, this book was copied by Jayakumāra, who is a *vāmatanaka* and a resident of the great Āpanaka monastery.

Commentary
The meaning of the word *vāmatanaka* is not known and may denote a lay administrator of the monastery.

P.P.

7

PANCHARAKSHA MANUSCRIPT

Inscription
deyadharmo='yaṃ pravara-mahāyāna-yāyinaḥ mahāsāmantādhipati-mahārājādhirāja-mahāmāṇḍalika-śrī-rudramāna-suta-paramopāsaka-rājaputra-vikramamānasya | yad=atra [etc.] || śrīman-madanapāla-devasya rājya-samvat 17 |

Translation
This is the pious gift of Prince Vikramamāna, who is steadfast in the excellent Mahāyāna and a devout worshipper, and the son of Rudramāna, the chief of the feudatories, the great king of kings and the provincial governor. Whatever merit there is in this gift [etc., same invocation as in the previous colophons]. In the seventeenth regnal year of Śrī Madanapāladeva.

15

KALPASUTRA AND KALAKACHARYAKATHA MANUSCRIPT

Inscription
Folio 97
LINE 1
dasasuaskaṁdhassa atthamam=ajha||yanaṃ||cha|| graṃ 1216 arhanmūlaḥ sudharmmādi-
LINE 2
ka-gaṇadhara-ja skaṃdha-baṃdh-ābhirāmaḥ sphūrjat-śrī-saṃghaśākhaḥ sthavira-vara-dala||-
LINE 3
ś=cāru-cāritra-puṣpaḥ| dan-ādyair-nīra|pūraiḥ sakala-sura-varaiḥ saṃtataṃ sicyamānaḥ
LINE 4
sacchāy-āpāsta-tāpaḥ śiva-gati-pha||ladaḥ kalpa-kalpadrumo vaḥ||1||cha||śrīḥ||
LINE 5
||saṃO 1499 varṣc śrī-satyapura-vāstavya-ūkeśa-jñātīya-mahaṃ-nāmasi-putra-mahaṃ-
LINE 6
sāmala-bhāryā-vaïjala-de-putra-mahaṃ-pāsā-suśrāvakeṇa bhāryā-maO-meghā-de|-
LINE 7
putra-maO-rūpā-madā-kolā-sahite|na śrī-aṃcala-gaccha-nāyaka-śrī-Jayakīrtti|
LINE 8
sūrīṃdra-su-gurūṇām=upadeśam-āsā|dya mahaṃ meghā-de śreyase śrī-kalpasūtra-pu|
LINE 9
stakaṃ lekhitaṃ|munijanaiḥ pravacya|mānaṃ ciraṃ vijayatāṁ||cha|| śrīḥ|| ||śrīḥ||

Translation
The eighth chapter of the Daśāśrutaskandha. Grantha 1216. Let the Kalpasūtra like the wish-granting tree grant you all the merit of auspicious end, [the Kalpasūtra] has as its root the Arhats, which is produced by Sudharma and other heads of assemblages of the holy ones (*gaṇadharas*), which is agreeable with the division of chapters, with bursting out branches of the holy monasteries (*saṃghas*), with leaves of excellent elders (*sthavira*), with flowers of pleasing narratives, which is always being watered by the prominent gods with streams of waters in the form of charity etc. [and] which removes the affliction with its comfortable shade.

In the Vikrama year 1499 [A.D. 1442] the manuscript of the Kalpasūtra is being caused to be written for the merit of the noble Meghādevī, having obtained the advice of the good teacher, the holy Jayakīrtti-Sūrīṃdra, the chief of the holy Aṃcala-gaccha, by the noble Pāsā, the good disciple, the son of the noble Sāmala and his wife Vaïjala-devī, the grandson of the noble Namasī, belonging to the Ūkeśa-gaccha and a resident of the holy Satyapura, with his wife Meghādevī and with the sons, Rupā, Madā and Kolā.

Let the sayings of the monks be ever victorious!

Commentary
On folio 103 of this manuscript occurs the statement that Dharma-prabhasūri's version of the *Kālakācāryakathā* was composed in V.S. 1389 (A.D. 1332). For the relevant extract see N. Brown 1933, pp. 96–97.
P.P.

18

KALPASUTRA MANUSCRIPT

Inscription
Earlier writing
Folio 103r
LINE 6
graṃtha 1216 || ba || ḥ ||
LINE 7
arhan-mūlaḥ [etc.]

Folio 103v
LINE 3
In a different and later hand
saṃ 1701 varṣa-posa-vadi 11 dine bhaṃdāramukīyāṃ gaṃ 2 sonerīca 5 udasva anāṃḍomāla 2 nīlāre samībaï
LINE 4
śrī-vijayasiṃha-sūribhiḥ ||

Translation
Earlier writing
Number of the manuscript 1216
Let the Kalpasūtra like the wish-granting tree [etc., same eulogy as in the previous colophon].

In a different and later hand
In the Vikrama year 1701 [A.D. 1644], in the eleventh day of the bright half of the month of Pauṣa [December–January] the text was recited by (the monks) Vijayasiṃha Sūri and others.

26

KALPASUTRA MANUSCRIPT

Inscription
Folio 75
graṃtha 1216
In a later hand than the text
iti kalpasūtra-sampūrṇaṃ
1559 viśākha-sudi 7|

Translation
Number of the manuscript
1216.
In a later hand than the text
Here ends the Kalpasūtra text, Vikrama year 1559 [A.D. 1502], the seventh day of the bright half of the month Vaiśākha [April–May].

27

KALPASUTRA MANUSCRIPT

Inscription
Folio 146r
LINE 3
ūkeśa-vaṃśe prasṛta-
pras[e]śa ||
LINE 4
deve gurau bhakti-rataḥ
kṛpāluḥ || maṃtrīśvaro
Jāvaḍa-nāmadheyo
LINE 5
babhūva bhūpāla-kuleṣu
mānya ||1|| tasya daṃtigatiḥ
kāṃtā ||
LINE 6
pativrata-ratā rati | taj-jjātau
ddhosuto khyātā | vati-prīti-
yutau
LINE 7
mithaḥ || 2 || ādyaḥ kaḍu-
ākhya iti prasiddho | bhīm-
ābhidhāno

Folio 146v
LINE 1
hy=aparo vabuddhaḥ | ādyasya
patnī sakalemḍu-vakrā |
sīlaṃkitā k-
LINE 2
āmalade prasiddhā||3||
sodarasya dvitīyasya |
bhīmāde viśrutā pri-
LINE 3
yā | tat-putro varddhamān-
ākhyo varddhamāna-
guṇoccayaḥ ||4|| kaḍū-ā-
LINE 4
ṅkaḥ sa maṃtrīśo lekhayitvā
vicitratāt | haya-ṣaṭ-śara
caṃdr-ā-
LINE 5
khye | varṣe śrī-kalpa-
pustakān||5| varecaṃpaka-
durgge=ṣṭa | paṃcāśa-
LINE 6
t-taṃga-samyutān | samagra-
muni-śālāsu | vācayāmāsa
sotsavaṃ |
LINE 7
6 vṛhat-kharatara-gacche |
svacche sal-laṣṭi-sāgarāḥ |
purā babhūva śrī-

Folio 147r
LINE 1
maṃto jinasāgara-sūrayaḥ |
7 | tat-paṭṭaṃbuja-ravayo
jinasuṃdara-
LINE 2
sūrayo guṇair guravaḥ | tat-
paṭṭa-kumada-caṃdraḥ | śrī |
ma | j-jina—harṣa-
LINE 3
sūrīṃdrāḥ | 8 | siddhāṃta-
dugdhāṃbudhi-pāragāmimaḥ
| sanmānaso |
LINE 4
llāsa-daśo .. lāśvinaḥ | tat-
paṭṭa-pūrvācala-navya-helayo|
LINE 5
jayaṃty=amī śrī-jinacaṃdra-
sūrayaḥ | 9 | upadeśa-
vaśāt=teṣṣāṃ | sa
LINE 6
śrāddhaḥ kaḍu-ābhidhaḥ||
imāṃ tu lekhayāṃcakre |
sārāṃ śrī-ka-
LINE 7
lpa-pustikāṃ| 10 |
aṇahillapur-ābhikhye |
pattane puṇya-śā ||

Folio 147v
LINE 1
lani | śrīmat-kamala-
saṃyama-pāvakānāṃ
samudyamāt || 11 nidhi
LINE 2
ṣaṭ-vāraṇa-caṃdr-ākhye varṣe
sādhubhur=uttamaiḥ |
sādaraṃ vācyamān=e-
LINE 3
yaṃ ciraṃ nandadu pustikā ||
iti praśasti || ba ||

Translation
In the Ūkeśa lineage was born a person called Jāvaḍa, the lord of the ministers, who was respected by royalty. His wife was Rati, who was beautiful and devoted to her husband. They had two sons, Kaḍūā and Bhīma. Kaḍūā's wife was the famous Kāmaladevī, and Bhīma's wife was the well-known Bhīmādevī. Their [Kaḍūā's and Kāmaladevī's] son was called Varddhamāna having the qualities of Varddhamāna [Mahāvīra]. Kaḍūā himself, the lord of the ministers, caused the Kalpa manuscript to be written in the [Vikrama] year 1567 [A.D. 1510]. And he caused the text to be recited in the whole assembly of monks in the fort called Varecaṃpaka.

In the great Kharatara clan belonged Jinacandrasūri to whose *paṭṭa* belonged Jinasundarasūri to whose *paṭṭa* belonged Jinasāgarasūri to whose *paṭṭa* belonged Jinaharṣasūri. Following the advice of Jinacandrasūri, Kaḍūā caused this manuscript of the Kalpa text to be written.

In the auspicious city of Aṇahillapura due to the effort of Śrīkamala in the [Vikrama] year 1868 [A.D. 1811] this manuscript was recited by the monks. Let this manuscript prosper forever.

28

KALPASUTRA MANUSCRIPT

Inscription

Folio 128v

LINE 1

|| Siddham || (symbol) śrīmad-vāyaḍa-vaṃśe saravaṇa-nāmā babhūva maṃtrīśaḥ | bharamuṃ nāmnā jāyā |

LINE 2

tayā tayā prasūtaṃ suta-dvaṃdvaṃ || 1 jyeṣṭo māṇikya-maṃtrī | vivekavān satya-śīla |

LINE 3

saṃvannaḥ | dvitīyo mādhava-maṃ | trī | dayāparo dharma-karma-rataḥ || 2 | taj-jā-

LINE 4

yā nirmāyā | pūtī-nāmnīti jaina-dharma-ratā satyānudāta-rasikā

LINE 5

|vinayaparā śīla-saṃpannā | 3 | tad-aṃga-jātāḥ saguṇair=anarghyās=tray-

LINE 6

o=py=abhūvan sukṛtaikasārāḥ | ādyaḥ sudhī ḍuṃgara-nāmadheyo | gallābhidhaḥ śrīpa-

LINE 7

ti ca prasiddhā | 4 sa tayā vināy-ān-āyānvitā dayā | dama-dākṣanya-

Folio 129r

LINE 1

yā | svajanābhimatā vacasvinaḥ | purusārthā iva rājate=niśaṃ || 5 tajāgamika-

LINE 2

suri-śrī-somaratna-guro | mukhāt | siddhāṃt-ārādhana-phalāṃ niśamya viśadāśay-

LINE 3

ā || 6 pūtī-nāmnayā taya śuddha-bhāva pūrita-cittayāṃvadhana-saphalīka-

LINE 4

rtuṃ | ramyaṃ śrī-kalpa-pustakaṃ || 7 || lekhitaṃ vikramād-varṣe daśa-paṃca-śate ga-

LINE 5

te sapta-saptatik-ādhikye | pakṣa-traya-viśuddhayā || 8 siddhāṃto bhava-

LINE 6

vāridhau nipatitāṃ potāyate dehināṃ | kṛtyākṛtya-vibhāga-dagdha-jalayo yo

LINE 7

rājahaṃsāyate | yasmāt-karma-gadā-pahaṃ vijayate vīrasya tīrthaṃkṛtau | dhanyāḥ ke-

LINE 8

|| pi hi lekhayaṃti kṛtin=āmmūṃ pustakaṃ dhīdhanā || 9 ||iti śrī-kālpa-pustikā praśasti ||

Translation

In the Vāyaḍa lineage the person called Saravaṇa was born. He was the lord of ministers and his wife's name was Bharamuṃ. From the couple two sons were born, Māṇikya-mantrī, the elder one, and Mādhava-mantrī, the younger one. Mādhava-mantrī was a very religious person. His wife was called Pūti, who also was attached to the Jain religion. They had three sons, Duṅgara, Gallā, and Śrīpati. Having heard about the merit of worshipping the holy scripture from the mouth of the preceptor Śrī Somaratna, Pūti caused the beautiful Kalpa manuscript to be written in the Vikrama year 1577 [A.D. 1520].

Bibliography

Ådahl, K. 1981. "A *Khamsa* of Nizāmī of 1439: Origin of the Miniatures—A Presentation and Analysis." Ph.D. diss., University of Uppsala.

Ardeshar, A.C. 1940. "Mughal Miniature Painting (with Illustrations from the Collection of Mr. A.C. Ardeshar of Bombay)." *Roopa Lekhā* 1, no. 2: 19–37.

Arnold, T.W., and J.V.S. Wilkinson. 1936. *The Library of A. Chester Beatty: A Catalogue of the Indian Miniatures.* 3 vols. London: Emery Walker.

Atil, E. 1975. *Art of the Arab World.* Exh. cat. Washington, D.C.: Freer Gallery of Art, Smithsonian Institution.

———. 1978. *The Brush of the Masters: Drawings from Iran and India.* Exh. cat. Washington, D.C.: Freer Gallery of Art, Smithsonian Institution.

Badiee, J. 1978. "Angels in an Islamic Heaven." *Los Angeles County Museum of Art Bulletin* 34: 50–59.

Barrett, D., and B. Gray. 1963. *Painting of India.* Lausanne: Skira.

Bautze, J. 1991. *Lotosmond und Löwenritt: Indische Miniaturmalerei.* Exh. cat. Stuttgart: Linden-Museum.

Beach, M.C. 1965. "The Gulshan Album and Its European Sources." *Museum of Fine Arts {Boston} Bulletin* 63, no. 332: 62–91.

———. 1966. Entries on Mughal, Rajput, and related paintings. In *Heeramaneck* 1966.

———. 1976–77. "The Mughal Painter Kesu Das." *Archives of Asian Art* 30: 34–52.

———. 1978. *The Grand Mogul: Imperial Painting in India, 1600–1660.* Exh. cat. Williamstown, Mass: Sterling and Francine Clark Art Institute.

———. 1980. "The Mughal Painter Abu'l Hasan and Some English Sources for His Style." *Journal of the Walters Art Gallery* 38: 7–33.

———. 1981. *The Imperial Image: Paintings for the Mughal Court.* Exh. cat. Washington, D.C.: Freer Gallery of Art, Smithsonian Institution.

———. 1987 *Early Mughal Painting.* Cambridge, Mass.: Harvard University Press.

Bernier, F. {1891} 1972. *Travels in the Mogul Empire A.D. 1656–1668.* Translated by A. Constable. New Delhi: S. Chand.

Beveridge, A.S., trans. {1922} 1969. *The* Bābur-nāma *in English: Memoirs of Bābur.* London: Luzac.

Beveridge, H., trans. {1902} 1972. *The* Akbarnāma *of Abul-Fazal.* 2 vols. Delhi: Rare Books.

Bhatia, U. 1990. *The Splendour of the Royal Ateliers.* New Delhi: Lalit Kalā Akademi.

Bhattacharyya, D.C. 1978. *Studies in Buddhist Iconography.* Delhi: Manohar.

Bhattasali, N.K. 1929. *Iconography of Buddhist and Brahmanical Sculptures in the Dacca Museum.* Dacca: Dacca Museum.

Binney, E., 3rd. 1973. *Indian Miniature Painting from the Collection of Edwin Binney, 3rd: The Mughal and Deccani Schools.* Exh. cat. Portland, Ore.: Portland Art Museum.

———. 1974. "The Arts of the Book." In Pal. 1974: 71–148.

———. 1979. "Indian Paintings from the Deccan." *Journal of the Royal Society of Arts* 3–4: 784–804.

———. 1981. "Sultanate Painting from the Collection of Edwin Binney, 3rd." In Krishna 1981a: 25–31.

Blair, S.S., and J.M. Bloom, eds. 1991. *Images of Paradise in Islamic Art.* Exh. cat. Hanover, N.H.: Hood Museum of Art, Dartmouth College.

Blochmann, H., trans. [1927] 1939. *The* Āʾīn-i Akbarī *of Abūʾl-Fazl ʿAllāmī.* Second edition revised by D.C. Phillott. 3 vols. Calcutta: Royal Asiatic Society of Bengal.

Brand, B. 1986. "The British Library's *Shahnama* of 1438 as a Sultanate Manuscript." In Skelton et al. 1986: 87–93.

Brand, M., and G.D. Lowry. 1985. *Akbar's India: Art from the Mughal City of Victory.* Exh. cat. New York: Asia Society Galleries.

Brown, P. 1924. *Indian Painting under the Mughals A.D. 1550–A.D. 1750.* Oxford: Clarendon Press.

Brown, W.N. 1930. "Early Vaishnava Miniature Paintings from Western India." *Eastern Art* 2: 167–206.

———. 1933. *The Story of Kālaka: Texts, History, Legends, and Miniature Paintings of the Śvetāmbara Jain Hagiographical Work.* Freer Gallery of Art Oriental Studies, no. 1. Washington, D.C.: Freer Gallery of Art, Smithsonian Institution.

———. 1934. *A Descriptive and Illustrated Catalogue of Miniature Paintings of the Jaina Kalpasutra as Executed in the Early Western Indian Style.* Freer Gallery of Art Oriental Studies, no. 2. Washington, D.C.: Freer Gallery of Art, Smithsonian Institution.

Bukhari, Y.K. 1967. "An Unpublished Illuminated Manuscript Entitled *Fawāid-ī-Quṭb Shāhī.*" *Lalit Kalā* 13: 8–10.

Caillat, C., and R. Kumar. 1981. *The Jain Cosmology.* Basel: Ravi Kumar.

Canby, S. 1983. *Indian Miniatures.* Exh. cat. San Francisco: Art Museum Association of America.

Carroll, D. 1972. *The Taj Mahal.* New York: Newsweek.

Chandra, M. 1953–54. "An Illustrated Manuscript of the *Kalpasūtra* and *Kālakāchāryakathā.*" *Prince of Wales Museum Bulletin* 4: 40–48.

Chandra, M., and U.P. Shah. 1975. *New Documents of Jaina Painting.* Bombay: Shri Mahavira Jaina Vidyalaya Publications.

Chandra, P. 1957–59. "A Series of *Rāmāyaṇa* Paintings of the Popular Mughal School." *Prince of Wales Museum Bulletin* 6: 64–70.

———. 1960. "Ustād Sālivāhana and the Development of Popular Mughal Art." *Lalit Kalā* 8: 25–46.

———. 1976. *The* Tuti-Nama *of the Cleveland Museum of Art and the Origins of Mughal Painting.* Codices Selecti, Commentarium vol. 55. Graz: Akademische Druck- und Verlagsanstalt.

Converse, H.S. 1986. "Selective Realism and Stylisation in Mughal Miniatures and Decorative Arts." In Skelton et al. 1986: 132–38.

Coomaraswamy, A.K. 1921. "An Illustrated Nepalese Manuscript." *Museum of Fine Arts {Boston} Bulletin* 19, no. 114: 47–49.

———. 1924. *Catalogue of the Indian Collections in the Museum of Fine Arts, Boston. Part 4, Jaina Paintings and Manuscripts.* Boston: Museum of Fine Arts.

Cort, J.E. 1989. "Liberation and Wellbeing: A Study of the Śvetāmbara Mūrtipūjak Jains of North Gujarat." Ph.D. diss., Harvard University.

Craven, R.C. 1976. *Indian Art: A Concise History.* London: Thames and Hudson.

Das, A.K. 1971. "Bis͟handās." In Krishna 1971a: 183–91.

———. 1978. *Mughal Painting during Jahangir's Time.* Calcutta: Asiatic Society.

———. 1981. "Calligraphers and Painters in Early Mughal Painting." In Krishna 1981a: 92–97.

———. 1986. *Splendour of Mughal Painting.* Bombay: Vakils, Feffer, & Simons.

Desai, V.N. 1985. *Life at Court: Art for India's Rulers, 16th–19th Centuries.* Exh. cat. Boston: Museum of Fine Arts.

Digby, S. 1967. "The Literary Evidence for Painting in the Delhi Sultanate." *Bulletin of the American Academy of Banaras* 1: 47–58.

Doshi, S. 1972. "An Illustrated Manuscript from Aurangabad Dated 1650 A.D." *Lalit Kalā* 15: 19–28.

———. 1985. *Masterpieces of Jain Painting.* Bombay: Marg Publications.

Dye, J.M., III. 1989. "Artists for the Emperor." In Pal et al. 1989: 88–127.

Ebeling, K. 1973. Ragamala *Paintings.* Basel: Ravi Kumar.

Ettinghausen, R. 1956. *An Exhibition of Islamic Art at the Ohio State Museum.* Exh. cat. Columbus: Ohio State University.

———. 1961. *Paintings of the Sultans and Emperors of India in American Collections.* Delhi: Lalit Kalā Akademi.

Falk, T., and M. Archer. 1981. *Indian Miniatures in the India Office Library.* London: Sotheby Parke Bernet.

Falk, T., S. Digby, and M. Goedhuis. n.d. *Paintings from Mughal India.* Exh. cat. London: Colnaghi.

Falk, T., E. Smart, and R. Skelton. 1978. *Indian Painting.* Exh. cat. London: P. & D. Colnaghi & Co.

Faridany-Akhavan, Z. 1989. "The Problems of the Mughal Manuscript of the *Hamza-nama* 1562–77: A Reconstruction." Ph.D. diss., Harvard University.

Fraad, I.L., and R. Ettinghausen. 1971. "Sultanate Painting in Persian Style, Primarily from the First Half of the Fifteenth Century: A Preliminary Study." In Krishna 1971a: 48–66.

Glynn, C. 1974. "An Early Mughal Landscape Painting and Related Works." *Los Angeles County Museum of Art Bulletin* 20, no. 2: 64–72.

Godard, Y. "Les Marges du Murakka Gulshan." *Athar-e-Iran* 1 (1936): 11–33.

Goetz, H. 1964. *The Art of India.* New York: Crown Books.

Gorakshkar, S., K. Desai, and M. Gandhi. 1987. *Skönhetens spegel: Konstskatter från Indien.* Exh. cat. Stockholm: Östasiatiska Museet.

Gorakshkar, S., and M.L. Nigam. 1988. *MṚIGA: Animal* [sic] *in Indian Art.* Exh. cat. Tokyo: Yomiuri Shimbun.

Goswamy, B.N. 1988. *A Jainesque Sultanate* Shahnama *and the Context of Pre-Mughal Painting in India.* Rietberg Series on Indian Art, no. 2. Zurich: Museum Rietberg.

Goswamy, B.N., and E. Fischer. 1987. *Wonders of a Golden Age: Indian Art of the 16th and 17th Centuries from Collections in Switzerland.* Zurich: Museum Rietberg.

Goswamy, B.N., V.C. Ohri, and A. Singh. 1985. "A 'Chaurpañchāśikā Style' Manuscript from the Pahāri Area." *Lalit Kalā* 21: 9–21.

Grube, E.J. 1968. *The Classical Style in Islamic Painting: The Early School of Herat and Its Impact on Islamic Painting of the Later 15th, the 16th, and 17th Centuries, Some Examples in American Collections.* Venice: Edizioni Oriens.

———, ed. 1991. *A Mirror for Princes from India.* Bombay: Marg Publications.

Gupta, S.P., ed. 1985. *Masterpieces from the National Museum Collection.* New Delhi: National Museum.

Guy, J., and D. Swallow, eds. 1990. *Arts of India: 1550–1990.* London: Victoria and Albert Museum.

Harle, J.C. 1986. *The Art and Architecture of the Indian Subcontinent.* New York: Viking Penguin.

Heeramaneck. 1966. *The Arts of India and Nepal: The Nasli and Alice Heeramaneck Collection.* Exh. cat. Boston: Museum of Fine Arts.

Heeramaneck, A.N. 1984. *Masterpieces of Indian Painting.* New York: Privately published.

Hodgkin, H., and T. McInerney. 1983. *Indian Drawing: An Exhibition.* Exh. cat. London: Arts Council of Great Britain.

Huntington, S.L. 1984. *The "Pāla-Sena" Schools of Sculpture.* Leiden: E. J. Brill.

———. 1985. *The Art of Ancient India: Hindu, Buddhist, Jain.* New York: Weatherhill.

Huntington, S.L., and J.C. Huntington. 1990. *Leaves from the Bodhi Tree.* Exh. cat. Dayton, Ohio: Dayton Art Institute.

Hutchins, F.G. 1980. *Young Krishna.* West Franklin, N.H.: Amarta Press.

L'Inde des légendes et des réalités: Miniatures indiennes et persanes de la Fondation Custodia Collection Frits Lugt. 1986. Exh. cat. Paris: Institut Neerlandais.

In the Image of Man: The Indian Perception of the Universe through 2000 Years of Painting and Sculpture. 1982. Exh. cat. Text by G. Michell, L. Leach, and T. Maxwell. London: Arts Council of Great Britain and Weidenfeld & Nicolson.

Jain, J., and E. Fischer. 1978. *Jaina Iconography.* 2 pts. Leiden. E.J. Brill.

James, D. 1988. *Qur'āns of the Mamlūks.* London: Alexandria Press.

Johnson, B.B. 1972. "Preliminary Study of the Technique of Indian Miniature Paintings." In Pal 1972: 139–46.

Kahlenberg, M.H. 1972. "A Study of the Development and Use of the Mughal *Patkā* (Sash) with Reference to the Los Angeles County Museum of Art Collection." In Pal 1972: 154–66.

Khandalavala, K. 1962. "Some Problems of Mughal Painting." *Lalit Kalā* 11: 9–13.

———. 1974. *The Development of Style in Indian Painting.* Delhi: Macmillan India.

———, ed. 1983. *An Age of Splendour: Islamic Art in India.* Bombay: Marg Publications.

———. 1985. "Deccani Painting: A Consideration of Mark Zebrowski—*Deccani Painting.*" *Lalit Kalā* 21: 35–52.

———. 1987. "Facets of Indian Miniature Painting." In Khandalavala & Doshi 1987: 77–164.

———. 1990. "The History and Dating of the Mahayana Caves at Ajanta." *Maharashtra Pathik* (Newsletter of the Maharashtra Tourism Development Corporation) 2, no. 1 (September): 18–21.

Khandalavala, K., and M. Chandra. 1965. *Miniatures and Sculptures from the Collection of the Late Sir Cowasji Jahangir, Bart.* Exh. cat. Bombay: Prince of Wales Museum.

———. 1969. *New Documents of Indian Painting.* Bombay: Prince of Wales Museum of Western India.

———. 1974. *An Illustrated* Aranyaka Parvan *in the Asiatic Society of Bombay.* Bombay: Asiatic Society of Bombay.

Khandalavala, K., M. Chandra, and P. Chandra. 1960. *Miniature Painting: A Catalogue of the Exhibition of the Sir Motichand Khajanchi Collection Held by the Lalit Kalā Akademi.* Exh. cat. New Delhi: Lalit Kalā Akademi.

Khandalavala, K., and S. Doshi. 1975. "Miniature Paintings." In A. Ghosh, ed. *Jaina Art and Architecture.* New Delhi: Bharatiya Jnanpith. 3: 393–427.

———. 1987. *A Collector's Dream.* Bombay: Marg Publications.

Khandalavala, K., and J. Mittal. 1969. "An Early Akbari Illustrated Manuscript of *Tilasm and Zodiac.*" *Lalit Kalā* 14: 9–21.

———. 1974. "The *Bhāgavatā* MSS from Palam and Isarda—A Consideration in Style." *Lalit Kalā* 16: 28–32.

Koch, E. 1982. "The Influence of the Jesuit Mission on Symbolic Representations of the Mughal Emperor." In *Islam in India: Studies and Commentaries.* Edited by C.W. Troll. New Delhi: Vikas Publishing House. 14–29.

Kramrisch, S. 1986. *Painted Delight: Indian Paintings from Philadelphia Collections.* Exh. cat. Philadelphia: Philadelphia Museum of Art.

Krishna, A., ed. 1971a. *Chhavi: Golden Jubilee Volume.* Banaras: Bharat Kala Bhanan.

———. 1971b. "A Study of the Akbari Artist: Farrukh Chela." In Krishna 1971a: 353–73.

———. 1973. "A Reassessment of the *Tuti-Nama* Illustrations in the Cleveland Museum of Art." *Artibus Asiæ* 35, no. 3: 241–68.

———, ed. 1981a. *Chhavi-2: Rai Krishnadasa Felicitation Volume.* Banaras: Bharat Kala Bhavan.

———. 1981b. "An Illustrated Manuscript of the *Laur-Chandā* in the Staatsbibliothek, Berlin." In Krishna 1981a: 275–89.

Kumar, L. n.d. "Dancers Costume and Provenance of the *Chaurapañchāśikā* Style." *Lalit Kalā* 25: 47–50.

Larson, G.J., P. Pal, and R.P. Gowen. 1980. *In Her Image: The Great Goddess in Indian Art and Medieval Christian Art.* Exh. cat. Santa Barbara: University of California Santa Barbara Art Museum.

Leach, L.Y. 1986. *Indian Miniature Paintings and Drawings; The Cleveland Museum of Art Catalogue of Oriental Art, Part 1.* Cleveland: Cleveland Museum of Art.

Lentz, T.W., and G.D. Lowry. 1989. *Timur and the Princely Vision: Persian Art and Culture in the Fifteenth Century.* Exh. cat. Los Angeles and Washington, D.C.: Los Angeles County Museum of Art, Arthur M. Sackler Gallery, and Smithsonian Institution Press.

Leoshko, J.L. 1990. "Selected Masterpiece: *Portrait of a Prince.*" *Los Angeles County Museum of Art Members' Calendar* 28, nos. 7–8: 17.

Levy, R., trans. 1967. *The Epic of the Kings: Shah-nama, the National Epic of Persia.* Chicago: University of Chicago Press.

Losty, J.P. 1982. *The Art of the Book in India.* Exh. cat. London: British Library.

———. 1985. "The 'Bute Hafiz' and the Development of Border Decoration in the Manuscript Studio of the Mughals." *Burlington Magazine* 27, no. 993: 855–70.

———. 1986. *Indian Paintings in the British Library.* New Delhi: Lalit Kalā Akademi.

Lowry, G.D., with S. Nemazee. 1988. *A Jeweler's Eye: Islamic Arts of the Book from the Vever Collection.* Washington, D.C., and Seattle: Arthur M. Sackler Gallery and University of Washington Press.

Majumdar, M.R. 1960. "Two Illustrated MSS of the *Bhāgavata Daśamaskandha.*" *Lalit Kalā* 8: 47–54.

Manucci, N. [1907] 1981. *Storia Do Mogor, or Mogul India, 1653–1708.* Translated by W. Irvine. 4 vols. New Delhi: Oriental Books Reprint Corporation.

Markel, S. 1987. "Carved Jades of the Mughal Period." *Arts of Asia* 17, no. 6: 123–30.

McInerney, T. 1982. *Indian Painting: 1525–1825.* Exh. cat. London: David Carritt Ltd.

———. 1991. "Manohar." In Pal 1991: 53–68.

Mehta, N.C., and M. Chandra. 1962. *The Golden Flute: Indian Painting and Poetry.* New Delhi: Lalit Kalā Akademi.

Meister, M.W. 1968. "The Arts of India and Nepal: The Nasli and Alice Heeramaneck Collection." *Oriental Art* n.s. 14, no. 2: 107–13.

Melikian Chirvani, A.S. 1969. "L'École de Shiraz et les origines de la miniature moghole." In *Painting from Islamic Lands.* Edited by R. Pinder-Wilson. Oriental Studies no. 4. Columbia: University of South Carolina Press. 124–41.

Mevissen, G.J.R. 1989. "Studies in Pañcarakṣā Manuscript Painting." *Berliner Indologische Studien* 4/5: 339–74.

Miller, B.S., trans. and ed. 1977. *Love Song of the Dark Lord: Jayadeva's* Gītagovinda. New York: Columbia University Press.

Milstein, R. 1984. *Islamic Painting in the Israel Museum.* Exh. cat. Jerusalem: Israel Museum.

Minorsky, V., trans. 1959. *Calligraphers and Painters: A Treatise by Qāḍī Aḥmad, Son of Mīr-Munshī, (circa* A.H. *1015/* A.D. *1606).* Freer Gallery of Art Occasional Papers, vol. 3, no. 2. Washington, D.C.: Freer Gallery of Art, Smithsonian Institution.

Nigam, M.L. n.d. "The 'Yoginīs' of the Deccani Miniatures." *Lalit Kalā* 23: 35–41.

Okada, A. 1986. "Cinq dessins de Basâwan au musée Guimet." *Arts asiatiques* 41: 82–88.

———. 1988. *Versprochene Unsterblichkeit: Bildnis vom Hofder Moghul-Kaiser des 17. Jarhunderts aus dem Musée Guimet in Paris.* Rietberg Series on Indian Art, no. 3. Zurich: Museum Rietberg.

———. 1989. *Miniatures de l'Inde impériale: Les peintres de la cour d'Akbar,* 1556–1605. Exh. cat. Paris: Éditions de la Réunion des musées nationaux.

———. 1991a. "Basawan." In Pal 1991: 1–16.

———. 1991b. "Miniatures of the Sultanates of Bijapur and Golconda in the Musée Guimet." *Orientations* 22, no. 5: 110–16.

———. 1991c. "La *Naissance de Tīmūr*: Une illustration inédite de *l'Akbar-nāme.*" *Arts asiatiques* 46: 34–38.

Pal, P. 1965. "A New Document of Indian Painting." *Journal of the Royal Asiatic Society* pts. 3/4: 103–11.

———. 1966. Entries on palm-leaf manuscripts and painted book covers. In *Heeramaneck* 1966.

———. 1971a. "Indian Art from the Paul Walter Collection: Catalogue." Exh. cat. *Allen Memorial Art Museum Bulletin* 28, no. 2: 67–103.

———. 1971b. *Indo-Asian Art from the John Gilmore Ford Collection.* Exh. cat. Baltimore: Walters Art Gallery.

———, ed. *Aspects of Asian Art.* Leiden: E.J. Brill.

———, ed. 1974. *Islamic Art: The Nasli M. Heeramaneck Collection.* Los Angeles: Los Angeles County Museum of Art.

———. 1978. *The Classical Tradition in Rajput Painting, from the Paul F. Walter Collection.* Exh. cat. New York: Pierpont Morgan Library and the Gallery Association of New York State.

———. 1982. *Indian Paintings in the Los Angeles Museum.* New Delhi: Lalit Kalā Akademi.

———. 1983. *Court Paintings of India: 16th–19th Centuries.* New York: Navin Kumar.

———, ed. 1984. *Light of Asia: Buddha Sakyamuni in Asian Art.* Exh. cat. Los Angeles: Los Angeles County Museum of Art.

———. 1986. "The Birth of the Celestial Twins." *Journal of the American Medical Association Southeast Asia* 2, no 9: 15.

———. 1987. "Muslim Patrons and Painting in India." *Arts of Asia* 17, no. 6: 113–22.

———. 1988. "A Forgotten Monastery of Bihar." *South Asian Studies* 4: 83–88.

———, ed. 1991. *Master Artists of the Imperial Mughal Court.* Bombay: Marg Publications.

Pal, P., and V. Dehejia. 1986. *From Merchants to Emperors: Britsh Artists and India, 1757–1930.* Exh. cat. Ithaca, N.Y.: Cornell University Press.

Pal, P., and C. Glynn. 1976. *The Sensuous Line: Indian Drawings from the Paul F. Walter Collection.* Exh. cat. Los Angeles: Los Angeles County Museum of Art.

Pal, P., J. Leoshko, J.M. Dye III, and S. Markel. 1989. *Romance of the Taj Mahal.* Los Angeles and London: Los Angeles County Museum of Art and Thames and Hudson.

Pal, P., and J. Meech-Pekarik. 1988. *Buddhist Book Illuminations.* New York: Ravi Kumar.

Perrot, M. 1987. "Une Série de portraits Deccani: La collection d'art indien du président de Robein au musée de Rennes." *La Revue du Louvre* 37, nos. 5/6: 379–88.

Persian and Mughal Art. 1976. Exh. cat. London: P. & D. Colnaghi & Co.

Pinder-Wilson, R. H. 1976. *Paintings from the Muslim Courts of India.* Exh. cat. London: World of Islam Festival Publishing Company.

Rehatsek, E., trans. 1966. *The* Gulistan *of Sa'di.* New York: Capricorn Books.

Robinson, B.W. 1980. *Persian Paintings in the John Rylands Library: A Descriptive Catalogue.* London: Sotheby Parke Bernet.

Rogers, A., trans., and H. Beveridge, ed. [1909–14] 1968. *The* Tūzuk-i-Jahāngīrī *or Memoirs of Jahāngīr.* 2 vols. Delhi: Munshiram Manoharlal.

Safadi, Y.H. 1979. *Islamic Calligraphy.* Boulder, Colo.: Shambhala.

Sanford, D.T. 1970. "Identification of Three Miniatures in the Nasli and Alice Heeramaneck Collection." *Artibus Asiæ* 32, no. 1: 42–46.

Saraswati, S.K. 1978. *Paljuger Chitrakala.* Calcutta: Ananda Publishers.

Schimmel, A. 1989. "Calligraphy." In *The Arts of Persia.* Edited by R.W. Ferrier. New Haven: Yale University Press. 306–14.

Schimmel, A., and S.C. Welch. 1983. *Anvari's* Divan: *A Pocket Book for Akbar.* New York: Metropolitan Museum of Art.

Schroeder, E. 1947. "The Troubled Image: An Essay upon Mughal Painting." In *Art and Thought: Issued in Honour of Dr. Ananda K. Coomaraswamy on the Occasion of His 70th Birthday.* Edited by K.B. Iyer. London: Luzac. 73–86.

Sen, G. 1984. *Paintings from the* Akbar Nama: *A Visual Chronicle of Mughal India.* Varanasi: Lustre Press.

Seyller, J. 1987. "Scribal Notes on Mughal Manuscript Illustrations." *Artibus Asiæ* 48, nos. 3/4: 247–77.

———. 1990. "Codicological Aspects of the Victoria & Albert Museum *Akbarnāma* and Their Historical Implications." *Art Journal* 49, no. 4: 379–87.

———. 1991. "Hashim." In Pal 1991: 105–18.

Shah, U.P. 1941. "Varddhamāna-Vidyā-Paṭa." *Journal of the Indian Society of Oriental Art* 9: 42–51.

———, ed. 1978. *Treasures of Jaina Bhaṇḍāras.* Ahmedabad: L.D. Institute of Indology.

Shiveshwarkar, L. 1967. *The Pictures of the Chaurpañchāśikā, A Sanskrit Love Lyric.* New Delhi: National Museum.

Singh, C. 1971. "European Themes in Early Mughal Miniatures." In Krishna 1971a: 401–10.

Skelton, R. 1970. "Mughal Paintings from Harivaṃśa Manuscript." In *Victoria and Albert Museum Year Book, Number Two.* London: Phaidon. 41–54.

———. 1976. "Indian Painting of the Mughal Period." In *Islamic Painting and the Arts of the Book in the Keir Collection.* Edited by B.W. Robinson. London: Faber and Faber. 231–74.

———. 1988. "Imperial Symbolism in Mughal Painting." In *Content and Context of Visual Arts in the Islamic World.* Edited by P.P. Soucek. College Art Association of America Monographs on the Fine Arts no. 44. University Park: Pennsylvania State University Press. 177–87.

Skelton, R., et al. 1982. *The Indian Heritage: Court Life & Arts under Mughal Rule.* Exh. cat. London: Victoria and Albert Museum.

Skelton, R., A. Topsfield, S. Stronge, R. Crill, eds. 1986. *Facets of Indian Art.* London: Victoria and Albert Museum.

Smart, E.S. 1973. "Four Illustrated Mughal *Baburnama* Manuscripts." *Art and Archaeology Research Papers* 3: 54–58.

———. 1978. "Six Folios from a Dispersed Manuscript of the *Baburnama.*" In Falk et al. 1978: 109–32.

———. 1991. "Balchand." In Pal 1991: 135–48.

Smart, E.S., and D.S. Walker. 1985. *Pride of the Princes: Indian Art of the Mughal Era in the Cincinnati Art Museum.* Cincinnati: Cincinnati Art Museum.

Soucek, P. 1985. "Abd-al-Samad Sirazi." In *Encyclopædia Iranica.* London: Routledge and Kegan Paul. 1: 162–67.

———. 1987. "Persian Artists in Mughal India: Influences and Transformations." *Muqarnas* 4: 166–81.

Spink, W. 1990. "Ajanta in a Historical and Political Context." *Maharashtra Pathik* (Newsletter of the Maharashtra Tourism Development Corporation) 2, no. 1 (September): 5–12, 16–17.

Stchoukine, I. 1929. *La Peinture indienne a l'époque des grands Moghols.* Paris: Ernest Leroux.

———. 1935. "Portraits Moghols IV." *Revue des arts asiatiques* 9: 167–76.

Stooke, H.J., and K. Khandalavala. 1953. *The Laud Ragamala Miniatures: A Study in Indian Painting and Music.* Oxford: Bruno Cassirer.

Strzygowski, J., ed. 1933. *Asiatische Miniaturenmalerei im Anschluss an Wesen und Werden der Mogulmalerei.* Klagenfurt, Austria: Kollitsch.

Tod, J. [1829, 1832] 1957. *Annals and Antiquities of Rajast'han, or the Central and Western Rajput States of India.* 2 vols. London: Routledge and Kegan Paul.

Topsfield, A., and M.C. Beach. 1991. *Indian Paintings and Drawings from the Collection of Howard Hodgkin.* Exh. cat. New York: Thames and Hudson.

Trabold, J.L. 1975. *The Art of India, an Historical Profile: Selections from the Los Angeles County Museum of Art.* Exh. cat. Northridge, Calif.: Fine Arts Gallery, California State University, Northridge.

Trubner, H., ed. 1950. *The Art of Greater India 3000 B.C.–1800 A.D.* Exh. cat. Los Angeles: Los Angeles County Museum.

Tucci, G. 1949. *Tibetan Painted Scrolls.* 2 vols. Rome: Libreria dello Stato.

Vaughn, P. 1991. "Miskin." In Pal 1991: 17–38.

Waldschmidt, E., and R.L. Waldschmidt. 1975. *Miniatures of Musical Inspiration in the Collection of the Berlin Museum of Indian Art.* Pt. 2, *Rāgamālā Pictures from Northern India and the Deccan.* Berlin: Museum für Indische Kunst.

Weber, R. 1982. *Porträts und historische Darstellungen in der Miniaturensammlung des Museums für Indische Kunst Berlin.* Berlin: Museum für Indische Kunst.

Welch, A. 1972. *Collection of Islamic Art: Prince Sadruddin Aga Khan, 1.* Geneva: Privately published.

———. 1975. "Islam in India." *Arts Victoria* 1, no. 2: n.p.

———. 1979. *Calligraphy in the Arts of the Muslim World.* Exh. cat. New York and Austin: Asia Society and University of Texas Press.

———. 1990. "The Worldly Vision of Mir Sayyid ʿAli." In *Persian Masters: Five Centuries of Painting.* Edited by S. R. Canby. Bombay: Marg Publications. 85–98.

Welch, A., and S.C. Welch. 1982. *Arts of the Islamic Book: The Collection of Prince Sadruddin Aga Khan.* Ithaca, N.Y.: Cornell University Press for the Asia Society.

Welch, S.C. 1961. "The Paintings of Basawan." *Lalit Kalā* 10: 7–18.

———. 1963. *The Art of Mughal India: Paintings and Precious Objects.* Exh. cat. New York: Asia Society.

———. 1972. *A King's Book of Kings: The Shah-Nameh of Shah Tahmasp.* New York: Metropolitan Museum of Art.

———. 1973. *A Flower from Every Meadow: Indian Paintings from American Collections.* Exh. cat. New York: Asia Society.

———. 1976. *Indian Drawings and Painted Sketches, 16th through 19th Centuries.* Exh. cat. New York: Asia Society.

———. 1978. *Imperial Mughal Painting.* New York: George Braziller.

———. 1985. *India: Art and Culture, 1300–1900.* Exh. cat. New York: Metropolitan Museum of Art and Holt, Rinehart, and Winston.

Wilkinson, J.V.S. n.d. *The Lights of Canopus: Anvār i Suhailī.* New York: William Edwin Rudge.

Zebrowski, M. 1981. "Transformations in Seventeenth-Century Deccani Painting at Bijapur." In Krishna 1981a: 170–81.

———. 1983. *Deccani Painting.* London, Berkeley, and Los Angeles: Sotheby Publications and University of California Press.

Index

Supervisors and Trustees